SILENT FILM PERFORMERS

SILENT FILM PERFORMERS

AN ANNOTATED BIBLIOGRAPHY OF PUBLISHED, UNPUBLISHED AND ARCHIVAL SOURCES FOR OVER 350 ACTORS AND ACTRESSES

BY Roy Liebman

McFarland & Company, Inc., Publishers
Jefferson, North Carolina, and London

Acknowledgments: This book would not have been possible without the generous and unstinting cooperation of people in almost 70 libraries, museums and archives. For those places I could not personally visit, the willingness of staff members to respond to my several surveys was most greatly appreciated. In the many places, on both coasts, which I did personally visit my reception was never less than cordial and sometimes far beyond that. Special thanks are due to Sam Gill at the Academy of Motion Picture Arts and Sciences for his gracious advice, assistance and broad knowledge and to my two young friends, Joel Tuchman and David Sigler, for their contributions.

British Library Cataloguing-in-Publication data are available

Library of Congress Cataloguing-in-Publication Data

Liebman, Roy.
    Silent film performers : an annotated bibliography of published, unpublished and archival sources for over 350 actors and actresses / by Roy Liebman.
      p. cm.
    Includes bibliographical references.
    ISBN 0-7864-0100-1 (lib. bdg. : 50# alk. paper) ∞
    1. Motion picture actors and actresses — Bibliography. 2. Silent films — History and criticism. I. Title.
Z5784.M9L54   1996
[PN1998.2]
016.79143'028'0922 — dc20   95-20915
                                                  CIP

Manufactured in the United States of America

McFarland & Company, Inc., Publishers
Box 611, Jefferson, North Carolina 28640

To my loving family
and to the memory of
my dear father-in-law, Jack Port,
who was so proud of this accomplishment

Table of Contents

Introduction

Silent Film Performers is intended for the growing number of scholars doing research into various aspects of film history, and also for the casual researcher who may just want to know more about a favorite performer.

Nearly all universities offer courses in film studies and there is ongoing rediscovery and restoration of older films, including silents. The increasing number of venues in which such films may be seen — festivals, universities, revival houses, cable TV — has enabled ever larger audiences to view films which were previously unavailable or rarely screened.

These activities have inevitably reawakened interest in many of the leading and supporting actors and actresses of silent film. Most of them made scores and even hundreds of films; some appeared in sound films as well. This book includes information on bibliographic and archival resources for more than 350 silent film performers, ranging from those who were in the very top rank of stardom to long-forgotten supporting players.

Although cinema studies was not considered a serious discipline for many years, there has not been a lack of published information about many who appeared in silent films. The lengthy selective bibliography in this book, arranged by title, contains many hundreds of books including full biographies, works of nostalgia, encyclopedic works, biographical and career overviews and lists of credits, although the latter sometimes may be incomplete. There is also a section on commercially available media materials.

For the major silent stars, the materials in the bibliography are intended to give a representative sampling of what is available, including books in foreign languages. For the less well-known performers, an effort was made to include all that was known to be available, although completeness is not claimed. Most of the entries in the bibliography include very brief and generally noncritical annotations which are intended to give a flavor of the works included.

There have been bibliographies

1

of books on film, although none of them provide as much information on each book as *Silent Film Performers* does. Among these are *The Film Book Bibliography, 1940–1975* by Jack C. Ellis, Charles Derry and Sharon Kern (Scarecrow Press, 1979), George Rehrauer's *Cinema Booklist* (Scarecrow Press, 1972–77) and the almost 6,800 titles in its successor *The Macmillan Film Bibliography* (Macmillan, 1982).

When it comes to primary research materials the unfortunate fact is that the majority of all films were allowed to disappear forever and so was much potential research material. Studios frequently discarded their "useless" records as they did their "useless" films. Performers who saved their memorabilia often found that no one was interested in preserving it for posterity.

Fortunately, there were some farseeing individuals and libraries and archives that collected — and, in some cases, rescued — materials and arranged them systematically. Many of these collections were made accessible to researchers. An important question became one of discovering where these resources were located.

Some libraries with special collections published their own catalogs, among them New York Public Library and the University of Southern California. William C. Young in his *American Theatrical Arts: A Guide to Manuscripts and Special Collections in the United States and Canada* (American Library Association, 1971) included brief descriptions of the holdings of some 138 American and Canadian theatrical (including film) collections. Linda Mehr in her *Motion Pictures, Television and Radio: A Union Catalogue of Manuscripts and Special Collections in the Western United States* (G.K. Hall, 1977) produced a fairly comprehensive listing of special collections in Western libraries.

Most of these publications are not arranged by performers' names but limited access is provided to some individual performers via indexes. However, the specificity of material about individual performers rarely goes beyond the collection level. Detailed information about "micro" level materials such as clipping files, correspondence, photographs and stills, and legal files has heretofore rarely been included in published sources. Some, but by no means all, libraries and archives have in-house catalogs to such materials but this is of no use unless researchers are on-site.

This lack of published access to a massive amount of potentially valuable research material has been redressed in large measure by this book. It provides access at the "micro" holdings level, including some resources not mentioned in any other publication, and in some cases, it describes them. To accomplish this, surveys were sent to numerous libraries, film archives and other known or possible repositories of primary materials. Personal visits were made to many collections on both coasts. Holdings of about 70 United States libraries, museums and archives as well as those of the British Film Institute and the National Archives of Canada are included in this book.

Among the resources included are clipping files, legal files, memorabilia (including scrapbooks), correspondence, privately printed or obscure published materials, stills and photographs, media materials and commercially published books and articles.

Some archives also have production files, scripts and other materials accessible only by film title. This material generally has not been included herein but a few collections not otherwise mentioned are listed in an Appendix. It may be assumed that many of the institutions included also have this type of material.

Capsule data is provided about each performer. It should be noted that accurate information about birth dates, real names and even home towns is sometimes difficult to find. When conflicting data was found, it has been provided. In the case of birthdates, it probably can be assumed that the earliest date is the accurate one but this is not always the case. Even when a single date is given it is not necessarily accurate. Perhaps by using this guide, future researchers will provide definitive answers to these questions.

THE ENTRIES

The performer entries in this book vary from a single page to many pages but each entry is constructed in a similar way:

Name (nickname or other "stage" name, if any), Real name(s), Place(s) of birth, Date(s) of birth and death
Brief biographical/career data.

Books (listed by title and arranged alphabetically within each category, except the first):

Books or parts of books which the performer wrote (or were ghostwritten) are always listed first. These books generally do *not* appear in the bibliography unless they actually provide some information about the performer. *Autobiographies are listed separately.*

As applicable, other books are divided into the following categories: General; Encyclopedic Works; Bibliography; Credits; Films (i.e., books primarily about the performer's films); Biography/Autobiography; Pictorial; Theses; Recordings; Catalogs, and Factoids. For full publication details and annotations about these books, the Bibliography must be consulted.

Because of the vast number of books written about Charles Chaplin, the general books in his entry are further divided into "Chaplin as Actor" and "Chaplin as Director/Writer/Producer."

Periodicals

For convenience, all items cited from periodicals are referred to as articles. Some are not full articles but may be parts of more extensive articles, obituaries, letters or merely very brief mentions of a performer. They have been included for their potential usefulness to a researcher.

Some clipping files contain periodical articles and these are included in the description of the files' contents. These articles are *not* then repeated in this section of the entry.

The periodical articles are listed chronologically by the first occurrence of a periodical title; all subsequent articles from the same periodical follow. For example: *Photoplay* (Jan. 1919, Sept. 1920, May 1923, Oct. 1967); *Motion Picture Classic* (Feb. 1919, Mar. 1922, Aug. 1925); *Newsweek* (Mar. 5, 1938, Sept. 2, 1946, Aug. 8, 1990).

In this way, researchers can see the dates of the articles from the same periodical without searching through the entire Periodicals section—but they should then also check the Clipping File section of each entry for additional articles.

When periodicals have changed their titles over the years, the title in use at the time the article was published is given; e.g., *8mm Collector* became *Classic Film Collector*, then *Classic Film/Video Images*, and finally *Classic Images*. *Film en Televisie* became *Film en Televisie + Video*. The *Motion Picture Classic* changed to *Movie Classic*. When title changes have been relatively minor and the titles have alternated at various times, e.g., *Motion Picture* and *Motion Picture Magazine*, one form generally has been used throughout.

Obscure Published Sources

This is a subjective category containing pamphlets and other brief works as well as some books produced by publishers about which little information is available.

Media

The videos, recordings, films, etc., in this section were all available from commercial vendors. Media materials recorded by individual institutions live or from broadcasts are listed under Archival Materials.

Archival Materials

As applicable in each entry, archival materials are divided into several categories: *Clipping File* (those files for which the contents are described); *Other Clipping File* (those files for which the content is *not* described); *Collection*; *Correspondence*; *Filmography*; *Interview*; *Legal File*; *Manuscript*; *Photograph/Still*; *Press Kit*; *Privately Printed Material*; *Program* (play or film); *Publicity Release*; *Reminiscence*; *Scrapbook*; *Studio Biography*. A few entries also contain other categories as appropriate.

A unique three- or four-letter code is assigned to each institution whose materials are included. (See the List of Institution Abbreviations for a complete listing.) The post office abbreviation for the state constitutes the first two letters; e.g., NYAM (American Museum of the Moving Image), NYPL (New York Public Library), OHCL (Cleveland Public Library). Canada's code is CND and Great Britain's is GB.

Clipping Files

Although clipping files contain some materials that were published at one time, for the purposes of this book they are considered archival materials. Generally these files contain contemporaneous newspaper clippings, obituaries, newsphotos (halftones) and almost anything else not otherwise housed on its own. Items like press releases or filmographies are separately listed (see below).

Some clipping files may only have one clipping, often an obituary; others may have hundreds of pieces. For those libraries personally visited, the contents of the clipping files are described under broad topics like legal problem, marriage/divorce and film appearance. The years in which the clip-

pings were published are supplied if known. Topics are not listed in any particular order, except that obituaries are always listed last. When an individual clipping touches upon many topics, it is listed as "article." As noted above, periodical articles found in clipping files are separately listed here by title.

Other Categories of Archival Materials (as listed above)

In general, some detail is provided for collections and, at the very least, dates of all materials are supplied when known, except for photographs and stills.

Some institutions have several collections of photographs or other materials. When only an institution symbol is provided, it indicates that the materials are not in a named collection or that the name was not known. When there are known named collections, the names are supplied. If there are both, the entry will read:

CAA (also in Hollywood Studio Museum Collection) (also in MGM collection).

This indicates that there is one unnamed collection, and two named ones, the MGM and the Hollywood Studio Museum.

This is a guide to *selected* published and archival materials. Although nearly every institution I contacted by survey or in person was most helpful, there were a relative few that did not respond. I would very much appreciate being informed about any sources that are not mentioned herein.

Selectivity was also applied to the number of silent film actors and actresses included. Most of the famous performers are here. The constraints of time on a project of this nature did not allow research on many hundreds of lesser known performers. These relatively obscure performers are good subjects for further research.

It should be noted that errors have no doubt occurred, given the magnitude of data assembled here; additionally, some old errors will inevitably have been repeated in cases where information has been garnered from previously published sources like periodical indexes. Although information was verified in multiple sources whenever possible, not all citations could be checked independently. Nevertheless, the errors remaining are probably minimal. The resulting compilation should provide researchers with much valuable and time-saving information.

Institutional Abbreviations

ARIZONA

AZSU   Arizona State University

CALIFORNIA

CAA   Academy of Motion Picture Arts and Sciences
CAFA   Ackerman Fantasy Archives
CAFI   American Film Institute
CAG   California State Library
CAH   Hollywood Studio Museum
CAHL   Huntington Library
CALM   Natural History Museum of Los Angeles County
CAOC   Occidental College
CAPH   Palm Springs Historical Society
CAPS   Palm Springs Public Library
CASF   San Francisco Performing Arts Library and Museum
CASP   San Francisco Public Library
CASU   Stanford University
CAUB   University of California, Berkeley
CAUC   University of California, Santa Cruz
CAUS   University of California, Los Angeles – Special Collections

CAUT   University of California, Los Angeles – Theater Arts Library
CAUU   University of Southern California – Cinema/TV Library
CAUW   University of Southern California – Warner Brothers Archive

CANADA

CNDA   National Archives of Canada

COLORADO

CODL   Denver Public Library
COPP   Pikes Peak Library District (Colorado Springs)

CONNECTICUT

CTW   Wesleyan University

DISTRICT OF COLUMBIA

DCG   Georgetown University
DCLC   Library of Congress – Manuscript Division

GREAT BRITAIN

GBBF   British Film Institute

ILLINOIS

ILHL Illinois State Historical Library

IOWA

IAU University of Iowa

KANSAS

KSWS Wichita State University

LOUISIANA

LANO New Orleans Public Library

MASSACHUSETTS

MABU Boston University
MAH Harvard University
MASC Smith College

MICHIGAN

MIDL Detroit Public Library
MISU Michigan State University – Voice Library

MINNESOTA

MNBH Blackwood Hall Memorial Library

MISSOURI

MOKC Kansas City Public Library
MOSL St. Louis Public Library

NEBRASKA

NEHS Nebraska State Historical Society

NEW JERSEY

NJFL Fort Lee Public Library
NJPT Princeton University – Theatre Collection

NEW YORK

NYAM American Museum of the Moving Image
NYB Bettmann
NYCO Columbia University – Oral History Research Office
NYCU Columbia University – Rare Books and Manuscripts
NYCZ Cornell University
NYEH International Museum of Photography, George Eastman House
NYMA Museum of Modern Art
NYMN Museum of the City of New York
NYPL New York Public Library – Performing Arts Research Center
NYSU State University of New York at Purchase
NYUR University of Rochester

OHIO

OHCI Public Library of Cincinnati and Hamilton County
OHCL Cleveland Public Library
OHKS Kent State University
OHSU Ohio State University

OKLAHOMA

OKTM Tom Mix Museum
OKU University of Oklahoma

PENNSYLVANIA

PAPL Free Library of Philadelphia
PAPT Carnegie Library of Pittsburgh

TENNESSEE

TNUT University of Tennessee, Knoxville

TEXAS

TXAC	Amon Carter Museum
TXSM	Southern Methodist University—Southwest Film/Video Archives
TXSO	Southern Methodist University—Oral History Collection
TXU	University of Texas–Austin

UTAH

UTBY	Brigham Young University

WISCONSIN

WICF	Wisconsin Center for Film and Theater Research
WIHS	State Historical Society of Wisconsin

WYOMING

WYU	University of Wyoming

Performers

ACORD, Art (also known as Buck Parvin), Stillwater, OK, 1890–1931.

One of the most popular of the silent Western stars, Art Acord made 90 films, beginning in 1911, for studios such as Bison, Mutual and Universal. Even earlier (about 1909) he was a stuntman. Among his films, some of which were made under the name of Buck Parvin, were several serials and the "Blue Streak" series. His greatest success came for Universal in the 1920s but his career effectively ended with the coming of sound.

Published Sources

• *Books – General*: *The BFI Companion to the Western*; *Eighty Silent Film Stars*; *The Hall of Fame of Western Film Stars*; *Winners of the West*. **Credits:** *Filmarama* (v. I and II); *Twenty Years of Silents*; *Who Was Who on Screen*. **Encyclopedic Works:** *Film Encyclopedia*; *Halliwell's Filmgoer's Companion*; *Who's Who in Hollywood*. **Pictorial:** *Silent Portraits*.

• *Periodicals* – The following periodical articles are in addition to those included in the library listings below: *Motion Picture Classic* (July 1931); *Films in Review* (Oct. 1962, Jan. 1963, Mar. 1963, Aug.-Sept. 1963); *Classic Film/Video Images* (Nov. 1979); *Classic Images* (Mar. 1982, Apr.-May 1991).

Archival Materials

• *Clipping File* – CAA: Injury (1922); excerpt from *Hall of Fame of Western Film Stars* (1969); obituary (1931). NYMA (also in Photoplay Collection): Article (1963); personal data summary. Periodical articles: *8mm Collector* (Spring 1966); *Classic Film Collector* (Fall 1974); *Classic Images* (Feb. 1982). NYPL: Rodeo contestant (1916); injury (1916); newsphotos; article (1916, 1919, 1922); signed by Fox (1916); returns to films (1919). Periodical articles: *Dramatic Mirror* (Dec. 11, 1915; Dec. 28, 1918). • *Other Clipping File* – AZSU (Jimmy Starr Collection), GBBF, WICF. • *Filmography* – CAA. • *Photograph/Still* – CAA, CAUT (Jessen Collection), DCG (Quigley Photographic Archives), NYPL, NYSU, TXU.

ADAMS, Claire, Winnipeg, Manitoba, Canada, 1898/ 1900–1978.

After making her debut about 1918, Claire Adams appeared in Westerns with Tom Mix and "supported" Rin Tin Tin in several films. She also had roles in such films as *The Penalty* (with Lon Chaney), *Souls for Sables*, *The Sea Wolf* and *The Big Parade*. Her career ended in the late 1920s.

Published Sources

• *Books – General*: *Blue Book of the Screen*; *Famous Film Folk*; *Who's Who on the Screen*. **Credits:** *Filmarama* (v. I and II); *Twenty Years of Silents*. **Encyclopedic Works:** *Film Encyclopedia*; *Filmlexicon degli Autori e delle Opere*; *Who's Who in Hollywood*.

11

• *Periodicals* — The following periodical articles are in addition to that included in the library listings below: *Motion Picture Classic* (May 1922); *Classic Images* (May 1990) (filmography).

ARCHIVAL MATERIALS

• *Clipping File* — CAA: Film appearance (1922); obituary (1978). NYMA: Marriage (1924); film appearance (1920-22); shares home with parents (1932); obituary (1978). NYPL: Newsphotos; accident (1920); article (1919); obituary (1978). Periodical article: *Motion Picture Classic* (Dec. 1920). • *Other Clipping File* — GBBF, NYSU, PAPL. • *Photograph/Still* — CAA, CAUT (Jessen Collection), CAUU, DCG (Quigley Photographic Archives), GBBF, NYCU (Dramatic Museum Portraits), NYPL, OHCL. • *Scrapbook* — NYPL. • *Studio Biography* — NYMA: Photoplay.

ADAMS, Kathryn, St. Louis, MO, ca. 1894-1959.

Blonde Kathryn Adams worked at Thanhouser, Metro and Universal, among others, and appeared in the 1914 version of *The Squaw Man* as well as in films such as *Riders of the Purple Sage*, *Little Brothers of the Rich* and *The Brute Breaker*. (Not to be confused with the actress of the same name who made films in the late 1930s and early 1940s.)

PUBLISHED SOURCES

• *Books* — Credits: *Filmarama* (v. I and II); *Who Was Who on Screen*. **Encyclopedic Works:** *Who's Who in Hollywood*.

ARCHIVAL MATERIALS

• *Clipping File* — CAA: Obituary (1959). Article: *Green Book Magazine* (Mar. 1916). CAUT: Obituary (1959). NYMA: Divorce (1928). NYPL: Article (undated). • *Other Clipping File* — GBBF, MAH, MIDL, OHCL. • *Photograph/Still* — CASF, DCG (Quigley Photographic Archives), NYPL, OHCL, WICF. • *Publicity Release* — NYMA: Thanhouser; Metro; Universal.

ADORÉE, Renée (Renée La Fonte or de la Fonte), Lille, France, 1896/98-1933.

Memorable as the French peasant girl who loved John Gilbert in *The Big Parade*, Renée Adorée appeared (from 1920) in U.S. films such as *Mr. Wu*, *On Ze Boulevard*, *Tin Gods*, *West of Chicago* and *La Bohème*. Although she had appeared in American stage musicals, the advent of talkies limited her roles and 1930 was the year that her final film, *Call of the Flesh*, was released. She was married to Tom Moore (q.v.).

PUBLISHED SOURCES

• *Books* — **Bibliography:** *The Idols of Silence*. **General:** *The Faces of Hollywood*; *Famous Film Folk*; *Hollywood Album*; *How I Broke Into the Movies*; *Immortals of the Screen*; *Twinkle, Twinkle, Movie Star*. **Credits:** *Filmarama* (v. II); *Twenty Years of Silents*; *Who Was Who on Screen*. **Encyclopedic Works:** *A Biographical Dictionary of Film*; *Film Encyclopedia*; *Filmlexicon degli Autori e delle Opere*; *Halliwell's Filmgoer's Companion*; *The Illustrated Who's Who of the Cinema*; *The Movie Makers*; *The Picturegoer's Who's Who and Encyclopedia of the Screen To-day*; *Quinlan's Illustrated Registry of Film Stars*; *Who's Who in Hollywood*; *The World Almanac Who's Who of Film*; *The World Encyclopedia of the Film*; *The World Film Encyclopedia*. **Pictorial:** *Silent Portraits*.

• *Periodicals* — *Fortnightly Review* (July 1920); *Motion Picture Classic* (May 1921, Sept. 1923, Oct. 1925, Apr. 1926, Dec. 1926); *Photoplay* (May 1921, June 1926, Nov. 1926, Jan. 1930); *Motion Picture Magazine* (Aug. 1926); *Silver Screen* (May 1931); *Movie Classic* (June 1932); *Cosmopolitan* (June 1933); *Films in Review* (June-Sept. 1968 (filmography), Jan. 1984).

ARCHIVAL MATERIALS

• *Clipping File* — CAA: Film appearance (1923); injury (1923-24); obituary (1933). NYPL: Newsphotos; film appearance (1920, 1923, 1927); illness (1930-31;

undated); returns to Hollywood (1932); will (1933); engagement to Tom Moore (1921); obituary (1933). • *Other Clipping File*—AZSU (Jimmy Starr Collection), GBBF, MAH, MIDL, NYMA (Photoplay Collection), OHCL, PAPL, WICF. • *Filmography*—NYMA. • *Oral History*—NYCO: Mentioned in: L. Gish interview. • *Photograph/Still*—AZSU (Jimmy Starr Collection), CAA, CAUU, CNDA, DCG (Quigley Photographic Archives), GBBF, NJPT, NYAM, NYB (Bettmann/UPI Collection) (Underwood Collection), NYCU (Dramatic Museum Portraits), NYEH, NYPL, NYSU, OHCL, TXSM, TXU, WICF. • *Publicity Release*—AZSU (Jimmy Starr Collection). • *Scrapbook*—NJPT (Yeandle Collection), NYPL. • *Studio Biography*—NYMA: Unknown studio (undated).

ALDEN, Mary, New Orleans, LA, 1883–1946.

Perhaps best remembered for one of her earlier roles as the housekeeper in *The Birth of a Nation*, Mary Alden appeared in several D. W. Griffith films. She went on to have a solid career as a supporting actress in numerous films of the silent era, frequently in mother roles. Her talkies were relatively few, the last one coming about 1937.

PUBLISHED SOURCES
• *Books*—General: *Famous Film Folk.* Credits: *Filmarama* (v. I and II); *Twenty Years of Silents*; *Who Was Who on Screen.* Encyclopedic Works: *Film Encyclopedia*; *Who's Who in Hollywood.* Pictorial: *Silent Portraits.*
• *Periodicals*—The following periodical articles are in addition to those included in the library listings below: *Motion Picture Magazine* (Nov. 1915, Mar. 1922); *Motion Picture Classic* (Dec. 1921, Jan. 1923, Aug. 1923); *Photoplay* (Feb. 1922, May 1924, Dec. 1928).

ARCHIVAL MATERIALS
• *Clipping File*—CAA: Film appearance (1922). NYMA: Film appearance (1920s); stage appearance; article (1920s?);

draft of newspaper article. Periodical article: *Photoplay* (Dec. 1931). NYPL: Newsphotos; film appearance (1916); article (1915–16; 1923; undated); stage appearance (1910s). Periodical articles: *Reel Life* (Apr. 24, 1915); *Photoplay* (May 1917, July 1919); *Motion Picture Classic* (Aug. 1919). • *Other Clipping File*—GBBF, PAPL, WICF. • *Correspondence*—NYMA: Note (1921). • *Photograph/Still*—CAA, CAUT (Jessen Collection), DCG (Quigley Photographic Archives), GBBF, NJFL, NYAM, NYCU (Palmer Collection), NYPL, NYSU, OHCL, TXU, WICF. • *Program*—CAA: Revival of *Birth of a Nation.* • *Scrapbook*—NYPL. • *Studio Biography*—NYMA: Mutual (1915); Allied (1922); Triangle; Photoplay.

ALLISON, May, Rising Farm, GA, 1895/98–1989.

Very pretty blonde May Allison was best known for her teaming with Harold Lockwood (q.v.) in a series of popular films in the mid-1910s. Her career began in New York around 1914 and it ended, after some time off the screen, with her retirement in 1927. Among her films were *River of Romance, The Testing of Mildred Vane, Castles in the Air, Men of Steel* and *The Woman Who Fooled Herself.*

PUBLISHED SOURCES
• *Books*—General: *Famous Film Folk; First One Hundred Noted Men and Women of the Screen; From Hollywood; Life Stories of the Movie Stars; Who's Who on the Screen.* Credits: *Filmarama* (v. I and II); *Twenty Years of Silents.* Encyclopedic Works: *Film Encyclopedia; Who's Who in Hollywood.* Pictorial: *Silent Portraits.*
• *Periodicals*—The following periodical articles are in addition to those included in the library listings below: *Theatre* (Sept. 1914); *Strand Magazine* (NY) (Oct. 1914); *Feature Movie Magazine* (Oct. 10, 1915); *Film Players Herald and Movie Pictorial* (Feb. 1916); *Motion Picture Magazine* (Mar. 1917, Dec. 1917, July 1918, Apr. 1921); *Motion Picture*

Classic (May 1917, July 1917, Dec. 1918, Jan. 1925, Aug. 1925); *Photoplay* (Sept. 1918, Jan. 1921, July 1921, Feb. 1922, July 1923, Nov. 1923, Nov. 1924, Apr. 1925, Oct. 1930); *Picture Play Magazine* (Jan. 1920); *Picture Show* (Jan. 17, 1920); *Films in Review* (May 1971 (team of MA and Harold Lockwood) (filmography), Oct. 1972).

ARCHIVAL MATERIALS
• *Clipping File* — CAA: Marriage (1927, 1934); newsphotos; film appearance (1921, 1923, 1926); article (1914); stage appearance (1913); obituary (1989). Periodical article: *Moving Picture World* (Mar. 1916). NYMA: Marriage/divorce (1924–26); editor of *Photoplay* (1932); film appearance (1920s); retires from films; newsphotos; "spirit" bride (1919); signs with Metro (1918); article (undated); draft periodical article. Periodical articles: *Photo-play World* (Mar. 1918, Dec. 1918). NYPL: Newsphotos; article (undated); marriage/divorce (1923, 1926–27, 1931–32); obituary (1989). Periodical articles: *Motion Picture Magazine* (May 1916); *Quirk's Reviews* (July 1989). • *Other Clipping File* — GBBF, NYSU, OHCL, OHSU, WICF. • *Filmography* — NYMA. • *Photograph/ Still* — CAA (also in Hollywood Studio Museum Collection), CALM, CAUT (Jessen Collection), CAUU, DCG (Quigley Photographic Archives), GBBF, IAU (Junkin Collection), NJFL, NYB (Springer Collection), NYPL, NYSU, OHCL, TXU, WICF. • *Publicity Release* — NYMA: Metro. • *Scrapbook* — NYPL (also in R. Locke Collection). • *Studio Biography* — NYMA: Metro (1916); Photoplay.

ALVARADO, Don (also known as Don Page) (Jose Page or Paige), Albuquerque, NM, 1900/04–1967.

Beginning his career as an extra about 1924, Don Alvarado became a second-string "Latin lover," playing roles in films such as *Loves of Carmen*, *Drums of Love*, *Rio Rita* and *The Bridge of San Luis Rey*. His appear-

ances continued into the 1950s, and in 1937 he also began working as an assistant director at Warner Bros.

PUBLISHED SOURCES
• *Books* — General: *Alice in Movieland*. Credits: *Filmarama* (v. II); *Forty Years of Screen Credits*; *Twenty Years of Silents*; *Who Was Who on Screen*. Encyclopedic Works: *Film Encyclopedia*; *Filmlexicon degli Autori e delle Opere*; *Halliwell's Filmgoer's Companion*; *The Movie Makers*; *The Picturegoer's Who's Who and Encyclopedia of the Screen To-day*; *Who's Who in Hollywood*; *The World Film Encyclopedia*. Pictorial: *Silent Portraits*.
• *Periodicals* — The following periodical articles are in addition to those included in the library listings below: *Motion Picture Magazine* (Dec. 1929); *Screen World* (no. 228, 1968).

ARCHIVAL MATERIALS
• *Clipping File* — CAA: Marriage/divorce (1932, undated); film appearance (1956); obituary (1967). NYPL: Newsphotos; engagement (1932); article (undated); obituary (1967). Periodical articles: *Hollywood* (June 15, 1928); *Photoplay* (June 1929); *Screen Secrets* (Apr. 1930). • *Other Clipping File* — AZSU (Jimmy Starr Collection), CASP, GBBF, MAH, PAPL, WICF. • *Legal File* — CAUW: Contract (1930); letter (1925, 1931); agreement (1925, 1931); option (1925); talent agreement (1925, 1930–31). • *Photograph/Still* — CAA (also in MGM Collection), CASP, CAUT (Jessen Collection), CAUU, CNDA, DCG (Quigley Photographic Archives), GBBF, NYPL, TXU, WICF. • *Scrapbook* — NYPL. • *Studio Biography* — CAA: RKO (1930s).

AMES, Robert, Hartford, CT, 1889–1931.

Robert Ames was a suave leading man of the stage who appeared in silent films beginning in 1925 and made a smooth transition to talkies. His films included *Three Faces East*, *A Lady to Love*, *Marianne*, *The Crown of Lies* and *Smart Woman*.

PUBLISHED SOURCES

• *Books*—Credits: *Filmarama* (v. II); *Forty Years of Screen Credits*; *Who Was Who on Screen.* **Encyclopedic Works:** *Filmlexicon degli Autori e delle Opere*; *Who Was Who in the Theatre*; *Who's Who in Hollywood*; *The World Film Encyclopedia.*

ARCHIVAL MATERIALS

• *Clipping File*—CAA: Divorce (1930); estate (1931); obituary (1931). NYMA (also in Photoplay Collection): Personal data summary. NYPL: Stage appearance (1920s); career (1921, 1930); newsphotos; film review (1920s, 1930s); play review (1920s); breach-of-promise suit (1927); marriage/divorce (1926-27); article (1929, 1931, undated); film appearance (1922); investigation of death (1931); obituary (1931). • *Other Clipping File*—GBBF, MAH, MIDL, OHCL, WICF. • *Legal File*—CAUT (Twentieth Century-Fox Collection): Memo, letter (1929-30); loanout (1930); agreement (1929-30); contract summary (1930). • *Photograph/Still*—CAA (also in Hollywood Studio Museum Collection), DCG (Quigley Photographic Archives), NYPL, NYSU, OHCL, TXU, WICF. • *Press Kit*—OHCL. • *Scrapbook*—NYPL (also in C. & L. Brown Collection).

ANDERSON, G(ilbert) M(axwell), ("Broncho Billy") (Max Aronson), Little Rock, AR, 1882-1971.

A true pioneer of film, G. M. Anderson made his debut in 1903 (perhaps in *The Messenger Boy's Mistake*) and soon after appeared in the seminal film *The Great Train Robbery.* Between 1908 and 1915 he directed and starred in hundreds of Broncho Billy one- and two-reel Western films. He was also the co-founder of Essanay studio (the "ay" standing for the "A" of Anderson). Although he appeared in over 320 films, only a few were made after 1915 and he did not make his talkie debut until 1965! He also produced some comedy films in the late 1910s.

PUBLISHED SOURCES

• *Books*—General: *The BFI Companion to the Western*; *Classics of the Silent Screen*; *Early American Cinema*; *The Fifty-Year Decline and Fall of Hollywood*; *The Golden Gate and the Silver Screen*; *The Hall of Fame of Western Film Stars*; *Hollywood Album*; *"Image" on the Art and Evolution of the Film*; *Life Stories of the Movie Stars*; *A Pictorial History of Westerns*; *The Rise of the American Film*; *They Went Thataway*; *The War, the West and the Wilderness*; *The Western* (Eyles); *The Western* (Fenin); *Wild West Characters*; *Winners of the West.* **Credits:** *Filmarama* (v. I and II); *Twenty Years of Silents*; *Who Was Who on Screen.* **Encyclopedic Works:** *A Companion to the Movies*; *Film Encyclopedia*; *Filmlexicon degli Autori e delle Opere*; *Halliwell's Filmgoer's Companion*; *The Illustrated Encyclopedia of the World's Great Movie Stars and Their Films*; *The Illustrated Who's Who of the Cinema*; *International Dictionary of Films and Filmmakers* (v. 3); *Who's Who in Hollywood*; *The World Almanac Who's Who of Film.* **Biography/Autobiography:** *My Autobiography* (Chaplin). **Pictorial:** *Silent Portraits.* **Factoids:** *Star Stats.*

• *Periodicals*—The following periodical articles are in addition to those included in the library listings below: *Motography* (Dec. 21, 1912); *Motion Pictures* (June 1913, June 1915); *Photoplay* (May 1915, July 1924); *Technical World* (June 1915); *Moving Picture World* (June 8, 1915); *Essanay News* (Sept. 11, 1915); *Dramatic Mirror* (Feb. 5, 1916); *Motion Picture Classic* (Mar. 1916); *Show* (Sept. 1962); *Newsweek* (Aug. 19, 1963); *8mm Film Collector* (May 1964); *Newsweek* (Feb. 1, 1971); *Time* (Feb. 1, 1971); *Classic Film Collector* (Spring 1971); *Film Culture* (Spring 1972); *Views and Reviews* (Fall 1972); *University Film Association Journal* (no. 1, 1978); *Pacific Historian* (Winter 1982); *Classic Images* (Aug.-Sept. 1983).

ARCHIVAL MATERIALS

• *Clipping File*—CAA: Nostalgia (1943, 1948, 1958, 1963-64); legal problem

(1946); producer (1950); Academy Award (1958); article (1958, 1989); film appearance (1964–65); American Film Institute program notes (1973); obituary (1971). CAFI: Obituary (1971). CAUT: Obituary (1971). NYMA: Synopses of Broncho Billy films (1913–15); comeback (1918, 1921); article (1917, 1925, 1948, 1961, 1971); obituary (1971). Periodical articles: *Motion Picture Magazine* (Jan. 1915, Mar. 1916); *Motion Picture Story Magazine* (Mar. 1916); *AFI Report* (Nov. 1972); *Memory Lane* (Feb. 1980); *Classic Film/Video Images* (May 1980, Sept. 1980); *Classic Images* (June–Oct. 1987). NYPL: Film synopsis (1910s); escapes injury (1914); article (1912–14, 1951, 1961, 1963); film appearance (1910s); nostalgia (1936, 1963); newsphotos (numerous); musical stock company (1915); Essanay (1912, 1916); returns to films (1918); talkie debut (1965); obituary (1971). Periodical articles: *Motography* (Apr. 5, 1913); *Motion Picture Magazine* (Jan. 1915); *Photoplay* (Mar. 1915); *Motion Pictures* (Mar. 1916); *AFI Report* (Nov. 1972); *Classic Film Collector* (Spring 1973). • *Other Clipping File*—AZSU (Jimmy Starr Collection), GBBF, MIDL, NYSU, OHCL, PAPL, WICF. • *Filmography*—CAA. • *Interview*—CAUT. • *Oral History*—NYCO: Interviewed in 1958. Also mentioned in the following interviews: Louella Parsons, Gloria Swanson, Carey Wilson. • *Photograph/Still*—CAA (also in Hollywood Studio Museum Collection), CALM, CAUT (Jessen Collection), GBBF, NJFL, NYB (Penguin Collection), NYEH, NYPL, NYSU, OHCL, WICF. • *Press Kit*—NYSU, OHCL.

ARBUCKLE, Roscoe ("Fatty"), Smith Center, KS, 1887–1933.

Roscoe Arbuckle was a very successful comic actor (making a million dollars a year in the 1910s) in numerous two reelers and features, including *The Last Round Up, Brewster's Millions* and *The Life of the Party*. His starring career ended following the scandal caused by the death of bit player Virginia Rappe, although he was ultimately acquitted of any crime. He eventually came back to direct (under a pseudonym) and appeared in comedy shorts in the early 1930s.

PUBLISHED SOURCES
• *Books*—Encyclopedic Works: *A Biographical Dictionary of Film; Film Encyclopedia; Filmlexicon degli Autori e delle Opere; Halliwell's Filmgoer's Companion; The Illustrated Encyclopedia of the World's Great Movie Stars and Their Films; The Illustrated Who's Who of the Cinema; International Dictionary of Films and Filmmakers* (v. 3); *The International Encyclopedia of Film; Joe Franklin's Encyclopedia of Comedians; The Movie Makers; The Oxford Companion to Film; The Picturegoer's Who's Who and Encyclopedia of the Screen To-day; Quinlan's Illustrated Directory of Film Comedy Actors; Quinlan's Illustrated Registry of Film Stars; Who's Who in Hollywood; The World Almanac Who's Who of Film; The World Encyclopedia of the Film; The World Film Encyclopedia.* **General:** *Clown Princes and Court Jesters; The Crazy Mirror; The Day the Laughter Stopped; Fallen Angels; Father Goose; Fatti* (i.e., Fatty); *The Fatty Arbuckle Case; The Fatty Arbuckle Scandal; First One Hundred Men and Women of the Screen; Frame Up!; The Funsters; The Great Movie Comedians; The Great Movie Stars; Hollywood Album; Hollywood Hall of Fame; Hollywood Heaven; The Hollywood Murder Casebook; Hollywood R.I.P.; Hollywood Tragedy; Hollywood's Unsolved Mysteries; Immortals of the Screen; Kings of Tragedy; Kops and Custards; Life Stories of the Movie Stars; Love, Laughter and Tears; Mack Sennett's Keystone; The Movie Stars Story; Scandal!* (Lebrow); *Scandal!* (Wilson); *Struck; Those Scandalous Sheets of Hollywood; Whodunit? Hollywood Style; Who's Who in the Film World; Who's Who on the Screen; You Must Remember This.* **Credits:** *Filmarama* (v. I and II); *Twenty Years of Silents; Who Was Who on Screen.* **Biography/Autobiography:** *Fatty; My Wonderful World of Slapstick; Roscoe "Fatty" Arbuckle*

(Fine); *Roscoe "Fatty" Arbuckle* (Oderman). **Films:** *Keaton et Cie.* **Pictorial:** *Life and Death in Hollywood; Silent Portraits.* **Factoids:** *Star Stats.*

• *Periodicals* — The following periodical articles are in addition to those included in the library listings below: *Motion Picture Magazine* (July 1915, Dec. 1915, June 1917, Sept. 1917, Mar. 1918, Sept. 1931, Nov. 1931); *Picture Play* (Apr. 1916); *Photoplay* (Aug. 1916, Apr. 1918, Nov. 1918, June 1919, Sept.–Oct. 1921, Aug. 1925, Mar. 1931, July 1931); *Motion Picture Classic* (Nov. 1916, July 1918, July 1927, July 1931); *Literary Digest* (July 14, 1917, Jan. 13, 1923); *Pantomime* (Sept. 28, 1921); *Outlook* (Jan. 3, 1923); *Good Housekeeping* (Mar. 1923); *American Projectionist* (Apr. 1927); *Movie Classic* (Sept. 1932); *Films and Filming* (July 1965–Jan. 1966, Dec. 1987); *Classic Film Collector* (Summer 1966, July 1979, Sept. 1979, Nov. 1979); *Films in Review* (Feb. 1973, Aug.–Sept. 1985); *After Dark* (Nov. 1974); *Action* (Mar.-Apr. 1978); *American Film* (May 1978); *Classic Film/Video Images* (Dec. 1979–Jan. 1980); *Segnocinema* (Jan. 1984); *Classic Images* (Oct. 1987, Mar. 1988, June 1990); *Cineforum* (Nov. 1987); *Sight and Sound* (Winter 1987/88); *Screen* (no. 2, 1988); *Positif* (June 1988); *Journal of Popular Film and Television* (Winter 1988).

ARCHIVAL MATERIALS

• *Clipping File* — CAA: Directs film (1924, 1927); film appearance (1921-22); article (1922, 1950, 1955, 1959, 1964, 1971); review of *Frame Up!* (1991); Paramount contract (1917); films shelved (1922); trial (1922); review of *The Day the Laughter Stopped* (1976); mock trial (1985); obituary (1933). Periodical articles: *Photoplay* (Aug. 1915, Apr. 1916); *True Mystery* (Feb. 1955); *Real* (Aug. 1955); *Men's Pictorial* (Apr. 1957); *Hollywood Studio Magazine* (June 1971); *Film Collector's World* (June 1977); *American Classic Screen* (Nov.-Dec. 1977). CAFI: Biographical play (1981, 1985); article (1985); biographical film (1984); film festival (1979). CAUT: Article (1975); review of *The Day the Laughter Stopped* (1976); scandal (1979);

divorce (1929). NYMA: Personal data summary; article (1919, 1921, undated); ban lifted on films (1922); scandal (1921, 1991); trial (1922); comeback (1923-24, 1927, 1929); review of *Frame Up!*; divorce (1923-24, 1928-29); returns to stage (1923-24); legal problem (1929-30); review of *The Day the Laughter Stopped* (1976); film appearance (1910s); signs with Paramount (1920); contract renewed (1919); mock trial (1985); *Arbuckle* (one-man show). Periodical articles: *Photoplay* (undated); *True Mystery* (Fall 1955); *Classic Film Collector* (Winter-Spring 1967, Fall-Winter 1968, Summer 1974); *Classic Film/Video Images* (July–Nov. 1979, May 1980–Dec. 1981); *Classic Images* (Jan. 1982, Nov. 1983). NYPL: PARTIAL CONTENTS: Newsphotos; scandal (1921, 1991, undated); review of *Frame Up!* (1991). Periodical article: *American Classic Screen* (Mar.-June 1978). • *Other Clipping File* — AZSU (Jimmy Starr Collection), CASF, CNDA, GBBF, MAH, MIDL, OHCL, WICF. • *Correspondence* — CAA (Adolph Zukor Collection): 1921–22. • *Filmography* — CAA (Paramount films only), NYEH, NYMA. • *Manuscript* — CAUT: *Trials of Fatty Arbuckle* (undated). • *Oral History* — NYCO: Mentioned in the following interviews: Sheilah Graham, Albert Hackett, Buster Keaton, Lila Lee, Harold Lloyd, Arthur Mayer, Conrad Nagel, Elliot Nugent, Louella Parsons, Otto Preminger, Sam Spewack, Blanche Sweet, Bert Wheeler, Adolph Zukor. • *Photograph/Still* — CAA (also in Hollywood Studio Museum Collection), CALM, CAOC (Kiesling Collection), CASF, CAUT (Jessen Collection), CNDA, DCG (Quigley Photographic Archives), IAU, NJFL, NYAM, NYB (Bettmann/UPI Collection) (Penguin Collection) (Springer Collection) (Underwood Collection), NYEH, NYPL, NYSU, OHCL, TXU, WICF. • *Publicity Release* — NYMA: Paramount (1917). • *Scrapbook* — NYPL (also C. & L. Brown Collection).

ARLEN, Richard (Richard Van Mattimore), Charlottesville, VA, 1898/1900-1976.

Although Richard Arlen made over 130 films (his final appearance coming in a cameo role in 1976), he probably reached his apex in the 1927 classic, *Wings*. He had already been in films as an extra or bit player since 1920. His somewhat bland acting style and all-American good looks were enough to keep him appearing in "B" films, including a string of Westerns, but he never found major stardom. He was married to Jobyna Ralston (q.v.).

PUBLISHED SOURCES

• *Books—General: Heroes, Heavies and Sagebrush; Hollywood Album; The Movie Stars Story; Screen Personalities; Universal Pictures; The Western* (Eyles); *You Must Remember This.* **Credits:** *Filmarama* (v. II); *Forty Years of Screen Credits; Twenty Years of Silents.* **Encyclopedic Works:** *Film Encyclopedia; Filmlexicon degli Autori e delle Opere; Halliwell's Filmgoer's Companion; The Illustrated Who's Who of the Cinema; International Motion Picture Almanac* (1975-76); *The Movie Makers; The Picturegoer's Who's Who and Encyclopedia of the Screen To-day; Quinlan's Illustrated Registry of Film Stars; Who's Who in Hollywood; Who's Who of the Horrors and Other Fantasy Films; The World Almanac Who's Who of Film; The World Film Encyclopedia.* **Nostalgia:** *Whatever Became of...* (1st, 7th). **Pictorial:** *The Image Makers; Silent Portraits.*

• *Periodicals—* The following periodical articles are in addition to those included in the library listings below: *Photoplay* (Apr. 1927, Sept. 1927, July 1928, Oct. 1929, May 1945); *Motion Picture Classic* (Oct. 1927); *Motion Picture Magazine* (Aug. 1929, May 1937); *Silver Screen* (May 1944); *Movie Classic* (Apr. 1933); *Films in Review* (Oct. 1968, June-July 1976); *Newsweek* (Apr. 12, 1976); *Time* (Apr. 12, 1976); *Cinema* (France) (May 1976); *Classic Images* (July-Aug. 1990) (filmography).

ARCHIVAL MATERIALS

• *Caricature—*NYMN. • *Clipping File—*CAA: Article (1961, 1963); TV ap-

pearance (1954, 1965-66, 1968); nostalgia (1969, 1972); legal problem (1947, 1955, 1963); marriage/divorce/children (1927, 1932-33, 1945-46); illness (1965); film appearance (1936, 1963-67); home (1939); induction into Aviation Hall of Fame (1973); kidnap plot (1932); injury (1928, 1930); obituary (1976). Periodical articles: *Screen Classics* (Feb. 1969); *Films in Review* (June-July 1979). CAFI: Obituary (1976). CAUT: Divorce (1945); legal problem (1950s); article (undated); obituary (1976). CAUU: Obituary (1976). NYMA: Obituary (1976). NYPL: Newsphotos; film appearance (1927-36, 1941, undated); marriage/divorce/children (1929, 1931-32, 1930s, 1945); career (1927-28, 1936); article (1933, 1943, 1951, 1955, 1958-59, undated); pilots plane (1928, 1942); injury (1932); comeback (1943); stage appearance (1945); assault (1940s?); TV appearance (1961); drunk driving (1963); obituary (1976). Periodical articles: *Picture Play* (Dec. 1928, June 1930, Dec. ?); *Photoplay* (Apr. 1929); *Motion Picture Classic* (Mar. 1931); *Silver Screen* (July 1931); *Screenland* (Oct. 1935). • *Other Clipping File—*AZSU (Jimmy Starr Collection), CALM, CNDA, GBBF, MAH, MIDL, OHCL, WICF. • *Correspondence—* NYPL (C. & L. Brown Collection): 1940s, 1950s. • *Legal File—*CAUW: Letter, memo (1932); personnel, payroll record (1932-60) communication (1932). • *Photograph/Still—*AZSU (Jimmy Starr Collection), CAA (also in Hollywood Studio Museum Collection), CAFA, CAHL, CASF, CAUT (Jessen Collection), CNDA, DCG (Quigley Photographic Archives), GBBF, MIDL, NJPT, NYAM, NYB (Bettmann/UPI Collection) (Penguin Collection) (Springer Collection) (Underwood Collection), NYCU (Dramatic Museum Portraits) (Palmer Collection), NYEH, NYPL, NYSU, OHCL, PAPL, TXU, WICF. • *Play Program—*CAHL: 1960. NYPL: 1947, 1953. • *Publicity Release—* CAA: Paramount (numerous) (1941-43). NYPL: Paramount (?) (numerous) (undated). • *Scrapbook—*NJPT (Yeandle Collection), NYAM, NYPL. • *Studio Biography—*CAA: Paramount (1941,

1951–52, 1956, 1960, 1966); Universal (1940). CAUT: Paramount (1952). NYPL: Paramount (1931).

ARLISS, George (George Andrews), London, England, 1868–1946.

Monocled George Arliss had a lengthy stage career and a film career that began with *The Devil* (1921) and included both the silent and sound versions of *The Green Goddess*. His greatest film fame came with the talkies (he won an Academy Award for 1929's *Disraeli*) and his impersonations of various historical characters were popular for a time. Indeed, he was dubbed "The First Gentleman of the Talking Screen." He returned to England in 1935, his last film appearance being *Doctor Syn* in 1937.

PUBLISHED SOURCES

• *Books* – **General:** *Actorviews*; *Famous Stars of Filmdom (Men)*; *The Great Movie Stars*; *Hollywood Album*; *Hollywood Greats of the Golden Years*; *Immortals of the Screen*; *The Movie Stars Story*; *The Oscar People*; *Screen Personalities* **Credits:** *British Film Actors' Credits*; *Filmarama* (v. II); *Twenty Years of Silents*; *Who Was Who on Screen.* **Encyclopedic Works:** *Dictionary of National Biography* (1941-50); *The Encyclopedia of World Theater*; *Famous Actors and Actresses on the American Stage*; *Film Encyclopedia*; *Filmlexicon degli Autori e delle Opere*; *Halliwell's Filmgoer's Companion*; *The Illustrated Who's Who of the Cinema*; *International Dictionary of Films and Filmmakers* (v. 3); *The International Encyclopedia of Film*; *The Movie Makers*; *Notable Names in the American Theatre*; *The Oxford Companion to Film*; *The Oxford Companion to the Theatre*; *The Picturegoer's Who's Who and Encyclopedia of the Screen To-day*; *Quinlan's Illustrated Registry of Film Stars*; *Who Was Who in the Theatre*; *Who's Who in Hollywood*; *Who's Who on the Stage* (1908); *The World Almanac Who's Who of Film*; *The World Encyclopedia of the Film*;

The World Film Encyclopedia. **Pictorial:** *Great Stars of the American Stage.* **Biography/Autobiography:** *My Ten Years in the Studios*; *Up the Years From Bloomsbury.* **Factoids:** *Star Stats.*
• *Periodicals* – The following periodical articles are in addition to those included in the library listings below: *Theatre* (Dec. 1909, Oct. 1925, Feb. 1929); *Green Book Album* (July 1910); *Current Literature* (Nov. 1911); *American Magazine* (Jan. 1912, Dec. 1921); *Munsey's Magazine* (May 1912); *Theatre Arts Magazine* (Apr. 1919); *Shadowland* (Jan. 1921); *Arts & Decoration* (Mar. 1921); *Motion Picture Classic* (Oct. 1922, Oct. 1929); *Atlantic Monthly* (Apr. 1923, Feb. 1931); *Collier's* (July 11, 1925, Aug. 29, 1925); *Vanity Fair* (Feb. 1928); *Literary Digest* (Apr. 12, 1930, July 11, 1931); *Motion Picture Magazine* (Sept. 1930, Sept. 1931); *Photo-Era* (Sept. 1930); *Fortune* (Oct. 1930); *Strand Magazine* (1932); *Windsor Magazine* (Aug. 1932); *Good Housekeeping* (June 1932); *Windsor* (Aug. 1932); *Cinema Digest* (Oct. 31, 1932, Jan. 9, 1933, Apr. 3, 1933, May 1, 1933); *Movie Classic* (Feb. 1933); *Photoplay* (June 1933, July 1934); *Theatre World* (Aug. 1934); *Newsweek* (Feb. 2, 1935, Feb. 18, 1946); *The Stage* (June 1935); *Current History* (Mar. 1940); *Saturday Review* (Mar. 30, 1940); *Time* (Feb. 18, 1946); *Films in Review* (Nov. 1985); *Classic Images* (May 1990) (filmography).

ARCHIVAL MATERIALS

• *Caricature* – NYMN, NYPL. • *Clipping File* – CAA: Film appearance (1924, 1933); stage appearance (1930); article (1922, 1941); salary reduced (1932); knighthood (1934); newsphotos; nostalgia (1971); obituary (1946). Periodical article: *Films in Review* (Apr. 1979). CAUT: Film appearance (1928). NYMA: Legal problem (1941); film appearance (1931); talkies (1931); pay cut (1932); article (1931-32); stage fright (1932); newsphotos; review of *My Ten Years in the Studios* (1940); film review (1930s?); obituary (1946). Periodical articles: *Equity* (Mar. 1923); *New Movie* (Mar. 1931); *Photoplay* (May 1931); *Film Weekly*

(Aug. 8, 1931, Aug. 29, 1931, Aug. 19, 1932); *Movie Mirror* (Jan. 1932); *Screenland* (Jan. 1932, Apr. 1932); *Movie Classic* (June 1932); *Woman's Home Companion* (Aug. 1932); *Classic Film Collector* (Spring 1971, Winter 1973, Sept. 1980). NYMN: Newsphotos; play review; obituary (1946). NYPL: PARTIAL CONTENTS: Newsphotos (numerous); film review (1920s, 1930s); stage appearance (1910s, 1920s); article (1930, 1940, undated); antivivisectionist (1922); legal problem (1930s); review of *My Ten Years in the Studios* (1940); stardom (1940); obituary (1946). Periodical articles: *Pearson's Magazine* (Oct. 1911); *McClure's* (Feb. 1914?); *Ladies' Home Journal* (May 1927); *Current Literature* (Feb. 16-20, 1931); *Classic Film Collector* (Winter 1973). • *Other Clipping File* — AZSU (Jimmy Starr Collection), CAFA, CASF, CAUB, CNDA, DCG, GBBF, MAH, MIDL, NYMN, NYPL, NYSU, OHCL, OHSU, PAPL, WICF. • *Correspondence* — CAHL: 2 letters (Max Farrand Papers) (1931-32); 24 letters (Edwin and Grace Hubble Papers) (1931-45); 8 letters (Mr. and Mrs. Hooper Papers) (1932-44); 19 letters (Godfrey Davies Papers) (1938-45). CAOC (Kiesling Collection). CASF. CAUB (Dobie Papers): Housed in Bancroft Library. CAUS. GBBF (Balcon Collection): Letters and telegrams pertaining to film work in England (1934-35). ILHL (Kohlsaat Papers). MABU (Bette Davis Collection) (Ellswyth Thane Collection) (Edmund Fuller Collection) (Alice H. Spaulding Collection). NYCU: 32 letters (Brander Matthews Collection) (1903-26, undated); letter (St. Cyr Collection) (1916); 2 letters (Hibbitt Collection) (1920); 10 letters (Dramatic Museum Collection) (1921-38, undated); 2 letters (Westervelt Collection) (1923, 1937); 2 letters (Thorndike Collection) (1925); letter (Belmont Collection) (1937). NYMA (Jacob Wilk Collection). NYMN. NYPL: 1918, 1921-24, 1927, 1931, 1934, undated. Includes three letters to Aileen Pringle (1921-27). WIHS (George S. Kaufman Papers): Letter about giving money to a mutual friend (1939). • *Filmography* — CAA. • *Legal File* — CAUT

(Twentieth Century-Fox Collection): Agreement (1933-34); letter, memo (1933-37); accident report (1936). Studio was asked to pay medical bills when GA's wife and sister-in-law were injured in an auto accident. CAUW: Letter, memo (1928-61); literary rights (1933); payroll record (1928-61); contract summary (1928-61); contract (1928); agreement (1931-32); talent agreement (1931). • *Memorabilia* — NYCU (Wheeler Theatrical Memorabilia), NYMN. • *Oral History* — CAUS: Mentioned in: Nunnally Johnson interview. NYCO: Mentioned in the following interviews: James Cagney, William Everson, Albert Howson, M. Young. • *Photograph/Still* — CAA (also in Hollywood Studio Museum Collection), CAHL, CALM, CASF, CAUS, CAUT (Jessen Collection), CAUU, DCG (Quigley Photographic Archives), GBBF, IAU (Blees Collection), MABU (Bette Davis Collection), NJFL, NYAM, NYB (Bettmann/UPI Collection) (Springer Collection) (Underwood Collection), NYCU (Bulliet Collection) (Dramatic Museum Portraits) (Palmer Collection), NYEH, NYMN (also in Jane Douglas Collection), NYPL, NYSU, OHCL, TXSM, TXU, WICF. • *Play Program* — CAHL: 1914, 1926, 1928. NYCU (Dramatic Museum Collection). NYPL. • *Press Kit* — CAFA. • *Print* — CAHL: 2 prints (1932, undated). • *Program* — NYPL: Film (1929). • *Reminiscence* — MISU. • *Scrapbook* — NYPL, WICF.

ARTHUR, George K. (Arthur George Brest), Littlehampton, Surrey or Aberdeen, Scotland, 1899- 1985

Diminutive comedian George K. Arthur scored a success in British films as H.G. Wells's Kipps. At MGM from the mid-1920s, his greatest success came in a series of popular comedies (including *Rookies* and *Detectives*) with hulking Karl Dane. Although his acting career ended in the mid-1930s he went on to become a successful award-winning producer of short films and features.

• *Books* — Encyclopedic Works: *Encyclopedia of Comedians; Film Encylopedia*; *Filmlexicon degli Autori e delle Opere*; *Halliwell's Filmgoer's Companion*; *Illustrated Who's Who In British Films*; *Joe Franklin's Encyclopedia of Comedians* (with Karl Dane); *The Picturegoer's Who's Who and Encyclopedia of the Screen To-day*; *Quinlan's Illustrated Directory of Film Comedy Actors* (with K. Dane); *Who's Who in Hollywood*; *The World Film Encyclopedia*. **Credits:** *British Film Actors' Credits*; *Filmarama* (v. II); *Forty Years of Screen Credits*; *Twenty Years of Silents*. **Pictorial:** *Silent Portraits*.
• *Periodicals* — The following periodical articles are in addition to those included in the library listings below: *Photoplay* (Jan. 1925); *Motion Picture Classic* (Dec. 1925, Sept. 1927).

ARCHIVAL MATERIALS
• *Clipping File* — CAA: Begins U.S. film career (1923); film producer (1952-58). Periodical article: *Films in Review* (Mar. 1962) (filmography). CAUT: Film producer (1954). NYMA: Smuggling charge; film appearance (1931); article (1932); injury (1932). Periodical article: *Picture Play* (May 1928). NYPL: Producer (1933-35); newsphotos; smuggling charge; nostalgia (1936); makes short films (1960); draft article by GKA (undated); comeback (1930s, 1933); film review (1929); article (undated). • *Other Clipping File* — GBBF, MIDL, OHCL, PAPL, WICF. • *Correspondence* — NYPL (C. & L. Brown Collection). • *Filmography* — NYPL (films *produced* by GKA). • *Oral History* — NYCO: Interviewed in 1957. • *Photograph/Still* — CAA (also in Hollywood Studio Museum Collection), CAUU, GBBF, NJPT, NYCU (Dramatic Museum Portraits) (Palmer Collection), NYEH, NYPL, NYSU, OHCL, PAPL, TXSM, TXU (A. Davis Collection), WICF. • *Publicity Release* — NYMA: MGM (1925). NYPL: 1958. • *Scrapbook* — NYPL.

ARVIDSON, Linda (also known as Mrs. D. W. Griffith and Linda Griffith) (Linda Johnson?), Stockholm, Sweden, 1884-1949.

From 1908 Linda Arvidson appeared in many of her then-husband D. W. Griffith's one- and two-reelers, including *Lines of White on a Sullen Sea*, *Enoch Arden*, *The Scarlet Letter* and *The Adventures of Dollie*. Her film career ended about 1915.

PUBLISHED SOURCES
• *Books* — Credits: *Filmarama* (v. I); *Twenty Years of Silents*; *Who Was Who on Screen*. **Encyclopedic Works:** *Film Encyclopedia*; *Filmlexicon degli Autori e delle Opere*; *Halliwell's Filmgoer's Companion*; *Who's Who in Hollywood*. **Biography/Autobiography:** *When the Movies Were Young*.

ARCHIVAL MATERIALS
• *Clipping File* — NYMA: Sues for alimony; article (1933); obituary (1949). NYPL: Newsphotos; obituary (1949). • *Photograph/Still* — NJFL, NYEH, NYPL, WICF. • *Scrapbook* — NYPL.

ASTHER, Nils, Hellerup, Denmark or Malmo, Sweden, 1897-1981.

Dubbed the "Masculine Garbo," handsome Nils Asther was a popular leading man at MGM from 1927, where he appeared in films such as *Sorrell and Son, Laugh Clown Laugh, Our Dancing Daughters, Wild Orchids* and *The Single Standard* (the latter two with the "feminine" Garbo). He came to the United States already an established film actor, having starred in Swedish, Danish and German films since about 1916. He went on to appear in sound films, including some British films in the 1930s; his most memorable role was in *The Bitter Tea of General Yen*. His American career lasted until 1950 and he was seen in a few Swedish films in the early 1960s.

PUBLISHED SOURCES

• **Books – General:** *Popular Men of the Screen*; *Strangers in Hollywood.* **Credits:** *Filmarama* (v. II); *Forty Years of Screen Credits*; *Twenty Years of Silents.* **Encyclopedic Works:** *Film Encyclopedia*; *Filmlexicon degli Autori e delle Opere*; *Halliwell's Filmgoer's Companion*; *The Illustrated Who's Who of the Cinema*; *The Movie Makers*; *The Picturegoer's Who's Who and Encyclopedia of the Screen To-day*; *Quinlan's Illustrated Registry of Film Stars*; *Who's Who in Hollywood*; *Who's Who of the Horrors and Other Fantasy Films*; *The World Almanac Who's Who of Film*; *The World Film Encyclopedia.* **Nostalgia:** *Whatever Became of...* (5th). **Pictorial:** *The Image Makers*; *Leading Men*; *Silent Portraits.*

• *Periodicals* – The following periodical articles are in addition to those included in the library listings below: *Cinema Art* (Oct. 1927); *Photoplay* (Oct. 1928, Feb.-Mar. 1929, Jan. 1930, Aug. 1930, Dec. 1941); *Motion Picture Magazine* (Aug. 1929, July 1932); *Motion Picture Classic* (Aug. 1931); *Silver Screen* (Oct. 1933); *Films in Review* (Feb. 1973, Jan. 1980); *Cine Revue* (Dec. 17, 1981); *Cinematographe* (Jan. 1982).

ARCHIVAL MATERIALS

• *Caricature* – NYMN. • *Clipping File* – CAA: Engagement/marriage/divorce (1927, 1929, 1930, 1932); legal problem (1931-34); stage appearance (1930); returns to U.S. (1941); newsphotos; MGM contract (1930-31); film appearance (1928, 1963); nostalgia (1949); article (1949, 1959); obituary (1981-82). Periodical article: *Films in Review* (Aug.-Sept. 1979). CAFI: Obituary (1981). NYMA (also in Photoplay Collection): Obituary (1981). NYPL: Newsphotos; film review (1920s, 1930s, 1942); returns to Hollywood; film appearance (1932-33); article (1929, 1932-33, undated); returns to Denmark; divorce (1932); Broadway debut (1952); obituary (1981). Periodical articles: *Screen Secrets* (undated); *Hollywood* (Dec. 15, 1928); *Motion Picture Magazine* (Mar. 1929); *Picture Play* (Oct. 1932); *American Weekly* (July 17, 1949).

• *Other Clipping File* – MIDL, OHCL, PAPL, WICF. • *Correspondence* – CAA (Hedda Hopper Collection): Letter from a friend about NA's current activities in Sweden (1965). • *Filmography* – CAA. • *Photograph/Still* – AZSU (Jimmy Starr Collection), CAA (also in Hollywood Studio Museum Collection) (also in MGM Collection), CAFA, DCG (Quigley Photographic Archives), NYCU (Dramatic Museum Portraits) (Palmer Collection), NYEH, NYPL, NYSU, OHCL, TNUT (Clarence Brown Collection), TXU, WICF. • *Publicity Release* – CAA: RKO; Paramount (1940s). • *Scrapbook* – NYPL. • *Studio Biography* – NYMA: Photoplay.

ASTOR, Gertrude, Lima, Ohio, 1887-1977.

Appearing in films from 1914, and one of the first actresses to become a Universal contract player, blonde Gertrude Astor had a lengthy career in films. Her statuesque figure largely limited her to "other woman" and supporting roles in films such as *Lorna Doone*, *The Strong Man*, *Kiki*, *Uncle Tom's Cabin* and *The Cat and the Canary.* The coming of sound relegated her to shorts and small roles in which she continued to appear off and on until the early 1960s.

PUBLISHED SOURCES

• *Books* – **Encyclopedic Works:** *Film Encyclopedia*; *Halliwell's Filmgoer's Companion*; *The Picturegoer's Who's Who and Encyclopedia of the Screen To-day*; *Who's Who in Hollywood*; *The World Film Encyclopedia.* **Credits:** *Filmarama* (v. I and II); *Forty Years of Screen Credits*; *Twenty Years of Silents.* **Pictorial:** *Silent Portraits.*

• *Periodicals* – The following periodical articles are in addition to that included in the library listings below: *Photoplay* (July 1927); *Classic Images* (May-June 1991).

ARCHIVAL MATERIALS

• *Clipping File* – AZSU (Jimmy Starr Collection): Obituary (1977). CAA: Film appearance (numerous) (1920s, 1963); marriage (1925); home (1926); nostalgia (1970); article (1972); honored by Universal (1975); obituary (1977). Periodical article: *Motion Picture Classic* (1927). CAUT: Obituary (1977). CAUU: Nostalgia (1970); honored by Universal (1975); obituary (1977). NYMA: Sues Vivian Duncan; honored by Universal (1975); film appearance (1920s); obituary (1977). NYPL: Article (undated); honored by Universal (1975); newsphotos; film appearance (1940s); obituary (1977). • *Other Clipping File* — CNDA, GBBF, MIDL, OHCL, PAPL. • *Correspondence* — CAHL: Letter (1927). • *Legal File* — CAA (Sennett Collection): Contract (1922). CAUW: Talent agreement (1927–29); contract (1929). • *Photograph/Still* — CAA (also in Hollywood Studio Museum Collection), CAFA, DCG (Quigley Photographic Archives), GBBF, NJPT, NYAM, NYCU (Dramatic Museum Portraits), NYEH, NYPL, NYSU, OHCL, PAPL, TXU (A. Davis Collection), WICF. • *Studio Biography* — NYMA: Inspiration (1928).

ASTOR, Mary (Lucille Langehanke), Quincy, IL, 1906–1987.

One of the most serenely beautiful actresses of the silent screen, Mary Astor began her 100+ film career in two-reelers and progressed to features by 1922. Her appearances in films like *Don Juan* and *Beau Brummell* brought her increasing popularity which continued into the sound period, beginning with *Ladies Love Brutes*. She continued working steadily in leading and character roles in films such as *Red Dust*, *Dodsworth* and *The Maltese Falcon* through the 1940s, then sporadically into the mid-1960s. She won an Academy Award for Best Supporting Actress in *The Great Lie*.

PUBLISHED SOURCES

• *Books* — Wrote novels, including *Goodbye Darling, Be Happy* (1965), *The Image of Kate* (1962), *The Incredible Charlie Carewe* (1960), *The O'Conners*

(1964) and *A Place Called Saturday* (1968). **Encyclopedic Works:** *A Biographical Dictionary of Film*; *The Biographical Encyclopaedia and Who's Who of the American Theatre*; *Current Biography Yearbook* (1961, 1987); *Film Encyclopedia*; *Filmlexicon degli Autori e delle Opere*; *Halliwell's Filmgoer's Companion*; *The Illustrated Encyclopedia of the World's Great Movie Stars and Their Films*; *The Illustrated Who's Who of the Cinema*; *International Dictionary of Films and Filmmakers* (v. 3); *The International Encyclopedia of Film*; *International Motion Picture Almananc* (1975–80); *The Movie Makers*; *The Oxford Companion to Film*; *The Picturegoer's Who's Who and Encyclopedia of the Screen To-day*; *Quinlan's Illustrated Registry of Film Stars*; *Variety Who's Who in Show Business*; *Who's Who in Hollywood*; *The World Almanac Who's Who of Film*; *The World Encyclopedia of the Film*; *The World Film Encyclopedia*. **General:** *Co-Starring Famous Women and Alcohol*; *Debrett Goes to Hollywood*; *Famous Film Folk*; *The Great Movie Stars*; *Headline Happy*; *Hollywood Greats of the Golden Years*; *Hollywood Kids*; *Hollywood R.I.P.*; *Hollywood Tragedy*; *Hollywood's Other Women*; *Ladies in Distress*; *The MGM Stock Company*; *The MGM Years*; *The Movie Stars Story*; *Return Engagement*; *Scandal!*; *The Truth About the Movies*; *Zanies.* **Credits:** *Filmarama* (v. II); *Forty Years of Screen Credits*; *Twenty Years of Silents.* **Nostalgia:** *Whatever Became of...* (4th). **Biography/Autobiography:** *A Life on Film*; *My Story.* **Pictorial:** *The Image Makers*; *Leading Ladies*; *Silent Portraits*; *They Had Faces Then.* **Recordings:** *Hollywood on Record.* **Factoids:** *Star Stats.*

• *Periodicals* — The following periodical articles are in addition to those included in the library listings below: *Metropolitan Magazine* (June 1923); *Photoplay* (June 1924, May 1930, Nov. 1931, June 1934, Mar. 1943, May 1945); *Motion Picture Magazine* (Oct. 1925, Feb. 1926, Apr. 1930, Jan. 1931, Feb. 1932, Nov. 1936, July 1937); *Motion Picture Classic* (May 1931); *Silver Screen*

(July 1931, Dec. 1941); *Newsweek* (Aug. 22, 1936, Jan. 12, 1959, Oct. 5, 1987); *Time* (Aug. 24, 1936, Oct. 5, 1987); *Lion's Roar* (Sept. 1943, Jan. 1944, Feb. 1945); *Cosmopolitan* (Nov. 1943); *Sequence* (Summer 1948); *Saturday Review* (Jan. 17, 1959); *Films and Filming* (Feb. 1961); *Sight and Sound* (Spring 1964, Autumn 1990); *Reader's Digest* (June 1969); *Films in Review* (Feb. 1970) (Wampas Baby Stars); *Classic Film Collector* (Summer 1972); *Film Dope* (Mar. 1973, Mar. 1988); *Films Illustrated* (Aug. 1974); *Cine Revue* (Oct. 13, 1977, Mar. 13, 1980, Oct. 8, 1987); *Esquire* (Nov. 1983); *Classic Images* (Oct. 1987); *U.S. News and World Report* (Oct. 5, 1987); *EPD Film* (Nov. 1987); *Revue du Cinema* (Dec. 1987); *Premiere* (Feb. 1988); *Hollywood Studio Magazine* (Nov. 1988, Sept. 1989); *Stars* (Mar. 1990, (biofilmography), Sept. 1990).

ARCHIVAL MATERIALS
• *Caricature* — NYPL. • *Clipping File* — CAA: Suicide attempt (1951); film appearance (1922, 1961); marriage/divorce/children (1926, 1928, 1931–32, 1935, 1937, 1942, 1944–45, 1953, 1955); legal problem (1934, 1936, 1938); home (1934); illness (1936); custody fight (1936); diary (1936, 1952, 1959); article (1936, 1940, 1942, 1946, 1949, 1957–1961, 1963, 1965, 1987); injury (1938); stage appearance (1953); reviews of *My Story* (1959); review of *A Life on Film* (1971); Academy Award (1972); obituary (1987). Periodical articles: *Time* (Aug. 17, 1936); *Life* (Feb. 1980). CAFI: Academy Award (1972); article (1987); obituary (1987). CAUT: Suicide attempt (1951); diary (1936, 1950s?); article (1955, 1961, 1980); Academy Award (1972); marriage/divorce (1937, 1942). CAUU (also in McCormick Collection): Article (1967, 1987). NYMA: 1936 custody fight (1959); article (1937, 1987); talkies (1967); review of *My Story* (1959); excerpt from *Current Biography* (1961); newsphotos; obituary (1987). Periodical articles *Pic* (Jan. 7, 1941); *McCall's* (June 1945). NYMN: Marriage (1937). NYPL: PARTIAL CONTENTS: Academy Award (1972); review of *A Life on Film* (1971);

biography (1974); newsphotos; obituary (1987). Periodical articles: *Jump Cut* (no. 32); *Films and Filming* (Nov. 1987). • *Other Clipping File* — AZSU (Jimmy Starr Collection), CASF, CNDA, GBBF, MAH, MIDL, OHCL, WICF. • *Collection* — MABU: Proof sheets, reviews, galleys, drafts, correspondence and typescripts of MA's books, including *The O'Conners*, *The Incredible Charlie Carewe*, *A Life on Film*, *My Story*, etc. Typescripts for published articles, unpublished works, and unproduced TV scripts; business correspondence (1960s–1970s); fan letters; stills; film program (1926). • *Correspondence* — CAA (Hedda Hopper Collection): Letters about appearance in *Return to Peyton Place* (1961). MABU (also in Collection): 5 letters (Sumner Locke-Elliott Collection) (1963–81). NYPL (C. & L. Brown Collection): 1945–46. • *Filmography* — CAA, NYMA. • *Interview* — GBBF (Hollywood Collection): Transcript of interview for *Hollywood* (TV series). • *Legal File* — CAUT (Twentieth Century-Fox Collection): Memo (1928–29, 1946); agreement (1928); option (1928); loanout (1946). CAUW: Contract (1930, 1933, 1940); subpoena (1934–35); memo, letter (1925–42); agreement (1925, 1927, 1930, 1934, 1941); personnel, payroll record (1926–42, 1964); contract summary (1926–42); option (1926–42); document (1926, 1943); talent agreement (1925–26, 1933–34, 1940–42); loanout (1934). • *Oral History* — NYCO: Mentioned in the following interviews: Bennett Cerf, Kitty Carlisle Hart, Henry Hathaway, Elliot Nugent, Richard Quine. • *Photograph/ Still* — CAA (also in Hollywood Studio Museum Collection) (also in MGM Collection), CAPH, CAUS, CAUT (Jessen Collection) (Portrait File), CAUU, CNDA, DCG (Quigley Photographic Archives), MABU (see Collection), NYAM, NYB (Bettmann/UPI Collection) (Penguin Collection) (Springer Collection) (Underwood Collection), NYCU (Dramatic Museum Portraits), NYEH, NYMN, NYPL, NYSU, OHCL, TXU, WICF. • *Program* — CASF, MABU (see Collection). • *Press Kit* — OHCL. • *Publicity Release* — CAA: Warner (1933);

Fox (1940s). • *Reminiscence* — MISU: Recording.   • *Scrapbook* — NYAM, NYPL. • *Studio Biography* — CAA: Columbia (1936); Paramount (1946, 1957); Fox (1946, 1960s). NYMA: MGM (1948).

AUGUST, Edwin (Edwin von der Butz), 1883-1964.

Known as "The Biograph Man," Edwin August appeared in over 300 silent films including *City of Tears*, *The Lesser Evil*, *The Idol of the North* and *A Broadway Scandal*, as well as in several directed by D. W. Griffith. His career as a leading man did not fare well after the mid-1920s but he continued playing sporadic small parts until the 1940s.

PUBLISHED SOURCES

• *Books* — Credits: *Filmarama* (v. I and II); *Twenty Years of Silents*; *Who Was Who on Screen*. Encyclopedic Works: *Film Encyclopedia*; *Who's Who in Hollywood*.
• *Periodicals* — The following periodical articles are in addition to those included in the library listings below: *Photoplay* (Jan. 1914, Jan. 1915); *Motion Picture Magazine* (Mar. 1915, Dec. 1915).

ARCHIVAL MATERIALS

• *Clipping File* — CAA: Obituary (1964). NYMA (also in Photoplay Collection): Personal data summary. NYPL: Newsphotos; career (1912); article (1908, 1913-14, 1916); film review (1910s). Periodical articles: *Moving Picture Magazine* (Dec. 1912); *Motion Pictures* (June 1914). • *Other Clipping File* — MAH, NYSU, PAPL, WICF. • *Correspondence* — NYPL (C. & L. Brown Collection): 1946, undated. • *Filmography* — NYMA. • *Legal File* — CAUW: Story digest (1919); rights (1919). • *Photograph/Still* — CAA (Hollywood Studio Museum Collection), DCG (Quigley Photographic Archives), GBBF, NJFL, NYPL, TXU.

AYRES, Agnes (Agnes Hinkle), Carbondale, IL, 1898-1940.

Forever to be remembered as the object of Rudolph Valentino's fevered advances in *The Sheik* (1921), Agnes Ayres did little else of note in her screen career. She had leading roles in programmers and small roles in major films such as *The Ten Commandments*, *Son of the Sheik* and *The Affairs of Anatol*. She left films in the late 1920s but returned for some bit parts in 1936.

PUBLISHED SOURCES

• *Books* — General: *Blue Book of the Screen*; *Famous Film Folk*; *The Truth About the Movies*; *Who's Who on Screen*. Credits: *Filmarama* (v. I and II); *Twenty Years of Silents*; *Who Was Who on Screen*. Encyclopedic Works: *Film Encyclopedia*; *Filmlexicon degli Autori e delle Opere*; *Halliwell's Filmgoer's Companion*; *The Movie Makers*; *Quinlan's Illustrated Registry of Film Stars*; *Who's Who in Hollywood*; *The World Almanac Who's Who of Film*. Pictorial: *Silent Portraits*.
• *Periodicals* — The following periodical articles are in addition to those included in the library listings below: *Motion Picture Classic* (Dec. 1918, Aug. 1920, Nov. 1921); *Motion Picture Magazine* (May 1921, Nov. 1922, Jan. 1926); *Photoplay* (Aug. 1921, Nov. 1921, Nov. 1924, May 1930); *Cinema Digest* (May 22, 1933); *Films in Review* (Apr. 1986).

ARCHIVAL MATERIALS

• *Clipping File* — CAA: Film appearance (1921, 1923, 1936); divorce (1921); obituary (1940). NYMA (also in Photoplay Collection): Personal data summary; newsphotos; obituary (1940). NYPL: Comeback (1930s); newsphotos; funeral (1940); article (1916, 1923, undated); divorce (1921, 1934); nostalgia (1936); film review (1920s); obituary (1940). Periodical articles: *Photoplay* (Nov. 1918, Apr. 1920); *Photo-play Journal* (Nov. 1919). • *Other Clipping File* — AZSU (Jimmy Starr Collection), GBBF, MAH, NYSU, PAPL, WICF. • *Correspondence* — CAA (Adolph Zukor Collection): 1922. • *Filmography* — NYMA.

• *Photograph/Still* — CAA (also in Hollywood Studio Museum Collection), CAUT (Jessen Collection), DCG (Quigley Photographic Archives), GBBF, NJFL, NYAM, NYCU (Dramatic Museum Portraits), NYEH, NYPL, NYSU, TXSM, TXU, WICF. • *Scrapbook* — NYPL.

BACLANOVA, Olga, Moscow, Russia, 1896/99–1974.

A graduate of the Moscow Art Theatre, and grandly billed just as Baclanova, blonde Olga Baclanova's appearances in films such as *Docks of New York* and *Street of Sin* (with Emil Jannings) made her popular for a brief time. The end of the silent era saw her career decline, although one of her last films, *Freaks* (1932), is no doubt her best remembered. She later returned to the stage.

PUBLISHED SOURCES

• *Books* — General: *People Will Talk*; *Scream Queens*. **Encyclopedic Works:** *Film Encyclopedia*; *Filmlexicon degli Autori e delle Opere*; *Halliwell's Filmgoer's Companion*; *The Illustrated Who's Who of the Cinema*; *The Picturegoer's Who's Who and Encyclopedia of the Screen To-day*; *Quinlan's Illustrated Registry of Film Stars*; *Who's Who in Hollywood*; *Who's Who in the Theatre*; *Who's Who of the Horrors and Other Fantasy Films*; *The World Film Encyclopedia*. **Credits:** *Filmarama* (v. II); *Forty Years of Screen Credits*; *Twenty Years of Silents*; *Who Was Who on Screen*. **Pictorial:** *Silent Portraits*; *They Had Faces Then*.

• *Periodicals* — *Photoplay* (Aug. 1928); *Motion Picture Magazine* (Sept. 1928); *Midnight Marquee* (Fall 1989).

ARCHIVAL MATERIALS

• *Clipping File* — AZSU (Jimmy Starr Collection): Obituary (1974). CAA: Legal problem (1929–31); film appearance (1928, 1930); divorce/marriage/childbirth (1929–30); stage appearance (1929, 1931); obituary (1974). CAUT: Legal problem (1929); marriage/divorce

(1929); article (1929). CAUU: Obituary (1974). NYMA (also in Photoplay Collection): Obituary (1974). NYPL: Stage appearance (1932–35); article (1929, 1941, undated); newsphotos; divorce; biography; obituary (1974). • *Other Clipping Files* — MIDL, OHCL, PAPL, WICF. • *Filmography* — NYMA. • *Interview* — CAUU (R. Lamparski Collection). • *Oral History* — NYCO: Mentioned in: Joshua Logan interview. • *Photograph/Still* — CAA (also in Hollywood Studio Museum Collection) (also in MGM Collection), CAFA, CNDA, DCG, GBBF, NJPT, NYCU (Dramatic Museum Portraits), NYEH, NYPL, NYSU, OHCL, PAPL, TXU (A. Davis Collection), WICF. • *Play Program* — NYPL. • *Scrapbook* — NYPL. • *Studio Biography* — NYMA: Photoplay.

BAGGOTT (sometimes Baggot), King, St. Louis, MO, 1874–1948.

From about 1909, King Baggott was a matinee idol who appeared in over 200 silent films and was called "The Most Photographed Man in the World." (He once played ten parts in a single film.) Among his films were *The Scarlet Letter*, *Ivanhoe* and *Dr. Jekyll and Mr. Hyde*, and he remained active into the 1940s albeit in bit and extra parts. He also directed.

PUBLISHED SOURCES

• *Books* — General: *Gentlemen to the Rescue*; *Life Stories of the Movie Stars*; *The Truth About the Movies*; *Who's Who on the Screen*. **Credits:** *Filmarama* (v. I and II); *Forty Years of Screen Credits*; *Twenty Years of Silents*; *Who Was Who on Screen*. **Encyclopedic Works:** *Film Encyclopedia*; *Filmlexicon degli Autori e delle Opere*; *Halliwell's Filmgoer's Companion*; *The Illustrated Who's Who of the Cinema*; *The Picturegoer's Who's Who and Encyclopedia of the Screen To-day*; *Who's Who in Hollywood*; *The World Almanac Who's Who of Film*. **Pictorial:** *Silent Portraits*.

• *Periodicals* — The following periodical articles are in addition to that included in the library listings below: *Photoplay* (Nov. 1913, Mar. 1919, July 1924); *Blue Book Magazine* (July 1914); *Moving Picture World* (Sept. 5, 1914); *Picture Play Weekly* (Aug. 28, 1915); *Filmplay Journal* (Oct. 1915); *Moving Picture Weekly* (Apr. 15, 1916); *Motion Picture Classic* (Oct. 1921); *Film Dope* (Mar. 1973).

ARCHIVAL MATERIALS

• *Clipping File* — CAA: Film appearance (1921–23); obituary (1948). NYMA: Article (1913); newsphotos; stage appearance; film appearance (1910s, 1920s); divorce (1930s). Periodical article: *Photoplay* (Oct. 1912). • *Other Clipping File* — CNDA, GBBF, NYSU, PAPL, WICF. • *Filmography* — CAA: Silent films only. • *Photograph/Still* — CAA (also in Hollywood Studio Museum Collection) (also in MGM Collection), DCG (Quigley Photographic Archives), GBBF, NJFL, NYEH, NYPL, NYSU, OHCL, WICF. • *Scrapbook* — NYPL. • *Studio Biography* — NYMA: Photoplay.

BAIRD, Leah, Chicago, IL, 1883/91–1971.

Stage-trained Leah Baird starred for studios such as Vitagraph in New York as early as 1909, and played a role in Carl Laemmle's first production, *Hiawatha*. The major part of her career ended before 1920 but she made sporadic appearances throughout the 1920s and returned for some supporting roles in the 1940s. Her films included *When Husbands Deceive*, *The Volcano*, *Neptune's Daughter*, *The Primrose Path* and *Souls in Bondage*.

PUBLISHED SOURCES

• *Books* — **General:** *The Big V*; *First One Hundred Noted Men and Women of the Screen*; *Life Stories of the Movie Stars*; *Who's Who on the Screen*. **Credits:** *Filmarama* (v. I and II); *Twenty Years of Silents*; *Who Was Who on Screen*. **Encyclopedic Works:** *Film Encyclopedia*; *Filmlexicon degli Autori e delle Opere*;

Who's Who in Hollywood. **Pictorial:** *Silent Portraits*.

• *Periodicals* — The following periodical articles are in addition to those included in the library listings below: *Motion Picture Magazine* (Jan. 1915); *Movie Pictorial* (Dec. 1915); *Moving Picture Weekly* (Sept. 30, 1916); *Motion Picture Classic* (Sept. 1917); *Photoplay* (Mar. 1924); *Classic Images* (July 1991).

ARCHIVAL MATERIALS

• *Clipping File* — CAA: Film appearance (1922–23, 1950); obituary (1971). CAUT: 50th wedding anniversary (1964). CAUU: Obituary (1971). NYMA: Article (1910s, 1915, 1917); returns to films (1925); film appearances (1910s, 1920s); obituary (1971). Periodical articles: *Photoplay* (Dec. 1913); *Classic Images* (June 1991). NYPL: Article (1913–14, 1916–18, 1920, 1924, undated); film review (1910s, 1920s); newsphotos. Periodical articles: *Motion Picture Story Magazine* (Sept. 1912); *Moving Picture World* (July 4, 1913); *Green Book Magazine* (Feb. 1915); *Photo-play Journal* (Nov. 1919, Jan. 1920); *Motion Picture Magazine* (Dec. 1919). • *Other Clipping File* — GBBF, MAH, NYSU, WICF. • *Correspondence* — CAA (Selig Collection): 1913. • *Legal File* — CAUW: Option (1941–48); contract (1941–43, 1945–46, 1948); letter, memo (1941–48); release (1945); story digest (1912–13, 1915, 1930); rights (1912–13, 1915, 1930); manuscript (1930). • *Photograph/Still* — CAA (also in Hollywood Studio Museum Collection), CAUT (Jessen Collection), DCG (Quigley Photographic Archives), GBBF, NJFL, NYPL, NYSU, OHCL, TXU, WICF. • *Publicity Release* — NYMA: Western Photoplays (1918). • *Studio Biography* — NYMA: Photoplay.

BAKEWELL, William, Los Angeles, CA, 1908–1993.

Entering films as a juvenile lead about 1926, William Bakewell experienced the highpoints of his 100-plus film career in 1929 with Douglas Fairbanks's *The Iron Mask* and the next year with *All Quiet on the Western Front*. He also appeared in D. W. Griffith's *The Battle of the Sexes*, *West Point*, *Annapolis* and *Harold Teen*. In talkies, he was a leading man in "B" movies and a supporting actor in major films like *Gone with the Wind* and *Seven Sinners*. He later appeared in numerous television character roles.

PUBLISHED SOURCES

• *Books—General:* *Broken Silence*. **Credits:** *Filmarama* (v. II); *Forty Years of Screen Credits*; *Twenty Years of Silents*. **Encyclopedic Works:** *Film Encyclopedia*; *Filmlexicon degli Autori e delle Opere*; *Halliwell's Filmgoer's Companion*; *The Movie Makers*; *The Picturegoer's Who's Who and Encyclopedia of the Screen To-day*; *Who's Who in Hollywood*; *The World Film Encyclopedia*. **Biography/Autobiography:** *Hollywood Be Thy Name*. **Pictorial:** *Silent Portraits*.

• *Periodicals*—The following periodical articles are in addition to those included in the library listings below: *Motion Picture Classic* (Jan. 1929, Mar. 1930, Mar. 1931); *Photoplay* (Dec. 1929); *Silver Screen* (May 1931, Apr. 1933); *Films in Review* (Mar.-Apr. 1991).

ARCHIVAL MATERIALS

• *Clipping File*—CAA: Marriage (1946, 1954); nostalgia (1969, 1980); obituary (1993). Periodical article: *Filmfax* (Mar. 1990). NYMA (also in Photoplay Collection). Periodical article: *Classic Images* (Nov. 1989). NYPL: Newsphotos; film appearance (1932, undated); article (1930, undated). Periodical articles: *Films in Review* (Mar. 1980, Nov.-Dec. 1990). • *Other Clipping File*—GBBF, MAH, OHCL, PAPL, WICF. • *Filmography*—CAA. • *Legal File*—CAUW: Contract summary (1931); letter, memo (1929); talent agreement (1929); personnel, payroll record (1931, 1951-66); contract (1947). • *Photograph/ Still*—CAA (also in Hollywood Studio Museum Collection) (also in MGM Collection), DCG (Quigley Photographic Archives), GBBF, NJPT, NYAM, NYEH, NYPL, NYSU, OHCL, TXU, WICF. • *Privately Printed Materials*— *The Silent Stars Speak*. AMPAS, 1979. • *Scrapbook*—NYPL. • *Studio Biography*—CAA: RKO (1932). NYMA: Photoplay.

BALLIN, Mabel (Mabel Croft), Philadelphia, PA, 1885/87–1958.

Wife of director Hugo Ballin, and his sometime star, Mabel Ballin appeared from 1917 in films like *Vanity Fair*, *Jane Eyre* and *East Lynne* for Goldwyn, Triangle and other studios. She also supported Tom Mix in *Riders of the Purple Sage* and *The Beauty and the Bad Man*. She retired from acting in 1925.

PUBLISHED SOURCES

• *Books—General:* *Blue Book of the Screen*; *Famous Film Folk*. **Credits:** *Filmarama* (v. I and II); *Twenty Years of Silents*; *Who Was Who on Screen*. **Encyclopedic Works:** *Film Encyclopedia*; *Filmlexicon degli Autori e delle Opere*; *Who's Who in Hollywood*. **Pictorial:** *Silent Portrait*.

• *Periodicals*—The following periodical articles are in addition to that included in the library listings below: *Motion Picture Magazine* (June 1921, Nov. 1922, Nov. 1926); *Motion Picture Classic* (Oct. 1921); *Photoplay* (Apr. 1922); *Screen World* (no. 10, 1959); *Classic Images* (Oct. 1989).

ARCHIVAL MATERIALS

• *Clipping File*—CAA: Newsphotos; film appearance (1922); home (1980); obituary (1958). NYMA: Signs with Vitagraph; film appearance (1920). Periodical article: *Classic Images* (Mar. 1992). NYPL: Newsphotos (numerous); career (1922); film appearance (1919, 1921); builds home (1917); obituary (1958). • *Other Clipping File*—CAUS (See Collection), GBBF, MIDL, NYSU, PAPL, WICF. • *Collection*—CAUS (Hugo and Mabel Ballin Collection): Scrapbooks, correspondence, photographs, clippings. • *Correspondence*—

CAHL: 1922. CAUS (See Collection). NYMA (Photoplay Collection): 1910s?. • *Photograph/Still* — CAA (also in Hollywood Studio Museum Collection) (also in MGM Collection), CAUS (see Collection), CAUT (Jessen Collection), CNDA, DCG (Quigley Photographic Archives), GBBF, NJFL, NYCU (Dramatic Museum Portraits), NYPL, NYSU, OHCL, TXU, WICF. • *Scrapbook* — CAUS (see Collection). • *Studio Biography* — NYMA: Photoplay.

BANCROFT, George, Philadelphia, PA, 1882-1956.

In films since the early 1920s, 6'2″ George Bancroft hit his film stride as a gangster in Josef von Sternberg's 1927 success *Underworld*. He portrayed similar characters in *Docks of New York* and *The Drag Net*. Although his career as a leading man peaked in the early 1930s, he continued to appear in character roles in many films through 1942.

PUBLISHED SOURCES

• *Books* — **General:** *Eighty Silent Film Stars*; *Hollywood Album 2*; *Immortals of the Screen*; *More Character People*; *Screen Personalities*; *Twinkle Twinkle Movie Star*; *The Versatiles*; *The Western* (Eyles). **Credits:** *Filmarama* (v. II); *Forty Years of Screen Credits*; *Twenty Years of Silents*; *Who Was Who on Screen*. **Encyclopedic Works:** *A Companion to the Movies*; *Film Encyclopedia*; *Filmlexicon degli Autori e delle Opere*; *Halliwell's Filmgoer's Companion*; *Hollywood Character Actors*; *The Illustrated Who's Who of the Cinema*; *The Movie Makers*; *The Picturegoer's Who's Who and Encyclopedia of the Screen To-day*; *Quinlan's Illustrated Registry of Film Stars*; *Who's Who in Hollywood*; *The World Almanac Who's Who of Film*; *The World Encyclopedia of the Film*; *The World Film Encyclopedia*. **Pictorial:** *Silent Portraits*.

• *Periodicals* — The following periodical articles are in addition to those included in the library listings below: *Motion Picture Classic* (Jan. 1926); *Mo-* *tion Picture Magazine* (Nov. 1927, Dec. 1928, Mar. 1930, Dec. 1930); *Photoplay* (Oct. 1930, Sept. 1931); *Silver Screen* (Apr. 1931); *Cinema Digest* (June 13, 1932); *Screen Book* (Aug. 1937); *Newsweek* (Oct. 15, 1956); *Film Dope* (Mar. 1973) (filmography).

ARCHIVAL MATERIALS

• *Clipping File* — CAA: Film appearance (1927); obituary (1956). Periodical article: *American Classic Screen* (Nov./Dec. 1982). CAUT: Obituary (1956). NYMA: Periodical article: *Classic Images* (Dec. 1985). NYMN: Newsphotos; comeback; divorce (1934, 1936, undated); obituary (1956). NYPL: Legal problem (1934, undated); article (1932, 1981, undated); newsphotos; film appearance (1933-34, undated); stage appearance (1911, 1913-15, 1918, 1933, 1935); comeback (1930s); obituary (1956). • *Other Clipping File* — GBBF, MAH, MIDL, OHCL, PAPL, WICF. • *Filmography* — CAA. • *Legal File* — CAUW: Contract (1938); talent agreement (1939). • *Oral History* — NYCO: Mentioned in the following interviews: John Cromwell, Andy Devine, August Heckscher, Helen Kirkpatrick, Morris Strauss. • *Photograph/Still* — AZSU (Jimmy Starr Collection), CAA (also in Hollywood Studio Museum Collection), CAUS, CAUT (Jessen Collection), CAUU, CNDA, DCG (Quigley Photographic Archives), GBBF, MIDL, NJPT, NYAM, NYB (Bettmann/UPI Collection), NYCU (Dramatic Museum Portraits), NYEH, NYMN, NYPL, NYSU, OHCL, TXU, WICF. • *Scrapbook* — NJPT (Yeandle Collection), NYPL. • *Studio Biography* — CAA: Columbia (1936); Paramount (1942). NYPL: Paramount (1931).

BANKY, Vilma (Vilma Baulsy, Konsics or Lonchit), 1898/1904-1991.

Blonde and beauteous Vilma Banky became a Goldwyn star in the mid-1920s, being teamed several times with Ronald Colman and with Rudolph Valentino (q.v.) in *The Eagle* and *The*

Son of the Sheik. Her first American film was *The Dark Angel* (1925); she had appeared previously in the German and Hungarian cinema. Her accent was not suitable for the talkies and she settled into married life with Rod La Rocque (q.v.).

PUBLISHED SOURCES

• *Books*—Bibliography: *The Idols of Silence.* General: *Alice in Movieland; Classics of the Silent Screen; Hollywood's Great Love Teams; The Movie Stars Story; Venus in Hollywood.* Credits: *Filmarama* (v. II); *Twenty Years of Silents.* Encyclopedic Works: *Film Encyclopedia; Filmlexicon degli Autori e delle Opère; Halliwell's Filmgoer's Companion; The Illustrated Who's Who of the Cinema; International Dictionary of Films and Filmmakers* (v. 3); *The Movie Makers; The Picturegoer's Who's Who and Encyclopedia of the Screen To-day; Quinlan's Illustrated Registry of Film Stars; Variety Who's Who in Show Business; Who's Who in Hollywood; The World Almanac Who's Who of Film; The World Encyclopedia of the Film; The World Film Encyclopedia.* Nostalgia: *Whatever Became of...* (1st, 10th). Pictorial: *Silent Portraits; They Had Faces Then.* Factoids: *Star Stats.*

• *Periodicals*—The following periodical articles are in addition to those included in the library listings below: *Motion Picture Magazine* (Nov. 1925, Apr. 1928); *Motion Picture Classic* (Dec. 1925, Jan. 1927, Aug. 1929); *Photoplay* (Dec. 1925, Apr. 1926, Nov. 1926, Apr. 1927, Mar. 1928, July 1932); *Pictures and Picturegoer* (May 1929); *Films in Review* (May 1974, Aug.-Sept. 1977, Feb. 1978).

ARCHIVAL MATERIALS

• *Clipping File*—CAA: Film appearance (1927-28, 1930, 1932); stage appearance (1930); marriage (1927, 1930); Goldwyn contract (1929); citizenship (1927, 1929); legal problem (1927); article (1925, 1950, 1961, 1984); retires from films (1930); injury (1926); returns to Hungary (1928); newsphotos; home (1970). Periodical article: *World of Yesterday* (Aug. 1979). CAFI: Newsphotos (numerous);

tribute (1984); nostalgia (1976). CAUT: Article (1920s, 1984); marriage (1927); film appearance (1928, 1930); legal problem (1920s); return from trip (1928); injury (1928); retires from films (1930); stage appearance (1930); Goldwyn contract (1929); citizenship (1929); newsphotos. NYMA: Nostalgia; newsphotos; obituary (1991). NYMN: Newsphotos; obituary (1991). NYPL: Newsphotos; engagement/marriage (1927); article (1926, 1928, undated); film appearance (1933); film review (1920s); dropped by Goldwyn (1930); signed by Laemmle (1932); nostalgia. Periodical articles: *Photoplay* (undated); *Screen Secrets Magazine* (undated); *Films in Review* (Feb. 1973); *Classic Images* (Oct. 1992). • *Other Clipping File*—AZSU (Jimmy Starr Collection), GBBF, MAH, NYSU, OHCL, PAPL, TXU, WICF. • *Correspondence*—CAA (Hedda Hopper Collection): Letter from HH to a friend about the wedding of VB and Rod LaRocque (1927). • *Oral History*—NYCO: Mentioned in: Conrad Nagel interview. • *Photograph/Still*—CAA (also in Hollywood Studio Museum Collection) (also in MGM Collection), CAOC (Kiesling Collection), CAUS, CAUT (Portrait File), CAUU, CNDA, DCG (Quigley Photographic Archives), GBBF, NYAM, NYB (Bettmann/UPI Collection) (Springer Collection) (Underwood Collection), NYCU (Dramatic Museum Portraits) (Palmer Collection), NYEH, NYMN, NYPL, NYSU, OHCL, TNUT (Clarence Brown Collection), TXSM, TXU, WICF. • *Scrapbook*—NYPL, TNUT (Clarence Brown Collection). • *Studio Biography*—AZSU (Jimmy Starr Collection).

BARA, Theda (Theodosia Goodman), Cincinnati, Ohio, 1885/90-1955.

Black-eyed Theda Bara became the personification of female evil after her role as the enchantress in *A Fool There Was* (1914). The film brought the word "vampire" into fashionable usage (shortened to "vamp") to describe women who made helpless slaves of men. She was "bad" in films like *The Tiger Woman, Destruction, Sin, The Devil's Daughter* and *The Serpent*, but she also essayed several sympathetic roles. By 1919, after 39 films, her vogue was over and only two more appearances followed in the 1920s, one in a self-parodying comedy short. An effort to bring her screen persona to Broadway in *The Blue Flame* (1920) was unsuccessful.

PUBLISHED SOURCES

• *Books*—Bibliography: *The Idols of Silence.* • *Filmography*—*Hollywood on the Palisades.* **General:** *Blue Book of the Screen; The Celluloid Sacrifice; Classics of the Silent Screen; Close Ups; Early American Cinema; Famous Film Folk; Fifty Super Stars; The Fox Girls; From Hollywood; Gentlemen to the Rescue; The Great Movie Stars: the Golden Years; History of the American Cinema* (v. 3); *Hollywood Album; Hollywood Hall of Fame; Immortals of the Screen; Ladies in Distress; Life Stories of the Movie Stars; Love Goddesses of the Movies; Movie Star; The Movie Stars; The Movie Stars Story; Sex Goddesses of the Silent Screen; Spellbound in Darkness; The Stars* (Schickel); *The Stars Appear; Virgins, Vamps and Flappers; Wicked Women of the Screen.* **Credits:** *Filmarama* (v. I and II); *Twenty Years of Silents; Who Was Who on Screen.* **Encyclopedic Works:** *A Biographical Dictionary of Film; Film Encyclopedia; Filmlexicon degli Autori e delle Opere; Halliwell's Filmgoer's Companion; The Illustrated Encyclopedia of the World's Great Movie Stars and Their Films; The Illustrated Who's Who of the Cinema; International Dictionary of Films and Filmmakers* (v. 3); *The International Encyclopedia of Film; The Movie Makers; Notable American Women: the Modern Period; The Oxford Companion to Film; Quinlan's Illustrated Registry of Film Stars; Who's Who in Hollywood; The World Almanac Who's Who of Film; The World Encyclopedia of the Film.* **Pictorial:** *The Image Makers; Leading Ladies; Silent Portraits.* **Thesis:** *Theda Bara and the Vamp Phenomenon, 1915–1920.* **Factoids:** *Star Stats.*

• *Periodicals*—The following periodical articles are in addition to those included in the library listings below: *Photoplay* (Sept. 1915, May 1917, Oct. 1917, May 1918, June 1920, Feb. 1923, Aug. 1929); *Green Book* (Feb. 1916); *Motion Picture Magazine* (Feb. 1916, July-Aug. 1916, Apr. 1917, Nov. 1922, June 1928); *Motion Picture Classic* (Apr. 1916, Oct. 1916, Apr. 1917, Dec. 1917, Sept. 1918, Feb. 1919, Dec. 1920-Jan. 1921); *Theatre* (Oct. 1918); *Forum* (June-July 1919); *Picture Show* (Feb. 7, 1920); *Shadowland* (Mar.-Apr. 1920); *Life* (Apr. 1, 1920); *American Magazine* (Sept. 1920); *Cue* (Aug. 19, 1936); *Harper's Bazaar* (Sept. 1948); *Newsweek* (Apr. 18, 1955); *Time* (Apr. 18, 1955); *Cinema* (Beverly Hills) (July 1966); *Films in Review* (Aug.-Sept. 1968); *Cine Revue* (July 30, 1981) (filmography); *Classic Images* (May 1986).

ARCHIVAL MATERIALS

• *Clipping File*—CAA: Newsphotos; film appearance (1924–25); article (1925, 1931, 1933–34, 1950–51); illness (1925, 1954–55); stage appearance (1929); film vampires (1934); nostalgia (1953, 1961); honor (1953); estate (1955); obituary (1955). Periodical articles: *Life* (Dec. 1958); *Films in Review* (May 1968) (filmography); *Classic Film Collector* (Fall 1970); *Horizon* (Jan. 1981). CAUT: Newsphotos; honor (1953); stage appearance (1929); illness (1955); estate (1955); obituary (1955). CAUU: Article (1950). Periodical article: *Classic Film Collector* (Fall 1970). NYMA: Review of *Theda Bara and the Frontier Rabbi* (musical) (1992); newsphotos; marriage (1921); leaves Fox (1919); returns to films (1924–25); legal problem (1919); stage appearance (1920, 1929, 1931, 1934); vampires (1936); article (1915, 1933, 1939); film appearance (1922); name legalized; production company (1923); obituary (1955). Periodical articles: *Theatre* (Nov. 1915); *Screen Weekly* (Aug. 6, 1932); *New Movie Magazine* (Mar. 1933); *New Yorker* (Oct. 18, 1952); *Classic Film Collector* (Fall 1970). NYMN: Newsphotos; obituary (1955). NYPL: *The Great Vampire* (film); stage appearance (1920); article (undated); comeback; sister (1933); obituary (1955). Periodical article: *Films in Review* (May 1968). • *Other Clipping File*—AZSU (Jimmy Starr Collection), CAUB, CNDA, GBBF, MAH, MIDL, NYSU, OHCI, OHCL, OHSU, PAPL, WICF. • *Correspondence*—CAA (Hedda Hopper Collection): 2 letters from TB (1948); letter about TB (1965). NYMA (Photoplay Collection): 1925. NYPL (C. & L. Brown Collection): 1939. • *Filmography*—CAA, NYMA. • *Oral History*—NYCO: Mentioned in the following interviews: Frances Marion, Nita Naldi, David Selznick, Carl Van Vechten. • *Photograph/Still*—CAA (also in Hollywood Studio Museum Collection), CAHL, CALM, CAPH, CASF, CAUT (Jessen Collection), CAUU, CNDA, DCG (Quigley Photographic Archives), GBBF, NJFL, NYB (Penguin Collection) (Springer Collection) (Underwood Collection), NYCU (Dramatic Museum Portraits), NYEH, NYMN, NYPL, NYSU, OHCL, TXU, WICF. • *Program*—NYMA (Film Study Center Special Collection): *Cleopatra* (film) (1917). • *Scrapbook*—NYPL (also in R. Locke collection).

BARNES, T(homas) Roy, England, 1880–1937.

A leading man in comedies and other films from 1920, T. Roy Barnes had roles in *Adam and Eva, Ladies of Leisure, Souls for Sale* and *The Go-Getter*. He turned to supporting roles in the latter 1920s and continued playing small parts in talkies, one notable appearance being in W. C. Fields's *It's a Gift* (1934).

PUBLISHED SOURCES
• *Books*—General: *The Truth About the Movies; Who's Who on the Screen.* Credits: *British Film Actors' Credits; Filmarama* (v. II); *Forty Years of Screen Credits; Twenty Years of Silents; Who Was Who on Screen.* Encyclopedic Works: *Film Encyclopedia; The Picturegoer's Who's Who and Encyclopedia of the Screen To-day; Who's Who in Hollywood.*

• *Periodicals*—*Motion Picture Classic* (May 1922); *Photoplay* (Oct. 1922).

ARCHIVAL MATERIALS
• *Clipping File*—NYMA (also in Photoplay Collection): Personal data summary. NYPL: Newsphotos; article (1913, undated); stage appearance (1926); film appearance; film reviews (1920s); obituary (1937). • *Other Clipping File*—GBBF, MAH, MIDL, OHCL. • *Legal File*—CAUW: Talent agreement (1929, 1934); personnel, pay record (1934). NYPL: Contract (1911, 1914–15). • *Photograph/Still*—CAA (also in Hollywood Studio Museum Collection), CAUU, DCG (Quigley Photographic Archives), NYPL, NYSU, OHCL, TXU. • *Scrapbook*—NYPL.

BARRISCALE, Bessie, New York, NY, ca. 1884–1965.

Stage actress Bessie Barriscale became a silent star with the Ince Studio about 1914. Among the many films in which she appeared until 1920 were *Brewster's Millions, Not My Sister, Tangled Threads, Rose of the Rancho* and *Girl of the Golden West*. After her screen career declined she turned to vaudeville.

PUBLISHED SOURCES
• *Books*—General: *First One Hundred Noted Men and Women of the Screen; Life Stories of the Movie Stars; Who's Who on the Screen.* Credits: *Filmarama* (v. I and II); *Twenty Years of Silents; Who Was Who on Screen.* Encyclopedic Works: *Film Encyclopedia; Filmlexicon degli Autori e delle Opere; Who's Who in Hollywood; Women Who Make Movies.* Pictorial: *Silent Portraits.*

• *Periodicals*—The following periodical articles are in addition to that included in the library listings below: *Motion Picture Magazine* (June 1915, Sept. 1915, Jan. 1916, Sept. 1916, Jan. 1919, Mar. 1920); *Motion Picture Classic* (Sept. 1917); *Photoplay* (Mar. 1918); *Silent Picture* (Spring 1972).

ARCHIVAL MATERIALS
• *Clipping File*—CAA: Film appear-

ance (1919); stage appearance (1921); obituary (1965). Periodical article: *Films in Review* (June-July 1961). NYMA: Comeback (1933); own production company (1917); article (undated); contract (1918); obituary (1965). NYPL: Newsphotos; obituary (1965). • *Other Clipping File*—GBBF, MAH, OHCL, PAPL, WICF. • *Photograph/Still*—CAA (also in Hollywood Studio Museum Collection), CAHL, CAUT (Jessen Collection), CAUU, DCG (Quigley Photographic Archives), GBBF, NYPL, NYSU, OHCL, WICF. • *Play Program*—CAHL: 1913. NYPL. • *Scrapbook*—NYPL (also in R. Locke Collection). • *Studio Biography*—NYMA: Ince (1915); Photoplay.

BARRY, Viola (later known as Peggy Pearce), 1894–1964.

From 1913 pretty Viola Barry appeared in D.W. Griffith films and many others including a version of *The Sea Wolf* (1918). She was one of the screen's earliest "vamps" and also was seen in numerous one- and two-reel comedies as well as Westerns later on in her fairly brief career. Most of her film appearances were made under the name of Peggy Pearce.

PUBLISHED SOURCES

• *Books*—Credits: *Filmarama* (v. I); *Who Was Who on Screen*. **Encyclopedic Works:** *Who's Who in Hollywood*.

ARCHIVAL MATERIALS

• *Clipping File*—CAA: Obituary (1964). CAUT: Obituary (1964). NYMA: Obituary (1964). NYPL: Film appearance (1916); newsphotos; obituary (1964). • *Legal File*—CAHL: Affidavit (1913). • *Photograph/Still*—CAA (under Peggy Pearce) (also Hollywood Studio Museum Collection), CAUT (Jessen Collection), NYPL.

BARRYMORE, John (family name was originally Blythe), Philadelphia, PA, 1882–1942.

The youngest scion of a distin-guished stage family, John Barrymore had a fabled theatrical career and a film career which began in 1914. His acclaimed Broadway *Hamlet* and films such as *Beau Brummell, Doctor Jekyll and Mr. Hyde, Sherlock Holmes* and *Don Juan* came in the 1920s. Other notable films followed in the 1930s, including *Grand Hotel, Counsellor at Law* and *Dinner at Eight*. Finally his roles began to mirror his rapidly deteriorating personal life and his last were mere parodies of his once distinguished persona.

PUBLISHED SOURCES

• *Books*—**Encyclopedic Works:** *A Biographical Dictionary of Film*; *A Companion to the Movies*; *A Concise Encyclopedia of the Theatre*; *The Encyclopedia of World Theater*; *The Entertainers*; *Famous Actors and Actresses on the American Stage*; *Film Encyclopedia*; *Filmlexicon degli Autori e delle Opere*; *Halliwell's Filmgoer's Companion*; *The Illustrated Encyclopedia of the World's Great Movie Stars and Their Films*; *The Illustrated Who's Who of the Cinema*; *International Dictionary of Films and Filmmakers* (v. 3); *The International Encyclopedia of Film*; *The Movie Makers*; *National Cyclopedia of American Biography* (1981); *The Oxford Companion to Film*; *The Oxford Companion to the Theatre*; *The Picturegoer's Who's Who and Encyclopedia of the Screen To-day*; *Quinlan's Illustrated Registry of Film Stars*; *Who Was Who in the Theatre*; *Who's Who in Hollywood*; *Who's Who of the Horrors and Other Fantasy Films*; *The World Almanac Who's Who of Film*; *The World Encyclopedia of the Film*; *The World Film Encyclopedia*. **General:** *Actorviews*; *America*; *Cads and Cavaliers*; *Classics of the Silent Screen*; *Close Ups*; *Dale Carnegie's Biographical Roundup*; *Debrett Goes to Hollywood*; *Doug and Mary and Others*; *Las Estrellas* (v. 5); *The Faces of Hollywood*; *Famous Film Folk*; *Famous Stars of Filmdom (Men)*; *From Hollywood*; *Gentlemen to the Rescue*; *Great Lovers of the Movies*; *The Great Movie Stars*; *Great Stars of Hollywood's Golden Age*; *Holly-*

wood (Kanin); *Hollywood Album*; *Hollywood Greats of the Golden Years*; *Hollywood Hall of Fame*; *The Hollywood Reporter Star Profiles*; *The Hollywood Style*; *I Love You, Clark Gable, Etc.*; *Immortals of the Screen*; *The Intimate Sex Lives of Famous People*; *Kings of Tragedy*; *The Matinee Idols*; *The MGM Stock Company*; *More Memorable Americans, 1750-1950*; *The Movie Stars Story*; *The National Society of Film Critics on the Movie Star*; *Personal Glimpses of Famous Folks*; *Popular Men of the Screen*; *Reference Point*; *Screen Personalities*; *Sherlock Holmes on the Screen*; *The Stars* (Schickel); *Then Came Each Actor*; *Tribute to John Barrymore*; *Twinkle, Twinkle, Movie Star*; *Who's Who on the Screen*; *Zanies*. **Credits:** *Filmarama* (v. I and II); *Forty Years of Screen Credits*; *Twenty Years of Silents*. **Biography/Autobiography:** *All My Sins Remembered*; *The Barrymores* (Alpert); *The Barrymores* (Kotsilibas-Davis); *A Child of the Century*; *Confessions of an Actor*; *Damned in Paradise*; *Good Night, Sweet Prince*; *Great Times, Good Times*; *The House of Barrymore*; *John Barrymore* (Power-Waters); *Minutes of the Last Meeting*; *Too Much, Too Soon*; *We Barrymores*; *We Three*. **Films:** *The Films of John Barrymore*. **Thesis:** *The Film Acting of John Barrymore*. **Pictorial:** *Great Stars of the American Stage*; *The Image Makers*; *Leading Men*; *Silent Portraits*. **Recordings:** *Hollywood on Record*. **Factoids:** *Star Stats*.

• *Periodicals* — The following periodical articles are in addition to those included in the library listings below: *Cosmopolitan* (Jan. 1902); *Green Book Album* (Mar. 1909, Nov. 1910); *Theatre* (June 1914, July 1916, Sept. 1919, June 1920); *Moving Picture World* (Dec. 5, 1914); *Everybody's Magazine* (July 1916, Aug. 1919, June 1920); *Photoplay* (Feb. 1919, June-July 1920, Nov. 1920, June 1924, Aug. 1925, Dec. 1926, Aug. 1928, Feb. 1929, July 1930, Jan. 1931, Mar. 1931, Aug. 1933, Feb. 1934, May 1934, Apr. 1936, Mar. 1938, June 1940); *American Magazine* (June 1919); *New Republic* (Mar. 24, 1920, Dec. 6, 1922, Sept. 14, 1927, Jan. 28, 1991); *Picture Play Magazine* (Apr. 1920); *The Nation* (Nov. 17, 1920); *Ladies' Home Journal* (Aug. 1922, Oct.-Nov. 1925, Jan.-Feb. 1926, July 1927, Jan. 1928); *Drama* (Mar. 1923); *Theatre Arts Magazine* (Apr. 1923, Jan. 1930, June 1954); *Motion Picture Magazine* (Aug. 1925, July 1934, Apr. 1937); *World's Work* (Sept. 1925); *Motion Picture Classic* (Apr. 1926, Sept. 1927, Feb. 1928, Apr. 1928, Nov. 1930, Mar. 1931); *Collier's* (Feb. 16, 1929); *Woman's Home Companion* (Apr. 1929); *Commonweal* (Apr. 9, 1930, Feb. 16, 1940); *Vanity Fair* (Sept. 1930); *Fortune* (Oct. 1930); *Movie Classic* (Feb. 1932); *Silver Screen* (Oct. 1932); *Cinema Digest* (Jan. 9, 1933, Apr. 7, 1933, May 8, 1933); *Literary Digest* (Nov. 21, 1936); *Newsweek* (June 26, 1937, Feb. 12, 1940, June 8, 1942, Jan. 10, 1944, Aug. 7, 1950, Apr. 5, 1954, Apr. 8, 1957, May 20, 1991); *Time* (Nov. 6, 1939, June 8, 1942, Apr. 5, 1954); *Life* (Feb. 12, 1940, Sept. 30, 1940, Mar. 9, 1942); *Movies and the People Who Make Them* (no. 2, 1940); *Stage* (Jan. 1941); *Lion's Roar* (Jan. 1944); *Irish Monthly* (May 1948); *Coronet* (Sept. 1951); *American Mercury* (Aug. 1957); *Players Showcase* (Spring 1965); *Film Fan Monthly* (July-Aug. 1966); *Films in Review* (May 1970, Dec. 1985); *Focus on Film* (Winter 1972); *Film Dope* (Mar. 1973); *People* (Aug. 26, 1974); *Classic Images* (June-July 1982); *Atlantic Monthly* (Jan. 1983); *New York* (Mar. 7, 1983); *Vogue* (July 1989); *New Theatre Quarterly* (Aug. 1991); *American Heritage* (Dec. 1991); *Hollywood Studio Magazine* (May 1992).

MEDIA

Grace Kelly, Will Rogers, John Barrymore (video); *Heroes* (video); *Irving Berlin, John Barrymore, Rudolph Valentino* (video); *John Barrymore: from Matinee Idol to Buffoon* (video).

ARCHIVAL MATERIALS

• *Caricature* — NYMN, NYPL. • *Clipping File* — CAA: Article (1935, 1951, 1960, 1962, 1982, 1990, 1992); review of *The House of Barrymore* (1990); spirit (1991); newsphotos; marriage/divorce/children (1926, 1928-30, 1932, 1935-37,

1939-40); home (1927, 1938, 1950, 1972-74, 1978; fight (1928, 1941); yacht (1930, 1935, 1937, 1944); illness (1930-31, 1934, 1936, 1938-39, 1941); stage appearance (1931, 1940); taxes (1933, 1937, 1940); Elaine Barrie (1935-36, 1940, 1964); missing papers (1936); legal problem (1936); debts (1940); estate (1942); sale of effects (1943); reviews of *Good Night, Sweet Prince* (1944); serialization of *Good Night, Sweet Prince*; biographical film (1954); film rights (1959); films (1970); reburial (1980); reviews of *The Barrymores* (Kotsilibas-Davis) (1981); review of *Ned and Jack* (play) (1981); postage stamp (1982); centenary (1982); *Hamlet* (play) (1982); obituary (1942). Periodical articles: *Green Book Magazine* (Jan. 1915); *Ladies' Home Journal* (Dec. 1925); *Liberty* (Mar. 2, 1929, July 19-26, 1936, Oct. 3-31, 1936, Apr. 15, 1939); *American Magazine* (Feb.-May 1933); *Look* (May 10, 1938); *Life* (Dec. 4, 1939); *Films in Review* (Dec. 1952); *Sir Knight* (1960s); *Architectural Digest* (Nov.-Dec. 1971, Apr. 1979); *Hollywood Studio Magazine* (June 1981, Oct. 1982); *American Classic Screen* (Nov.-Dec. 1981). CAUU (also in McCormick Collection): Home (1950, 1973); centenary (1982); *Hamlet* (play) (1982). Periodical articles: *Modern Maturity* (Aug.-Sept. 1974); *People* (Apr. 12, 1976); *American Film* (Oct. 1980); *Hollywood Studio Magazine* (Nov. 1983); *Newsweek* (Apr. 30, 1990). NYMA: Newsphotos; review of *The Films of John Barrymore*; booklet for tribute to JB (1969); career (1942); mass (1942); article (1944, 1977, 1982, 1992, undated); funeral (1942); *Hamlet* (play) (1982); sale of effects; review of *The Barrymores* (Kotsilibas-Davis) (1981); review of *We Barrymores* (1951); review of *Damned in Paradise* (1977); centenary of birth (1982); ashes moved to Philadelphia (1980); review of *The House of Barrymore*; review of *I Hate Hamlet* (play); personal data summary; obituary (1942). Periodical articles: *Photo-play World* (1918); *Theatre Magazine* (Apr. 1928); *American Magazine* (Feb.-May 1933): *Image* (Jan. 1957); *8mm Collector* (Sept. 1964); *Classic Images* (May 1982). NYMN: Newsphotos (numerous); review

of *Good Night, Sweet Prince* (1944); review of *Confessions of an Actor* (1926); illness (1939); career (1939); article (1932, 1940, undated [numerous]); souvenir booklet; tribute (1982); divorce/separation (1935, 1937); Elaine Barrie (1930s); *Hamlet* (play); stage appearance (1939); bankruptcy (1936); obituary (1942). Periodical article: *Ladies' Home Journal* (June 1927). NYPL: PARTIAL CONTENTS: Review of *Damned in Paradise* (1978); film festival (1982); biography (1981); centenary (1982); ashes moved (1980); *Hamlet* (1982); article (1982); newsphotos; review of *The House of Barrymore* (1990); home (1990). Periodical article: *Hollywood Studio Magazine* (Oct. 1982). • *Other Clipping File*—AZSU (Jimmy Starr Collection), CAFA, CASF, CNDA, GBBF, MAH, MIDL, OHCL, WICF. • *Correspondence*—CAA: Notes, telegrams (Hedda Hopper Collection) (1941-42); 2 letters (Adolph Zukor Collection) (1919, 1925). CAUS (R.G. Bright Collection). DCLC (George Middleton Papers). MABU (G.B. Stern Papers). NYCU: 1 letter (Bulliet Collection) (1939); 2 letters (Erskine Collection) (undated); 2 letters (A. Strong Collection) (1926, 1939). NYPL: Letters to various individuals including Katharine Cornell (1939, undated). • *Costume*—NYMN: Richard III. • *Filmography*—CAA. • *Legal File*—CAUW: Letter (1926, 1928-58, undated); payroll, personnel record (1928-58); contract (1931); authorization (1931); agreement (1931); talent agreement (1925, 1928-29, 1931). • *Memorabilia*—NYCU (Roger Wheeler Theatrical Memorabilia, 1770-1940). NYMN: Oil painting, bust. • *Oral History*—CAUS: Mentioned in the following interviews: Fred K. Klebingat, Ben Carre. NYCO: Mentioned in the following interviews: Sidney Blackmer, Harold Clurman, Ted Cott, George Cukor, Reginald Denny, Andy Devine, Melvyn Douglas, Jose Ferrer, Lillian Gish, Albert Howson, Fritz Lang, Lila Lee, Myrna Loy, Chester Morris, Nita Naldi, Frances Nalle, Geraldine Page, Richard Quine, Tony Randall, Blanche Ring, Vincent Sherman, Potter Stewart, Albert (Eddie) Sutherland, Blanche Sweet, King

Vidor, John H. Wheelock, Jack Yellers, Jerome Zerbe, Adolph Zukor. • *Photograph/Still* – CAA (also in Hollywood Studio Museum Collection) (also in MGM Collection), CAFA, CAHL, CALM, CASF, CAUS, CAUT (Jessen Collection) (Portrait File), CAUU, CNDA, MABU (Douglas Fairbanks Jr. Collection), NYAM, NYB (Bettmann/UPI Collection) (Penguin Collection) (Springer Collection) (Underwood Collection), NYCU (Bulliet Collection) (Dramatic Museum Portraits) (Palmer Collection), NYEH, NYMN, NYPL, NYSU, OHCL, OHSU, TXU, WICF. • *Play Program* – NYCU (Dramatic Museum Collection). NYPL: 1912. • *Press Kit* – OHCL. • *Publicity Release* – AZSU (Jimmy Starr Collection): Schenck. CAA: Paramount (1939); Fox (1940). • *Reminiscence* – MISU. • *Scrapbook* – CASU (Stark Collection), NYPL (also M. Altman Collection) (also Winthrop Ames Collection) (also C. & L. Brown Collection) (also R. Locke Collection) (also Players Collection), WICF. • *Studio Biography* – CAA: MGM (1933).

BARTHELMESS, Richard,
New York, NY, 1895–1963.

Richard Barthelmess came to filmgoers' attention in 1916's *War Brides* but his roles in the 1919–1921 trio of *Broken Blossoms*, *Way Down East* and *Tol'able David* made him a superstar for the rest of the silent era. Although he had success with such sound films as *The Dawn Patrol*, his youthful looks faded and his somewhat unsuitable voice further diminished his stardom. He ended his career in 1942 having played several character roles.

PUBLISHED SOURCES

• *Books* – **Bibliography:** *The Idols of Silence.* **General:** *Blue Book of the Screen*; *Classics of the Silent Screen*; *Eighty Silent Film Stars*; *Famous Film Folk*; *Famous Stars of Filmdom (Men)*; *Gentlemen To the Rescue*; *The Great Movie Stars: the Golden Years*; *Hollywood Album*; *Hollywood Exiles*; *Hollywood Hall of Fame*; *How I Broke Into the Movies*; *Immortals of the Screen*; *Intimate Talks With Movie Stars*; *Leading Men*; *The Movie Stars Story*; *Popular Men of the Screen*; *Screen Personalities*; *Stardom*; *The Stars Appear*; *Who's Who on the Screen.* **Credits:** *Filmarama* (v. I and II); *Forty Years of Screen Credits*; *Twenty Years of Silents*; *Who Was Who on Screen.* **Encyclopedic Works:** *A Biographical Directory of Film*; *Film Encyclopedia*; *Filmlexicon degli Autori e delle Opere*; *Halliwell's Filmgoer's Companion*; *The Illustrated Encyclopedia of the World's Great Movie Stars and Their Films*; *The Illustrated Who's Who of the Cinema*; *International Dictionary of Films and Filmmakers* (v. 3); *The Movie Makers*; *The Oxford Companion to Film*; *The Picturegoer's Who's Who and Encyclopedia of the Screen To-day*; *Quinlan's Illustrated Registry of Film Stars*; *Who's Who in Hollywood*; *The World Almanac Who's Who of Film*; *The World Encyclopedia of the Film*; *The World Film Encyclopedia.* **Pictorial:** *The Image Makers*; *Leading Men*; *The Revealing Eye*; *Silent Portraits.* **Factoids:** *Star Stats.*
• *Periodicals* – The following periodical articles are in addition to those included in the library listings below: *Photoplay* (Sept. 1919, Sept. 1923, Feb. 1924, Aug. 1924, May 1925, Sept. 1928, Mar. 1930, July 1938); *Motion Picture Magazine* (Feb. 1920, Apr. 1921, Oct. 1922, Feb. 1925, Jan. 1926, Nov. 1927, Feb. 1930, July 1930, Mar. 1931, Jan. 1932, May 1934); *Motion Picture Classic* (Feb. 1919, Jan. 1920, June 1922, Jan. 1924, Aug. 1924); *Photo-Play Journal* (June 1919); *Moving Picture World* (July 26, 1919); *Picture Play* (Aug. 1920, Nov. 1920); *Shadowland* (Oct. 1920); *Cinema Art* (Apr. 1926); *Pictures and Picturegoer* (June 1929); *Silver Screen* (Jan. 1931, Sept. 1931, June 1933); *Vanity Fair* (Mar. 1932); *Life* (Jan. 23, 1956); *Films in Review* (Jan. 1958) (filmography); *Time* (Aug. 23, 1963); *Newsweek* (Aug. 26, 1963); *8mm Collector* (Nov. 1963); *Films and Filming* (Sept. 1971); *Film Dope* (Aug. 1973); *Virginia Quarterly Review*

(Autumn 1982) (about *Tol'able David*); *Hollywood Studio Magazine* (no. 5, 1988).

ARCHIVAL MATERIALS
• *Caricature*—NYMN. • *Clipping File*—CAA (also in Collection): Film appearance (1921–22, 1924, 1930); legal problem (1932–33); article (1922, 1926, 1944); engagement/marriage/divorce/children (1925–28, 1930); injury (1927, 1929); obituary (1963). Periodical articles: *Motion Picture Classic* (Dec. 1922); *Cine Revue* (March 1979). CAFI: Article (1987). CAUT: Article (1929); estate (1963); obituary (1963). CAUU: Nostalgia (1963); obituary (1963). NYMA: Newsphotos; obituary (1963). Periodical articles: *Photoplay* (Sept. 1920); *Classic Images* (May 1985, May 1989) (filmography). NYMN: Newsphotos; career; stage appearance (1937); obituary (1963). NYPL (also in C. & L. Brown Collection): Article (1918, 1932, undated); stage appearance (1936, undated); film appearance (1919–22, 1927, 1932–34); newsphotos; career (1930, 1934, undated); leaves Warner Bros. (1930s?); marriage/divorce/children (1923, 1926–27, undated); obituary (1963). Periodical articles: *Movie Weekly* (1910s?); *Photoplay* (Apr. 1918); *Motion Picture Magazine* (June 1918); *Screen Secrets* (Feb. 1929); *Picture Play* (May 1929); *Motion Picture Classic* (May 1929, undated); *Films and Filming* (May 1972). • *Other Clipping File*—CNDA, GBBF, MAH, MIDL, OHCL, PAPL, WICF. • *Collection*—CAA: 48 scrapbooks containing reviews, programs and clippings on films beginning with *War Brides* (1916). NYMA (D.W. Griffith Collection): Reminiscence. • *Correspondence*—CAHL (A.B. Paine Collection): 1930. MABU: Few letters, telegram (in restricted collection; needs donor approval) (1957). NYPL: Letters (C. & L. Brown Collection) (1940, undated); others (1937, 1944, 1960). • *Filmography*—CAA, NYMA, NYPL. • *Interview*—CAUS. CAUU (Hollywood Museum Collection): 1957. • *Legal File*—CAUW: Letter, memo (1924, 1926–34); personnel, payroll record

(1926–40); contract summary (1926–32); note (undated); document (1929–31, 1933–34); contract (1921–22, 1926–32, 1940); release (1934); talent agreement (1921, 1923–24, 1926, 1928–30, 1933); letter (1924, 1932–33). • *Oral History*—NYCO: Interviewed in the 1950s. Also mentioned in the following interviews: Lila Lee, Frances Marion, Nita Naldi. • *Photograph/Still*—CAA, CAHL, CALM, CAPH, CASU, CAUB, CAUT (Jessen Collection), CNDA, DCG (Quigley Photographic Archives), GBBF, MIDL, NJFL, NJPT, NYAM, NYB (Bettmann/UPI Collection) (Springer Collection) (Underwood Collection), NYCU (Dramatic Museum Portraits) (Palmer Collection), NYEH, NYMN, NYPL, OHCL, TXSM, TXU, WICF. • *Program*—CAA (see Collection). NYMA: Toronto Film Society festival (contains biography of RB). • *Scrapbook*—CAA (See Collection), CASU (Stark Collection), NJPT (Yeandle Collection), NYMA, NYMN, NYPL. • *Studio Biography*—CAA: RKO (1939).

BASQUETTE, Lina (Lena Baskett or Baskette, some sources say Belcher), San Mateo, CA, 1907–1994.
Beginning as a child actress in a series of Universal shorts in 1916, brunette Lina Basquette appeared in several silent films and starred in Cecil B. DeMille's part-talkie *The Godless Girl* (1929). Her private life was tempestuous and her career declined in the early 1930s, relegating her to westerns and other "B" films. Until her appearance in a 1991 film, her last performance had been in 1942's *A Night for Crime*.

PUBLISHED SOURCES
• *Books*—LB, who raised dogs professionally, wrote two dog care books: *How to Raise and Train a Great Dane* (1961) and *Your Great Dane* (1972). **General:** *Broken Silence; Sweethearts of the Sage.* **Encyclopedic Works:** *Film Encyclopedia; Filmlexicon degli Autori e delle*

Opere; *The Picturegoer's Who's Who and Encyclopedia of the Screen To-day*; *Who's Who in Hollywood*; *The World Film Encyclopedia*. **Credits:** *Filmarama* (v. I and II); *Forty Years of Screen Credits*; *Twenty Years of Silents*. **Biography/Autobiography:** *Lina, De Mille's Godless Girl*. **Nostalgia:** *Whatever Became of...* (4th). **Pictorial:** *Silent Portraits*.

• *Periodicals* — The following periodical articles are in addition to those included in the library listings below: *Films in Review* (February 1970) (Wampas Baby Stars); *Classic Images* (Apr. 1989); *American Film* (Jan.-Feb. 1992).

ARCHIVAL MATERIALS

• *Clipping File* — AZSU: Suicide attempt (1930s); assault trial. CAA: Career as child actress (1916); film appearance (1920s, 1991); marriage/divorce/childbirth (1929, 1930s, 1940s); legal problem (1929, 1930s, 1940s); illness; suicide attempt (1928–32); romance with Jack Dempsey (1932); dog raising (1963, 1980); career (1970). CAUT: Marriage (1920s, 1929). CAUU: Article (1985). Periodical article: *New Yorker* (Feb. 13, 1989). NYMA (also in Photoplay Collection): Suicide attempt (1930, 1932); marriage/divorce/children (1926, 1930, 1933–35); rape (1943); legal problem (1936); romance with Jack Dempsey (1932); film appearance (1917); writes book; injury (1932); article (1916, 1930, 1932, 1970); raises dogs (1983); stage appearance (1932). Periodical articles: *Motion Picture Magazine* (Mar. 1928); *Hollywood* (Aug. 1928); *Photoplay* (Aug. 1928); *Screen Play Secrets* (Dec. 1931); *Movie Classic* (Aug. 1932, Oct. 1932); *Popular Dogs Magazine* (May 1969); *Classic Images* (May-June 1983); *New Yorker* (Feb. 13, 1989). NYPL: Newsphotos; dancer; film review (1917); writes novel (1932); rape (1943); marriage/divorce/children (1932, 1934, undated); raises dogs (1959–60, 1963, 1983); romance (1944); injury (1932, 1935); article (1916, 1944); stage appearance (1927, 1932, undated); suicide attempt (1932); film appearance (1917). Periodical articles: *Picture Play* (Jan. 1917); *TV Guide* (July 22, 1961); *Big Reel*

(Sept. 1980); *New Yorker* (Feb. 13, 1989). • *Other Clipping File* — CASP, CAUC, GBBF, MIDL, OHCL, PAPL, WICF. • *Correspondence* — NYPL (Lamparski Collection): 1972. • *Interview* — CAUU (R. Lamparski Collection). • *Legal File* — CAUW: Talent agreement (1928). • *Photograph/Still* — CAA (also in Hollywood Studio Museum Collection), CAH, CASP, CAUT (Portrait File), CAUU, DCG (Quigley Photographic Archives), GBBF, NJPT, NYB (Bettmann/UPI Collection), NYCU (Palmer Collection), NYEH, NYMN, NYPL, NYSU, OHCL, PAPL, TXSM, TXU (A. Davis Collection), WICF. • *Publicity Release* — NYPL: Unknown studio (1932). • *Scrapbook* — UTBY (DeMille Archives). • *Studio Biography* — NYMA: Photoplay (undated).

BAXTER, Warner, Columbus, Ohio, 1889/91–1951.

Probably best remembered as the hard-driving director in *42nd Street*, Warner Baxter's career spanned 32 years, from 1918 to 1950. His sound career proved more notable than his silent one; he received an Academy Award as best actor in 1929's *In Old Arizona*. Despite some noteworthy 1930s films, such as *The Prisoner of Shark Island*, his career gradually declined to "B" status in the 1940s and he finished his career in the low-budget *Crime Doctor* series.

PUBLISHED SOURCES

• *Books* — **General:** *Blue Book Of the Screen*; *Eighty Silent Film Stars*; *Famous Film Folk*; *Famous Movie Detectives*; *Famous Stars of Filmdom (Men)*; *The Great Movie Stars: The Golden Years*; *The Hall of Fame of Western Film Stars*; *Heroes, Heavies and Sagebrush*; *Hollywood Album*; *Hollywood Greats of the Golden Years*; *Immortals of the Screen*; *The Movie Stars Story*; *The Oscar People*; *A Pictorial History of Westerns*; *Saturday Afternoon at the Bijou*; *Screen Personalities*; *The Truth About the Movies*; *The Western* (Eyles); *What Actors Eat When They Eat*. **Credits:** *Filma-*

rama (v. I and II); *Forty Years of Screen Credits*; *Twenty Years of Silents*; *Who Was Who on Screen.* **Encyclopedic Works:** *A Biographical Dictionary of Film*; *A Companion to the Movies*; *Film Encyclopedia*; *Filmlexicon degli Autori e delle Opere*; *Halliwell's Filmgoer's Companion*; *The Illustrated Encyclopedia of the World's Great Movie Stars and Their Films*; *The Illustrated Who's Who of the Cinema*; *The Movie Makers*; *National Cyclopedia of American Biography* (1954); *The Oxford Companion to Film*; *The Picturegoer's Who's Who and Encyclopedia of the Screen To-day*; *Quinlan's Illustrated Registry of Film Stars*; *Who's Who in Hollywood*; *The World Almanac Who's Who of Film*; *The World Encyclopedia of the Film*; *The World Film Encyclopedia.* **Pictorial:** *Pictures of Movie Stars, with Stories.* **Factoids:** *Star Stats.*

• *Periodicals* — The following periodical articles are in addition to those included in the library listings below: *Motion Picture Classic* (Apr. 1922, July 1923); *Photoplay* (Mar. 1925, Apr. 1929, Feb. 1938, July 1938, Dec. 1940); *Motion Picture Magazine* (May 1926, May 1929, May 1930, Dec. 1932, Mar. 1936, Dec. 1936); *Screen Mirror* (Oct. 1930); *Movie Classic* (Jan. 1934, Apr. 1934, Feb. 1935, Jan. 1936); *Silver Screen* (Feb. 1934); *Photoplay* (Feb. 1938, July 1938); *Newsweek* (May 14, 1951); *Time* (May 21, 1951); *Filmograph* (no. 1-2, 1970); *Cine Revue* (Mar. 31, 1977); *American Classic Screen* (Jan.-Feb. 1983); *Classic Images* (Nov. 1989) (filmography).

ARCHIVAL MATERIALS

• *Caricature* — NYPL (Sardi Collection). • *Clipping File* — CAA: Film appearance (1923, 1930, 1933, 1938); article (1929-30); illness (1935, 1951); article by WB (1948); excerpt from *National Cyclopedia of American Biography* (1954); obituary (1951). Periodical article: *Architectural Digest* (April 1990). CAFI: Draft article by WB about director Herbert Brenon. CAUU: Nostalgia (1970); obituary (1951). NYMA: Career (1938). Periodical articles: *Motion Picture Magazine* (Apr. 1934); *Screenland* (1937);

Hollywood (Dec. 1937); *Classic Film Collector* (Winter 1970); *Classic Images* (Dec. 1984, Sept.-Oct. 1989). NYPL: Newsphotos (numerous); article (1938); film appearance (1933); film reviews (numerous); film synopses (numerous); injury (1935); obituary (1951). • *Other Clipping File* — AZSU (Jimmy Starr Collection), GBBF, MAH, MIDL, OHCL, PAPL, WICF. • *Correspondence* — NYPL (C. & L. Brown Collection) (1924, 1930s, 1940s). • *Filmography* — CAA, NYPL (incomplete). • *Legal File* — CAA (Vertical File Collection): Agreement (Fox, Paramount, American Federation of Radio Artists, Columbia) (1928-1944). CAUW: Payroll, personnel record (1932); letter (1936-38). • *Oral History* — CAUS: Mentioned in: Edward Anhalt interview. • *Photograph/Still* — AZSU (Jimmy Starr Collection), CAA (also in Hollywood Studio Museum Collection) (also in MGM Collection), CAFA, CAFI, CAHL, CALM, CAUT (Jessen Collection), CAUU, CNDA, DCG (Quigley Photographic Archives), GBBF, MIDL, NJPT, NYAM, NYB (Bettmann/UPI Collection) (Penguin Collection) (Underwood Collection), NYCU (Dramatic Museum Portraits), NYEH, NYPL, NYSU, OHCL, TXSM, TXU, WICF. • *Publicity Release* — CAA: Fox (1938). • *Scrapbook* — NJPT (Yeandle Collection), NYAM. • *Studio Biography* — CAA: Fox (1936-38, 1940, 1943); Columbia (1949). CAFI: Unknown studio. NYMA: Unknown studio.

BAYNE, Beverly (Pearl Bain), Minneapolis, MN, 1894-1982.

Appearing in nearly 400 films, mostly one- and two- reelers beginning about 1912, Beverly Bayne was best known as half of a romantic film (and later real life) duo with Francis X. Bushman. Among their films together was *Romeo and Juliet.* Her career tapered off in the 1920s and her final silent film was *Who Cares?* (1925). She remained active on the stage thereafter and essayed a few supporting roles in early 1930s films.

PUBLISHED SOURCES
• *Books* – Bibliography: *The Idols of Silence*. General: *Famous Film Folk*; *Ladies in Distress*; *Life Stories of the Movie Stars*; *Who's Who on the Screen*. Credits: *Filmarama* (v. I and II); *Twenty Years of Silents*. Encyclopedic Works: *Film Encyclopedia*; *Filmlexicon degli Autori e delle Opere*; *Halliwell's Filmgoer's Companion*; *Who's Who in Hollywood*. Nostalgia: *Whatever Became of...* (2nd). Pictorial: *Silent Portraits*.
• *Periodicals* – The following periodical articles are in addition to those included in the library listings below: *Motion Picture Magazine* (Sept. 1915); *Photoplay* (Mar. 1917, May 1918); *Cine Revue* (Sept. 30, 1982).

ARCHIVAL MATERIALS
• *Clipping File* – CAA: Donates memorabilia (1964); nostalgia (1970); obituary (1982). Periodical articles: *Photoplay* (Oct. 1915); *Classic Film Collector* (Fall/Winter 1968, Winter 1970-Fall 1971, Spring-Summer 1972). CAFI: Article (1968); obituary (1982). CAUT: Stage appearance (1928?); newsphoto; obituary (1982). NYMA: Periodical article: *Photo-play World* (Mar. 1918). NYPL: Stage appearance (1929, 1930s, 1940s, undated); nostalgia (1970); newsphotos; article (1940, undated); career (1941, 1967); obituary (1982). Periodical article: *Classic Film Collector* (Winter 1970-Fall 1971). • *Other Clipping File* – GBBF, MAH, MIDL, PAPL, WICF, WYU (see Collection). • *Collection* – WYU: Newspaper clippings (1931-66, undated); over 135 photographs and stills (some with Francis X. Bushman); play programs (1931-55); scrapbooks (1930-1950s). • *Correspondence* – NYPL (C. & L. Brown Collection). • *Legal File* – CAUW: Agreement (1924); talent agreement (1924). • *Photograph/Still* – CAA (also in Hollywood Studio Museum Collection), CAUT (Jessen Collection), CAUU, DCG (Quigley Photographic Archives), GBBF, IAU (Junkin Collection), NYPL, OHCL, WICF, WYU (see Collection). • *Play Program* – WYU (see Collection). • *Publicity Release* – NYPL: CBS (1940); unknown studio.

• *Scrapbook* – NYPL (also in C. & L. Brown Collection), WYU (see Collection).

BEDFORD, Barbara (Violet Rose – ?), Prairie du Chien, WI, 1900?-1981

A star after one of her first films, *The Last of the Mohicans* (1920), Barbara Bedford made numerous films for Fox and other companies throughout the 1920s. Among these was *Tumbleweeds*, William S. Hart's final film in 1925. She appeared in a variety of film genres including westerns, melodrama and comedies. Her pleasantly low-pitched voice was suitable for talkies and her career continued, albeit mainly in supporting roles and shorts, until about 1944.

PUBLISHED SOURCES
• *Books* – General: *Famous Film Folk*; *Sweethearts of the Sage*. Credits: *Filmarama* (v. II); *Forty Years of Screen Credits*; *Twenty Years of Silents*. Encyclopedic Works: *Film Encyclopedia*; *Filmlexicon degli Autori e delle Opere*. Pictorial: *Silent Portraits*.
• *Periodicals* – The following periodical article is in addition to those included in the library listings below: *Classic Images* (Oct. 1989).

ARCHIVAL MATERIALS
• *Clipping File* – CAA: Elevation to stardom (1921); newsphotos. NYMA: Film appearance (1920s); marriage/divorce (1921, 1928, 1930). Periodical articles: *Classic Images* (Nov.-Dec. 1984). NYPL: Newsphotos; article (1923). • *Other Clipping File* – GBBF, PAPL. • *Filmography* – NYMA. • *Legal File* – CAUW: Contract (1928, 1930); talent agreement (1930). • *Photograph/Still* – CAA (also in Hollywood Studio Museum Collection) (also in MGM Collection), CAUU, DCG (Quigley Photographic Archives), GBBF, NJPT, NYEH, NYPL, NYSU, OHCL, PAPL, TNUT (Clarence Brown Collection), TXU (A. Davis Collection), WICF. • *Publicity Release* –

NYMA: Unknown studio (undated). • *Scrapbook* – NYPL, TNUT (Clarence Brown Collection).

BEERY, Noah (in some early sources he is called Noah Beery *Jr.*, the name by which his actor son was later known), Kansas City, MO, 1883/84–1946.

With his basso profundo voice, craggy-faced Noah Beery (brother of Wallace) was made for talkie villainy but he enjoyed a lengthy career in silent films as well, beginning about 1920. Among his better-remembered were *The Coming of Amos* and *Beau Geste*. His career continued in westerns and melodramas as well as a stage appearance in a Broadway musical up to the time of his death.

PUBLISHED SOURCES

• *Books* – **General:** *Blue Book of the Screen*; *Eighty Silent Film Stars*; *Famous Film Folk*; *The Hall of Fame of Western Film Stars*; *Heroes, Heavies and Sagebrush*; *Hollywood Album*; *How I Broke Into the Movies*; *The Truth About the Movies*; *Who's Who on the Screen.* **Credits:** *Filmarama* (v. I and II); *Forty Years of Screen Credits*; *Twenty Years of Silents*; *Who Was Who on Screen.* **Encyclopedic Works:** *B Western Actors Encyclopedia*; *A Companion to the Movies*; *Film Encyclopedia*; *Filmlexicon degli Autori e delle Opere*; *Halliwell's Filmgoer's Companion*; *Hollywood Character Actors*; *The Illustrated Encyclopedia of Movie Character Actors*; *The Illustrated Who's Who of Cinema*; *The Movie Makers*; *The Oxford Companion to Film*; *The Picturegoer's Who's Who and Encyclopedia of the Screen To-day*; *Who's Who in Hollywood*; *The World Almanac Who's Who of Film*; *The World Film Encyclopedia.* **Pictorial:** *Silent Portraits.*

• *Periodicals* – The following periodical articles are in addition to that included in the library listings below: *Motion Picture Magazine* (Jan. 1922);
Photoplay (Dec. 1926); *Time* (Apr. 8, 1946).

MEDIA
Why Ever Did They? (CD recording).

OBSCURE PUBLISHED SOURCES
CAA (Pat O'Malley Collection): *The Cast* (v. 1).

ARCHIVAL MATERIALS
• *Caricature* – NYMN. • *Clipping File* – CAA: Separation/divorce (1927–28, 1930); resort (1927); legal problem (1928–32, 1941); illness (1930, 1939); bankruptcy (1935); obituary (1946). NYMA: Obituary (1946). Periodical article: *Classic Film/Video Images* (Sept. 1980). NYMN: Stage appearance (1945); legal problem (1935); newsphotos; obituary (1946). NYPL: Article (1928, 1937, undated); newsphotos; stage appearance (1945); vaudeville appearance; film review (1910s, 1920s, 1930s); characterization (1920); debt (1935); obituary (1946). • *Other Clipping File* – CNDA, GBBF, MAH, MIDL, NYSU, OHCL, PAPL, WICF. • *Correspondence* – GBBF (Balcon Collection): 1935. • *Legal File* – CAUT (Twentieth Century–Fox Collection): Loanout (1930); letter, memo (1930). CAUW: Personnel, payroll record (1931); letter, memo (1929–31); document (undated); agreement (1929); release (1931); loanout (1930); contract (1929); talent agreement (1927–30, 1932). • *Oral History* – NYCO: Mentioned in the following interviews: Dorothy Fields, Albert Hackett. • *Photograph/Still* – CAA (also in Hollywood Studio Museum Collection), CAUB, CAUC (Motion Picture Photograph Collection), CAUT (Jessen Collection), CAUU, CNDA, DCG (Quigley Photographic Archives), GBBF, NJFL, NYB (Bettmann/UPI Collection), NYCU (Dramatic Museum Portraits) (Palmer Collection), NYEH, NYMN, NYPL, NYSU, OHCL, TXU, WICF. • *Publicity Release* – CAA: Paramount (1925–29, 1934). • *Scrapbook* – UTBY (DeMille Archives).

BELLAMY, Madge (Margaret Philpott), Hillsboro, TX, 1900/04–1990.

Onscreen from about 1919, pretty Madge Bellamy appeared in over 80 films during the course of her career. A very popular silent star, she is probably best remembered for John Ford's *The Iron Horse* (1924) and the cult film *The White Zombie* made in 1932. She appeared in only a handful of talkies, some in small supporting roles, and her career was essentially over by 1935.

PUBLISHED SOURCES

• *Books*—Bibliography: *The Idols of Silence*. **General:** *Blue Book of the Screen*; *Broken Silence*; *Famous Film Folk*; *How I Broke Into the Movies*; *Speaking of Silents*; *Sweethearts of the Sage*. **Credits:** *Filmarama* (v. II); *Forty Years of Screen Credits*; *Twenty Years of Silents*. **Encyclopedic Works:** *Film Encyclopedia*; *Filmlexicon degli Autori e delle Opere*; *Halliwell's Filmgoer's Companion*; *The Movie Makers*; *The Picturegoer's Who's Who and Encyclopedia of the Screen To-day*; *Who's Who in Hollywood*; *The World Almanac Who's Who of Film*; *The World Film Encyclopedia*. **Biography/Autobiography:** *A Darling of the Twenties*. **Nostalgia:** *Is That Who I Think It Is?* (v. 3); *Whatever Became of . . .* (11th). **Pictorial:** *The Image Makers*; *Silent Portraits*; *They Had Faces Then*.

• *Periodicals*—The following periodical articles are in addition to those included in the library listings below: *Motion Picture Classic* (Jan. 1921, Mar. 1922, Apr. 1927, July 1931); *Photoplay* (Mar. 1921, Oct. 1926, Mar. 1929, May 1930, July 1931); *Motion Picture Magazine* (Apr. 1922); *Films in Review* (April-July 1970); *Classic Film Collector* (Winter 1970); *Classic Images* (Oct. 1989, Mar. 1990) (filmography); *Skoop* (Apr. 1990).

ARCHIVAL MATERIALS

• *Clipping File*—AZSU (Jimmy Starr Collection): Legal problem (1943). CAA: Film appearance (1922); interview (1923); legal problem (1943); stage appearance (1946); nostalgia (1975, 1979); obituary (1990). CAFI: Obituary (1990). CAUT: Divorce (1943). CAUU: Nostalgia

(1974-75). NYMA: Obituary (1990). Periodical articles: *Classic Images* (Sept.-Oct. 1983, Mar. 1988, Dec. 1989, Feb. 1990). NYPL: Film appearance (1920s, 1930s); newsphotos (numerous); stage appearance (1918-20, 1934); comeback (1930s); assaults boyfriend (1944); divorce (1928); film review (1920s); article (1922, 1926). • *Other Clipping File*—GBBF, MAH, MIDL, OHCL, PAPL, WICF. • *Correspondence*—CAA (Hedda Hopper Collection): 1964. • *Filmography*—NYMA, NYPL. • *Interview*—NYAM: Videotape interview (1975). • *Manuscript*—GBBF: Original unedited typescript of *A Darling of the Twenties*. • *Photograph/Still*—CAA (also in Hollywood Studio Museum Collection) (also in MGM Collection), CAFA, CAH, CASF, CASU, CAUB, CAUC (Motion Picture Photograph Collection), CAUU, CNDA, DCG (Quigley Photographic Archives), GBBF, MIDL, NJPT, NYAM, NYB (Bettmann/UPI Collection), NYCU (Dramatic Museum Portraits) (Palmer Collection), NYEH, NYMA, NYMN, NYPL, NYSU, OHCL, PAPL, TXSM, TXU (Robbins Collection), WICF. • *Scrapbook*—NYPL.

BENNETT, Alma, Seattle, WA, 1889-1958.

Pretty Alma Bennett exerted her screen wiles against many an unwary hero in numerous film roles as the other woman or "vamp." The films included *Why Men Leave Home*, *A Fool and His Money*, *Don Juan's Three Nights* and *My Lady's Past*. She also appeared in westerns and comedies such as *Long Pants*. Her career did not survive the early sound period.

PUBLISHED SOURCES

• *Books*—Credits: *Filmarama* (v. II); *Twenty Years of Screen Credits*; *Who Was Who on Screen*. **Encyclopedic Works:** *Film Encyclopedia*; *Halliwell's Filmgoer's Companion*; *Who's Who in Hollywood*. **Pictorial:** *Silent Portraits*.

• *Periodicals*—*Classic Images* (Aug. 1990) (filmography).

ARCHIVAL MATERIALS
• *Clipping File*—CAA: Newsphotos. CAUT: Legal problem (1929). NYMA: Marriage (1929); film appearance (1921); legal problem (1929–30); vamp roles (1929); career (1923); signs with Goldwyn (1922); obituary (1958). • *Other Clipping File*—PAPL. • *Filmography*—GBBF. • *Legal File*—CAA (Sennett Collection): Talent agreement (1926); letter/telegram (1927–29). • *Photograph/Still*—CAA (Hollywood Studio Museum Collection), CAUT (Jessen Collection), DCG (Quigley Photographic Archives), GBBF, NJPT, NYEH, NYPL, NYSU, OHCL, WICF. • *Publicity Release*—CAA (Mack Sennett Collection): 1926. • *Studio Biography*—CAA (Mack Sennett Collection): 1927. NYMA: Fox (undated).

BENNETT, Belle, Milaca, MN, 1890/91–1932.
After performing on her family's showboat, Belle Bennett began her screen career about 1916. Her roles gradually improved and she went on to portray the title role in Hollywood's first version of *Stella Dallas* (1925). She was a well-regarded actress whose other films included *The Battle of the Sexes*, *Mother Machree* and *The Way of All Flesh*. She also was seen in some early talkies, the last of which was 1931's *The Big Shot*.

PUBLISHED SOURCES
• *Books*—Credits: *Filmarama* (v. I and II); *Forty Years of Screen Credits*; *Twenty Years of Silents*; *Who Was Who on Screen.* **Encyclopedic Works:** *Film Encyclopedia*; *Filmlexicon degli Autori e delle Opere*; *Halliwell's Filmgoer's Companion*; *Who's Who in Hollywood.* **Pictorial:** *Silent Portraits.*
• *Periodicals*—*Photoplay* (Jan. 1926, Nov. 1926); *Motion Picture Magazine* (Feb. 1926, Dec. 1928); *Motion Picture Classic* (Feb. 1926); *Movie Classic* (Jan. 1933).

ARCHIVAL MATERIALS
• *Clipping File*—CAA: Film appear-

ance (1924); estate (1932–33). CAUT: Legal problem (1920s?); newsphotos. NYMA (also in Photoplay Collection): Newsphotos; obituary (1932). NYPL: Film appearance (1917–18); estate (1932); newsphotos; contract dispute (1927); illness (1932); article (1918, 1920–21); obituary (1932). Periodical article: *Photoplay Journal* (May 1918). • *Other Clipping File*—GBBF, MAH, MIDL, OHCL, PAPL, WICF. • *Correspondence*—NYPL (C. & L. Brown Collection): 1924. • *Filmography*—NYMA, NYPL (incomplete). • *Photograph/Still*—CAA (also in Hollywood Studio Museum Collection), CAUU, DCG (Quigley Photographic Archives), GBBF, NJPT, NYCU (Dramatic Museum Portraits) (Palmer Collection), NYEH, NYPL, NYSU, OHCL, TXU, WICF. • *Scrapbook*—NJPT (Yeandle Collection). • *Studio Biography*—NYPL: Unknown studio (1931).

BENNETT, Enid, Australia, 1895/98–1969.
After a film career which began about 1917, popular Enid Bennett left films in 1927 but she returned for a few supporting roles in 1931 and 1939. Among the films in which she appeared were Douglas Fairbanks's *Robin Hood*, *The Courtship of Miles Standish* and the first version of *Waterloo Bridge* (1931).

PUBLISHED SOURCES
• *Books*—**General:** *Blue Book of the Screen*; *Famous Film Folk*; *First One Hundred Noted Men and Women of the Screen*; *The Truth About the Movies*; *Who's Who on the Screen.* **Credits:** *British Film Actors' Credits*; *Filmarama* (v. I and II); *Forty Years of Screen Credits*; *Twenty Years of Silents*; *Who Was Who on Screen.* **Encyclopedic Works:** *Film Encyclopedia*; *Filmlexicon degli Autori e delle Opere*; *Halliwell's Filmgoer's Companion*; *Who's Who in Hollywood*; *The World Film Encyclopedia.* **Pictorial:** *Silent Portraits.*
• *Periodicals*—The following periodical articles are in addition to those in-

cluded in the library listings below: *Motion Picture Classic* (July 1920, Feb. 1922, Mar. 1923); *Motion Picture Magazine* (Dec. 1920, July 1922); *Photoplay* (Jan. 1921, Sept. 1922, Sept.-Oct. 1923).

ARCHIVAL MATERIALS
• *Clipping File* — CAA: Marriage/children (1921, 1963); film appearance (1922); comeback (1939); obituary (1969). CAUT: Obituary (1969). NYMA: Obituary (1969). NYPL: Film appearance (1910s, 1920s); newsphotos (numerous); article (1916–20); legal problem (1914); marriage/children (1918, 1920); Ince star (1916); comeback (1930s); obituary (1969). Periodical articles: *Motion Picture Classic* (Aug. 1918); *Photoplay Journal* (Oct.-Nov. 1919); *Picture Play* (Feb. 1920); *Photoplay* (Mar. 1920). • *Other Clipping File* — GBBF, MAH, NYSU, OHCL, PAPL, WICF. • *Filmography* — NYPL. • *Legal File* — CAA (Mack Sennett Collection): Contract (1926–29). • *Photograph/Still* — CAA (also in Hollywood Studio Museum Collection), CAUT (Jessen Collection), CAUU, CNDA, DCG (Quigley Photographic Archives), GBBF, NYMA, NYPL, NYSU, OHCL, TXU, WICF. • *Press Release* — CAA (Mack Sennett Collection): 1926–27. • *Scrapbook* — NYPL (also in R. Locke Collection).

BESSERER, Eugenie, Marseilles, France, 1870–1934.

Another of the silent screen's archetypal mothers was Eugenie Besserer. Dubbed the "Ellen Terry of the Screen," she was already mature when she entered films in 1911 as a leading lady with Selig. She later appeared in several D. W. Griffith films (e.g., *The Greatest Question*) and numerous others like *Anna Christie* (1923 version), *The Coast of Folly*, *Flesh and the Devil* and *Lilac Time*. It is, of course, for her role as Al Jolson's "Momma" in *The Jazz Singer* that she is remembered.

PUBLISHED SOURCES
• *Books* — General: *Who's Who in the Film World*. Credits: *Filmarama* (v. I and II); *Forty Years of Screen Credits*; *Twenty Years of Silents*; *Who Was Who on Screen*. Encyclopedic Works: *Film Encyclopedia*; *Filmlexicon degli Autori e delle Opere*; *Halliwell's Filmgoer's Companion*; *The Picturegoer's Who's Who and Encyclopedia of the Screen To-day*; *Who's Who in Hollywood*.

ARCHIVAL MATERIALS
• *Clipping File* — CAA: Obituary (1934). NYMA (also in Photoplay Collection): Personal data summary. NYPL: Newsphotos; film appearance (1910s); article (1912–13, 1915–17); injury (1912); biography (1906); obituary (1934). • *Other Clipping File* — MIDL. • *Legal File* — CAUT (Twentieth Century–Fox Collection): Memo (1929); loanout (1929). CAUW: Talent agreement (1925, 1927). • *Photograph/Still* — CAA, CAUT (Jessen Collection), DCG (Quigley Photographic Archives), NYPL. • *Scrapbook* — NYPL, WICF.

BILLINGTON, Francelia, Dallas, TX, 1895–1934.

In a 35-film career which spanned the years 1912–1930, Francelia Billington worked for several studios including Majestic, Kalem, Thanhouser, Reliance and Universal. She appeared steadily in films until about 1922; her roles during the remainder of the decade were sparse. Among her leading men were William Russell (q.v.) and Tom Mix (q.v.); her films included *Blue Blazes*, *What a Wife Learned*, *Blind Husbands*, *Hearts Are Trumps*, *Shackles of Truth* and her final film, *The Mounted Stranger*.

PUBLISHED SOURCES
• *Books* — General: *Who's Who in the Film World*. Credits: *Filmarama* (v. I). Encyclopedic Works: *Who's Who in Hollywood*. Pictorial: *Silent Portraits*. • *Periodicals* — *Photoplay* (Dec. 1914); *Motion Picture Classic* (Apr./May 1920); *Classic Images* (Aug. 1988, Oct. 1989).

ARCHIVAL MATERIALS

• *Clipping File* — CAA: Article (1988).
• *Other Clipping File* — GBBF. • *Filmography* — CAA. • *Photograph/Still* — CAA Hollywood Studio Museum Collection), CAUT (Jessen Collection), DCG (Quigley Photographic Archives), NYPL, NYSU, WICF. • *Scrapbook* — NYPL.

BINNEY, Constance, 1900– 1989

In 1920 popular Constance Binney was the runner-up to Mary Pickford for the title of "America's Sweetheart." Her films included *Sporting Life, A Bill of Divorcement, Erstwhile Susan* and *39 East.* Her career was brief and her final film role came when she was still in her early twenties, although she later made some stage appearances. Her sister, Faire, was also a silent screen actress.

PUBLISHED SOURCES

• *Books* — General: *Who's Who on the Screen.* Credits: *Filmarama* (v. I and II); *Twenty Years of Silents.* Encyclopedic Works: *Filmlexicon degli Autori e delle Opere*; *Who Was Who in the Theatre*; *Who's Who in Hollywood.* Pictorial: *Silent Portraits.*
• *Periodicals* — The following periodical articles are in addition to those included in the library listings below: *Photoplay* (Mar. 1919, Apr. 1920, Sept. 1920); *Motion Picture Magazine* (Mar. 1920, Nov. 1920, May 1922); *Picture Play* (Sept. 1920); *Motion Picture Classic* (Jan. 1921); *Filmplay Journal* (Sept. 1921, June 1922); *Delineator* (Oct. 1921); *Classic Film Collector* (Summer 1974).

ARCHIVAL MATERIALS

• *Clipping File* — CAA: Divorce (1932, 1936); newsphotos; article (undated). NYMA: Signs with Lasky (1919); film review (1919); signs with Realart; film appearance (1921, 1923); article (1919, 1932); marriage/divorce (1923, 1926, 1932); stage comeback (1932); Rosemary Award (1973–74). Periodical articles: *Photoplay* (Sept. 1919); *Classic Film Collector* (Summer 1973?). NYMN: Newsphotos (numerous). NYPL: Play appearance

(1932); most popular star; newsphotos; article (1950). Periodical article: *Classic Film Collector* (Summer 1973). • *Other Clipping File* — GBBF, MAH, MIDL, OHCL, WICF. • *Correspondence* — CAHL: 1919. • *Interview* — NYAM. • *Photograph/Still* — CAA (also in Hollywood Studio Museum Collection), DCG (Quigley Photographic Archives), NYAM, NYEH, NYMN, NYPL, OHCL, TXU, WICF. • *Scrapbook* — NYPL. • *Speech* — CAUU (A. Slide Collection): A speech given by CB on the occasion of the Rosemary Award presentation (1973).

BLACKWELL, Carlyle, Troy, PA, 1888–1955.

Known for his chiseled profile, matinee idol Carlyle Blackwell made numerous films in his U.S. and British career. At one time he was known as "Picture-a-Day" Blackwell because he sometimes completed a film in one day. His American career lasted until about 1920 and he spent much of the 1920s and early '30s in England where his final films were completed.

PUBLISHED SOURCES

• *Books* — General: *Gentlemen to the Rescue*; *Life Stories of the Movie Stars*; *Sherlock Holmes on the Screen*; *Who's Who in the Film World.* Credits: *British Film Actors' Credits*; *Filmarama* (v. I and II); *Twenty Years of Silents*; *Who Was Who on Screen.* Encyclopedic Works: *Film Encyclopedia*; *Filmlexicon degli Autori e delle Opere*; *Halliwell's Filmgoer's Companion*; *The Illustrated Who's Who in British Films*; *The Picturegoer's Who's Who and Encyclopedia of the Screen To-day*; *Who's Who in Hollywood*; *The World Film Encyclopedia.* Pictorial: *Silent Portraits.*
• *Periodicals* — The following periodical articles are in addition to those included in the library listings below: *Blue Book Magazine* (May 1914); *Photoplay* (June 1914); *Motion Picture Magazine* (Feb. 1915, Mar. 1916, July 1916, Apr. 1917); *Feature Movie* (Apr. 15, 1915); *Movie Pictorial* (Oct. 1915); *Motion Pic-*

ture Classic (June 1918); *Time* (June 27, 1955).

ARCHIVAL MATERIALS
• *Clipping File*—CAA: Article (1955); divorce (1933); obituary (1955). NYMA: Newsphotos; article (1917–18, undated); signed by Lasky; marriage/divorce (1917, 1922, 1925–26, 1933); film appearance (1922); returns to U.S. films (1931); makes English films (1923); career (1918); own production company (1919). Periodical articles: *Screen Book Tabloid* (Aug. 1933); *Classic Images* (May 1988). NYPL: Marriage/divorce (1926, 1933, 1948, undated); newsphotos; article (undated); film review (1913, 1920); handwriting analyzed; obituary (1955). Periodical articles: *Picturegoer* (Dec. 1928); *Pic* (Mar. 7, 1939); *Films in Review* (Nov. 1971). • *Other Clipping File*—GBBF, MAH, MIDL, NYSU, OHCL, PAPL, WICF. • *Correspondence*—CAA (Adolph Zukor collection): 1927. GBBF (Balcon Collection): 1931, 1933. NYPL (C. & L. Brown Collection): 1921–40. • *Photograph/Still*—CAA (also in Hollywood Studio Museum Collection), CAUT (Jessen Collection), DCG (Quigley Photographic Archives), GBBF, NJFL, NYB (Bettmann/UPI Collection), NYEH, NYPL, NYSU, OHCL, WICF. • *Scrapbook*—NYPL. • *Studio Biography*—NYMA: Photoplay.

BLANE, Sally (Elizabeth Jane Jung or Young), Salida, CO, 1910– \ ۹ ۹ ٦

One of three actress sisters (Polly Ann and Loretta Young were the other two), Sally Blane's career began late in the silent era with *The Collegians* series. Her films included *Rolled Stockings*, *Wolves of the City*, *Her Summer Hero*, *King Cowboy* and the early talkie *The Vagabond Lover*. She continued on through the thirties, generally in "B" films with an occasional supporting role in a major film (e.g., *Alexander Graham Bell*).

PUBLISHED SOURCES
• *Books*—General: *Hollywood Kids*;

Sweethearts of the Sage. **Credits:** *Filmarama* (v. II); *Forty Years of Screen Credits*; *Twenty Years of Silents.* **Encyclopedic Works:** *Film Encyclopedia*; *Filmlexicon degli Autori e delle Opere*; *Halliwell's Filmgoer's Companion*; *The Movie Makers*; *The Picturegoer's Who's Who and Encyclopedia of the Screen To-day*; *Variety Who's Who in Show Business*; *Who's Who in Hollywood*; *The World Film Encyclopedia.* **Nostalgia:** *Whatever Became of...* (3rd, 8th). **Pictorial:** *The Revealing Eye*; *They Had Faces Then.*
• *Periodicals*—The following periodical articles are in addition to that included in the library listings below: *Motion Picture Magazine* (July 1929); *Photoplay* (Mar. 1930); *Films in Review* (Feb. 1970) (Wampas Baby Stars); *Classic Images* (Oct. 1989).

ARCHIVAL MATERIALS
• *Clipping File*—CAA: Film appearance (1932); marriage (1933, 1935). CAUT: Legalizes name (1930s?). CAUU: Periodical article: *Tribute* (Mar.-Apr. 1984). NYMA: Periodical article: *Classic Images* (Sept. 1982). NYPL: Newsphotos; marriage; return from England; makes Mexican film; film appearance (1933–34). • *Other Clipping File*—CODL, GBBF, MIDL, NYMA (Photoplay Collection), PAPL, WICF. • *Legal File*—CAUW: Payroll record (undated); contract (1931); talent agreement (1931); memo (1931). • *Photograph/Still*—AZSU (Jimmy Starr Collection), CAA (also in Hollywood Studio Museum Collection), CAOC (Kiesling Collection), CAUT (Jessen Collection), DCG (Quigley Photographic Archives), GBBF, MIDL, NJPT, NYAM, NYCU (Palmer Collection), NYEH, NYPL, NYSU, OHCL, TXU, WICF. • *Scrapbook*—NJPT (Yeandle Collection). • *Studio Biography*—CAA: Fox (1935). CAUU: Fox (1935). NYMA: Photoplay.

BLETCHER, William ("Billy"), Lancaster, PA, 1894–1979.

Billy Bletcher was more fortunate than many of his contemporaries; his career continued well into the talkie era. It was, however, his voice rather than his person which was generally featured. He supplied the voices in many an animated film and was featured on the radio. His "visible" career was as an original member of the Mack Sennett team, in Christie two-reel comedies of the 1920s, Hal Roach comedies of the '30s and roles for DeMille and Universal.

PUBLISHED SOURCES

• *Books* — **General:** *Clown Princes and Court Jesters*; *The Real Tinsel*. **Credits:** *Filmarama* (v. II). **Encyclopedic Works:** *Film Encyclopedia*; *The Picturegoer's Who's Who and Encyclopedia of the Screen To-day*; *Who's Who in Hollywood*.
• *Periodicals* — The following periodical article is in addition to those included in the library listings below: *Funnyworld* (Summer 1978).

ARCHIVAL MATERIALS

• *Clipping File* — CAA: Obituary (1979). NYMA: Periodical articles: *Classic Images* (Oct. 1985, June 1990). NYPL: Periodical article: *Films in Review* (May 1970). • *Other Clipping File* — GBBF. • *Legal File* — CAUW: Talent agreement 1929-30. • *Photograph/Still* — CAA (MGM Collection).

BLUE, Monte (Gerard Montgomery Blue), Indianapolis, IN, 1887/90–1963.

Monte Blue's lengthy career lasted into the television era from his beginnings as a stunt man in films like *Birth of a Nation*. He was a leading man in the 1920s and then slipped into character parts. Among the better known of his approximately 200 films were *Peacock Alley*, *Orphans of the Storm* and *White Shadows in the South Seas*.

PUBLISHED SOURCES

• *Books* — **General:** *Blue Book of the Screen*; *Eighty Silent Film Stars*; *Famous Film Folk*; *Heroes, Heavies and Sagebrush*; *Hollywood Album 2*; *How I*

Broke Into the Movies; *Immortals of the Screen*; *The Kindergarten of the Movies*; *More Character People*; *Stunt*; *The Truth About the Movies*; *Twinkle, Twinkle, Movie Star*; *The Versatiles*; *Who's Who on the Screen*. **Credits:** *Filmarama* (v. I and II); *Forty Years of Screen Credits*; *Twenty Years of Silents*; *Who Was Who on Screen*. **Encyclopedic Works:** *Film Encyclopedia*; *Filmlexicon degli Autori e delle Opere*; *Halliwell's Filmgoer's Companion*; *The Illustrated Encyclopedia of Movie Character Actors*; *The Illustrated Who's Who of the Cinema*; *The Movie Makers*; *The Picturegoer's Who's Who and Encyclopedia of the Screen To-day*; *Who's Who in Hollywood*; *The World Almanac Who's Who of Film*; *The World Film Encyclopedia*. **Pictorial:** *Silent Portraits*.
• *Periodicals* — The following periodical articles are in addition to those included in the library listings below: *Motion Picture Classic* (Jan. 1921, Dec. 1927); *Motion Picture Magazine* (Feb. 1921, Aug. 1922, Sept. 1924, July 1925, Aug. 1928); *Photoplay* (June-July 1924, Feb. 1925, May 1926, July 1926, Oct. 1930); *Theatre* (Dec. 1926); *Newsweek* (Mar. 4, 1963); *Films in Review* (May 1963) (filmography); *Classic Film Collector* (Spring 1971) (filmography); *Classic Images* (Jan. 1986).

ARCHIVAL MATERIALS

• *Clipping File* — CAA: Illness (1921, 1954, 1963); marriage (1959); article (1958); honors (1945, 1951); nostalgia (1961); obituary (1961). Periodical article: *Classic Film Collector* (Summer 1971). CAUT: Marriage/children (1928, 1959); film appearance (1959); obituary (1963). CAUU: Obituary (1963). Periodical article: *Cinema Trails* (no. 2). NYMA: Comeback (1944); obituary (1963). Periodical article: *Classic Film Collector* (Summer 1971). NYPL: Film appearance (1919, 1930, 1934, undated); marriage (1959); newsphotos; comeback (1944, undated); article (1926-27, 1929); career (1948); home (1926); interview (1931). Periodical articles: *Photoplay* (Mar. 1919); *Motion Picture Magazine* (Oct. 1919); *Motion Picture Classic* (May

1929); *Films in Review* (Oct. 1963). • *Other Clipping File* – CNDA, GBBF, MAH, MIDL, OHCL, PAPL, WICF. • *Correspondence* – NYPL: Letters (C. &. L. Brown Collection) (1930s); others (1957, 1959). OHCL: 2 letters, 2 cards. • *Legal File* – CAUW: Letter, memo (1926–30, 1941–49); document (1930, 1949); option (1928–30, 1943–48); contract (1927, 1942–47); authorization (1943–44); contract summary (1944–47); agreement (1929); talent agreement (1922–27, 1935, 1938, 1942). • *Oral History* – NYCO: Mentioned in: Albert Howson interview. • *Photograph/Still* – CAA (also in Hollywood Studio Museum Collection) (also in MGM Collection), CASF, CAUS, CAUT (Jessen Collection), CNDA, DCG (Quigley Photographic Archives), GBBF, NJFL, NJPT, NYAM, NYB (Underwood Collection), NYCU (Bulliet Collection), NYEH, NYPL, NYSU, OHCL, TXSM, TXU, WICF. • *Publicity Release* – CAA: Warner (undated). • *Scrapbook* – NJPT (Yeandle Collection), NYPL. • *Studio Biography* – CAA: Paramount (1940); Warner (1945?).

BLYTHE, Betty (Elizabeth Blythe Slaughter), Los Angeles, CA, 1893–1972.

Tall and lithe Betty Blythe made a great success in her scantily-clad 1921 interpretation of the title role, *Queen of Sheba*, giving rise to the slang expression "Sheba" as the female counterpart of "Sheik." Although she was to continue in films for many more years (over 120 films in all), by the 1930s she was in supporting roles which she continued to play off and on until the 1960s. Her final film was *My Fair Lady* (1964), in which she appeared as an extra.

PUBLISHED SOURCES

• *Books* – **Bibliography:** *The Idols of Silence*. **General:** *Blue Book of the Screen*; *Famous Film Folk*; *It Was Fun While It Lasted*; *The Parade's Gone By*; *Who's Who on the Screen*. **Credits:** *British Film Actors' Credits*; *Filmarama* (v. I and II); *Forty Years of Screen Credits*; *Twenty Years of Silents*; *Who Was Who on Screen*. **Encyclopedic Works:** *Film Encyclopedia*; *Filmlexicon degli Autori e delle Opere*; *Halliwell's Filmgoer's Companion*; *The Illustrated Who's Who of the Cinema*; *The Movie Makers*; *The Picturegoer's Who's Who and Encyclopedia of the Screen To-day*; *Who's Who in Hollywood*; *The World Film Encyclopedia*. **Nostalgia:** *Whatever Became of...* (3rd). **Pictorial:** *The Image Makers*; *Silent Portraits*.

• *Periodicals* – The following periodical articles are in addition to those included in the library listings below: *Photoplay* (Dec. 1919, Jan. 1921, Dec. 1921, Nov. 1924); *Picture Show* (Jan. 3, 1920); *Picture Play* (Aug. 1920); *Motion Picture Magazine* (Feb. 1921, Aug. 1921, Feb. 1925); *Motion Picture Classic* (Aug. 1921, Apr. 1922); *Classic Film Collector* (Summer 1972).

ARCHIVAL MATERIALS

• *Caricature* – NYPL (Sardi Collection). • *Clipping File* – CAA: Film appearance (1920s); stage appearance (1944); interview (1962); marriage (1967); obituary (1972). Periodical articles: *Hollywood Studio Magazine* (Dec. 1975, Mar. 1976). CAUT: Newsphotos; nostalgia (1962); marriage (1967); film appearance (1962–63); article (1967); obituary (1972). CAUU: Newsphotos; obituary (1972). NYMA: Article (1923); stage appearance (1934); film appearance (1920s); sues producer (1926); tax problem (1929); bankruptcy (1933); goes to England (1923); career wanes (1931); obituary (1972). Periodical article: *Photo-play World* (Apr. 1918); *Screenland* (Mar. 1940). NYMN: Newsphotos (numerous). NYPL: Film review (1934); returns to films (1933); stage appearance (1914, 1926, 1929, 1931, 1935, undated); newsphotos; article (1923, undated); bankruptcy (1933); obituary (1972). Periodical articles: *Photoplay* (Sept. 1918); *Motion Picture Magazine* (Dec. 1918, Oct. 1919); *Photo-play Journal* (Jan. 1919, June 1919, Dec. 1919); *Picture Play* (Dec. 1919); *Motion Picture Classic* (Feb. 1920); *Movie Weekly* (July 19,

1924). • *Other Clipping File* – CNDA, GBBF, MIDL, OHCL, PAPL, TXU, WICF. • *Correspondence* – CAA (Hedda Hopper Collection): (1954, undated). CAHL: 1 letter (1918). NYMA (Photoplay Collection). NYPL: Letters (C. & L. Brown Collection); others, including to M. Davies (1931, 1944, undated). • *Interview* – CAUU (R. Lamparski Collection). • *Legal File* – CAUT (Twentieth Century-Fox Collection): Talent agreement (1921). CAUU (Universal Pictures Collection): Contract summary (1951). CAUW: Publicity photo (1964; last film appearance). • *Photograph/Still* – CAA (also in Hollywood Studio Museum Collection), CAFA, CAH, CNDA, DCG (Quigley Photographic Archives), GBBF, MIDL, NJPT, NYB (Bettmann/UPI Collection), NYEH, NYPL, NYSU, OHCL, PAPL, TXSM, WICF. • *Publicity Release* – CAA: Monogram (1945); Demille (1955). • *Scrapbook* – NYPL. • *Studio Biography* – NYMA: Photoplay.

BOARDMAN, Eleanor, Philadelphia, PA, 1898/99–1991.

Aristocratically beautiful Eleanor Boardman had her one memorable screen role playing against type in the 1928 silent classic *The Crowd*, directed by her then-husband King Vidor. In films since 1922 (the year she was named a Wampas Baby Star), her silent films were mostly routine melodramas at MGM. She appeared in only a handful of talkies and her final film, made in Spain about 1934, was not released in the United States.

PUBLISHED SOURCES

• *Books* – **General:** *Blue Book of the Screen; Broken Silence; Famous Film Folk; Let Me Entertain You; The Movie Stars Story; People Will Talk; Return Engagement; Screen Album; Speaking of Silents.* **Credits:** *Filmarama* (v. II); *Forty Years of Screen Credits; Twenty Years of Silents.* **Encyclopedic Works:** *Film Encyclopedia; Filmlexicon degli Autori e delle Opere; Halliwell's Filmgoer's Companion; The Movie Makers;*

The Picturegoer's Who's Who and Encyclopedia of the Screen To-day; Who's Who in Hollywood; The World Film Encyclopedia. **Nostalgia:** *Whatever Became Of...* (7th). **Pictorial:** *Leading Ladies; Silent Portraits; They Had Faces Then.* • *Oral History* – Eleanor Boardman d'Arrast. **Factoids:** *Star Stats.*
• *Periodicals* – The following periodical articles are in addition to those included in the library listings below: *Photoplay* (Sept. 1923); *Motion Picture Classic* (Feb. 1924, Aug. 1925); *Motion Picture Magazine* (July 1925, July 1926); *Films in Review* (Feb. 1970) (Wampas Baby Stars), (Dec. 1973).

ARCHIVAL MATERIALS

• *Clipping File* – CAA: Film appearance (1922); legal problem (1926-41); marriage/divorce/children (1926-33); Beverly Hills home (1949); nostalgia (1974, 1980). CAUU: Nostalgia (1974). NYMA: Marriage/divorce/children (1926, 1930-31, 1933); sues for support (1935); tax problem (1929-30); article (1931); legal problem (1928); film appearance (1920s). Periodical articles: *Theatre Magazine* (Aug. 1927); *Photoplay* (Feb. 1931); *Screen Play* (Feb. 1932); *Movie Classic* (Sept. 1932); *Classic Images* (July 1983, June 1989). NYPL: Marriage/divorce (1932-33, undated); legal problem (1933, 1935, undated); newsphotos; signs with MGM (1922); article (1923); film review (1923); obituary (1991). • *Other Clipping File* – GBBF, OHCL, PAPL, TXU, WICF. • *Collection* – CAUU (King Vidor Collection): Various letters and documents. • *Correspondence* – CAUU: See Collection. NYPL: 18 letters (Herman Weinberg Collection) (1971-79); 1 letter (Lamparski Collection) (1972). • *Photograph/Still* – CAA (also in Hollywood Studio Museum Collection) (also in MGM Collection), CAH, CASU, CAUT (Portrait File), CAUU, CNDA, DCG (Quigley Photographic Archives), GBBF, NJPT, NYB (Bettmann/UPI Collection), NYCU (Palmer Collection), NYEH, NYPL, NYSU, OHCL, PAPL, TNUT (Clarence Brown Collection), TXU (A. Davis Collection) (Robbins Collection), WICF.

• *Scrapbook* – NYPL. • *Studio Biography* – NYMA: MGM (1925); Photoplay (undated); Paramount (undated).

BOARDMAN, True (William True Boardman), Oakland, CA, 1882–1918.

Formerly an actor in stock companies, True Boardman starred mainly in action films and serials (including the *Stingaree* series) from 1911. Among the studios at which he worked were Selig, Essanay and Kalem. He appeared in such films as *Tarzan of the Apes* (not as the title character), *The False Clue*, *The Man in Irons* and some episodes of *The Hazards of Helen*. His son True, Jr., and wife Virginia True Boardman also appeared in films.

PUBLISHED SOURCES

• *Books* – Credits: *Filmarama* (v. I); *Who Was Who on Screen*. Encyclopedic Works: *Film Encyclopedia*; *Who's Who in Hollywood*.

ARCHIVAL MATERIALS

• *Clipping File* – NYMA: Obituary (1918). Periodical article: *Classic Images* (Oct. 1989). NYPL: Newsphotos; film appearance (1914, 1916–17); obituary (1918). Periodical article: *Motion Picture Classic* (Feb. 1917). • *Other Clipping File* – WICF. • *Photograph/Still* – CAA, DCG (Quigley Photographic Archives), NYPL, WYU (True Boardman, Jr. Collection).

BOLES, John, Greenville, TX, 1895/1900–1969.

Stage-trained John Boles's film career began in the late silent era with *The Love of Sunya* (1927), but it was his singing voice which brought him his greatest fame. He warbled through such early talkies as *The Desert Song* and *Rio Rita* and later became a competent, if rather bland, leading man in such 1930s films as *Back Street*, *Stella Dallas* and *Craig's Wife*. His career lasted until the early 1950s, although the films became increasingly less prestigious.

PUBLISHED SOURCES

• *Books* – General: *Hollywood Players: the Thirties*; *Hollywood Songsters*; *The MGM Years*; *The Movie Musical from Vitaphone to 42nd Street*. Credits: *Filmarama* (v. II); *Forty Years of Screen Credits*; *Twenty Years of Silents*; *Who Was Who on Screen*. Encyclopedic Works: *The Biographical Encyclopaedia and Who's Who of the American Theatre*; *The Complete Encyclopedia of Popular Music and Jazz*; *Encyclopedia of the Musical Theatre*; *Film Encyclopedia*; *Filmlexicon degli Autori e delle Opere*; *Halliwell's Filmgoer's Companion*; *The Illustrated Who's Who of the Cinema*; *The Movie Makers*; *The Picturegoer's Who's Who and Encyclopedia of the Screen To-day*; *Quinlan's Illustrated Registry of Film Stars*; *Who Was Who in the Theatre*; *Who's Who in Hollywood*; *The World Almanac Who's Who of Film*; *The World Film Encyclopedia*. Nostalgia: *Whatever Became of. . .* (2nd). Pictorial: *The Image Makers*; *Pictures of Movie Stars, with Stories*. Recordings: *Hollywood on Record*.

• *Periodicals* – The following periodical articles are in addition to those included in the library listings below: *Motion Picture Magazine* (July 1928, Dec. 1929, Mar. 1931, Sept.-Oct. 1935, Feb. 1936, Apr. 1937); *Photoplay* (Sept. 1929, Apr. 1934, Aug. 1934); *Motion Picture Classic* (July 1930); *Silver Screen* (June 1931, Feb. 1933, Mar. 1936); *Movie Classic* (Nov. 1932, July 1934, Dec. 1934, Nov. 1935); *Lion's Roar* (Jan. 1944); *Time* (Mar. 7, 1969); *Newsweek* (Mar. 10, 1969); *Classic Film Collector* (Spring 1969); *Classic Images* (Dec. 1989).

ARCHIVAL MATERIALS

• *Caricature* – NYMN. • *Clipping File* – AZSU (Jimmy Starr Collection): Advertisement (1930). CAA: Article (1929, 1931, 1944, 1951, 1961); interview (1961); release from Fox (1936); film appearance (1961); obituary (1969). CAFI: Newsphotos; article (1960); obituary (1969). CAUT: Film appearance (1962);

obituary (1969). CAUU: Obituary (1969). NYMA: Obituary (1969). NYMN: Extortion plot (1937); newsphotos (numerous). NYPL: Film appearance (1920s, 1930s [numerous]); career (1930, undated); newsphotos (numerous); article (1944, undated [numerous]); stage appearance (numerous); exercise regimen; obituary (1969). Periodical articles: *Screen Secrets* (Nov. 1929); *Motion Picture Classic* (Dec. 1929); *Universal Weekly* (Dec. 21, 1929); *Cinelandia* (Mar. 1930); *Motion Picture Magazine* (July 1930); *Screenland* (Nov. 1930); *Photoplay* (Jan. 1931, Sept. 1931); *Picture Play* (Mar. 1931); *Screen Romances* (Apr. 1931); *Screen Play* (Apr. 1931). • *Other Clipping File*— CNDA, GBBF, MAH, MIDL, OHCL, PAPL, WICF. • *Collection*— CAUU (King Vidor Collection): Documents. • *Correspondence*— OHCL. NYPL (C. & L. Brown Collection): 1939. • *Legal File*— CAUT (Twentieth Century-Fox Collection): Letter (1931-36); contract (1931); loanout (1932-35); talent agreement (1936); option (1931). CAUW: Payroll record (1927); contract summary (1927); contract (1927); talent agreement (1927, 1929). • *Oral History*— NYCO: Mentioned in: Gloria Swanson interview. • *Photograph/Still*— AZSU (Jimmy Starr Collection), CAA (also in Hollywood Studio Museum Collection) (also in MGM Collection), CAFA, CALM, CAUT (Jessen Collection) (Portrait File), CAUU, CNDA, DCG (Quigley Photographic Archives), GBBF, MIDL, NJPT, NYAM, NYB (Bettmann/UPI Collection), NYCU (Dramatic Museum Portraits) (Palmer Collection), NYEH, NYMN, NYPL, NYSU, OHCL, TXSM, TXU, WICF. • *Publicity Release*— AZSU (Jimmy Starr Collection). CAA: Paramount (1938). NYPL: Universal (numerous).   • *Scrapbook*— NJPT (Yeandle Collection), NYAM, NYPL. • *Studio Biography*— AZSU: Universal. CAA: Fox (1933); RKO (1933); Paramount (1936). CAFI: Paramount (1933).

BONNER, Priscilla, Adrian, MI, 1904– *1996*

Winsome Priscilla Bonner's first film

was *Homer Come Home*, with Charles Ray (q.v.), and she appeared with Harry Langdon (q.v.) in the films *Long Pants* and *The Strong Man*. A popular leading lady during the 1920s, her other films included *Shadows, It* and *The Red Kimono*. She retired at the dawn of the sound era.

PUBLISHED SOURCES

• *Books* – **General:** *The Idols of Silence.* **Credits:** *Filmarama* (v. II); *Twenty Years of Silents.* **Encyclopedic Works:** *Who's Who in Hollywood.* **Nostalgia:** *Whatever Became of...* (9th). **Pictorial:** *Silent Portraits.*

• *Periodicals*—The following periodical articles are in addition to that included in the library listings below: *Motion Picture Classic* (Jan. 1921, Aug. 1927); *Motion Picture Magazine* (Oct. 1921).

ARCHIVAL MATERIALS

• *Clipping File*— CAA: Marriage (1921); article (1979). Periodical article: *Films in Review* (Mar. 1980). • *Other Clipping File*— GBBF. • *Collection*— CAUT: Over 120 stills.• *Correspondence*— CAUU (A. Slide Collection): 1974. • *Interview*— CAUU (A. Slide Collection): 1973. • *Legal File*— CAUW: Release (1926). • *Photograph/Still*— CAA (also in Hollywood Studio Museum Collection), CAUT (Jessen Collection) (Portrait File) (also in Collection), CAUU (A. Slide Collection), NYPL, NYSU, OHCL, TXU. • *Privately Printed Material*— CAA: *The Silent Stars Speak.* AMPAS, 1979.

BORDEN, Olive (Sybil Tinkle), Timpson, TX or Richmond, VA, 1906/07–1947.

Olive Borden was a smoldering brunette who had a brief popularity in the last years of the silents. Named a Wampas Baby Star in 1925, she appeared in films such as *Virgin Lips, Fig Leaves* and *Joy Girl*, but there was far more drama in her unfortunate private life. The advent of talkies and her release from Fox about 1928 for "temperament" tarnished her career. After several sound films, her final film came in 1934.

PUBLISHED SOURCES
• *Books* — **General:** *How I Broke Into the Movies.* **Credits:** *Filmarama* (v. II); *Forty Years of Screen Credits*; *Twenty Years of Silents*; *Who Was Who on Screen.* **Encyclopedic Works:** *Film Encyclopedia*; *Filmlexicon degli Autori e delle Opere*; *Halliwell's Filmgoer's Companion*; *The Movie Makers*; *Who's Who in Hollywood.* **Pictorial:** *They Had Faces Then.*
• *Periodicals* — The following periodical articles are in addition to those included in the library listings below: *Photoplay* (May 1926, Jan. 1927, May 1927, Dec. 1927); *Motion Picture Magazine* (June 1926, July 1927); *Motion Picture Classic* (July 1929, Nov. 1929); *Time* (Oct. 13, 1947); *Films in Review* (Feb. 1970) (Wampas Baby Stars); *Classic Images* (Nov. 1990, Feb. 1991) (filmography).

ARCHIVAL MATERIALS
• *Caricature* — NYPL (Sardi Collection). • *Clipping File* — CAA: Film appearance (1926); husband sued by ex-wife (1932); work in Los Angeles mission (1946); career (1948); obituary (1947). CAUT: Obituary (1947). NYMA: Newsphotos; marriage/divorce (1931–32); article (1926, 1932); signs with Fox (1925); film appearance (1920s); comeback (1929); husband sued for bigamy (1932); obituary (1947). Periodical articles: *Photoplay* (Dec. 1929, July 1931); *Classic Images* (Jan. 1991). NYPL: Newsphotos; career (1948); article (undated); divorce (1932); film review (1920s); obituary (1947). • *Other Clipping File* — GBBF, MIDL, OHCL, PAPL, WICF. • *Legal File* — CAUT (Twentieth Century–Fox Collection): Memo (1947); talent agreement (1925); assignment (1927). CAUW: Contract (1929). • *Photograph/Still* — CAA (also in Hollywood Studio Museum Collection) (also in MGM Collection), CAH, CAUT (Jessen Collection), DCG (Quigley Photographic Archives), GBBF, MIDL, NJPT, NYCU (Dramatic Museum Portraits) (Palmer Collection), NYEH, NYPL, NYSU, OHCL, TXSM, TXU (A. Davis Collection), WICF, WYU. • *Publicity Release* — NYMA: Paramount (1925).

BOSWORTH, Hobart, Marietta, Ohio, 1867–1943.

"The Grand Old Man of the Movies" and "The Dean of Hollywood" were one and the same person: much beloved Hobart Bosworth. In a career going back to 1909, he appeared in hundreds of films, including perhaps the first one-reeler made in Hollywood, *The Power of the Sultan.* At one point he had his own film company, Bosworth Inc., which ultimately merged with Famous Players and Lasky Film Co. to form Paramount. He made his final film appearances in the early 1940s.

PUBLISHED SOURCES
• *Books* — **General:** *Blue Book of the Screen*; *Character People*; *Eighty Silent Film Stars*; *Famous Film Folk*; *The Golden Gate and the Silver Screen*; *The Idols of Silence*; *Life Stories of the Movie Stars*; *The Truth About the Movies*; *Who's Who in the Film World*; *Who's Who on the Screen.* **Credits:** *Filmarama* (v. I and II); *Forty Years of Screen Credits*; *Twenty Years of Silents*; *Who Was Who on Screen.* **Encyclopedic Works:** *Film Encyclopedia*; *Filmlexicon degli Autori e delle Opere*; *Halliwell's Filmgoer's Companion*; *International Dictionary of Films and Filmmakers* (v. 3); *The Movie Makers*; *The Picturegoer's Who's Who and Encyclopedia of the Screen To-day*; *Who's Who in Hollywood*; *The World Almanac Who's Who of Film*; *The World Film Encyclopedia.* **Pictorial:** *Silent Portraits.*
• *Periodicals* — The following periodical articles are in addition to those included in the library listings below: *Motion Picture Magazine* (Feb. 1915, Feb. 1922, Apr. 1928); *Moving Picture Weekly* (Sept. 18, 1915); *Photoplay* (Dec. 1915, Apr. 1920); *The Nation* (May 1918); *Motion Picture Classic* (Dec. 1919);

National Magazine (June 1925); *Cinema Digest* (Sept. 19, 1932); *Mark Twain Quarterly* (Fall-Winter 1942-1943) (article by HB about Jack London); *Newsweek* (Jan. 10, 1944); *Time* (Jan. 10, 1944); *Classic Film/Video Images* (July 1981); *Film History* (no. 3, 1990).

OBSCURE PUBLISHED SOURCES
CAA (Pat O'Malley Collection): *The Cast* (v. 1).

ARCHIVAL MATERIALS
• *Clipping File* — CAA: Film appearance (1920, 1927, 1929); marriage (1921); program of exhibit (1950); article (1939-40, 1957); obituary (1943). CAFI: Article (1980); home (1981). CAUT: Article (1920s?); donation (1929); estate (1981). NYMA: Signs with Ince (1919); signs with Universal; article (1931-32, 1934, 1941); illness; film appearance (1920s, 1930s). Periodical articles: *Classic Images* (June-Sept. 1985, Apr. 1988, Mar. 1992). NYMN: Newsphotos. NYPL: Film appearance (1930s); newsphotos. • *Other Clipping File* — GBBF, MAH, MIDL, OHCL, PAPL, WICF. • *Correspondence* — CAA (Selig Collection): 1911. CAHL (Jack, Charmian and Eliza London Papers): More than 100 letters and telegrams (1913-55). • *Legal File* — CAHL: Affidavit (1913). CAUW: Option (1942); letter, memo (1941-42); personnel, payroll record (1941-42); talent agreement (1929-30); contract (1930). • *Oral History* — CAUS: Mentioned in: Harry Oliver interview. NYCO: Mentioned in the following interviews: Mrs. H.E. Erskine, Chester Morris. • *Photograph/Still* — CAA (also in MGM collection), CAFA, CALM, CAUT (Jessen Collection), CAUU, DCG (Quigley Photographic Archives), GBBF, NJFL, NYAM, NYCU (Dramatic Museum Portraits), NYEH, NYMN, NYPL, NYSU, OHCL, TNUT (Clarence Brown Collection), TXSM, TXU, WICF. • *Play Program* — NYPL: 1890s, 1903. • *Publicity Release* — CAA: Warner (1941). NYMA: Bosworth Productions (1921). • *Scrapbook* — NYPL, WICF. • *Studio Biography* — NYMA: Photoplay.

BOW, Clara, Brooklyn, NY, 1905-1965.
From her first (minor) role in *Down to the Sea in Ships* (1923), it was an ever-upward path to the heights of stardom for Clara Bow. Dubbed the "It Girl," she became an enduring symbol of the Jazz Age in Paramount films such as *It, Hula, Fascinating Youth, Dancing Mothers* and *Children of Divorce.* At the end of the silent era, however, changing tastes and her own troubled private life combined to undermine her career. Although she made a relatively successful talkie debut with her not-unpleasant low-pitched voice, her career ended in 1933 with the supposed comeback film *Hoopla.*

PUBLISHED SOURCES
• *Books* — **Bibliography:** *The Idols of Silence.* **General:** *Alice in Movieland; The Celluloid Sacrifice; Clara Bow* (Noe); *Classics of the Silent Screen; Co-Starring Famous Women and Alcohol; Famous Film Folk; Fifty Super Stars; The Great Movie Stars: the Golden Years; History of the American Cinema* (v. 3); *Hollywood Album; Hollywood Hall of Fame; Hollywood Heartbreak; The Hollywood Reporter Star Profiles; Hollywood R.I.P.; How I Broke Into the Movies; Ladies in Distress; Love Goddesses of the Movies; Love, Laughter and Tears; Movie Star; The Movie Stars; The Movie Stars Story; The Paramount Pretties; Personal Glimpses of Famous Folks; Popcorn Venus; The Public is Never Wrong; Screen Personalities; Sex Goddesses of the Silent Screen; The Stars* (Schickel); *The Stars Appear; Stars of the Silents; Those Scandalous Sheets of Hollywood; The Truth About the Movies; Tres Comicos del Cine; Twinkle, Twinkle, Movie Star; Zanies.* **Credits:** *Filmarama* (v. II); *Forty Years of Screen Credits; Twenty Years of Silents; Who Was Who on Screen.* **Encyclopedic Works:** *A Biographical Dictionary of Film; A Dictionary of the Cinema; Film Encyclopedia; Filmlexicon degli Autori e delle Opere; Halliwell's Filmgoer's Com-*

panion; *The Illustrated Encyclopedia of the World's Great Movie Stars and Their Films*; *The Illustrated Who's Who of the Cinema*; *International Dictionary of Films and Filmmakers* (v. 3); *The International Encyclopedia of Film*; *The Movie Makers*; *Notable American Women: the Modern Period*; *The Oxford Companion to Film*; *The Picturegoer's Who's Who and Encyclopedia of the Screen To-day*; *Quinlan's Illustrated Registry of Film Stars*; *Who's Who in Hollywood*; *The World Almanac Who's Who of Film*; *The World Encyclopedia of the Film*; *The World Film Encyclopedia*. **Biography/Autobiography:** *Clara Bow* (Stenn); *The "It" Girl*; *Secret Love-Life of Clara*. **Pictorial:** *The Image Makers*; *Leading Ladies*; *Life and Death in Hollywood*; *The Revealing Eye*; *Silent Portraits*; *They Had Faces Then*. **Factoids:** *Star Stats*.

• *Periodicals*—The following periodical articles are in addition to those included in the library listings below: *Motion Picture Classic* (Jan. 1922, Sept. 1922, June 1925, June 1926, Feb. 1927, Aug. 1928, Dec. 1928, Sept. 1930, Nov. 1930, Apr.-May 1931, Aug. 1931); *Photoplay* (June 1925, Mar. 1926, Feb.-Apr. 1928, Sept.-Oct. 1929, Jan. 1930, May 1930, July 1930, Sept.-Oct. 1930, Jan. 1931, July-Sept. 1931, July 1932, Nov. 1932, May 1933, Nov. 1933, Feb. 1934); *Motion Picture Magazine* (Aug. 1927, Nov. 1928, Mar. 1930, Sept. 1930, Jan. 1931, Apr. 1931, Aug. 1932, Nov. 1932); *Theatre World* (Nov. 1927); *Pictorial Review* (Nov. 1927); *Fortune* (Oct. 1930); *Silver Screen* (Nov. 1930, Apr. 1931, Sept. 1931, Jan. 1933, Dec. 1933); *Movie Classic* (Sept. 1931, Feb. 1932, Apr. 1932, July 1932, Apr. 1933, Aug. 1934); *Cinema Digest* (Sept. 19, 1932, Jan. 9, 1933); *Pictures and Picturegoer* (Dec. 3, 1932); *Life* (Mar. 31, 1947, Oct. 8, 1965); *Show* (June 1962); *Films in Review* (Nov. 1963 (filmography), Feb. 1970) (Wampas Baby Stars); *8mm Collector* (Spring 1965, Fall/Winter 1965); *Newsweek* (Oct. 11, 1965); *Film Dope* (Mar. 1974); *Cine Revue* (June 5, 1975); *Classic Images* (May 1981); *Hollywood Studio Magazine* (Nov. 1985); *Film Comment* (Nov.-Dec. 1988).

ARCHIVAL MATERIALS

• *Clipping File*—CAA: Fame and Fortune Contest (1921); romance (1926, 1929-30); Paramount contract (1927, 1931); "It" (1927); marriage/children (1931, 1934); legal problem (1928-31); illness (1928, 1931); film appearance (1931-32); radio appearance (1947); article (1950, 1953, 1957, 1964); death of husband (1962); Academy of Motion Picture Arts and Sciences tribute (1981); obituary (1965). Periodical articles: *Motion Picture Classic* (numerous 1920s-early 30s); *Films in Review* (Oct. 1963); *Sight and Sound* (Autumn 1968); *Classic Film Collector* (May 1970); *Hollywood Studio Magazine* (Mar. 1972, Aug. 1981); *Liberty* (Spring 1975); *Cosmopolitan* (Oct. 1980); *Premiere* (Sept. 1982); *Nevada* (July-Aug. 1985). CAFI: Newsphotos (numerous); review of *Clara Bow: Running Wild* (1988); obituary (1965). Periodical articles: *Look* (Dec. 21, 1937); *Time* (Oct. 8, 1965). CAUT: Engagement (1929); newsphotos; article (1981); film festival (1980s?) CAUU: Article (1929, 1953, 1976, 1980-81); program from Tribute to Clara Bow (1981). Periodical article: *Classic Film Collector* (Spring/Summer 1970). NYMN: Children (1935); article (1920s); obituary (1965). NYPL: Newsphotos; biography (1950, 1957); article (1927, 1932, 1953, 1988, undated); sex symbol (1976, 1981); illness (1953, 1956, 1961); obituary (1965). Periodical articles: *Films in Review* (Oct. 1963); *Liberty Magazine* (Spring 1975); *Interview* (Sept. 1988); *Big Reel* (Jan. 1991). • *Other Clipping File*—AZSU (Jimmy Starr Collection), CASF, CAUB, CNDA, GBBF, MAH, MIDL, NYMA, OHCL, PAPL, WICF. • *Correspondence*—CAA (Hedda Hopper Collection): Letters (1950, 1959, 1962); telegram about the acting ambitions of her son Tony (1963); several Christmas cards. MABU (Anthony Glyn Collection). • *Film Program*—CAHL: (1928). • *Filmography*—CAA, NYPL. • *Legal File*—CAUT (Twentieth Century-Fox Collection): Letter, memo (1932-35); agreement (1931-32). CAUW: Loanout (1924); talent agreement (1924); breach of contract (undated). • *Memorabilia*—NYCU

(Bennett Cerf Collection). • *Oral History*—CAUS: Mentioned in: Edward A. Dickson interview. NYCO: Mentioned in the following interviews: Joseph Mankiewicz, A. Mayer, Henry Myers, Elliot Nugent, Geraldine Page, Charles Ruggles, Adela St. Johns, Albert (Eddie) Sutherland. • *Photograph/Still*—CAA (also in Hollywood Studio Museum Collection), CAHL, CALM, CASF, CAUB, CAUS, CAUT (Jessen Collection) (Portrait File), CNDA, GBBF, IAU (Junkin Collection), NYAM, NYB (Bettmann/UPI Collection) (Penguin Collection) (Springer Collection) (Underwood Collection), NYCU (Dramatic Museum Portraits) (Palmer Collection), NYEH, NYMN, NYPL, OHCL, TXSU, TXU, WICF. • *Press Kit*—OHCL. • *Scrapbook*—NYAM, NYPL. • *Studio Biography*—CAA: Fox (1932).

BOWERS, John, Garrett, IN, 1899-1936.

John Bowers had a relatively successful career throughout the 1920s as a leading man in films such as *Lorna Doone*, *Richard the Lion-Hearted*, *Whispering Smith* and *When a Man's a Man*. He was virtually finished with the coming of sound, however, and appeared in only a couple of talkies. His mode of suicide (drowning in the ocean) was supposedly the inspiration for the similar demise of the ex-star in *A Star Is Born*. He was married to Marguerite de la Motte (q.v.).

PUBLISHED SOURCES
• *Books*—General: *Famous Film Folk*. Credits: *Filmarama* (v. I and II); *Twenty Years of Silents*; *Who Was Who on Screen*. Encyclopedic Works: *Film Encyclopedia*; *Filmlexicon degli Autori e delle Opere*; *The Picturegoer's Who's Who and Encyclopedia of the Screen To-day*; *Who's Who in Hollywood*. Pictorial: *Silent Portraits*.
• *Periodicals*—The following periodical articles are in addition to those included in the library listings below: *Motion Picture Magazine* (Aug. 1919,

Jan. 1921); *Motion Picture Classic* (Aug. 1921).

ARCHIVAL MATERIALS
• *Clipping File*—CAA: Article (1922); obituary (1936). NYMA (also in Photoplay Collection): Personal data summary. NYPL: Newsphotos; article (1918, 1921, 1923); obituary (1936). Periodical articles: *Photoplay* (Aug. 1919); *Motion Picture Classic* (Jan. 1920). • *Other Clipping File*—GBBF, MAH, MIDL, OHCL, PAPL, WICF. • *Legal File*—CAUW: Talent agreement (1928-29). • *Photograph/Still*—CAA (also in Hollywood Studio Museum Collection), CAUU, DCG (Quigley Photographic Archives), GBBF, NJFL, NJPT, NYAM, NYEH, NYPL, NYSU, OHCL, TXSM, TXU, WICF. • *Scrapbook*—NYPL. • *Studio Biography*—CAA: Metropolitan (1926).

BRACY (sometimes Bracey), Sidney, Melbourne, Australia, 1877-1942.

Sidney Bracy was in films by 1910 and he appeared in serials such as *The Invisible Ray* and *Zudora* and features including *The Merry Widow* and *The Cameraman*. Although his starring career did not survive the early 1920s, he went on to play numerous character roles until the time of his death.

PUBLISHED SOURCES
• *Books*—Credits: *British Film Actors' Credits*; *Filmarama* (v. I and II); *Forty Years of Screen Credits*; *Twenty Years of Silents*; *Who Was Who on Screen*. Encyclopedic Works: *Film Encyclopedia*; *The Picturegoer's Who's Who and Encyclopedia of the Screen To-day*; *Who's Who in Hollywood*.
• *Periodicals*—The following periodical article is in addition to that included in the library listings below: *Motion Picture Magazine* (Oct. 1915).

ARCHIVAL MATERIALS
• *Clipping File*—NYPL: Film review; newsphotos; article (1916, undated). Periodical article: *Green Book Magazine* (Feb. 1914). • *Other Clipping File*—

GBBF, WICF. • *Legal File* – CAUW: Contract summary (1939); option (1938–42); contract (1938–41); letter, memo (1938–42); talent agreement (1938–40); communication (1940). • *Photograph/ Still* – DCG (Quigley Photographic Archives), NYAM, NYPL, WICF. • *Publicity Release* – NYPL: Famous Players.

BRENT, Evelyn (Mary Elizabeth Riggs), Tampa, FL, 1899–1975.

After doing extra work in Fort Lee, New Jersey, from about 1914, Evelyn Brent made several films in England between 1920 and 1922, then, after returning to the United States, was named a Wampas Baby Star of 1923. Her real fame came near the end of the silent era with a role in von Sternberg's *Underworld*. The success of this film somewhat typed her as a "moll," a box from which she found it difficult to break out. Although she continued to appear in films until 1948's *The Golden Eye*, her roles grew fewer. Her last appearances were in the 1950s television show "Wagon Train."

PUBLISHED SOURCES

• *Books* – Bibliography: *The Idols of Silence.* General: *Famous Film Folk*; *Motion Picture News Booking Guide and Studio Directory* (1927); *People Will Talk*; *Screen Album*; *Sweethearts of the Sage.* Credits: *British Film Actors' Credits*; *Filmarama* (v. I and II); *Forty Years of Screen Credits*; *Twenty Years of Silents*; *Who Was Who on Screen.* Encyclopedic Works: *Film Encyclopedia*; *Filmlexicon degli Autori e delle Opere*; *Halliwell's Filmgoer's Companion*; *The Illustrated Who's Who in British Films*; *The Illustrated Who's Who of the Cinema*; *The Movie Makers*; *The Picturegoer's Who's Who and Encyclopedia of the Screen To-day*; *Quinlan's Illustrated Registry of Film Stars*; *Who's Who in Hollywood*; *The World Almanac Who's Who of Film*; *The World Film Encyclopedia.* Pictorial: *The Image Makers*; *Leading Ladies*; *Silent Portraits*; *They Had Faces Then.* Nostalgia: *Whatever Became of . . .* (3rd).

• *Periodicals* – The following periodical articles are in addition to those included in the library listings below: *Motion Picture Classic* (Sept. 1917, July 1929, Aug. 1931); *Motion Picture Magazine* (Feb. 1928, Mar. 1930, Dec. 1930); *Photoplay* (May 1928, Jan. 1931); *Films in Review* (Feb. 1970) (Wampas Baby Stars), (June-July 1976); *Avant-Scene* (Mar. 15, 1980).

ARCHIVAL MATERIALS

• *Clipping File* – AZSU (Jimmy Starr Collection): Obituary (1975). CAA: Film appearance (1926, 1929); divorce (1947); newsphotos; interview (1960); TV appearance (1958); nostalgia (1972, undated); obituary (1975). CAFI: Newsphotos (numerous); article (1970s, 1975). Periodical article: *Films in Review* (April 1970). CAUT: Newsphotos; article (1929). NYMA (also in Photoplay Collection): Changes name (1916); obituary (1975). Periodical articles: *Monthly Film Bulletin* (May 1966) (filmography); *Classic Images* (Jan.-Feb. 1983). NYMN: Newsphotos; bankruptcy. NYPL: Newsphotos; article (1916, 1918, 1926, 1932, undated); comeback (1930s); film review (1920s, 1930s); signs with Metro (1917); obituary (1975). • *Other Clipping File* – CAUB, GBBF, MIDL, OHCL, PAPL, TXU, WICF. • *Correspondence* – OHCL: Few items. • *Filmography* – NYMA, NYPL. • *Interview* – CAUU (R. Lamparski Collection). • *Legal File* – CAUW: Talent agreement (1932). • *Photograph/Still* – CAA (also in Hollywood Studio Museum Collection), CAFI, CAH, CASF, CASU, CAUU, CNDA, DCG (Quigley Photographic Archives), GBBF, MIDL, NJPT, NYAM, NYB (Bettmann/UPI Collection) (Penguin Collection), NYCU (Dramatic Museum Portraits) (Palmer Collection), NYEH, NYMN, NYPL, NYSU, OHCL, PAPL, TXU (A. Davis Collection) (Robbins Collection), WICF. • *Play Program* – CAHL: (1931). • *Press Kit* – OHCL. • *Scrapbook* – NYPL. • *Studio Biography* – CAA: RKO (1938?); Paramount (1938).

BRIAN, Mary (Louise Dantzler), Corsicana, TX, 1908–

Appearing as a teenager in the silents (e.g., Wendy in *Peter Pan*) and an adult actress in talkies (mainly "B"s), winsome Mary Brian was seen in such films as *The Virginian*, *Alias the Deacon*, *Brown of Harvard*, *Paris at Midnight* and *Beau Geste*. Her American career was basically over by the mid-1930s but she made some British films, had a couple of roles in 1940s quickies and later was seen on television.

PUBLISHED SOURCES

• *Books* – **General:** *Hollywood Players: the Thirties*; *Return Engagement*; *Sweethearts of the Sage*; *Twinkle, Twinkle, Movie Star.* **Credits:** *Filmarama* (v. II); *Forty Years of Screen Credits*; *Twenty Years of Silents.* **Encyclopedic Works:** *Film Encyclopedia*; *Filmlexicon degli Autori e delle Opere*; *Halliwell's Filmgoer's Companion*; *The Movie Makers*; *The Picturegoer's Who's Who and Encyclopedia of the Screen To-day*; *Quinlan's Illustrated Registry of Film Stars*; *Who's Who in Hollywood*; *The World Film Encyclopedia.* **Nostalgia:** *Whatever Became of...* (4th, 8th). **Pictorial:** *The Image Makers*; *Silent Portraits*; *They Had Faces Then.*

• *Periodicals* – The following periodical articles are in addition to those included in the library listings below: *Motion Picture Magazine* (July 1925, Mar. 1929, Aug. 1930, July 1931, Jan. 1934, Nov. 1934); *Photoplay* (May 1930); *Silver Screen* (Apr. 1931, Sept. 1933); *Films in Review* (Feb. 1970) (Wampas Baby Stars); *Classic Images* (Dec. 1982); *Hollywood Studio Magazine* (Nov. 1984).

ARCHIVAL MATERIALS

• *Clipping File* – CAA: Wartime entertaining (1942?, 1945); marriage (1941, 1947); nostalgia (1975, 1980). CAFI: Newsphotos; nostalgia (1975). CAUU: Nostalgia (1975). NYMA: Periodical articles: *Classic Images* (Nov. 1981, Mar. 1984). NYMN: Newsphotos; article (1930). Periodical article: *New Movie Magazine* (undated). NYPL: Stage appearance; newsphotos; article (1926, 1955, undated); film appearance (1926, 1932–33, 1936); marriage/divorce (1941, undated); film reviews (numerous). • *Other Clipping File* – GBBF, MAH, MIDL, OHCL, PAPL, WICF. • *Interview* – CAUU (R. Lamparski Collection), NYAM. • *Legal File* – CAUW: Personnel, payroll record (1932); talent agreement (1930–32); document (1931–32). • *Photograph/Still* – CAA (also in Hollywood Studio Museum Collection), CASF, CAUT (Jessen Collection), CAUU, DCG (Quigley Photographic Archives), GBBF, MIDL, NJPT, NYAM, NYB (Bettmann/UPI Collection), NYCU (Dramatic Museum Portraits), NYEH, NYMN, NYPL, NYSU, OHCL, TXSM, TXU, WICF. • *Scrapbook* – NJPT (Yeandle Collection), NYPL. • *Studio Biography* – CAA: Paramount (1920s, early 1930s?).

BROCKWELL, Gladys (Gladys Lindeman), Brooklyn, NY, 1894–1929.

After a successful career in silent films beginning about 1913, Gladys Brockwell was also finding talkie success at the time of her death. Her debut was made in one- and two-reelers but she ultimately appeared in such features as *Oliver Twist*, *The Hunchback of Notre Dame*, *So Big* and *Seventh Heaven*. She was also in the first alltalkie, *The Lights of New York*.

PUBLISHED SOURCES

• *Books* – Written by (or ghostwritten for) GB: *Cinema* (one part). **Bibliography:** *The Idols of Silence.* **Credits:** *Filmarama* (v. I and II); *Forty Years of Screen Credits*; *Twenty Years of Silents*; *Who Was Who on Screen.* **Encyclopedic Works:** *Film Encyclopedia*; *Filmlexicon degli Autori e delle Opere*; *Who's Who in Hollywood.* **Pictorial:** *Silent Portraits.*

• *Periodicals* – The following periodical articles are in addition to that included in the library listings below: *Photoplay* (Apr. 1917, June 1917, July 1918); *Motion Picture Magazine* (July

1917, June 1919); *Motion Picture Classic* (Oct. 1917, Sept. 1922).

ARCHIVAL MATERIALS
• *Clipping File*—CAA: Engagement (1921); film appearance (1927); obituary (1929). CAUT: Obituary (1929). NYMA (also in Photoplay Collection): Personal data summary. Periodical article: *Classic Images* (Oct. 1987). NYPL: Newsphotos; film review (1916); obituary (1929). • *Other Clipping File*—GBBF, MAH, NYSU, PAPL, WICF. • *Filmography*— CAA, NYMA. • *Legal File*—CAUT (Twentieth Century-Fox Collection): Agreement (1917). CAUW: Contract (1929); talent agreement (1926, 1928). • *Photograph/Still*—CAA (also in Hollywood Studio Museum Collection), CAUB, CAUT (Jessen Collection), CNDA, DCG (Quigley Photographic Archives), GBBF, NJFL, NYB (Bettmann/UPI Collection), NYEH, NYPL, NYSU, OHCL, TXSM, TXU, WICF. • *Scrapbook*—NYPL.

BRONSON, Betty (Elizabeth Bronson), Trenton, NJ, 1906/07–1971.

"Fey" is probably the best word to describe petite Betty Bronson's screen persona at the height of her fame in films such as *Peter Pan* (1924) and *A Kiss for Cinderella*. Her later "adult" roles were not as well received and by the time sound came in her career was already faltering, although she appeared in the phenomenally successful talkie *The Singing Fool*. After a few films in the 1930s, she essayed some character roles in the '60s and also appeared on television.

PUBLISHED SOURCES
• *Books*—**Bibliography:** *The Idols of Silence*. **General:** *Classics of the Silent Screen*; *Famous Film Folk*; *Motion Picture News Booking Guide and Studio Directory* (1927); *Movie Star*. **Credits:** *Filmarama* (v. II); *Forty Years of Screen Credits*; *Twenty Years of Silents*; *Who Was Who on Screen*. **Encyclopedic Works:** *Film Encyclopedia*; *Filmlexicon*

degli Autori e delle Opere; *Halliwell's Filmgoer's Companion*; *The Illustrated Encyclopedia of the World's Great Movie Stars and Their Films*; *The Illustrated Who's Who of the Cinema*; *The Movie Makers*; *The Picturegoer's Who's Who and Encyclopedia of the Screen To-day*; *Who's Who in Hollywood*; *The World Film Encyclopedia*. **Pictorial:** *The Image Makers*; *Silent Portraits*; *They Had Faces Then*. **Nostalgia:** *Whatever Became Of...* (3rd).
• *Periodicals*—*Photoplay* (Oct. 1924, Jan. 1926, Mar. 1927, July 1931); *Motion Picture Classic* (Nov. 1924, Dec. 1925); *Motion Picture Magazine* (July 1928); *Classic Film Collector* (Winter 1971); *Films in Review* (May 1972, Dec. 1974).

ARCHIVAL MATERIALS
• *Clipping File*—CAA: Draft articles by BB on clothes and grooming (1920s); marriage (1932); film appearance (1961–65); nostalgia (1969); obituary (1971). CAFI: Article (1975). CAUT (also in Collection): Obituary (1971). CAUU: Obituary (1971). NYMA: Article (1924, 1964); film festival (1964); obituary (1971). NYMN: Newsphotos; article (1930?). NYPL: *Peter Pan* (1926); stage appearance (1933, 1935); newsphotos; engagement/marriage (1932); film appearance (1926); article (undated); comeback (1930s, 1962); obituary (1971). Periodical articles: *TV Guide* (Mar. 2, 1963); *Film Fan Monthly* (Nov. 1971). • *Other Clipping File*—CNDA, GBBF, MAH, MIDL, OHCL, PAPL, TXU, WICF. • *Collection*—CAUT: 1100 clippings (including numerous film reviews), 370 photographs, 40 playbills, scripts, scrapbooks, sheet music, correspondence, legal papers, diaries, manuscripts. • *Correspondence*—CAUT (see Collection). NYMA: 1969. NYPL (C. & L. Brown Collection): 1933. • *Filmography*—NYMA. • *Interview*—CAUU (R. Lamparski Collection). • *Legal File*—CAUT (see Collection). CAUW: Contract (1928); talent agreement (1929). • *Oral History*—NYCO: Mentioned in: William K. Everson interview. • *Photograph/Still*—CAA (also in Hollywood Studio Museum Collection), CAFA,

CAFI, CAH, CASF, CAUT (see also Collection), CNDA, DCG (Quigley Photographic Archives), GBBF, NJPT, NYAM, NYB (Underwood Collection), NYEH, NYMN, NYPL, NYSU, OHCL, OHSU, PAPL, TXSM, TXU (A. Davis Collection), WICF. • *Play Program* – CAHL: 1931. CAUT (see Collection). • *Scrapbook* – CAUT (see Collection), NYPL.

BROOKS, Louise, Cherryvale, KS, 1906–1985.

Louise Brooks became somewhat of a cult figure in the 1970s and 1980s with her perceptive writings on cinema and the revival of her German films (*Pandora's Box, Diary of a Lost Girl*) made in the late 1920s. Her brief American career was mostly in program films like *Love 'Em and Leave 'Em* and *Rolled Stockings*, although one like *Beggars of Life* occasionally came along. Although she could be seen as late as 1938 in a "B" western, she had been long forgotten until her renaissance as *The Girl in the Black Helmet* decades later.

PUBLISHED SOURCES

• *Books* – **General:** *Classics of the Silent Screen*; *Close Ups*; *Co-Starring Famous Women and Alcohol*; *The Great Movie Stars*; *The Haunted Screen*; *History of the American Cinema* (v. 3); *"Image" on the Art and Evolution of the Film*; *Ladies in Distress*; *The Movie Stars Story*; *The Parade's Gone By*; *People Will Talk*; *Return Engagement*; *Show People*; *Women and the Cinema*. **Credits:** *Filmarama* (v. II); *Forty Years of Screen Credits*; *Twenty Years of Silents*. **Encyclopedic Works:** *A Biographical Dictionary of Film*; *Current Biography* (1984); *A Dictionary of the Cinema*; *Film Encyclopedia*; *Filmlexicon degli Autori e delle Opere*; *Halliwell's Filmgoer's Companion*; *The Illustrated Encyclopedia of the World's Great Movie Stars and Their Films*; *The Illustrated Who's Who of the Cinema*; *International Dictionary of Films and Filmmakers* (v. 3); *The International En-cyclopedia of Film*; *The Movie Makers*; *The Oxford Companion to Film*; *The Picturegoer's Who's Who and Encyclopedia of the Screen To-day*; *Quinlan's Illustrated Registry of Film Stars*; *Variety Who's Who in Show Business*; *Who's Who in Hollywood*; *The World Almanac Who's Who of Film*; *The World Encyclopedia of the Film*; *The World Film Encyclopedia*. **Pictorial:** *Leading Ladies*; *Silent Portraits*; *They Had Faces Then*. **Nostalgia:** *Whatever Became of...* (3rd). **Biography/Autobiography:** *Louise Brooks* (Paris); *Lulu in Hollywood*. **Films:** *Louise Brooks* (Jaccard).

• *Periodicals* – The following periodical articles are in addition to those included in the library listings below: *Photoplay* (Apr. 1926, Feb. 1927); *Motion Picture Classic* (Sept. 1927); *Image* (Sept. 1956); *Sight and Sound* (Summer 1958, Winter 1958/59, Summer 1965, Winter 1966/67, Spring 1971, Spring 1986); *Monthly Film Bulletin Checklist* (July 1965) (filmography); *8mm Collector* (Summer 1965); *Film Culture* (Spring 1966, Spring 1972, nos. 58-60, 1974, nos. 67-69, 1979); *Positif* (Mar. 1970, Dec. 1977-Jan. 1978, Dec. 1983, Nov. 1985); *Focus on Film* (Winter 1972, Mar. 1978); *Film Dope* (July 1974); *Ecran* (Sept.-Oct. 1974); *Film* (London) (May 1975); *Observer Magazine* (Nov. 11, 1979); *Jeune Cinema* (June 1980); *Film und Fernsehen* (no. 12, 1980); *Avant-Scene du Cinema* (Dec. 1, 1980); *Frauen und Film* (Dec. 1980, Dec. 1985); *Cahiers du Cinema* (Jan. 1981); *Cine Revue* (Jan. 1, 1981, Aug. 22, 1985); *Esquire* (May 1982); *Newsweek* (May 24, 1982, Aug. 19, 1985); *Films in Review* (June-July 1982, Nov. 1985); *New Leader* (Aug. 9-23, 1982); *Cineaste* (Sept.-Dec. 1982); *American Film* (Oct. 1982); *Visions* (Nov. 15, 1982, Oct. 1985); *Film Comment* (Nov.-Dec. 1982); *Classic Images* (Feb. 1983, Apr.-May 1983, Oct. 1983); *Andere Sinema* (May 1983, Nov.-Dec. 1990); *Screen* (July-Oct. 1983); *Missouri Review* (Summer 1983); *Skrien* (Sept. 1983); *Horizon* (Jan.-Feb. 1984); *Filmcritica* (July 1984); *Time* (Aug. 19, 1985); *Cinematographe* (Sept. 1985); *Revue du Cinema* (Oct.

1985); *Sequences* (Nov. 1985); *Grand Angle* (Dec. 1985); *Skoop* (June 1986); *Hollywood Studio Magazine* (July 1988); *Film Criticism* (Winter 1989/90); *New Republic* (Dec. 25, 1989); *Artforum* (Apr. 1990); *Filmvilag* (no. 4, 1991).

MEDIA

Lulu in Berlin (video).

ARCHIVAL MATERIALS

• *Clipping File* — CAA: Nostalgia (1969, 1975); marriage/divorce (1933–34, 1937); illness (1979); film appearance (1937); article (1926, 1979, 1982–83, 1989); review of *Lulu in Hollywood* (1982); film festival (1983, 1989); review of *Louise Brooks* (1989); articles by LB; obituary (1985). Periodical articles: *New Yorker* (June 11, 1979); *Imagenes* (Nov. 1979); *Life* (Feb. 1980); *Cine Revue* (Jan. 8, 1981); *Vogue* (Sept. 1981, May 1982); *Paris Match* (Sept. 1985); *Vanity Fair* (Oct. 1989). CAFI: Review of *Louise Brooks* (1989); film festival (1983, 1985); review of *Lulu in Hollywood* (1982); article on *Pandora's Box* (film); excerpt from *Current Biography* (1984); obituary (1985). Periodical articles: *New Yorker* (June 1989); *American Film* (Nov. 1989). CAUT: Article (1983); review of *Lulu in Hollywood* (1982); obituary (1985). Periodical articles: *New Yorker* (June 11, 1979); *American Film* (Sept. 1986). CAUU (Also in McCormick Collection): Film festival (1983); nostalgia (1969, 1975); review of *Lulu in Hollywood* (1982); article (1985); obituary (1985). Periodical article: *Vogue* (Sept. 1981). NYMN: Newsphotos; dancer (1930s); divorce (1934); singer (1930s?); obituary (1985). NYPL: PARTIAL CONTENTS: Newsphotos; review of *Louise Brooks* (Paris) (1983); article (1985); obituary (1985). • *Other Clipping File* — AZSU (Jimmy Starr Collection), CAUB, CNDA, GBBF, MAH, MIDL, NYEH, NYMA (also in Film Study Center Special Collection), OHSU, PAPL, WICF. • *Correspondence* — CAA (Adolph Zukor Collection). NYMA (Film Study Center Special Collection): 1966. NYPL: 206 letters (Herman Weinberg Collection) (1962–83); letter(s) (C. & L. Brown Collection) (undated); 8 letters

(Fitzroy Davis Collection) (1966–69). • *Interview* — GBBF (Hollywood Collection): Transcript of interview for *Hollywood* (TV series). NYAM. • *Legal File* — CAUW: Talent agreement (1930). • *Manuscript* — NYEH. • *Oral History* — NYCO: Mentioned in: Jay Leyda interview. • *Photograph/Still* — CAA, CASF, CAUB, CAUU, CNDA, DCG (Quigley Photographic Archives), GBBF, NYAM, NYB (Bettmann/UPI Collection) (Springer Collection), NYEH, NYMN, NYPL, OHCL, TXU, WICF. • *Publicity Release* — CAA: Paramount (1920s). • *Remininscence* — MISU: Kenneth Tynan relates stories about LB: 1984 (recording). • *Scrapbook* — NYPL.

BRUNETTE, Fritzi (sometimes Fritzie) (Freda Samuels), New Orleans, LA?, 1890–1943.

Beginning about 1913, Fritzi(e) Brunette appeared in films including *Annie Laurie* (early version), *The Devil to Pay*, *The Woman Thou Gavest Me* and *The Green Flame*. Several of her films co-starred popular J. Warren Kerrigan (q.v.). Her period of stardom was not lengthy; she played supporting roles later in the silent days and continued in bit roles until at least 1940.

PUBLISHED SOURCES

• *Books* — Credits: *Filmarama* (v. I and II); *Twenty Years of Silents*; *Who Was Who on Screen*. **Encyclopedic Works:** *Film Encyclopedia*; *Film Lexicon degli Autori e delle Opere*; *Who's Who in Hollywood*.

ARCHIVAL MATERIALS

• *Clipping File* — CAA: Excerpt from *Film Daily Year Book* (1944). NYMA: Vaudeville appearance (1923); film appearance (1915, 1918, 1920–21); article (1910s); signs with Santa Barbara Film Company. NYPL: Newsphotos; film appearance (1910s, 1922); article (1913–14); signs with Universal (1913); marriage (1914); obituary (1943). Periodical articles: *Photoplay* (May 1917); *Theatre Magazine* (Apr. 1919). • *Other Clipping File* — MAH, PAPL, WICF. • *Photo-*

graph/Still—CAA, DCG (Quigley Photographic Archives), GBBF, NYPL, NYSU, OHCL, TXU, WICF. • *Publicity Release*—NYMA: Unknown studio (1919); American Releasing Corporation (1923); Universal.

BUNNY, John, Brooklyn, NY, 1863-1915.

Cherubic John Bunny was wildly popular during his relatively brief, though prolific, film career which began about 1910. His almost 200 films consisted largely of one- and two-reelers ("Bunnygrams") in which he frequently appeared with acerbic Flora Finch and which sometimes bore his name in the title (e.g., *Bunny's Honeymoon*). Other films included *A Cure for Pokeritis, John Tobin's Sweetheart* and *Chumps*. He also appeared in a few dramatic roles such as *Vanity Fair* and *Pickwick Papers*.

PUBLISHED SOURCES
• *Books*—Bibliography: *The Idols of Silence*. General: *The Big V*; *Classics of the Silent Screen*; *Clown Princes and Court Jesters*; *Early American Cinema*; *Two Reels and a Crank*; *World of Laughter*. Credits: *British Film Actors' Credits*; *Filmarama* (v. I); *Twenty Years of Silents*; *Who Was Who on Screen*. Encyclopedic Works: *Film Encyclopedia*; *Filmlexicon degli Autori e delle Opere*; *Halliwell's Filmgoer's Companion*; *The Illustrated Who's Who of the Cinema*; *International Dictionary of Films and Filmmakers* (v. 3); *The International Encyclopedia of Film*; *Joe Franklin's Encyclopedia of Comedians*; *Quinlan's Illustrated Directory of Film Comedy Actors*; *Who's Who in Hollywood*; *The World Almanac Who's Who of Film*.
• *Periodicals*—The following periodical articles are in addition to those included in the library listings below: *Moving Picture World* (Oct. 14, 1911, Sept. 21, 1912, Feb. 15, 1913); *Saturday Review* (England) (Apr. 11, 1914); *Blue Book Magazine* (May 1914, Sept. 1914); *American Magazine* (Aug. 1914); *World's Work* (Mar. 1915); *Motion Picture Mag-*

azine (May 1915, Feb. 1925); *Bioscope* (May 6, 1915); *Photoplay* (Mar. 1926); *Motion Picture Classic* (Oct. 1926); *Good Housekeeping* (Aug. 1932); *Silent Picture* (Winter 1968/1969, Summer 1972).

ARCHIVAL MATERIALS
• *Clipping File*—CAA: Article (1931). Periodical article: 1915 (no title); *World of Yesterday* (Oct. 1977). CAUT: Periodical article: *Photoplay* (Oct. 1914). NYMA (also in Photoplay Collection): Personal data summary. Periodical articles: *Moving Picture World* (May 8, 1915); *Classic Images* (Jan. 1992). NYPL: Newsphotos; pie eating contest (1903); biography (1914). • *Other Clipping File*—CNDA, GBBF, WICF. • *Biography*—CAUU (A. Slide Collection). • *Correspondence*—NYMA (Film Study Center Special Collection): Postcard. • *Filmography*—NYEH, NYPL. • *Oral History*—NYCO: Mentioned in the following interviews: Harry Brandt, Ross Browne, Arthur Hornblow Jr., Buster Keaton, Elliot Nugent. • *Photograph/Still*—CAA (also in Hollywood Studio Museum Collection), CALM, CASF, DCG (Quigley Photographic Archives), NYB (Bettmann/UPI Collection) (Underwood Collection), NYEH, NYPL, NYSU, OHCL, WICF. • *Program*—CASF, NYPL. • *Scrapbook*—NYPL.

BURNS, Edmund (Edward Burns), Philadelphia, PA, 1892-1980.

Popular DeMille star Edmund Burns appeared in *Male and Female* and also in many programmers with titles like *Jazzmania, The Princess from Hoboken* and *The Manicure Girl*. He was a dependable lead and supporting player throughout his career, which ended in the mid-1930s.

PUBLISHED SOURCES
• *Books*—Credits: *Filmarama* (v. I and II); *Forty Years of Screen Credits*; *Twenty Years of Silents*. Encyclopedic Works: *Film Encyclopedia*; *Film Lexicon degli Autori e delle Opere*; *Who's*

Who in Hollywood. **Pictorial:** *Silent Portraits*.

ARCHIVAL MATERIALS

• *Clipping File* – CAA: Marriage (1934); obituary (1980). CAFI: Obituary (1980). CAUT: Obituary (1980). NYMA: Film appearance (1920-24). NYPL: Newsphotos (numerous); film appearance (1920s, 1930s). • *Other Clipping File* – GBBF, PAPL, WICF. • *Filmography* – NYPL (incomplete). • *Legal File* – CAUW: Talent agreement (1928-29). • *Photograph/Still* – CAA, DCG (Quigley Photographic Archives), GBBF, NJFL, NYAM, NYPL, OHCL, TXU, WICF. • *Publicity Release* – NYMA: DeMille (1926). • *Scrapbook* – NYPL. • *Studio Biography* – CAA: DeMille (1926). NYMA: Photoplay.

BUSCH, Mae, Melbourne, Australia, 1891/1897-1946.

Despite her flippant latter-day designation (by Jackie Gleason) as the "ever-popular" Mae Busch, the actress had many respectable roles. She had a successful career in the 1920s with such films as *Foolish Wives*, *The Christian* and *The Unholy Three*, but is perhaps best remembered as the frequent foil to Laurel and Hardy in their comedy shorts and features of the 1930s.

PUBLISHED SOURCES

• *Books* – **General:** *Famous Film Folk*; *Hollywood Album 2*; *The Laurel and Hardy Book*; *The Truth About the Movies*; *Twinkle, Twinkle, Movie Star*. **Credits:** *Filmarama* (v. I and II); *Forty Years of Screen Credits*; *Twenty Years of Silents*; *Who Was Who on Screen*. **Encyclopedic Works:** *Film Encyclopedia*; *Filmlexicon degli Autori e delle Opere*; *Halliwell's Filmgoer's Companion*; *The Illustrated Who's Who of the Cinema*; *The Movie Makers*; *The Picturegoer's Who's Who and Encyclopedia of the Screen To-day*; *Who's Who in Hollywood*; *The World Almanac Who's Who of Film*; *The World Film Encyclopedia*. **Pictorial:** *The Image Makers*; *Silent Portraits*; *They Had Faces Then*.

• *Periodicals* – The following periodical articles are in addition to those included in the library listings below: *Motion Picture Classic* (Apr. 1921); *Motion Picture Magazine* (Nov. 1921, Nov. 1924, Aug. 1925); *Photoplay* (Mar. 1922); *Time* (Apr. 29, 1946); *Films in Review* (Mar. 1956, May 1976, Aug.-Sept. 1986); *Classic Images* (Feb. 1985).

ARCHIVAL MATERIALS

• *Clipping File* – CAA: Newsphotos; marriage/divorce (1923, 1936); film appearance (1921-22, 1924); obituary (1946). Periodical article: *Filmograph* (no. 1-1, 1970). NYMA (also in Photoplay Collection): Marriage/divorce (1926, 1928-29, undated); film appearance (1920s); comeback (1932); expenses; signs with Goldwyn (1923). NYPL: Newsphotos; film appearance (1932, 1935); article (1916); career (1922); marriage (1916, 1930s); fight with a bear (1916); obituary (1946). Periodical article: *Motion Picture Classic* (Sept. 1916). • *Other Clipping File* – AZSU (Jimmy Starr Collection), GBBF, MAH, MIDL, NYSU, OHCL, WICF. • *Correspondence* – NYMA (Film Study Center Special Collection). • *Legal File* – CAUW: Personnel, payroll record (1932-38); talent agreement (1932). • *Photograph/Still* – CAA (also in Hollywood Studio Museum Collection) (also in MGM Collection), CAUU, CNDA, DCG (Quigley Photographic Archives), NYB (Bettmann/UPI Collection), NYCU (Dramatic Museum Portraits), NYEH, NYPL, NYSU, OHCL, TXSM, TXU, WICF. • *Press Kit* – OHCL. • *Publicity Release* – AZSU (Jimmy Starr Collection): Cameron. NYMA: MGM (1925). • *Reminiscence* – MISU: Recording. • *Scrapbook* – NYPL. • *Studio Biography* – NYMA: Photoplay (undated).

BUSHMAN, Francis X., Baltimore, MD, 1883-1966.

One of the great matinee idols of his day was Francis X. Bushman. During a career that began around 1910, he made hundreds of films and was elected "King of the Movies" in 1915. Unfortunately, when his fans learned he had divorced his hitherto un-publicized wife and the mother of his five children, his career nosedived. There was a brief comeback with *Ben-Hur* in 1927, but it was in a supporting role. He continued in radio and small movie character parts well into the 1960s. He was married to Beverly Bayne (q.v.) with whom he made numerous pictures.

PUBLISHED SOURCES

• *Books*—**Bibliography:** *The Idols of Silence.* **Credits:** *Filmarama* (v. I and II); *Forty Years of Screen Credits*; *Twenty Years of Silents*; *Who Was Who on Screen.* **Encyclopedic Works:** *Film Encyclopedia*; *Filmlexicon degli Autori e delle Opere*; *Halliwell's Filmgoer's Companion*; *The Illustrated Encyclopedia of the World's Great Movie Stars and Their Films*; *The Illustrated Who's Who of the Cinema*; *International Dictionary of Films and Filmmakers* (v. 3); *The Movie Makers*; *The Oxford Companion to Film*; *The Picturegoer's Who's Who and Encyclopedia of the Screen To-day*; *Who's Who in Hollywood*; *Who's Who of the Horrors and Other Fantasy Films*; *The World Almanac Who's Who of Film*; *The World Film Encyclopedia.* **General:** *Classics of the Silent Screen*; *Early American Cinema*; *Gentlemen to the Rescue*; *Hollywood Album*; *Hollywood Hall of Fame*; *Hollywood Without Makeup*; *Life Stories of the Movie Stars*; *The Matinee Idols*; *The Movie Stars Story*; *Pete Martin Calls on...*; *Who's Who on the Screen.* **Pictorial:** *The Image Makers*; *Silent Portraits.* **Recordings:** *Hollywood on Record.* **Factoids:** *Star Stats.*

• *Periodicals*—The following period-ical articles are in addition to those in-cluded in the library listings below: *Moving Picture World* (May 23, 1914); *Motion Picture Magazine* (Jan. 1915, July 1916, Sept. 1916); *Feature Movie* (Mar. 15, 1915); *Photoplay* (June 1915, July 1924, Mar. 1925, Jan. 1928, Jan. 1931); *Motography* (Aug. 1915); *Motion Picture Classic* (Dec. 1916, Mar. 1917,

June 1923); *Time* (Sept. 22, 1947, Sept. 2, 1966); *Coronet* (Sept. 1952); *Saturday Review* (Oct. 13, 1956); *Show* (Aug. 1962); *Newsweek* (Sept. 5, 1966); *Classic Film Collector* (Fall 1966, Spring 1972); *Films in Review* (Mar. 1978).

MEDIA

Feinstein and Francis X. Bushman (recording); *Francis X. Bushman* (re-cording).

ARCHIVAL MATERIALS

• *Clipping File*—CAA: Film ap-pearance (1915, 1923, 1951, 1953, 1961, 1965–66); article (1931, 1944, 1947, 1950–52, 1957–59, 1961, 1963–64, 1966, 1972); nostalgia (1948, 1956, 1961); newsphotos; legal problem (1943); marriage (1956); honor (1959, 1963–64); invention (1934); TV appearance (1965); memorial plaque (1970); obituary (1966). Periodical ar-ticles: *Saturday Evening Post* (Apr. 28, 1945); *Life* (Feb. 2, 1948). CAUU: Article (1966); memorial (1970); obituary (1966). NYMA: Marriage (1956); article (1961); obituary (1966). Periodical articles: *Photo-play World* (Apr. 1918); *Saturday Evening Post* (Apr. 28, 1945); *Classic Images* (Aug. 1992). NYPL: Article (1913, 1915–17, 1944, 1947, 1951, 1954, 1956–57, 1959, undated [numerous]); newsphotos (numerous); engagement/marriage/rec-onciliation/divorce (1918, 1956, un-dated); film appearances (numerous); film synopses (numerous); injury (1912); wins American Hero contest (1914); stage appearance (1921); bankruptcy (1933); buys mansion (1916); obituary (1966). Periodical articles: *Motion Pictures* (Feb. 1912); *Motography* (Nov. 9, 1912); *Photoplay* (July 1914, May 1915, Mar. 1916, Apr. 1917); *Moving Picture World* (Feb. 27, 1915); *Motion Picture Magazine* (Feb. 1915, May 1915, Dec. 1916); *Picture Play Weekly* (Apr. 10, 1915); *Picture Play* (May 1916); *Photo-play Journal* (Sept. 1917, Dec. 1917, June-July 1918, Sept. 1918, Nov. 1918). • *Other Clipping File*—CAUB, CNDA, GBFF, MAH, MIDL, OHCL, PAPL, WICF. • *Correspon-dence*—DCLC (Lillian Gish Papers). NYPL (C. & L. Brown Collection): 1932. • *Filmography*—CAA, NYMA, NYPL. • *Legal File*—CAUU (Universal Pictures

Collection): Payroll record (1951); publicity. CAUW: Personnel, payroll record (1958). • *Oral History* — NYCO: Mentioned in the following interviews: G.M. Anderson, Lila Lee, Conrad Nagel, Louella Parsons, Gloria Swanson. • *Photograph/Still* — CAA (also in Hollywood Studio Museum Collection) (also in MGM Collection), CAHL, CALM, CASF, CAUT (Jessen Collection), CNDA, DCG (Quigley Photographic Archives), GBBF, IAU (Junkin Collection), MIDL, NJPT, NYB (Bettmann/UPI Collection) (Springer Collection), NYCU (Dramatic Museum Portraits), NYEH, NYPL, NYSU, OHCL, TXSM, TXU, WICF. • *Play Program* — CAUT: 1929. • *Publicity Release* — CAA: Fox (1950s, 1963–64). NYMA: American-International (1965). NYPL: Columbia (1938–39); American-International (1965). • *Scrapbook* — NJPT (Yeandle Collection), NYPL. • *Studio Biography* — CAA: Columbia (1959); Universal.

CALHOUN, Alice, Cleveland, Ohio, 1904–1966.

Vitagraph was one of the studios for which pretty Alice Calhoun made her 52 films between 1916 and 1929. One of her major roles was in *The Little Minister*; other films included *Between Friends*, *The Man on the Box*, *The Part Time Wife* and *Savage Passions*.

PUBLISHED SOURCES
• *Books* — General: *The Big V*; *Blue Book of the Screen*; *Famous Film Folk*; *Intimate Talks with Movie Stars*; *Who's Who on the Screen*. Credits: *Filmarama* (v. I and II); *Twenty Years of Silents*; *Who Was Who on Screen*. Encyclopedic Works: *Film Encyclopedia*; *Who's Who in Hollywood*. Pictorial: *Silent Portraits*.
• *Periodicals* — The following periodical articles are in addition to those included in the library listings below: *Motion Picture Classic* (June 1920, Oct. 1921); *Moving Picture World* (Oct. 23, 1920); *Photoplay* (May 1921); *Motion Picture Magazine* (July 1921, Oct. 1921,

July 1922); *Pantomime* (Dec. 31, 1921); *Classic Images* (May 1988, Oct. 1990).

ARCHIVAL MATERIALS
• *Clipping File* — CAA: Marriage/divorce (1938, 1948); home (1922); film appearance (1922–23); obituary (1966). NYMA: Marriage (1926–27); film appearance (1921); Vitagraph star (1920). Periodical articles: *Moving Picture World* (Feb. 12, 1921); *Classic Film Collector* (Spring 1976). NYPL: Newsphotos; injury (1926); article (1921, undated). • *Other Clipping File* — AZSU (Jimmy Starr Collection), GBBF, MAH, PAPL, WICF. • *Correspondence* — NYMA (Photoplay Collection). • *Legal File* — CAUW: Contract (1920); letter, memo (1922–23); talent agreement (1920). • *Photograph/Still* — CAA (also Hollywood Studio Museum Collection), DCG (Quigley Photographic Archives), GBBF, NYCU (Dramatic Museum Portraits), NYEH, NYPL, NYSU, OHCL, TXU, WICF. • *Publicity Release* — NYMA: Vitagraph. • *Studio Biography* — NYMA: Photoplay.

CALVERT, Catherine (Catherine Cassidy), Baltimore, MD, 1891–1971.

Catherine Calvert came to films after a fairly distinguished stage career and she had a brief but respectable screen career as well between 1917 and 1922. Among her efforts were *Fires of Faith*, *The Heart of Maryland* and *That Woman*.

PUBLISHED SOURCES
• *Books* — General: *Who's Who on the Screen*. Credits: *British Film Actors' Credits*; *Filmarama* (v. I and II); *Twenty Years of Silents*; *Who Was Who on Screen*. Encyclopedic Works: *Film Encyclopedia*; *Filmlexicon degli Autori e delle Opere*; *Who Was Who in the Theatre*; *Who's Who in Hollywood*. Pictorial: *Silent Portraits*.
• *Periodicals* — The following periodical articles are in addition to those included in the library listings below: *Motion Picture Magazine* (Apr. 1918,

Dec. 1920); *Photoplay* (May 1921); *Motion Picture Classic* (June 1921).

ARCHIVAL MATERIALS

• *Clipping File* — CAA: Obituary (1971). NYMA: Film appearance (1921-23); signs with Vitagraph (1920); signs with Famous Players-Lasky; signs with U. S. Amusement (1917); marriage (1925); film review (1919); newsphotos; article (undated); obituary (1971). NYMN: Newsphotos; marriage (1934). Periodical article: *Collier's* (undated). NYPL: Stage appearance (1910s); film appearance (1910s); newsphotos; career (1910); article (1909, 1919); signs with Famous Players-Lasky (1919); signs with Films Inc. (1919); marriage (1913). Periodical articles: *Green Book Magazine* (Sept. 1912); *Photoplay* (Mar. 1919). • *Other Clipping File* — CAH, GBBF, MIDL, NYSU, PAPL, WICF. • *Correspondence* — NYPL (C. & L. Brown Collection): 1923. • *Photograph/Still* — CAA (also in Hollywood Studio Museum Collection), GBBF, NJFL, NYMN, NYPL, NYSU, OHCL, WICF. • *Play Program* — NYPL. • *Publicity Release* — NYMA: Keeney (1917); Famous Players-Lasky. • *Scrapbook* — NYPL (also in R. Locke Collection).

CAPRICE, June (Betty Lawton or June Millarde), Arlington or Boston, MA, 1899-1936.

June Caprice's film career was a short one, lasting approximately five years from 1916 to 1921. She was a popular star, however, and the winner of a Mary Pickford lookalike contest. Her first film was *Caprice of the Mountains* and she appeared in such other films as *A Modern Cinderella* and *Small Town Girl* before her last prominent role in the serial *Sky Rangers*.

PUBLISHED SOURCES

• *Books* — Filmography: *Hollywood on the Palisades*. General: *Who's Who on the Screen*. Credits: *Filmarama* (v. I and II); *Twenty Years of Silents*; *Who Was Who on Screen*. Encyclopedic Works: *Film Encyclopedia*; *Filmlexicon*

degli Autori e delle Opere; *Who's Who in Hollywood*. Pictorial: *Silent Portraits*.

• *Periodicals* — The following periodical articles are in addition to those included in the library listings below: *Motion Picture Magazine* (Jan. 1917, June 1917, May 1921); *Motion Picture Classic* (Dec. 1917); *Photoplay* (Jan. 1920); *Picture Show* (Jan. 31, 1920); *Classic Images* (Dec. 1985).

ARCHIVAL MATERIALS

• *Clipping File* — CAA: Article (1917); nostalgia (1987). NYMA (also in Photoplay Collection): Personal data summary. Periodical articles: *Exhibitors' Bulletin* (Feb. 1918, June 1918); *Classic Images* (Sept. 1987). NYPL: Newsphotos; obituary (1936). • *Other Clipping File* — OHCL, PAPL. • *Correspondence* — CAA: Fan letter. • *Filmography* — GBBF, NYMA. • *Photograph/Still* — CAA (also in Hollywood Studio Museum Collection), CNDA, DCG (Quigley Photographic Archives), GBBF, NJFL, NYPL, NYSU, OHCL. • *Scrapbook* — NYPL (R. Locke Collection).

CAREWE (sometimes Carew), Arthur Edmund, Trebizond, Armenia, 1894-1937.

Arthur Edmund Carew(e) had the kind of dark brooding looks which could portray either villany or romantic intensity. He came to Hollywood about 1920 and played numerous, usually supporting, roles in such films as *The Torrent*, *The Cat and the Canary*, *Phantom of the Opera* and *Uncle Tom's Cabin*. He continued into talkies, his final appearance coming in a Charlie Chan movie. (Not to be confused with director Edwin Carewe.)

PUBLISHED SOURCES

• *Books* — Credits: *Filmarama* (v. II); *Twenty Years of Silents*. Encyclopedic Works: *The Picturegoer's Who's Who and Encyclopedia of the Screen To-day*; *Who's Who in Hollywood*. Pictorial: *Silent Portraits*.

• *Periodicals* — *Midnight Marquee* (Fall 1986).

• *Clipping File* — CAA: Article (1924); obituary (1937). • *Other Clipping File* — CAFA, MAH, NYMA, (Photoplay Collection), PAPL. • *Correspondence* — NYMA. • *Legal File* — CAUW: Personnel, payroll record; talent agreement (1930-32); document (1932); loanout (1926); letter (1926). • *Photograph/Still* — CAA, CAFA, GBBF, NJFL, NYEH, NYPL, OHCL, TXU.

CAROL, Sue (Evelyn Lederer), Chicago, IL, 1907/1910-1982.

Although later (and perhaps better) known as a Hollywood agent (her major client being her husband Alan Ladd), Sue Carol had a 26-film career after her initial role in *Slaves of Beauty* (1927). She appeared in collegiate flapper roles in silents and in musicals during the early sound era. Her filmography included *The Exalted Flapper*, *Girls Gone Wild*, *Dancing Sweeties* and *Chasing Through Europe*. Legend has it that she inspired the popular tune "Sweet Sue." She was earlier married to Nick Stuart (q.v.).

PUBLISHED SOURCES
• *Books* — General: *Debrett Goes to Hollywood*; *Hollywood Dynasties*; *Return Engagement*; *You Must Remember This*. **Credits:** *Filmarama* (v. II); *Forty Years of Screen Credits*; *Twenty Years of Silents*. **Encyclopedic Works:** *Film Encyclopedia*; *Filmlexicon degli Autori e delle Opere*; *Halliwell's Filmgoer's Companion*; *The Movie Makers*; *The Picturegoer's Who's Who and Encyclopedia of the Screen To-day*; *Who's Who in Hollywood*; *The World Film Encyclopedia*. **Biography/Autobiography:** *Ladd*. **Nostalgia:** *Is That Who I Think It Is?* (v. 2); *Whatever Became of...* (5th). **Pictorial:** *They Had Faces Then*.
• *Periodicals* — The following periodical articles are in addition to those included in the library listings below: *Photoplay* (Mar. 1928, Dec. 1929, Nov. 1930, Jan. 1931, Dec. 1942, July 1943, Sept. 1948); *Motion Picture Magazine* (Mar. 1928, Feb. 1930, Nov. 1930); *Motion Picture Classic* (Aug. 1928, Oct. 1929); *American Hebrew* (Mar. 16, 1928); *Silver Screen* (Feb. 1945); *Films in Review* (Feb. 1970) (Wampas Baby Stars).

ARCHIVAL MATERIALS
• *Clipping File* — CAA: Engagement/marriage/divorce (1934, 1936, 1942); article (1951, 1976); newsphoto (1928); producer (1965); obituary (1982). Periodical article: *Liberty* (June 1928). CAFI: Obituary (1982). CAPS: Obituary (1982). Periodical article: *Palm Springs Villager* (Jan. 1956). CAUT: Legal problem (1928-29); divorce (1929); obituary (1982). NYMA (also in Photoplay Collection): Obituary (1982). NYPL: Newsphotos; divorce (1933-34, 1942); legal problem (1935); article (1979, undated); film appearance (1933); obituary (1982). Periodical article: *Hollywood Reporter* (1976 anniversary issue). • *Other Clipping File* — MAH, MIDL, PAPL, WICF. • *Correspondence* — NYPL: Letters (C. & L. Brown Collection) (1943-44); others (undated). • *Legal File* — CAUT (Twentieth Century-Fox Collection). Letter, memo (1928-30); lawsuit (1928); loanout (1929-30); contract (1928); agreement (1928). • *Photograph/Still* — CAA (also in Hollywood Studio Museum Collection), CASF, CAUU, DCG (Quigley Photographic Archives), GBBF, MIDL, NJPT, NYB (Penguin Collection), NYCU (Dramatic Museum Collection) (Palmer Collection), NYEH, NYPL, NYSU, OHCL, TXU, WICF. • *Scrapbook* — NJPT (Yeandle Collection), NYPL.

CARR, Mary (Mary Kennevan?), Philadelphia, PA, 1874-1973.

Mary Carr specialized in playing mothers and elderly women but she was not really so old when she appeared in her most famous role: 1920's *Over the Hill (To the Poorhouse)*. Among the early studios for which she worked was Lubin and her first screen appearance may have been as far back as 1905. She appeared in numerous silent and talking films, including *Go Straight, Silver Wings, The Red Kimono* and *Frenzied Flames* and, after a long absence, returned for her final role in *Friendly Persuasion* (1956).

PUBLISHED SOURCES
• *Books* – General: *Famous Film Folk; The Truth About the Movies.* Credits: *Filmarama* (v. I and II); *Forty Years of Screen Credits; Twenty Years of Silents; Who Was Who on Screen.* Encyclopedic Works: *Film Encyclopedia; Filmlexicon degli Autori e delle Opere; Halliwell's Filmgoer's Companion; The Movie Makers; The Picturegoer's Who's Who and Encyclopedia of the Screen To-day; Who's Who in Hollywood.* Pictorial: *Silent Portraits.*
• *Periodicals* – *Photoplay* (Mar. 1921, July 1923, May 1925); *Motion Picture Magazine* (Mar. 1921, Sept. 1924); *Classic Film Collector* (Fall 1973); *Classic Images* (Jan. 1985).

ARCHIVAL MATERIALS
• *Clipping File* – CAA: Radio appearance (1951); film appearance (1955); birthday (1958, 1964). NYMA (also in Photoplay Collection): Obituary (1973). NYPL: Newsphotos; article (1920); film appearance (1921, 1927); evicted from home (1933). • *Other Clipping File* – GBBF, MAH, NYSU, OHCL, PAPL, WICF. • *Correspondence* – CAA (Hedda Hopper Collection): 1962–64. One letter is about the beginning of her career. • *Legal File* – CAA (J. Searle Dawley Collection): Agreement (1922). CAUW: Contract (1928); contract summary (1927); talent agreement (1924, 1937). • *Photograph/Still* – CAA (also in Hollywood Studio Museum Collection), CAUT (Jessen Collection), CAUU, DCG (Quigley Photographic Archives), GBBF, NJFL, NYPL, NYSU, OHCL, TXU, WICF. • *Scrapbook* – NYPL (R. Locke Collection). • *Studio Biography* – CAA: RKO (1920s).

CHADWICK, Helene, Chadwicks, NY, 1897–1940.
Helene Chadwick's career began in

1916 with *The Angel Factory* and she had many credits during the silent era, among them *An Adventure in Hearts, Confessions of a Wife, Quicksands* and *The Sin Flood.* There were also occasional westerns. Her appearances in talkies were sporadic but she was seen onscreen until 1935, sometimes as an extra.

PUBLISHED SOURCES
• *Books* – General: *Blue Book of the Screen; Famous Film Folk; Intimate Talks with Movie Stars; The Truth About the Movies; Who's Who on the Screen.* Credits: *Filmarama* (v. I and II); *Twenty Years of Silents; Who Was Who on Screen.* Encyclopedic Works: *Film Encyclopedia; Filmlexicon degli Autori e delle Opere; The Picturegoer's Who's Who and Encyclopedia of the Screen To-day; Who's Who in Hollywood.* Pictorial: *Silent Portraits.*
• *Periodicals* – The following periodical articles are in addition to that included in the library listings below: *Filmplay Journal* (Jan. 1919); *Motion Picture Classic* (Jan. 1919, Jan. 1921); *Motion Picture Magazine* (Aug. 1920, July 1921, Mar. 1922, Aug. 1922); *Photoplay* (Aug. 1920, Aug. 1922).

ARCHIVAL MATERIALS
• *Clipping File* – CAA: Newsphoto (1920s, 1926); illness (1921); film appearance (1924); extra work (1935). NYMA (also in Photoplay Collection). Periodical article: *Photo-play World* (Apr. 1918). NYPL: Article (1920, 1923); newsphotos; obituary (1940). • *Other Clipping File* – GBBF, MAH, OHCL, PAPL, WICF. • *Legal File* – CAUW: Talent agreement (1926). • *Photograph/Still* – CAA (also in Hollywood Studio Museum Collection) (also in MGM Collection), CAUT (Jessen Collection), CAUU, DCG (Quigley Photographic Archives), GBBF, NJPT, NYAM, NYB (Bettmann/UPI Collection) (Underwood Collection), NYEH, NYMN, NYPL, NYSU, OHCL, TXSM, TXU, WICF. • *Scrapbook* – NYPL (also in R. Locke Collection).

CHANEY, Lon (later known as Lon Chaney Sr.) (Alonso or Alonzo Chaney), Colorado Springs, CO, 1883/86–1930.

Lon Chaney labored in relative movie obscurity from about 1912 to 1919 when *The Miracle Man* catapulted him to fame. (Previous films like *Riddle Gawne* had brought him some notice as well.) At Universal and MGM he became the renowned "Man of a Thousand Faces," appearing in roles where frequently his makeup ability was almost as important as his acting ability. Prominent roles included *The Penalty, The Unholy Three, Phantom of the Opera, The Hunchback of Notre Dame, London After Midnight* and *Tell It to the Marines.* His talkie debut in a 1930 remake of *The Unholy Three* was successful, but by that time he was mortally ill.

PUBLISHED SOURCES

• *Books* — **Bibliography:** *The Idols of Silence.* **Credits:** *Filmarama* (v. I and II); *Twenty Years of Silents.* **Encyclopedic Works:** *A Biographical Dictionary of Film; A Companion to the Movies; A Dictionary of the Cinema; Film Encyclopedia; Filmlexicon degli Autori e delle Opere; Halliwell's Filmgoer's Companion; The Illustrated Encyclopedia of the World's Great Movie Stars and Their Films; The Illustrated Who's Who of the Cinema; International Dictionary of Films and Filmmakers* (v. 3); *The International Encyclopedia of Film; The Movie Makers; The Oxford Companion to Film; The Penguin Encyclopedia of Horror and the Supernatural; Quinlan's Illustrated Registry of Film Stars; Who's Who in Hollywood; Who's Who of the Horrors and Other Fantasy Films; The World Almanac Who's Who of Film; The World Encyclopedia of the Film; The World Film Encyclopedia.* **General:** *America; Blue Book of the Screen; Classics of the Silent Screen; Faces, Forms, Films; The Faces of Hollywood; Famous Film Folk; Fant'America 1; From Hollywood; Gentlemen to the Rescue; The Great Movie Stars: the Golden Years; Heroes of the Horrors; History of the American Cinema* (v. 3); *Hollywood Album; Hollywood and the Great Stars; Hollywood Hall of Fame; Horror Film Stars; The Horror People; How I Broke Into the Movies; An Illustrated History of the Horror Films; Immortals of the Screen; Love, Laughter and Tears; The Movie Stars Story; Popular Men of the Screen; The Stars* (Schickel); *The Truth About the Movies; Twinkle, Twinkle, Movie Star; Universal Pictures; What the Stars Told Me; Who's Who on the Screen.* **Biography/Autobiography:** *Lon Chaney* (Blake); *Lon Chaney* (Ross). **Films:** *Lon of 1000 Faces!* **Pictorial:** *Silent Portraits.* **Factoids:** *Star Stats.*

• *Periodicals* — The following periodical articles are in addition to those included in the library listings below: *Motion Picture Magazine* (Mar. 1920, Dec. 1922-Jan. 1923, Sept. 1925, Aug. 1927, July 1930, June 1933); *Picture Play* (Mar. 1920); *California Theatre Program* (Sept. 19, 1920); *Photoplay* (July 1921, Mar. 1922, Feb. 1927, Dec. 1927-Feb. 1928, May-June 1930); *Motion Picture Classic* (Sept. 1922, Nov. 1923, Mar. 1926, May 1928, Mar. 1929, June 1930, Oct. 1930); *Pictures and Picturegoer* (Mar. 1926, Dec. 1927); *Collier's* (May 8, 1926); *World Today* (Feb. 7, 1929); *National Board of Review Magazine* (Sept. 1930); *Silver Screen* (Nov. 1930); *Movie Classic* (Apr. 1932, Jan. 1933); *Good Housekeeping* (Aug. 1932); *Films in Review* (Dec. 1953) (filmography), (Apr.-May 1970, Oct. 1970, Feb.-Mar. 1971); *Coronet* (Dec. 1955); *Saturday Review* (Aug. 17, 1957); *Newsweek* (Aug. 19, 1957); *Life* (Sept. 2, 1957); *8mm Collector* (Winter 1964); *Film Fan Monthly* (July/Aug. 1966); *Focus on Film* (May-Aug. 1970); *Famous Monsters* (Sept. 1970); *Lon Chaney* (1971- an entire periodical devoted to LC); *Gore Creatures* (Sept. 1971); *Classic Film/Video Images* (July 1979); *Filmcritica* (Sept. 1977); *Cine Revue* (Nov. 3, 1977); *Positif* (July-Aug. 1978); *Celuloide* (Feb. 1983); *Ecran Fantastique* (July-Sept. 1983); *American Cinematographer* (June 1985); *Filmhaftet* (Dec. 1989).

ARCHIVAL MATERIALS

• *Clipping File* — CAA: Anderson contract (1923); newsphotos; film festival (1938, 1983, undated); honor (1985); review of *Lon of a Thousand Faces* (1983); article (1924, 1928, 1930, 1950, 1979); obituary (1930). Periodical articles: *Vanity Fair* (Feb. 1928); *American Cinematographer* (Jan. 1930); *Photoplay* (Nov. 1930); *New Movie* (Nov. 1930); *Liberty* (May 2-23, 1931); *Hollywood Studio Magazine* (Oct. 1973). CAUU: Film festival (undated, 1983). Periodical article: *Photoplay* (Nov. 1930). NYMA (also in Photoplay Collection). Film review (1920s); personal data summary; newsphotos; Lon Chaney's influence (1983); article (1983); obituary (1930). Periodical articles: *Theatre Magazine* (Oct. 1927); *Motion Picture Magazine* (Dec. 1930); *Films in Review* (May 1970); *Classic Film Collector* (Spring 1973, Winter 1975). NYMN: Newsphotos; obituary (1930). NYPL: Funeral (1930); newsphotos; article (1950); death of wife (1933); obituary (1930). Periodical articles: *Motion Picture Classic* (Mar. 1920); *Picturegoer* (Mar. 1921); *Literary Digest* (Sept. 13, 1930); *Fangoria* (Feb. 1984); *Focus on Film* (undated); *Classic Film Collector* (undated). • *Other Clipping File* — CAFA, CNDA, CODL, COPP, GBBF, MAH, MIDL, NYSU, OHCL, WICF. • *Filmography* — CAA, CAUU, NYEH, NYMA. • *Legal File* — CAFA. • *Oral History* — NYCO: Mentioned in the following interviews: James Agee, Lew Ayres, James Cagney, Conrad Nagel, Elliot Nugent, George Seaton, Carey Wilson. • *Photograph/Still* — CAA (also in MGM Collection), CAFA, CALM, CAUS, CAUT (Jessen Collection), CAUU, CNDA, DCG (Quigley Photographic Archives), NYB (Bettmann/UPI Collection) (Penguin Collection) (Springer Collection) (Underwood Collection), NYCU (Dramatic Museum Portraits), NYEH, NYMN, NYPL, NYSU, OHCL, OHSU, TNUT (Clarence Brown Collection), TXU, WICF. • *Press Kit* — CAFA. • *Reminiscence* — MISU: Recording. • *Scrapbook* — COPP, NYPL (also in R. Locke Collection), WICF. • *Studio Biography* — CAA: MGM.

CHAPLIN, Charles (Charlie), London, England, 1889-1977.

Long considered the preeminent genius of film comedy, Charlie Chaplin came out of the English music halls to begin his film career with Mack Sennett in 1914's *Making a Living*. His persona as the "little fellow" tramp character became one of the most recognized in the world in the 1910s and 1920s. He was a founder of United Artists and had his own studio, directing nearly all of his films, including classics like *The Gold Rush*, *City Lights* and *Modern Times*. Although personal and political travails in the 1940s and '50s made his later films less popular, at least in the United States, his career continued, with increasingly greater intervals between films. In the mid-1960s he directed his final one, the unsuccessful *A Countess from Hong Kong*.

PUBLISHED SOURCES

• *Books* — Written by (or ghostwritten for) CC: *Charlie Chaplin's Chatter and Funny Sayings*; one part of *Cinema*. **Bibliography:** *Books On/By Chaplin*; *Charles Chaplin: a Bio-Bibliography*; *Charles Chaplin: a Guide to References and Resources*; *The Idols of Silence*. **Credits:** *British Film Actors' Credits*; *Filmarama* (v. I and II); *Forty Years of Screen Credits*; *Twenty Years of Silents*. **Encyclopedic Works:** *American Screenwriters*; *A Biographical Dictionary of Film*; *Cinema, a Critical Dictionary*; *Collier's Yearbook* (1953); *A Companion to the Movies*; *Contemporary Dramatists*; *Contemporary Literary Criticism* (v. 16); *Current Biography* (1940, 1962, 1979); *Dictionary of Film Makers*; *A Dictionary of the Cinema*; *Film Encyclopedia*; *Film Lexicon degli Autori e delle Opere*; *Halliwell's Filmgoer's Companion*; *The Illustrated Encyclopedia of the World's Great Movie Stars and Their Films*; *The Illustrated Who's Who of the Cinema*; *International Dictionary of Films and Filmmakers* (v. 2); *The International Encyclopedia of Film*; *International Motion Picture Almanac* (1975-78); *Joe Franklin's Encyclopedia of*

Comedians; The Movie Makers; The Oxford Companion to Film; The Picturegoer's Who's Who and Encyclopedia of the Screen To-day; Quinlan's Illustrated Directory of Film Comedy Actors; Quinlan's Illustrated Registry of Film Stars; St. James Guide to Biography; Who Was Who in the Theatre; Who's Who in Hollywood; The World Almanac Who's Who of Film; The World Encyclopedia of the Film; World Film Directors; The World Film Encyclopedia. **Chaplin as Director/Writer/Producer:** The American Cinema; American Directors; American Film Directors; American Visions; Authors on Film; Behind the Screen; Beyond the Image; Charles Chaplin (Silver); Charles Spencer Chaplin; Cinema Stylists; The Classic Cinema; Close-Ups; Comedy/Cinema/Theory; Comic Technique of Pathos-Humor; Contemporary Dramatists; The Early Work of Charles Chaplin; Film Biographies; Film Essays; The Film Handbook; Film Makers on Film Making; Great Film Directors; History of the American Film Industry; Hollywood as Historian; Hollywood Directors, 1914–1940; An Hour With the Movies and the Talkies; The "I" of the Camera; The Immediate Experience; Interviews with Film Directors; The Legend of Charlie Chaplin; Major Film Directors of the American and British Cinema; A Million and One Nights; The Movie Makers; Passport to Hollywood; Religion in Film; The Rise of the American Film; Saint Cinema; Schickel on Film; Sex Psyche Etcetera in the Film; Tout Chaplin; United Artists; What is Cinema?; With Eisenstein in Hollywood. **Chaplin as Actor:** Acting in the Cinema; L'Age d'Or du Comique; Agee on Film; Alice in Movieland; The Art of Charlie Chaplin; Before My Eyes; Beverly Hills is My Beat; Blue Book of the Screen; Chaplin (Gifford); Chaplin (Smith); Chaplin (Sobel/Francis); Chaplin (Tyler); Chaplin and American Culture; Chapliniana; Charlie Chaplin's One-Man Show; Cinema; Le Cinéma Burlesque Américain au Temps du Muet; Cinema Stylists; Classic Movie Comedians; Classics of the Silent Screen; Come to Judgment; Comedy Films, 1894–1954; The Comic Mind; The Crazy Mirror; D. Quixote e Carlito; A Dozen and One; Early American Cinema; Las Estrellas (v. 6); Famous Film Folk; Famous Stars of Filmdom (Men); Father Goose; Fifty Super Stars; Film: an Anthology; The Film Answers Back; Focus on Chaplin; Four Great Comedians; Funniest Man in the World; Funny Men of the Movies; The Funsters; "Get Me Geisler"; The Golden Age of Sound Comedy; Great Companions; The Great Funnies; Great God Pan; The Great Movie Comedians; The Great Movie Stars: the Golden Years; Great Stars of Hollywood's Golden Age; Harlequin's Stick-Charlie's Cane; Headline Happy; Here Come the Clowns; L'Histoire de l'Art Cinématographique; The History of Motion Pictures; History of the American Cinema (v. 3); Hollywood (Kanin); Hollywood: the Golden Era; Hollywood Album 2; Hollywood and the Great Stars; Hollywood Exiles; Hollywood Greats of the Golden Years; Hollywood Hall of Fame; The Hollywood Reporter Star Profiles; Hollywood R.I.P.; Hollywood Tragedy; Hommage à Charles Chaplin; How I Broke Into the Movies; Les Immortels du Cinéma; The Intimate Sex Lives of Famous People; Kops and Custards; Laugh Makers; Life Stories of the Movie Stars; Love, Laughter and Tears; Mack Sennett's Keystone; Masters of the American Cinema; Movie Comedians; The Movie Stars; The Movie Stars Story; The Movies Come From America; The National Society of Film Critics on Movie Comedy; The National Society of Film Critics on the Movie Star; New York Times Great Lives of the Twentieth Century; The Parade's Gone By; The Reverend Goes to Hollywood; The Saturday Evening Post Movie Book; Screen Personalities; The Seven Lively Arts; The Silent Clowns; Six Men; Spellbound in Darkness; Star Profiles; Stardom; The Stars (Morin); The Stars (Schickel); Stars!; Stars of the Silents; Starstruck; Those Scandalous Sheets of Hollywood; The Truth About the Movies; Tres Comicos del Cine; Unholy Fools; Vie de Charlot; The War, the

West and the Wilderness; What the Stars Told Me; Who's Who in the Film World; Who's Who on the Screen; The World of Comedy; World of Laughter; Yesterday's Clowns; Zanies. **Films:** Chaplin's Films; Charles Chaplin's City Lights; Charlie Chaplin: an Illustrated History of the Movies; The Complete Films of Charlie Chaplin; An Index to the Films of Charles Chaplin. **Pictorial:** Charlie Chaplin in the Movies; Charlie Chaplin's Funny Stunts; Cinema Star Albums (A Series); The Comic Art of Charlie Chaplin; The Image Makers; The Laugh Makers; Life and Death in Hollywood; The Picture History of Charlie Chaplin; The Revealing Eye; Silent Portraits; Wallace Neff. **Thesis:** Chaplin Imitators and Their Films; Charles Chaplin and the Tradition of the Commedia Dell'Arte; Charles Chaplin, Film Author; Charles Chaplin's Limelight; Five Films By Charles Chaplin; Reinhold Niebuhr and Charles Chaplin; A Study of the Satire of Charles Chaplin. **Biography/Autobiography:** Chaplin (Dell Publishing); Chaplin (Manvell); Chaplin: His Life and Art (Robinson); Chaplin: the Immortal Tramp; Chaplin: the Mirror of Opinion (Robinson); Chaplin, the Movies and Charlie; Chaplin vs. Chaplin; Charles Chaplin (Lepronhon); Charles Chaplin (Martin); Charlie Chaplin (Bessy); Charlie Chaplin (Bowman); Charlie Chaplin (Brasey); Charlie Chaplin (Brown); Charlie Chaplin (Delluc); Charlie Chaplin (Haining); Charlie Chaplin (Huff); Charlie Chaplin (McCabe); Charlie Chaplin (Moss); Charlie Chaplin (Quigly); Charlie Chaplin (Riess); Charlie Chaplin (Sokolov); Charlie Chaplin (Villegas Lopez); Charlie Chaplin (Von Ulm); Charlie Chaplin Story; Charlie Chaplin's Own Story; I Couldn't Smoke the Grass on My Father's Lawn; King of Comedy; The Little Fellow; Memoirs of a Star; Moments with Chaplin; Monsieur Chaplin; My Autobiography; My Father, Charlie Chaplin; My Life in Pictures; My Life With Chaplin; My Trip Abroad; La Passion de Charlie Chaplin; Remembering Charlie; Sir Charlie; When the Moon Shone Bright on Charlie Chaplin. Re-

cordings: Hollywood on Record. **Catalog:** Charlie Chaplin Sale. **Factoids:** Star Stats.

• **Periodicals**—The following periodical articles are in addition to those included in the library listings below: Motion Picture News (Mar. 21, 1914); Photoplay (Feb. 1915, Aug.-Oct. 1915, May 1916, Mar. 1917, June 1917, Sept. 1917, Mar. 1918, Feb. 1919, Apr. 1919, May 1920, July 1921, Nov. 1921-Feb. 1922, Nov. 1922, Feb. 1923, May 1923, May 1924, Oct. 1924, Feb. 1925, Feb. 1926, Dec. 1926-Jan. 1927, Jan. 1929, June 1929, May 1930, Mar. 1931, May 1933, Aug. 1934, Apr. 1935, Oct. 1935, Sept. 1936, Apr. 1939, Dec. 1940-Jan. 1941, June 1943, Sept. 1943, May 1961); Motion Picture Magazine (Mar. 1915, July-Aug. 1915, Oct.-Nov. 1915, Jan. 1916, Apr. 1916, Feb.-Apr. 1917, Nov. 1917, May 1922, Nov. 1922, Dec. 1923, Feb. 1924, Nov. 1925, Sept. 1926, Mar. 1927, Dec. 1928, May 1929, June 1931, Sept. 1931, Jan. 1933, Oct. 1933, Jan. 1934, July 1935, May 1936); McClure's Magazine (July 1915, July 1916); Essanay News (Aug. 14, 1915); Theatre Magazine (Sept. 1915, July 1917, Oct. 1919, Jan. 1924, Sept. 1928); Picture Play (Dec. 1915-Apr. 1916); Harper's Weekly (Mar. 25, 1916, May 6, 1916); Motography (July 22, 1916); Green Book Magazine (Aug. 1916); Motion Picture Classic (Sept. 1916, Nov.-Dec. 1916, Feb. 1917, Apr. 1919, Mar. 1924, Jan. 1928, Jan. 1931); New Republic (Feb. 3, 1917, Aug. 23, 1922, Sept. 2, 1925, Oct. 13, 1926, Feb. 8, 1928, Feb. 25, 1931, May 4, 1942, Nov. 17, 1952, Nov. 22, 1954, Oct. 5, 1957, Oct. 3, 1964, May 6, 1978); Moving Picture World (July 21, 1917); Ladies' Home Journal (Aug. 1918, Oct. 1922, Oct. 1923, Oct. 1924); American Magazine (Nov. 1918, Oct. 1931); Landmark (no. 1, 1919); Literary Digest (May 3, 1919, Oct. 8, 1921, Jan. 28, 1922, Feb. 2, 1924, Mar. 24, 1928, Feb. 28, 1931, Mar. 18, 1931, May 23, 1931, Sept. 12, 1931); Picture Show (Nov. 8-15, 1919); Living Age (Apr. 9, 1921, Nov. 14, 1925, July 1928, Oct. 15, 1929, Mar. 1931, June 1931, June 1934); Graphic (Sept. 10, 1921, Oct. 15, 1921, Mar. 29; 1930, Mar. 7,

72   Chaplin

1931); *Saturday Review* (Oct. 1, 1921,
Feb. 28, 1931, May 3, 1947, Oct. 15, 1956,
Sept. 28, 1957, Oct. 10, 1964, May 6,
1972); *Shadowland* (Nov. 1921, Oct.
1923); *Outlook* (Jan. 18, 1922, Feb. 18,
1931); *World's Work* (Feb. 1922);
Metropolitan Magazine (Feb. 1922); *Current Opinion* (Feb. 1922, Dec. 1923);
Canadian Bookman (Apr. 1922);
Screenland (June 1922); *Collier's* (Nov.
11, 1922, Aug. 15, 1925, Jan. 30, 1926,
Mar. 28, 1931, Oct. 26, 1935, Mar. 16,
1940, Apr. 12, 1947); *Sunset* (July 1923);
Spectator (Sept. 8, 1923); *Pictorial
Review* (Jan-Apr. 1927); *Arts* (Feb.
1927); *Transition* (France) (Sept. 1927);
The Nation (Feb. 29, 1928, Mar. 4, 1931,
Feb. 19, 1936, Oct. 4, 1952, Nov. 15, 1952,
Jan. 31, 1953, Mar. 21, 1953, Oct. 12,
1964, Apr. 24, 1972); *Dial* (May 1928);
Harper's Magazine (Dec. 1928, Oct.
1964); *North American Review* (July
1930); *Nation and Atheneum* (July 19,
1930); *Vanity Fair* (Aug. 1930); *Silver
Screen* (Nov. 1930); *Theatre Arts
Monthly* (Nov. 1930, Nov. 1952); *Delineator* (Dec. 1930); *Close-Up* (Mar. 1931);
Weekend Review (Mar. 7, 1931); *Review
of Reviews* (Mar. 1931); *Commonweal*
(Mar. 18, 1931, Feb. 6, 1953, Oct. 16,
1964, June 2, 1972, Feb. 8, 1974); *Correspondent* (Apr. 25, 1931); *Nouvelle
Revue* (June 1, 1931); *Millgate* (Aug.
1931); *Movie Classic* (Nov. 1931, June
1932, Sept.-Nov. 1932, Aug. 1933, June
1934, Oct. 1935); *Scenario* (July 1932);
Cinema Digest (Jan. 9, 1933); *Woman's
Home Companion* (Nov.-Dec. 1933);
Good Housekeeping (Jan. 1934); *New
Yorker* (May 23, 1935, Nov. 15, 1952,
Apr. 15, 1972, Apr. 29, 1972, Jan. 9,
1989); *New Theatre* (Nov. 1935);
Newsweek (Feb. 8, 1936, June 21-28,
1943, Feb. 21, 1944, Apr. 10, 1944, May
15, 1944, Jan. 15, 1945, Apr. 30, 1945,
Apr. 28, 1947, Apr. 27, 1953, June 14,
1954, Nov. 21, 1955, Sept. 9, 1957, Jan.
12, 1959, Nov. 9, 1959, July 27, 1964, Oct.
5, 1964, Feb. 21, 1972, Apr. 17, 1972,
Mar. 17, 1975, Mar. 28, 1977, Mar. 13,
1978, May 29, 1978, Nov. 19, 1979);
Windsor Magazine (Sept. 1936); *Reader's
Digest* (Dec. 1938); *Cue* (Apr. 15, 1939);
Atlantic (Aug. 1939, May 1982); *Time*

(Aug. 7, 1939, June 28, 1943, Apr. 3,
1944, Jan. 1, 1945, May 5, 1947, Sept. 23,
1957, May 4, 1962, Oct. 2, 1964, Jan. 5,
1970, Feb. 21, 1972, Apr. 10-17, 1972,
Mar. 17, 1975, Mar. 3, 1978, May 29,
1978); *Current History* (Sept. 1939);
Screen Book (Jan. 1940); *National Board
of Review Magazine* (Feb. 1940); *Christian Century* (June 16, 1940, Feb. 22,
1978); *Sequence* (1940, Spring 1949); *Life*
(Sept. 2, 1940, June 28, 1943, Jan. 8,
1945, Nov. 17, 1952, Jan. 23, 1956, Oct.
2, 1964, Dec. 3, 1971); *Decision* (Mar.
1941); *French Forum* (no. 2, 1941); *Canadian Forum* (Aug. 1941); *Listener* (1941);
New Statesman (Oct. 9, 1943, May 16,
1953, Sept. 14, 1957); *Jewish Social
Studies* (1944); *Sight and Sound* (Spring-
Summer 1946, Jan.-Mar. 1953, Jan-Mar.
1954, July-Sept. 1954, Autumn 1957,
Winter 1965/66, Spring 1978, Fall 1980,
Spring 1983, Spring 1985, Spring 1989);
Screen Writer (July 1947); *Mainstream*
(Summer 1947); *Here and Now* (Dec.
1947); *World Review* (Apr. 1949); *Films
in Review* (Sept. 1950, Aug.-Sept. 1959,
Jan. 1962, Dec. 1964, Jan. 1981, Nov.
1981, Nov. 1989); *Dance Magazine* (May
1952); *Journal of Aesthetics and Art
Criticism* (June 1952); *American Mercury* (Nov. 1952); *Commentary* (Mar.
1953); *Western Review* (Autumn 1953);
U.S. News and World Report (Feb. 19,
1954, Apr. 24, 1989); *Saturday Evening
Post* (Sept. 4, 1954, Mar. 22, 1958, Nov.
21, 1959, Summer 1972); *Film* (Feb. 1955,
Summer 1964, Summer 1966, Oct. 1983);
Films and Filming (Aug. 1957, Sept.
1958, May 1966, May 1972, Feb. 1978,
June 1983, May-June 1985); *America*
(Oct. 5, 1957, Aug. 4, 1962, Mar. 11,
1972); *Reporter* (Oct. 17, 1957); *Playboy*
(Mar. 1960); *Coronet* (June 1960); *The
Floating Bear* (no. 21, 1962); *Film
Culture* (Spring 1963, Spring 1966,
Spring 1972); *Vogue* (Nov. 15, 1964, July
1966, Apr. 1, 1972, Dec. 1992); *National
Review* (Dec. 1, 1964, Jan. 26, 1965, May
30, 1967, Jan. 20, 1978); *Esquire* (Feb.
1965, Apr. 1965); *Filmcritica* (Feb. 1965);
Cinema Studies (June 1966); *Moviegoer*
(Summer 1966); *Tulane Drama Review*
(Fall 1966); *Cinema* (Beverly Hills) (Summer 1968); *Film Quarterly* (Fall 1968, Fall

1981, Winter 1984/85); *Dramma* (May 1969); *Cine Cubano* (no. 56-57, 1969, no. 99, 1981, no. 102, 1982, no. 106, 1983, no. 111, 1985, no. 116, 1986, no. 122, 126, 1989); *Cinema Journal* (Fall 1969, Fall 1987); *Film Comment* (Winter 1969, Sept.-Oct. 1972, Mar.-Apr. 1978, July-Aug. 1982, Mar.-Apr. 1988); *Telecine* (Jan. 1972, Apr. 1977); *Image et Son* (Jan. 1972, Nov. 1972, Jan. 1977, Feb. 1978); *Velvet Light Trap Review of Cinema* (Winter 1971/72); *Action* (Jan./Feb. 1972); *Focus* (Spring 1972); *Cinema Nuovo* (May-June 1972, May-Aug. 1975, July-Oct. 1976, Oct. 1979, Feb. 1981, Dec. 1982, Feb. 1984, Nov.-Dec. 1985, Mar.-Oct. 1989, Jan-Apr. 1991); *Filmograph* (no. 3-1, 1972); *Cinema Que* (Oct. 1972); *Classic Film Collector* (Winter 1972, Fall 1974-Spring 1976, Fall-Winter 1976, Summer 1977, Winter 1977-Spring 1978, Fall 1978, Sept. 1979); *Horizon* (no. 3, 1973); *Filmihullu* (no. 3, no. 5, nos. 7-8, 1973, no. 1, 1974, no. 8, 1975, no. 2, 1979, no. 1, 1982); *Bianco e Nero* (Jan.-Feb. 1973, Jan.-Feb. 1979); *English Journal* (May 1973); *Filmkritik* (July 1973, Nov. 1973, May 1979); *Positif* (July-Aug. 1973, Nov. 1983, Nov. 1985, June 1989); *Kosmodrama* (Aug. 1973); *Filmkultura* (Nov.-Dec. 1973, Jan.-Feb. 1978); *Yale Review* (Dec. 1974); *Film und Fernsehen* (Apr. 1974, no. 10, 1976, Feb.-Mar. 1978, Apr. 1983, Dec. 1983, no. 2, 1984, no. 5, 1989); *Ecran* (July 1974, Dec. 1975, June 15, 1977, Dec. 15, 1977, Feb. 15, 1978, Mar. 15, 1978, Oct. 1978, Feb. 15, 1979); *Film Library Quarterly* (no. 7-2, 1974); *Cinema* (Romania) (Sept. 1974, Dec. 1977-Jan. 1978); *Kinoizkustvo* (Oct. 1974, Feb. 1978); *Film a Doba* (Oct. 1974, Nov. 1975, Apr. 1978, Apr. 1989); *Film Dope* (Nov. 1974, Dec. 1983); *Literature/Film Quarterly* (Spring 1975, no. 3, 1980, July 1984, no. 1, 1989, no. 3, 1989, no. 2, 1991); *Thousand Eyes Magazine* (Jan. 1976); *Critical Inquiry* (no. 2, 1976); *Iskusstvo Kino* (June 1976, no. 6, 1978, no. 4, 1989); *Cinématographe* (Aug.-Sept. 1976, Jan.-Feb. 1978, Nov. 1980, Jan. 1981, July-Aug. 1983, Mar. 1985); *Revue du Cinéma* (Jan. 1977, Feb. 1978, Mar. 1982); *American Classic Screen* (Jan.-Feb.

1977, July-Aug. 1983); *University Film Association Journal* (no. 1, 1977, Winter 1979); *Lumière du Cinéma* (Mar. 1977); *Quarterly Review of Film Studies* (Nov. 1977) (bibliography); *Revue Belge du Cinéma* (Oct. 1977, Dec. 1980-Feb. 1981); *Ecran* (no. 1, 1978, nos. 1-2, 1981, nos. 3-4, 1989) (filmography); *Avant-Scène du Cinema* (Jan. 1, 1978, May 1, 1978, Jan. 1, 1979, Feb. 15, 1980, May 15, 1980, June 15, 1981); *Cine Revue* (Jan. 5, 1978, Mar. 12, 1981, July 11, 1985); *New Times* (Jan. 23, 1978); *Amis du Film et de la Télévision* (Feb.-Mar. 1978); *Film & Kino* (Feb. 1978, no. 5, 1983); *Skrien* (Feb. 1978); *Cinéma* (France) (Feb.-Mar. 1978, Oct.-Nov. 1987, Mar. 1989); *Cahiers du Cinéma* (Feb. 1978, Feb. 1979, June 1980, Aug. 1983, May 1991); *Skoop* (Feb. 1978, July 1979, Apr. 1981, Sept.-Oct. 1985); *Take One* (Mar. 1978); *Film und Ton* (Mar. 1978); *Boxoffice* (Mar. 6, 1978); *Film en Televisie* (Mar. 1978); *American Film* (May 1978, Apr. 1986, Apr. 1989, June 1989); *Encounter* (June 1978, May 1983); *Kino* (July 1978, Oct. 1989); *Panorama* (Autumn 1978); *Chaplin* (no. 154, 1978, nos. 194-195, 1984, no. 196, 1985, no. 211, 1987, no. 219, 1988); *Wide Angle* (no. 2, 1979, nos. 3-4, 1986, no. 4, 1987); *Metro* (Winter 1979); *Salmagundi* (Winter 1979); *Classic Film/Video Images* (May 1980, Nov. 1981); *Film Criticism* (Fall 1980); *Classic Images* (Jan.-Feb. 1982, Aug. 1982, Nov. 1982, Mar. 1983, June 1983; Apr. 1984, Jan. 1986, July 1986, July 1988, Oct. 1988, Apr. 1989, Nov. 1989, June 1990); *Contracampo* (June 1980); *Levende Billeder* (Nov. 1980); *Cinemateca* (Mar. 1981); *Celuloide* (Mar. 7-9, 1981, June 24, 1981, Aug. 15-17, 1981, Sept. 2-3, 1981, Aug. 1982, Jan. 1983); *Semiotica* (nos. 3-4, 1981); *Cineforum* (Jan.-Feb. 1982, July-Aug. 1983, Nov. 1989, Nov. 1990); *Post Script* (no. 2, 1982, Spring-Summer 1984); *Film Reader* (no. 5, 1982); *Pacific Historian* (Winter 1982); *Millimeter* (Dec. 1982); *Historical Journal of Film, Radio and Television* (Mar. 1983, no. 1, 1984, nos. 1-2, 1985); *Hollywood Studio Magazine* (Mar. 1983); *Casablanca* (Apr. 1983); *Film Exchange* (Spring 1983, no. 4, 1988); *Western Humanities Review* (no. 4, 1983); *On Location* (Apr. 1984); *Cineaste* (Oct. 1984, May 1986); *Film Directions* (no. 28, 1985); *Partisan Review* (no. 3, 1985); *Motion Picture* (no. 1, 1986); *Journal of Popular Film and Television* (Summer 1986, no. 3, 1988); *New Criterion* (June 1986); *East-West Film Journal* (Dec. 1987); *Soviet Film* (no. 366, 1987, no. 383, 1989); *Artforum* (Nov. 1, 1987); *North Dakota Quarterly* (no. 1, 1988); *Radical History Review* (Spring 1988); *Cinema India-International* (no. 2, 1988); *Zelluloid* (Spring 1988); *Griffithiana* (Sept. 1988, Oct.-Nov. 1989, Oct. 1991); *Humanist* (Jan.-Feb. 1989); *CICIM* (Jan. 1989); *People Weekly* (Mar. 20, 1989); *Interview* (Sept. 1989); *Cahiers Cinématheque* (nos. 51/52, 1989); *Unesco Courier* (Oct. 1989); *Filmhaftet* (Dec. 1989); *Jump Cut* (Apr. 1990); *New German Critique* (Fall 1990).

OBSCURE PUBLISHED SOURCES
CAA: *Chaplin paa Jagt efter Lykken* (included in CC clipping files). DCG: (Terry Ramsaye Papers): *A Comedian Sees the World.*

MEDIA
Chaplin: a Character Is Born (video); *Comedy—a Serious Business* (video); *The Gentleman Tramp* (film); *Unknown Chaplin* (video); *Wm. S. Hart and the Sad Clowns* (video).

ARCHIVAL MATERIALS
• *Caricature*—NYPL.   • *Clipping File*—CAA: Review of *Charlie Chaplin* (McCabe) (1978); excerpt from *The Reel Revolution* (1978); review of *The Kid* (1981); review of *Chaplin, His Life and Art* (1985); review of *Charlie Chaplin* (Bessy) (1985); article (1930-31, 1937, 1939-42, 1950-54, 1957-60, 1962, 1964-67, 1970-72, 1974, 1976, 1978, 1982, 1984-87, 1989); excerpt from *Musical Scene* (Thomson) (1945); trip (1931, 1936); honor (1931, 1952); newsphotos; sons' careers (1932); death threat (1933); second front crusade (1942); citizenship (1942); paternity trial (1943-46, 1954); injury (1921, 1945); deportation (1945, 1947, 1949-50); communism (1947); review of *Chaplin: Last of the Clowns* (1948); relation with Pola Negri (1922-

23); Chaplin Studio (1953); program from Toronto Film society (1986/87); centenary (1989); review of *Chaplin and American Culture* (1989); Vevey, Switzerland (1990); Oona Chaplin's death (1991); biographical film (1991); photo exhibit (1989); sale of effects (1986-87); TV documentary (1986); United Artists (1949, 1955); review of *Charlie Chaplin* (Huff) (1951); review of *The Little Fellow* (1951); leaves U.S. (1952); banned from U.S. (1952-53); peace prize (1954); review of *My Father Charlie Chaplin* (1961); Oxford degree (1962); review of *My Autobiography* (1964); directs film (1966-67); 80th birthday (1969); film festival (1969, 1971, 1981, 1989); Academy Award (1972); returns to U.S. (1972); 85th birthday (1974); review of *My Life in Pictures* (1975); stage appearance (1909-13); fitness (1920); marriage/divorce/children (1924-28, 1932-33, 1935-36, 1938, 1941-44, 1949, 1951, 1953, 1957, 1959, 1962); legal problem (1922, 1925, 1931, 1933, 1935, 1937, 1939, 1941, 1943, 1947, 1952); lost films (1925, 1989); film appearance (1925-26, 1931-32, 1935-36, 1939-40, 1947); tax problem (1927-28, 1932, 1937-38, 1941, 1943, 1955-56, 1958); knighthood (1928, 1975); Chaplin image (1928, 1991); illness (1929, 1932, 1977); talkies (1929-30, 1932); body stolen (1978); obituary (1977). Periodical articles: *Scribner's Magazine* (Sept. 1929); *Woman's Home Companion* (Sept.-Oct. 1933, Jan. 1934); *Film Pictorial* (Dec. 22, 1934); *InterCine* (Oct. 1935); *Literary Digest* (Nov. 2, 1935); *New Theatre* (Mar. 1936); *Sight and Sound* (Spring 1938); *Cine-Club* (Jan.-Feb. 1948); *Life* (Sept. 5, 1949, Mar. 17, 1952, Apr. 1, 1966, Mar. 10, 1967, Apr. 21, 1972, Sept. 1989); *New Yorker* (Feb. 25, 1950, May 22, 1978); *Atlantic* (Feb. 1950); *American Legion Magazine* (Dec. 1952); *Saturday Evening Post* (Mar. 8-15, 1958); *Playboy* (Mar. 1959); *Redbook* (Sept. 1959); *MD* (1960s); *Offbeat* (1960?); *Photoplay* (July 1961); *Films and Filming* (Nov.-Dec. 1964); *Ramparts* (Mar. 1965); *Ladies' Home Journal* (May 1965); *Look* (Apr. 19, 1966); *Newsweek* (June 6, 1966); *Cue* (Mar. 28, 1970, Mar. 18, 1972); *Applause* (Dec. 22, 1971);

Harper's Bazaar (Apr. 1972); Liberty (Winter 1972); Show (1972); McCall's (Mar. 1978); Reader's Digest (May 1978); Hollywood Studio Magazine (Sept. 1978); Blackhawk Film Digest (Feb.-Mar. 1980, Fall 1981); Vogue (Mar. 1981); Ballet News (Aug. 1981); Scott Stamp Monthly (Oct. 1985); Smithsonian (July 1986); People (Mar. 20, 1989); British Heritage (Aug.-Sept. 1989); Cable Guide (Sept. 1989); Architectural Digest (Apr. 1990). CAFI: Paternity suit (1943-46); legal problem (1930, 1947, 1952, 1954); film studio (1930, 1954-55, 1980, 1984); peace prize (1954); departs U.S. (1952-53); article (1947, 1950, 1952-54, 1956, 1959, 1963, 1967, 1969, 1971-74, 1977-79, 1981, 1984, 1989); attacked by crowd (1952); film appearance (1951, 1953, 1957, 1970); lost film (1978, 1982); biographical play (1981, 1983); Chaplin image (1984); knighthood (1975); catalog from sale of effects (1987); newsphotos; biography (1930s or '40s); economic theory (1932); sons' careers (1932, 1953); taxes (1951, 1955-56); returns to U.S. (1972); attacks U.S. (1955); film copyright (1978); children (1948-49, 1962); directs film (1965-66); deportation (1945, 1949); review of Charlie Chaplin (Huff) (1951); review of Charlie Chaplin (McCabe) (1978); review of Moments With Chaplin (1980); review of The Kid (1981); review of Chaplin (Robinson) (1985); review of Charlie Chaplin (Bessy) (1985); review of Chaplin and American Culture (1989-90); synopses of films; accused of Communism (1947); film festival (1973-75, 1984); obituary (1977). Periodical articles: Atlantic (Feb. 1950); Saturday Evening Post (Mar. 8, 1958); Positif (Feb. 1962), Cue (Mar. 28, 1970); Applause (Dec. 22, 1971); Life (Apr. 21, 1972); New Yorker (May 22, 1978); Z Magazine (Sept. 1985). CALM: Periodical article: Liberty (Aug. 12, 1933). CAUT: Proposed peace prize (1949); political views (1942); article (1916, 1939-40, 1953-54, 1961, 1972, 1977-78, 1984); communism (1947); film sale (1941); marriage (1943); security risk (1952); Chaplin studio (1954); newsphotos; films on TV (1971, 1986); honor (1971); returns to U.S. (1972); film festival (1971-72, 1977);

Academy Award (1972); body stolen (1978); knighthood (1975); returns to Paris (1976); illness (1976-77); review of Chaplin (Robinson) (1984-85); lost films (1978, 1982); review of Moments with Chaplin (1980); home (1982); obituary (1977). Periodical articles: The Adelphi (Jan. 1924); Theatre Guild Magazine (Sept. 1930); New Pioneer (Mar. 1936); Ladies' Home Journal (July 1940); Life (Dec. 3, 1941); Theatre Arts (June 1947); Atlantic (Feb. 1950); The Nation (Aug. 4, 1956); Ramparts (Mar. 1965); Newsweek (June 6, 1966); Smithsonian (July 1986). CAUU (also in McCormick Collection): Film festival (1938, 1963-64, 1975-76, 1978-79, 1984); marriage (1943, undated); films (1947, 1950, 1958-59, 1971-72, 1978, 1983); citizenship (1950, undated); romance (1943); article (1953, 1971-73, 1976, 1978, 1984, undated); paternity suit (1943, 1953); United Artists (1957); Communism (1953); TV series (1950); leaves U.S. (1950); Jerome Epstein (producer) (1967); returns to U.S. (1972); body stolen (1978); knighthood (1975); visits London (1972); review of Moments With Chaplin (1980); TV documentary (1983); obituary (1977). Periodical articles: Living Age (Aug. 15, 1927); Life (Mar. 10, 1967); Academy Leader (Apr. 1972); Movie Classics (June 1973); Newsweek (Jan. 9, 1978); Reader's Digest (May 1978); Time (June 6, 1983); Quarterly Journal of the Library of Congress (Summer 1983); American Film (Sept. 1984). NYMN: Program from film festival; films buried (1985); article (1915, undated [numerous]); newsphotos; marriage (1953); tax claim (1964); honor (1962); 80th birthday (1969); review of My Father Charlie Chaplin (1960); paternity case (1940s); review of My Autobiography; receives medal (1972); review of Chaplin (Robinson); films revived (1959); review of Charlie Chaplin (Huff). Periodical articles: Photoplay (July 1915); New Movie Magazine (Nov. 1931). NYPL: PARTIAL CONTENTS: Films (1978); funeral (1977); article (1977-78, 1989, 1992); review of Chaplin (Robinson) and The Complete Films of Charlie Chaplin (1989); estate (1978); body recovered (1978); review of Chaplin and

American Culture (1990); centenary; denies being a Communist (1951); not returning to U.S. (1953); review of *Charlie Chaplin's Own Story* and *Chapliniana* (1989); review of *Remembering Charlie* (1989); newsphotos; body stolen (1978); death of wife (1991); obituary (1978). Periodical articles: *Esquire* (Nov. 1962); *Films and Filming* (Oct. 1965); *Show* (June 1972); *Film News* (Jan.-Feb. 1978); *Time* (Jan. 2, 1978); *Newsweek* (Jan. 9, 1978); *New Yorker* (May 2, 1978); *Quest* (Apr. 1989); *Big Reel* (Apr. 1991). • *Other Clipping File* – AZSU (Jimmy Starr Collection), CASF, CNDA, GBBF, MAH, MIDL, NYMA, NYSU, OHCL, WICF. • *Collection* – The extensive Chaplin archives containing clippings, correspondence, studio records, programs, etc., going back to the 1890s, are being processed in Switzerland. As of 1993 the archives were not open to researchers but it is anticipated that a study center and/or museum will someday be open for research. The Archive may be contacted at the following address: Pamela Paumier, Roy Export Company Establishment, 4 Impasse des Peintres, 75002 Paris, France, (022) 731 96 10; Fax: (022) 731 96 51. • *Correspondence* – CAUS: Letter(s) (Rob Wagner Collection) relating to *Rob Wagner's Script* (periodical); 4 letters (Preston Sturges Collection). DCLC (George Kleine Collection): 1918-21. (May also contain other materials.) GBBF (Ivor Montagu Collection). NYCU: Letter (Meloney Collection) (1918); letter (Random House Collection) (1960); letter (Winter Collection) (1953). • *Discussion* – GBBF (Hollywood Collection): Transcript of interview for *Hollywood* (TV series). MISU: Charles Chaplin Jr. discusses the autobiography of his father (recording) (1964); Marcel Marceau discusses the art of silent comedy, including CC, Buster Keaton and others (recording) (1974). • *Filmography* – CAA, CAFI, CAUT, NYEH, NYMN. • *Interview* – MISU: CC talks to reporters after being knighted (recording) (1975). • *Legal File* – CAUW: Contract (1917); license agreement (1963); checklist (1922); letter, memo (1924-25,

1962); agreement (1917-18, 1920, 1929); royalty payment (1920-27); document (1921). • *Manuscript* – CAA: *Charlie Chaplin Secrets: Intimate Facts Pertinent to His Life Not Revealed in His Own Autobiography* (Edward Manson) (undated). CAUT: *Charlie Chaplin and Mack Sennett* (1951). • *Oral History* – CAUS: Mentioned in the following interviews: Louis Epstein, Marta L. Feuchtwanger, Richard Huemer, Albert Maltz. NYCO: Mentioned in the following interviews: James Agee, G. M. Anderson, George K. Arthur, Bruce Bliven, James Cagney, Harold Clurman, Marc Connelly, Eddie Dowling, Paul Fejos, Gracie Fields, Moe Foner, Waldo Frank, Lillian Gish, Louis Goldblatt, Dorothy Gordon, Robert Indiana, Buster Keaton, Lila Lee, Jay Leyda, Harold Lloyd, Josh Logan, Anita Loos, Samuel Loveman, Don Malkames, Frances Marion, Arthur Mayer, Joel McCrea, Conrad Nagel, Elliot Nugent, Louella Parsons, Charles Poletti, Otto Preminger, Tony Randall, Basil Rathbone, Max Schuster, David Selznick, Upton Sinclair, Albert (Eddie) Sutherland, Gloria Swanson, Blanche Sweet, Carey Wilson, M. Wilson, F.L. Wright, Max Youngstein, Adolph Zukor. • *Photograph/Still* – CAA (also in Hollywood Studio Museum Collection), CAHL, CALM, CASF, CAUS, CAUT (Jessen Collection) (Portrait File), CAUU, CNDA, IAU, MABU (Douglas Fairbanks Jr. Collection), NYAM, NYB (Bettmann/UPI Collection) (Penguin Collection) (Springer Collection) (Underwood Collection), NYCU (Bulliet Collection) (Dramatic Museum Portraits), NYEH, NYMN, NYPL, NYSU, OHCL, OHSU, TXSM, TXU, WICF. • *Press Kit* – OHCL. • *Program* – NYMN: *Great Dictator* (1940). • *Publicity Release* – CAUU: Columbia (1972). • *Reminiscence* – MISU: Honorary Academy Award presentation to CC, with remarks by CC (recording) (1972); portrait of CC as he returned for the special Academy Award, including comments from Sydney and Geraldine Chaplin (recording) (1972); Adolph Green and others talk about CC and his films (recording) (1977); Nancy Pogel discusses CC (recording) (1980); David Robinson (biographer), Jerry Epstein (friend) and Claire Bloom (co-star) remember CC on his 100th birthday (recording) (1989). • *Scrapbook* — CALM: 1931. Clippings from European newspapers relating to the European release of *City Lights*. CASU (Stark Collection), NYAM, NYPL (also in D. Stickney Collection) (also in R. Locke Collection), WICF. • *Studio Biography* — CAA: Unknown studio (United Artists?) (1928); Columbia (1972).

CHASE, Charley (sometimes Charlie) (Charles Parrott), Baltimore, MD, 1893–1940.

Slim, dapper Charley Chase mainly appeared in two-reelers and shorts throughout his career which began about 1914. He had supporting roles in relatively few features (the last made in the late 1930s). In his best work, the humor depended on his earnest but usually frustrated efforts to stay out of trouble. He also was a most competent director of other comedians' work and now has been accorded the appreciation that he did not have during his lifetime.

PUBLISHED SOURCES

• *Books* — **General:** *Clown Princes and Court Jesters*; *The Funsters*; *The Great Movie Comedians*; *Immortals of the Screen*; *Movie Comedians*; *The Truth About the Movies*. **Credits:** *Filmarama* (v. I and II); *Forty Years of Screen Credits*; *Twenty Years of Silents*; *Who Was Who on Screen*. **Encyclopedic Works:** *Film Encyclopedia*; *Filmlexicon degli Autori e delle Opere*; *Halliwell's Filmgoer's Companion*; *The Illustrated Who's Who of the Cinema*; *Joe Franklin's Encyclopedia of Comedians*; *The Oxford Companion to Film*; *The Picturegoer's Who's Who and Encyclopedia of the Screen To-day*; *Quinlan's Illustrated Directory of Film Comedy Actors*; *Who's Who in Hollywood*; *Who's Who of the Horrors and Other Fantasy Films*; *The World Encyclopedia of the Film*; *The World Film Encyclopedia*. **Films:** *Selected Short Subjects*;

Keaton et Cie. **Pictorial:** *Silent Portraits.*
• *Periodicals* — The following periodical articles are in addition to those included in the library listings below: *Cinema Art* (Apr. 1926); *Films in Review* (May 1975); *Classic Images* (Jan. 1982, June 1987).

ARCHIVAL MATERIALS

• *Clipping File* — CAA: Article (1979); obituary (1940). CAFI: Film festival (1979). CAUU: Article (1979). NYMA (also in Photoplay Collection): Separation (1934); surgery (1929); article (1928); film synopses; personal data summary; obituary (1940). Periodical articles: *8mm Collector* (Spring-Summer 1965); *Film Fan Monthly* (July-Aug. 1969); *Classic Images* (Feb.-Mar. 1986, Oct. 1986). NYPL: Tribute (1979); newsphotos; film appearance (1937); obituary (1940). • *Other Clipping File* — CASF, GBBF, MAH, MIDL, OHCL, WICF. • *Manuscript* — NYMA: *The Mystery of the Parrotts*. A compilation of articles which comprise a brief discussion of the Parrott brothers. • *Photograph/Still* — CAA (also in Hollywood Studio Museum Collection) (also in MGM Collection), CALM, CAUT (Jessen Collection), CAUU, CNDA, DCG (Quigley Photographic Archives), NYB (Bettmann/UPI Collection), (Penguin Collection) (Underwood Collection), NYCU (Dramatic Museum Portraits), NYEH, NYPL, NYSU, OHCL, TXU, WICF. • *Publicity Release* — NYMA: Roach.

CLARK, Marguerite (Helen M. Clark), Avondale, Ohio, 1882/87–1940.

For a time, Famous Players' star Marguerite Clark was a rival to Mary Pickford in film popularity. Although the petite (4'10") stage-trained actress did not prove to have Pickford's staying power, she appeared in well-received films such as the *Babs* series, *The Goose Girl*, *Mrs. Wiggs of the Cabbage Patch* and *Snow White*. Her film career ended in 1921.

PUBLISHED SOURCES

• *Books* — **Bibliography:** *The Idols of*

Silence. **General:** *Behind the Screen*; *Classics of the Silent Screen*; *From Hollywood*; *Life Stories of the Movie Stars.* **Credits:** *Filmarama* (v. I and II); *Twenty Years of Silents*; *Who Was Who on Screen.* **Encyclopedic Works:** *Film Encyclopedia*; *Filmlexicon degli Autori e delle Opere*; *Halliwell's Filmgoer's Companion*; *Notable American Women, 1607-1950*; *Who Was Who in the Theatre*; *Who's Who in Hollywood*; *Who's Who on the Stage* (1908). **Filmography:** *Hollywood on the Palisades.* **Biography/Autobiography:** *Marguerite Clark, America's Darling, The Public Is Never Wrong.*

• *Periodicals* — The following periodical articles are in addition to those included in the library listings below: *Pearson's Magazine* (NY) (Aug. 1909); *Cosmopolitan* (Sept. 1912, June 1915); *Green Book Magazine* (May 1913, Mar. 1914, July 1916); *Theatre* (Apr. 1914, Nov. 1917, June 1919, Aug. 1919); *Cosmopolitan* (June 1915); *Motion Picture Magazine* (July 1915, Aug. 1916, Feb. 1917, Aug. 1917, Nov. 1917, July 1918, Aug. 1919); *Photoplay* (Mar. 1916, Dec. 1916, Jan. 1918, July 1918, June 1919, Jan. 1920, Apr. 1921, July 1924, Apr. 1925); *Everybody's* (June 1916, Sept. 1918); *Motion Picture Classic* (Oct. 1917, July 1921); *American Magazine* (Dec. 1917); *Picture Play Magazine* (Nov. 1919); *Films in Review* (Mar. 1965, Apr. 1975, June-July 1975).

ARCHIVAL MATERIALS
• *Clipping File* — CAA: Newsphotos; obituary (1940). Periodical article: *Films in Review* (Oct. 1966). NYMA (also in Photoplay collection): Newsphotos; personal data summary; obituary (1940). Periodical article: *Photo-play Journal* (Dec. 1918). NYMN: Article (1932, undated); death of husband; aids Huey Long (1935); newsphotos; obituary (1940). Periodical article: *New Movie Magazine* (Nov. 1934). NYPL: Funeral (1940); newsphotos (numerous); article (1910s, 1932, 1934-35, 1940); sells Liberty bonds (1917); retirement (1934); death of husband (1936); nostalgia (1936); obituary (1940). Periodical articles: *Picturegoer* (Apr. 1921); *Films in Review* (Dec.

1964). • *Other Clipping File* — AZSU (Jimmy Starr Collection), GBBF, MAH, MIDL, NYSU, OHCI, OHSU, PAPL, WICF.   • *Correspondence* — CAA (Adolph Zukor Collection): 1919-20. • *Filmography* — CAA (incomplete), NYMA, NYPL. • *Oral History* — NYCO: Mentioned in the following interviews: Preston Bassett, Jean Dalrymple, Moe Foner, Adolph Zukor. • *Manuscript* — CAA (Searle Dawley Collection): Notes by SD about directing MC. • *Photograph/Still* — CAA (also in Hollywood Studio Museum Collection), CALM, CAUS, CAUT (Jessen Collection), CAUU, DCG (Quigley Photographic Archives), GBBF, IAU (Junkin Collection), NJFL, NYB (Underwood Collection), NYCU (Dramatic Museum Portraits), NYEH, NYMN, NYPL, NYSU, OHCL, TXU, WICF. • *Play Program* — NYPL: 1910s. • *Publicity Release* — CAA: Paramount (1936). • *Scrapbook* — NYPL (also in R. Locke Collection) (also in Players Collection).

CLAYTON, Ethel, Champaign, IL, 1884-1966.

Lubin star Ethel Clayton was a popular actress from about 1910. She was seen in numerous films including *Sunny Side Up*, *Easy Money*, *The Girl Who Came Back*, *Whims of Society* and *Mother Machree*. As time went on her roles became supporting ones and in the talkies her appearances were in bit parts until at least the 1940s. She was married to Ian Keith (q.v.).

PUBLISHED SOURCES
• *Books* — **General:** *Blue Book of the Screen*; *Famous Film Folk*; *First One Hundred Noted Men and Women of the Screen*; *Who's Who on the Screen.* **Credits:** *Filmarama* (v. I and II); *Forty Years of Screen Credits*; *Twenty Years of Silents*; *Who Was Who on Screen.* **Encyclopedic Works:** *Film Encyclopedia*; *Filmlexicon degli Autori e delle Opere*; *Halliwell's Filmgoer's Companion*; *Who's Who in Hollywood.* **Filmography:** *Hollywood on the Palisades.* **Pictorial:** *Silent Portraits.*

• *Periodicals—New England Magazine* (Feb. 1912); *Photoplay* (Jan. 1915, June-July 1915, Aug. 1916, Apr. 1917, May 1919, Apr. 1920, Jan. 1921); *Motion Picture Magazine* (Aug. 1916, Nov. 1918, Apr.-May 1920, Apr. 1921); *Motion Picture Classic* (Mar. 1919, Oct. 1921, Mar. 1923).

ARCHIVAL MATERIALS

• *Clipping File*—CAA: Newsphoto; divorce (1932); film appearance (1917); obituary (1966). NYMA (also in Photoplay Collection): Obituary (1966). NYMN: Divorce (1932); newsphotos. NYPL: Newsphotos (numerous); divorce (1932); works as extra (1936); film review (1920s); article (undated); obituary (1966). • *Other Clipping File*—CNDA, GBBF, MAH, MIDL, NYSU, OHCL, PAPL, WICF. • *Correspondence*—NYPL (C. & L. Brown Collection): 1953. • *Filmography*—CAA (silent films only). • *Legal File*—CAUW: Talent agreement (1928, 1930). • *Photograph/Still*—CAA (also in Hollywood Studio Museum Collection), CASF, CAUT (Jessen Collection), CAUU, DCG (Quigley Photographic Archives), GBBF, NJFL, NYAM, NYCU (Palmer Collection), NYMN, NYPL, NYSU, OHCL, TXU, WICF. • *Play Program*—NYPL: 1927. • *Scrapbook*—NYPL (also in R. Locke Collection), WICF. • *Studio Biography*—NYMA: Photoplay.

CLAYTON, Marguerite, Salt Lake City or Ogden, Utah, 1891/1900-1968.

Among beautiful Marguerite Clayton's films were *Hit-the-Trail Holiday*, *The Pleasure Seekers*, *Wolf Blood*, *The Circus Cowboy* and *The New Moon*. She was primarily a star of serials and "actioners," including many with "Broncho Billy" Anderson (q.v.). Her career continued until the end of the silent era with such studios as Pathé, Fox, Essanay and Paramount.

PUBLISHED SOURCES

• *Books—General: Sweethearts of the Sage*; *Who's Who in the Film World*.

Credits: *Filmarama* (v. I and II); *Twenty Years of Silents*; *Who Was Who on Screen*. **Encyclopedic Works:** *Film Encyclopedia*; *Who's Who in Hollywood*. **Pictorial:** *Silent Portraits*.

• *Periodicals—Motion Picture Magazine* (Jan. 1915, Jan. 1916); *Motion Picture Classic* (Oct. 1916, Oct. 1917, May 1918); *Photoplay* (Mar. 1917, Oct. 1918); *Classic Images* (May 1988, Nov. 1989).

ARCHIVAL MATERIALS

• *Clipping File*—NYPL: Newsphotos. • *Other Clipping File*—NYMA (Photoplay Collection), PAPL, WICF. • *Filmography*—GBBF. • *Photograph/Still*—CAA, CAUT (Jessen Collection), DCG (Quigley Photographic Archives), GBBF, NJFL, NYEH, NYPL, OHCL, WICF. • *Scrapbook*—NYPL (R. Locke Collection). • *Studio Biography*—CAA: Paramount (1920s); Fox (1931, 1940s); Columbia (1944).

CLIFFORD, Ruth, Pawtucket, RI, 1900- 1998

Ruth Clifford was still appearing in small roles through the 1950s (e.g., *The Man in the Gray Flannel Suit*) and she also could be seen on television. Her films for Edison, Universal and other studios, beginning in 1915, included *The Face on the Barroom Floor*, *Butterfly*, *Abraham Lincoln* (1924), *A Kentucky Cinderella* and *The Dangerous Age*. Among her later films were *How Green Was My Valley*, *My Darling Clementine* and *The Searchers*.

PUBLISHED SOURCES

• *Books—General: Blue Book of the Screen*; *Famous Film Folk*; *The Truth About the Movies*; *Who's Who on the Screen*. **Credits:** *Filmarama* (v. I and II); *Forty Years of Screen Credits*; *Twenty Years of Silents*. **Encyclopedic Works:** *Film Encyclopedia*; *Filmlexicon degli Autori e delle Opere*; *Who's Who in Hollywood*. **Pictorial:** *Silent Portraits*.

• *Periodicals—Photoplay* (Aug. 1917, Apr. 1918); *Moving Picture Weekly* (Oct.

13, 1917); *Motion Picture Magazine* (May 1919); *Classic Images* (July 1990).

ARCHIVAL MATERIALS

• *Clipping File*—CAA: Article (1922, 1924, 1933, 1989); marriage/divorce (1934, 1938, 1953); Academy of Motion Picture Arts and Sciences symposium (1979). CAUT: Stage appearance (1966). NYPL: Newsphotos (numerous); divorce. • *Other Clipping File*—GBBF, MIDL, NYMA (Photoplay Collection), PAPL, WICF. • *Photograph/Still*—CAA (also in Hollywood Studio Museum Collection), CAUT (Jessen Collection) (Portrait File), CAUU, CNDA, DCG (Quigley Photographic Archives), GBBF, IAU (Junkin Collection), NYCU (Dramatic Museum Portraits), NYPL, NYSU, OHCL, TXU, WICF. • *Scrapbook*—NYPL (R. Locke Collection)

CODY, Lew (also known as Lewis J. Cody) (Louis Cote), Berlin, NH or Waterville, ME, 1884/1887–1934.

Mustachioed Lew Cody was a popular MGM star of the 1920s, appearing in a series of marital comedies with Aileen Pringle (q.v.) as well as in melodramas like *Rupert of Hentzau*. His films included *So This Is Marriage*, *Valley of Silent Men*, *Revelation* and *Wickedness Preferred*. After his first talkie, *What a Widow*, he was successfully cast in numerous sound films as well. He was married to Mabel Normand (q.v.) and Dorothy Dalton (q.v.).

PUBLISHED SOURCES

• *Books*—General: *Blue Book of the Screen*; *Famous Film Folk*; *Immortals of the Screen*; *Who's Who on the Screen*. **Credits:** *Filmarama* (v. I and II); *Forty Years of Screen Credits*; *Twenty Years of Silents*; *Who Was Who on Screen*. **Encyclopedic Works:** *Film Encyclopedia*; *Filmlexicon degli Autori e delle Opere*; *Halliwell's Filmgoer's Companion*; *The Illustrated Who's Who of the Cinema*; *The Movie Makers*; *The Picturegoer's Who's Who and Encyclopedia of the Screen To-day*; *Who's Who in Hollywood*; *The World Film Encyclopedia*. • *Periodicals*—*Photoplay* (Mar. 1919, May 1920, July 1922, June 1924, Jan. 1927, July 1929, June 1931); *Motion Picture Classic* (Feb. 1920, June 1921, Nov. 1921, Feb. 1923, Dec. 1923, May 1929, Nov. 1930); *Picture Show* (Feb. 28, 1920); *Motion Picture Magazine* (June 1921, Mar. 1924, Oct. 1924, June 1926); *Theatre* (Feb. 1928).

ARCHIVAL MATERIALS

• *Clipping File*—CAA: Film appearance (1922, undated); newsphotos; obituary (1934). CAUT: Biography. NYMN: Estate; obituary (1934). NYPL: Marriage (1926); estate; career (1932); funeral (1934); film reviews (several); article (1933, undated); obituary (1934). • *Other Clipping File*—GBBF, MAH, MIDL, NYMA (Photoplay Collection), OHCL, PAPL, WICF. • *Legal File*—CAUW: Document (1924); talent agreement (1924, 1930, 1932); contract (1930); personnel, payroll record (1932). • *Oral History*—NYCO: Mentioned in: Joseph Mankiewicz interview. • *Photograph/Still*—AZSU (Jimmy Starr Collection), CAA (also in Hollywood Studio Museum Collection) (also in MGM Collection), CAHL, CAUT (Jessen Collection), CAUU, DCG (Quigley Photographic Archives), GBBF, MIDL, NJFL, NJPT, NYAM, NYB (Underwood Collection), NYCU (Dramatic Museum Portraits) (Palmer Collection), NYEH, NYMN, NYPL, NYSU, OHCL, TXU, WICF. • *Scrapbook*—NJPT (Yeandle Collection), NYPL (also in R. Locke Collection). • *Studio Biography*—CAA: Paramount (early 1930s); C.B. Rogers (1933).

COLLIER, William, Jr. ("Buster"), New York, NY, 1900–1987.

Son of famous character actor William Collier, Sr., "Buster" Collier was a popular young juvenile star in silent films, having begun as a teenager in 1914. Among his 100 films were *College Widow*, *Two Men and a Maid* and *The Devil's Cargo*. His more prestigious sound films included *Cimarron*, *Little Caesar* and *Street Scene*. By 1935, his acting career had run its course and he eventually became an agent.

PUBLISHED SOURCES

• *Books*—Credits: *Filmarama* (v. I and II); *Forty Years of Screen Credits*; *Twenty Years of Silents*. Encyclopedic Works: *Film Encyclopedia*; *Filmlexicon degli Autori e delle Opere*; *The Picturegoer's Who's Who and Encyclopedia of the Screen To-day*; *Who's Who in Hollywood*; *The World Film Encyclopedia*. Pictorial: *Silent Portraits*.
• *Periodicals*—*Motion Picture Classic* (Oct. 1920, Oct. 1925); *Motion Picture Magazine* (May 1928, Sept. 1928).

ARCHIVAL MATERIALS

• *Caricature*—NYPL. • *Clipping File*—CAA (also in Collection): Marriage (1934); obituary (1987). CAFI: Obituary (1987). NYPL: Newsphotos; engagement/marriage (1934, undated); obituary (1987). • *Other Clipping File*—CASF, GBBF, MAH, MIDL, NYMA (Photoplay Collection), PAPL, WICF.
• *Collection*—CAA: Legal files, clippings, correspondence, programs, press books, scrapbooks, photographs relating to William Collier Sr. and Jr. (1900–1987). • *Correspondence*—CAA (see Collection). • *Filmography*—NYPL (incomplete). • *Legal File*—CAA (see Collection). CAUW: Talent agreement (1924, 1926–27, 1930); memo (1928); communication (1928); document (1926).
• *Photograph/Still*—CAA (also in Collection) (also in Hollywood Studio Museum Collection), CAH, CASF, CAUT (Jessen Collection), DCG (Quigley Photographic Archives), GBBF, MIDL, NJPT, NYAM, NYEH, NYMN, NYPL, NYSU, TXU, WICF.
• *Program*—CAA (see Collection).
• *Scrapbook*—CAA (see Collection), NYPL (also in R. Locke Collection).
• *Studio Biography*—CAA: Paramount (1932–33). NYMA: Photoplay.

COMPSON, Betty (Eleanor Luicime Compson), Beaver, UT, 1897–1974.

In films since 1915, Betty Compson became one of the major stars of silent cinema after her appearance in *The Miracle Man* (1919). She survived career declines and was nominated in 1928 for the first Academy Award as best actress for her role in *The Barker*. She made a successful transition to sound films and worked steadily, though in increasingly less significant vehicles and smaller roles, through the 1930s and 1940s. Her final film came in 1948.

PUBLISHED SOURCES

• *Books*—Bibliography: *The Idols of Silence*. General: *Blue Book of the Screen*; *Famous Film Folk*; *From Hollywood*; *Personal Glimpses of Famous Folks*; *Sweethearts of the Sage*; *The Truth About the Movies*; *Twinkle, Twinkle, Movie Star*; *Who's Who on the Screen*. Credits: *Filmarama* (v. I and II); *Forty Years of Screen Credits*; *Twenty Years of Silents*; *Who Was Who on Screen*. Encyclopedic Works: *Film Encyclopedia*; *Filmlexicon degli Autori e delle Opere*; *Halliwell's Filmgoer's Companion*; *The Illustrated Who's Who of the Cinema*; *The Movie Makers*; *The Picturegoer's Who's Who and Encyclopedia of the Screen To-day*; *Quinlan's Illustrated Registry of Film Stars*; *Who's Who in Hollywood*; *The World Film Encyclopedia*. Nostalgia: *Whatever Became Of...* (2nd). Pictorial: *Silent Portraits*; *They Had Faces Then*.
• *Periodicals*—The following periodical articles are in addition to those included in the library listings below: *Motion Picture Classic* (Dec. 1919, June 1921, July 1928, Dec. 1928, June 1931); *Photoplay* (Dec. 1919, Oct.-Nov. 1921, Nov.-Dec. 1923, June-July 1924, Nov. 1924, Apr. 1929, Aug.-Sept. 1930, Nov. 1930, Mar. 1931); *Picture Play Magazine* (Jan. 1920); *Shadowland* (Mar.-Apr. 1920); *Dramatic Mirror* (Nov. 13, 1920); *Motion Picture Magazine* (Mar. 1921, June 1921, Mar. 1922, May 1923, Jan. 1930, July 1931); *Pantomime* (Sept. 28, 1921); *Pictorial Review* (Jan. 1928); *Silver Screen* (Mar. 1931); *Cinema Digest*

(Aug. 22, 1932); *Films in Review* (Oct. 1966, Dec. 1968); *Classic Film Collector* (Spring 1971, Winter 1971-Spring 1972, Summer 1974); *Time* (May 6, 1974); *Classic Images* (Mar.-Apr. 1985).

OBSCURE PUBLISHED SOURCES
CAA: *How Talkies Are Made*; *Life Story of Betty Compson*.

ARCHIVAL MATERIALS
• *Clipping File* — AZSU (Jimmy Starr Collection): Wedding announcement; draft article by BC congratulating Wampas Baby Stars (1930). CAA: Film appearance (1920s, 1930s, 1940s); legal problem (1927–34); marriage/divorce (1930–44); stage appearance (1934); nostalgia (1969); obituary (1974). Periodical article: *Films in Review* (Aug.-Sept. 1966). CAFI: Periodical article: *Films in Review* (Aug.-Sept. 1966). CAUT: Robbery (1933); legal problem (1929–30); obituary (1974). CAUU: Obituary (1974). NYMA: Article (1928, 1930, 1971); excerpt from *Whatever Became of...*; obituary (1974). Periodical articles: *Motion Picture Classic* (June 1920); *Classic Film Collector* (Fall-Winter 1972); *Classic Images* (Feb. 1985). NYMN: Newsphotos; divorce (1937). NYPL: Article (1923, undated); newsphotos (numerous); dancer (1930s?); biography (1933); robbery (1933); named in divorce suit (1934); stage appearance (1933, undated); career (1927); returns to films (1932); marriage/divorce (1933–34); film appearance (1930s); obituary (1974). Periodical articles: *Pictures and Picturegoer* (July 1923); *Hollywood* (May 1930); *Liberty* (July 12, 1930); *Screen Romances* (Sept. 1930); *Films in Review* (Aug.-Sept. 1966). • *Other Clipping File* — GBBF, MIDL, OHCL, PAPL, TXU, WICF. • *Correspondence* — NYPL: Letter(s) (C. & L. Brown Collection) (1933); 2 letters in response to fans (1928, 1935). • *Filmography* — CAA: Incomplete to 1941 (includes excerpts from two books (1930–31) about BC career. NYMA. • *Oral History* — NYCO: Mentioned in: David Dressler interview. • *Photograph/Still* — CAA (also in Hollywood Studio Museum Collection), CAFA, CASU, CAUT (Jessen Collection), CAUU, CNDA, DCG (Quigley Photographic Archives), GBBF, MIDL, NJPT, NYB (Bettmann/UPI Collection) (Springer Collection) (Underwood Collection), NYCU (Dramatic Museum Portraits), NYEH, NYMN, NYPL, NYSU, OHCL, PAPL, TXSM, TXU (Robbins Collection), WICF, WYU. • *Scrapbook* — NYMA, NYPL (also in R. Locke Collection), WICF, WYU. • *Studio Biography* — CAA: Paramount (1933).

COOPER, Miriam, Baltimore, MD, 1891/94–1976.

A contrast to the fair-haired actresses whom D.W. Griffith seemed to favor was dark-eyed Miriam Cooper. She appeared in *Birth of a Nation, Intolerance* and many other films including *Serenade, The Oath, Should a Husband Forgive?* and *Evangeline,* but she never became a major star. Her appearances were few after 1920 and the end of her film career came early in that decade.

PUBLISHED SOURCES
• *Books* — **Bibliography:** *The Idols of Silence.* **General:** *Blue Book of the Screen; The Griffith Actresses; Who's Who in the Film World.* **Credits:** *Filmarama* (v. I and II); *Twenty Years of Silents.* **Encyclopedic Works:** *Film Encyclopedia; Filmlexicon degli Autori e delle Opere; Who's Who in Hollywood.* **Biography/Autobiography:** *Dark Lady of the Silents.* **Pictorial:** *Silent Portraits.*
• *Periodicals* — The following periodical articles are in addition to those included in the library listings below: *Motion Picture Magazine* (Mar. 1920, Sept. 1920, Aug. 1921, Nov. 1921, June 1922); *New York Dramatic Mirror* (May 15, 1920); *Photoplay* (Sept. 1920); *American Magazine* (Feb. 1937); *Silent Picture* (Autumn 1969, Spring 1970) *Classic Film Collector* (Winter 1970, Spring 1974); *Quarterly Journal of the Library of Congress* (Summer/Fall 1980).

ARCHIVAL MATERIALS
• *Clipping File* — CAA: Illness (1970); newsphotos; obituary (1976). Periodical

article: *Cinephile Newsletter* (June 1976). CAUU: Obituary (1976). NYMA: Illness (1970); article (1970); obituary (1976). Periodical articles: *Films in Review* (Apr. 1970); *Classic Film Collector* (Fall 1974). NYPL: Marriage/divorce (1927, undated); film review (1919); film appearance (1922); obituary (1976). Periodical articles: *Silent Picture* (Winter 1969, Summer 1970, Winter(?) 1974). • *Other Clipping File* — DCLC (see Collection), GBBF, MAH, NYSU, PAPL, TXU, WICF. • *Collection* — DCLC: Correspondence, including telegrams; clippings; writings; miscellany (1915–76). Collection relates chiefly to MC's marriage to director Raoul Walsh and her career, especially her work with D.W. Griffith. • *Correspondence* — DCLC (see Collection). • *Filmography* — TXU: Kalem films only. • *Photograph/Still* — CAA, CAH, CAUT (Jessen Collection), DCG (Quigley Photographic Archives), GBBF, NYEH, NYPL, NYSU, OHCL, TXSM, TXU, WICF. • *Scrapbook* — NYPL (also in R. Locke Collection).

CORTEZ, Ricardo (Jacob Krantz or Kranze), Vienna, Austria or Alsace-Lorraine, France, 1899–1977.

An extra from about 1916, Ricardo Cortez came into his own with the vogue for "Latin lover" types in the 1920s. He was a popular leading man during the silent era, co-starring with Greta Garbo (q.v.) in one of her earliest films. His career continued through the thirties and forties with roles in such films as the original *Maltese Falcon* and *Wonder Bar*, but mainly he labored in the "B" vineyards where he often played villains. His last film was *The Last Hurrah*. He was married to Alma Rubens (q.v.).

PUBLISHED SOURCES

• *Books* — **General:** *Eighty Silent Film Stars; Famous Film Folk; The Movie Stars Story; Screen Personalities; The Truth About the Movies.* **Credits:** *Filmarama* (v. II); *Forty Years of Screen Credits; Twenty Years of Silents.* **Encyclopedic Works:** *The "B" Directors; Film Encyclopedia; Filmlexicon degli Autori e delle Opere; Halliwell's Filmgoer's Companion; The Movie Makers; The Picturegoer's Who's Who and Encyclopedia of the Screen To-day; Quinlan's Illustrated Registry of Film Stars; Who's Who in Hollywood; The World Almanac Who's Who of Film; The World Film Encyclopedia.* **Nostalgia:** *Whatever Became of...* (2nd). **Pictorial:** *Silent Portraits.* **Factoids:** *Star Stats.*
• *Periodicals* — The following periodical articles are in addition to those included in the library listings below: *Photoplay* (Sept. 1925, Apr. 1930); *Motion Picture Classic* (July 1931); *Movie Mirror* (Dec. 1931); *Movie Classic* (Apr. 1932); *Silver Screen* (May 1934); *Newsweek* (Aug. 4, 1934, May 9, 1977); *Motion Picture Magazine* (July 1935); *Films in Review* (June-July 1984); *Classic Images* (Oct. 1990) (filmography).

ARCHIVAL MATERIALS

• *Clipping File* — CAA: Marriage, divorce (1925, 1928, 1930, 1933–34, 1937, 1940, 1950); RKO contract (1930); film appearance (1928); legal problem (1932); article (1932, 1958); nostalgia (1969); obituary (1977). CAUT: Divorce (1940); obituary (1977). CAUU: Obituary (1977). NYMA: Retirement (1959); newsphotos; obituary (1977). Periodical article: *Classic Images* (Sept. 1987). NYMN: Career; newsphotos. NYPL: Newsphotos (numerous); article (1926, early 1930s, 1930, 1932, 1934, undated); film review (1920s, 1930s); marriage/divorce (1929–30, 1933–34, 1939); film appearance (1930s); relationship with Alma Rubens (1930); career (1933); director (early 1940s); obituary (1977). Periodical articles: *Hollywood* (undated); *Photoplay* (June 1929, Dec. 1931, Nov. 1932); *Modern Screen* (Aug. 1932); *Shadowplay* (Sept. 1933); *New Movie Magazine* (Sept. 1934). • *Other Clipping File* — AZSU (Jimmy Starr Collection), CNDA, GBBF, MAH, MIDL, OHCL, PAPL, WICF. • *Correspondence* — NYPL (C. & L. Brown Collection): 1939. • *Filmog-*

raphy—CAA. • *Legal File*—CAUW: Letter, memo (1933–37); document (1933); loanout (1931, 1933–37); personnel, payroll record (1933–37); contract summary (1933–37); option (1933–37); agreement (1934); contract (1930, 1933, 1936, 1943); release (1937); talent agreement (1924, 1927, 1930, 1933–37). • *Photograph/Still*—CAA (also in Hollywood Studio Museum Collection), CAHL, CALM, CAUT (Jessen Collection) (Portrait File), CAUU, CNDA, DCG (Quigley Photographic Archives), GBBF, MIDL, NJPT, NYAM, NYB (Bettmann/UPI Collection) (Underwood Collection), NYCU (Dramatic Museum Portraits), NYEH, NYMN, NYPL, NYSU, OHCL, TXU, WICF. • *Publicity release*—CAA: Paramount (several) (1930s). NYPL: Warner (1935). • *Scrapbook*—NJPT (Yeandle Collection), UTBY (DeMille Archives). • *Studio biography*—CAA: Paramount (1933); RKO (1930?); Columbia (1958).

COSTELLO, Dolores, Pittsburgh, PA, 1904/05–1979.

Daughter of early matinee idol Maurice Costello (q.v.) (and wife to a later one, John Barrymore [q.v.]), blonde beauty Dolores Costello appeared in some of her father's films as early as 1909. Often joining her was her sister Helen(e) (q.v.). Her first adult film was *Glimpses of the Moon* (1923); others in the silent era included *Glorious Betsy* and *The Sea Beast*. She continued sporadically into the 1930s but her roles were generally not strong ones. Her penultimate effort, in Orson Welles's *The Magnificent Ambersons* (1942), was undoubtedly her best.

PUBLISHED SOURCES

• *Books*—**Bibliography:** *The Idols of Silence*. **General:** *Classics of the Silent Screen*; *Famous Stars of Filmdom (Women)*; *From Hollywood*; *Hollywood Album 2*; *Hollywood Kids*; *How I Broke Into the Movies*; *The Stars* (Schickel). **Credits:** *Filmarama* (v. I and II); *Forty Years of Screen Credits*; *Twenty Years of Silents*. **Encyclopedic Works:** *Film En-*

cyclopedia; *Filmlexicon degli Autori e delle Opere*; *Halliwell's Filmgoer's Companion*; *The Illustrated Who's Who of the Cinema*; *International Dictionary of Film and Filmmakers* (v. 3); *The Movie Makers*; *The Picturegoer's Who's Who and Encyclopedia of the Screen To-day*; *Quinlan's Illustrated Registry of Film Stars*; *Who's Who in Hollywood*; *The World Almanac Who's Who of Film*; *The World Film Encyclopedia*. **Nostalgia:** *Whatever Became of...* (2nd). **Biography/Autobiography:** *The Barrymores* (Alpert); *Good Night, Sweet Prince*; *The House of Barrymore*. **Pictorial:** *The Image Makers*; *Silent Portraits*; *They Had Faces Then*. **Factoids:** *Star Stats*.

• *Periodicals*—The following periodical articles are in addition to that included in the library listings below: *Photoplay* (Sept. 1923, Apr. 1926, Feb. 1929, Feb. 1936); *Motion Picture Classic* (Nov. 1925, Oct. 1927); *Motion Picture Magazine* (May 1926, Apr. 1936); *Time* (Mar. 23, 1936); *Films in Review* (Feb. 1970) (Wampas Baby Stars); *Film Comment* (Summer 1971); *Cine Revue* (Mar. 15, 1979); *Cinématographe* (Apr. 1979); *Cinéma* (France) (July-Aug. 1979).

ARCHIVAL MATERIALS

• *Caricature*—NYPL. • *Clipping File*—CAA: Stage appearance (1925, 1951); film appearance (1928, 1930, 1935); marriage/divorce/children (1928–29, 1935, 1951–52); robbery (1929); article (1927, 1947, 1949); legal problem (1947, 1953–54, 1958); nostalgia (1969); obituary (1979). CAUT: Legal problem (1958); children (1929); obituary (1979). CAUU: Article (1971); obituary (1979). NYMA: Divorce (1951); stage appearance (1951); newsphotos; obituary (1979). NYMN: Comeback (1938); career; newsphotos; obituary (1979). NYPL: Newsphotos (numerous); father sues for support (1938); article (1979, undated); biography (1948–49); returns to screen (1935–36, 1942?); marriage/separation/divorce (1926, 1935, 1952); film review (1920s, 1930s); stage appearance (1951); sues for alimony (1940); nostalgia (1936); illness (1935); drunken driving

(1950s); obituary (1979). Periodical article: *Focus On Film* (Winter 1972).
• *Other Clipping File*—AZSU (Jimmy Starr Collection), GBBF, MAH, MIDL, OHCL, PAPL, WICF. • *Correspondence*—CAA (Vertical File Collection): Letters from Mae Costello (mother) to Maurice Costello (father) which contain many mentions about DC at the start of her film career (1925). • *Filmography*—CAA: Through 1929. • *Interview*—GBBF (Hollywood Collection): Transcript of interview for *Hollywood* (TV series). • *Legal File*—CAUW: Notes (undated); contract summary (1927–29); personnel, payroll record (1927–29, 1937–43); agreement (1927–29); letter, memo (1927–31); document (1927, 1929, 1942); contract (1926, 1929); option (1927–28); talent agreement (1925–26, 1929–30, 1937). • *Oral History*—NYCO: Mentioned in the following interviews: Albert Howson, Conrad Nagel. • *Photograph/ Still*—CAA (also in Hollywood Studio Museum Collection), CAHL, CALM, CASF, CAUS, CAUT (Jessen Collection) (Portrait File), CAUU, CNDA, DCG (Quigley Photographic Archives), GBBF, MIDL, NJPT, NYAM, NYB (Bettmann/UPI Collection) (Underwood Collection), NYCU (Dramatic Museum Portraits) (Palmer Collection), NYEH, NYMN, NYPL, NYSU, OHCL, TXU, WICF. • *Scrapbook*—NJPT (Yeandle Collection), NYMA, NYPL (R. Locke Collection). • *Studio Biography*—CAA: RKO (1942); Warner (1940s). NYPL: Warner (1927, 1931).

COSTELLO, Helene (Helen Costello), New York, NY, 1903/04–1957.

Along with her sister Dolores (q.v.), pretty Helene Costello appeared in films with her father Maurice Costello (q.v.) as early as 1909. Her adult film career began in 1925 with Warner Bros. for whom she appeared during the remainder of the silent era. She was named a Wampas Baby Star in 1927. Her claim to fame is her leading role in the first all-talking film *The Lights of New York* in 1928, but her career did not prosper in the sound era. She was married to Lowell Sherman (q.v.).

PUBLISHED SOURCES
• *Books*—Credits: *Filmarama* (v. II); *Forty Years of Screen Credits*; *Twenty Years of Silents*; *Who Was Who on Screen*. Encyclopedic Works: *Film Encyclopedia*; *Filmlexicon degli Autori e delle Opere*; *The Picturegoer's Who's Who and Encyclopedia of the Screen To-day*; *Who's Who in Hollywood*; *The World Film Encyclopedia*. Pictorial: *Silent Portraits*; *They Had Faces Then*.
• *Periodicals*—*Photoplay* (May 1930); *Motion Picture Classic* (May 1930); *Movie Classic* (Feb. 1932, Aug. 1932); *Time* (Feb. 11, 1957); *Films in Review* (Feb. 1970) (Wampas Baby Stars); *Classic Images* (July 1985).

ARCHIVAL MATERIALS
• *Clipping File*—AZSU: Marriage; legal problem. CAA: Marriage/divorce (1927); custody fight (1947–48); desire to freelance (1928); robbery (1933); obituary (1957). CAUT: Custody fight (1947); return from trip (1929); obituary (1957). NYMA (also in Photoplay Collection): Funeral (1957); obituary (1957). NYMN: Newsphotos; obituary (1957). NYPL: Biography (1948); obituary (1957). • *Other Clipping File*—GBBF, MIDL, OHCL, PAPL, TXU, WICF. • *Correspondence*—CAA (Vertical File Collection): 1 letter from HC to Maurice Costello (father). Other letters from Mae Costello (mother) to Maurice Costello contain many mentions of HC (1925). • *Filmography*—CAA. • *Legal File*—CAUW: Talent agreement (1925–29); letter, memo (1926); loan out (1926); contract (1926–28). • *Photograph/Still*—CAA (also in Hollywood Studio Museum Collection), CAH, CAUU, CNDA, DCG (Quigley Photographic Archives), GBBF, NJPT, NYB (Bettmann/UPI Collection) (Underwood Collection), NYEH, NYPL, NYSU, OHCL, TXU (A. Davis Collection), WICF. • *Press Kit*—OHCL. • *Scrapbook*—NYPL (R. Locke Collection). • *Studio Biography*—NYMA: Photoplay.

COSTELLO, Maurice, Pittsburgh, PA, 1877-1950.

Maurice Costello was one of the earliest matinee idols, a leading man for Edison and Vitagraph, and one of the first stars to be billed by name. His starring career prospered from about 1907 to 1916 when his popularity began to diminish, but he played supporting roles well into the sound period. He was the father of Dolores (q.v.) and Helene Costello (q.v.).

PUBLISHED SOURCES

• *Books* – General: *The Big V*; *Classics of the Silent Screen*; *Gentlemen to the Rescue*; *Life Stories of the Movie Stars*. Credits: *Filmarama* (v. I and II); *Twenty Years of Silents*; *Who Was Who on Screen*. Encyclopedic Works: *Film Encyclopedia*; *Filmlexicon degli Autori e delle Opere*; *Halliwell's Filmgoer's Companion*; *The Illustrated Who's Who of the Cinema*; *International Dictionary of Films and Filmmakers* (v. 3); *Who's Who in Hollywood*.

• *Periodicals* – The following periodical articles are in addition to that included in the library listings below: *Blue Book Magazine* (Aug. 1914); *Motion Picture Magazine* (Jan. 1916); *Photoplay* (Jan. 1917, Sept. 1923, July 1924, May 1932); *Motion Picture Classic* (Oct. 1926, Jan. 1928); *Newsweek* (Nov. 6, 1950); *Time* (Nov. 6, 1950); *Films in Review* (Apr. 1971).

ARCHIVAL MATERIALS

• *Clipping File* – CAA (also in Collection): Marriage/divorce (1927, 1939, 1941); legal problem (1929–33); article (1929, 1948); illness (1932, 1950); obituary (1950). NYMA: Article (1939 [in Spanish], undated). NYMN: Reconciles with daughters (1935); obituary (1950). NYPL: Nostalgia (1939); reconciles with daughters (1935); divorce (1941); article (1923, 1939, 1943, undated); newsphotos; injury (1934); comeback (1938); obituary (1950). Periodical article: *New Movie Magazine* (undated). • *Other Clipping File* – AZSU (Jimmy Starr Collection), GBBF, MAH, MIDL, NYSU, OHCL, PAPL, PAPT, WICF. • *Collection* –

CAA (Vertical File Collection): Correspondence from wife Mae about daughters Dolores and Helen (Helene) and other matters (1916–25); contract (1925); photographs; clippings, and programs. • *Correspondence* – CAA (See Collection). • *Filmography* – CAA (silents only). • *Legal File* – CAA (See Collection). • *Photograph/Still* – CAA (also in Hollywood Studio Museum Collection) (also in Vertical File Collection), CALM, DCG (Quigley Photographic Archives), GBBF, NYAM, NYB (Bettmann/UPI Collection), NYEH, NYMN, NYPL, NYSU, OHCL, WICF. • *Program* – CAA (see Collection). • *Publicity Release* – CAA: Fox (1940); Paramount (1940). CAUU (A. Slide Collection): Fox (1941). • *Scrapbook* – NYPL (R. Locke Collection).

CRANE, Ward, Albany, NY, 1891-1928.

Entering films about 1919 or 1920, Ward Crane appeared in *The Phantom of the Opera* and many programmers like *The Luck of the Irish*, *French Heels*, *Risky Business* and *Honeymoon Flats*. If he is remembered today, it is undoubtedly as the rival for the affections of Buster Keaton's sweetheart in *Sherlock, Jr.*

PUBLISHED SOURCES

• *Books* – General: *Who's Who on the Screen*. Credits: *Filmarama* (v. I and II); *Twenty Years of Silents*; *Who Was Who on Screen*. Encyclopedic Works: *Film Encyclopedia*; *Who's Who in Hollywood*.

• *Periodicals* – *Motion Picture Magazine* (Dec. 1920); *Photoplay* (Dec. 1925).

ARCHIVAL MATERIALS

• *Clipping File* – NYMA (also in Photoplay Collection): Personal data summary. NYPL: Newsphotos; obituary (1928). • *Other Clipping File* – GBBF, MAH, NYSU, PAPL, WICF. • *Filmography* – NYMA. • *Photograph/Still* – CAA (also in Hollywood Studio Museum Collection), CAUT (Jessen Collection), DCG (Quigley Photographic Archives),

GBBF, NYAM, NYPL, NYSU, OHCL, WICF. • *Studio Biography*—NYMA: Photoplay.

CUMMINGS, Irving, New York, NY, 1888-1959.

From 1909, Irving Cummings was a leading man at studios such as Pathé. He starred in several serials, among which were *The Million Dollar Mystery* and *The Diamond from the Sky* (one of the longest serials ever made). His other starring films included *The Bells, The Gilded Cage, Jane Eyre* and *A Royal Romance.* In the 1920s he switched to directing, one of his films being *In Old Arizona* (1929).

PUBLISHED SOURCES

• *Books*—General: *Who's Who on the Screen.* Credits: *Filmarama* (v. I and II); *Twenty Years of Silents; Who Was Who on Screen.* Encyclopedic Works: *The "B" Directors; A Companion to the Movies; Film Encyclopedia; Filmlexicon degli Autori e delle Opere; Halliwell's Filmgoer's Companion; The Illustrated Who's Who of the Cinema; The Movie Makers; Who's Who in Hollywood.* Filmography: *Hollywood on the Palisades.*
• *Periodicals*—*Motion Picture Magazine* (Mar. 1922).

ARCHIVAL MATERIALS

• *Clipping File*—CAA: Anniversary in films (1945); directs film (1942, 1944); Edison Award (1944); 30th anniversary in show business (1939); article (1939); obituary (1959). CAUT: Obituary (1959). NYPL: Divorce (1930s, 1940s, undated); newsphotos; award (1940s); career; obituary (1959). • *Other Clipping File*—AZSU (Jimmy Starr Collection), CNDA, GBBF, MAH, MIDL, NYMA (Photoplay Collection), PAPL, WICF. • *Correspondence*—NYPL (C. & L. Brown Collection): 1915. • *Legal File:* CAUT (Twentieth Century-Fox Collection): Letter, memo (1928-31, 1933-47); loanout (1930); agreement (1933, 1935-36, 1938, 1941, 1943). CAUW: Talent agreement (1927); letter (1927); trans-

fer of rights (1923-27). • *Photograph/ Still*—CAA (also in Hollywood Studio Museum Collection), CAUT (Jessen Collection), DCG (Quigley Photographic Archives), GBBF, NJPT, NYEH, NYPL, NYSU, OHCL, WICF. • *Scrapbook*—NYPL (also in R. Locke Collection). • *Studio Biography*—CAUU: Fox (1940s?). NYMA: Photoplay.

CUNARD, Grace (Harriet Jeffries), Columbus, Ohio, 1893/94-1967.

Grace Cunard, one of the premiere serial queens of silent film, had an active career which lasted to the sound era. Among her serials were *Lucille Love (Girl of Mystery), The Broken Coin,* and *The Purple Mask.* Her features included *Society's Driftwood, Lady Raffles Returns* and *The Man Hater.* She played bits in sound films such as *The Bride of Frankenstein* and *The North Star.*

PUBLISHED SOURCES

• *Books*—General: *Continued Next Week; Early American Cinema; Ladies in Distress; Life Stories of the Movie Stars; Reel Women; Sweethearts of the Sage; Those Fabulous Serial Heroines; Who's Who in the Film World.* Credits: *Filmarama* (v. I and II); *Twenty Years of Silents; Who Was Who on Screen.* Encyclopedic Works: *Film Encyclopedia; Filmlexicon degli Autori e delle Opere; Halliwell's Filmgoer's Companion; Who's Who in Hollywood; Women Who Make Movies.* Pictorial: *Silent Portraits.*
• *Periodicals*—The following periodical articles are in addition to those included in the library listings below: *Motion Picture Magazine* (Mar. 1915, July 1915); *Feature Movie* (June 25, 1915); *Motion Picture Classic* (Jan. 1916, Aug. 1917); *Photoplay* (Apr. 1916); *Films in Review* (May 1967, Feb. 1972); *Film Comment* (Nov.-Dec. 1972, Nov. 1976).

ARCHIVAL MATERIALS

• *Clipping File*—CAA: Comeback (1941); obituary: (1967). CAUT: Obituary

(1967). NYMA (also in Photoplay Collection): Obituary (1967). Periodical article: *Classic Film Collector* (Summer 1973). NYPL: Film appearance (1933); newsphotos; obituary (1967). Periodical article: *New Movie Magazine* (Feb. 1932). • *Other Clipping File*—GBBF, MIDL, NYSU, OHCL, WICF. • *Correspondence*—CAA (Selig Collection): 1916. NYMA (Photoplay Collection). • *Filmography*—CAA, NYPL. • *Legal File*—CAUU (Universal Pictures Collection): Memo about finding extra work (1941). • *Photograph/Still*—CAA (also in Hollywood Studio Museum Collection), CAUT (Jessen Collection), DCG (Quigley Photographic Archives), NYPL, NYSU, OHCL, TXSM, WICF. • *Scrapbook*—NYPL (R. Locke Collection). • *Studio Biography*—NYMA: Photoplay.

DALTON, Dorothy, Chicago, IL, 1893/94–1972.

From 1914, Dorothy Dalton was a popular performer playing both "vamp" roles and romantic leads. She was a major Paramount star from 1921 to 1924, the year of her retirement from pictures. One of her later roles was in *Moran of the Lady Letty* opposite Rudolph Valentino (q.v.). Other appearances were in *The Disciple* (with W. S. Hart [q.v.]), *Flame of the Yukon* and *Fool's Paradise*. She also played on Broadway. She was married to Lew Cody (q.v.).

PUBLISHED SOURCES
• *Books*—General: *Blue Book of the Screen*; *Famous Film Folk*; *First One Hundred Noted Men and Women of the Screen*; *Who's Who on the Screen.* Credits: *Filmarama* (v. I and II); *Twenty Years of Silents*; *Who Was Who on Screen.* Encyclopedic Works: *Film Encyclopedia*; *Filmlexicon degli Autori e delle Opere*; *Halliwell's Filmgoer's Companion*; *Who Was Who in the Theatre*; *Who's Who in Hollywood.* Pictorial: *Silent Portraits.*
• *Periodicals*—The following periodical articles are in addition to those in-

cluded in the library listings below: *Motion Picture Magazine* (Sept. 1917, Nov. 1917, Oct. 1918, Nov. 1920, Feb. 1922, Sept. 1922); *Photoplay* (Aug. 1918, Mar. 1919, May 1920, Dec. 1921, Mar. 1922); *Motion Picture Classic* (Aug. 1919, Aug. 1921, May 1922); *Filmplay Journal* (Feb. 1922); *Silent Picture* (Spring 1972); *Classic Film Collector* (Summer 1972).

ARCHIVAL MATERIALS
• *Clipping File*—CAA: Film appearance (1921); newsphoto; article (1916, undated); obituary (1972). Periodical article: *Films in Review* (Oct. 1978). CAFI: Periodical article: *Films in Review* (Oct. 1978). CAUT: Obituary (1972). NYMA (also in Photoplay Collection): Film synopsis (1920); film appearance (1921); newsphotos. NYPL: Return to films (1929?); nostalgia (1936); newsphotos (numerous); legal problem (1939); article (1920, 1923, undated); stage appearance (1919); career (1921); marriage (1924); obituary (1972). Periodical articles: *Photoplay* (undated); *Movie Weekly* (1921). • *Other Clipping File*—GBBF, MAH, MIDL, NYSU, PAPL, WICF. • *Photograph/Still*—CAA (also in Hollywood Studio Museum Collection), CALM, CAUT (Jessen Collection), CAUU, DCG (Quigley Photographic Archives), GBBF, NJFL, NYAM, NYB (Bettmann/UPI Collection) (Underwood Collection), NYEH, NYPL, NYSU, OHCL, TXU, WICF. • *Scrapbook*—NYPL (also in R. Locke Collection). • *Studio Biography*—CAUT. NYMA: Photoplay.

DANA, Viola (Violet or Virginia Flugrath), Brooklyn, NY, 1897–1987.

One of three actress sisters (Shirley Mason [q.v.] and Edna Flugrath were the others), petite (4'11″) Viola Dana was a child actress who appeared on Broadway and in Edison films. Her success in the play *Poor Little Rich Girl* brought her to film fame and she became a star for Metro and Paramount. Among her films were *Kosher Kitty Kelly*, *Naughty Nanette*, *Glass*

Houses and *Flowers of the Dusk*. Her final screen—and only talkie—appearance was in a musical number from *The Show of Shows* with her sister Shirley Mason.

PUBLISHED SOURCES

• *Books*—General: *Blue Book of the Screen*; *Famous Film Folk*; *First One Hundred Noted Men and Women of the Screen*; *The Movie Stars Story*; *Who's Who on the Screen*. **Credits:** *Filmarama* (v. I and II); *Twenty Years of Silents*. **Encyclopedic Works:** *Film Encyclopedia*; *Filmlexicon degli Autori e delle Opere*; *Halliwell's Filmgoer's Companion*; *The Illustrated Who's Who of the Cinema*; *The Picturegoer's Who's Who and Encyclopedia of the Screen To-day*; *Variety Who's Who in Show Business*; *Who's Who in Hollywood*. **Nostalgia:** *Whatever Became of...* (5th). **Biography/Autobiography:** *Locklear*. **Pictorial:** *Silent Portraits*.

• *Periodicals*—The following periodical articles are in addition to that included in the library listings below: *Munsey's Magazine* (May 1913); *Cosmopolitan* (June 1913); *Green Book Magazine* (Nov. 1913); *Theatre* (Aug. 1914); *Weekly Movie Record* (May 10, 1915); *Motion Picture Magazine* (Aug. 1915, Sept. 1916, Oct. 1917, Sept. 1919, Feb. 1922, Dec. 1924, June 1925); *Picture Play Magazine* (May 1916); *Photoplay* (Feb. 1917, Oct. 1917, June 1919, Feb. 1920, May 1923, June 1924, July 1925, June 1926); *Motion Picture Classic* (July 1918, Jan. 1919, Oct. 1919, Nov. 1920, June 1921, Apr. 1922); *Films in Review* (Mar. 1976); *Cine Revue* (July 20, 1987); *Classic Images* (Aug. 1987).

OBSCURE PUBLISHED SOURCES

CAA, NYMA: *Viola Dana*.

MEDIA

Vi, Portait of a Silent Star (video).

ARCHIVAL MATERIALS

• *Clipping File*—CAA: Newsphotos; nostalgia (1975, 1980); divorce (1945); film appearance (1920); article (1975); obituary (1987). CAFI: Obituary (1987). NYMA (also in Photoplay Collection):

Obituary (1987). Periodical article: *Photo-play Journal* (Dec. 1918). NYMN: Newsphotos. NYPL: Newsphotos (numerous); film review (1917); obituary (1987). • *Other Clipping File*—CAUB, GBBF, MAH, MIDL, NYSU, OHCL, PAPL, WICF. • *Filmography*—NYPL. • *Interview*—CAUU (Hollywood Studio Museum Collection) (R. Lamparski Collection). GBBF (Hollywood Collection): Transcript of interview for *Hollywood* (TV series). MISU: Recorded from a telephone interview. • *Legal File*—CAUW: Talent agreement (1926); agreement (1929). • *Photograph/Still*—CAA (also in Hollywood Studio Museum Collection) (also in MGM Collection), CAUB, CAUC (Motion Picture Photograph Collection), CAUT (Jessen Collection), DCG (Quigley Photographic Archives), GBBF, IAU (Junkin Collection), NJFL, NYAM, NYEH, NYMN, NYPL, NYSU, OHCL, TXSM, TXU, WICF. • *Play Program*—NYPL: (1913?). • *Scrapbook*—NYPL (also in R. Locke Collection). • *Studio Biography*—CAA: Metropolitan (1924). NYMA: Photoplay.

DANIELS, Bebe (Virginia Daniels), Dallas, TX, 1901–1971.
Bebe Daniels entered films as a child and eventually served an apprenticeship of several years with Harold Lloyd in numerous comedy shorts. Her appearances in DeMille films like *Male and Female* were her entree to major stardom at Paramount throughout the 1920s. She had a brief popularity in talkies when her singing voice was heard in such musicals as *Rio Rita*, *Dixiana* and *42nd Street* but she eventually went to England to re-establish her career. She and husband Ben Lyon (q.v.) found fame there in long-running radio and television series.

PUBLISHED SOURCES

• *Books*—Wrote *282 Ways of Making a Salad* (1950). **General:** *Alice in Movieland*; *Blue Book of the Screen*; *Famous Film Folk*; *Famous Stars of Filmdom (Women)*; *From Hollywood*; *The Great*

Movie Stars: the Golden Years; *Harold Lloyd* (Reilly); *Hollywood Album 2*; *Hollywood Kids*; *How I Broke Into the Movies*; *The Idols of Silence*; *Love, Laughter and Tears*; *The Movie Musical from Vitaphone to 42nd Street*; *The Movie Stars Story*; *Screen Personalities*; *The Truth About the Movies*; *Who's Who on the Screen*. **Credits:** *Filmarama* (v. I and II); *Forty Years of Screen Credits*; *Twenty Years of Silents*; *Who Was Who on Screen*. **Encyclopedic Works:** *A Biographical Dictionary of Film*; *The Complete Encyclopedia of Popular Music and Jazz*; *Film Encyclopedia*; *Filmlexicon degli Autori e delle Opere*; *Halliwell's Filmgoer's Companion*; *The Illustrated Encyclopedia of the World's Great Movie Stars and Their Films*; *The Illustrated Who's Who in British Films*; *The Illustrated Who's Who of the Cinema*; *International Dictionary of Films and Filmmakers* (v. 3); *The Movie Makers*; *The Oxford Companion to Film*; *The Picturegoer's Who's Who and Encyclopedia of the Screen To-day*; *Quinlan's Illustrated Directory of Film Comedy Actors*; *Quinlan's Illustrated Registry of Film Stars*; *Who Was Who in the Theatre*; *Who's Who in Hollywood*; *The World Almanac Who's Who of Film*; *The World Film Encyclopedia*. **Nostalgia:** *Whatever Became of...* (1st, 8th). **Biography/Autobiography:** *Bebe and Ben*; *Life with the Lyons*. **Pictorial:** *The Revealing Eye*; *Silent Portraits*; *They Had Faces Then*. **Recordings:** *Hollywood on Record*. **Factoids:** *Star Stats*.

• *Periodicals* — The following periodical articles are in addition to those included in the library listings below: *Photoplay* (Dec. 1913, Nov. 1918, July 1919, Sept. 1919, Jan. 1921, July 1921, Nov. 1921, Nov. 1922, Jan. 1924, July 1924, Nov. 1924, Nov. 1925, Feb. 1926, Sept. 1928, July 1930, Oct. 1930); *Motion Picture Classic* (May 1919, Sept. 1921, Mar. 1923, Nov. 1923, Sept. 1924, Dec. 1928-Jan. 1929, Nov. 1929, Aug. 1931); *Photo-play World* (June 1919); *Motion Picture Magazine* (Nov. 1919, Sept. 1920, Sept. 1921, Nov. 1921, Apr. 1922, Jan.-Feb. 1925, Feb. 1926, May 1926, May 1928, Dec. 1929, Aug.-Sept. 1930, May 1931, Jan. 1933); *Picture Play Magazine* (Nov. 1919, Sept. 1920); *Shadowland* (Mar.-Apr. 1920); *Theatre* (July 1928); *Newsweek* (May 6, 1957, Mar. 29, 1971); *Show* (Aug. 1962); *Films in Review* (Oct.-Dec. 1964) (filmography); *Films and Filming* (June 1970); *Time* (Mar. 29, 1971); *Classic Film Collector* (Spring 1971); *Silent Picture* (Summer-Autumn 1971); *Cine Revue* (Feb. 13, 1975).

MEDIA

Joe Louis/Bebe Daniels (video).

ARCHIVAL MATERIALS

• *Caricature* — NYMN. • *Clipping File* — CAA: Illness (1922, 1927-28, 1949, 1963); newsphotos; engagement/marriage/children (1926, 1929, 1930-31); film appearance (1934); injury (1928); article (1924, 1931-32, 1946, 1960s, 1962, 1979); threatened by fan (1931-33); legal problem (1921, 1934, 1936); return from England (1939, 1941, 1945); producer (1946); robbery (1952); nostalgia (1954, 1957, 1969, 1970); TV appearance (*This Is Your Life*) (1954); obituary (1971). CAFI: Article (1984). CAUT: Injury (1958); newsphotos; obituary (1971). CAUU: Threatened by fan (1932-33); marriage (1930); nostalgia (1966?); obituary (1971). NYMA: Newsphotos; excerpt from *Love, Laughter and Tears*; article (1946); war service (1945); obituary (1971). NYMN: Newsphotos. NYPL: Newsphotos; article (1922, 1933, 1940s, 1946, 1954, undated); threatened by fan (1932, undated); life in England (1941); film review (1920s, 1930s); stage appearance (1940s?); marriage; producer; signs with Paramount (1926); film appearance (1930s); film synopses (1930s); war correspondent (1944); comeback (1954); illness (1963, 1967); obituary (1971). Periodical articles: *Film Fans Magazine* (Sept. 1925); *TV Guide* (Nov. 20, 1954); *Films in Review* (Aug.-Sept. 1964); *Silent Picture* (Spring 1971); *Hollywood Studio Magazine* (Dec. 1979). • *Other Clipping File* — AZSU (Jimmy Starr Collection), CAUB, CNDA, GBBF, MAH, MIDL, OHCL, PAPL, WICF. • *Correspondence* — CAA (Adolph Zukor Collection): 1922, undated. CAUS (Rob Wagner Collection): Letter(s) pertaining to *Rob Wagner Script* (periodical). NYPL: 1930, undated. • *Filmography*—NYMA, NYPL. • *Interview*—CAUU (A. Slide Collection): 1970 (joint interview with B. Lyon). • *Legal File*—CAUW: Personnel, payroll record (1931-34); contract summary (1931-34); agreement (1930-34); waiver (1931-34); letter, memo (1930-34); loanout (1931); contract (1931); document (1932); talent agreement (1931). • *Oral History*—NYCO: Mentioned in the following interviews: Albert (Eddie) Sutherland, Bert Wheeler, Carey Wilson. • *Photograph/Still*—AZSU (Jimmy Starr Collection), CAA (also in Hollywood Studio Museum Collection), CAHL, CALM, CAOC (Kiesling Collection), CAUB, CAUS, CAUT (Jessen Collection), CAUU, CNDA, GBBF, MABU (Douglas Fairbanks Jr. Collection), MIDL, NJPT, NYAM, NYB (Bettmann/UPI Collection) (Springer Collection) (Underwood Collection), NYCU (Dramatic Museum Portraits) (Palmer Collection), NYEH, NYPL, NYSU, OHCL, TXAC (Struss Collection), TXSM, WICF. • *Publicity Release*—AZSU (Jimmy Starr Collection). • *Scrapbook*—GBBF, NJPT (Yeandle Collection), NYMA, NYPL (R. Locke Collection), UTBY (DeMille Archives). • *Studio Biography*—CAA: Paramount (1927-28); Fox (1935).

D'ARCY, Roy (Roy Giusti), San Francisco, CA, 1894-1969.

One of the most villainous of the silent villains you loved to hate was Roy D'Arcy, especially in his early film *The Merry Widow* (1925). He continued his evil ways in such silent movies as *Bardelys the Magnificent* and *La Bohème*, as well as in talkies like *Flying Down to Rio* and, later in the 1930s, a few "B" efforts.

PUBLISHED SOURCES
• *Books*—Credits: *Filmarama* (v. I and II); *Forty Years of Screen Credits*; *Twenty Years of Silents*; *Who Was Who*

on Screen. **Encyclopedic Works:** *Film Encyclopedia*; *Filmlexicon degli Autori e delle Opere*; *The Picturegoer's Who's Who and Encyclopedia of the Screen To-day*; *Who's Who in Hollywood*; *The World Film Encyclopedia*. **Pictorial:** *Silent Portraits*. • *Periodicals*—*Motion Picture Classic* (Nov. 1925, Aug. 1926); *Cinema Art* (Sept. 1926); *Photoplay* (Jan. 1927); *Theatre* (Jan. 1927); *Motion Picture Magazine* (Apr. 1927).

ARCHIVAL MATERIALS
• *Caricature*—NYPL (Sardi Collection). • *Clipping File*—CAA: Film appearance (1933); legal problem (1932); divorce (1933); obituary (1969). CAUT: Obituary (1969). NYMA (also in Photoplay Collection): Obituary (1969). NYPL: Newsphotos; marriage (1929); film review (1920s); stage appearance (1930); obituary (1969). • *Other Clipping File*—CASP, GBBF, MIDL. • *Correspondence*—NYPL (C. & L. Brown Collection): (1931-36). • *Photograph/Still*—CAA (also in Hollywood Studio Museum Collection) (also in MGM Collection), CALM, CASP, DCG (Quigley Photographic Archives), NYB (Underwood Collection), NYCU (Dramatic Museum Portraits), NYPL, TXU, WICF. • *Scrapbook*—NYPL.

DARMOND, Grace, Toronto, Canada, 1898-1963.

Grace Darmond was another of the popular serial queens. She made her way intrepidly through such chapterplays as *The Shielding Shadow*, *The Hawk's Trail*, *The Hope Diamond Mystery* and *A Dangerous Adventure*. She appeared in numerous other films as well, making her final one in 1928.

PUBLISHED SOURCES
• *Books*—General: *Those Fabulous Serial Heroines*; *The Truth About the Movies*. **Credits:** *Filmarama* (v. I and II); *Twenty Years of Silents*; *Who Was Who on Screen*. **Encyclopedic Works:** *Film Encyclopedia*; *Filmlexicon delle Autori e delle Opere*; *Who's Who in*

Hollywood. **Pictorial:** *Silent Portraits.*

• *Periodicals* — The following periodical articles are in addition to that included in the library listings below: *Photoplay* (June 1915); *Feature Movie* (Jan. 1916); *Film Players Herald & Movie Pictorial* (Feb. 1916); *Motion Picture Classic* (Feb. 1916, Apr. 1919); *Motion Picture Magazine* (Dec. 1917, July 1921).

ARCHIVAL MATERIALS

• *Clipping File* — CAA: Divorce (1937); film appearance (1920); obituary (1963). NYMA (also in Photoplay Collection). Periodical article: *Classic Images* (Aug. 1986). NYPL: Newsphotos; divorce (1933). • *Other Clipping File* — GBBF, MAH, OHCL, WICF. • *Correspondence* — NYMA (Photoplay Collection). • *Photograph/Still* — CAA (Hollywood Studio Museum Collection), CAFA, CALM, CAUT (Jessen Collection), DCG (Quigley Photographic Archives), NYPL, NYSU, OHCL, WICF. • *Scrapbook* — NYPL (R. Locke collection), WICF.

DAVENPORT, Dorothy (also known as Mrs. Wallace Reid), Boston, MA, 1895–1977.

Versatile Dorothy Davenport was actress, producer and scriptwriter at various times during her career. The bulk of her film appearances came between 1909 and 1923, her producing years were 1926 through 1942 and she wrote actively until about 1968. She was a popular star in her own right and often appeared with husband Wallace Reid (q.v.). After his death she produced and starred in *Human Wreckage*, a cautionary tale about drug abuse, the addiction from which he died. She made her sound film debut in 1932.

PUBLISHED SOURCES

• *Books* — **General:** *Early Women Directors*; *Famous Film Folk*; *Reel Women*; *Who's Who in the Film World*. **Credits:** *Filmarama* (v. I and II); *Twenty Years of Silents*. **Encyclopedic Works:**

Film Encyclopedia; *Filmlexicon degli Autori e delle Opere*; *Halliwell's Filmgoer's Companion*; *Who's Who in Hollywood*. **Nostalgia:** *Whatever Became of...* (10th). **Pictorial:** *Silent Portraits.*

• *Periodicals* — *Moving Picture Stories* (Jan. 3, 1913); *Motion Picture Magazine* (Dec. 1915, Feb. 1922); *Motion Picture Classic* (July 1916); *Photoplay* (Nov. 1921, Sept. 1924); *Shadowplay* (Dec. 1934); *Films in Review* (Apr. 1966).

ARCHIVAL MATERIALS

• *Clipping File* — CAA: Film appearance (1921, 1932); article (1916); obituary (1977). NYPL (also in Locke Collection): Producer; writes screen plays; newsphotos; director (1934). • *Other Clipping File* — GBBF, NYMA (Photoplay Collection), WICF. • *Correspondence* — CAA (Wallace Reid Jr. Collection): 1922, 1926, 1938, 1941, 1966. • *Interview* — CAUU (A. Slide Collection). • *Photograph/Still* — CAA (also in Hollywood Studio Museum Collection), CAHL, CAUT (Jessen Collection), CAUU, CNDA, DCG (Quigley Photographic Archives), GBBF, NYCU (Dramatic Museum Portraits), NYEH, NYPL, WICF. • *Scrapbook* — NYPL (R. Locke Collection).

DAVIES, Marion (Marion Douras), Brooklyn, NY, 1897–1961.

Whatever talents blonde Marion Davies may have possessed were always to be overshadowed by her relationship with publishing magnate William Randolph Hearst. In a film career that stretched from *Runaway Romany* (1918) to 1937's *Ever Since Eve*, she showed considerable comedic ability but was frequently in overproduced films like *Janice Meredith*, *Little Old New York* and *When Knighthood Was in Flower*. There were other films where she did shine (e.g., *Show People*) but these were rare.

PUBLISHED SOURCES

• *Books* — **Bibliography:** *The Idols of*

Silence. **General:** *Alice in Movieland; Classics of the Silent Screen; Co-Starring Famous Women and Alcohol; Debrett Goes to Hollywood; Famous Film Folk; The Golden Days of San Simeon; The Great Lovers; The Great Movie Stars; History of the American Cinema* (v. 3); *Hollywood Album; Hollywood Greats of the Golden Years; How I Broke Into the Movies; Immortals of the Screen; Ladies in Distress; The MGM Girls; The MGM Stock Company; The MGM Years; More of Hollywood's Unsolved Mysteries; Movie Star; The Movie Stars Story; Scandal!; Screen Personalities; Some Are Born Great; The Truth About the Movies; Who's Who on the Screen.* **Credits:** *Filmarama* (v. I and II); *Forty Years of Screen Credits; Twenty Years of Silents; Who Was Who on Screen.* **Encyclopedic Works:** *A Biographical Dictionary of Film; Film Encyclopedia; Filmlexicon degli Autori e delle Opere; Halliwell's Filmgoer's Companion; The Illustrated Encyclopedia of the World's Great Movie Stars and Their Films; The Illustrated Who's Who of the Cinema; International Dictionary of Films and Filmmakers* (v. 3); *The Movie Makers; The Oxford Companion to Film; The Picturegoer's Who's Who and Encyclopedia of the Screen To-day; Quinlan's Illustrated Registry of Film Stars; Who Was Who in the Theatre; Who's Who in Hollywood; The World Almanac Who's Who of Film; The World Encyclopedia of the Film; The World Film Encyclopedia.* **Biography/Autobiography:** *Citizen Hearst; The Hearsts; Marion Davies; My Autobiography* (Chaplin); *The Times We Had.* **Pictorial:** *The Image Makers; Leading Ladies; Silent Portraits; They Had Faces Then.* • *Oral History* — *NOTE:* The following oral histories are placed in this section because they are readily available from the issuer. For other oral histories on MD, see the Oral History section under Archival Materials. *Aileen Pringle, Silent Movie Actress and Frequent Guest; Arthur and Pat Lake; Dalmacio Carpio, Hearst Chef...; Eleanor Boardman d'Arrast; The Eubanks Family and San Simeon; Hearst and Davies at St. Donat's Castle;*

Hearst as a Host; King Vidor; Remembering Aunt Marion; Serving Hearst and Davies as a Waiter and Butler; Vera Burnett (Shaw), Marion Davies' Movie Double. NOTE: All these oral histories can be found at California State Polytechnic University, San Luis Obispo and most are available at other libraries as well. **Factoids:** *Star Stats.*
• *Periodicals* — The following periodical articles are in addition to those included in the library listings below: *Motion Picture Magazine* (Aug. 1918, Dec. 1918, Aug. 1919, Mar. 1920, June 1920, Sept. 1920, Aug. 1925, June 1926, Jan. 1928, Sept. 1931, Aug. 1933, Jan. 1935); *Photoplay* (Feb. 1919, Oct. 1919, Sept. 1921, Jan. 1922, Apr. 1922, Jan. 1925, May 1926, Sept. 1926, July 1928, Feb. 1932, June 1933, Jan. 1934, Feb. 1935); *Motion Picture Classic* (Sept. 1919, Sept. 1922, Feb. 1926, Mar. 1927); *(New York) Dramatic Mirror* (May 8, 1920, Dec. 25, 1920); *Theatre* (Jan. 1927); *Cinema Digest* (July 25, 1932); *Vanity Fair* (Nov. 1932); *Silver Screen* (July 1933); *Movie Classic* (Sept. 1933, Sept. 1935); *Shadowplay* (Aug. 1934); *Cinema Arts* (June 1937); *Time* (Nov. 5, 1951, Nov. 24, 1952, Aug. 1, 1955, Sept. 29, 1961); *Life* (Nov. 12, 1951); *Newsweek* (Nov. 12, 1951); *Sight and Sound* (Autumn 1968); *Films and Filming* (Feb. 1971); *Films in Review* (June-Sept. 1972); *Film Culture* (nos. 58-60, 1974); *Cine Revue* (Apr. 17, 1975, Apr. 18, 1985); *Film Dope* (Apr. 1976); *Hollywood Studio Magazine* (Feb. 1992).

MEDIA
A Very Public Private Affair (video).

ARCHIVAL MATERIALS
• *Clipping File* — CAA: Legal problem (1931, 1953, 1955, 1958); article (1935, 1951, 1954, 1969, 1974); ends career (1937); marriage/divorce (1951–52, 1954); film appearance (1922–24, 1927); gift to UCLA (1958, 1988); party (1922–23, 1930, 1934, 1951–52); home (1947, 1949, 1955, 1957, 1981–82, 1986–87, 1990); Hearst Trust (1951); extortion attempt (1937); honor (1928, 1932, 1947, 1951, 1954, 1958); Foundation (1933, 1935, 1937, 1939, 1949, 1952, 1957); sale of

effects (1953); Desert Inn, Las Vegas (1955, 1960); illness (1955); review of *Marion Davies* (1972); review of *The Times We Had* (1975); estate (1961); obituary (1961). Periodical articles: *Life* (Oct. 20, 1952); *Newsweek* (Oct. 2, 1961). CAFI: Article (1951); film festival (1979); marriage/divorce (1951–52); Desert Inn, Las Vegas (1955); honor (1932); newsphotos; obituary (1961). Periodical articles: *Screenland* (July 1935); *Los Angeles Magazine* (Feb. 1981). CAUT: Award (1958); sale of jewelry (1963); estate (1961); review of *The Times We Had*; home (1957); obituary (1961). Periodical article: *Life* (Oct. 20, 1952). CAUU (also in McCormick Collection): Newsphotos; film appearance (1929, 1972). NYMA: Review of *Marion Davies*; newsphotos; film review (1929); illness; article (1961, 1972); review of *The Times We Had*; obituary (1961). Periodical articles: *Movie Mirror* (June 1934); *Picturegoer* (Sept. 21, 1935); *Classic Images* (Nov.-Dec. 1982). NYPL: PARTIAL CONTENTS: Illness (1956, 1961); will; newsphotos; Hearst empire (1951); review of *The Times We Had*; article (1954, 1972, undated); marriage/divorce (1951, 1954); review of *Marion Davies* (1973); film appearance (1920s); lives in Japan (1951); fortune (1948); beach house (1960, undated); extortion threat (1937); *Maggie* (novel) (1971); legal problem; Desert Inn, Las Vegas (1955); surgery (1961); sale of effects (1951); honor (1942); charity work; biography (1975); San Simeon (1978); film roles (1979); obituary (1961). Periodical article: *Silent Picture* (Summer 1970). • *Other Clipping File* — AZSU (Jimmy Starr Collection), CALM (see Collection), CNDA, GBBF, MAH, MIDL, OHCL, WICF. • *Collection* — CALM: 10 scrapbooks with clippings about several 1920s films such as *Little Old New York, The Fair Co-Ed, The Patsy* and *Zander the Great*. • *Correspondence* — CAA: Notes, telegrams (Hedda Hopper Collection) (1940–59); letter (Adolph Zukor Collection) (1919). • *Filmography* — CAA, CAFI, CAUT. • *Interview* — CAA (Hedda Hopper Collection): Proposed divorce (1952). GBBF (Hollywood Collection). • *Memora-*

bilia — CASF. • *Oral History* — CAUS: Mentioned in the following interviews: Edward A. Dickson, Ivan N. Mensh, George Tarjan. NYCO: Mentioned in the following interviews: Bennett Cerf, Marc Connelly, Thomas Cowan, J. P. Getty, Douglass Montgomery, Elliot Nugent, William Perlberg, Boris Shishkin, W.A. Swanberg, Blanche Sweet, Carl Van Vechten, Burton Wheeler, Jerome Zerbe. • *Photograph/Still* — CAA (also in Hollywood Studio Museum Collection) (also in MGM Collection), CAFA, CALM, CAOC (Kiesling Collection), CASF, CAUS, CAUT (Jessen Collection) (Portrait File), CAUU (A. Slide Collection), CNDA, DCG (Quigley Photographic Archives) (Terry Ramsaye Papers), NJFL, NYAM, NYB (Bettmann/UPI Collection) (Underwood Collection), NYCU (Dramatic Museum Portraits) (Palmer Collection), NYEH, NYPL, NYSU, OHCL, TXSM, TXU, WICF. • *Press Kit* — CAFA, OHCL. • *Publicity Release* — NYMA: Warner (1930s). • *Scrapbook* — CALM (see Collection), NYMA, NYPL (also in R. Locke Collection). • *Studio Biography* — CAA: MGM (1929). NYPL: Warner (1936?).

DAW, Marjorie (Marjorie House), Colorado Springs, CO, 1902–1977.

Among pretty Marjorie Daw's films were *The River's End, Rupert of Hentzau, Going Up, The Warrens of Virginia* and *Experience*, but the highlights of her career undoubtedly were her co-starring appearances with Douglas Fairbanks in breezy comedies of the mid-1910s like *His Majesty the American* and *The Knickerbocker Buckaroo*. Her career did not survive the silent era.

PUBLISHED SOURCES
• *Books* — **General:** *Blue Book of the Screen; Famous Film Folk; Sweethearts of the Sage; Who's Who on the Screen.* **Credits:** *Filmarama* (v. I and II); *Twenty Years of Silents.* **Encyclopedic Works:** *Film Encyclopedia; Filmlexicon degli*

Autori e delle Opere; *Who's Who in Hollywood*. **Biography/Autobiography:** *Showman*. **Pictorial:** *Silent Portraits*.

• *Periodicals* — The following periodical articles are in addition to those included in the library listings below: *Photoplay* (Jan. 1916, July 1918, Feb. 1920); *Motion Picture Magazine* (Apr. 1919, Sept. 1920); *Motion Picture Classic* (Apr. 1919, Mar. 1920, July 1921); *Everybody's* (June 1920); *Classic Images* (Sept. 1983, Apr. 1991).

ARCHIVAL MATERIALS

• *Clipping File* — CAA: Film appearance (1921); article (1924). NYMA (also in Photoplay Collection): Periodical article: *Classic Images* (June 1987). NYPL: Divorce; inherits millions; legal problem (1949); newsphotos; film appearance (1923). Periodical article: *Hollywood Life* (Oct. 1929). • *Other Clipping File* — GBBF, MAH, NYSU, OHCL, PAPL, TXU, WICF. • *Oral History* — NYCO: Mentioned in: Nita Naldi interview. • *Scrapbook* — NYPL (R. Locke Collection), TNUT (Clarence Brown Collection). • *Studio Biography* — CAA: Paramount. NYMA: Photoplay.

DAY, **Alice,** Pueblo, CO, 1905-1995

Pretty Alice Day's film career started a bit earlier than that of her sister Marceline (q.v.) and lasted from about 1923 to 1932. She began as a Sennett bathing beauty and then was groomed to be a major Sennett star. Her films included *Drag, The Gorilla, Viennese Nights* and *Phyllis of the Follies*. None of her roles were substantial enough to prolong her time in the limelight past the early sound period.

PUBLISHED SOURCES

• *Books* — **Credits:** *Filmarama* (v. II); *Forty Years of Screen Credits*; *Twenty Years of Silents*. **Encyclopedic Works:** *Film Encyclopedia*; *Filmlexicon degli Autori e delle Opere*; *The Picturegoer's Who's Who and Encyclopedia of the Screen To-day*; *Who's Who in Hollywood*; *The World Film Encyclopedia*.

• *Periodicals* — *Motion Picture Classic* (Dec. 1927, Feb. 1929); *Films in Review* (Feb. 1970) (Wampas Baby Stars).

ARCHIVAL MATERIALS

• *Clipping File* — CAA: Divorce (1938-39). CAA (Sennett Collection): Newsphotos; marriage (1926); film appearance (1927). CAUT: Marriage (1920s?). NYPL: Article (1926); alimony.
• *Other Clipping File* — AZSU (Jimmy Starr Collection), GBBF, NYMA (Photoplay Collection), OHCL, PAPL.
• *Legal File* — CAA (Mack Sennett Collection): Contract (1923-25); letter (1924). CAUW: Talent agreement (1927, 1929-30). • *Photograph/Still* — CAA (also in Hollywood Studio Museum Collection) (also in MGM Collection), CAUU, DCG (Quigley Photographic Archives), GBBF, MIDL, NJPT, NYB (Underwood Collection), NYEH, NYPL, OHCL, TXU. • *Press Release* — CAA (Mack Sennett Collection): 1925-27 (numerous). • *Studio Biography* — CAA (Sennett Collection).

DAY, **Marceline,** Colorado Springs, CO, 1907/08-

Winsome Marceline Day entered films about 1925, a bit later than her older sister Alice (q.v.). She was cast mostly in minor films but a few were memorable, among them *London After Midnight, The Beloved Rogue* and *The Cameraman*. After her transition to talkies, the roles were mundane and the westerns and other quickies in which she appeared did nothing to sustain her career after 1933.

PUBLISHED SOURCES

• *Books* — **General:** *Sweethearts of the Sage*. **Credits:** *Filmarama* (v. II); *Forty Years of Screen Credits*; *Twenty Years of Silents*. **Encyclopedic Works:** *Film Encyclopedia*; *Filmlexicon degli Autori e delle Opere*; *The Picturegoer's Who's Who and Encyclopedia of the Screen To-day*; *Who's Who in Hollywood*; *The World Film Encyclopedia*. **Pictorial:** *Silent Portraits*.

• *Periodicals* — *Motion Picture Classic*

(Dec. 1927); *Motion Picture Magazine* (Feb. 1928, Jan. 1929); *Films in Review* (Feb. 1970) (Wampas Baby Stars).

ARCHIVAL MATERIALS
• *Clipping File* — NYPL: Newsphotos. • *Other Clipping File* — GBBF, MIDL, NYMA (Photoplay Collection), PAPL. • *Photograph/Still* — CAA (also in Hollywood Studio Museum Collection) (also in MGM Collection), CAFI, CAH, CASF, CASU, CAUU, CNDA, DCG (Quigley Photographic Archives), GBBF, NJPT, NYB (Bettmann/UPI Collection) (Underwood Collection), NYCU (Dramatic Museum Portraits), NYEH, NYPL, NYSU, OHCL, PAPL, TXU (A. Davis Collection), WICF. • *Publicity Release* — CAA (Mack Sennett Collection): 1920s. • *Scrapbook* — NYPL. • *Studio Biography* — CAA: Paramount. NYMA: Photoplay.

DEAN, Priscilla (Priscilla Fitzpatrick?), New York, NY, 1896-1987.

Beginning as a Biograph extra about 1914, vibrant Priscilla Dean became a very popular star who eventually had her own production company and appeared in films like *The Hand That Rocks the Cradle*, *Outside the Law* (with Lon Chaney), *The Virgin of Stamboul* and *Under Two Flags*. Her career had virtually ended before sound came in but she appeared in three talkies after a five-year hiatus.

PUBLISHED SOURCES
• *Books* — General: *Blue Book of the Screen*; *Famous Film Folk*; *Ladies in Distress*; *The Truth About the Movies*; *Who's Who on the Screen*. Credits: *Filmarama* (v. I and II); *Twenty Years of Silents*. Encyclopedic Works: *Film Encyclopedia*; *Filmlexicon degli Autori e delle Opere*; *The Picturegoer's Who's Who and Encyclopedia of the Screen To-day*; *Who's Who in Hollywood*. Nostalgia: *Whatever Became of...* (7th). Pictorial: *Silent Portraits*.
• *Periodicals* — The following periodical articles are in addition to those in-

cluded in the library listings below: *Photoplay* (Nov. 1918, Oct. 1919, Oct. 1920, Sept. 1923, Mar. 1924, Aug. 1925); *Motion Picture Classic* (Feb. 1919, June 1920, Oct. 1922); *Picture Play Magazine* (Oct. 1919); *Motion Picture Magazine* (Oct. 1919, Mar. 1920, Dec. 1921, July 1925); *Filmograph* (no. 1-2, 1970, no. 1-4, 1970); *Classic Film/Video Images* (Jan. 1980); *Films in Review* (Aug.-Sept. 1984); *Cine Revue* (Mar. 3, 1988); *Classic Images* (Mar.-Apr. 1988).

ARCHIVAL MATERIALS
• *Clipping File* — CAA: Nostalgia (1969, 1977, 1981); article (undated, 1972); obituary (1988). Periodical article: *Classic Film Collector* (Spring 1971). CAFI: Obituary (1988). CAUT: Newsphoto; legal problem (1927, 1929). NYMA (also in Photoplay Collection): Newsphotos; article (undated); obituary (1988). Periodical article: *Classic Film Collector* (undated). NYPL: Newsphotos; film appearance (1924); obituary (1988). • *Other Clipping File* — CAUB, GBBF, MIDL, NYSU, PAPL, WICF. • *Filmography* — NYMA. • *Interview* — CAUU (R. Lamparski Collection). • *Photograph/Still* — CAA (also in Hollywood Studio Museum Collection), CAFA, CAUT (Jessen Collection) (Portrait File), CNDA, DCG (Quigley Photographic Archives), GBBF, IAU (Junkin Collection), NJFL, NYCU (Bulliet Collection), NYEH, NYMN, NYPL, NYSU, OHCL, TXSM, TXU, WICF. • *Scrapbook* — NYPL (R. Locke Collection). • *Studio Biography* — CAA: MGM (1926). NYMA: Photoplay.

DEGRASSE, Sam, Bathhurst, New Brunswick, Canada, 1875-1953.

Another dependable silent villain was Sam DeGrasse whose appearances in major films like *Robin Hood*, *King of Kings* and *The Black Pirate* could not help but enliven the proceedings. In films since 1912, his first feature was *Birth of a Nation* and he remained in front of the cameras until the early talkie period (1930).

PUBLISHED SOURCES

• **Books**—General: *The Truth About the Movies*. **Credits:** *Filmarama* (v. I and II); *Forty Years of Screen Credits*; *Twenty Years of Silents*; *Who Was Who on Screen*. **Encyclopedic Works:** *Film Encyclopedia*; *Filmlexicon degli Autori e delle Opere*; *The Picturegoer's Who's Who and Encyclopedia of the Screen To-day*; *Who's Who in Hollywood*. **Pictorial:** *Silent Portraits*.
• **Periodicals**—*Classic Images* (Sept. 1991).

ARCHIVAL MATERIALS

• *Clipping File*—CAA: Film appearance (1927); legal problem (1937); article (1991); obituary (1953). NYPL: Article (1923). • *Other Clipping File*—NYMA (Photoplay Collection), WICF. • *Photograph/Still*—CAA, DCG (Quigley Photographic Archives), NJFL, NYPL, OHCL, WICF. • *Scrapbook*—NYPL (R. Locke Collection), UTBY (DeMille Archives).

DE LA MOTTE, Marguerite, Duluth, MN, 1902/1904-50.

The lovely leading lady of Douglas Fairbanks in his epics *The Three Musketeers* and *The Mark of Zorro*, Marguerite de la Motte had a modestly successful career in the silents. Her other films included *The Beloved Brute*, *Children of the Whirlwind*, *Just Like a Woman* and *Wandering Daughters*. There were also scattered sound film appearances as late as the early 1940s. She was married to John Bowers (q.v.).

PUBLISHED SOURCES

• **Books**—General: *Blue Book of the Screen*; *Famous Film Folk*; *Who's Who on the Screen*. **Credits:** *Filmarama* (v. I and II); *Twenty Years of Silents*; *Who Was Who on Screen*. **Encyclopedic Works:** *Film Encyclopedia*; *Filmlexicon degli Autori e delle Opere*; *Halliwell's Filmgoer's Companion*; *The Picturegoer's Who's Who and Encyclopedia of the Screen To-day*; *Who's Who in Hollywood*. **Pictorial:** *Silent Portraits*.

• **Periodicals**—*Photoplay* (July 1919, Apr. 1922); *Motion Picture Magazine* (Aug. 1919, July 1922); *Picture Play* (Aug. 1920); *Motion Picture Classic* (Jan. 1921, June 1922, Sept. 1924); *Time* (Mar. 20, 1950).

ARCHIVAL MATERIALS

• *Clipping File*—CAA: Film appearance (1924); newsphotos; divorce (1943); obituary (1950). CAUU: Obituary (1950). NYPL: Newsphotos (numerous); dancer; Fairbanks contract (1921); article (undated). • *Other Clipping File*—CNDA, GBBF, MIDL, NYMA (Photoplay Collection), OHCL, PAPL. • *Photograph/Still*—AZSU (Jimmy Starr Collection), CAA (also in Hollywood Studio Museum Collection), CAUT (Jessen Collection), CNDA, DCG (Quigley Photographic Archives), GBBF, NJPT, NYCU (Dramatic Museum Portraits), NYEH, NYPL, NYSU, OHCL, TXSM, TXU. • *Scrapbook*—NYPL (R. Locke Collection). • *Studio Biography*—CAA: Metropolitan (1921).

DEL RIO, Dolores (Dolores Martinez Asunsolo Lopez Negrette), Durango, Mexico, 1904/05-1983.

For a while, Dolores Del Rio was Hollywood's all-purpose "exotic" leading lady, a stereotype her dark beauty and her accent consigned her to. This unfortunately limited her screen possibilities for she was a fine actress as is apparent from her later Mexican films. After a couple of perfunctory films in 1926, *What Price Glory?* brought her to public notice. She remained in Hollywood until 1942 and then returned to Mexico where she became one of that country's leading actresses in films like *Maria Candelaria* and *Flor Silvestre*. In the 1960s and 1970s she made a few more American film appearances.

PUBLISHED SOURCES

• **Books**—Written by (or ghostwritten for) DDR: a chapter in *Breaking into the Movies*. **General:** *Celebrity Homes*;

Dolores Del Rio (IMEN); *Dolores Del Rio* (Monsivais); *Dolores Del Rio* (Wilson); *From Hollywood*; *The Great Movie Stars: the Golden Years*; *The Hollywood Beauties*; *How I Broke Into the Movies*; *Las Estrellas* (v. 3); *Ladies in Distress*; *Mexican Cinema*; *The Movie Stars Story*; *Notable Hispanic American Women*; *Screen Personalities*; *The Stars* (Schickel); *What the Stars Told Me.* **Credits:** *Filmarama* (v. I and II); *Forty Years of Screen Credits*; *Twenty Years of Silents.* **Encyclopedic Works:** *A Biographical Dictionary of Film*; *Film Encyclopedia*; *Filmlexicon degli Autori e delle Opere*; *Halliwell's Filmgoer's Companion*; *The Illustrated Who's Who of the Cinema*; *International Dictionary of Films and Filmmakers* (v. 3); *International Motion Picture Almanac* (1975-80); *The Movie Makers*; *The Oxford Companion to Film*; *The Picturegoer's Who's Who and Encyclopedia of the Screen To-day*; *Quinlan's Illustrated Registry of Film Stars*; *Variety Who's Who in Show Business*; *Who's Who in Hollywood*; *The World Almanac Who's Who of Film*; *The World Encyclopedia of the Film*; *The World Film Encyclopedia.* **Nostalgia:** *Is That Who I Think It Is?* (v. 3); *Whatever Became of...* (3rd, 8th). **Pictorial:** *The Image Makers*; *Leading Ladies*; *More Fabulous Faces*; *Silent Portraits*; *They Had Faces Then.* **Biography/Autobiography:** *Dolores Del Rio* (Martinez Gandia). **Films:** *The Films of Dolores del Rio.* **Recordings:** *Hollywood on Record.* **Factoids:** *Star Stats.*

• *Periodicals*—The following periodical articles are in addition to those included in the library listings below: *Motion Picture Classic* (Mar. 1927, Aug. 1928, Apr. 1931); *Photoplay* (June 1927, Feb. 1929, Aug. 1931, Sept. 1932, Oct. 1933, Apr. 1934, Dec. 1934, Nov. 1935, Feb. 1936, Sept. 1936, Mar. 1938, July 1983); *Motion Picture Magazine* (Sept. 1927, Mar. 1929, June 1930, Apr. 1931, Oct. 1931, July 1932, Nov. 1934, Feb. 1936); *Theatre* (Feb. 1928); *Movie Classic* (Sept. 1931, Oct. 1935); *True Confession* (Mar. 1934); *Silver Screen* (Nov. 1935, Apr. 1940); *Films in Review* (May 1951,

May 1967 [filmography], Aug.-Sept. 1967, Nov. 1967, Feb. 1970 [Wampas Baby Stars]); *Newsweek* (Apr. 28, 1958, Apr. 25, 1983); *Film Quarterly* (Summer 1965); *Classic Film Collector* (Fall/Winter 1967); *Films and Filming* (July-Aug. 1972, July 1983); *Cine Revue* (July 8, 1974, June 13, 1985, Dec. 1, 1988); *Macleans* (Apr. 25, 1983); *Time* (Apr. 25, 1983); *Hollywood Studio Magazine* (Mar. 1983); *Cinematographe* (May 1983); *Revue du Cinema* (May 1983); *Cinema* (France) (Sept. 1983); *Architectural Digest* (Apr. 1992).

MEDIA
Why Ever Did They? (CD recording).

ARCHIVAL MATERIALS
• *Clipping File*—CAA: Article (1925, 1928, 1947, 1958, 1960, 1963-64, 1970, 1976, 1978, 1983); mural (1990); marriage/divorce (1928-31, 1940-41, 1959); kidnap plot (1928); legal problem (1929-32, 1954); illness (1930); romance with Orson Welles (1942); newsphotos; nostalgia (1947, 1969, 1973, 1981); film appearance (1953, 1960, 1963, 1965-66, 1977); stage appearance (1961); honor (1967); TV appearance (1969, 1975); film festival (1981); obituary (1983). Periodical articles: *Silver Screen* (June 1934); *Hollywood Studio Magazine* (Apr. 1974, Sept. 1977, Mar. 1978); *Women's Wear Daily* (Jan. 1975); *People* (Aug. 1976); *Architectural Digest* (Nov.-Dec. 1976); *Celebrity Pictorial* (Feb. 1978); *Modern Maturity* (Feb.-Mar. 1981); *Cine Revue* (Apr. 1983); *Vanity Fair* (Aug. 1989). CAFI: Newsphoto; article (1978, 1983); film festival (1981); mural (1990); obituary (1983). CAUT: Article (1929, 1960, 1963, 1974-75, 1978, 1982); newsphotos; marriage (1959); trip (1928); illness (1929, 1955); obituary (1983). CAUU: Article (1958, 1964, 1978, 1981); nostalgia (1974); obituary (1983). Periodical articles: *Modern Maturity* (Feb.-Mar. 1981); *Hollywood Studio Magazine* (Oct. 1983). NYMA: Film festival (1981); article (1975, 1981); manages nursery; film appearance (1977); review of *Orchids in the Moonlight* (play); obituary (1983). Periodical articles: *Norte* (Apr. 1946); *Americas* (Nov. 1967); *Art of the Amer-*

icas *Bulletin* (v. 3, 1968); *Classic Film/Video Images* (July 1981). NYMN: Newsphotos; obituary (1983). Periodical article: *Vanity Fair* (Oct. 1930). NYPL: PARTIAL CONTENTS: Article (1974-75, 1981, undated); TV appearance (1975); runs nursery (1976); film appearance (1977); film festival (1976, 1981-82); obituary (1983). Periodical articles: *Modern Maturity* (Feb.-Mar. 1981); *American Film* (Sept. 1983); *Quirk's Reviews* (Sept. 1983). • *Other Clipping File* – AZSU (Jimmy Starr Collection), CNDA, GBBF, MAH, MIDL, NYSU, OHCL, PAPL, WICF. • *Correspondence* – NYPL (C. & L. Brown Collection): 1940, 1942, 1950. • *Filmography* – CAA, NYMA, NYPL. • *Legal File* – CAUT (Twentieth Century-Fox Collection): Affidavit (1960); letter, memo (1926-28, 1960); loanout (1960). CAUW: Agreement (1933-34, 1947); talent agreement (1926, 1933-34); document (1949); contract summary (1934-35); personnel, payroll record (1933-35); contract (1934-35); letter, memo (1934-35, 1947, 1949-51); release (1949); magazine, newspaper clipping (1947). NYPL (T. Ratcliffe, Jr. Collection): Contract; letter (1956). • *Oral History* – NYCO: Mentioned in the following interviews: Joel McCrea, Jerome Zerbe. • *Photograph/Still* – CAA (also in Hollywood Studio Museum Collection) (also in MGM Collection), CALM, CAUB, CAUS, CAUT (Portrait File), CAUU, CNDA, DCG (Quigley Photographic Archives), GBBF, NJFL, NYAM, NYB (Penguin Collection) (Springer Collection) (Underwood Collection), NYCU (Dramatic Museum Portraits), NYEH, NYMN, NYPL, NYSU, OHCL, TNUT (Clarence Brown Collection), TXU, WICF. • *Press Kit* – OHCL. • *Publicity Release* – CAA: Fox (1937). NYPL: ABC (1970). • *Scrapbook* – NYAM, WICF. • *Studio Biography* – CAA: Fox (1937, 1943, 1961); Warner (1963). CAFI. CAUU: Fox (1930s?); Warner (1960s?, undated). NYMA: Warner (1963).

DEMPSTER, Carol, Duluth, MN, 1902-1991.

Carol Dempster was D. W. Griffith's last major film discovery/protégée and her reputation generally has suffered the fate of those films in which she appeared; they are considered to be less noteworthy than his earlier works. He tried to make her a major star in films like *Dream Street, The White Rose, America, Sorrows of Satan* and *Isn't Life Wonderful?* but she never achieved real popularity and her career was over by 1926.

PUBLISHED SOURCES

• *Books* – **Bibliography:** *The Idols of Silence.* **General:** *Classics of the Silent Screen; Famous Film Folk; The Griffith Actresses; Who's Who on the Screen.* **Credits:** *Filmarama* (v. I and II); *Twenty Years of Silents.* **Encyclopedic Works:** *Film Encyclopedia; Filmlexicon degli Autori e delle Opere; Halliwell's Filmgoer's Companion; The Illustrated Who's Who of the Cinema; Who's Who in Hollywood.* **Nostalgia:** *Whatever Became of...* (2nd). **Pictorial:** *Silent Portraits.*

• *Periodicals* – The following periodical articles are in addition to those included in the library listings below: *Photoplay* (Aug. 1919, Feb. 1922, July 1925, Mar. 1926, Aug. 1928); *Motion Picture Classic* (Oct. 1920, Dec. 1925, Oct. 1926); *Motion Picture Magazine* (July 1922, July 1925, Jan. 1927, Apr. 1927); *Cinema* (Beverly Hills) (Fall 1971); *Film Dope* (Oct. 1980); *Classic Images* (Apr. 1991).

ARCHIVAL MATERIALS

• *Clipping File* – CAA: United Kingdom film offer (1923); newsphoto; bequest (1991); obituary (1991). NYMA (also in Photoplay Collection): Booklet *The Movies, Mr. Griffith and Carol Dempster* (possibly a supplement or reprint from *Cinema*?). Periodical article: *Classic Film Collector* (Spring 1975). NYPL: Article (1931); newsphotos; film appearance (1923); estate (1991); obituary (1991). Periodical article: *Film Fan Monthly* (Nov. 1991). • *Other Clipping File* – CAUB, GBBF, MAH, PAPL, WICF. • *Collection* – NYMA (D.W.

Griffith Collection): Includes papers and scrapbooks of CD. • *Filmography* — CAA. • *Photograph/Still* — CAA (also in Hollywood Studio Museum Collection), CALM, CAUT (Jessen Collection), CAUU, CNDA, DCG (Quigley Photographic Archives), GBBF, NYAM, NYB (Underwood Collection), NYEH, NYPL, NYSU, OHCL, TXU, WICF. • *Scrapbook* — NYMA (see Collection), NYPL (also in R. Locke Collection). • *Studio Biography* — NYMA: Photoplay.

DESMOND, William, Dublin, Ireland, 1878–1949.

William Desmond seemed built for rugged roles and he appeared in numerous popular westerns, serials and melodramas in a career which began about 1915 and lasted, albeit latterly in bit parts, until the late 1940s. He also was seen in more mainstream films like *Ben Hur*, *Ruggles of Red Gap* and *Romeo and Juliet*.

PUBLISHED SOURCES

• *Books* — **General:** *Blue Book of the Screen*; *Bound and Gagged*; *Buster Crabbe*; *Eighty Silent Film Stars*; *Famous Film Folk*; *The Hall of Fame of Western Film Stars*; *Heroes, Heavies and Sagebrush*; *Hollywood Album 2*; *The Truth About the Movies*; *Viliam* (i.e., William) *Desmond*; *Who's Who on the Screen*; *Winners of the West*. **Credits:** *Filmarama* (v. I and II); *Forty Years of Screen Credits*; *Twenty Years of Silents*; *Who Was Who on Screen*. **Encyclopedic Works:** *Film Encyclopedia*; *Filmlexicon degli Autori e delle Opere*; *Halliwell's Filmgoer's Companion*; *Who's Who in Hollywood*. **Pictorial:** *Silent Portraits*.

• *Periodicals* — The following periodical articles are in addition to those included in the library listings below: *Photoplay* (Aug. 1917, Feb. 1919, Sept. 1919, Sept. 1920); *Motion Picture Magazine* (Feb. 1918); *Motion Picture Classic* (July 1918, Jan. 1919); *Picture Play* (Jan. 1920, Sept. 1920); *Picture Show* (Feb. 7, 1920); *Silent Picture* (Spring 1972); *Cinema Trails* (no. 2).

ARCHIVAL MATERIALS

• *Clipping File* — CAA: Injury (1922); obituary (1949). NYMA (also in Photoplay Collection): Periodical articles: *Classic Images* (Mar. 1983, Sept. 1986, Dec. 1988). NYPL: Newsphotos; children (1932); stage appearance (1905, 1928, 1932); illness; obituary (1949). Periodical article: *Motion Picture Classic* (Jan. 1920). • *Other Clipping File* — GBBF, MAH, MIDL, NYSU, OHCL, PAPL, WICF. • *Correspondence* — NYPL (C. & L. Brown Collection): 1948. • *Filmography* — NYPL. • *Legal File* — CAUW: Talent agreement (1928). • *Oral History* — NYCO: Mentioned in: Blanche Sweet interview. • *Photograph/Still* — CAA (also in Hollywood Studio Museum Collection), CAUS, CAUT (Jessen Collection), CAUU, DCG (Quigley Photographic Archives), GBBF, IAU (Junkin Collection), NYB (Underwood Collection), NYCU (Palmer Collection), NYPL, NYSU, OHCL, TXU, WICF. • *Scrapbook* — NYPL (R. Locke Collection).

DEVORE, Dorothy (Alma Williams), Fort Worth, TX, 1899–1976.

A popular comic actress of the 1920s, Dorothy Devore appeared in Christie comedies and features which included *A Broadway Butterfly*, *His Majesty*, *Bunker Bean* and *Money to Burn*. Although she supposedly was one of the more highly paid performers of that decade, her career did not survive the coming of sound.

PUBLISHED SOURCES

• *Books* — **Bibliography:** *The Idols of Silence*. **General:** *Blue Book of the Screen*; *Clown Princes and Court Jesters*; *Famous Film Folk*; *The Truth About the Movies*. **Credits:** *Filmarama* (v. I and II); *Twenty Years of Silents*. **Encyclopedic Works:** *Film Encyclopedia*; *Filmlexicon degli Autori e delle Opere*. **Pictorial:** *Silent Portraits*.

• *Periodicals* — The following periodical articles are in addition to that included in the library listings below:

Motion Picture Magazine (Mar. 1921, Jan. 1926); *Motion Picture Classic* (Dec. 1921); *Films in Review* (Feb. 1970) (Wampas Baby Stars).

ARCHIVAL MATERIALS

• *Clipping File* – CAA: Divorce (1933–35); film appearance (1920); obituary (1976). CAUT: Legal problem (1929). NYPL: Newsphotos; divorce (1933); obituary (1976). Periodical article: *Silent Picture* (Summer 1972). • *Other Clipping File* – GBBF, MAH, NYMA (Photoplay Collection), NYSU, PAPL. • *Correspondence* – CAUU (A. Slide Collection): 1973. • *Interview* – CAUU (A. Slide Collection): 1971. • *Legal File* – CAUW: Letter, memo (1924–25, 1935); talent agreement (1924–26); document (1925–26, 1935). • *Photograph/Still* – CAA (also in Hollywood Studio Museum Collection), CAUS, CAUT (Jessen Collection), CAUU (Also in A. Slide Collection), DCG (Quigley Photographic Archives), GBBF, NYB (Underwood Collection), NYCU (Bulliet Collection) (Dramatic Museum Portraits), NYEH, NYPL, NYSU, OHCL, TXSM, TXU, WICF. • *Scrapbook* – NYPL.

DEXTER, Elliott, Galveston, TX, 1870–1946.

Among the screen's handsome and popular matinee idols, and a C.B. DeMille favorite, was former stage actor Elliott Dexter. In his ten-year career his films included *The Squaw Man* (1919 version), *Don't Change Your Husband*, *Adam's Rib*, *Behold My Wife*, *Capital Punishment* and *The Fast Set*.

PUBLISHED SOURCES

• *Books* – **General:** *Blue Book of the Screen*; *Famous Film Folk*; *Who's Who on the Screen.* **Credits:** *Filmarama* (v. I and II); *Twenty Years of Silents*; *Who Was Who on Screen.* **Encyclopedic Works:** *Film Encyclopedia*; *Filmlexicon degli Autori e delle Opere*; *Who's Who in Hollywood.* **Pictorial:** *Silent Portraits.*

• *Periodicals* – The following periodical articles are in addition to that included in the library listings below:

Theatre (Dec. 1917); *Photoplay* (May 1918, Nov. 1918, May 1920); *Motion Picture Magazine* (Feb. 1919, Dec. 1922); *Motion Picture Classic* (Jan. 1920, Oct. 1921).

ARCHIVAL MATERIALS

• *Clipping File* – CAA: Film appearance (1922); obituary (1946). NYPL: Newsphotos (numerous); article (1923, 1928, undated); stage appearance (1914); divorce (1921, undated); film review (numerous) (1920s); stage appearance (1920s); nostalgia (1936); obituary (1946). Periodical article: *Movie Weekly* (June 10, 1922?). • *Other Clipping File* – GBBF, NYMA (Photoplay Collection), NYSU, OHCL, PAPL, WICF. • *Legal File* – CAUW: Talent agreement (1924). • *Oral History* – NYCO: Mentioned in: Albert (Eddie) Sutherland interview. • *Photograph/Still* – CAA (also in Hollywood Studio Museum Collection), CASF, CAUT (Jessen Collection), CAUU, DCG (Quigley Photographic Archives), GBBF, IAU (Junkin Collection), NJFL, NYPL, NYSU, OHCL, TXAC (Struss Collection), TXU, WICF. • *Scrapbook* – NYAM, NYPL (also in R. Locke Collection), WICF.

DIX, Richard (Ernest Brimmer), St. Paul, MN, 1894–1949.

Rugged Richard Dix's career was a long one, beginning in 1921 and lasting almost to the time of his death. His era of major stardom was, however, relatively brief (late 1920s to the early 1930s). He was sometimes cast as a Native American (*The Redskin*, *The Vanishing American*) or westerner (*Cimarron*) but was equally at home in films like *The Ten Commandments*. In the 1940s he was seen mainly in minor "A" westerns and the low-budget series *The Whistler*.

PUBLISHED SOURCES

• *Books* – **General:** *Alice in Movieland*; *The BFI Companion to the Western*; *Blue Book of the Screen*; *Classics of the Silent Screen*; *Eighty Silent Film Stars*; *Famous Film Folk*;

From Hollywood; Gentlemen to the Rescue; The Great Cowboy Stars of Movies & Television; The Great Movie Stars; Great Western Stars; The Hall of Fame of Western Film Stars; How I Broke Into the Movies; Immortals of the Screen; Motion Picture News Booking Guide and Studio Directory (1927); The Movie Stars Story; Popular Men of the Screen; Richard Diks (i.e., Dix); Screen Personalities; The Truth About the Movies; Twinkle, Twinkle, Movie Star; The Western (Eyles); What the Stars Told Me. **Credits:** Filmarama (v. I and II); Forty Years of Screen Credits; Twenty Years of Silents; Who Was Who on Screen. **Encyclopedic Works:** A Biographical Dictionary of Film; A Companion to the Movies; Film Encyclopedia; Filmlexicon degli Autori e delle Opere; Halliwell's Filmgoer's Companion; The Illustrated Who's Who of the Cinema; The Movie Makers; National Cyclopedia of American Biography (1951); The Picturegoer's Who's Who and Encyclopedia of the Screen To-day; Quinlan's Illustrated Registry of Film Stars; Who's Who in Hollywood; Who's Who of the Horrors and Other Fantasy Films; The World Almanac Who's Who of Film; The World Film Encyclopedia. **Pictorial:** Silent Portraits.

• *Periodicals* — The following periodical articles are in addition to those included in the library listings below: Motion Picture Magazine (Jan. 1922, Feb. 1923, Nov. 1924, Oct. 1925, Dec. 1925, Mar. 1927, Dec. 1927, Mar. 1930, June 1932, Dec. 1935); Motion Picture Classic (Feb. 1922, Jan. 1923, Feb. 1924, July 1926, Jan. 1927, Aug. 1927, Mar. 1937); Photoplay (Jan. 1924, May-July 1924, Nov. 1924, Jan.-Feb. 1925, Aug. 1925, July 1926, Sept. 1926, Feb. 1927, Jan. 1932); Cinema Art (July 1926, Mar. 1927); Theatre (May 1929); American Magazine (Sept. 1929); Movie Classic (Jan. 1932, Mar. 1936); Newsweek (Oct. 3, 1949); Time (Oct. 3, 1949); Films in Review (Nov. 1966, Feb. 1968).

OBSCURE PUBLISHED SOURCES
CAA: *Life Story of Richard Dix.*

ARCHIVAL MATERIALS
• *Caricature* — NYMN. • *Clipping File* — CAA: Film appearance (1921); marriage/divorce/childbirth (1929, 1931, 1933–35); article (1924); threatened by fan (1927); walks off set (1927); Paramount contract (1928); illness (1928–29, 1933, 1948–49); leaves Paramount (1929); RKO contract (1929); legal problem (1930–32, 1934); stage appearance (1939); obituary (1949). CAUU: Estate (1949); obituary (1949). NYMA: Newsphotos; career (1926, undated); tax problem (1930–31); new contract (1921, 1931); article (1928, 1930–31); film appearance (1921–22); director (1931); notes for entry in *National Cyclopedia of American Biography*; obituary (1949). Periodical articles: *Photoplay* (July 1928, June 1930); *Hollywood* (Oct. 1928, Feb. 1932); *Screenland* (June 1930); *Motion Picture Magazine* (July 1930); *Motion Picture Classic* (Jan. 1931); *Picture Play* (Nov. 1931); *Screen Play Secrets* (1931?); *Classic Film Collector* (Summer 1978); *Classic Images* (June 1982, Apr. 1989). NYMN: Newsphotos; marriage/divorce/children (1933–35); article (1936); obituary (1949). NYPL: Newsphotos (numerous); article (1928, 1941–42, undated); breaking into films (1933); drunken driving (1937); illness (1928); biography (1930); film review (1920s, 1930s); threat against life (1925); film synopses (1920s); film appearance (1930s); engagement/marriage/divorce/children (1930–31, 1933–35); obituary (1949). Periodical articles: *New Movie Magazine* (undated); *Films in Review* (Oct. 1966). • *Other Clipping File* — AZSU (Jimmy Starr Collection), GBBF, MAH, MIDL, OHCL, PAPL, WICF. • *Collection* — CAUT: 13 boxes of stills from numerous films. • *Correspondence* — NYPL (C. & L. Brown Collection): 1940s. • *Filmography* — CAA. • *Legal File* — CAUT (Twentieth Century-Fox Collection): Letter, memo (1939); contract (1939). CAUW: Talent agreement (1929). • *Oral History* — CAUS: Mentioned in: Edward Anhalt interview. NYCO: Mentioned in the following interviews: Gabby Hayes, James Wong Howe, Jeanette MacDonald, Joel McCrea. • *Photograph/Still* — AZSU

(Jimmy Starr Collection), CAA (also in Hollywood Studio Museum Collection) (also in MGM Collection), CAFA, CALM, CAPH, CAUS, CAUT (Prinz Collection) (Jessen Collection) (Portrait File) (also in Collection), CAUU, CNDA, DCG (Quigley Photographic Archives), GBBF, IAU (Junkin Collection), MIDL, NJPT, NYAM, NYB (Bettmann/UPI Collection) (Springer Collection) (Underwood Collection), NYCU (Dramatic Museum Portraits) (Palmer Collection), NYEH, NYMN, NYPL, NYSU, OHCL, TXSM, TXU, WICF. • *Press Kit* — CAFA. • *Publicity Release* — NYMA: Unknown studio (1927). • *Scrapbook* — NJPT (Yeandle Collection), NYAM, NYMA, NYPL (also in R. Locke Collection), UTBY (DeMille Archives). • *Studio Biography* — CAA: Paramount (1940); unknown studio (1943); Columbia (1944). NYMA: Photoplay (undated).

DOVE, Billie (Lillian Bohny or Bohney), New York, NY, 1900/04– 1997

Although she made few films which were memorable, Billie Dove was renowned for her great beauty and, possibly, for her relationship with Howard Hughes. The actress who was dubbed the "All-American Beauty" came to films in the early 1920s and appeared to advantage in two silent color films, one of which was Fairbanks's *The Black Pirate*. Her talkie career was mediocre and after she appeared in two poorly-received Hughes productions her career ended in 1932.

PUBLISHED SOURCES

• *Books* — Written by (or ghostwritten for) BD: a chapter of *Breaking into the Movies*. **General:** *Blue Book of the Screen*; *Famous Film Folk*; *How I Broke Into the Movies*; *Return Engagement*; *Some Are Born Great*. **Credits:** *Filmarama* (v. II); *Forty Years of Screen Credits*; *Twenty Years of Silents*. **Encyclopedic Works:** *Film Encyclopedia*; *Filmlexicon degli Autori e delle Opere*; *Halliwell's Filmgoer's Companion*; *The*

Movie Makers; *The Picturegoer's Who's Who and Encyclopedia of the Screen To-day*; *Variety Who's Who in Show Business*; *Who's Who in Hollywood*; *The World Almanac Who's Who of Film*; *The World Film Encyclopedia*. **Nostalgia:** *Whatever Became of...* (2nd). **Pictorial:** *Silent Portraits*; *They Had Faces Then*. **Factoids:** *Star Stats.*

• *Periodicals* — The following periodical articles are in addition to those included in the library listings below: *National Magazine* (June 1922); *Motion Picture Classic* (Nov. 1922, Dec. 1927, Apr. 1931); *Photoplay* (Apr. 1927, Oct. 1933); *Motion Picture Magazine* (June 1928, Feb. 1929, Nov. 1929, May 1930, Dec. 1931); *Show* (Aug. 1962); *Films in Review* (Jan.-Feb. 1968, Oct. 1970); *Hollywood Studio Magazine* (Dec. 1971); *Classic Images* (Apr. 1991).

ARCHIVAL MATERIALS

• *Clipping File* — AZSU: Marriage. CAA: Film appearance (1922); marriage/divorce/children (1930–34); romance with Howard Hughes (1931); wins jingle contest (1962); nostalgia (1969, 1980); interview (1984). Periodical articles: *Films in Review* (April 1979); *Life* (1980). CAUT: Film appearance (1961); divorce (1930); home (1929). NYMA (also in Photoplay Collection): Newsphotos. Periodical article: *Los Angeles* (Jan. 1984). NYMN: Newsphotos (numerous); illness (1933). NYPL: Article (1958, 1990); newsphotos (numerous); film review (1920s); illness (1933); marriage/children (1933–34, undated); film appearance (1927). Periodical article: *Dance Magazine* (Aug. 1929). • *Other Clipping File* — CNDA, GBBF, MIDL, OHCL, PAPL, TXU, WICF. • *Interview* — MISU: Recorded from a telephone interview. • *Legal File* — CAUW: Talent agreement (1926–30); letter, memo (1926–30); payroll record (1926–30); contract summary (1926, 1930); contract (1926–30); document (1926). • *Photograph/Still* — CAA (also in Hollywood Studio Museum Collection) (also in MGM Collection), CAH, CASU, CAUB, CAUT (Jessen Collection), CAUU, CNDA, DCG (Quigley Photographic Archives), GBBF, MIDL, NJPT, NYB (Bettmann/UPI Collection) (Penguin Collection) (Springer Collection) (Underwood Collection), NYEH, NYPL, NYSU, OHCL, PAPL, TXSM, TXU (A. Davis Collection), WICF. • *Scrapbook*—NYMA, NYPL, WICF. • *Studio Biography*—CAA: United Artists (1932); Paramount (1920s?). NYMA: Photoplay.

DUNN, Josephine (Mary J. Dunn), New York, NY, 1906–1983.

Josephine Dunn first appeared in *Fascinating Youth* (1926), after a stage career, and was cast in a rapid succession of films thereafter for MGM and other studios. Among them were *She's a Sheik*, *Love's Greatest Mistake*, *Sin Sister* and the early talkie *The Singing Fool*. She was a Wampas Baby Star of 1929. Her eventual typecasting in icy "other woman" roles limited her screen possibilities, even though she made a number of films following her transition to the talkies. By 1933 the very pretty blonde had returned to the stage although there were rare screen roles thereafter.

PUBLISHED SOURCES
• *Books*—Credits: *Filmarama* (v. II); *Forty Years of Screen Credits*; *Twenty Years of Silents*. **Encyclopedic Works:** *Film Encyclopedia*; *Filmlexicon degli Autori e delle Opere*; *The Movie Makers*; *The Picturegoer's Who's Who and Encyclopedia of the Screen To-day*; *Who's Who in Hollywood*; *The World Film Encyclopedia*. **Pictorial:** *They Had Faces Then*.
• *Periodicals*—*Motion Picture Magazine* (Dec. 1928); *Films in Review* (Feb. 1970) (Wampas Baby Stars); *Classic Film Collector* (Fall 1978); *Cine Revue* (May 26, 1983).

OBSCURE PUBLISHED SOURCES
CAA: *Graduating Exercises of the Paramount Pictures School Class of 1926*.

ARCHIVAL MATERIALS
• *Clipping File*—AZSU (Jimmy Starr Collection): Obituary (1983). CAA: Marriage (1932); obituary (1983). CAFI: Obituary (1983). CAUT: Newsphotos. NYMA (also in Photoplay Collection): Obituary (1983). NYPL: Newsphotos; stage appearance (1932, 1940s); marriage (1933). • *Other Clipping File*—CNDA, GBBF, WICF. • *Correspondence*—NYPL (C. & L. Brown Collection): 1944. • *Legal File*—CAUT (Twentieth Century-Fox Collection): Letter, memo (1928–30); loanout (1928–29). CAUW: Contract (1927); document (1928, 1932); talent agreement (1928–29, 1932). NYPL (C. & L. Brown Collection): Contract (1944). • *Photograph/Still*—CAA (also in Hollywood Studio Museum Collection) (also in MGM Collection), CAH, CAOC (Kiesling Collection), CASF, CAUT (Jessen Collection), DCG (Quigley Photographic Archives), GBBF, MIDL, NJPT, NYAM, NYB (Underwood Collection), NYCU (Dramatic Museum Portraits), NYEH, NYPL, NYSU, OHCL, PAPL, TXSM, TXU (A. Davis Collection), WICF. • *Publicity Release*—CAA: Paramount (numerous). • *Scrapbook*—NYPL. • *Studio Biography*—CAA: Paramount. NYMA: Photoplay.

DWAN, Dorothy (Dorothy Smith?), 1907–1970.

Pretty Dorothy Dwan made almost 25 films, some of which were with her husband Larry Semon (q.v.), including *Spuds* and *The Wizard of Oz*. She also appeared in melodramas like *Sinners in Silk* but the majority of her output was in westerns including five with Tom Mix (q.v.) and several with Ken Maynard. Her last film was *The Fighting Legion* (1930).

PUBLISHED SOURCES
• *Books*—General: *Sweethearts of the Sage*. **Credits:** *Filmarama* (v. II); *Forty Years of Screen Credits*; *Twenty Years of Silents*. **Encyclopedic Works:** *Who's Who in Hollywood*. **Pictorial:** *Silent Portraits*.

• *Periodicals* — *Motion Picture Magazine* (Dec. 1926, May 1928); *Classic Images* (Nov. 1989).

ARCHIVAL MATERIALS

• *Clipping File* — CAA: Marriage/divorce (1930, 1935). CAUT: Legal problem (1929). NYPL: Newsphotos. • *Other Clipping File* — GBBF, NYMA (Photoplay Collection), WICF. • *Legal File* — CAUW: Talent agreement (1926). • *Photograph/Still* — CAA (also in Hollywood Studio Museum Collection) (also in MGM Collection), DCG (Quigley Photographic Archives), NYB (Underwood Collection), NYPL, NYSU, OHCL, WICF.

EDESON, Robert, New Orleans, LA, 1868-1931.

Stage actor Robert Edeson was a popular, if mature, leading man of silents and, after the mid-1920s, an equally successful character actor in numerous films, including several directed by DeMille. He continued his appearances up to the time of his death. Among his roles were those in *The Spoilers* (1923 version), *The Light That Failed*, *Extravagance*, *Feet of Clay*, *The Ten Commandments* and *The Volga Boatman*.

PUBLISHED SOURCES

• *Books* — Credits: *Filmarama* (v. I and II); *Forty Years of Screen Credits*; *Twenty Years of Silents*; *Who Was Who on Screen*. **Encyclopedic Works:** *Film Encyclopedia*; *Filmlexicon degli Autori e delle Opere*; *The Movie Makers*; *The Oxford Companion to Film*; *Who Was Who in the Theatre*; *Who's Who in Hollywood*; *Who's Who on the Stage* (1908). **Pictorial:** *Silent Portraits*.
• *Periodicals* — The following periodical article is in addition to that included in the library listings below: *Classic Images* (Nov. 1989).

ARCHIVAL MATERIALS

• *Caricature* — NYPL.   • *Clipping File* — CAUT: Article (1928). LANO: Obituary. NYMA (also in Photoplay collection): Personal data summary.

NYMN: Marriage; newsphotos; obituary (1931). NYPL: Newsphotos; article (1902-03, 1914); film review (1920s); stage appearance (1900s, 1920s); obituary (1931). Periodical article: *Green Book Magazine* (Aug. 1912). • *Other Clipping File* — GBBF, MAH, MIDL, NYSU, WICF. • *Correspondence* — NYMN: Note. NYPL (C. & L. Brown Collection): 1907, 1912, undated. • *Filmography* — NYMA. • *Legal File* — CAUT (Twentieth Century-Fox Collection): Memo, letter (1930-31); agreement (1930-31). CAUW: Talent agreement (1928-30); document (1930). • *Photograph/Still* — CAA (also in Hollywood Studio Museum Collection), CAHL, CASF, CAUS, CAUT (Jessen Collection), DCG (Quigley Photographic Archives), GBBF, NYAM, NYCU (Bulliet Collection) (Dramatic Museum Collection), NYEH, NYMN, NYPL, OHCL, TXU, WICF. • *Play Program* — CAHL: (1906). NYPL: • *Poster* — NYPL. • *Print* — CAHL. • *Press Kit* — OHCL. • *Scrapbook* — NYPL (also in C. & L. Brown Collection) (also in Locke Collection), UTBY (DeMille Archives). • *Studio Biography* — CAA: Paramount (1928, 1931).

ELLIS, Robert, Brooklyn, NY, 1892-1935.

Following a stage career, Robert Ellis became a very popular matinee idol at MGM and other studios after his first appearances in 1919. His films included *Upstairs and Down*, *For Sale*, *The Girl from Montmartre* and *Perils of the Sea*. He was married to May Allison (q.v.) and Vera Reynolds (q.v.). *NOTE:* He is sometimes confused with a screenwriter of the same name (also known as Robert Reel Ellis) but they appear to be different people.

PUBLISHED SOURCES

• *Books* — General: *Who's Who on the Screen*. **Credits:** *Filmarama* (v. I and II); *Forty Years of Screen Credits*; *Twenty Years of Silents*; *Who Was Who on Screen*. **Encyclopedic Works:** *Film Encyclopedia*; *Filmlexicon degli Autori e delle Opere*; *The Picturegoer's Who's*

Who and Encyclopedia of the Screen To-day; Who's Who in Hollywood. • Periodicals — Motion Picture Classic (Sept. 1919); Photoplay (Feb. 1922).

ARCHIVAL MATERIALS

• Clipping File — CAA: Film appearance (1922). NYPL: Marriage (1929); newsphotos; screenwriter; article (1931, undated); film reviews; obituary (1935). • Other Clipping File — GBBF, MIDL, NYMA (Photoplay Collection), OHCL, PAPL. • Collection — WYU: 27 photographs from film A Modern Jeckyll (sic) and Hyde (1913); playbill (1918). • Legal File — CAA: Legal notice (Selznick) (1920). CAUW: Document (1933); talent agreement (1924). • Photograph/Still — CAA (also in Hollywood Studio Museum Collection), CNDA, DCG (Quigley Photographic Archives), GBBF, NJPT, NYAM, NYEH, NYPL, NYSU, TXU, WICF, WYU (see Collection). • Play Program — WYU (see Collection). • Scrapbook — NYPL (also in R. Locke Collection). • Studio Biography — CAA: Paramount (undated); Fox (1930s). CAUU: Fox (1930s?). NYMA: Photoplay.

ELVIDGE, June, ca. 1893–1965.

June Elvidge was a popular leading lady and supporting player from about 1915 to 1923 in films like The Lure of Women, Poison Pen, The Man Who Saw Tomorrow, Call of the Yukon and The Quickening Flame.

PUBLISHED SOURCES

• Books — Filmography: Hollywood on the Palisades. General: Who's Who on the Screen. Credits: Filmarama (v. I and II); Twenty Years of Silents; Who Was Who on Screen. Encyclopedic Works: Who's Who in Hollywood. • Periodicals — Green Book Magazine (June 1915); Photoplay (Feb. 1919); Motion Picture Classic (July 1919); Motion Picture Magazine (Oct. 1920).

ARCHIVAL MATERIALS

• Clipping File — CAA: Film appearance (1921); obituary (1965). NYMN: Newsphotos. NYPL: Newsphotos; di-

vorce (1920); article (1919); stage appearance (1920–21); obituary (1965). • Other Clipping File — GBBF, NYMA (Photoplay Collection), OHCL, WICF. • Photograph/Still — CAA, CAUT (Jessen Collection), DCG (Quigley Photographic Archives), NJFL, NYPL, NYSU, OHCL, TXU, WICF. • Publicity Release — NYPL: Unknown studio (1914?). • Scrapbook — NYPL (R. Locke Collection).

EVANS, Madge (Margherita Evans), New York, NY, 1909–1981.

Pretty Madge Evans was a talented child actress in silent films from 1915 until 1924. In the early days of talkies, she returned for supporting roles in prestigious MGM films like Dinner at Eight and David Copperfield and in leading roles in lesser films. Although her screen career petered out in the late 1930s after a series of low-budget efforts, she made many stage appearances.

PUBLISHED SOURCES

• Books — General: Hollywood Kids; The MGM Stock Company; Their Hearts Were Young and Gay. Credits: Filmarama (v. I and II); Forty Years of Screen Credits; Twenty Years of Silents. Encyclopedic Works: The Biographical Encyclopaedia and Who's Who of the American Theatre; Film Encyclopedia; Filmlexicon degli Autori e delle Opere; Halliwell's Filmgoer's Companion; The Movie Makers; The Picturegoer's Who's Who and Encyclopedia of the Screen To-day; Quinlan's Illustrated Registry of Film Stars; Who Was Who in the Theatre; Who's Who in Hollywood; The World Almanac Who's Who of Film; The World Film Encyclopedia. • Filmography — Hollywood on the Palisades. Nostalgia: Whatever Became of... (1st). Pictorial: They Had Faces Then.

• Periodicals — The following periodical articles are in addition to those included in the library listings below: Photoplay (June 1915, Sept. 1918, Nov.- Dec. 1931, Jan. 1933, Nov. 1933, July

1936); *Silver Screen* (Oct. 1931, June 1933, Jan. 1937); *Motion Picture Magazine* (Dec. 1931, Sept. 1932, May 1934, Jan. 1935, July 1935); *Movie Classic* (Mar. 1934); *Literary Digest* (July 13, 1935); *Films in Review* (Oct. 1973, Dec. 1973-Jan. 1974); *Cine Revue* (May 14, 1981).

ARCHIVAL MATERIALS

• *Caricature* – NYMN. • *Clipping File* – CAA: Article (1932, 1975-76); marriage (1939); nostalgia (1969, 1981); stage appearance (1933); obituary (1981). Periodical article: *Film Fan Monthly* (Dec. 1972-Jan. 1973) (filmography). CAFI: Obituary (1981). CAUT: Obituary (1981). CAUU: Obituary (1981). NYMA: Obituary (1981). Periodical article: *Classic Film Collector* (Summer 1977). NYMN: Newsphotos; marriage (1939); returns to New York (1937); career (1933); obituary (1981). NYPL: Newsphotos (numerous); article (1934, 1938, undated); extortion threat (1930s); child star; tax problem (1939); stage appearance (1930s, 1939); marriage (1939); film review (1930s); film appearance (1930s); illness; nostalgia (1969); obituary (1981). Periodical articles: *Film Fan Monthly* (Jan. 1973); *New Yorker* (undated). • *Other Clipping File* – CAFA, GBBF, MAH, MIDL, NYSU, PAPL, OHCL. • *Correspondence* – NYPL: Letters (C. & L. Brown Collection) (1936-46); other (1966). • *Filmography* – NYPL (silents only). • *Legal File* – CAUW: Personnel, payroll record (1933); talent agreement (1933). NYPL (C. & L. Brown Collection): (1944). • *Oral History* – NYCO: Mentioned in: P.C. Wagner interview. • *Photograph/Still* – CAA (also in Hollywood Studio Museum Collection) (also in MGM Collection), CAFA, CAUB, CAUU, CNDA, DCG (Quigley Photographic Archives), GBBF, NJFL, NYAM, NYB (Bettmann/UPI Collection) (Springer Collection) (Underwood Collection), NYCU (Dramatic Museum Portraits), NYEH, NYMN, NYPL, NYSU, OHCL, TXU, WICF. • *Press Kit* – CAFA, OHCL. • *Scrapbook* – NYAM, NYPL (also in R. Locke Collection) (also in Playwrights Company Collection). • *Studio Biography* – NYMN: Frohman.

EYTON, Bessie (Bessie Harrison), Santa Barbara, CA, 1890-? (Miss Eyton's whereabouts after 1935 are unknown).

Among redhaired Bessie Eyton's films, made for Selig and other studios beginning in 1910, were *The Smoldering Spark*, *The Heart of Texas Ryan*, *Sole Survivor*, *The Still Alarm* and *City of Purple Dreams*. She also appeared in the first version of *The Spoilers* (1914) and was frequently teamed with its co-star Tom Santschi (q.v.). Her starring career declined after 1919 and she appeared in supporting roles until 1921, returning as a bit player in talkies.

PUBLISHED SOURCES

• *Books* – **General:** *Sweethearts of the Sage*; *Who's Who in the Film World.* **Credits:** *Filmarama* (v. I and II); *Twenty Years of Silents.* **Pictorial:** *Silent Portraits.*
• *Periodicals* – The following periodical articles are in addition to that included in the library listings below: *Motion Picture Magazine* (Jan. 1916); *Picture Play Magazine* (Apr. 1916); *Photoplay* (July 1916).

ARCHIVAL MATERIALS

• *Clipping File* – NYMA (also in Photoplay Collection): Periodical article: *Classic Images* (Apr. 1989). NYPL: Newsphotos; film review. • *Other Clipping File* – GBBF, MAH, WICF. • *Photograph/Still* – CAA, DCG (Quigley Photographic Archives), IAU (Junkin Collection), NYPL, NYSU, OHCL, TXU, WICF. • *Scrapbook* – NYPL.

FAIRBANKS, Douglas (Douglas Ullman), Denver, CO, 1883-1939.

After stage experience, Douglas

Fairbanks attained his first screen popularity playing a series of optimistic "all-American boy" roles during the mid- and late 1910s. A switch to swashbucklers beginning with *The Mark of Zorro* (1920) and his marriage to reigning movie queen Mary Pickford (q.v.) made him a worldwide icon. His fame continued unabated through the 1920s with films such as *The Black Pirate, Robin Hood* and *The Three Musketeers* but his talkie career was brief and not comparably successful.

PUBLISHED SOURCES

• *Books* – A series of books which would be deemed pop psychology by a later generation were written by (or ghostwritten for) DF, including *Assuming Responsibilities; Initiative and Self-Reliance; Laugh and Live; Making Life Worthwhile; Profiting By Experience; Youth Points the Way.* **Bibliography:** *The Idols of Silence.* **General:** *Alice in Movieland; Behind the Screen; Blue Book of the Screen; Cads and Cavaliers; Cinq Mois à Hollywood avec Douglas Fairbanks; Classics of the Silent Screen; Close Ups; Debrett Goes to Hollywood; Doug and Mary and Others; Douglas Fairbanks* (Cooke); *Douglas Fairbanks, 1883-1939* (Fairbanks); *Duglas Ferbenks* (i.e., Douglas Fairbanks); *Las Estrellas* (v.3); *Famous Film Folk; Famous Stars of Filmdom (Men); Fifty Super Stars; First One Hundred Noted Men and Women of the Screen; From Hollywood; Gentlemen to the Rescue; Great Lovers of the Movies; The Great Movie Stars; His Picture in the Papers; History of the American Cinema (v. 3); History of the American Film Industry; The History of Motion Pictures; Hollywood Album; Hollywood Hall of Fame; Hollywood Love Stories; The Hollywood Style; How I Broke Into the Movies; I Love You, Clark Gable, Etc.; Immortals of the Screen; Intimate Talks With Movie Stars; The Kindergarten of the Movies; Leading Men; Love, Laughter and Tears; The Matinee Idols; More Memorable Americans, 1750-1950; The Movie Stars; The Movie Stars Story; The National Society of Film Critics on the Movie Star; The Parade's Gone By; Pickfair; The Public is Never Wrong; The Saturday Evening Post Movie Book; Schickel on Film; Screen Personalities; Screening Out the Past; The Silent Voice; Stardom; The Stars* (Schickel); *The Stars Appear; Stunt; The Swashbucklers; Swordsmen of the Screen; The Truth About the Movies; Twinkle, Twinkle, Movie Star; United Artists; The Western; Who's Who on the Screen; With Eisenstein in Hollywood; You Must Remember This.* **Credits:** *Filmarama* (v. I and II); *Twenty Years of Silents; Who Was Who on Screen.* **Encyclopedic Works:** *A Biographical Dictionary of Film; Cinema, a Critical Dictionary; A Companion to the Movies; Dictionary of American Biography* (Supplement 2); *A Dictionary of the Cinema; Film Encyclopedia; Filmlexicon degli Autori e delle Opere; Halliwell's Filmgoer's Companion; The Illustrated Encyclopedia of the World's Great Movie Stars and Their Films; The Illustrated Who's Who of the Cinema; International Dictionary of Films and Filmmaking* (v. 3); *The International Encyclopedia of Film; The Movie Makers; The Oxford Companion to Film; The Picturegoer's Who's Who and Encyclopedia of the Screen To-day; Quinlan's Illustrated Registry of Film Stars; Who Was Who in the Theatre; Who's Who in Hollywood; The World Almanac Who's Who of Film; The World Encyclopedia of the Film; The World Film Encyclopedia.* **Filmography:** *Hollywood on the Palisades.* **Biography/ Autobiography:** *Doug and Mary; Douglas Fairbanks* (Ford); *Douglas Fairbanks* (Hancock); *Douglas Fairbanks* (Schickel); *Douglas Fairbanks* (Wilson); *Douglas Fairbanks, 1883-1939* (Eisenschitz); *His Majesty the American; Mary Pickford and Douglas Fairbanks; My Autobiography* (Chaplin); *The Salad Days.* **Pictorial:** *The Fairbanks Album; Leading Men; The Revealing Eye; Silent Portraits; Wallace Neff.* **Films:** *His Majesty the American; The Thief of Bagdad.* **Recording:** *Hollywood on Record.* **Factoids:** *Star Stats.*

• *Periodicals* – The following periodical articles are in addition to those included in the library listings below: *Green Book Album* (Dec. 1910); *Theatre* (Nov. 1911, Apr. 1917, Dec. 1928); *Green Book Magazine* (Jan. 1913, Oct. 1914, July 1916); *Film Players Herald & Movie Pictorial* (Feb. 1916); *Photoplay* (July 1916, Dec. 1916, Mar. 1917, May-June 1917, Oct. 1917, Jan.-Mar. 1918, Apr. 1919, Nov. 1919, June 1920, Nov. 1921, Sept. 1923, Dec. 1923, June 1924, Nov. 1924, Jan.-Feb. 1925, Jan. 1926, Feb. 1927, May 1929, Aug. 1930, Apr. 1932, Feb. 1933, Sept. 1933, Nov. 1933, Feb. 1934, Aug. 1936); *Motion Picture Classic* (July 1916, Mar. 1917, Sept. 1917, Dec. 1917, Aug. 1922, Nov. 1928, Mar. 1930, Mar. 1931); *Everybody's* (Dec. 1916, Nov. 1920); *Motion Picture Magazine* (Dec. 1916, Nov. 1917, Apr. 1918, Feb. 1919, Nov. 1920, Nov. 1922, Jan. 1925, Oct. 1925, Aug. 1926, Feb. 1931, July 1931, Jan. 1932, Apr.-May 1932, Feb-Mar. 1934); *American Magazine* (July 1917, Aug. 1922); *Moving Picture World* (July 21, 1917); *Hearst's Magazine* (Nov. 1917); *Sunset* (Apr. 1918, Oct. 1928); *Woman's Home Companion* (July 1919, Feb. 1929); *Picture Show* (Mar. 13, 1920); *Collier's* (June 18, 1921, Nov. 28, 1931); *Pantomime* (Sept. 28, 1921); *Ladies' Home Journal* (Sept. 1922, Apr.-May 1924, Sept. 1924); *National Magazine* (Jan. 1923); *Outlook* (Dec. 24, 1924, Apr. 14, 1926); *National Board of Review Magazine* (Jan. 1928); *Nation* (Jan. 25, 1928); *World Today* (Dec. 1928); *Vanity Fair* (May 1930); *Close-Up* (no. 6, 1930); *Cinema Digest* (July 25, 1932); *Movie Classic* (Mar. 1933, Sept. 1933, Oct.-Nov. 1934); *Pictures and Picturegoer* (Mar. 18-Apr. 1, 1933); *Shadowplay* (Apr. 1934); *Time* (Dec. 25, 1939); *Newsweek* (Dec. 25, 1939, May 11, 1953, Nov. 28, 1977); *Sequence* (Summer 1949); *Films in Review* (Aug.-Sept. 1959, June-July 1965, May 1976; *Films and Filming* (Feb. 1961, Sept. 1976); *Cinema* (Beverly Hills) (v. 1, no. 3, 1963); *8mm Collector* (Fall/Winter 1965); *Granta* (May 3, 1967); *Classic Film Collector* (Summer 1967 [filmography], Summer 1977); *Focus on Film* (Winter 1970); *Screen Greats* (Summer 1971); *American Heritage* (Dec.

1971); *Liberty* (Spring 1972); *Positif* (Nov.-Dec. 1972); *Sight and Sound* (Spring 1973); *Filmkritik* (Oct. 1973); *Travelling* (Feb./Mar. 1974); *Cine Revue* (Jan. 9, 1975); *Literature/Film Quarterly* (no. 2, 1975); *American Classic Screen* (Jan.-Feb. 1977); *Film Dope* (Sept. 1978); *Wide Angle* (no. 1, 1979); *Revue du Cinéma* (May 1980, Apr. 1982); *Cinéma* (France) (Jan. 1982); *Jeune Cinéma* (Feb. 1982); *Classic Images* (Apr. 1982, Dec. 1982, July 1984, Apr. 1985); *Journal of Popular Film and Television* (Fall 1983); *Esquire* (Nov. 1983); *Listener* (Jan. 16 or 26, 1984); *Hollywood Studio Magazine* (July 1989); *Filmfax* (Mar. 1990).

ARCHIVAL MATERIALS

• *Clipping File*—CAA (also in Collection under entry for Mary Pickford): Article (1950, 1953, 1978, 1988); film appearance (1920-22, 1933); newsphotos (numerous); legal problem (1928, 1932–34, 1939); producer (1935); excerpt from *Hollywood Be Thy Name*; film festival (1979, 1983, 1990); home (1926, 1952, 1980–82, 1985); rodeo (1918); death threat (1927); talkies (1929–30); robbery (1930); marriage/divorce (1933); estate (1940); travels (1931–33); nostalgia (1959); tribute (1941); reviews of *Douglas Fairbanks* (1953); reviews of *Mary Pickford and Douglas Fairbanks* (1977); obituary (1939). Periodical articles: *Photoplay* (1920s); *Shadowland* (June 1922); *Liberty* (1926, Nov. 1929, Feb. 1934); *Saturday Review* (July 10, 1954, Feb. 1968); *Films and Filming* (Dec. 1954, May 1973); *National Aeronautics* (July-Aug. 1974); *Architectural Digest* (Apr. 1990). CAFI: Article (1974, 1977, 1981, 1983); tribute (1983). CAUT: Article (undated, 1978, 1983); ranch (undated, 1980); review of *Douglas Fairbanks* (1953); joint review of *Douglas Fairbanks* and *The Fairbanks Album* (1976); film festival (1940?-41); obituary (1939). Periodical articles: *Photoplay* (Nov.-Dec. 1917, Apr. 1918). CAUU: Review of *Fairbanks Album* (1976); article (1983); review of *His Picture in the Papers* (1974). DCG: Retirement (1930s?). NYMA (also in Photoplay Collection). PARTIAL CON-

110   Faire

TENTS: Periodical article: *Photo-play World* (1918). NYMN: Newsphotos; marriage (1936); romance with Sylvia Ashley (1930s); obituary (1939). Periodical article: *Ladies' Home Journal* (Aug. 1926). NYPL (also in C. & L. Brown Collection): PARTIAL CONTENTS: Booklet *Douglas Fairbanks: 1883-1939*; film festival (1965, 1983); sale of effects (1981); review of *The Fairbanks Family Album*; newsphotos; article (1977). Periodical articles: *Films and Filming* (May 1973); *Liberty* (Spring 1975). • *Other Clipping File* — CAFA, CAUB, CNDA, CODL, GBBF, MABU (see also Douglas Fairbanks Jr. Collection), MAH, MIDL, NYSU, OHCL, PAPL, TXU, WICF. • *Collection* — CAA (see Collection under entry for Mary Pickford). • *Correspondence* — CAA (Adolph Zukor Collection): 1923. CAUS (Rob Wagner Collection); DCLC (George Middleton Papers) (Thomas J. Geraghty Papers) (Owen Wister Papers). NYMN: 1917. NYPL: Letters (C. & L. Brown Collection) (1909); others (various dates, undated). • *Filmography* — CAA. • *Legal File* — CAUW: Copyright (1923, 1926); letter, memo (1917-23); agreement (1917-23). • *Oral History* — NYCO: Mentioned in the following interviews: George K. Arthur, Marc Connelly, Jackie Cooper, J.F. Curtis, Albert Delacorte, Lillian Gish, Buster Keaton, Jay Leyda, Harold Lloyd, Anita Loos, Frances Marion, Mae Murray, Conrad Nagel, Elliot Nugent, Adela St. Johns, Max Schuster, David Selznick, Albert (Eddie) Sutherland, Gloria Swanson, Blanche Sweet, A. Wallander, L.G. White, Max Youngstein, Jerome Zerbe, Adolph Zukor. • *Manuscript* — CAA (Searle Dawley Collection): Notes about SD's experiences directing DF. • *Photograph/Still* — CAA (also in Hollywood Studio Museum Collection) (also in Mary Pickford Collection), CAFA, CAUB, CAUS (also in Eddie Cantor Collection), CAUT (Jessen Collection), CAUU, CODL, GBBF, IAU (Junkin Collection), MABU (also in Douglas Fairbanks Jr. Collection), NJFL, NYAM, NYB (Bettmann/UPI Collection) (Springer Collection) (Underwood Collection),

NYCU (Dramatic Museum Portraits) (Preston Gibson Collection) (Palmer Collection), NYEH, NYMN, NYPL, NYSU, OHCL, TXSM, TXU, WICF. • *Play Program* — MABU (Douglas Fairbanks Jr. Collection). • *Press Kit* — WICF. • *Scrapbook* — CASU (Stark Collection), MABU (Douglas Fairbanks Jr. Collection), NYMA, NYPL (also in R. Locke Collection) (also in Players Collection), WICF. • *Studio Biography* — AZSU (Jimmy Starr Collection): Unknown studio.

FAIRE, Virginia Brown (Virginia LaBuna), Brooklyn, NY, 1904-1980.

Virginia Brown Faire's first role, after having been an extra, was in 1919's *Without Benefit of Clergy*. A 50-film career followed with roles in *The Count of Monte Cristo*, *The Temptress* and *Peter Pan*. She made the transition to talkies and had a lead in Frank Capra's first talkie, *The Donovan Affair*, before her appearances in a series of "B" westerns starring John Wayne, Hoot Gibson and Buck Jones. The last came in 1935.

PUBLISHED SOURCES

• *Books* — General: *Sweethearts of the Sage*; *Who's Who on the Screen*. Credits: *Filmarama* (v. II); *Forty Years of Screen Credits*; *Twenty Years of Silents*; *Who Was Who on Screen*. Encyclopedic Works: *B Western Actors Encyclopedia*; *Filmlexicon degli Autori e delle Opere*; *Picturegoer's Who's Who and Encyclopedia of the Screen To-day*; *Who's Who in Hollywood*. Pictorial: *Silent Portraits*.
• *Periodicals* — The following periodical articles are in addition to that included in the library listings below: *Motion Picture Classic* (June 1920); *Motion Picture Magazine* (July 1921); *Films in Review* (Feb. 1970 [Wampas Baby Stars], Nov. 1977).

ARCHIVAL MATERIALS

• *Clipping File* — CAA: Film appearance (1922); marriage (1930); obituary (1980). CAFI: Obituary (1980). CAUT

Marriage (1929); obituary (1980). NYMA (also in Photoplay Collection): Obituary (1980). Periodical article: *Classic Images* (Apr. 1987). NYPL: Film appearance (1922-23); obituary (1980). • *Other Clipping File* — GBBF, MIDL. • *Legal File* — CAUW: Contract (1923); release (1924); talent agreement (1923-24, 1927). • *Photograph/Still* — CAA (also in Hollywood Studio Museum Collection), DCG (Quigley Photographic Archives), NYPL, NYSU, TXSM, TXU, WICF. • *Scrapbook* — NYPL (also in R. Locke Collection). • *Studio Biography* — NYMA: Photoplay.

FARNUM, Dustin, Hampton Beach, NH, 1874-1929.

After his debut in *The Squaw Man* (1914), stage actor Dustin Farnum became a very popular star of action films and westerns for Fox and other studios. Among his films were *The Scarlet Pimpernel*, *The Corsican Brothers* and an early version of *The Virginian*. His career declined somewhat during the mid-1920s. He was the brother of William Farnum (q.v.).

PUBLISHED SOURCES

• *Books* — **General:** *The BFI Companion to the Western*; *Classics of the Silent Screen*; *Eighty Silent Film Stars*; *First One Hundred Noted Men and Women of the Screen*; *The Hall of Fame of Western Film Stars*; *Hollywood Album 2*; *Immortals of the Screen*; *Who's Who in the Film World*; *Who's Who on the Screen*. **Credits:** *Filmarama* (v. I and II); *Twenty Years of Silents*; *Who Was Who on Screen*. **Encyclopedic Works:** *Film Encyclopedia*; *Filmlexicon degli Autori e delle Opere*; *Halliwell's Filmgoer's Companion*; *The Illustrated Who's Who of the Cinema*; *Who Was Who in the Theatre*; *Who's Who in Hollywood*; *The World Almanac Who's Who of Film*. **Pictorial:** *Silent Portraits*. **Factoids:** *Star Stats*.

• *Periodicals* — The following periodical articles are in addition to those included in the library listings below: *Theatre* (Oct. 1906); *Photoplay* (July

1915, June 1916, Nov. 1919); *Motion Picture Classic* (Apr. 1916, Aug. 1916, Dec. 1916, Sept. 1917, Dec. 1919, Apr. 1922); *Picture Play Magazine* (May 1916, Oct. 1919); *Motion Picture Magazine* (Nov. 1916, Mar. 1919, Feb. 1920); *Classic Film Collector* (Spring 1979); *Films in Review* (Nov. 1983).

ARCHIVAL MATERIALS

• *Clipping File* — CAA: Marriage/divorce (1924, 1926); estate (1930); article (1916); newsphoto; obituary (1929). CAUT: Obituary (1929). NYMA (also in Photoplay Collection): Personal data summary; obituary (1929). Periodical article: *Classic Images* (Apr. 1982). NYPL: PARTIAL CONTENTS: Newsphotos; article (undated). Periodical article: *Photo-play Journal* (Sept. 1919). • *Other Clipping File* — AZSU (Jimmy Starr Collection), MAH, MIDL, NYSU, PAPL, WICF. • *Collection* — CAUU (see Collection entry under entry for William Farnum). • *Correspondence* — DCLC (Owen Wister Papers): Some items related to *The Virginian*. NYPL (C. & L. Brown Collection): 1916. • *Filmography* — NYMA. • *Legal File* — CAUT (Twentieth Century-Fox Collection): Talent agreement (1921). • *Oral History* — NYCO: Mentioned in the following interviews: G.M. Anderson, Conrad Nagel, Blanche Sweet. • *Photograph/Still* — CAA (also in Hollywood Studio Museum Collection), CAHL, CALM, CASF, CAUT (Jessen Collection), CAUU, DCG (Quigley Photographic Archives), GBBF, NJFL, NYAM, NYB (Bettmann/UPI Collection), NYCU (Dramatic Museum Portraits), NYEH, NYPL, NYSU, OHCL, TXSM, TXU, WICF. • *Play Program* — CAHL: 1907, 1915. • *Scrapbook* — NYPL (also in R. Locke Collection) (also in Players Collection), WICF.

FARNUM, William, Boston, MA, 1876-1953.

At one time burly William Farnum was the highest paid actor in films. His memorable first film, coming after a stage career, was *The Spoilers* (1914). Although he was seriously injured in the mid-1920s while making a film, he countinued sporadic appearances in lesser roles. His attempt to regain his star status in 1931 was unsuccessful but he was seen in character parts until the 1950s. Among his films were *Les Misérables, A Tale of Two Cities, The Scarlet Letter* and *Samson and Delilah.* His brother was Dustin Farnum (q.v.).

PUBLISHED SOURCES

• *Books* — **General:** *Classics of the Silent Screen; Eighty Silent Film Stars; Famous Film Folk; First One Hundred Noted Men and Women of the Screen; Gentlemen to the Rescue; The Hall of Fame of Western Film Stars; Heroes, Heavies and Sagebrush; Hollywood Album 2; The Truth About the Movies; Who's Who on the Screen.* **Credits:** *Filmarama* (v. I and II); *Forty Years of Screen Credits; Twenty Years of Silents; Who Was Who on Screen.* **Encyclopedic Works:** *Film Encyclopedia; Filmlexicon degli Autori e delle Opere; Halliwell's Filmgoer's Companion; The Illustrated Who's Who of the Cinema; The Movie Makers; The Picturegoer's Who's Who and Encyclopedia of the Screen To-day; Who Was Who in the Theatre; Who's Who in Hollywood; The World Almanac Who's Who of Film; The World Film Encyclopedia.* **Pictorial:** *Silent Portraits.* **Factoids:** *Star Stats.*

• *Periodicals* — The following periodical articles are in addition to those included in the library listings below: *Photoplay* (Oct. 1915, Nov. 1917, Nov. 1919, Jan. 1928); *Motion Picture Magazine* (Dec. 1915, Sept. 1916, June 1918, Feb. 1919, Sept. 1920, June 1922, Dec. 1924); *Picture Show* (Nov. 8, 1919); *Time* (June 15, 1953); *Newsweek* (June 15, 1953); *Classic Film Collector* (Fall 1960); *Films in Review* (Nov. 1983); *Classic Images* (Sept. 1991).

ARCHIVAL MATERIALS

• *Clipping File* — CAA: Marriage/divorce (1928-32); film appearance (1930, 1952); stage appearance (1928, 1949); newsphoto; illness (1953); honor (1940, 1948, 1950); article (1950, undated); nostalgia (1947, 1950); 50th anniversary in show business (1941); obituary (1953). Periodical article: *Moving Picture World* (Mar. 1914). CAUT: Newsphotos. NYMA (also in Photoplay Collection): Film review (1920). Periodical articles: *Classic Film Collector* (Spring 1969); *Classic Film/Video Images* (May 1980). NYPL: Bankruptcy (1933); article (1934, 1941, undated); newsphotos; play review (1909, 1928); marriage/divorce (1929, 1932); film appearance (1920s, 1930s, 1940s); radio appearance (1936); film review (1910s, 1920s, 1930s, 1940s); fight in *The Spoilers* (film) (1942); obituary (1953). • *Other Clipping File* — AZSU (Jimmy Starr Collection), CAUU (see Collection), GBBF, MAH, MIDL, NYSU, OHCL, PAPL. • *Collection* — CAUU: Materials covering the years 1897-1953, including photographs and stills; interviews (1939-40); scrapbooks; correspondence; objects; newspaper clippings; publicity releases, and play programs relating to WF and Dustin Farnum. • *Correspondence* — CAA (Selig Collection). CAOC (B. Henry Collection): Letter (from Mrs. W. Farnum about WF) (1958). CAUU (see Collection). NYPL: Letters (C. & L. Brown Collection) (1933, 1944); others (1909-10). • *Interview* — CAUU (See Collection). • *Legal File* — CAUT (Twentieth Century-Fox Collection): Letter (1916, 1921); real estate appraisal (1921); income tax return (1916?). • *Oral History* — NYCO: Mentioned in: Conrad Nagel interview. • *Photograph/Still* — CAA (also Hollywood Studio Museum Collection), CALM, CAPH, CASF, CAUT (Jessen Collection), CAUU (also in Collection), DCG (Quigley Photographic Archives), GBBF, NJFL, NYAM, NYB (Bettmann/UPI Collection) (Underwood Collection), NYCU (Dramatic Museum Portraits) (Palmer Collection), NYEH, NYPL, NYSU, OHCL, TXU, WICF. • *Play Program* — CAUU (see Collection). • *Publicity Release* — CAA: Paramount (1940s); Fox (1941). CAUU (see Collection). • *Scrapbook* — CAUU (see Collection), NYPL (also in Locke Collection) (also in Players Collection). • *Studio Biography* — CAA: Paramount (1920s?, 1947); RKO (1934). NYMA: Photoplay.

FARRELL, Charles, Onset Bay, MA, 1900/01-1990.

Charles Farrell began his film career in 1923 playing small parts in films like *The Cheat*. It was his teaming with Janet Gaynor (q.v.) in the wildly popular *Seventh Heaven* (1927) which made them one of the premiere romantic teams of the latter 1920s. They appeared in many films together, including some early sound musicals. His efforts without her were not as successful and he gradually drifted into "B" films. His final roles came in the early 1940s but he enjoyed a brief rebirth of popularity in the 1950s television show *My Little Margie*. He was married to Virginia Valli (q.v.).

PUBLISHED SOURCES

• *Books* – **Bibliography:** *The Idols of Silence.* **General:** *Alice in Movieland; Hollywood's Great Love Teams; Popular Men of the Screen; Screen Album; Screen Personalities; The Stars Appear; Twinkle, Twinkle, Movie Star.* **Credits:** *Filmarama* (v. I and II); *Forty Years of Film Credits; Twenty Years of Silents.* **Encylopedic Works:** *The Complete Encyclopedia of Popular Music and Jazz; Contemporary Theatre, Film and Television* (v. 9); *Film Encyclopedia; Filmlexicon degli Autori e delle Opere; Halliwell's Filmgoer's Companion; The Illustrated Who's Who of the Cinema; International Motion Picture Almanac* (1975-80); *The Movie Makers; The Picturegoer's Who's Who and Encyclopedia of the Screen To-day; Quinlan's Illustrated Registry of Film Stars; Variety Who's Who in Show Business; Who's Who in Hollywood; Who's Who in the Theatre; The World Almanac Who's Who of Film; The World Film Encyclopedia.* **Nostalgia:** *Whatever Became of...* (2nd). **Pictorial:** *The Image Makers.* **Factoids:** *Star Stats.*
• *Periodicals* – The following periodical articles are in addition to those included in the library listings below: *Motion Picture Classic* (July 1926, Nov. 1926, Sept. 1931); *Photoplay* (June 1927, Jan. 1931, July 1931, Feb. 1933, Dec.

1933, June 1974); *Motion Picture Magazine* (Nov. 1927, May 1928, Dec. 1928, July 1929, Dec. 1929, Sept. 1931, Oct. 1933, Feb. 1935); *Screen Mirror* (Jan. 1931); *Silver Screen* (Nov. 1931, Oct. 1938); *Movie Classic* (Nov. 1932, Feb. 1933); *Cinema Digest* (Jan. 9, 1933); *Shadowplay* (Feb. 1934); *Screen Book* (Nov. 1938); *TV Guide* (Aug. 22, 1952, Mar. 12, 1954); *Cosmopolitan* (Dec. 1953); *Show* (Aug. 1962); *Sports Illustrated* (Apr. 15, 1963); *Films in Review* (Oct. 1976); *Film Dope* (Sept. 1978); *Classic Images* (June 1990); *Skoop* (July-Aug. 1990).

ARCHIVAL MATERIALS

• *Clipping File* – CAA: Newsphotos; home (1928, 1930, 1934); film appearance (1926, 1932-33, 1938); release from Fox (1932); Fox contract (1929); comeback (1938); article (1927, 1930, 1930s, 1948, 1951, 1953-54, 1976-77, undated); marriage (1930-31); nostalgia (1969, 1980-81); Racquet Club (1964-65, 1967-68); mayor of Palm Springs (1952); obituary (1990). Periodical articles: *Racquet Club* (Oct. 1963); *Hollywood Studio Magazine* (Mar. 1972). CAPH: Obituary (1990). Periodical article: *Desert Magazine* (Mar. 1963). CAPS: Article (1968, 1977, 1980); honor (1968, 1978); newsphotos; obituary (1990). CAUU: Article (1950s, 1977). NYMA (also in Photoplay Collection): Newsphotos; article (1975); obituary (1990). NYPL (also in C. & L. Brown Collection): Newsphotos (numerous); article (1935, 1953-56); Palm Springs (1963); stage appearance (1939, 1952, undated); film appearance (1920s, 1930s); home destroyed (1935); *My Little Margie* (TV show) (1953); returns from WWII (1940s); obituary (1990). Periodical articles: *Motion Picture Classic* (Feb. 1930); *New Movie Magazine* (1931).
• *Other Clipping File* – AZSU (Jimmy Starr Collection), CASF, CAUB, GBBF, MAH, MIDL, OHCL, PAPL, WICF.
• *Correspondence* – CAA (Hedda Hopper Collection): Letters about Racquet Club (1954-55). CAOC (B. Henry Collection). NYPL: Letters (C. & L. Brown Collection) (1935, 1937-40); other (1939).
• *Filmography* – CAA. • *Legal File* –

CAUT (Twentieth Century-Fox Collection): Letter, memo, telegram (1928–34, 1938, 1962); contract (1932); talent agreement (1926, 1928–29, 1933, 1938); release (1934); loanout (1932). CAUW: Personnel, payroll record (1933); talent agreement (1933). • *Oral History*—NYCO: Mentioned in the following interviews: William Couch, Janet Gaynor. • *Photograph/Still*—CAA (also in Hollywood Studio Museum Collection), CASF, CAUS, CAUT (Jessen Collection), CAUU, CNDA, DCG (Quigley Photographic Archives), GBBF, MIDL, NJPT, NYB (Bettmann/UPI Collection), NYCU (Dramatic Museum Portraits) (Palmer Collection), NYEH, NYPL, NYSU, OHCL, TXU, WICF. • *Publicity Release*—AZSU (Jimmy Starr Collection). CAA: Fox (numerous) (1920s–30s); Paramount (1920s–30s); RKO (1933); unknown studio (1938). • *Scrapbook*—NJPT (Yeandle Collection), NYMA. • *Studio Biography*—NYPL: Fox (1938).

FAZENDA, Louise, Lafayette, IN, 1889/1896–1962.

In her early career, Louise Fazenda's persona was that of a raucous country girl, a role she played in such features as *Down on the Farm*, the remake of *Tillie's Punctured Romance* and in numerous two-reelers. Her range gradually expanded in the 1920s and until the end of the 1930s she had supporting parts in numerous comic and dramatic films, the last being *The Old Maid* (1939). She was married to producer Hal Wallis.

PUBLISHED SOURCES

• *Books*—Written by (or ghostwritten for) LF: a chapter of *Breaking into the Movies*. **General:** *Blue Book of the Screen*; *Character People*; *Clown Princes and Court Jesters*; *Famous Film Folk*; *Keaton et Cie*; *Mack Sennett's Keystone*; *The Truth About the Movies*; *Who's Who in the Film World*; *Who's Who on the Screen*; *Women in Comedy*. **Credits:** *Filmarama* (v. I and II); *Forty Years of Screen Credits*; *Twenty Years of Silents*;

Who Was Who on Screen. **Encyclopedic Works:** *Dictionary of American Biography* (Supplement 7); *Film Encyclopedia*; *Filmlexicon degli Autori e delle Opere*; *Halliwell's Filmgoer's Companion*; *The Illustrated Who's Who of the Cinema*; *The Movie Makers*; *The Picturegoer's Who's Who and Encyclopedia of the Screen To-day*; *Quinlan's Illustrated Directory of Film Comedy Actors*; *Who's Who in Hollywood*; *The World Almanac Who's Who of Film*; *The World Encyclopedia of the Film*; *The World Film Encyclopedia*. **Pictorial:** *Silent Portraits*; *They Had Faces Then*. **Factoids:** *Star Stats*.

• *Periodicals*—The following periodical articles are in addition to those included in the library listings below: *Motion Picture Magazine* (Dec. 1916, Dec. 1917, Jan. 1919, Nov. 1921, Mar. 1926, Sept. 1928, Oct. 1929, Jan. 1930); *Photoplay* (Aug. 1917, Apr. 1918, Nov. 1919); *Motion Picture Classic* (May 1919, Feb. 1921, Apr. 1925); *Pantomime* (Oct. 5, 1921); *Picture Play* (Jan. 1924); *Collier's* (June 11, 1938); *Time* (Apr. 27, 1962); *Films in Review* (Aug.-Sept. 1962).

ARCHIVAL MATERIALS

• *Clipping File*—CAA (also in Collection): Film appearance (1921, 1923–24, 1928); marriage/divorce/children (1926–27, 1932–33); Sennett contract (1920); legal problem (1922); injury (1927); illness (1932); article (1930); stage appearance (1932); estate (1962); excerpt from *Dictionary of American Biography*; newsphotos; obituary (1962). CAUU: Periodical article: *American Dancer* (Nov. 1930). NYMA (also in Photoplay Collection): Article (1916, 1928–32, 1936–37, undated); film appearance (1921, 1923–24); signs with Educational (1922); signs with Special Pictures (1920); marriage/divorce/children (1926, 1933–34); obituary (1962). Periodical articles: *Screen Secrets* (Nov. 1929); *Photoplay* (Jan. 1930, June 1931); *Picture Play* (Oct. 1930); *Motion Picture Classic* (Mar. 1931); *Screen Play* (Nov. 1934); *Screenland* (Nov. 1934). NYPL: Newsphotos (numerous); career (1936–38); article (1930, undated); film review (1920s,

1930s); film appearance (1930s); stage appearance (1932); birth of son (1933); obituary (1962). Periodical articles: *Photoplay* (June 1925, Aug. 1933). • *Other Clipping File* – AZSU (Jimmy Starr Collection), CAG (see Collection), GBBF, MAH, MIDL, OHCL, PAPL, WICF. • *Collection* – CAA (Vertical File Collection): Numerous clippings and a manuscript *The Life Story of Louise Fazenda* (MGM, 1940), all collected for LF's entry in *The Dictionary of American Biography*. CAG (Albert Dressler Collection): 55 letters, greeting cards and telegrams (1926–59); newspaper and periodical clippings. Mainly pertains to LF's interest in purchasing antiques and collectibles from Mr. Dressler. • *Correspondence* – CAA (Hedda Hopper Collection): Letters about the Louise Fazenda Wallis Memorial Fund at UCLA Medical Center (1962). CAG (see Collection). • *Filmography* – CAA: Silent films only. • *Legal File* – CAA (Sennett Collection): Contract (1919). CAUT (Twentieth Century-Fox Collection): Letter, memo (1934–35); contract summary (1935); loanout (1934). CAUW: Letter, memo (1924–27, 1935); talent agreement (1924–30, 1933, 1935–37, 1939); loanout (1924–27, 1935–36); personnel, payroll record (1927, 1933–39); contract (1929, 1936). • *Oral History* – NYCO: Mentioned in: Hal Wallis interview. • *Photograph/Still* – AZSU (Jimmy Starr Collection), CAA (also in Hollywood Studio Museum Collection) (also in MGM Collection), CAFA, CAG (see Collection), CAUT (Jessen Collection), CAUW, CNDA, DCG (Quigley Photographic Archives), GBBF, MIDL, NJPT, NYAM, NYB (Bettmann/UPI Collection), NYCU (Bulliet Collection) (Dramatic Museum Portraits) (Palmer Collection), NYEH, NYPL, NYSU, OHCL, TXSM, TXU, WICF. • *Press Release* – AZSU (Jimmy Starr Collection). • *Publicity Release* – NYMA: Sennett (undated); unknown studio (undated). • *Scrapbook* – NJPT (Yeandle Collection), NYPL (also in R. Locke Collection). • *Studio Biography* – CAA: Paramount (1931); MGM (1940). NYMA: Photoplay.

FELLOWES, Rockliffe, Ottawa, Canada, 1885–1950.

In films from the early 'teens and a popular star from his appearance in *The Easiest Way* (1917), Rockliffe Fellowes worked for no fewer than 14 studios during his career, generally in dramatic roles. He also essayed an occasional western film. He continued in character roles in early talkies, the final one coming in 1934. Among his films were *Declasse*, *Taxi Driver*, *East of Suez* and the Marx Brothers' *Monkey Business*.

PUBLISHED SOURCES

• *Books* – General: *Famous Film Folk*; *The Truth About the Movies*. **Credits:** *Filmarama* (v. I and II); *Forty Years of Screen Credits*; *Twenty Years of Silents*; *Who Was Who on Screen*. **Encyclopedic Works:** *Filmlexicon degli Autori e delle Opere*; *Halliwell's Filmgoer's Companion*; *The Picturegoer's Who's Who and Encyclopedia of the Screen To-day*; *Who's Who in Hollywood*.
• *Periodicals* – *Motion Picture Magazine* (Apr.-May 1920); *Photoplay* (Feb. 1925).

ARCHIVAL MATERIALS

• *Clipping File* – CAA: Film appearance (1921); obituary (1950). NYPL (also in C. & L. Brown Collection): Film appearance (1932); film review; newsphotos; obituary (1950). • *Other Clipping File* – CNDA, GBBF, MAH, NYMA (Photoplay Collection), OHCL, WICF. • *Correspondence* – NYPL (C. & L. Brown Collection): ca. 1911-12. • *Legal File* – CAUW: Contract (1927); talent agreement (1926). • *Photograph/Still* – CAA (Hollywood Studio Museum Collection), DCG (Quigley Photographic Archives), NJFL, NYPL, NYSU, OHCL, TNUT (Clarence Brown Collection), TXU, WICF. • *Scrapbook* – NYPL (also in R. Locke Collection), TNUT (Clarence Brown Collection), WICF. • *Studio Biography* – CAA: Paramount (1931).

FERGUSON, Elsie, New York, NY, 1883–1961.

Popular stage star Elsie Ferguson transferred her fame to silent movies for a relatively brief period from 1917 to the early 1920s. She began as one of the Famous Players and her appearances included *A Doll's House, Eyes of the Soul, Footlights* and *Sacred and Profane Love.* She made a single talkie appearance in 1930.

PUBLISHED SOURCES

• *Books*—**General:** *Actorviews; Famous Film Folk; Intimate Talks with Movie Stars; More From Hollywood; Who's Who on the Screen.* **Credits:** *Filmarama* (v. I and II); *Twenty Years of Silents; Who Was Who on Screen.* **Encyclopedic Works:** *Current Biography* (1944, 1963); *Film Encyclopedia; Filmlexicon degli Autori e delle Opere; Halliwell's Filmgoer's Companion; The Movie Makers; Who Was Who in the Theatre; Who's Who in Hollywood.* **Filmography:** *Hollywood on the Palisades.* **Pictorial:** *Great Stars of the American Stage; The Image Makers; Silent Portraits.*

• *Periodicals*—The following periodical articles are in addition to those included in the library listings below: *Theatre* (Feb. 1909, Nov. 1909, May 1919, July-Aug. 1920, Mar. 1926); *Pearson* (NY) (Oct.-Nov. 1909); *Green Book Album* (Feb. 1910); *Cosmpolitan* (Jan. 1913, Mar. 1915); *Green Book Magazine* (Apr. 1913, Aug. 1915); *Motion Picture Classic* (Feb. 1918, June 1919, Mar. 1921); *Motion Picture Magazine* (Sept. 1918, June 1919, Feb. 1920, May 1921, Oct. 1921); *Photoplay* (Apr. 1918, Aug. 1919, Mar. 1920, Jan. 1922); *Picture Play Magazine* (Oct. 1919); *Shadowland* (Feb. 1920); *Filmplay Journal* (Apr. 1922); *Ladies' Home Journal* (June 1927); *Films in Review* (Jan. 1965, Apr. 1966).

ARCHIVAL MATERIALS

• *Caricature*—NYMN. • *Clipping File*—CAA: Film appearance (1921); newsphotos; marriage (1934); obituary (1961). Periodical article: *Theatre Arts* (Dec. 1952). CAUT: Obituary (1961).

NYMA (also in Photoplay Collection): Newsphotos; obituary (1961). Periodical article: *Green Book Magazine* (May 1915). NYMN: Newsphotos (numerous); marriage (1934); obituary (1961). NYPL: PARTIAL CONTENTS: Newsphotos; return to stage (1930, 1934, 1943, 1940s?); film appearance (1930); play review (1920s); article (1925, 1980); obituary (1961). Periodical article: *Films in Review* (Nov. 1964). • *Other Clipping File*—GBBF, MAH, MIDL, NYSU, OHCL, PAPL, WICF. • *Correspondence*—CAA (Adolph Zukor Collection): 1919, 1922. NYPL: Letters (C. & L. Brown Collection) (1944, 1946); others (1913–20, 1925, 1943, 1947, undated). • *Filmography*—NYMA. • *Legal File*—CAUW: Letter (1930); contract (1930); payroll record (1930); contract summary (1930). • *Manuscript*—CAA (Searle Dawley Collection): Notes by SD about directing EF. • *Oral History*—NYCO: Mentioned in: Nita Naldi interview. • *Photograph/Still*—CAA (also in Hollywood Studio Museum Collection), CAHL, CAOC (Kiesling Collection), CAUS, CAUT (Jessen Collection), CAUU, DCG (Quigley Photographic Archives), GBBF, IAU (Junkin Collection), NJFL, NYAM, NYB (Bettmann/UPI Collection), NYCU (Bulliet Collection) (Dramatic Museum Portraits) (Palmer Collection), NYEH, NYMA, NYMN, NYPL, NYSU, OHCL, TXSM, TXU, WICF. • *Play Program*—CAHL: 1915, 1923. NYPL: 1922–24. • *Scrapbook*—NYPL (also in Locke Collection) (also in Players Collection). • *Studio Biography*—NYMA: Photoplay.

FERGUSON, Helen, Decatur, IL, 1901–1977.

Helen Ferguson was a serial queen who, after her screen career ended, became a Hollywood press agent. Beginning with Essanay, she remained a popular star, often in action roles, throughout the 1920s, and in 1922 was dubbed a Wampas Baby Star. Her serials included *Casey of the Coast Guard* and *Fire Fighters;* among her other films were *Just Pals, Call of the*

North, Hungry Hearts and *Miss Lulu Bett*. She was married to William Russell (q.v.).

PUBLISHED SOURCES

• *Books* – **General:** *Blue Book of the Screen*; *Famous Film Folk*; *Sweethearts of the Sage*; *Those Fabulous Serial Heroines*; *The Truth About the Movies*. **Credits:** *Filmarama* (v. I and II); *Twenty Years of Silents*. **Encyclopedic Works:** *Film Encyclopedia*; *Filmlexicon degli Autori e delle Opere*; *International Motion Picture Almanac* (1975–80); *Who's Who in Hollywood*.
• *Pictorial* – *Silent Portraits*.
• *Periodicals* – The following periodical articles are in addition to those included in the library listings below: *Motion Picture Magazine* (Oct. 1920, May 1922); *Filmplay Journal* (Sept. 1921); *Photoplay* (Dec. 1921, Aug. 1924); *Motion Picture Classic* (Apr. 1922); *Films in Review* (Feb. 1970) (Wampas Baby Stars).

ARCHIVAL MATERIALS

• *Clipping File* – CAA: Newsphoto; home (1954); obituary (1977). Periodical article: *TV Guide* (Nov. 4, 1961). NYPL: Newsphotos; legal problem (1936); article (1951); film appearance (1923); article (undated); obituary (1977). Periodical articles: *Pic* (Jan. 24, 1939); *TV Guide* (Nov. 4, 1961). • *Other Clipping File* – GBBF, MAH, MIDL, NYMA (Photoplay Collection), NYSU, OHCL, PAPL, WICF. • *Correspondence* – NYMA (Photoplay collection). NYPL: 1954. • *Legal File* – CAUW: Agreement (1927); talent agreement (1929–30). • *Oral History* – NYCO: Mentioned in the following interviews: Marie Anderson, Albert Delacorte. • *Photograph/ Still* – CAA (also in Hollywood Studio Museum Collection), CAUT (Jessen Collection), DCG (Quigley Photographic Archives), GBBF, NYB (Underwood Collection), NYEH, NYPL, NYSU, OHCL, TXSM, TXU, WICF. • *Scrapbook* – NYPL (also in R. Locke Collection). • *Studio Biography* – NYMA: Photoplay.

FISCHER (later Fisher), **Margarita,** Missouri Valley, IA, 1886–1973.

After much stage experience, beginning as a child, Margarita Fischer's film career commenced in 1910 with Selig Polyscope. She ultimately appeared in over 90 silent films, including *Uncle Tom's Cabin* (1913), *Withering Roses*, *The Dragon*, *The Miracle of Life*, *Any Woman* and *The Pearl of Paradise* (in which her nude scenes caused a stir). She finished out her career in a 1927 remake of *Uncle Tom's Cabin*. In 1914 she had been named America's Most Popular Star in a Photoplay contest.

PUBLISHED SOURCES

• *Books* – **General:** *Who's Who on the Screen*. **Credits:** *Filmarama* (v. I and II); *Twenty Years of Silents*; *Who Was Who on Screen*. **Encyclopedic Works:** *Filmlexicon degli Autori e delle Opere*; *Who's Who in Hollywood*. **Pictorial:** *Silent Portraits*.
• *Periodicals* – The following periodical articles are in addition to that included in the library listings below: *Movie Pictorial* (July 1915); *Photoplay* (Feb. 1917); *Motion Picture Classic* (May 1917, Sept. 1917, Mar. 1927); *Motion Picture Magazine* (May 1919); *Picture Show* (Dec. 20, 1919); *Classic Images* (Nov. 1990).

ARCHIVAL MATERIALS

• *Clipping File* – CAA: Sells home (1952). NYMA (also in Photoplay Collection): Periodical article: *Universal Weekly* (Sept. 20, 1913). NYPL: Newsphotos. • *Other Clipping File* – WICF. • *Collection* – KSWS: Photographs (1899–1961); a filmography; correspondence (mainly fan letters) (1917–69); contracts (1911–18); scrapbooks (1904–20); and travel mementos and other miscellany covering MF's career on stage and screen (1917–60). • *Filmography* – CAFI, KSWS (see Collection). • *Legal File* – KSWS (see Collection). • *Photograph/Still* – CAA (also in Hollywood Studio Museum Collection), DCG (Quigley Photographic Archives), KSWS (see Collection), NYCU (Dramatic Museum Portraits), NYPL, NYSU, OHCL, TXSM, TXU, WICF. • *Scrapbook*—KSWS (see Collection), NYPL (R. Locke Collection). • *Studio Biography*—NYMA: Photoplay.

FORBES, Ralph (Ralph Taylor), London, England, 1902/05–1951.

Member of a well-known English acting family, Ralph Forbes entered British films in 1921 and came to Hollywood in 1926. His first film there was the popular *Beau Geste*. After he made the transition to talkies, Ralph Forbes's roles became mostly supporting ones, but he was cast in a large number of prestigious films, including *Twentieth Century*, *The Barretts of Wimpole Street*, *Romeo and Juliet*, *Stage Door* and *The Private Lives of Elizabeth and Essex*. His final appearance was in 1944's *Frenchman's Creek*.

PUBLISHED SOURCES

• *Books*—General: *Alice in Movieland*. **Credits:** *British Film Actors' Credits*; *Filmarama* (v. II); *Forty Years of Screen Credits*; *Twenty Years of Silents*; *Who Was Who on Screen*. **Encyclopedic Works:** *Film Encyclopedia*; *Filmlexicon degli Autori e delle Opere*; *Halliwell's Filmgoer's Companion*; *The Movie Makers*; *The Picturegoer's Who's Who and Encyclopedia of the Screen To-day*; *Who Was Who in the Theatre*; *Who's Who in Hollywood*; *The World Almanac Who's Who of Film*; *The World Film Encyclopedia*. **Pictorial:** *Silent Portraits*.

• *Periodicals*—The following periodical articles are in addition to those included in the library listings below: *Photoplay* (Dec. 1926); *Motion Picture Classic* (Feb. 1928, Mar. 1930, Jan. 1931); *Motion Picture Magazine* (May 1931); *Movie Classic* (May 1932, Mar. 1933, Nov. 1934); *Newsweek* (Apr. 9, 1951); *Time* (Apr. 9, 1951).

ARCHIVAL MATERIALS

• *Caricature*—NYMN. • *Clipping File*—CAA: Illness (1928); divorce (1932); career overview (1943); obituary (1951). NYMN: Marriage; newsphotos; obituary (1951). NYPL: Newsphotos (numerous); stage appearance (1930s?, 1940s?); play review (1940s); article (1927–28, undated); film review (1933); film appearance (1930s); career (1948); marriage/separation/divorce (1926–27, 1929, 1932, undated); film contract (1926); obituary (1951). Periodical articles: *Cinema Art* (July 1927); *Silver Screen* (May 1931). • *Other Clipping File*—GBBF, MIDL, MNBH (see Collection), NYMA (Photoplay Collection), OHCL, PAPL, TXU, WICF. • *Collection*—MNBH: Photographs, clippings, filmography and possibly other materials. • *Correspondence*—NYPL: Letters (C. & L. Brown Collection) (1939–41, undated); others (1926, 1928, 1947). • *Filmography*—MNBH (see Collection). • *Legal File*—CAUW: Personnel, payroll record (1935–39); talent agreement (1928–30, 1934, 1939); contract (1937); document, letter, memo (1929–30). • *Oral History*—NYCO: Mentioned in: Kitty Carlisle Hart interview. • *Photograph/Still*—CAA (also in Hollywood Studio Museum Collection) (also in MGM Collection), CAH, CASU, CAUT (Portrait File), CAUU, DCG (Quigley Photographic Archives), GBBF, MNBH (see Collection), NJPT, NYAM, NYB (Underwood Collection), NYCU (Palmer Collection), NYEH, NYMN, NYPL, NYSU, OHCL, OHSU, PAPL, TNUT (Clarence Brown Collection), TXU (A. Davis Collection), WICF. • *Play Program*—NYPL: 1944. • *Reminiscence*—MISU. • *Scrapbook*—NYPL. • *Studio Biography*—CAA: Paramount (1943). NYMA: Photoplay.

FORD, Harrison, Kansas City, MO, 1884/94–1957.

The "original" Harrison Ford was a popular matinee idol and light comedian who appeared with many of the leading actresses of his day in numerous films beginning in 1917. Among them were *The Passion Flower*, *Vanity Fair*, *Little Old New York*, *Janice*

Meredith (both with Marion Davies [q.v.]) and *The Marriage Whirl*. His best known performance was probably in *Smilin' Through* opposite Norma Talmadge (q.v.). He apparently made only a single talkie in 1932.

PUBLISHED SOURCES

• *Books*—General: *Famous Film Folk*; *Motion Picture News Booking Guide and Studio Directory* (1927); *Who's Who on the Screen*. Credits: *Filmarama* (v. I and II); *Twenty Years of Silents*; *Who Was Who on Screen*. Encyclopedic Works: *Film Encyclopedia*; *Filmlexicon degli Autori e delle Opere*; *Halliwell's Filmgoer's Companion*; *Who's Who in Hollywood*. Pictorial: *Silent Portraits*.

• *Periodicals*—The following periodical articles are in addition to those included in the library listings below: *Motion Picture Classic* (Dec. 1918, Feb. 1922, Oct. 1925); *Photoplay* (Jan. 1920, Nov. 1920, May 1926); *Motion Picture Magazine* (Mar. 1920, May 1921, Nov. 1922).

ARCHIVAL MATERIALS

• *Clipping File*—CAA: Newsphoto; injury (1951); film appearance (1923); obituary (1957). CAUT: Newsphotos. NYMA (also in Photoplay Collection). Periodical article: *Classic Images* (July 1988). NYMN: Newsphotos. NYPL: Newsphotos (numerous); injury; article (1925-26, undated); career; Paramount contract (1925); stage appearance (1929); film appearance (1925, 1929); film reviews (numerous) (1920s). Periodical article: *Picture Show* (Nov. 5, 1927). • *Other Clipping File*—CNDA, GBBF, MAH, MIDL, OHCL, PAPL, WICF. • *Correspondence*—NYPL: Letters (C. & L. Brown Collection) (undated); others (1940, 1942, undated). • *Legal File*—CAUW: Talent agreement (1929). • *Photograph/still*—CAA (also in Hollywood Studio Museum Collection), CAUB, CNDA, DCG (Quigley Photographic Archives), GBBF, NJFL, NJPT, NYAM, NYCU (Bulliet Collection), NYEH, NYPL, NYSU, OHCL, TXSM, TXU, WICF. • *Play Program*—CAHL:

1931. • *Scrapbook*—NYAM, NYPL (also in R. Locke Collection). • *Studio Biography*—CAA: MGM (1926); Paramount (1928).

FRAZER, Robert, Worcester, MA, 1890/91-1944.

Robert Frazer appeared in a very large number of films during a career which began with romantic leads as far back as 1912 and extended to 1944 in character roles. He was equally at home as hero or heavy and also was seen on the stage. Among his movies were *Fascination*, *Jazzmania*, *As a Man Loves* and the cult film *The White Zombie*.

PUBLISHED SOURCES

• *Books*—General: *Eighty Silent Film Stars*; *Heroes, Heavies and Sagebrush*. Credits: *Filmarama* (v. II); *Forty Years of Screen Credits*; *Twenty Years of Silents*; *Who Was Who on Screen*. Encyclopedic Works: *Film Encyclopedia*; *Hollywood Character Actors*; *The Picturegoer's Who's Who and Encyclopedia of the Screen To-day*; *Who's Who in Hollywood*.

• *Periodicals*—The following periodical articles are in addition to those included in the library listings below: *Photoplay* (June-July 1924, Sept. 1924).

ARCHIVAL MATERIALS

• *Clipping File*—CAA: Newsphoto; obituary (1944). NYMA (also in Photoplay Collection): Periodical articles: *Classic Images* (June-July 1986). NYPL: Newsphotos; film review (1920s); film appearance (1934); career (1928-29); article (undated); obituary (1944). • *Other Clipping File*—GBBF, PAPL, WICF. • *Legal File*—CAUW: Letter, memo (1925); contract (1925); agreement (1925); talent agreement (1925, 1927-29). • *Photograph/Still*—CAA, CAUT (Jessen Collection), DCG (Quigley Photographic Archives), GBBF, NJFL, NYAM, NYPL, WICF. • *Publicity Release*—CAA: Unknown studio (1924). • *Scrapbook*—NYPL (also in R. Locke Collection). • *Studio Biography*—CAA: Paramount.

FREDERICK, Pauline (Beatrice Pauline or Pauline Beatrice Libbey), Boston, MA, 1881/85-1938.

Renowned stage actress Pauline Frederick was one of the Famous Players who established a firm foothold in movies with roles in such films as *The Eternal City, Zaza, Sapho* and *Madame X.* After appearing somewhat less frequently during the latter 1920s, "The Girl with the Topaz Eyes" brought her commanding presence and low-pitched voice to the talkies where she appeared in many supporting roles.

PUBLISHED SOURCES

• *Books*—Bibliography: *The Idols of Silence.* General: *Behind the Screen; Blue Book of the Screen; Famous Film Folk; Immortals of the Screen; Ladies in Distress; More From Hollywood; Who's Who on the Screen.* Credits: *Filmarama* (v. I and II); *Forty Years of Screen Credits; Twenty Years of Silents; Who Was Who on the Screen.* Biography/Autobiography: *Pauline Frederick.* Encyclopedic Works: *Film Encyclopedia; Filmlexicon degli Autori e delle Opere; Halliwell's Filmgoer's Companion; The Illustrated Who's Who of the Cinema; The Movie Makers; Notable American Women, 1607-1950; The Oxford Companion to Film; The Picturegoer's Who's Who and Encyclopedia of the Screen To-day; Quinlan's Illustrated Registry of Film Stars; Who Was Who in the Theatre; Who's Who in Hollywood; Who's Who on the Stage* (1908); *The World Almanac Who's Who of Film; The World Film Encyclopedia.* Pictorial: *Silent Portraits; They Had Faces Then.* Filmography: *Hollywood on the Palisades.*

• *Periodicals*—The following periodical articles are in addition to those included in the library listings below: *Cosmopolitan* (May 1913, Dec. 1914); *Green Book Magazine* (May 1913); *Theatre* (June 1913, Nov. 1915, Apr. 1923); *National Magazine* (Jan. 1915); *Photoplay* (Feb. 1915, Oct. 1915, Jan. 1917, June 1917, May 1919, May 1920, Sept. 1921, Apr. 1923, Sept. 1926); *Motion Picture Classic* (June 1916, Oct. 1916, Jan. 1917, Sept. 1917, Nov. 1917, May 1922, Mar. 1929); *Motion Picture Magazine* (Dec. 1918, Oct. 1919, Feb. 1922); *Pantomime* (Dec. 17, 1921); *Theatre Guild Magazine* (Apr. 1932); *Films in Review* (Mar. 1965); *Avant-Scene* (Jan. 1-15, 1981).

ARCHIVAL MATERIALS

• *Caricature*—NYPL. • *Clipping File*—CAA: Marriage/divorce (1922, 1930, 1934, undated); Warner contract (1928); newsphoto; article (1927); film appearance (1919, 1928, 1930); stage appearance (1926, 1929); bankruptcy (1933-34); legal problem (1930, 1933); illness (1929, 1936-37); article (1935, 1983); accident (1932); obituary (1938). CAUT: PF's ghost haunts theater (1984). NYMA: Obituary (1938). Periodical article: *Classic Film/Video Images* (May 1979). NYMN: Newsphotos; article (1935); illness (1936); marriage (1934); obituary (1938). NYPL (also in C. & L. Brown Collection): Newsphotos (numerous); biography (1927); stage appearance (1920s, 1930s); article (1936, 1938); review of *Pauline Frederick* (1940); legal problem (1923); marriage/separation (1922, 1934); returns to stage (1932); obituary (1938). Periodical article: *Films in Review* (Feb. 1965) (filmography). • *Other Clipping File*—AZSU (Jimmy Starr Collection), CASF, CAUB, GBBF, MAH, MIDL, OHCL, OHSU, PAPL, WICF. • *Correspondence*—NYPL. • *Filmography*—NYMA, NYPL (incomplete). • *Legal File*—CAUW: Talent agreement (1924); document (1929); release (1928); contract (1928); letter (1928). • *Oral History*—NYCO: Mentioned in the following interviews: Katherine Beebe, Dana Carver, Lila Lee. • *Photograph/Still*—AZSU (Jimmy Starr Collection), CAA (also in Hollywood Studio Museum Collection), CAHL, CALM, CASF, CASU, CAUT (Jessen Collection), CAUU, CNDA, DCG (Quigley Photographic Archives), GBBF, IAU (Junkin Collection), MIDL, NJFL, NJPT, NYAM, NYB (Underwood Collection), NYCU (Bulliet Collection) (Dramatic

Museum Portraits), NYEH, NYMN, NYPL, NYSU, OHCL, TNUT (Clarence Brown Collection), TXSM, TXU, WICF. • *Play Program* – CAHL: 1926, 1928-29, 1931. CASF. • *Publicity Release* – AZSU (Jimmy Starr Collection). NYMA: Unknown studio. • *Scrapbook* – CASU (Stark Collection), NJPT (Yeandle Collection), NYPL (also in C. & L. Brown Collection) (also in R. Locke Collection) (also in Players Collection), TNUT (Clarence Brown Collection). • *Studio Biography* – CAA: Paramount (1931).

GARBO, Greta (Greta Gustafsson), Stockholm, Sweden, 1905-1990.

Considered the premiere film actress of the 1930s, Greta Garbo came to MGM in 1926 after a brief European career. It was her teaming with top romantic star John Gilbert (q.v.) in *Flesh and the Devil* (1927) which propelled her to stardom and began her rise to the status of Hollywood icon. The lushly mounted melodramas in which she appeared (*Mata Hari*, *Anna Karenina*, *Camille*) were enough to keep her legions of fans happy through the mid-1930s but a change of image was thought to be advisable. Her first comedy, 1939's *Ninotchka*, was a success but her second, *Two-Faced Woman* (1941), marked the end of her legendary career.

PUBLISHED SOURCES

• *Books* – **Bibliography:** *The Idols of Silence*. **General:** *The American Movie Goddess*; *The Book of People*; *Cecil Beaton*; *The Celluloid Sacrifice*; *Classics of the Silent Screen*; *Close Ups*; *Conversations With Greta Garbo*; *Co-Starring Famous Women and Alcohol*; *Curtains*; *Customs and Characters*; *The Faces of Hollywood*; *Famous Stars of Filmdom (Women)*; *Fifty Super Stars*; *Garbo* (Screen Greats); *Garbo* (Steiger); *The Great Movie Stars*; *Great Stars of Hollywood's Golden Age*; *Greta Garbo* (Durgnat/Kobal); *Greta Garbo* (Kuhn);

Hollywood (Kanin); *Hollywood: the Pioneers*; *Hollywood and the Great Stars*; *Hollywood Exiles*; *Hollywood Goddesses*; *Hollywood Hall of Fame*; *The Hollywood Reporter Star Profiles*; *Hollywood's Great Love Teams*; *How I Broke Into the Movies*; *Les Immortels du Cinema*; *Ladies in Distress*; *The Legend of Garbo*; *The Lion's Share*; *Love Goddesses of the Movies*; *Love, Laughter and Tears*; *Mae West, Greta Garbo*; *Mayer and Thalberg*; *The MGM Girls*; *The MGM Stock Company*; *More From Hollywood*; *Movie Star*; *The Movie Stars*; *The Movie Stars Story*; *The National Society of Film Critics on the Movie Star*; *Popcorn Venus*; *The Saturday Evening Post Movie Book*; *Screen Personalities*; *Star Acting*; *Stardom*; *The Stars* (Schickel); *Stars!*; *The Stars Appear*; *Starstruck*; *Strangers in Hollywood*; *Those Fabulous Movie Years*; *Venus in Hollywood*; *Walking With Garbo*; *What the Stars Told Me*; *Who's Who at Metro Goldwyn Mayer*; *Women and the Cinema*. **Credits:** *Filmarama* (v. II); *Forty Years of Screen Credits*; *Twenty Years of Silents*. **Encyclopedic Works:** *A Biographical Dictionary of Film*; *Cinema, a Critical Dictionary*; *A Companion to the Movies*; *Contemporary Theatre, Film, and Television* (v. 9); *Current Biography* (1956, 1990); *A Dictionary of the Cinema*; *Film Encyclopedia*; *Filmlexicon degli Autori e delle Opere*; *Halliwell's Filmgoer's Companion*; *The Illustrated Encyclopedia of the World's Great Movie Stars and Their Films*; *The Illustrated Who's Who of the Cinema*; *International Dictionary of Films and Filmmakers* (v. 3); *The International Encyclopedia of Film*; *The International Motion Picture Almanac* (1975-80); *The Movie Makers*; *The Oxford Companion to Film*; *The Picturegoer's Who's Who and Encyclopedia of the Screen To-day*; *Quinlan's Illustrated Registry of Film Stars*; *Who's Who in Hollywood*; *The World Almanac Who's Who of Film*; *The World Encyclopedia of the Film*; *The World Film Encyclopedia*. **Biography/Autobiography:** *The Divine Garbo*; *Garbo* (Bainbridge); *Garbo* (Billquist); *Garbo*

(Brion); *Garbo* (Gronowicz); *Garbo* (Paris); *Garbo* (Walker); *Garbo* (Zierold); *Greta Garbo* (Agel); *Greta Garbo* (Ducout); *Greta Garbo* (Laing); *Greta Garbo* (Wild); *Greta Garbo's Saga*; *Here Lies the Heart*; *The Life Story of Greta Garbo*; *People in a Diary*; *The Private Life of Greta Garbo*; *Vida de Greta Garbo*. **Pictorial:** *Cinema Star Albums* (A Series); *Four Fabulous Faces*; *Garbo* (Sjolander); *Greta Garbo* (Rizzoli); *The Image Makers*; *Leading Ladies*; *Life and Death in Hollywood*; *The Revealing Eye*; *Silent Portraits*; *They Had Faces Then*. **Catalog:** *The Greta Garbo Collection.* **Films:** *The Complete Films of Greta Garbo*; *Die Gottliche Garbo*; *The Great Garbo*; *Greta Garbo* (Corliss); *What a Bunch of Characters*. **Recordings:** *Hollywood on Record.* **Thesis:** *Greta Garbo* (Winstead); *Greta Garbo's Film Transformation of the Femme Fatale*. **Factoids:** *Star Stats.*

• *Periodicals* — The following periodical articles are in addition to those included in the library listings below: *Motion Picture Classic* (May 1926, Aug. 1927, Feb. 1929, Jan. 1930, Mar. 1931, June 1931); *Motion Picture Magazine* (May 1926, Dec. 1926, Feb. 1928, Aug. 1931, Oct. 1931, Jan. 1932, Mar. 1932, May-July 1932, May 1933, July 1933, Oct. 1933, Mar. 1934, June 1934, Dec. 1934, Apr. 1935, July 1935, Sept. 1935, Dec. 1935, Aug. 1936, Dec. 1936, Sept. 1937); *Photoplay* (May 1926, Feb. 1927, Apr. 1927, Apr.-June 1928, Jan. 1930, Apr.-June 1930, Aug.-Oct. 1930, Feb.-Apr. 1931, July 1931, Sept. 1931, Dec. 1931-Mar. 1932, Apr.-May 1932, Aug.-Nov. 1932, Jan. 1933, Apr. 1933, July-Aug. 1933, Oct. 1933, Dec. 1933-Jan. 1934, Mar. 1934, May 1934, Sept. 1934, Nov. 1934, May 1935, Sept. 1935, July 1936, Sept. 1936, Dec. 1936, Jan. 1938, July 1939, Mar. 1942, Aug. 1944, Nov. 1957, Apr. 1958, June 1961); *Theatre* (Dec. 1927); *Vanity Fair* (June 1928, Feb. 1932, June 1934); *Pictorial Review* (Oct. 1929, Jan. 1935); *Atlántico* (Feb. 16, 1930); *Commonweal* (Mar. 26, 1930); *Fortune* (Oct. 1930); *Silver Screen* (Jan. 1931, May 1931, June 1931, Oct. 1931, Mar. 1932, June 1932, Mar. 1933, May

1933, Sept. 1933, Nov. 1933, Dec. 1934, Aug. 1935, May 1936, Dec. 1936, Oct. 1939, Mar. 1940); *New Yorker* (Mar. 7, 1931); *Saturday Evening Post* (May 30, 1931, Mar. 26, 1932); *Living Age* (June 1931); *Saturday Review* (June 13, 1931); *Movie Classic* (Sept.-Oct. 1931, Feb.-Mar. 1932, July-Aug. 1932, July 1933, Sept. 1933, Nov. 1933, Feb.-Mar. 1934, June 1934, July 1935, Oct. 1935, Feb. 1937); *The Nation* (Nov. 11, 1931, Jan. 24, 1934, Dec. 19, 1934); *Literary Digest* (May 7, 1932, Jan. 13, 1934, Sept. 21, 1935); *Cinema Digest* (Aug. 22, 1932, Jan. 9, 1933, Apr. 10, 1933, May 8, 1933); *New Republic* (Sept. 28, 1932, May 7, 1990); *Close-Up* (Dec. 1932); *Delineator* (Oct. 1933); *True Confessions* (Feb. 1935); *Stage* (Oct. 1935); *Visages et Contes du Cinema* (May 15, 1936); *Theatre World* (Apr. 1937); *Life* (Sept. 29, 1941, Feb. 19, 1951, Oct. 8, 1951, Apr. 5, 1963); *Theatre Arts Magazine* (Dec. 1937); *American-Scandinavian Review* (1938); *Screen Book* (Jan. 1940); *Movies and the People Who Make Them* (no. 2, 1940); *Lion's Roar* (Nov. 1941); *Good Housekeeping* (Jan. 1942); *Newsweek* (Sept. 8, 1947, Jan. 16, 1961, Mar. 11, 1963, Mar. 29, 1976, July 17, 1978); *Time* (Aug. 30, 1948, June 6, 1949, Sept. 21, 1977); *Arizona Quarterly* (Spring 1949); *Coronet* (July 1949); *Screen Guide* (Oct. 1949); *Harper's Bazaar* (Oct. 1949); *World Review* (Dec. 1949); *Reader's Digest* (July 1952); *New Statesman and Nation* (Dec. 13, 1952); *Films and Filming* (Mar. 1955, July 1955, Sept. 1955, Aug. 1956, Dec. 1956, June 1959, Mar. 1962, Oct. 1979, May 1984); *Cosmopolitan* (Oct. 1956); *Sight and Sound* (Winter 1958/59); *Contemporary Review* (Dec. 1960); *McCall's* (Aug. 1962); *Show* (June 1963); *Screen Education Studies* (Sept./Oct. 1963); *Seventeen* (Jan. 1964); *December* (Spring 1965); *Cinema* (France) (May 1965, May 1984, May 1990); *Players Showcase* (Summer 1965); *Moviegoer* (Summer 1966); *Journal of Popular Culture* (Summer 1968); *Arts in Society* (Fall-Winter 1968); *Film Comment* (Summer 1970, July-Aug. 1990); *Film* (London) (Spring 1971, Nov. 1980); *Cinema Que* (Sept. 1972);

Silent Picture (Autumn 1972); *Focus on Film* (Summer 1973); *Liberty* (Fall 1973); *Viva* (Jan. 1974); *Ecran* (Aug.-Sept. 1974, June 1976); *Kinoizkustvo* (Oct. 1974); *Biography News* (Oct. 1974); *Films in Review* (Feb. 1975, Nov.-Dec. 1991); *American Film* (Oct. 1975, May 1984, Nov. 1987, Aug. 1990); *Telecine* (Apr. 1976); *Cinéma d'Aujourd'hui* (May-June 1976); *Kino* (June 1976); *Cinema* (Romania) (June 1976); *Film und Fernsehen* (no. 7, 1979, no. 9, 1980, no. 9, 1985); *Image* (no. 1, 1979); *Film Dope* (Sept. 1979) (filmography); *Cinema 2002* (Jan. 1980); *Cine* (May 1980); *American Classic Screen* (Summer 1980); *Cinema Nuovo* (Aug. 1980, Mar.-Apr. 1990); *Avant-Scène* (Mar. 15, 1981); *Screen Actor* (no. 2, 1981/82); *Deux Ecrans* (Apr. 1982); *Cult Movie* (Nov.-Dec. 1982); *Cinématographe* (Jan. 1983, Jan. 1986); *Atlantic Monthly* (Jan. 1983); *Skoop* (Feb.-Mar. 1983, June 1990); *Esquire* (Mar. 1983); *Skrien* (Sept. 1983, June-July 1990); *Hollywood Studio Magazine* (Sept. 1984, Nov. 1987, May 1989, Sept. 1990); *Classic Images* (Dec. 1984, Mar. 1986, Nov. 1986, May 1990); *Positif* (June 1985); *Critical Inquiry* (June 1985); *Segnocinema* (Sept. 1985); *TV World* (Oct. 1985); *Filmfaust* (Dec. 1985-Jan. 1986); *Chaplin* (no. 208, 1987, no. 228, 1990); *Screen* (Summer 1988); *Yale Review* (no. 4, 1988); *Filmkunst* (no. 121, 1989); *Film & Kino* (no. 3, 1990); *Quaderni di Cinema* (Mar.-June 1990); *Z Filmtidsskrift* (no. 33, 1990); *Filmnews* (no. 4, 1990); *Imagine* (Spring 1990); *New Statesman and Society* (Apr. 20, 1990); *U.S. News and World Report* (Apr. 30, 1990); *National Review* (May 14, 1990); *EPD Film* (June 1990); *Revue du Cinema* (June 1990); *Film Monthly* (July 1990); *Film en Televisie + Video* (July-Aug. 1990); *Stars* (Sept. 1990) (filmography); *Business Week* (Nov. 5, 1990); *Premiere* (Winter 1991); *Art and Antiques* (Feb. 1991); *Architectural Digest* (Apr. 1992); *Bulletin of Bibliography* (Mar. 1993).

MEDIA

The Divine Garbo (video).

ARCHIVAL MATERIALS

• *Caricature* — NYMN, OHCL. • *Clip-*

ping File — CAA: Marriage (1927); MGM contract (1927); illness (1927); reclusive nature (1930, 1932); newsphotos; citizenship (1932, 1948, 1950-51); return to Sweden (1932, 1946); return to Hollywood (1932, 1953); romance (1934, 1937, 1951, 1954); leading men (1934); article (1936, 1938, 1949, 1951, 1954, 1956, 1960, 1962-63, 1965, 1970, 1973, 1980-83, 1985, 1990); inherits estate (1947); comeback (1948-51, 1955, 1963, 1966-67, 1969); travels to Paris (1952); wealth (1953); review of *Garbo* (Bainbridge) (1955); excerpt from *Current Biography* (1955); 60th birthday (1965); film festival (1966, 1968-70, 1980, 1983, 1990); memoirs (1972); walks in New York (1977); repudiates biography (1978, 1990); review of *Garbo* (Walker) (1981); secret agent (1980); 75th birthday (1980); 80th birthday (1985); autograph (1982); review of *Garbo* (Gronowicz) (1990); sale of effects (1990); estate (1990); biography (1990); obituary (1990). Periodical articles: *Vanity Fair* (July 1927, Sept. 1930); *Photoplay* (July-Aug. 1929); *Movie Mirror* (Dec. 1931); *Pictorial Review* (July 1933); *Liberty* (July 27, 1929, Oct. 22, 1932, Aug. 25, 1934, May 30, 1936); *Look* (Mar. 1937, Sept. 6, 1955, Sept. 8, 1970); *Coronet* (July 1951); *Films in Review* (Dec. 1951 [filmography], Jan. 1952, Nov. 1979); *Collier's* (Mar. 1, 1952); *Harper's Bazaar* (Apr. 1952); *Life* (Jan. 10-24, 1955, Nov. 12, 1971, Spring 1989); *Pix* (Sept. 10, 1955); *Show* (June 1963); *Films and Filming* (Sept. 1963, Nov. 1964, Aug. 1965, Sept. 1985); *MD* (July 1964); *Diners' Club Magazine* (Dec. 1964); *Newsweek* (July 22, 1968); *Vogue* (Nov. 1, 1968, Dec. 1981); *McCall's* (Aug. 1969, Dec. 1971); *Hollywood Studio Magazine* (Nov. 1971, May 1973, May 1978); *Screen Greats* (no. 8, 1972); *W* (July 26, 1974); *Modern Maturity* (Aug.-Sept. 1974, Feb.-Mar. 1980); *Cosmopolitan* (Dec. 1974); *Esquire* (Sept. 1975); *People* (Apr. 12, 1976, Apr. 30, 1990); *Ladies' Home Journal* (Apr. 1976); *Viva* (May 1976); *Books Digest* (July 1976); *Cine Revue* (Oct. 25, 1979, Apr. 25, 1985); *American Film* (Oct. 1980); *Saturday Review* (Mar.-Apr. 1985); *New York Magazine* (May 21,

1990). CAFI: Article (1974, 1977, 1979–80, 1984–86, 1990); film festival (1968, 1970, 1979–80, 1983, 1985, 1990); biography (1978); sale of effects (1990); home (1983); 80th birthday (1985); newsphoto; review of *Garbo* (Walker) (1980–81); review of *Garbo* (Gronowicz) (1990); obituary (1990). Periodical articles: *Look* (Sept. 8, 1970); *Harper's Bazaar* (Nov. 1972); *McCall's* (Aug. 1979) *American Film* (Oct. 1980); *Saturday Review* (Mar.-Apr. 1985); *American Movie Classics* (June 1988); *Life* (Spring 1989). CAUT: Article (1954, 1965–66, 1975, 1978–80, 1985); newsphotos (numerous); film appearance (1980); biography (1978); film festival (1980). Periodical articles: *Time* (Mar. 14, 1938); *Sight and Sound* (Apr.-June 1954) *Life* (Jan. 10-31, 1955); *Look* (Sept. 8, 1970). CAUU (also in McCormick Collection): Article (1953, 1977, 1979–80, 1985–86, undated); citizenship (1951); film festival (1980); denounces Gronowicz book (1978); newsphotos; review of *Garbo* (Gronowicz) (1990); obituary (1990). Periodical articles: *Photoplay Studies* (1937); *Collier's* (Mar. 1, 1952); *Life* (Jan. 10, 1955). NYMN: Newsphotos; honor; article (1936–37, 1940); marriage (1937); legal problem (1937); buys home; review of *Garbo* (Bainbridge); 80th birthday (1985); obituary (1990). Periodical articles: *Life* (Nov. 8, 1937, Jan. 10, 1955); *Look* (Sept. 8, 1970). NYPL: PARTIAL CONTENTS: Sale of effects (1990); article (1970–71, 1974–75?, 1977, 1979, 1984–85, 1990); review of *Garbo* (Gronowicz) (1990); estate (1990–91); privacy (1990); newsphotos; biography (1980); silent films (1978); review of *Conversations with Greta Garbo* (1992); Gronowicz biography (1977–79); review of *Garbo* (Walker) (1981); 80th birthday (1985); obituary (1990). Periodical articles: *Liberty* (Summer 1971, Summer 1974); *Classic Film Collector* (Spring 1973); *Modern Maturity* (Feb.-Mar. 1980); *People* (Apr. 30, 1990); *Newsweek* (Apr. 30, 1990); *Time* (Apr. 30, 1990); *New York* (May 21, 1990); *Quest* (Summer 1990); *Screen* (undated). • *Other Clipping File* – AZSU (Jimmy Starr Collection), CNDA, GBBF, MAH, MIDL, NYMA, OHCL, WICF. • *Correspondence* – NYPL (C. & L. Brown Collection): 1930. • *Filmography* – CAA, NYEH. • *Lecture* – CAUS: Discussed in Christopher Isherwood's *Six Lectures* (recording). • *Oral History* – CAUS: Mentioned in: C.E. Carle interview. NYCO: Mentioned in the following interviews: Walter Abel, Lew Ayres, Pandro Berman, Charles Brackett, Johnny Mack Brown, Bennett Cerf, Delmer Daves, Reginald Denny, Melvyn Douglas, Jessica Dragonette, Lillian Gish, James Wong Howe, Nunnally Johnson, Lila Lee, Josh Logan, Anita Loos, Myrna Loy, Jeanette MacDonald, Rouben Mamoulian, Joseph Mankiewicz, Frances Marion, Joel McCrea, Conrad Nagel, Reginald Owen, Geraldine Page, Charles Poletti, Otto Preminger, Greta Rapper, Richard Rodgers, Adela St. Johns, Roger Straus, Blanche Sweet, Carey Wilson, Jerome Zerbe. • *Photograph/Still* – CAA (also in Hollywood Studio Museum Collection) (also in MGM Collection), CAHL, CALM, CAUS, CAUT (Jessen Collection) (Portrait File), CAUU, CNDA, DCG (Quigley Photographic Archives), IAU (Blees Collection), NYAM, NYB (Bettmann/UPI Collection) (Penguin Collection) (Springer Collection) (Underwood Collection), NYCU (Dramatic Museum Portraits) (Palmer Collection), NYEH, NYMN, NYPL, OHCL, OHSU, TNUT (Clarence Brown Collection), TXSM, TXU, WICF. • *Press Kit* – OHCL. • *Reminiscence* – MISU: John Gielgud and Ruth Gordon talk about GG (recording). • *Scrapbook* – NYMA, NYPL, WICF. • *Studio Biography* – CAA: MGM (1930, 1932-33, 1939-41). • *Telephone Calls* – CTW (Sam Green Collection): About 100 hours of recorded conversations between GG and Green, circa 1970s. *NOTE*: Only transcriptions will be available for researchers beginning in late 1995.

GARDNER, Helen, ca. 1880s–1968.

A screen star from about 1911 in vehicles like *Cleopatra*, *Vanity Fair* (also known as *Becky Sharp*) and *A*

Sister to Carmen, Helen Gardner was one of the earliest "vamps" and a pioneer woman producer with her own production company. Her period of stardom was brief but she continued to make sporadic appearances in supporting roles through the mid-1920s.

PUBLISHED SOURCES

• *Books – General: The Big V.* **Credits:** *Filmarama* (v. I and II); *Who Was Who on Screen.* **Encyclopedic Works:** *Film Encyclopedia; Who's Who in Hollywood.* **Pictorial:** *Silent Portraits.*
• *Periodicals – Photoplay* (Jan. 1914); *Motography* (Dec. 26, 1914); *Motion Picture Magazine* (Apr. 1915); *New Yorker* (Jan. 9, 1960).

ARCHIVAL MATERIALS

• *Clipping File* – CAA: Obituary (1969). NYPL: Newsphotos; obituary (1968). • *Other Clipping File* – MAH, MIDL, NYMA (Photoplay Collection), TXU. • *Photograph/Still* – CAA (Hollywood Studio Museum Collection), CAUT (Jessen Collection), DCG (Quigley Photographic Archives), GBBF, NYB (Bettmann/UPI Collection), NYEH, NYPL, TXU. • *Scrapbook* – NYPL (R. Locke Collection).

GARON, Pauline (Marie P. Garon), Montreal, Canada, 1900/04-1965.

After appearing in DeMille's *Adam's Rib* near the beginning of her film career, blonde and perky Pauline Garon's screen persona was that of the liberated flapper. Although a popular star when the silents ended, her type of role was passé and she was relegated to lesser roles in a number of talkies until about 1938. She was married to Lowell Sherman (q.v.).

PUBLISHED SOURCES

• *Books – General: Blue Book of the Screen; Famous Film Folk.* **Credits:** *Filmarama* (v. I and II); *Forty Years of Screen Credits; Twenty Years of Silents; Who Was Who on Screen.* **Encyclopedic Works:** *Film Encyclopedia; Filmlexicon*

degli Autori e delle Opere; Who's Who in Hollywood. **Pictorial:** *Silent Portraits.*
• *Periodicals – Photoplay* (Jan. 1923); *Motion Picture Classic* (May 1923); *Films in Review* (Feb. 1970) (Wampas Baby Stars).

ARCHIVAL MATERIALS

• *Clipping File* – CAA: Film appearance (1922-24); marriage (1953); obituary (1965). CAUT: Injury (1920s); divorce (1929). NYMN: Newsphotos; article (1937); stage appearance (1959); injury; obituary (1965). NYPL: Marriage (1920s, 1930s); works as extra (1930s); article (1923, undated); newsphotos; career (1923). • *Other Clipping File* – GBBF, NYMA (Photoplay Collection), OHCL, PAPL, WICF. • *Correspondence* – NYPL (C. & L. Brown Collection): 1929. • *Legal File* – CAUW: Talent agreement (1929). • *Photograph/Still* – CAA (also in Hollywood Studio Museum Collection) (also in MGM Collection), CAOC (Kiesling Collection), CNDA, DCG (Quigley Photographic Archives), GBBF, NJFL, NJPT, NYB (Underwood Collection), NYEH, NYPL, NYSU, OHCL, TXU (A. Davis Collection), WICF. • *Studio Biography* – NYMA: Photoplay.

GAYNOR, Janet (Laura Gainer), Philadelphia, PA, 1906-1984.

Redhaired Janet Gaynor began as an extra in 1924, progressed to her first major role in *The Johnstown Flood* (1925), and thence to stardom in 1927's *Seventh Heaven* and *Sunrise.* For the latter two (as well as *Street Angel*), she won the first Best Actress Academy Award. She and Charles Farrell (q.v.) became one of the major romantic teams of the late silents and early talkie period in a dozen films, including musicals. She made some successful films during the 1930s but her career was winding down when she appeared in the first version of *A Star Is Born* (1937). She left Hollywood soon thereafter, to return only once for a minor film in 1957, but she subsequently made stage appearances.

PUBLISHED SOURCES

• *Books*—**Bibliography:** *The Idols of Silence*; *Janet Gaynor*. **General:** *Famous Stars of Filmdom (Women)*; *The Fox Girls*; *The Great Movie Stars*; *Hollywood Greats of the Golden Years*; *Hollywood's Great Love Teams*; *Movie Star*; *The Movie Stars Story*; *The Oscar People*; *Return Engagement*; *Screen Personalities*; *Showcase*. **Credits:** *Filmarama* (v. II); *Forty Years of Screen Credits*; *Twenty Years of Silents*. **Encyclopedic Works:** *A Biographical Dictionary of Film*; *A Companion to the Movies*; *The Complete Encyclopedia of Popular Music and Jazz*; *Film Encyclopedia*; *Filmlexicon degli Autori e delle Opere*; *Halliwell's Filmgoer's Companion*; *The Illustrated Encyclopedia of the World's Great Movie Stars and Their Films*; *The Illustrated Who's Who of the Cinema*; *International Dictionary of Films and Filmmakers* (v. 3); *The Movie Makers*; *The Oxford Companion to Film*; *The Picturegoer's Who's Who and Encyclopedia of the Screen To-day*; *Quinlan's Illustrated Registry of Film Stars*; *Variety Who's Who in Show Business*; *Who's Who in Hollywood*; *The World Almanac Who's Who of Film*; *The World Encyclopedia of the Film*; *The World Film Encyclopedia*. **Nostalgia:** *Whatever Became of...* (2nd). **Pictorial:** *The Image Makers*; *Leading Ladies*; *Pictures of Movie Stars, with Stories*; *Silent Portraits*; *They Had Faces Then*. **Factoids:** *Star Stats*.

• *Periodicals*—The following periodical articles are in addition to those included in the library listings below: *Photoplay* (Jan. 1927, Oct. 1927, Dec. 1928-Jan. 1929; Aug. 1930, Nov. 1930, Apr. 1931, July 1932, Mar.-Apr. 1933, Aug. 1933, Nov. 1933, July 1937, Jan. 1938, Nov. 1939, June 1974); *Motion Picture Magazine* (Aug. 1927, Feb. 1928, Apr. 1930, Feb. 1931, June 1931, Dec. 1931, June 1932, Nov. 1932, Mar. 1933, Nov. 1934, Aug.-Sept. 1936, Sept. 1937); *Motion Picture Classic* (Sept. 1927); *Pictorial Review* (Mar. 1928, Dec. 1936);

Fortune (Oct. 1930); *Silver Screen* (Nov. 1930, Nov. 1931, Nov. 1932, July 1933, Dec. 1934, Nov. 1939); *Pictures and Picturegoer* (Aug. 8, 1931, Apr. 6-20, 1935); *Movie Classic* (Dec. 1932, Mar. 1933, Sept. 1933, Sept.-Oct. 1934, Sept. 1935, May 1936); *Cinema Digest* (Jan. 16, 1933, June 5, 1933); *Shadowplay* (Feb. 1934); *Screen Book* (Aug. 1937, Nov. 1938); *Vogue* (Jan. 1, 1945); *House and Garden* (Oct. 1949); *Films in Review* (Mar. 1960, May 1965, Feb. 1970 [Wampas Baby Stars], Nov. 1984); *Newsweek* (Apr. 15, 1963, Sept. 24, 1984); *Look* (Nov. 3, 1970); *Film Comment* (Jan.-Feb. 1974); *Films Illustrated* (Oct. 1979); *Film Dope* (Dec. 1979); *Time* (Sept. 24, 1984); *Cinematographe* (Sept.-Oct. 1984); *Cine Revue* (Oct. 4, 1984) *Celuloide* (Oct.-Dec. 1984); *Revue du Cinema* (Nov. 1984); *Architectural Digest* (Apr. 1992).

ARCHIVAL MATERIALS

• *Clipping File*—CAA: Film appearance (1925-27, 1930, 1936, 1956-57); ranch in Brazil (1955-56, 1959, undated); engagement/marriage/divorce (1927, 1929, 1932, 1939, 1964); salary (1927); illness (1928, 1930, 1932, 1984); article (1930-31, 1934-35, 1949, 1963, 1973, 1980); Fox contract (1933); rescued from drowning (1936); home (1971, 1973); film festival (1979); draft article by JG (1936); radio appearance (1951); TV appearance (1953-54, 1961, 1965, 1980); stage appearance (1959, 1968, 1979-81); nostalgia (1962, 1981); paintings (1974, 1976); honor (1978); review of *Harold and Maude* (play) (1980); interview (1982); accident (1982-83); obituary (1984). Periodical articles: *Film Pictorial* (Jan. 1936); *Screen and Radio Weekly* (1936?); *Life* (May 1937); *Films in Review* (Oct. 1959). CAFI: Article (1976, 1979-80, 1982, undated); accident (1982); newsphotos; obituary (1984). CAPS: Accident (1982); article (1973, 1980-81); Palm Springs ranch (1971); paintings (1973, 1982); obituary (1984). Periodical article: *American Artist* (Feb. 1982). CAUT: Article (1929, 1973, 1976); residence in Brazil (1950s); marriage (1929); accident (1982); newsphotos; stage appearance (1979-80); obituary (1984). CAUU: Accident (1982); article (1973, 1980, 1984); honor (1978); stage appearance (1979); obituary (1984). NYMA (also in Photoplay Collection): Injury (1982-83); newsphotos (numerous); paintings (1976); film festival (1979); booklet for film festival (1979); stage appearance (1979-80); article (1954, 1977, 1979-81); review of *Harold and Maude* (play) (1980); honor (1978); illness (1930); obituary (1984). Periodical articles: *Film Fan Monthly* (Sept. 1982); *After Dark* (Feb. 1980). NYPL: PARTIAL CONTENTS: Article (1984); obituary (1984). • *Other Clipping File*—AZSU (Jimmy Starr Collection), CAUB, CNDA, GBBF, MABU (see Collection), MAH, MIDL, NYSU, OCHL, PAPL, TXU, WICF. • *Collection*—MABU: Over 50 scrapbooks containing clippings and stills. • *Correspondence*—CAA (Hedda Hopper Collection): 1940, 1956. MABU (Robert Carson Collection). NYMN: 1964. NYPL: Letters (C. & L. Brown Collection) (1940s); other (1971, undated). • *Interview*—GBBF (Hollywood Collection): Transcript of interview for *Hollywood* (TV series). • *Legal File*—CAUT (Twentieth Century-Fox Collection): Letter, memo (1926-27, 1929-36, 1957, 1962); birth certificate (1906); option (1928, 1935); agreement (1925-27, 1929, 1933, 1935, 1957); loanout (1935); contract summary (1957). Matters of interest in this collection include an intensive search by the studio for JG's birth certificate to determine her true age, and her desire for better billing, compensation and choice of roles. • *Oral History*—NYCO: Interviewed in 1958. Also mentioned in the following interviews: Marc Connelly, George Cukor, Kitty Carlisle Hart, Joel McCrea, Ginger Rogers, David Selznick. • *Photograph/Still*—CAA (also in Hollywood Studio Museum Collection) (also in MGM Collection), CAHL, CALM, CAOC (Kiesling Collection), CAPH, CASF, CAUB, CAUS, CAUT (Jessen Collection) (Portrait File), CAUU (also in A. Slide Collection), CNDA, DCG (Quigley Photographic Archives), GBBF, MABU (see Collection), NYAM, NYB (Bettmann/ UPI Collection) (Penguin Collection)

(Springer Collection) (Underwood Collection), NYCU (Dramatic Museum Portraits) (Palmer Collection), NYEH, NYMN, NYPL, NYSU, OHCL, TXU, WICF. • *Publicity Release*—CAA: Fox (1933-36, 1957). CAUT: Fox (1957). CAUU: American Broadcasting Company (1980). • *Reminiscence*—MISU: JG discusses her acting career and her life as a painter (1976 [recording]). • *Scrapbook*—MABU (see Collection), NYAM, NYMA, NYPL, WICF. • *Studio Biography*—CAA: Fox (1927-28, 1930-31, 1936). CAFI: 1954. CAUT: Fox (1936). CAUU. NYMA: Photoplay.

GERAGHTY, Carmelita, Rushville, IN, 1901-1966.

Vivacious Carmelita Geraghty was a dependable leading lady or second lead of 1920s films like *Black Oxen, The Great Gatsby, My Best Girl* and *Passionate Youth*. Her transition to talkies was made smoothly enough and she continued to appear in films, mostly of the "B" variety, until 1935.

PUBLISHED SOURCES

• *Books*—**General:** *Sweethearts of the Sage; The Truth About the Movies.* **Credits:** *Filmarama* (v. II); *Forty Years of Screen Credits; Twenty Years of Silents; Who Was Who on Screen.* **Encyclopedic Works:** *Filmlexicon degli Autori e delle Opere; The Picturegoer's Who's Who and Encyclopedia of the Screen To-day; Who's Who in Hollywood.* • *Periodicals*—*Photoplay* (July 1924, Sept. 1928); *Films in Review* (Feb. 1970) (Wampas Baby Stars); *Classic Images* (May 1991).

ARCHIVAL MATERIALS

• *Clipping File*—CAA: Marriage (1934); obituary (1966). CAUT: Obituary (1966). NYMA (also in Photoplay Collection): Obituary (1966). NYMN: Newsphotos; obituary (1966). NYPL: Injury; newsphotos; marriage; obituary (1966). • *Other Clipping File*—GBBF, PAPL, WICF. • *Legal File*—CAA (Sennett Collection): Contract (1927); option (1927); release (1928). CAUW: Talent agreement

(1930). • *Photograph/Still* — AZSU (Jimmy Starr Collection), CAA (also in Hollywood Studio Museum Collection), CAUT (Jessen Collection), DCG (Quigley Photographic Archives), GBBF, NJPT, NYEH, NYPL, OHCL, TXU, WICF. • *Publicity Release* — CAA (Mack Sennett Collection): (1927). • *Studio Biography* — CAA (Mack Sennett Collection): (1927, undated). NYMA: Photoplay.

GIBSON, Helen (Rose H. Wenger), 1892/94–1977.

Helen Gibson (wife of cowboy star Hoot) was yet another of the 1910s and '20s serial queens whose appearances in chapterplays like the railroad-themed *The Hazards of Helen* and *The Vanishing West* thrilled audiences. She also appeared in other "actioner" roles and then slipped into bit and extra work which continued into the 1960s.

PUBLISHED SOURCES
• *Books* — General: *Reel Women*; *Sweethearts of the Sage*. Credits: *Filmarama* (v. I and II); *Twenty Years of Silents*. Encyclopedic Works: *Film Encyclopedia*; *Halliwell's Filmgoer's Companion*; *Who's Who in Hollywood*.
• *Periodicals* — *Motion Picture Magazine* (Feb. 1916, June 1917); *Films in Review* (Jan. 1968); *Silent Picture* (Winter 1968/69); *Classic Images* (June 1989).

ARCHIVAL MATERIALS
• *Clipping File* — CAA: 50th anniversary in films (1965?); film appearance (1950, 1952, 1961); 44th anniversary in films (1959); article (1962). NYPL: Career (1938); newsphotos. • *Other Clipping File* — GBBF, NYMA (Photoplay Collection), WICF. • *Photograph/Still* — CAA (also in Hollywood Studio Museum Collection), CAUT (Jessen Collection), DCG (Quigley Photographic Archives), GBBF, NYPL. • *Scrapbook* — NYPL (R. Locke Collection).

GILBERT, John (John Pringle), Logan, Utah, 1895/99–1936.

A popular favorite in romantic and action roles for First National, Fox and MGM since 1916, John Gilbert gained superstardom with *The Big Parade* (1925). His subsequent teaming with Greta Garbo (q.v.) in *Flesh and the Devil* and other silent dramas solidified his lofty place. However, his transition to sound films in 1929's *His Glorious Night* was mishandled (perhaps deliberately) and his fame dissipated in a series of poorly scripted films in the early 1930s. A supporting role in *The Captain Hates the Sea* (1934) was his final effort. He was married to Leatrice Joy (q.v.).

PUBLISHED SOURCES
• *Books* — Bibliography: *The Idols of Silence*. General: *Classics of the Silent Screen*; *Famous Film Folk*; *Gentlemen to the Rescue*; *Great Lovers of the Movies*; *The Great Movie Stars*; *History of the American Cinema* (v. 3); *Hollywood: the Pioneers*; *Hollywood Album*; *Hollywood Hall of Fame*; *Hollywood Heaven*; *Hollywood's Great Love Teams*; *How I Broke Into the Movies*; *I Love You, Clark Gable, Etc.*; *Immortals of the Screen*; *Kings of Tragedy*; *The Lion's Share*; *Love, Laughter and Tears*; *The Matinee Idols*; *Mayer and Thalberg*; *The Movie Stars Story*; *Popular Men of the Screen*; *Screen Personalities*; *Stardom*; *The Stars* (Schickel); *The Stars Appear*; *Starstruck*; *The Truth About the Movies*; *Venus in Hollywood*; *What the Stars Told Me*. Credits: *Filmarama* (v. I and II); *Forty Years of Screen Credits*; *Twenty Years of Silents*; *Who Was Who on Screen*. Encyclopedic Works: *A Biographical Dictionary of Film*; *A Companion to the Movies*; *Dictionary of American Biography* (Supplement 2); *Film Encyclopedia*; *Filmlexicon degli Autori e delle Opere*; *Halliwell's Filmgoer's Companion*; *The Illustrated Encyclopedia of the World's Great Movie Stars and Their Films*; *The Illustrated Who's Who of the Cinema*; *International Dictionary of Films and Filmmakers* (v. 3); *The International Encyclopedia of Film*; *The Movie Makers*; *The Oxford Companion to Film*; *The Picturegoer's*

Who's Who and Encyclopedia of the Screen To-day; *Quinlan's Illustrated Registry of Film Stars*; *Who's Who in Hollywood*; *The World Almanac Who's Who of Film*; *The World Encyclopedia of the Film*; *The World Film Encyclopedia*. **Biography/Autobiography:** *Dark Star*. **Pictorial:** *Leading Men*; *Silent Portraits*. **Recordings:** *Hollywood on Record*. **Factoids:** *Star Stats*.

• *Periodicals*—The following periodical articles are in addition to those included in the library listings below: *Motion Picture Classic* (Dec. 1921, Nov. 1925, Jan. 1926, Dec. 1926, May 1931, Aug. 1932); *Photoplay* (Feb.-Mar. 1925, Oct. 1925, Mar. 1926, June 1926, Feb. 1927, July-Aug. 1929, Feb. 1930, June 1930, Oct. 1931, Oct.-Nov. 1933, Jan. 1934, Apr. 1934, June 1935, Sept. 1936); *Motion Picture Magazine* (May 1925, Mar. 1926, July 1926, Apr. 1927, Nov. 1927, Sept. 1929, Dec. 1930, Apr. 1931, Nov. 1931, Jan. 1933); *Cinema Art* (Apr. 1926); *Theatre Magazine* (July 1926, Mar. 1927); *Vanity Fair* (May 1928); *Silver Screen* (Oct. 1931, Aug. 1932); *Movie Classic* (Oct. 1931, Dec. 1931, Aug. 1932, Nov. 1933, Sept. 1934); *Cinema Digest* (Sept. 5, 1932, Oct. 3, 1932, Jan. 9, 1933); *Shadowplay* (Mar. 1934); *Time* (Jan. 20, 1936); *Films in Review* (Oct. 1962); *Saturday Review* (Oct. 13, 1956); *Classic Film Collector* (Fall 1969); *Films and Filming* (Oct. 1972); *Cine Revue* (Oct. 10, 1974); *Film Dope* (Dec. 1979); *Classic Images* (Aug.-Nov. 1985).

MEDIA
Star Treatment (video).

ARCHIVAL MATERIALS
• *Clipping File*—CAA: Romance with Garbo (1927, 1991); newsphotos; film appearance (1925, 1927, 1933); accident (1927); illness (1927); legal problem (1927, 1933); MGM contract (1928); fight (1930); marriage/divorce (1929-32, 1934); article (1920s, 1929, 1936, 1951, 1980); auction catalog (1936); home (1940, 1987); review of *Dark Star* (1985); obituary (1936). Periodical articles: *Motion Picture Director* (Dec. 1926); *Photoplay* (June-Sept. 1928); *Films in Review* (Mar. 1956); *Cine Revue* (Dec. 31, 1987).

CAFI: Article (1985-86); review of *Dark Star* (1985). CAUT: Marriage (1929). CAUU: Review of *Dark Star* (1985). NYMA (also in Photoplay Collection): Review of *Dark Star*; newsphotos; *The Big Parade* (film); article (1985, undated); jail term (1927); personal data summary; program for film festival (including filmography). Periodical articles: *Photoplay* (June-Aug. 1928); *Greenwich Review* (Sept. 1984). NYPL: PARTIAL CONTENTS: Newsphotos; article (1923, 1933, undated); film review (1910s, 1920s); review of *Dark Star* (1985); marriage/divorce (1933-34); sues MGM (1934). Periodical articles: *Picture Show* (Dec. 21, 1929); *Photoplay* (Mar. 1936).
• *Other Clipping File*—CALM, CAUB, GBBF, MAH, MIDL, NYSU, OHCL, PAPL, WICF. • *Correspondence*—CAHL (A. B. Paine Papers): 1931. NYMA (Photoplay Collection). NYPL: Letters (C. & L. Brown Collection) (1930s); others (1934). • *Filmography*—CAA, NYMA. • *Interview*—CAUU (R. Lamparski Collection): Interview is a discussion with author Charles Higham about JG. • *Legal File*—CAUT (Twentieth Century-Fox Collection): Letter (1924); talent agreement (1921-22).
• *Oral History*—NYCO: Mentioned in the following interviews: Ralph Bellamy, John Cromwell, Delmer Daves, Reginald Denny, Albert Hackett, Lila Lee, Don Malkaures, Frances Marion, King Vidor, Mahonri Young, Jerome Zerbe. • *Photograph/Still*—CAA (also in Hollywood Studio Museum Collection), CAUT (Jessen Collection) (Portrait File), CAUU, CNDA, DCG (Quigley Photographic Archives), GBBF, IAU (Blees Collection), NYAM, NYB (Bettmann/UPI Collection) (Springer Collection) (Underwood Collection), NYCU (Dramatic Museum Portraits) (Palmer Collection), NYEH, NYPL, NYSU, OHCL, TNUT (Clarence Brown Collection), TXU, WICF. • *Publicity Release*—NYPL: MGM. • *Reminiscence*—MISU. • *Scrapbook*—NYPL, WICF. • *Studio Biography*—CAA: Unknown studio. NYMA: Photoplay.

GILMORE, Douglas (Harris A. Gilmore), Marion, IA, 1903–1950.

Douglas Gilmore was a dependable leading man and second lead for MGM and other studios beginning with *His Buddy's Wife* (1925) to 1931. Among the films in which he appeared were *Sally, Irene and Mary*, *The Taxi Dancer*, *Rough House Rosie*, *Song of Kentucky* and *Hell's Angels*. After his film career ended he found some success in the theater, on radio and then on television.

PUBLISHED SOURCES

• *Books* — Credits: *Filmarama* (v. II). Encyclopedic Works: *The Picturegoer's Who's Who and Encyclopedia of the Screen To-day*; *Who's Who in Hollywood*.

ARCHIVAL MATERIALS

• *Clipping File* — CAA: Obituary (1950). NYMA (also in Photoplay Collection): Periodical article: *Classic Images* (Dec. 1983). NYPL: Newsphotos; stage appearance (1930s, 1940s); biography. • *Other Clipping File* — GBBF, MIDL. • *Correspondence* — NYPL (J. Golden Collection): 1938. • *Filmography* — CAA. • *Legal File* — CAUT (Twentieth Century–Fox Collection): Letter, memo (1929–30); option (1929); agreement (1929); talent agreement (1930). • *Photograph/Still* — CAA (also in MGM Collection), CALM, DCG (Quigley Photographic Archives), NYPL, NYSU, TXU, WICF. • *Studio Biography* — CAA: Paramount (1930s). NYMA: Photoplay.

GISH, Dorothy (original family name is believed to be Guiche or de Guiche), Masillon, Ohio, 1898–1968.

Dorothy Gish and her sister Lillian (q.v.) were D. W. Griffith actresses by 1912. For most of her career she appeared in comedies, although she did play dramatic roles such as the one in 1922's *Orphans of the Storm*. By the mid-1920s, she was onscreen infre-quently and the talkie era found her primarily a stage performer. She returned for occasional roles as late as 1964.

PUBLISHED SOURCES

• *Books* — Bibliography: *The Idols of Silence*. General: *Classics of the Silent Screen*; *Famous Film Folk*; *The Griffith Actresses*; *Hollywood Album*; *Hollywood Kids*; *Intimate Talks with Movie Stars*; *The Kindergarten of the Movies*; *More From Hollywood*; *People Will Talk*; *Remembering Dorothy Gish*; *Who's Who in the Film World*; *Who's Who on the Screen*. Credits: *Filmarama* (v. I and II); *Forty Years of Screen Credits*; *Twenty Years of Silents*. Encyclopedic Works: *The Biographical Encyclopaedia and Who's Who of the American Theatre*; *Current Biography* (1944, 1969); *Famous Actors and Actresses on the American Stage*; *Film Encyclopedia*; *Filmlexicon degli Autori e delle Opere*; *Halliwell's Filmgoer's Companion*; *The Illustrated Who's Who of the Cinema*; *The Movie Makers*; *Notable American Women: the Modern Period*; *Notable Women in the American Theatre*; *The Oxford Companion to Film*; *The Picturegoer's Who's Who and Encyclopedia of the Screen To-day*; *Quinlan's Illustrated Registry of Film Stars*; *Who Was Who in the Theatre*; *Who's Who in Hollywood*; *Women Who Make Movies*; *The World Almanac Who's Who of Film*; *The World Encyclopedia of the Film*; *The World Film Encyclopedia*. Pictorial: *Dorothy and Lillian Gish*; *Great Stars of the American Stage*; *The Image Makers*; *The Revealing Eye*; *Silent Portraits*. Factoids: *Star Stats*. Biography/Autobiography: *When the Movies Were Young*.

• *Periodicals* — The following periodical articles are in addition to those included in the library listings below: *Photoplay* (Dec. 1914, Sept. 1918, Jan. 1919, Mar. 1920, Nov. 1920, Mar. 1921, June 1921, Mar. 1922, Nov. 1922, Apr. 1923, Sept. 1923, Aug. 1925, Aug. 1930); *Motion Picture Magazine* (June 1915, June 1917, Feb. 1919, Aug. 1919, July 1921, May 1922, Aug. 1923, Oct.-Nov.

1924, June 1925, Apr. 1929); *Film Players Herald & Movie Pictorial* (Feb. 1916); *Theatre* (Nov. 1917); *Motion Picture Classic* (May 1918, Jan. 1919, Nov. 1919); *Picture Show* (Sept. 1, 1919); *Filmplay Journal* (Apr. 1922); *Ladies' Home Journal* (July 1925); *Literary Digest* (Mar. 17, 1934); *Cue* (Nov. 14, 1942, Dec. 4, 1943, Feb. 25, 1950); *National Review* (June 18, 1963); *Time* (June 14, 1968); *Newsweek* (June 17, 1968); *Films in Review* (Aug.-Sept. 1968); *Film Dope* (Dec. 1979); *Cinematographe* (Oct. 1983); *Classic Images* (Sept. 1985, Nov.-Dec. 1987, Feb. 1988, Apr. 1988); *Interview* (Sept. 1987).

MEDIA
Dorothy Gish (filmstrip).

ARCHIVAL MATERIALS
• *Caricature* – NYMN. • *Clipping File* – CAA: Film appearance (1919, 1922, 1943, 1951); marriage/divorce (1921, 1935); article (1943, 1951, 1955); estate (1968); review of *The Man* (play) (1955); stage appearance (1947, 1955); newsphotos; obituary (1968). Periodical articles: *Life* (Aug. 20, 1951); *Cine Revue* (Oct. 23, 1980). CAFI: Film festival (1968); estate (1968); obituary (1968). CAUT: Film appearance (1951). Periodical articles: *Motion Picture Classic* (Sept. 1925); *Life* (Aug. 20, 1951). CAUU: Obituary (1968). NYMA: Booklet for a tribute to DG; newsphotos; article (undated); obituary (1968). Periodical articles: *Theatre Magazine* (Nov. 1927); *Classic Film Collector* (Summer 1968); *Classic Images* (Jan. 1988, Mar. 1988). NYMN: Newsphotos; film appearance (1951); illness; divorce (1935); stage appearance (1946); obituary (1968). NYPL (also in C. & L. Brown Collection): PARTIAL CONTENTS: Honor (1986); stage appearance (1930, 1946, 1956, undated); newsphotos; illness; article (1945, 1950–51, 1956, 1963); film appearance (1951); divorce (1935); obituary (1968). Periodical article: *Life* (Aug. 20, 1951). • *Other Clipping File* – CNDA, GBBF, MAH, MIDL, WICF. • *Correspondence* – CAA (Adolph Zukor Collection): 1919. DCG (Terry Ramsaye Papers); DCLC (Ruth Gordon Papers).

NYPL: Letters (C. & L. Brown Collection) (1928, 1940s); others (undated). • *Costume* – NYMN. • *Filmography* – CAA, CAUT, NYEH, NYMA, NYPL. • *Interview* – CAUU (Hollywood Studio Museum Collection): 1957. • *Legal File* – CAUT (Twentieth Century-Fox Collection): Letter, memo (1945, 1973 [from L. Gish]); agreement (1945); distribution agreement (1922). • *Oral History* – NYCO: Mentioned in the following interviews: Richard Boone, William Everson, Lillian Gish, Lila Lee, Anita Loos, Frances Marion, E.M. Plant, Blanche Sweet, E.L. Tyson. • *Photograph/Still* – CAA (also in Hollywood Studio Museum Collection) (also in MGM Collection), CAHL, CALM, CASF, CAUS, CAUT (Jessen Collection), CAUU, CNDA, DCG (Quigley Photographic Archives), MASC (Sophia Smith Collection), NJFL, NYB (Bettmann/UPI Collection) (Penguin Collection) (Springer Collection) (Underwood Collection), NYCU (Dramatic Museum Portraits) (Palmer Collection), NYEH, NYMN, NYPL, NYSU, OHCL, OHSU, TXSM, TXU, WICF. • *Program* – CASF. • *Scrapbook* – CASU (Stark Collection), NYAM, NYPL (also in R. Locke Collection), WICF. • *Studio Biography* – Paramount: 1943, 1944.

GISH, Lillian (family name is originally believed to be Guiche or de Guiche), Masillon or Springfield, Ohio, 1893/98-1993.

By dint of sheer longevity, as well as talent, Lillian Gish carved a unique place in the history of cinema, appearing in films over a 75-year period. Beginning with D.W. Griffith in 1912, along with her sister Dorothy (q.v.), she had a notable silent career playing fragile (but often determined) heroines in films like *Birth of a Nation, Broken Blossoms, The White Sister, La Bohème* and *The Wind*. She went on to a less exalted place in sound films but continued to appear sporadically in character roles until 1987. Besides appearing in over 100 screen roles, she was also an acclaimed stage actress.

PUBLISHED SOURCES

• *Books* — **Bibliography:** *The Idols of Silence.* **General:** *Acting in the Cinema; Analiz Igry Kino-aktera; The Celluloid Mistress; Classics of the Silent Screen; Close Ups; Doug and Mary and Others; Famous Film Folk; Fifty Super Stars; The Great Movie Stars; Great Names; The Griffith Actresses; History of the American Cinema* (v. 3); *Hollywood Hall of Fame; Hollywood Kids; Hollywood Lolitas; The Hollywood Reporter Star Profiles; Hommage à Lillian Gish; Intimate Talks with Movie Stars; The Kindergarten of the Movies; Ladies in Distress; Life Stories of the Movie Stars; Lillian Gish* (American Film Institute); *Lillian Gish* (Museum of Modern Art); *Lillian Gish, an Interpretation; Movie Star; The Movie Stars Story; The Movies in the Age of Innocence; The National Society of Film Critics on the Movie Star; Popcorn Venus; Reel Women; Return Engagement; The Rise and Fall of the Matinee Idol; Spellbound in Darkness; Star Acting; Stardom; Stars of the Silents; Virgins, Vamps and Flappers; Who's Who in the Film World; Who's Who on the Screen.* **Credits:** *Filmarama* (v. I and II); *Forty Years of Screen Credits; Motion Picture Players' Credits; Twenty Years of Silents.* **Encyclopedic Works:** *The Biographical Encyclopaedia and Who's Who of the American Theatre; A Biographical Dictionary of Film; A Companion to the Movies; Contemporary Theatre, Film and Television* (v.4); *Current Biography* (1944, 1979); *A Dictionary of the Cinema; Famous Actors and Actresses on the American Stage; Film Encyclopedia; Filmlexicon degli Autori e delle Opere; Halliwell's Filmgoer's Companion; The Illustrated Encyclopedia of the World's Great Movie Stars and Their Films; The Illustrated Who's Who of the Cinema; International Dictionary of Films and Filmmakers* (v. 3); *The International Encyclopedia of Film; International Motion Picture Almanac* (1975–80); *Magill's Cinema Annual* (1983); *The Movie Makers; Notable Women in the American Theatre; The Oxford Companion to Film; The Picturegoer's Who's Who and Encyclopedia of the Screen To-day; Quinlan's Illustrated Registry of Film Stars; Variety Who's Who in Show Business; Who's Who in Hollywood; Who's Who in the Theatre; Women Who Make Movies; The World Almanac Who's Who of Film; The World Encyclopedia of the Film; The World Film Encyclopedia.* **Pictorial:** *Dorothy and Lillian Gish; Great Stars of the American Stage; The Image Makers; Leading Ladies; The Revealing Eye; Silent Portraits; They Had Faces Then.* **Biography/Autobiography:** *Life and Lillian Gish; Lillian Gish: The Movies, Mr. Griffith and Me; When the Movies Were Young.* **Recordings:** *Hollywood on Record.* **Factoids:** *Star Stats.*

• *Periodicals* — The following periodical articles are in addition to those included in the library listings below: *Moving Picture World* (June 20, 1914); *Photoplay* (June 1914, Dec. 1914, July 1916, Nov. 1919, Mar. 1920, Dec. 1921, May 1922, June 1924, Mar. 1926, Aug. 1930, Oct. 1979, Oct. 1986); *Motion Picture Magazine* (Jan. 1915, Aug. 1916, Oct. 1916, Aug. 1918, May 1922, Dec. 1923, Oct.-Nov. 1924, Jan. 1925, Dec. 1925, Feb. 1926, May 1930); *Picture Play Magazine* (May 1916, Nov. 1920); *Motion Picture Classic* (Jan. 1919, Sept. 1919, Nov. 1921, Dec. 1922, Feb. 1923, Apr. 1927); *New York Dramatic Mirror* (Apr. 3, 1920); *Filmplay Journal* (Apr. 1922); *Ladies' Home Journal* (Sept. 1925); *Nation* (May 7, 1930); *Cinema Digest* (Aug. 8, 1932); *New Republic* (Jan. 4, 1933); *Newsweek* (May 6, 1933, Mar. 15, 1993); *Cue* (Nov. 27, 1937, Nov. 14, 1942); *Harper's Bazaar* (Oct. 1940); *Cosmopolitan* (Feb. 1946); *Films and Filming* (Jan. 1955, Aug. 1963, Sept. 1971, Nov. 1983, Aug. 1987); *Life* (Jan. 23, 1956); *Screen Facts* (May-June 1963); *Films in Review* (Apr. 1964, Mar. 1975, Oct. 1975, Oct. 1980); *Film Culture* (Spring/Summer 1965); *8mm Collector* (Fall/Winter 1965); *Classic Film Collector* (Summer-Fall 1966, Summer-Fall 1969, Summer

1973); *Filmcritica* (Nov.-Dec. 1967); *Silent Picture* (Autumn 1969); *Horizon* (Spring 1972); *Film Comment* (Nov.-Dec. 1972); *Ecran* (Aug.-Sept. 1974); *Time* (Feb. 3, 1975, Mar. 15, 1993); *Cine Revue* (Mar. 13, 1975); *Boxoffice* (Apr. 25, 1977); *Opera News* (Dec. 24, 1977); *Soviet Literature* (no. 2, 1978); *Andy Warhol's Interview* (Dec. 1978); *Filmkultura* (July-Aug. 1979); *Film Dope* (Dec. 1979); *Quarterly Journal of the Library of Congress* (Summer/Fall 1980); *Classic Film/Video Images* (Jan. 1981); *Cinématographe* (June 1981, Oct. 1983); *Classic Images* (Mar. 1982, Jan. 1984, Sept. 1984, Nov.-Dec. 1987, Feb. 1988, Apr. 1988); *Cahiers du Cinéma* (Nov. 1983, May 1988); *Sight and Sound* (Spring 1984); *Chaplin* (no. 210, 1987); *Sequences* (Apr. 1987); *Soviet Film* (no. 361, 1987); *Positif* (July-Aug. 1987, June 1989); *Hollywood Studio Magazine* (May 1988, May 1990); *Grand Angle* (June 1988); *Film & Kino* (no. 8, 1988); *Film en Televisie + Video* (Nov. 1988); *American Scholar* (Spring 1990); *Griffithiana* (Oct. 1991).

OBSCURE PUBLISHED SOURCES
CAA, NYMA: *Lillian Gish: As She Is to Those Who Know Her.*

MEDIA
Early Women Directors on Directing (video); *Focus on Lillian Gish* (recording); *Lillian Gish* (video); *Lillian Gish — the Actor's Life For Me* (video).

ARCHIVAL MATERIALS
• *Caricature* — NYMN, OHCL. • *Clipping File* — CAA: Newsphotos; stage appearance (1932, 1950-51, 1953, 1965, 1967); film appearance (1923, 1945, 1954-55, 1965-66, 1976-77); legal problem (1945); marriage (1930); article (1940s, 1949, 1950-51, 1954-55, 1960-61, 1963, 1965-66, 1968-69, 1973-74, 1977-79, 1984, 1987); Lillian and Dorothy Gish (1951, 1955-56); TV appearance (1951, 1975); review of The *Movies, Mr. Griffith and Me* (1969); lecture (1968-69, 1971); donates papers to Library of Congress (1970); award (1973, 1978, 1984); review of *Dorothy and Lillian Gish* (1973); honor (1978); 100th film (1977); interview

with Andy Warhol (1978); obituary (1993). Periodical articles: *American Mercury* (Apr. 1924); *American Traveler* (Jan. 1935); *Rob Wagner's Script* (Oct. 10, 1942); *Life* (Aug. 20, 1951); *After Dark* (June 1969); *Films and Filming* (Jan. 1970); *Architectural Digest* (Apr. 1979, Apr. 1990); *Vogue* (Oct. 1981); *Emmy* (Jan.-Feb. 1984); *Drama-Logue* (Mar. 29-Apr. 4, 1984); *People* (Feb. 9, 1987). CAFI: Article (1968-69, 1974-75, 1978, 1980, 1982-84, 1988, undated); film festival (1958, 1970s?, 1975, 1980); award (1979, 1983-84); honor (1981-82); TV appearance (1980); review of *Lillian Gish and the Movies* (1969); film appearance (1985-86); review of *The Actor's Life for Me* (TV show); review of *Lillian Gish* (1969); lecture (1969, 1960s? [program from lecture]); excerpt from *The Spiritual Woman* (book edited by M. Turner) (1955); booklet from Museum of Modern Art's retrospective of LG films. Periodical articles: *Photoplay* (Aug. 1918, June 1921, Apr. 1929); *Motion Picture Magazine* (Apr.-May 1920): *Motion Picture Classic* (June 1921); *American Mercury* (Apr. 1924); *Pictures and Picturegoer* (Oct. 1924); *Theatre* (Nov.-Dec. 1927); *American Traveler* (Jan. 1935); *Stage* (Jan. 1937); *Theatre Arts* (Sept. 1949); *Life* (Aug. 20, 1951); *Films and Filming* (Dec. 1954, Dec. 1957, Jan. 1970); *Sight and Sound* (Winter 1957/58, Winter 1958/59); *Films in Review* (Dec. 1962, Oct. 1974); *After Dark* (June 1969); *Classic Film Collector* (Fall 1973, undated); *Rolling Stone* (Feb. 23, 1979); *Architectural Digest* (Apr. 1979); *Quarterly Review of Film Studies* (Winter 1981); *Vanity Fair* (Oct. 1983); *Film Dope* (undated); *Emmy Magazine* (Jan.-Feb. 1984); *American Film* (Mar. 1984); *Drama-Logue* (Mar.-Apr. 1984); *Interview* (Sept. 1987); *Premiere* (Oct. 1987). CAUT: Biography; excerpt from *Revolt in the Arts* (Sayler) (1930); interview (with A. Warhol) (1978); article (1943, 1968, 1973-75, 1978, 1981-84, undated); excerpt from *Spiritual Woman* (Sheehan) (1955); lecture (1969, 1973); booklet for Museum of Modern Art retrospective; TV appearance (1980); review of *The Movies, Mr. Griffith and Me* (1969);

134   Gish

honor (1979, 1982–84); film appearance (1986). Periodical articles: *Photoplay* (Apr. 1918, June 1921, Apr. 1929): *Motion Picture Magazine* (Apr.-May 1920); *Motion Picture Classic* (June 1921); *American Mercury* (Apr. 1924); *Theatre* (Dec. 1927); *American Traveler* (Jan. 1935); *Stage* (Jan. 1937); *Theatre Arts* (Sept. 1949); *Life* (Aug. 20, 1951); *Films and Filming* (Dec. 1954, Dec. 1957, Jan. 1970); *Sight and Sound* (Winter 1957/58, Winter 1958/59); *Films in Review* (Dec. 1962, Oct. 1974); *Silent Picture* (Spring 1970); *Architectural Digest* (Apr. 1979); *Quarterly Review of Film Studies* (Winter 1981); *Vogue* (Oct. 1981); *American Film* (Mar. 1984). CAUU (also in McCormick Collection): Program for lecture; article (1968, 1975, 1977, 1981, 1983–84); film festival (1975–76, 1978–79, 1980, 1983–84, 1989); award (1978–79, 1982–84); biography; newsphotos; TV appearance (1975); interview (1985); program for AFI Life Achievement Award (1984). Periodical articles: *Films and Filming* (Dec. 1957); *Rolling Stone* (Feb. 22, 1979); *American Film* (Mar. 1984). NYMA: Review of *Lillian Gish: the Movies, Mr. Griffith and Me* (1968); film retrospective (1980); newsphotos; 100th film (1977?); discussion of *Lillian and Dorothy Gish*; article (1971, 1979); film catalog. Periodical articles: *Classic Images* (Jan. 1988, Mar. 1988). NYMN: Newsphotos (numerous); award (1984); film appearance; review of *Lillian Gish: the Movies, Mr. Griffith and Me*; career; article (1937, 1975, 1982, 1984, undated [numerous]); film retrospective; TV appearance (1961); stage appearance (1973); draft article by LG. NYPL: PARTIAL CONTENTS: Article (1938, 1984, 1986–87); *Whales of August* (film) (1987); newsphotos; TV documentary (1988); obituary (1993). Periodical articles: *American Cinematographer* (June 1984); *Andy Warhol's Interview* (Sept. 1987); *Architectural Digest* (undated). • *Other Clipping File* – CASF, CNDA, GBBF, MAH, MIDL, OHCL, WICF. • *Collection* – DCLC: Play scripts, film synopses, film and TV scenarios (most of these for works in which LG did not appear); 400+ letters, most concerning the

America First Committee and a 1925 legal case (1924–78); interviews; financial records; legal papers; speeches; articles. • *Correspondence* – CAA: "Bread and butter" letters (Hedda Hopper Collection) (1942, 1954, 1957); letter (Adolph Zukor Collection) (1948). CAUU (A. Slide Collection): 1957, 1969. DCG (Terry Ramsaye Papers); DCLC (also in Collection) (Huntington Cairns Papers) (Ruth Gordon Papers) (George Middleton Papers). MABU (Frederick Fischer & Welthy Honsinger Papers): 1969. NYCU: Letter (J.D. Brown Collection) (1941); 4 letters (Erskine Collection) (1964–70); letter (Flaherty Collection) (1949); 2 letters (Macy Collection) (1943–44); letter (O'Brien Collection) (1965); letter (Palmer Collection) (1975); letter (Schang Collection) (undated). NYPL: Letters (C. & L. Brown Collection) (1948); others (1930, 1932, 1950, 1954–78). • *Costume* – NYMN. • *Filmography* – CAFI, NYEH, NYMA (incomplete). • *Interview* – CAA (Hedda Hopper Collection): 1963, 1965. CAFI: 1963, 1978, 1980. CAUU (A. Slide Collection): 1969, 1973. DCLC (see Collection). GBBF (Hollywood Collection): Transcript for an interview on *Hollywood* (TV series). MISU: Interview on the TV program *Sunday Morning* (1984); interview from the Kennedy Center Honors TV broadcast (1982); discusses her attempts to save old films and her work with D.W. Griffith on the TV program *Good Morning America* (1980); interview on the TV program *Speaking Freely* (1974); describes her work with D.W. Griffith on the TV program *Camera Three* (1975 [recordings]). NYMN: Interview by Tony Randall (video). • *Legal File* – DCLC (see Collection). • *Manuscript* – NYMA: Draft lecture. • *Memorabilia* – NYMN. • *Miscellaneous* – NYMN: Highlights from Star Award luncheon (1986). • *Oral History* – CAUS: Mentioned in: Ray Rennahan interview. NYCO: Interviewed in 1978. Also mentioned in the following interviews: James Barco, Lyman Bryson, Eddie Dowling, William Everson, Sessue Hayakawa, Leo Hurwitz, Lila Lee, Anita Loos, Frances Marion, E.M. Plant, Kim

Stanley, Michael Straight, Blanche Sweet, E.L. Tyson, King Vidor. TXSO: 1979. • *Photograph/Still* – CAA (also in Hollywood Studio Museum Collection) (also in MGM Collection), CAHL, CALM, CASF, CAUT (Jessen Collection) (Portrait File), CNDA, DCG (Quigley Photographic Archives), MASC (Sophia Smith Collection), NJFL, NYAM, NYB (Bettmann/UPI Collection) (Penguin Collection) (Springer Collection) (Underwood Collection), NYCU (Dramatic Museum Portraits) (Palmer Collection), NYEH, NYMN, NYPL, NYSU, OHCL, OHSU, TXSM, TXU, WICF. • *Press Kit* – OHCL. • *Program* – CAA: Play. CAFI, CAUU: AFI Life Achievement Award (1984). CAHL, CASF: Third Annual Crystal Awards, Women in Film (1979). NYMA: Play. • *Publicity Release* – CAFI: Fox (1977). CAUU: ABC (1979, 1984). NYMA: Fox; Scribner. NYPL: WNET. • *Scrapbook* – CASU (Stark Collection), NYAM, NYPL (also R. Locke Collection) (also Players Collection), WICF. • *Seminar* – CAFI. • *Speech* – CAA (Hedda Hopper Collection): Draft of LG speech to the American Institute of Architects centennial celebration (1957). • *Stageography* – CAUT. • *Studio Biography* – CAFI: Disney (1960s); Paramount (1966); Universal (1980s); American Film Institute (1984?). CAUT: Disney (1960s); CBS (1963). CAUU: Disney (1962?); Fox (1977); Universal (1980s).

GLAUM, Louise, Baltimore, MD or Washington, DC, 1890s/1900–1970.

In the wake of Theda Bara came several other actresses who sought to inherit the mantle of the screen's foremost "vamp." First, perhaps, among the pretenders was Louise Glaum in films like *The Tiger Lady*, *Sex*, and *The Leopard Woman*, as well as William S. Hart westerns (e.g., *Hell's Hinges* and *The Aryan*). She had previously played comedy and character parts for studios such as Pathé,

Nestor, Kay-Bee and Kalem. Her career waned with the decline of the "vampire" genre, her final film being 1925's *Fifty-Fifty*.

PUBLISHED SOURCES

• *Books* – Bibliography: *The Idols of Silence*. General: *First One Hundred Noted Men and Women of the Screen*; *Intimate Talks with Movie Stars*; *Who's Who on the Screen*. Credits: *Filmarama* (v. I and II); *Twenty Years of Silents*; *Who Was Who on Screen*. Encyclopedic Works: *Filmlexicon degli Autori e delle Opere*; *Who's Who in Hollywood*. Pictorial: *Silent Portraits*.

• *Periodicals* – The following periodical articles are in addition to those included in the library listings below: *Motion Picture Magazine* (May 1915); *Photoplay* (Dec. 1917, Aug. 1918); *Picture Show* (Feb. 14, 1920); *Classic Film Collector* (Spring 1971); *Silent Picture* (Spring 1972); *Films in Review* (May 1978).

ARCHIVAL MATERIALS

• *Clipping File* – CAA: Film appearance (1920); produces play (1952); obituary (1970). Periodical articles: *Motion Picture Classic* (Mar. 1917, Dec. 1917, Apr. 1918, June 1919); *Photoplay* (Apr. 1918, July 1924); *Motion Picture Magazine* (Sept. 1920, Mar. 1922). CAUT: Obituary (1970). NYMA: Film appearance (1910s, 1920s); personal data summary; sues producer (1925); marriage/divorce (1926, undated); signs with Paralta (1918); obituary (1970). NYPL: Article (1916, 1926, undated); runs theater; newsphotos; obituary (1970). • *Other Clipping File* – GBBF, WICF. • *Correspondence* – NYMA (Photoplay Collection). • *Filmography* – NYMA, NYPL. • *Photograph/Still* – CAA (also in Hollywood Studio Museum Collection), CALM, CASF, CAUT (Jessen Collection) (Portrait File), CAUU, DCG (Quigley Photographic Archives), NYPL, NYSU, OHCL, TXSM, TXU, WICF. • *Publicity Release* – NYMA: Paralta (1918). • *Scrapbook* – NYPL (also in R. Locke Collection).

GODOWSKY, Dagmar, Vilna, Lithuania, 1897–1975.

"Flamboyant" was the word for Dagmar Godowsky both on and off the screen. Her onscreen career was brief, lasting only four or five years and it consisted largely of fervid melodramas in which she generally played the "vamp." Such titles as *The Sainted Devil* with Rudolph Valentino (q.v.), *Red Lights*, *Virtuous Liars*, *Playthings of Desire* and *In Borrowed Plumes* vividly describe her film métier.

PUBLISHED SOURCES

• *Books* – General: *Famous Film Folk*; *Giving Up the Ghost*; *People Will Talk*; *The Real Tinsel*. Credits: *Filmarama* (v. II); *Twenty Years of Silents*; *Who Was Who on Screen*. Encyclopedic Works: *Film Encyclopedia*; *Who's Who in Hollywood*. Nostalgia: *Whatever Became of...* (1st). Biography/Autobiography: *First Person Plural*.

• *Periodicals* – The following periodical articles are in addition to that included in the library listings below: *Picture Play Magazine* (Nov. 1920); *Motion Picture Classic* (Jan. 1921); *Photoplay* (June 1922, May 1924, Oct.-Nov. 1924); *Motion Picture Magazine* (July 1922); *American Mercury* (Mar. 1943); *Time* (Feb. 24, 1958); *Silent Picture* (Summer 1970).

ARCHIVAL MATERIALS

• *Clipping File* – CAA: Newsphotos; article (1924, 1970); obituary (1975). Periodical article: *Guideposts* (Aug. 1975). CAFI: Obituary (1975). CAUT: Obituary (1975). CAUU: Obituary (1975). NYMA (also in Photoplay Collection): Obituary (1975). NYMN: Nostalgia (1962); review of *First Person Plural*. NYPL: Newsphotos; article (1935, 1957–58, 1970, undated); diet (1971); review of *First Person Plural* (1958); nostalgia (1936, 1962); obituary (1975). • *Other Clipping File* – CAUB, GBBF, MIDL, NYSU, PAPL, WICF. • *Correspondence* – NYMA (Photoplay Collection). NYPL: 1931. • *Interview* – CAUU (R. Lamparski Collection) (A. Slide Collection) (1969). • *Photograph/*

Still – CAA (also in Hollywood Studio Museum Collection), DCG (Quigley Photographic Archives), GBBF, NYAM, NYMN, NYPL, NYSU, TXU, WICF. • *Studio Biography* – NYMA: Photoplay.

GOUDAL, Jetta (Jetje Goudeket), Amsterdam, The Netherlands, (older sources say Versailles, France), 1891/98–1985.

During her film career of some seven or eight years, Jetta Goudal became as well known for her temperament as for her acting ability. Nevertheless, she lent her distinctive beauty to such films as *Lady of the Pavements*, *The Bright Shawl*, *Forbidden Woman*, *The Green Goddess* and *Three Faces East*. Because of her accent, her talkie debut did not come until 1932 and she made no more.

PUBLISHED SOURCES

• *Books* – General: *Famous Film Folk*; *The Idols of Silence*; *Return Engagement*. Credits: *Filmarama* (v. II); *Twenty Years of Screen Credits*. Encyclopedic Works: *Film Encyclopedia*; *Filmlexicon degli Autori e delle Opere*; *Halliwell's Filmgoer's Companion*; *The Movie Makers*; *The Picturegoer's Who's Who and Encyclopedia of the Screen To-day*; *Who's Who in Hollywood*; *The World Film Encyclopedia*. Nostalgia: *Whatever Became of...* (1st). Pictorial: *Silent Portraits*.

• *Periodicals* – The following periodical articles are in addition to those included in the library listings below: *Photoplay* (July-Aug. 1923, Oct. 1924, Aug. 1927, May 1930); *Motion Picture Classic* (Oct. 1924, Feb. 1926, Dec. 1928, Feb. 1929, July 1929); *Motion Picture Magazine* (Aug. 1925); *Movie Classic* (Nov. 1931); *Films in Review* (Mar. 1969, Oct. 1974, Dec. 1974-Jan. 1975, May 1986); *Cine Revue* (Feb. 7, 1985); *Classic Images* (Jan. 1990).

ARCHIVAL MATERIALS

• *Clipping File* – CAA (also in Vertical File Collection): Film appearance (1924,

1926–29, 1931, 1933); article (1923–25, 1927, 1973, 1976, 1980); legal problem (1926–29, 1931–32); signs contract (1923, 1927); marriage (1930); illness (1927, 1930); honor (1983); nostalgia (1972, 1981–82); home (1964); obituary (1985). Periodical articles: *Smart Set* (Jan. 1924); *Picture Play Magazine* (July 1929); *Films in Review* (Mar. 1980). CAFI: Obituary (1985). CAUT: Article (undated); legal problem (1929). CAUU: Article (1971). NYMA (also in Photoplay Collection): Obituary (1985). NYPL: Newsphotos; film appearance (1933); article (undated); obituary (1985). • *Other Clipping File* — AZSU (Jimmy Starr Collection), CAUB, GBBF, MIDL, PAPL, WICF. • *Correspondence* — CAA (Vertical File Collection): Letters, telegrams about film and stage career (1924–1980). NYMA (Photoplay Collection) (Film Study Center Special Collection). NYPL: Letter (C. & L. Brown Collection) (1924); letter (Herman Weinberg Collection) (1978). • *Filmography* — NYMA. • *Interview* — CAUU (A. Slide Collection), NYAM. • *Legal File* — CAA (Vertical File Collection): Contract (1928–29); complaint (1930?). CAUW: Contract (1929). • *Photograph/Still* — CAA (also in Hollywood Studio Museum Collection) (also in MGM Collection), DCG (Quigley Photographic Archives), GBBF, NJPT, NYAM, NYCU (Dramatic Museum Portraits), NYEH, NYPL, NYSU, OHCL, TXU, WICF. • *Privately Printed Material* — CAA: *The Silent Stars Speak.* AMPAS, 1979. • *Publicity Release* — CAUU (A. Slide Collection): DeMille (1926). • *Scrapbook* — NJPT (Yeandle Collection). • *Studio Biography* — CAA: Paramount; DeMille (1926).

GRAVES, Ralph, Cleveland, Ohio, 1900/03–1977.

Ralph Graves's square chin and strong profile helped make him a popular matinee idol. His career began about 1918, his first major role being in 1919's *Sporting Life.* Graves appeared in over 150 films (three by D.W. Griffith), many with prominent actresses of the silent screen. For a short while after the advent of talkies, he continued as a leading man but he slipped into character roles and turned to writing and directing films, including several in which he appeared. His active career ended in 1939, but he returned for a few small parts in 1949.

PUBLISHED SOURCES

• *Books* — **General:** *Famous Film Folk; The Idols of Silence.* **Credits:** *Filmarama* (v. I and II); *Forty Years of Screen Credits; Twenty Years of Silents.* **Encyclopedic Works:** *Film Encyclopedia; Filmlexicon degli Autori e delle Opere; Halliwell's Filmgoer's Companion; The Movie Makers; The Picturegoer's Who's Who and Encyclopedia of the Screen To-day; Who's Who in Hollywood; The World Film Encyclopedia.* **Pictorial:** *Silent Portraits.*

• *Periodicals* — The following periodical articles are in addition to those included in the library listings below: *Photoplay* (Oct. 1919, Mar. 1922); *Motion Picture Classic* (Nov. 1919); *Motion Picture Magazine* (June 1920, Apr. 1922); *Classic Images* (Sept. 1988).

ARCHIVAL MATERIALS

• *Clipping File* — AZSU (Jimmy Starr Collection): Obituary (1977). CAA: Film appearance (1920s); marriage/divorce (1928–34); death threats (1929); fight with director (1931); bankruptcy (1939); obituary (1977). CAUT: Death threat (1929); obituary (1977). Periodical article: *Motion Picture Classic* (Nov. 1929). NYMN: Marriage (1934). NYPL (also in Locke Collection): Film review (1920s); newsphotos; screenwriter (1933); article (1928–32, 1973, undated); marriage (1934); career (1927); obituary (1977). Periodical articles: *Screenland* (undated); *Screen Secrets* (Feb. 1930); *Cine-Mundial* (July 1930). TXU: Obituary (1977). • *Other Clipping File* — GBBF, NYMA (Photoplay Collection), OHCL, PAPL, WICF. • *Correspondence* — OHCL: Few letters. • *Filmography* — CAA. • *Interview* — CAUU (Anthony Slide Collection). • *Legal File* — CAA (Sennett Collection): Talent agreement

138   Gray; Griffith

(1923–25); pay record; option (1925). CAUW: Talent agreement (1927–28); story rights (as director) (1928); checklist (as writer) (1927). • *Oral History* — NYCO: Mentioned in the following interviews: R.L. Duffus, Robert Drew, Andrew Heiskell, Lila Lee. • *Photograph/ Still* — CAA (also in Hollywood Studio Museum Collection) (also in MGM Collection), CAFA, CAFI, CAH, CASU, CAUB, CAUT (Jessen Collection), CAUU (also in A. Slide Collection), DCG (Quigley Photographic Archives), GBBF, NJPT, NYEH, NYPL, NYSU, OHCL, PAPL, TXU (A. Davis Collection), WICF. • *Publicity Release* — CAA (Mack Sennett Collection): 1924, undated. • *Scrapbook* — NYPL (also in R. Locke Collection). • *Studio Biography* — NYMA: Photoplay.

GRAY, Lawrence, San Francisco, CA, 1898/1900–1970.

Lawrence Gray was an all-purpose leading man from Broadway who co-starred with many of the silent era's major actresses. Among his films were *Everybody's Acting, Diamond Handcuffs, Kid Boots* and *Oh Kay!* He could play both rugged and romantic leads, and in the early 1930s he also appeared in several screen musicals. After the end of his film career in the mid-1930s, he became the coordinator between the American and Mexican film industries.

PUBLISHED SOURCES
• *Books* — Credits: *Filmarama* (v. II); *Forty Years of Screen Credits*; *Twenty Years of Silents*; *Who Was Who on Screen*. Encyclopedic Works: *Film Encyclopedia*; *The Picturegoer's Who's Who and Encyclopedia of the Screen To-day*; *Who's Who in Hollywood*; *The World Film Encyclopedia*.
• *Periodicals* — *Motion Picture Classic* (Sept. 1925); *Films in Review* (Oct. 1966).

ARCHIVAL MATERIALS
• *Clipping File* — CAA: Nostalgia (1969); obituary (1970). CAFI: Obituary. NYMN: Marriage (1935); newsphotos. NYPL: Newsphotos; film review (1920s);

article (1928, 1930, undated); film synopses (1920s); engagement/marriage (1920s, 1926); career (1926, undated); obituary (1970). • *Other Clipping File* — CASP, GBBF, MIDL, NYMA (Photoplay Collection), PAPL, WICF. • *Legal File* — CAUW: Talent agreement (1928, 1930). • *Photograph/Still* — CAA (also in Hollywood Studio Museum Collection) (also in MGM Collection), CAH, CASP, DCG (Quigley Photographic Archives), GBBF, NJPT, NYAM, NYEH, NYMN, NYPL, NYSU, OHCL, PAPL, TXU (A. Davis Collection), WICF. • *Scrapbook* — NYPL. • *Studio Biography* — CAA: Paramount (1931, undated). NYMA: Photoplay.

GRIFFITH, Corinne (Corinne Griffin), Texarkana, TX, 1898/1906–1979.

In one of the more bizarre legal cases of modern times, Corinne Griffith claimed that the real star was deceased and she was either "her" own stand-in, sister or daughter. (Her identity as the real "Orchid Lady" was confirmed by several of her silent screen colleagues.) She was a major star during the 1920s appearing in (and producing some) films which included *Lilies of the Field, Declassée, The Lady in Ermine, Black Oxen* and *Infatuation*. Her foray into talkies was brief and ended in the early 1930s. Another film apparently made in 1958 was never released.

PUBLISHED SOURCES
• *Books* — Wrote fiction and other books on various topics, including *Abolish the Individual Federal Income Tax* (196-); *Antiques I Have Known* (1961); *Eggs I Have Known* (1955); *Hollywood Stories* (1955); *I Can't Boil Water* (a cookbook) (1963); *I'm Lucky at Cards*; *Not For Men Only — But Almost* (1969); *Papa's Delicate Condition* (1952); *This You Won't Believe* (1972); *Truth Is Stranger* (1964). Bibliography: *The Idols of Silence*. General: *Blue Book of the Screen*; *Classics of the Silent Screen*; *Famous Film Folk*; *How I Broke Into the Movies*; *The Truth About the Movies*;

Who's Who on the Screen. **Credits:** *Filmarama* (v. II); *Forty Years of Screen Credits*; *Twenty Years of Silents.* **Encyclopedic Works:** *Film Encyclopedia*; *Filmlexicon degli Autori e delle Opere*; *Halliwell's Filmgoer's Companion*; *The Illustrated Who's Who of the Cinema*; *The Movie Makers*; *The Picturegoer's Who's Who and Encyclopedia of the Screen To-day*; *Who's Who in Hollywood*; *The World Almanac Who's Who of Film*; *The World Film Encyclopedia.* **Nostalgia:** *Whatever Became of...* (2nd). **Pictorial:** *The Image Makers*; *Silent Portraits*; *They Had Faces Then.* **Recordings:** *Hollywood on Record.* **Factoids:** *Star Stats.* **Biography/Autobiography:** *My Life With the Redskins.*
• *Periodicals* — The following periodical articles are in addition to those included in the library listings below: *Photoplay* (Jan. 1919, July 1920, Nov. 1921, Jan. 1922, Dec. 1923, June-July 1924, Jan. 1926, July 1929, May 1932); *Motion Picture Classic* (Apr. 1919, Mar. 1921, June 1926, Aug. 1928, May 1929); *Picture Show* (Feb. 14, 1920); *Motion Picture Magazine* (Mar. 1920, Jan. 1922, Oct. 1924, Dec. 1924, Aug. 1925, July 1927, Dec. 1929, Apr.-May 1930); *Movie Classic* (June 1932); *Films in Review* (Nov. 1959-Jan. 1960, Nov. 1975); *Show* (Mar. 1962); *Classic Film Collector* (Summer 1966, Nov. 1975); *Cinematographe* (no. 50, 1979); *Cine Revue* (Aug. 2, 1979); *Time* (Aug. 6, 1979); *Bianco e Nero* (Sept.-Dec. 1983); *Classic Images* (Jan. 1990).

OBSCURE PUBLISHED SOURCES
CAA, NYMA, NYPL: *Corinne Griffith.*

ARCHIVAL MATERIALS
• *Clipping File* — CAA: Newsphotos; marriage/divorce (1924, 1934, 1936, 1958, 1965-66); home (1951, 1953-55); production company (1923); articles (1951, 1953, 1959-61, 1963, 1971); income tax (1951-53, 1956-57, 1960, 1962); film appearance (1922-23, 1932, 1950, 1957); honor (1959, 1961); robbery (1966); legal problem (1963, 1966); biography; obituary (1979). Periodical article: *Saturday Evening Post* (Dec. 14, ?). CAFI:

Obituary (1979). CAUT: Obituary (1979). CAUU: Income tax (1951); tests for film (1950); obituary (1979). NYMA: Divorce (1966); newsphotos; career (1961); the "other" CG (1966); obituary (1979). NYMN: Stage appearance (1933); makes speech (1959); newsphotos; obituary (1979). NYPL: Marriage/divorce (1934, 1936, 1938, 1958, 1965); newsphotos (numerous); nostalgia (1936); article (1951, 1953, undated); end of film career (1961); stage appearance (1933); review of *This You Won't Believe* (1972); career (1928); film review (1920s); income tax (1939, 1962); lectures (1951); obituary (1979). Periodical article: *Photoplay* (May 1930). • *Other Clipping File* — AZSU (Jimmy Starr Collection), CNDA, GBBF, MAH, MIDL, OHCL, PAPL, WICF. • *Correspondence* — CAA (Hedda Hopper Collection): Few letters relating to books written by CG, the Communist menace, and the income tax (1951, 1953, undated). • *Filmography* — NYPL (incomplete). • *Legal File* — CAUW: Contract (1927); payroll (1923-30); agreement (1923-30); contract summary (1923-30); document (1921-29); contract (1923-28, 1930); release (1930); communication (1928); letter (1923-30); rights transfer (1926-32); production agreement (1923). • *Oral History* — NYCO: Mentioned in: Reginald Denham interview. • *Photograph/Still* — AZSU (Jimmy Starr Collection), CAA (also in Hollywood Studio Museum Collection), CAPH, CAUS, CAUT (Jessen Collection), CAUU, DCG (Quigley Photographic Archives), GBBF, MIDL, NJPT, NYB (Bettmann/ UPI Collection) (Springer Collection) (Underwood Collection), NYCU (Palmer Collection), NYEH, NYMA, NYPL, NYSU, OHCL, TXU, WICF. • *Scrapbook* — NJPT (Yeandle Collection), NYMA, NYPL (R. Locke Collection).

GRIFFITH, Raymond, Boston, MA, 1890-1957.

Considered a most underrated comic actor today, Raymond Griffith started as an extra at Vitagraph in the mid-

1910s and had a moderately popular career for Paramount in such films as *Hands Up*, *Minnie*, *Wet Paint*, *Open All Night* and *Miss Bluebeard*. He became known for his persona as a "silk hat" comedian, his trademark being elegant nonchalance. Supposedly unable to speak above a whisper (although this is disputed), he played his only talkie role in *All Quiet on the Western Front* as a dying soldier. He later became a producer.

PUBLISHED SOURCES
• *Books—General:* *Famous Film Folk*; *The Great Movie Comedians*; *The Silent Clowns*. **Credits:** *Filmarama* (v. I and II); *Twenty Years of Silents*; *Who Was Who on Screen*. **Encyclopedic Works:** *Cinema, a Critical Dictionary*; *Film Encyclopedia*; *Filmlexicon degli Autori e delle Opere*; *Halliwell's Filmgoer's Companion*; *The Illustrated Who's Who of the Cinema*; *The Movie Makers*; *Quinlan's Illustrated Directory of Film Comedy Actors*; *Who's Who in Hollywood*. **Pictorial:** *Silent Portraits*.
• *Periodicals—* The following periodical articles are in addition to that included in the library listings below: *Photoplay* (May 1925, July 1930); *Motion Picture Magazine* (May 1926); *Film Dope* (Oct. 1980); *Classic Images* (Jan. 1982); *Positif* (Sept. 1991); *Griffithiana* (Oct. 1991).

ARCHIVAL MATERIALS
• *Clipping File—*CAA: Film appearance (1922); article (1991); obituary (1957). CAUT: Obituary (1957). NYMA (also in Photoplay Collection): Film appearance (1920s?); film synopsis (1925); article (undated); newsphotos. Periodical article: *Classic Film Collector* (Spring 1975). NYPL: Producer (1930s?, 1933); film review (1920s); newsphotos; article (1934); obituary (1957).• *Other Clipping File—*AZSU (Jimmy Starr Collection), GBBF, MAH, MIDL, PAPL, WICF. • *Correspondence—*CAHL: 1925. • *Filmography—*CAA, NYMA. • *Legal File—*CAA (Sennett Collection): Option (1919-20); talent agreement (as scenario writer) (1919). CAUT (Twen-

tieth Century-Fox Collection): Agreement (1933-35); memo, letter (1934-35, 1938-39, 1940); loanout (1929). • *Photograph/Still—*CAA (also in Hollywood Studio Museum Collection), CAUT (Jessen Collection), CAUU, DCG (Quigley Photographic Archives), GBBF, NYEH, NYPL, NYSU, OHCL, TXU, WICF. • *Studio Biography—*CAA: Paramount (1925, 1927).

GULLIVER, Dorothy, Salt Lake City, Utah, 1908/10-

Dorothy Gulliver's career began late in the silent era when she appeared in the *Collegians* series and was one of Rin Tin Tin's "co-stars." She was named a Wampas Baby Star in 1928. Her career continued on until 1933 in serials (*The Shadow of the Eagle*) and westerns, with an occasional later role, most notably in *Faces*.

PUBLISHED SOURCES
• *Books—General:* *Broken Silence*; *Sweethearts of the Sage*; *Those Fabulous Serial Heroines*. **Credits:** *Filmarama* (v. II); *Forty Years of Screen Credits*; *Twenty Years of Silents*. **Encyclopedic Works:** *Film Encyclopedia*; *The Picturegoer's Who's Who and Encyclopedia of the Screen To-day*; *Who's Who in Hollywood*; *The World Film Encyclopedia*. **Nostalgia:** *Whatever Became of...* (11th).
• *Periodicals—* The following periodical articles are in addition to those included in the library listings below: *Motion Picture Magazine* (Oct. 1928); *Films in Review* (Feb. 1970) (Wampas Baby Stars); *Classic Images* (Aug. 1984).

ARCHIVAL MATERIALS
• *Clipping File—*CAA: Nostalgia (1972). CAUT: Divorce (1929). NYMA: Periodical article: *Classic Images* (Nov. 1984). NYPL: Newsphotos. Periodical article: *Hollywood Studio Magazine* (June 1982). • *Other Clipping File—*AZSU (Jimmy Starr Collection), GBBF, PAPL. • *Correspondence—*CAFI: Letter (written by director John Cassavetes) concerning possible Oscar nomination

for DG's performance in *Faces*. • *Photograph/Still* — CAA (also in Hollywood Studio Museum Collection), CAUT (Jessen Collection) (Portrait File), CAUU, DCG (Quigley Photographic Archives), GBBF, NYAM, NYEH, NYPL, NYSU, TXU.

HACKETT, Raymond, New York, NY, 1902/03–1958.

After a lengthy Broadway career, Raymond Hackett returned to films, in which he also had appeared as a teenager. Beginning in the late 1920s he made several silents and talkies, mainly playing bland romantic or second leads in such films as *The Girl in the Show*, *Our Blushing Brides*, *The Love of Sunya*, *The Trial of Mary Dugan* and *Madame X*. By 1931 his film career had ended and he returned to Broadway. He was married to Blanche Sweet (q.v.).

PUBLISHED SOURCES

• *Books* — Credits: *Filmarama* (v. II); *Forty Years of Screen Credits*; *Who Was Who on Screen*. **Encyclopedic Works:** *Film Encyclopedia*; *Filmlexicon degli Autori e delle Opere*; *Halliwell's Filmgoer's Companion*; *The Picturegoer's Who's Who and Encyclopedia of the Screen To-day*; *Who's Who in Hollywood*; *Who Was Who in the Theatre*; *The World Film Encyclopedia*. **Factoids:** *Star Stats*.

• *Periodicals* — The following periodical articles are in addition to those included in the library listings below: *Motion Picture Magazine* (Oct. 1929); *Motion Picture Classic* (Apr. 1930).

ARCHIVAL MATERIALS

• *Clipping File* — CAA: Divorce (1935); obituary (1958). CAUT: Newsphotos; obituary (1958). NYMN: Newsphotos; marriage (1935). Periodical article: *Radio-Mirror* (undated). NYPL: Marriage; stage appearance (1910s, 1920s, 1930s, 1940s); film appearance (1929–30); obituary (1958). Periodical articles: *Photoplay* (July 1929); *Picture Play Magazine* (June 1930); *Star-Dust*

(Feb. 1932). • *Other Clipping File* — GBBF, MIDL, NYMA (Photoplay Collection), PAPL, WICF. • *Correspondence* — NYPL: Letters (C. & L. Brown Collection) (1931–41, various other dates); other (1936). • *Legal File* — CAUT (Twentieth Century–Fox Collection): Loanout (1930); letter, memo (1930). CAUW: Loanout (1929–30); talent agreement (1929–30). • *Oral History* — NYCO: Mentioned in the following interviews: Sessue Hayakawa, Elliott Nugent. • *Photograph/Still* — CAA (also in Hollywood Studio Museum Collection) (also in MGM Collection), CAUT (Jessen Collection), CAUU, DCG (Quigley Photographic Archives), GBBF, NJPT, NYEH, NYMN, NYPL, NYSU, OHCL, PAPL, TXU (A. Davis Collection), WICF. • *Play Program* — OHSU. • *Publicity Release* — NYPL: Unknown studio (undated). • *Scrapbook* — NYPL. • *Studio Biography* — NYMA: Photoplay.

HAINES, William, Staunton, VA, 1900–1973.

After winning a "New Faces" contest in 1922, William Haines came to Hollywood and within a couple of years was a popular MGM star. Although he appeared in various types of films, he was best known for light comedies. Among his hits were *Sally, Irene and Mary*, *Alias Jimmy Valentine*, *Tell It to the Marines* and *Brown of Harvard*. He made a relatively successful transition to talkies but his acting career ended by the mid–1930s.

PUBLISHED SOURCES

• *Books* — General: *Classics of the Silent Screen*; *The Funsters*; *How I Broke Into the Movies*; *Popular Men of the Screen*; *Screen Album*. **Credits:** *Filmarama* (v. II); *Forty Years of Screen Credits*; *Twenty Years of Silents*; *Who Was Who on Screen*. **Encyclopedic Works:** *Film Encyclopedia*; *Filmlexicon degli Autori e delle Opere*; *Halliwell's Filmgoer's Companion*; *The Movie Makers*; *The Picturegoer's Who's Who and Encyclopedia of the Screen To-day*;

Who's Who in Hollywood; *The World Film Encyclopedia*. **Nostalgia:** *Whatever Became of* . . . (4th, 7th). **Pictorial:** *Silent Portraits.*

• *Periodicals* — The following periodical articles are in addition to those included in the library listings below: *Photoplay* (Oct. 1924, Oct. 1926, Sept.-Oct. 1929, May 1931); *Motion Picture Magazine* (May 1926, Nov. 1929, Aug. 1930); *Motion Picture Classic* (Jan. 1927, Dec. 1927); *Vanity Fair* (Apr. 1932); *Filmograph* (nos. 3-4, 1973) (filmography); *Classic Film Collector* (Spring 1974); *Films in Review* (Dec. 1975); *Cine Revue* (Oct. 15, 1981).

ARCHIVAL MATERIALS

• *Clipping File* — CAA: Nostalgia (1969); interior decorator (1949–50, 1969–70); film appearance (1927); obituary (1974). CAFI: Article (1973). Periodical article: *Films in Review* (Mar. 1984). CAUT: Obituary (1973). NYMA (also in Photoplay collection): Interior decorator (1934); attacked by mob (1936); article (1932); obituary (1973). Periodical articles: *Movie Mirror* (Jan. 1932); *Picture Play Magazine* (Feb. 1932); *New Movie Mirror* (July 1932); *Filmograph* (no.3-3, 1973). NYMN: Newsphotos. NYPL: Attacked by mob (1936); newsphotos (numerous); interior decorator (1934, 1950); MGM contract; article (1932, undated [numerous]); film review; film appearance (1927, 1930, 1932, 1934); nostalgia; obituary (1973). Periodical articles: *Film Fun* (Jan. 1930); *Picture Play* (Feb. 1931); *Screen Romance* (Mar. 1931); *Movie Classic* (Apr. 1931); *Screenland* (Sept. 1931); *Photoplay* (Sept. 1931); *Architectural Digest* (Sept.-Oct. 1972). • *Other Clipping File* — CAH, GBBF, MIDL, OHCL, OHSU, PAPL, WICF. • *Filmography* — CAA. • *Photograph/ Still* — CAA (also in Hollywood Studio Museum Collection) (also in MGM Collection), CAUT (Jessen Collection) (Portrait File), CAUU, CNDA, DCG (Quigley Photographic Archives), GBBF, IAU (Junkin Collection), MIDL, NJPT, NYAM, NYB (Bettmann/UPI Collection), NYCU (Dramatic Museum Portraits) (Palmer Collection), NYEH,

NYPL, NYSU, OHCL, TNUT (Clarence Brown Collection), TXSM, TXU, WICF. • *Scrapbook* — NJPT (Yeandle Collection), NYMA, NYPL (also in R. Locke Collection). • *Studio Biography* — NYMA: Photoplay.

HALE, Creighton (Patrick Fitzgerald), Cork, Ireland, 1882–1965.

Perhaps best known for his roles in *Way Down East* (1920) and *The Cat and the Canary* (1927), Creighton Hale had a long career as a popular leading man and supporting player. He was Pearl White's co-star in several early serials and played in a variety of genres, including melodrama (*Orphans of the Storm*), comedy (*The Marriage Circle*) and mystery. His career continued through the late 1940s.

PUBLISHED SOURCES

• *Books* — **General:** *Life Stories of the Movie Stars*. **Credits:** *Filmarama* (v. I and II); *Forty Years of Screen Credits*; *Twenty Years of Silents*; *Who Was Who on Screen*. **Encyclopedic Works:** *Film Encyclopedia*; *Filmlexicon degli Autori e delle Opere*; *Halliwell's Filmgoer's Companion*; *The Movie Makers*; *The Picturegoer's Who's Who and Encyclopedia of the Screen To-day*; *Who's Who in Hollywood*; *The World Almanac Who's Who of Film*. **Pictorial:** *Silent Portraits.*

• *Periodicals* — The following periodical articles are in addition to that included in the library listings below: *Motion Picture Magazine* (Mar. 1916, Jan. 1917, Sept. 1917, June 1919); *Photoplay* (Nov. 1916); *Films in Review* (June-July 1969); *Classic Images* (Dec. 1985).

ARCHIVAL MATERIALS

• *Clipping File* — CAA: Film appearance (1953); obituary (1965). NYMA (also in Photoplay Collection). Periodical article: *Motion Picture Classic* (June 1919). NYMN: Newsphotos; obituary (1965). NYPL: Newsphotos; film reviews (numerous); marriage (1931); obituary

(1965). • *Other Clipping File* – GBBF, MAH, OHCL, PAPL, WICF. • *Correspondence* – CAHL: Letter in verse (1920). • *Filmography* – NYPL (incomplete). • *Legal File* – CAUW: Personnel, payroll record (1937–48); contract summary (1939–40); option (1939–48); letter, memo (1939–40, 1945, 1948); questionnaire (1945); release (1945); contract (1939–40, 1945–46, 1948); talent agreement (1925, 1928–29, 1939–40). • *Photograph/Still* – CAA (also in Hollywood Studio Museum Collection) (also in MGM Collection), CAFA, CAUT (Jessen Collection) (Portrait File), DCG (Quigley Photographic Archives), GBBF, NJPT, NYCZ (Ithaca Movie Industry Photograph Collection), NYEH, NYMN, NYPL, NYSU, OHCL, TXU, WICF. • *Play Program* – CAHL: 1923. • *Publicity Release* – NYPL: Chamberlain-Brown. • *Scrapbook* – NJPT (Yeandle Collection), NYAM, NYPL (also in Locke Collection). • *Studio Biography* – NYMA: Photoplay.

HALE, Georgia, St. Joseph, MO, 1906–1985.

The role of the dance hall girl in *The Gold Rush* (1925) has made Georgia Hale one of the most recognizable of the minor silent actresses. In her brief career it was her only film of note, with the possible exception of von Sternberg's oddity *The Salvation Hunters*. Others included *Floating College, Hills of Peril, The Last Moment* and *A Woman Against the World*. She apparently had only one sound role, in the 1931 serial *The Lightning Warrior*.

PUBLISHED SOURCES
• *Books* – Credits: *Filmarama* (v. II); *Twenty Years of Silents*. Encyclopedic Works: *Film Encyclopedia; Filmlexicon degli Autori e delle Opere; Halliwell's Filmgoer's Companion; The Illustrated Who's Who of the Cinema; The Movie Makers; Who's Who in Hollywood*. Nostalgia: *Whatever Became of...* (11th). • *Periodicals* – *Photoplay* (Aug. 1925,

Dec. 1925); *Films Illustrated* (May 1974); *Classic Images* (Apr. 1991).

ARCHIVAL MATERIALS
• *Clipping File* – CAUT: Marriage (1929). NYPL: Newsphotos; article (undated). • *Other Clipping File* – AZSU (Jimmy Starr Collection), NYMA (Photoplay Collection), PAPL, WICF. • *Filmography* – GBBF. • *Photograph/Still* – CAA (also in Hollywood Studio Museum Collection), DCG (Quigley Photographic Archives), GBBF, NYEH, NYPL, NYSU, OHCL, TXSM, TXU, WICF. • *Studio Biography* – CAA: Paramount (1920s).

HALL, James (James Brown), Dallas, TX, 1900–1940.

Best remembered as the "good" brother in *Hell's Angels*, James Hall's first starring film was *Campus Flirt* in 1926. He became a popular leading man and appeared in several well-regarded films like John Ford's *Four Sons* and von Sternberg's *The Case of Lena Smith*. Paramount released him in 1930 and adverse publicity about his stormy personal life finished his film career after a final role in 1933. At the time of his death he was working as master of ceremonies in a third-rate night club.

PUBLISHED SOURCES
• *Books* – General: *Immortals of the Screen*. Credits: *Filmarama* (v. II); *Forty Years of Screen Credits; Twenty Years of Silents; Who Was Who on Screen*. Encyclopedic Works: *Film Encyclopedia; Filmlexicon degli Autori e delle Opere; Halliwell's Filmgoer's Companion; The Movie Makers; The Picturegoer's Who's Who and Encyclopedia of the Screen To-day; Who's Who in Hollywood; The World Film Encyclopedia*. Pictorial: *Silent Portraits*. • *Periodicals* – The following periodical articles are in addition to those included in the library listings below: *Motion Picture Magazine* (Dec. 1926, Aug. 1928); *Motion Picture Classic* (Sept. 1928); *Films in Review* (Jan.-Feb. 1992).

ARCHIVAL MATERIALS

• *Clipping File*—CAA: Film appearance (1930); legal problem (1932). NYMA: Personal data summary. Periodical articles: *Classic Images* (Aug.-Sept. 1988). NYMN: Newsphotos; legal problem (1932–33); obituary (1940). NYPL: Newsphotos (numerous); legal problem (1932–33); film review (1920s); reconciliation with wife (1932); article (1927, 1929–30, undated); obituary (1940). Periodical articles: *Picture Play* (May 1928, Aug. 1931); *Screen Play* (Sept. 1930); *Radio Mirror* (1930s); *Quirk's Reviews* (Oct. 1987). • *Other Clipping File*—GBBF, MAH, MIDL, OHCL, PAPL, WICF. • *Filmography*—NYMA. • *Legal File*—CAUW: Contract (1930); memo (1930). • *Photograph/Still*—CAA (also in Hollywood Studio Museum Collection), CAH, CAUT (Portrait File), CAUU, DCG (Quigley Photographic Archives), GBBF, NJPT, NYB (Underwood Collection), NYCU (Dramatic Museum Portraits), NYEH, NYMN, NYPL, NYSU, OHCL, TXU (A. Davis Collection), WICF. • *Studio Biography*—CAA: Paramount (late 1920s?, 1930, undated).

HAMILTON, Hale, Fort Madison, IA, 1880–1942.

Hale Hamilton was a stage actor who had a successful career as a leading man in silent films and as a character actor in talkies. For Metro and other studios he appeared in silent films like *Opportunity* and *The Great Gatsby*. In the 1930s he was seen in many prestigious films such as *Susan Lenox: Her Fall and Rise*, *Grand Hotel* and *The Adventures of Marco Polo*.

PUBLISHED SOURCES

• *Books*—Credits: *Filmarama* (v. I and II); *Forty Years of Screen Credits*; *Twenty Years of Silents*; *Who Was Who on Screen*. Encyclopedic Works: *The Movie Makers*; *Who Was Who in the Theatre*; *Who's Who in Hollywood*; *The World Film Encyclopedia*.
• *Periodicals*—*Photoplay* (Mar. 1919);

Motion Picture Magazine (July 1919); *Classic Film Collector* (Spring 1978).

OBSCURE PUBLISHED SOURCES

CAA (Pat O'Malley Collection): *The Cast* (v. 1).

ARCHIVAL MATERIALS

• *Clipping File*—NYMA (also in Photoplay Collection): Personal data summary. NYPL: Newsphotos; film review (1920s); bankruptcy; stage appearance (1920s); film appearance (1928, 1930); article (1936); career (1928); obituary (1942). • *Other Clipping File*—GBBF, MAH, MIDL, WICF. • *Correspondence*—NYPL: 1935. • *Legal File*—CAUW: Talent agreement (1932); contract (1932, 1934); authorization (undated). • *Photograph/Still*—CASF, DCG (Quigley Photographic Archives), NYCU (Dramatic Museum Portraits), NYPL, NYSU, OHCL, WICF. • *Scrapbook*—NYPL (also in John Golden Collection) (also in R. Locke Collection) (also in Players Collection).

HAMILTON, Mahlon, 1883–1960.

Mahlon Hamilton was a popular leading man in silent films, appearing with many of the day's leading actresses including Mary Pickford and Marion Davies. Among his films were *A Fool There Was* (1922 remake), *Little Old New York*, *Daddy Long Legs*, *Peg O'My Heart* and *The Single Standard*. He was also seen in a few serial roles and went on to be a well-regarded supporting player in talkies.

PUBLISHED SOURCES

• *Books*—General: *Famous Film Folk*; *Who's Who on the Screen*. Credits: *Filmarama* (v. I and II); *Forty Years of Screen Credits*; *Twenty Years of Silents*; *Who Was Who in Hollywood*. Encyclopedic Works: *Filmlexicon degli Autori e delle Opere*; *The Picturegoer's Who's Who and Encyclopedia of the Screen To-day*; *Who's Who in Hollywood*.
• *Periodicals*—*Photoplay* (May 1917, Mar. 1921); *Motion Picture Magazine*

(Mar. 1919, Apr. 1921); *Classic Film Collector* (Spring 1978).

ARCHIVAL MATERIALS
• *Clipping File*—CAA: Obituary (1960). NYPL (also in Locke Collection): Newsphotos; film review (1920s); film appearance (1930, 1933). • *Other Clipping File*—GBBF, NYMA (Photoplay Collection), OHCL, WICF. • *Photograph/Still*—CAA (also in Hollywood Studio Museum Collection) (also in MGM Collection), CAUT (Jessen Collection), CAUU, DCG (Quigley Photographic Archives), NYPL, NYSU, OHCL, WICF. • *Studio Biography*—NYMA: Photoplay.

HAMILTON, Neil (James N. Hamilton), Lynn, MA, 1899–1984.

Looking like the clothing model he had been, Neil Hamilton played the stalwart leading man in films like Griffith's *America*, *The White Rose* (his first major role after doing extra work), *The Great Gatsby*, *Beau Geste* and *The Dawn Patrol*. By the early 1930s his career was sliding toward "B" films but he continued, off and on, as a character actor through the 1960s. His recurring role as Commissioner Gordon in *Batman*, the "camp" television series of the 1960s, is probably his best remembered.

PUBLISHED SOURCES
• *Books*—Wrote pamphlet *My Friend Don Bosco*. **General:** *Classics of the Silent Screen*. **Credits:** *Filmarama* (v. II); *Forty Years of Screen Credits*; *Twenty Years of Silents*. **Encyclopedic Works:** *The Biographical Encyclopaedia and Who's Who of the American Theatre*; *Film Encyclopedia*; *Filmlexicon degli Autori e delle Opere*; *Halliwell's Filmgoer's Companion*; *The Movie Makers*; *The Picturegoer's Who's Who and Encyclopedia of the Screen To-day*; *Quinlan's Illustrated Registry of Film Stars*; *Who Was Who in the Theatre*; *Who's Who in Hollywood*; *The World Almanac Who's Who of Film*; *The*

World Film Encyclopedia. **Nostalgia:** *Whatever Became of...* (5th). **Pictorial:** *Silent Portraits*.
• *Periodicals*—The following periodical articles are in addition to those included in the library listings below: *Photoplay* (July 1923); *Motion Picture Magazine* (Oct. 1925, Aug. 1931); *Motion Picture Classic* (Nov. 1925, May 1929, Aug. 1931); *Motion Picture Magazine* (May 1930); *Silver Screen* (July 1931); *Films in Review* (Mar. 1982, June-July 1982, Oct. 1982); *Newsweek* (Oct. 15, 1984); *Cine Revue* (Oct. 25, 1984); *Classic Images* (Apr. 1985, July 1988).

ARCHIVAL MATERIALS
• *Caricature*—NYMN. • *Clipping File*—CAA: Film appearance (1944, 1963, 1965, 1970); article (1958, 1965, 1980); illness (1965); bankruptcy (1940); nostalgia (1960s, 1971, 1976, 1979, 1981); TV appearance (1950, 1965); children (1931); leaves Paramount (1930); obituary (1984). Periodical articles: *Hollywood Studio Magazine* (Feb. 1975, Apr. 1975). CAFI: Periodical article (1974); obituary (1984). CAUT: Article (1976); play appearance (1958). Periodical article: *TV Guide* (June 4, 1966). CAUU: Nostalgia (1976); obituary (1984). Periodical article: *Hollywood Studio Magazine* (Sept. 1980). NYMA: Newsphotos; obituary (1984). NYMN: Newsphotos; article (undated); career. NYPL: Article (1927, 1931, undated); newsphotos (numerous); stage appearance (1930s, 1940s, 1953); prays for work (1943); returns to birthplace (1945); film appearance (1920s, 1930s); career (1926, 1929); marriage (1922); signs with Selznick (1940s); obituary (1984). Periodical articles: *Screen Play* (May 1931); *TV Guide* (June 4, 1966); *Hollywood Studio Magazine* (Sept. 1980). • *Other Clipping File*—AZSU (Jimmy Starr Collection), CAUB, GBBF, MAH, MIDL, OHCL, PAPL, WICF. • *Correspondence*—CAA: Fan letter (1927). NYPL: Letters (C. & L. Brown Collection) (1920s-40s); other (1965). • *Filmography*—CAA: To 1966. • *Interview*—CAUU (Hollywood Studio Museum Collection): 1964. GBBF (Hollywood Collection): Transcript of

interview for *Hollywood* (TV series).
• *Legal File*—CAUT (Twentieth Cen-
tury-Fox Collection): Loanout (1928).
CAUW: Document (undated, 1930); con-
tract (1930); talent agreement (1928,
1930, 1932–33). NYPL (C. & L. Brown
Collection): Contract (1944). • *Oral
History*—NYCO: Mentioned in: Mary
Ellen Leary interview. • *Photograph/
Still*—AZSU (Jimmy Starr Collection),
CAA (also in Hollywood Studio Museum
Collection) (also in MGM Collection),
CAHL, CASF, CAUT (Jessen Collec-
tion) (Portrait File), CAUU, CNDA,
DCG (Quigley Photographic Archives),
GBBF, MIDL, NJPT, NYAM, NYB
(Bettmann/UPI Collection) (Underwood
Collection), NYCU (Palmer Collection),
NYEH, NYMN, NYPL, NYSU, OHCL,
TXSM, TXU, WICF. • *Play Program*—
CAHL: 1958. NYPL: 1954. • *Publicity
Release*—CAA: Paramount (numerous)
(1930s). CAUT: Paramount (1929?).
NYMA: American Broadcasting Com-
pany (1968). NYPL: Unknown studio.
• *Scrapbook*—NJPT (Yeandle Collec-
tion), NYAM, NYMA, NYPL (also in R.
Locke Collection). • *Studio Biography*—
CAA: Paramount (1928, 1933); MGM
(1933). CAUT: American Broadcasting
Company (1965).

HAMMERSTEIN, Elaine,
Philadelphia, PA, 1897/98–
1948.
Pretty Elaine Hammerstein was, for
a time, a very popular leading lady in
films. She starred in about 30 films
from 1917, including *Reckless Youth*,
Rupert of Hentzau (probably her best
role), *Broadway Gold* and *Drums of
Jeopardy*. Her career ended in 1926.

PUBLISHED SOURCES
• *Books*—General: *Blue Book of the
Screen*; *Ladies in Distress*; *Who's Who
on the Screen*. Credits: *Filmarama* (v. I
and II); *Twenty Years of Silents*; *Who
Was Who on Screen*. Encyclopedic
Works: *Film Encyclopedia*; *Filmlexicon
degli Autori e delle Opere*; *Who's Who in
Hollywood*. Pictorial: *Silent Portraits*.
• *Periodicals*—*Photoplay* (Nov. 1919);

Motion Picture Classic (Jan. 1920);
Newsweek (Aug. 23, 1948).

ARCHIVAL MATERIALS
• *Clipping File*—CAA: Article (1924);
obituary (1948). NYMN: Newsphotos;
obituary (1948). NYPL (also in Locke
Collection): Newsphotos (numerous);
play review (1918); film appearance
(1920s); article (undated); obituary
(1948). • *Other Clipping File*—GBBF,
MIDL, NYMA (Photoplay Collection),
PAPL, WICF. • *Legal File*—CAUT
(Twentieth Century-Fox Collection):
Talent agreement (1923). • *Photograph/
Still*—CAA (also in Hollywood Studio
Museum Collection), CAHL, CNDA,
DCG (Quigley Photographic Archives),
GBBF, NJFL, NYMN, NYPL, NYSU,
OHCL, TXSM, TXU, WICF. • *Scrap-
book*—NYPL (R. Locke Collection).

HANSEN, Juanita, Des
Moines, IA, 1895/97–1961.
A popular serial queen, blonde
Juanita Hansen's exploits in serials like
Secret of the Submarine, *The Lost City*
and *The Brass Bullet* were eagerly
followed. She also appeared in comedy
(with the Keystone Kops) and in
various other roles. Her hour of fame
was brief, probably because of her
drug addiction, and by 1923 her starring career had ended. She apparently
also played some bits in the 1930s.

PUBLISHED SOURCES
• *Books*—Wrote with Preston L.
Hickey *The Conspiracy of Silence* (1938),
dealing with the drug traffic and addic-
tion. General: *Continued Next Week*;
Ladies in Distress; *Those Fabulous Serial
Heroines*; *The Truth About the Movies*;
Who's Who on the Screen. Credits: *Film-
arama* (v. I and II); *Twenty Years of
Silents*; *Who Was Who on Screen*. En-
cyclopedic Works: *Filmlexicon degli
Autori e delle Opere*; *Halliwell's Film-
goer's Companion*; *Who's Who in
Hollywood*. Pictorial: *Silent Portraits*.
• *Periodicals*—The following periodical articles are in addition to those in-
cluded in the library listings below:

Photoplay (May 1916, Sept. 1918, May 1920); *Motion Picture Magazine* (Aug. 1916, July 1919); *Motion Picture Classic* (Jan. 1917, Dec. 1920); *Time* (Oct. 6, 1961); *Films in Review* (Mar. 1962); *Classic Film Collector* (Spring 1978).

ARCHIVAL MATERIALS

• *Clipping File*—CAA: Drug habit (1951-52); article (1935, 1950); obituary (1961). CAUU: Article (1951). NYMA (also in Photoplay Collection): Periodical article: *Classic Film Collector* (Spring-Summer 1969). NYMN: Newsphotos; drug addiction (1934, undated); drug charges (1936-37); injury. NYPL (also in Locke Collection): Newsphotos; diet advertisement; drug arrest (1923, undated); article (1922, 1937); obituary (1961). • *Other Clipping File*—AZSU (Jimmy Starr Collection), GBBF, MAH, MIDL, OHCL, WICF. • *Photograph/Still*—CAA (also in Hollywood Studio Museum Collection), CAUT (Jessen Collection), CAUU, NYB (Bettmann/UPI Collection), NYPL, NYSU, OHCL, TXU, WICF. • *Press Kit*—OHCL. • *Studio Biography*—NYMA: Photoplay.

HARLAN, Kenneth, Boston, MA, 1895/98-1967.

Kenneth Harlan was an enormously popular matinee idol almost from the moment he entered films about 1917. During the course of his silent film career he partnered many of the leading actresses of the day. Although he appeared in more than 130 films, the advent of talkies saw his career in decline. He made few films until 1935 when he came back to appear in a long string of films through 1943. This time his roles were supporting ones, including numerous villains in westerns. He was married to Marie Prevost (q.v.), one of his seven marriages.

PUBLISHED SOURCES

• *Books*—Co-authored (with Rex Lease) a cookbook: *What Actors Eat—When They Eat* (1939). **General:** *Blue Book of the Screen*; *Character People*;

Eighty Silent Film Stars; *Famous Film Folk*; *The Truth About the Movies*; *Who's Who on the Screen*. **Credits:** *Filmarama* (v. I and II); *Forty Years of Screen Credits*; *Twenty Years of Silents*; *Who Was Who on Screen*. **Encyclopedic Works:** *Film Encyclopedia*; *Filmlexicon degli Autori e delle Opere*; *Halliwell's Filmgoer's Companion*; *The Movie Makers*; *The Picturegoer's Who's Who and Encyclopedia of the Screen To-day*; *Who's Who in Hollywood*; *The World Film Encyclopedia*. **Pictorial:** *Silent Portraits*.

• *Periodicals*—The following periodical articles are in addition to those included in the library listings below: *Motion Picture Magazine* (Dec. 1919); *Motion Picture Classic* (Dec. 1920, Oct. 1928); *Photoplay* (Nov. 1924); *Classic Images* (Sept. 1981, Aug.-Sept. 1990) (filmography).

ARCHIVAL MATERIALS

• *Caricature*—NYPL (Sardi Collection). • *Clipping File*—CAA: Marriage/divorce (1928, 1930, 1946, 1953, 1957); nostalgia (1950s?, 1956, 1961); obituary (1967). CAUT: Obituary (1967). NYMA (also in Photoplay Collection): Obituary (1967). Periodical article: *Classic Images* (Jan. 1984). NYMN: Newsphotos. NYPL (also in Locke Collection): Stage appearance (1929); newsphotos; marriage/divorce (1927, 1930, 1934); film appearance (1920s, 1930s); film synopsis (1920s); article (1928, undated); obituary (1967). Periodical articles: *Photoplay Art* (Dec. 1917); *Motion Picture Magazine* (Feb. 1929). TXU: Obituary (1967). • *Other Clipping File*—GBBF, MIDL, OHCL, PAPL, WICF. • *Correspondence*—NYMA (Photoplay Collection). NYPL (C. & L. Brown Collection): 1928-37. • *Filmography*—CAA. • *Legal File*—CAUW: Contract (1925-41); personnel, payroll record (1925-41); union agreement (1941); talent agreement (1926-27, 1936-37, 1939-40). • *Photograph/Still*—CAA (also in Hollywood Studio Museum Collection), CAH, CASF, CAUC, CAUT (Jessen Collection) (Portrait File), CAUU, DCG (Quigley Photographic Archives),

GBBF, NJPT, NYCU (Bulliet Collection), NYEH, NYMN, NYPL, OHCL, PAPL, TNUT (Clarence Brown Collection), TXSM, TXU (A. Davis Collection), WICF. • *Scrapbook*—NYPL, TNUT (Clarence Brown Collection). • *Studio Biography*—NYMA: Photoplay.

HARRIS, Mildred (also known as Mildred Harris Chaplin), Cheyenne, WY, 1901-1944.

Although pretty Mildred Harris was in films as a child before her marriage to Charles Chaplin (q.v.), it could reasonably be said that the liaison helped sustain her adult career. Throughout the 1920s she appeared in films such as *Fool's Paradise*, *Dangerous Traffic*, *The Desert Hawk* and *Frivolous Sal*. She was also seen in early talkies but by then the roles were decreasing and she eventually was reduced to bit parts.

PUBLISHED SOURCES

• *Books*—General: *Hollywood Kids*; *Who's Who in the Film World*; *Who's Who on the Screen*. Credits: *Filmarama* (v. I and II); *Forty Years of Screen Credits*; *Twenty Years of Silents*; *Who Was Who on Screen*. Encyclopedic Works: *Film Encyclopedia*; *Filmlexicon degli Autori e delle Opere*; *Who's Who in Hollywood*. Biography/Autobiography: *Charlie Chaplin* (Huff); *The Little Fellow*; *My Autobiography* (Chaplin). Pictorial: *Silent Portraits*.
• *Periodicals*—The following periodical articles are in addition to that included in the library listings below: *Moving Picture World* (Nov. 7, 1914); *Photoplay* (Oct. 1918, Feb. 1919, Dec. 1919, Apr. 1920, May 1924); *Motion Picture Magazine* (Nov. 1918, June 1920); *Picture Play Magazine* (July 1920); *Classic Film Collector* (Spring 1978).

ARCHIVAL MATERIALS

• *Clipping File*—CAA: Illness (1944); stage appearance (1937); legal problem (1933); home (1918?); obituary (1944). NYMN: Newsphotos; obituary (1944).

NYPL (also in Locke Collection): Newsphotos; article (undated); burlesque appearance; engagement/marriage (1933-34, undated); comeback; legal problem (1932); stage appearance; works as extra (1926); film appearance (1926, 1935); illness (1944); obituary (1944). Periodical article: *Film Culture* (Spring 1972). • *Other Clipping File*—GBBF, MAH, MIDL, NYMA (Photoplay Collection), WICF. • *Legal File*—CAUW: Contract (1927); talent agreement (1929-31). • *Oral History*—NYCO: Mentioned in: Albert (Eddie) Sutherland interview. • *Photograph/Still*—CAA (also in Hollywood Studio Museum Collection) (also in MGM Collection), CALM, CAUT (Jessen Collection), CAUU, DCG (Quigley Photographic Archives), IAU (Junkin Collection), NYEH, NYPL, NYSU, OHCL, TXSM, TXU, WICF. • *Scrapbook*—NYPL (R. Locke Collection). • *Studio Biography*—CAA: Paramount (1930s?, 1942).

HARRON, John (Johnny), New York, NY, 1903-1939.

John Harron was a serviceable leading man in many 1920s films, including *The Fire Patrol*, *Rose of the Tenements*, *Satan in Sables* and *Hell-Bent for Heaven*. He continued in minor films of the 1930s (e.g., *The White Zombie*, *Each Dawn I Die*) and was kept busy up to the time of his death. He was the brother of Robert Harron (q.v.).

PUBLISHED SOURCES

• *Books*—Credits: *Filmarama* (v. II); *Forty Years of Screen Credits*; *Twenty Years of Silents*; *Who Was Who on Screen*. Encyclopedic Works: *Film Encyclopedia*; *The Picturegoer's Who's Who and Encyclopedia of the Screen To-day*; *Who's Who in Hollywood*.
• *Periodicals*—*Motion Picture Classic* (June 1921).

ARCHIVAL MATERIALS

• *Clipping File*—CAA: Family tragedies (1960). • *Other Clipping File*—GBBF, NYMA (Photoplay Collection),

OHCL, WICF. • *Legal File* — CAUW: Contract summary (1937); option (1937-39); letter, memo (1937-39); contract (1937-39); personnel, payroll record (1932-39); talent agreement (1925, 1930, 1932, undated). • *Photograph/Still* — CAA (also in Hollywood Studio Museum Collection), CNDA, DCG (Quigley Photographic Archives), GBBF, NJPT, NYEH, NYPL, OHCL, TXSM, TXU, WICF. • *Studio Biography* — NYMA: Photoplay.

HARRON, Robert (Bobby), New York, NY, 1893/94-1920.

Robert Harron was a most popular D.W. Griffith leading man from the early 1910s — the epitome of the sensitive young hero — among whose films were *Intolerance* (the modern story), *Birth of a Nation*, *True Heart Susie* and *Hearts of the World*. He was the older brother of John Harron (q.v.).

PUBLISHED SOURCES

• *Books* — Bibliography: *The Idols of Silence.* General: *First One Hundred Noted Men and Women of the Screen*; *The Kindergarten of the Movies*; *Who's Who in the Film World*; *Who's Who on the Screen.* Credits: *Filmarama* (v. I and II); *Twenty Years of Silents*; *Who Was Who on Screen.* Encyclopedic Works: *Film Encyclopedia*; *Halliwell's Filmgoer's Companion*; *Who's Who in Hollywood*; *The World Almanac Who's Who of Film.* Pictorial: *Silent Portraits.*
• *Periodicals* — The following periodical articles are in addition to those included in the library listings below: *Photoplay* (Feb. 1915, Aug. 1917, Apr. 1918, Mar. 1926); *Motion Picture Magazine* (Sept. 1919, Dec. 1920); *Picture Show* (Nov. 1, 1919); *Motion Picture Classic* (July 1920); *Films in Review* (Apr. 1964, Apr. 1968, Oct. 1968); *Silent Picture* (Autumn 1969); *Film Dope* (Sept. 1981).

ARCHIVAL MATERIALS

• *Clipping File* — CAA: Harron family (1960). NYMA (also in Photoplay Collec-

tion): Personal data summary; autopsy report (1920); Harron family (1960). Periodical articles: *Photo-play Journal* (Aug. 1916); *Exhibitors' Trade Review* (Sept. 18, 1920); *Moving Picture World* (Sept. 25, 1920). NYMN: Newsphotos. NYPL (also in Locke Collection): Newsphotos. Periodical articles: *Films in Review* (Dec. 1963) (filmography); *Films and Filming* (May 1972). • *Other Clipping File* — GBBF, MAH, PAPL, WICF. • *Filmography* — NYMA. • *Oral History* — NYCO: Mentioned in: Grayson Kirk interview. • *Manuscript* — NYMA: *Griffith's Boy: an Introduction to the Career of Robert Harron* (Celia McGerr), 1978. Probably an unpublished thesis. • *Photograph/Still* — CAA (also in Hollywood Studio Museum Collection), CAUT (Jessen Collection), CNDA, DCG (Quigley Photographic Archives), GBBF, NJFL, NYEH, NYMN, NYPL, WICF. • *Program* — CAA: Revival of *Birth of a Nation.* • *Scrapbook* — NYPL (also in R. Locke Collection).

HART, William S(urrey), Newburgh, NY, 1864/70-1946.

Middle-aged stage actor William S. Hart went "West" in 1914 to become an unlikely western hero/anti-hero and one of the most popular stars of the 1910s. Some of his films like *Hell's Hinges* and *The Testing Block* are still highly regarded today. Others included *The Aryan*, *Singer Jim McKee*, and *The Narrow Trail*. There were also a few non-western appearances. In the 1920s his stardom waned but his last film *Tumbleweeds* (1925), for whose reissue he filmed an eloquent introduction in 1939, is considered a classic.

PUBLISHED SOURCES

• *Books* — Written by (or ghostwritten for) WSH were adventure stories for boys, and other fiction, including *A Lighter of Flames* (1923), *In the Days of '52* (1925), *Injun and Whitey* (1919), *Injun and Whitey Strike Out For Themselves* (1921), *The Golden West Boys, Injun and Whitey* (1919), *Pinto Ben* and Other Stories (1919), *Patrick Henry* (1920), *Hoofbeats* (1933), *The Law on Horseback* (1925), *Told Under a White Oak Tree* ("written" by WSH's pinto pony) (1922) and *Injun and Whitey to the Rescue* (1922). Wrote with his sister Mary Hart—*And All Points West!* (1940). Other books credited to WSH include *The Order of Chanta Sutas* (1925). **Bibliography:** *The Idols of Silence.* **General:** *The BFI Companion to the Western*; *Classics of the Silent Screen*; *Close Ups*; *The Cowboy*; *Famous Film Folk*; *The Filming of the West*; *The First Film Makers*; *The Great Cowboy Stars of Movies & Television*; *Great Western Stars*; *The Hall of Fame of Western Film Stars*; *The History of Motion Pictures*; *History of the American Cinema* (v. 3); *Hollywood Album*; *Hollywood Directors, 1914-1940*; *Hollywood Hall of Fame*; *"Image" on the Art and Evolution of the Film*; *Immortals of the Screen*; *Life Stories of the Movie Stars*; *The Matinee Idols*; *The Movie Stars*; *The Movie Stars Story*; *Personal Glimpses of Famous Folks*; *A Pictorial History of Westerns*; *Shooting Stars*; *The Stars* (Schickel); *The Stars Appear*; *They Went Thataway*; *The Truth About the Movies*; *The War, the West and the Wilderness*; *The Western* (Eyles); *The Western* (Fenin); *Who's Who on the Screen*; *Wild West Characters*; *Winners of the West.* **Credits:** *Filmarama* (v. I and II); *Twenty Years of Silents*; *Who Was Who on Screen.* **Encyclopedic Works:** *A Biographical Dictionary of Film*; *A Companion to the Movies*; *A Dictionary of the Cinema*; *Film Encyclopedia*; *Filmlexicon degli Autori e delle Opere*; *Halliwell's Filmgoer's Companion*; *The Illustrated Encyclopedia of the World's Great Movie Stars and Their Films*; *The Illustrated Who's Who of the Cinema*; *International Dictionary of Films and Filmmakers* (v. 3); *The International Encyclopedia of Film*; *The Movie Makers*; *The Oxford Companion to Film*; *The Picturegoer's Who's Who and Encyclopedia of the Screen To-day*; *Quinlan's Illustrated Registry of Film Stars*; *Who Was Who in the Theatre*; *Who's Who in Hollywood*; *The World Almanac Who's Who of Film*; *The World Encyclopedia of the Film.* **Films:** *The Complete Films of William S. Hart.* **Biography/Autobiography:** *My Life East and West.* **Pictorial:** *Silent Portraits.* **Factoids:** *Star Stats.*

• *Periodicals*—The following periodical articles are in addition to those included in the library listings below: *Moving Picture World* (Nov. 14, 1914); *Motion Picture Magazine* (May 1915, Jan. 1917, Apr. 1917, Dec. 1917, Sept. 1922, Nov. 1923, Oct. 1924); *Motion Picture Classic* (Mar. 1916, Oct. 1918, July 1922, Oct. 1927, Oct. 1929); *Picture Show* (Jan. 24, 1920); *Pictures and Picturegoer* (Apr. 1921, Sept. 1921); *American Magazine* (July 1921); *Photoplay* (Sept. 1925, Apr. 1928); *National Magazine* (Mar. 1926); *Newsweek* (July 1, 1946); *Time* (July 1, 1946); *Films in Review* (May 1955); *Image* (Mar. 1956) (filmography); *Show* (Sept. 1962); *8mm collector* (Aug. 1963); *Film Fan Monthly* (July-Aug. 1966); *Silent Picture* (Spring 1972); *Western Horseman* (Apr. 1973); *The Velvet Light Trap* (Spring 1974); *Classic Film Collector* (Fall 1974, May 1979); *Film and History* (Dec. 1977); *Classic Film/Video Images* (Jan. 1980, July 1980, Jan. 1981); *Cine Revue* (July 9, 1981); *Film Dope* (Sept. 1981); *Classic Images* (Oct. 1984); *Cineforum* (Nov. 1984); *Southwest Art* (Aug. 1986); *Ecran* (nos. 5/6, 1988); *Art and Antiques* (Sept. 1989).

OBSCURE PUBLISHED SOURCES
CAA, NYMA: *William S. Hart.*

MEDIA
Out West (video); *Saddle Up* (video); *William S. Hart* (film); *Wm. S. Hart and the Sad Clowns* (video).

ARCHIVAL MATERIALS
• *Clipping File*—CAA (also in Collection): Newsphotos; film appearance (1916, 1920-21, 1923, 1941); Hart Park (1944, 1964, 1976, 1989); marriage/divorce (1921-22); novel (1923-24); article (1918, 1920, 1922, 1929); horse (1919); legal problem (1926-27, 1931, 1934); comeback (1929); illness (1933, 1946); guardianship (1946); estate (1947, 1949–

51, 1953, 1955); ranch (1947, 1949, 1957–62, 1965, 1967–70, 1977, 1980, 1984, 1987); film festival (1965, 1978 [program notes]); obituary (1946). Periodical articles: *Photoplay* (Oct. 1915, Oct. 1916, May 1917, Sept. 1917, Apr. 1919, Feb. 1920, Jan. 1921, Apr. 1921, Feb. 1922, Apr.-May 1922, May 1923, Aug. 1923, May 1925, Oct. 1929, Dec. 1930); *Picture Play Magazine* (Sept. 1916, Dec. 1919, Sept. 1920); *Motion Picture Magazine* (Nov. 1916, May 1917, Jan. 1918, Sept. 1918, Mar. 1919, Aug. 1919, July 1920, Apr. 1921, Feb. 1922, June 1922); *Motion Picture Classic* (Nov. 1917, Aug. 1918, Dec. 1918, Jan. 1919, Aug. 1920); *Campfire Stories* (a series "by" WSH) (1920s); *Films in Review* (Apr. 1955, Aug.-Sept. 1962); *Westways* (July 1972); *Terra* (Nov.-Dec. 1987). CAFI: Film festival (1987); list of films in U.S. archives; look-alike contest (1986); home/ranch (1970, 1980, 1982, 1984, 1986). CAUT: Film appearance (1929); article (1929, 1936, 1940, 1946, 1972); ranch (1946, 1959, 1961, 1965, 1977–79, 1981, 1984); home (1966); newsphotos; illness (1946); obituary (1946). CAUU: Film festival (1978). NYMA: Biography (1965); excerpts of reviews for *Hoofbeats* (1933); career (1945); article (1936, 1939, 1940–41); newsphotos; obituary (1946). Periodical articles: *Photoplay* (Mar. 1917); *8mm Collector* (Spring 1965); *Classic Film Collector* (Fall 1966, Summer 1967); *Classic Film/Video Images* (May 1979, Nov. 1979); *Classic Images* (Jan. 1983, Mar. 1985). NYMN: Newsphotos; lawsuit against United Artists (1936); article (1934, 1936, 1940, undated); obituary (1946). NYPL (also in C. & L. Brown Collection) (also in Locke Collection): PARTIAL CONTENTS: Hart ranch (1968, 1970). Periodical articles: *Players Bulletin* (Spring 1960); *Silent Picture* (Summer-Autumn 1972). • *Other Clipping File*–AZSU (Jimmy Starr Collection), CALM (see Collection), CNDA, DCLC (see Collection), GBBF, MAH, MIDL, OHCL, WICF. • *Collection*–CAA: Typescript scenarios of films; several hundred clippings, mainly of film appearances (1918–21); *Campfire Boys* and other stories apparently ghostwritten for

WSH; publicity releases (W. S. Hart Company); draft press books for films, including *The Testing Block, The Whistle, O'Malley of the Mounted* and *Sand*. CALM: Business and personal correspondence (1916–40); fan mail (1917–26); books; photos; stories "by" WSH; financial records (including checks, statements, account books, bills, receipts, auditor's reports) (1916–43); clippings (1897–1946); scrapbooks (1891–1923); books and story manuscripts; poems; film scenarios; play programs (1889–1947); periodical articles (1895–1946); legal papers (lawsuits) (1917–28); drawings, posters. DCLC (Gatewood Dunston Collection): 63 letters discussing WSH's films and career (1929–46); miscellaneous correspondence; synopses of WSH's stories and scripts (1914–18); clippings regarding a lawsuit against United Artists (1940); publicity; materials about the efforts of WSH's son to contest his father's will (1946–50). • *Correspondence*–CAA (Adolf Zukor Collection): 9 letters relating to marriage, divorce, childbirth, etc. (1919–22). CAHL: 9 letters (1929–31). CALM (see Collection), DCLC (see Collection). NEHS (McKelvie Collection): 11 letters (1921–41). Includes a poem by WSH. NYMA: 1929, 1931. NYMN. NYPL: Letters (C. & L. Brown Collection) (1930s, 1938–45); others (1929, 1937, undated). NYUR: 5 letters relating to marriage, a surgery, etc. (1921–33). • *Filmography*–CAA, NYMA. • *Legal File*–CALM (see Collection), DCLC (see Collection). • *Oral History*–NYCO: Mentioned in the following interviews: G.M. Anderson, Robert Beard, Johnny Mack Brown, Jean Dalrymple, Sessue Hayakawa, Gabby Hayes, Ben Johnson, Joel McCrea, Louella Parsons, Adolph Zukor. • *Photograph/Still*–CAA (also in Hollywood Studio Museum Collection), CALM (also in Collection) (William S. Hart Photograph Collection), CASF, CAUC (Motion Picture Photograph Collection), CAUS, CAUT (Jessen Collection), CAUU, DCG (Quigley Photographic Archives), MABU (Douglas Fairbanks Jr. Collection), NYAM, NYB (Bettmann/UPI

Collection) (Penguin Collection) (Springer Collection) (Underwood Collection), NYCU (Dramatic Museum Portraits), NYEH, NYMN, NYPL, NYSU, OHCL, TXSM, TXU, WICF. • *Press Kit* — OHCL. • *Program* — CAA: Play program (*Ben-Hur*) (1901). CALM (see Collection). • *Publicity Release* — CAA (see Collection), DCLC (see Collection). • *Reminiscence* — MISU: Hart bids farewell to his fans, as broadcast on the HBO series *Remember When* (recording) (1984). • *Scrapbook* — CALM (see Collection), NYPL (also in C. & L. Brown Collection) (also in R. Locke Collection), WICF.

HAVER, Phyllis (Phyllis O'Haver), Douglas, KS, 1899–1960.

One of the better known alumna of the Mack Sennett bathing beauties was Phyllis Haver. A rather statuesque actress, she frequently found herself playing in comedies or as the "other woman" in melodramas (e.g., *The Battle of the Sexes*). When she did play a lead, as in *Chicago*, it was often as a somewhat tarnished heroine. She departed the screen after some 1929 films.

PUBLISHED SOURCES

• *Books* — General: *Blue Book of the Screen*; *Famous Film Folk*; *How I Broke Into the Movies*; *Who's Who on the Screen*. Credits: *Filmarama* (v. I and II); *Forty Years of Screen Credits*; *Twenty Years of Silents*; *Who Was Who on Screen*. Encyclopedic Works: *Film Encyclopedia*; *Filmlexicon degli Autori e delle Opere*; *Halliwell's Filmgoer's Companion*; *The Movie Makers*; *Who's Who in Hollywood*; *The World Film Encyclopedia*. Pictorial: *Silent Portraits*. • *Periodicals* — *Motion Picture Classic* (May 1921, Apr. 1922, Oct. 1928); *Photoplay* (Sept. 1921, Oct. 1927); *Motion Picture Magazine* (Apr. 1923, Sept. 1927, Feb. 1928, Apr. 1929); *Collier's* (Oct. 20, 1928); *Focus on Film* (Autumn 1974); *Classic Film Collector* (Spring 1978).

ARCHIVAL MATERIALS

• *Clipping File* — CAA: Divorce (1945); film appearance (1923); article (1945); obituary (1960). NYMA (also in Photoplay Collection): Newsphotos; obituary (1960). NYPL (also in Locke Collection): Newsphotos; nostalgia (1936?); career (1931); film appearance (1920s); article (1940); bitten by monkey (1930s?); marriage (1945); obituary (1960). • *Other Clipping File* — AZSU (Jimmy Starr Collection), GBBF, MAH, MIDL, NYSU, OHCL, PAPL, TXU, WICF. • *Legal File* — CAA (Sennett Collection): Contract (1919–21); option (1919–20). • *Photograph/Still* — CAA (also in Hollywood Studio Museum Collection) (also in MGM Collection), CAUT (Jessen Collection), CAUU, DCG (Quigley Photographic Archives), GBBF, NYB (Bettmann/UPI Collection), NYCU (Dramatic Museum Portraits) (Palmer Collection), NYEH, NYPL, NYSU, OHCL, TXSM, TXU, WICF. • *Scrapbook* — NYPL.

HAWLEY, Wanda (also known as Wanda Petit) (Wanda Pittack?), Scranton, PA, 1895/97–1963.

Working at Realart and other studios, as well as for C.B. DeMille, blonde Wanda Hawley made films like *The Affairs of Anatol*, *Old Wives for New*, *The Snob* and *Bobbed Hair*. She was a popular star from her debut around 1917 to the end of the '20s, co-starring with Rudolph Valentino (q. v.) and other major leading men.

PUBLISHED SOURCES

• *Books* — General: *Blue Book of the Screen*; *Famous Film Folk*; *Sweethearts of the Sage*; *The Truth About the Movies*; *Who's Who on the Screen*. Credits: *Filmarama* (v. I and II); *Twenty Years of Silents*. Encyclopedic Works: *Film Encyclopedia*; *Filmlexicon degli Autori e delle Opere*; *Who's Who in Hollywood*. Pictorial: *Silent Portraits*. • *Periodicals* — *Motion Picture Classic* (Oct. 1918, Sept. 1921); *Photoplay* (Apr. 1919, Jan. 1920, Sept. 1920); *Theatre* (May 1919); *Motion Picture Magazine* (Nov. 1919, Aug. 1920); *Picture Play*

Magazine (Nov. 1919); *Pantomime* (Oct. 29, 1921).

ARCHIVAL MATERIALS

• *Clipping File* — NYPL (also in Locke Collection): Newsphotos; stage appearance (1927); article (undated); divorce (1923). • *Other Clipping File* — GBBF, MAH, NYMA (Photoplay Collection), WICF. • *Correspondence* — NYPL (C. & L. Brown Collection): Various dates. • *Photograph/ Still* — CAA (also in Hollywood Studio Museum Collection), CALM, CAUT (Jessen Collection), CAUU, DCG (Quigley Photographic Archives), IAU (Junkin Collection), NYB (Springer Collection), NYCU (Dramatic Museum Portraits), NYPL, NYSU, OHCL, TXSM, TXU, WICF. • *Scrapbook* — NYPL (also in R. Locke Collection). • *Studio Biography* — CAA: Paramount (1922).

HAYAKAWA, Sessue (Kintaro Hayakawa), Chiba, Japan, 1886/90-1973.

Unlike most other "exotic" actors in Hollywood, Sessue Hayakawa was sometimes cast as a heroic leading man rather than being a perennial villain. From 1914 he appeared in a series of popular films, most of them melodramas like the sensational *The Cheat* (1915). He left Hollywood in 1923 to make films abroad but returned in 1931 for *Daughter of the Dragon*. His American talkie career did not prosper and it was not until 1949 that he returned for more films, among them his notable role in *The Bridge on the River Kwai* (1957).

PUBLISHED SOURCES

• *Books* — Wrote a novel *The Bandit Prince* (1926). **General:** *Character People*; *Classics of the Silent Screen*; *First One Hundred Noted Men and Women of the Screen*; *Gentlemen to the Rescue*; *Hollywood Album*; *The Movie Stars Story*; *Who's Who on the Screen*. **Credits:** *Filmarama* (v. I and II); *Forty Years of Screen Credits*; *Twenty Years of Silents*; *Who Was Who on Screen*. **Encyclopedic Works:** *Current Biography* (1944, 1963, 1975); *A Dictionary of the Cinema*; *Film Encyclopedia*; *Filmlexicon degli Autori e delle Opere*; *Halliwell's Filmgoer's Companion*; *The Illustrated Who's Who of the Cinema*; *International Dictionary of Films and Filmmakers* (v. 3); *The International Encyclopedia of Film*; *The Movie Makers*; *The Oxford Companion to Film*; *The Picturegoer's Who's Who and Encyclopedia of the Screen To-day*; *Quinlan's Illustrated Registry of Film Stars*; *Who's Who in Hollywood*; *The World Almanac Who's Who of Film*; *The World Film Encyclopedia*. **Biography/Autobiography:** *Zen Showed Me the Way to Peace, Happiness and Tranquility*. **Pictorial:** *Silent Portraits*. **Recordings:** *Hollywood on Record*. **Factoids:** *Star Stats*.

• *Periodicals* — The following periodical articles are in addition to those included in the library listings below: *Sunset* (July 1916); *Motion Picture Classic* (Dec. 1916, July 1922, May 1926); *Literary Digest* (Nov. 3, 1917); *Current Opinion* (Jan. 1918); *Picture Show* (Jan. 3, 1920); *Motion Picture Magazine* (Mar. 1921, Jan. 1929, Oct. 1931); *Filmplay Journal* (Sept. 1921); *Newsweek* (Nov. 14, 1949, Dec. 3, 1973); *Films in Review* (June-July 1966, Apr. 1976, Nov. 1976, June-July 1983); *Time* (Dec. 3, 1973); *Cinema 74* (Jan. 1974); *Cinéma* (France) (Jan. 1974); *Ecran* (Jan. 1974); *Classic Film Collector* (Spring 1974); *Cine Revue* (Nov. 5, 1981).

ARCHIVAL MATERIALS

• *Caricature* — NYMN.   • *Clipping File* — CAA: Home (1956); article (1957-58, 1966, 1987); Japanese biographical musical (1989); return to Hollywood (1948-49); film appearance (1960); practices Zen (1960); legal problem (1961); obituary (1973). Periodical articles: *Photoplay* (Oct. 1914, Mar. 1916, Nov. 1918, Dec. 1919); *Motion Picture Magazine* (Apr. 1918, Oct. 1920, Mar. 1922, May 1922); *Motion Picture Classic* (Nov. 1918, Jan. 1919, Sept. 1921); *Newsweek* (Mar. 17, 1958); *New Yorker* (Aug. 1, 1959); *Coronet* (May 1961). CAFI: Film festival (1979); obituary

(1973). Periodical article: *Classic Film Collector* (1969?). CAUT: Film appearance (1955); legal problem (1960); newsphotos; article (1949); obituary (1973). CAUU: Film festival (1979); article (1922, 1958, 1976); obituary (1973). NYMA: Article (1957, undated); newsphotos; biography (1982); obituary (1973). Periodical articles: *Newsweek* (Mar. 17, 1958); *Classic Film Collector* (Spring-Summer 1970). NYMN: Newsphotos; stage appearance (1959); film appearance (1949). NYPL (also in Locke Collection): Article (1949–50, 1957–58, 1963); stage appearance (1959); program for Asian-American International Film Festival (1982); film appearance (1949, undated); newsphotos; film review (1959); Buddhism (1960); play review (1959); TV appearance (1958); paternity case (1961); excerpt from *Current Biography* (1962); review of *Zen Showed Me the Way*; obituary (1974). Periodical article: *Bridge* (Winter 1982/83). • *Other Clipping File*—AZSU (Jimmy Starr Collection), CNDA, GBBF, MAH, MIDL, OHCL, WICF. • *Correspondence*—NYPL (C. & L. Brown Collection): 1949. • *Filmography*—CAA, NYEH, NYMA. • *Legal File*—CAUT (Twentieth Century-Fox Collection): Memo (1955); agreement (1955); affidavit (1955). • *Oral History*—NYCO: Interviewed in 1959. • *Photograph/Still*—CAA (also in Hollywood Studio Museum Collection), CALM, CAUT (Jessen Collection), CAUU, CNDA, DCG (Quigley Photographic Archives), IAU (Junkin Collection), NYB (Bettmann/UPI Collection) (Penguin Collection), NYEH, NYMN, NYPL, NYSU, OHCL, TXU, WICF. • *Press Kit*—OHCL. • *Publicity Release*—AZSU (Jimmy Starr Collection). • *Reminiscence*—MISU: Recording. • *Scrapbook*—NYPL (also in R. Locke Collection). • *Studio Biography*—CAA: Paramount (1931, 1958); Columbia (1956); Allied Artists (1960). CAFI: Allied Artists (1960). CAUT: Paramount (1958). CAUU: Paramount (1931); Columbia (1956).

HERSHOLT, Jean, Copenhagen, Denmark, 1886–1956.

Jean Hersholt switched from sometime silent villainy (e.g., *Greed*) to talkie kindliness as doctors Dafoe and Christian (the latter based on his radio program). He played a variety of roles in his hundreds of American and European films from the early 1910s to the 1950s, including one-reelers, and was always a dependable lead or supporting player. He was awarded two special Oscars for his work on Hollywood humanitarian causes.

PUBLISHED SOURCES
• *Books*—Edited and translated the *Complete Works of Hans Christian Andersen* and various other editions of Andersen, as well as individual fairy tales (1930s and 1940s); wrote *Report of the National America Denmark Association and Denmark Relief, Inc.* **General:** *Eighty Silent Film Stars*; *The Great Movie Series*; *Hollywood Album*; *How I Broke Into the Movies*; *Immortals of the Screen*; *The MGM Stock Company*; *More Character People*; *Motion Picture News Booking Guide and Studio Directory* (1927); *Saturday Afternoon at the Bijou*; *Strangers in Hollywood.* **Credits:** *Filmarama* (v. I and II); *Forty Years of Screen Credits*; *Twenty Years of Silents*; *Who Was Who on Screen.* **Encyclopedic Works:** *Current Biography* (1944); *Film Encyclopedia*; *Filmlexicon degli Autori e delle Opere*; *Halliwell's Filmgoer's Companion*; *Hollywood Character Actors*; *The Illustrated Who's Who of the Cinema*; *The Movie Makers*; *National Cyclopaedia of American Biography* (1942, 1958); *The Picturegoer's Who's Who and Encyclopedia of the Screen To-day*; *Quinlan's Illustrated Registry of Film Stars*; *Who's Who in Hollywood*; *The World Almanac Who's Who of Film*; *The World Encyclopedia of the Film*; *The World Film Encyclopedia.* **Catalog:** *Catalog of the Jean Hersholt Collection of Hans Christian Andersen.* **Pictorial:** *Silent Portraits.* **Factoids:** *Star Stats.*
• *Periodicals*—The following periodical articles are in addition to those included in the library listings below: *Photoplay* (Sept. 1925, Dec. 1926);

Motion Picture Magazine (Jan. 1926, Feb. 1930); *Motion Picture Classic* (Feb. 1927, Aug. 1928, Apr. 1929, Jan. 1931, Apr. 1931); *Close-Up* (June 1928); *Silver Screen* (July 1936, May 1941); *Woman's Home Companion* (June 1939); *Screen Book* (Nov. 1939); *Horn Book* (May 1944); *Saturday Review* (Feb. 14, 1948); *Newsweek* (June 11, 1956); *Time* (June 11, 1956); *Classic Images* (Mar. 1991) (filmography).

ARCHIVAL MATERIALS

• *Clipping File* — CAA (also in Collection): Special Academy Award (1949); TV appearance (1955); President of Academy of Motion Picture Arts and Sciences (1948); honor (1947–49, 1954–56); newsphotos; production company (1944); gift to Library of Congress (1944); 40th year in films (1946); President of Motion Picture Relief Fund (1945, 1947, 1949, 1950–52, 1954–55); surgery (1946, 1955–56); film appearance (1947, 1954); memorial (1958); tribute (1956–57); 40th wedding anniversary (1954); 30th wedding anniversary (1944); radio appearance (1950, 1953); 50 years in films (1955); plans Hollywood Museum (1953); heads Hollywood Bowl Association (1951); obituary (1956). Periodical articles: *Vore Damer* (Apr. 1930) (in Danish); *Screen and Radio Weekly* (1930s); *American-Scandinavian Review* (June 1944); *Cue* (June 29, 1946); *Saturday Review of Literature* (Dec. 21, 1946); *Atlantic Monthly* (May 1948); *Classic Film Collector* (Fall 1969). CAFI: Article (1988). CAUU: Tribute (undated). Periodical article: *Classic Film Collector* (Fall 1969). NYMA: Excerpt from *Current Biography* (1944); article (1983); newsphotos; obituary (1956). Periodical articles: *Classic Film Collector* (Fall 1969); *Classic Images* (Mar. 1987). NYMN: Career; article (undated); obituary (1956). NYPL: Career (1955); article (1926, 1936–37, 1940, undated); newsphotos; Andersen fairy tales (1942); home for aged actors; film review (1930s); work with Dionne Quintuplets (1930s, 1938); returns to films (1950); Dr. Christian (1952, undated); radio appearance (1930s); funeral (1956); war

work (1940s); obituary (1956). Periodical articles: *Collier's* (Apr. 4, 1936); *Look* (Oct. 11, 1938). • *Other Clipping File* — CNDA, GBBF, MAH, OHCL, WICF. • *Collection* — CAA: 32 scrapbooks containing clippings and reviews (1916–43); photographs (1927–54); stills (1915–54); Academy of Motion Picture Arts and Sciences publicity (1945–47); Motion Picture Relief Fund publicity (1938–54); clippings about *Dr. Christian* radio series (1937–48). Also separate bound scripts. • *Correspondence* — CAUS (Hugo Ballin Collection) (Rob Wagner Collection) (Preston Sturges Collection) (Paul J. Smith Collection). MABU (Kate Smith Papers): 1933. NYCU: Letter (Brand collection) (1946); letter (Grauer Collection) (1950); letters (House of Books Collection) (1948). NYMN: 1932–54. NYPL: Letters (C. & L. Brown Collection) (1941); others (1940, 1946, 1951, undated). • *Filmography* — CAA, NYPL. • *Legal File* — CAUT (Twentieth Century-Fox Collection): Letter, memo (1931, 1935–37, 1946); loanout (1935); agreement (1934–38); pay record (1938); contract (1937); contract summary (1937). CAUW: Letter (1948); document (1949); talent agreement (1926, 1929–30). • *Oral History* — NYCO: Mentioned in: Helen Macy interview. • *Photograph/Still* — CAA (also in Collection) (also in Hollywood Studio Museum Collection) (also in MGM Collection), CAFA, CALM, CAOC (Kiesling Collection), CASF, CAUT (Jessen Collection) (Portrait File), CAUU, CNDA, DCG (Quigley Photographic Archives), NYAM, NYB (Bettmann/UPI Collection) (Underwood Collection), NYCU (Palmer Collection), NYEH, NYMN, NYPL, NYSU, OHCL, TXU, WICF. • *Press Kit* — OHCL. • *Publicity Release* — CAA (see Collection). NYPL: Columbia Broadcasting System (1939–40, 1945). • *Reminiscence* — MISU: Recording. • *Scrapbook* — CAA (see Collection), NYAM, NYPL. • *Studio Biography* — CAA: Paramount (1932, 1954); Fox (1930s?); RKO (1939); MGM (1950s). CAUT: Paramount (1954).

HINES, Johnny, Golden, CO, 1895/97–1970.

The brash, cocky characters played by comic actor Johnny Hines can be gleaned from the titles of some of his films: *Burn 'Em Up Barnes, The Crackerjack, Sure-Fire Flint, The Live Wire*. Films like these, and the "Torchy" series in which he appeared from 1920 to 1923, made Hines a popular comedian in the 1920s. His screen appearances began in 1914 but it was with *Alias Jimmy Valentine* in 1920 that he came into his own. By 1928 his appeal was beginning to ebb and his talkie career consisted of scattered supporting roles until 1938.

PUBLISHED SOURCES

• *Books*—General: *Blue Book of the Screen; Eighty Silent Film Stars; Famous Film Folk; Gentlemen to the Rescue; Silent Clowns*. Credits: *Filmarama* (v. I and II); *Twenty Years of Silents; Who Was Who on Screen*. Encyclopedic Works: *Halliwell's Filmgoer's Companion; Filmlexicon degli Autori e delle Opere; The Picturegoer's Who's Who and Encyclopedia of the Screen To-day; Who's Who in Hollywood*. Filmography: *Hollywood on the Palisades*. Pictorial: *Silent Portraits*.

• *Periodicals*—The following periodical articles are in addition to those included in the library listings below: *Motion Picture Magazine* (July 1916, Mar. 1919, Aug. 1926); *Photoplay* (Apr. 1919, Aug. 1925); *Cinema Art* (Mar. 1926); *Motion Picture Classic* (July 1928).

ARCHIVAL MATERIALS

• *Clipping File*—CAA: Obituary (1970). NYMA (also in Photoplay Collection): Film review (1921). Periodical articles: *Classic Film Collector* (Fall 1966, Winter 1970, Fall 1974); *Classic Images* (Sept. 1981, Apr. 1987, July 1987). NYPL (also in Locke Collection): Newsphotos (numerous); film review (1920s); signs with First National; article (undated); freelances (1929); film synopses; stage appearance (1928); obituary (1970). • *Other Clipping File*—GBBF, OHCL, PAPL, WICF. • *Filmography*—CAA, NJFL, NYMA. • *Legal File*—CAUW: Letter,

memo, communication (1927–29, 1947–49); option (1927); payroll record (1947–49); contract (1947–49); document (1923, 1928). • *Photograph/Still*—CAA (also in Hollywood Studio Museum Collection), CAH, CAUU, DCG (Quigley Photographic Archives), GBBF, MIDL, NJFL, NJPT, NYB (Underwood Collection), NYCU (Bulliet Collection) (Dramatic Museum Portraits), NYEH, NYPL, NYSU, OHCL, PAPL, TXSM, TXU (A. Davis Collection), WICF. • *Scrapbook*—NYPL (also in R. Locke Collection). • *Studio Biography*—CAA (also in Mack Sennett Collection): Paramount.

HOLMES, Helen, Chicago, IL, 1892–1950.

Helen Holmes was the original heroine of the lengthy railroad serial *The Hazards of Helen* (later replaced by Helen Gibson [q.v.]) and she also was seen in several other serials and features, many with a railroad theme. She began in films with Mack Sennett (which was perhaps where she developed her ability for stuntwork). Her roles declined to supporting ones in the mid-1920s and she returned, after a long screen absence, to play small parts in the late 1930s and early '40s.

PUBLISHED SOURCES

• *Books*—General: *Continued Next Week; Early American Cinema; Life Stories of the Movie Stars; Reel Women; Sweethearts of the Sage; Those Fabulous Serial Heroines; Who's Who in the Film World; Winners of the West*. Credits: *Filmarama* (v. I and II); *Twenty Years of Silents; Who Was Who on Screen*. Encyclopedic Works: *Film Encyclopedia; Who Was Who in the Theatre; Who's Who in Hollywood*. Pictorial: *Silent Portraits*.

• *Periodicals*—The following periodical articles are in addition to those included in the library listings below: *Green Book Album* (Apr. 1910); *Photoplay* (Mar. 1915, July 1915, June 1916, Oct. 1916, Mar. 1917, June 1917, July 1924); *Motion Picture Magazine* (Apr. 1915, Mar. 1917, July 1917, Nov.

1917); *Feature Movie* (July 25, 1915); *Green Book Magazine* (Apr. 1916); *Motion Picture Classic* (Aug. 1917); *School and Society* (Dec. 3, 1938); *Silent Picture* (Winter 1968-69); *Classic Film Collector* (Spring 1978); *Classic Images* (July 1982).

ARCHIVAL MATERIALS

• *Clipping File* – CAA: Film appearance (1936); animal trainer (1945); obituary (1950). NYMA (also in Photoplay Collection): Periodical articles: *Classic Film Collector* (Winter 1973); *Classic Film/Video Images* (Sept. 1981); *Classic Images* (Aug. 1982, June 1988). NYPL (also in Locke Collection): Newsphotos; comeback (1930s); career (1973); obituary (1950). Periodical article: *Classic Film Collector* (Winter 1973). • *Other Clipping File* – GBBF, MAH, NYSU, PAPL, WICF. • *Correspondence* – NYPL (C. & L. Brown Collection): 1929-50. • *Oral History* – NYCO: Mentioned in: Albert (Eddie) Sutherland interview. • *Photograph/Still* – CAA (also in Hollywood Studio Museum Collection), CAHL, CAUT (Jessen Collection), CAUU, DCG (Quigley Photographic Archives), GBBF, NYEH, NYPL, NYSU, OHCL, WICF. • *Publicity Release* – Paramount (1936). • *Scrapbook* – NYPL (C. & L. Brown Collection) (Locke Collection). • *Studio Biography* – NYMA: Photoplay.

HOLMES, Stuart (Joseph Liebschen?), Chicago, IL or Germany, 1887-1971.

Beginning in films with Edison about 1910, Stuart Holmes had a huge number of films to his credit (some sources say over 600) and was one of the silent screen's busiest villains. He had roles in such movies as *The Four Horsemen of the Apocalypse*, *The Prisoner of Zenda* and *Tess of the D'Urbervilles*. His career continued well into the sound era; he was onscreen as late as 1962.

PUBLISHED SOURCES

• *Books* – **General:** *Blue Book of the Screen*; *Famous Film Folk*. **Credits:**

Filmarama (v. I and II); *Forty Years of Screen Credits*; *Twenty Years of Silents*; *Who Was Who on Screen*. **Encyclopedic Works:** *Film Encyclopedia*; *Filmlexicon degli Autori e delle Opere*; *The Picturegoer's Who's Who and Encyclopedia of the Screen To-day*; *Who's Who in Hollywood*. **Pictorial:** *Silent Portraits*.

• *Periodicals* – The following periodical articles are in addition to that included in the library listings below: *Photoplay* (Dec. 1916); *Motion Picture Classic* (July 1917).

ARCHIVAL MATERIALS

• *Clipping File* – CAA: Film appearance (1961-62); article (1961); obituary (1971). Periodical article: *Classic Film Collector* (Fall 1970). CAUT: Film appearance (1956, 1961-62); obituary (1971). NYMA (also in Photoplay Collection): Periodical article: *Classic Film Collector* (Fall 1970). NYPL (also in Locke Collection): Newsphotos; film appearance (1933, 1961); film review (1916); obituary (1972). • *Other Clipping File* – CAFA, GBBF, MAH, MIDL, PAPL, WICF. • *Legal File* – CAUW: Option (1937-42); letter, memo (1937-42); contract (1937-40, 1942); release (1937-42); contract summary (1937-42); talent agreement (1926-27, 1937-40, undated). • *Oral History* – NYCO: Mentioned in: George K. Arthur interview. • *Photograph/Still* – CAA (also in Hollywood Studio Museum Collection), CAFA, DCG (Quigley Photographic Archives), NJFL, NYCU (Dramatic Museum Portraits), NYEH, NYPL, NYSU, OHCL, TXU, WICF. • *Scrapbook* – NYPL (R. Locke collection). • *Studio Biography* – CAA: Paramount (1933, 1954). NYMA: Photoplay.

HOLT, Jack (Charles J. Holt), The Bronx, NY or Winchester, VA, 1888-1951.

Mustachioed Jack Holt was not a typically handsome leading man but he appeared as the rugged lead in numerous silent and sound films from 1915. Many of them were westerns and serials. Others included *The Woman*

Thou Gavest Me, Kitty Kelly, M.D.,
Eve's Secret and *The Tigress.* He was
kept busy throughout the 1920s and
'30s and returned, after World War II,
to a career in supporting roles which
lasted up to the time of his death.

PUBLISHED SOURCES

• *Books* – Wrote *Desert Poems* (1933).
General: *The BFI Companion to the
Western*; *Blue Book of the Screen*;
Famous Film Folk; *Gentlemen to the
Rescue*; *The Hall of Fame of Western
Film Stars*; *Heroes, Heavies and Sage-
brush*; *Saddle Aces of the Cinema*;
Screen Personalities; *The Truth About
the Movies*; *The Western* (Eyles); *Who's
Who on the Screen.* **Credits:** *Filmarama*
(v. I and II); *Forty Years of Screen
Credits*; *Twenty Years of Silents*; *Who
Was Who on Screen.* **Encyclopedic
Works:** *Film Encyclopedia*; *Filmlexicon
degli Autori e delle Opere*; *Halliwell's
Filmgoer's Companion*; *The Illustrated
Who's Who of the Cinema*; *The Movie
Makers*; *The Picturegoer's Who's Who
and Encyclopedia of the Screen To-day*;
Who's Who in Hollywood; *The World
Almanac Who's Who of Film*; *The
World Film Encyclopedia.* **Biography/
Autobiography:** *The Fabulous Holts*;
The Wizard of Mordialloc. **Pictorial:**
Silent Portraits.
• *Periodicals* – *Photoplay* (Aug. 1918,
Aug. 1921, Nov. 1922, July 1924, July
1926); *Motion Picture Classic* (Jan. 1919,
July 1925, Mar. 1927, July 1928);
Filmplay Journal (Sept. 1921); *Motion
Picture Magazine* (Nov. 1921, Jan. 1925);
Movie Classic (Nov. 1936); *Newsweek*
(Jan. 29, 1951) *Time* (Jan. 29, 1951);
Views and Reviews (no. 4, 1974); *Classic
Images* (Mar.-Apr. 1982).

ARCHIVAL MATERIALS

• *Clipping File* – CAA: Divorce (1933,
1939-40); ranch (1932); film appearance
(1921, 1945); article (1941); newsphotos;
radio appearance (1948); Paramount
contract (1927); illness (1927); legal problem (1928); obituary (1951). NYMA: Divorce (1933); signs with Columbia (1929);
signs with Famous Players-Lasky (1920);
article (1929, 1931-32); film review

(1930s); film appearance (1910s, 1920s);
obituary (1951). Periodical articles:
Modern Screen (July 1931, Aug. 1933);
Photoplay (Sept. 1932, Nov. 1942); *Picture Play* (Dec. 1933); *Classic Film/
Video Images* (Jan. 1981, Mar. 1981, May
1981). NYMN: Obituary (1951). NYPL
(also in Locke Collection): PARTIAL
CONTENTS: Newsphotos; article (un-
dated); divorce (1933, 1939); film ap-
pearance (1920s, 1930s); film review
(1920s, 1930s); signs with Columbia
(1933); career (1937); family (1942);
funeral (1951); illness; obituary (1951).
• *Other Clipping File* – AZSU (Jimmy
Starr Collection), CNDA, GBBF, MAH,
MIDL, NYSU, OHCL, PAPL, WICF.
• *Filmography* – CAA, NYMA, NYPL.
• *Legal File* – CAUW: Talent agreement
(1948-49). • *Oral History* – NYCO:
Mentioned in the following interviews:
Ralph Bellamy, Lila Lee. • *Photograph/
Still* – CAA (also in Hollywood Studio
Museum Collection), CAFA, CALM,
CAUT (Jessen Collection) (Portrait
File), CAUU, CNDA, DCG (Quigley
Photographic Archives), GBBF, NJFL,
NYAM, NYCU (Dramatic Museum Por-
traits) (Palmer Collection), NYEH,
NYMN, NYPL, NYSU, OHCL, TXU,
WICF. • *Publicity Release* – CAA: Para-
mount (numerous) (1930s); Warner
(1940s). NYMA: Famous Players-Lasky
(1922). • *Scrapbook* – NYAM, NYPL
(also in R. Locke Collection). • *Studio
Biography* – AZSU (Jimmy Starr Collec-
tion). CAA: Paramount (1930); RKO
(1940s). NYMA: Columbia (1935); Paramount. NYPL: Columbia (1935).

HOWES, Reed, Ogden, UT or
Washington, DC, 1900-1964.
Reed Howes was one of the Arrow
Collar men of magazine advertisement
fame. This was the springboard to his
film career which lasted for some 35
years, the last 25 in supporting roles
and stunt work. His starring career
began in 1923 with his own series, the
Rayart-Reed Howes films. For the remainder of the decade he played the
dashing romantic hero but by the early

1930s he was seen mainly as a villain in westerns.

PUBLISHED SOURCES

• *Books* – **General:** *The Hall of Fame of Western Film Stars*; *Heroes, Heavies and Sagebrush.* **Credits:** *Filmarama* (v. II); *Forty Years of Screen Credits*; *Twenty Years of Silents*; *Who Was Who on Screen.* **Encyclopedic Works:** *Film Encyclopedia*; *Filmlexicon degli Autori e delle Opere*; *The Picturegoer's Who's Who and Encyclopedia of the Screen To-day*; *Who's Who in Hollywood.*

ARCHIVAL MATERIALS

• *Clipping File* – CAA: Film appearance (1927); obituary (1964). Periodical article: *Motion Picture Magazine* (1944). NYPL: Newsphotos (numerous); comeback (1940s); film review (1920s); career (1926). Periodical article: *Cinema Art* (Apr. 1926). • *Other Clipping File* – GBBF, WICF. • *Correspondence* – NYPL (C.& L. Brown Collection): 1922. • *Legal File* – CAUW: Talent agreement (1928–30, 1939). • *Photograph/Still* – CAA (Hollywood Studio Museum Collection), CNDA, DCG (Quigley Photographic Archives), GBBF, NJPT, NYCU (Palmer Collection), NYEH, NYPL, NYSU, OHCL, PAPL, TXSM, WICF. • *Scrapbook* – NYPL.

HUGHES, Gareth, Llanelly, Wales, 1894–1965.

Best known for his 1921 film *Sentimental Tommy*, Gareth Hughes was a youthful-looking leading man who made his debut in 1919 and appeared in films like *Mrs. Wiggs of the Cabbage Patch*, *The Christian* and *The Lure of Youth.* He was also a Broadway actor. In later life he worked as a missionary (renamed Brother David) with the Paiute Indians.

PUBLISHED SOURCES

• *Books* – **General:** *Blue Book of the Screen.* **Credits:** *Filmarama* (v. I and II); *Twenty Years of Silents*; *Who Was Who on Screen.* **Encyclopedic Works:** *Film Encyclopedia*; *Filmlexicon degli Autori e delle Opere*; *Who's Who in Hollywood.*

• *Periodicals* – *Motion Picture Classic* (Feb. 1921, Aug. 1921); *Motion Picture Magazine* (Jan. 1922); *Reader's Digest* (Mar. 1952).

OBSCURE PUBLISHED SOURCES

AZSU (Jimmy Starr Collection), NYPL: Booklet about GH's acting career with a selection of reviews and a filmography (possibly a funeral memento?).

ARCHIVAL MATERIALS

• *Clipping File* – CAA: Article (1953); missionary work (1947, 1952–53, 1955–56, 1963); obituary (1965). NYMA (also in Photoplay Collection): Film appearance (1910s, 1920s); works for the WPA (1936). NYMN: Newsphotos; works for the WPA (1930s). NYPL (also in Locke Collection): Newsphotos; missionary (1946–47, 1952–54); film review (1920s); stage appearance (1925–26, 1937); obituary (1965). • *Other Clipping File* – AZSU (Jimmy Starr Collection), CNDA, GBBF, MAH, MIDL, NYSU, OHCL, WICF.   • *Correspondence* – AZSU (Jimmy Starr Collection): Letter concerning his ministry as Brother David (1946?). CAA (Hedda Hopper Collection): Several letters from "Brother David" (1951, 1954, 1964, undated). NYMA (Photoplay Collection). NYPL: Letters (C. & L. Brown Collection) (1920s–40s); others (various dates). • *Filmography* – NYMA (also includes a stageography), NYPL. • *Oral History* – NYCO: Mentioned in: Ernest Gross interview. • *Photograph/Still* – CAA (also in Hollywood Studio Museum Collection), CAUT (Jessen Collection), DCG (Quigley Photographic Archives), GBBF, NYMN, NYPL, NYSU, OHCL, TXU, WICF. • *Press Kit* – OHCL. • *Scrapbook* – NYPL (also in Locke Collection), WICF. • *Studio Biography* – CAA: Paramount (1920s). NYMA: Photoplay.

HUGHES, Lloyd, Bisbee, AZ, 1896/99–1958.

Lloyd Hughes entered films as an extra about 1917, his first known film being *Impossible Susan.* In time, the handsome leading man had co-starring roles with many well-known actresses such as Mary Pickford, Colleen Moore and Billie Dove, and he made eight films with Mary Astor. Although he made the transition to talkies, he was a somewhat bland actor and his roles were largely of the "B" variety. His final film appearance came in 1940's *Vengeance of the Deep*.

PUBLISHED SOURCES

• *Books* – **General:** *Blue Book of the Screen*; *Famous Film Folk*; *Who's Who on the Screen*. **Credits:** *Filmarama* (v. I and II); *Forty Years of Screen Credits*; *Twenty Years of Silents*; *Who Was Who on Screen*. **Encyclopedic Works:** *Filmlexicon degli Autori e delle Opere*; *Halliwell's Filmgoer's Companion*; *The Movie Makers*; *The Picturegoer's Who's Who and Encyclopedia of the Screen To-day*; *Who's Who in Hollywood*; *The World Film Encyclopedia*. **Pictorial:** *Silent Portraits*.

• *Periodicals* – The following periodical articles are in addition to those included in the library listings below: *Motion Picture Classic* (Apr.-May 1920); *Motion Picture Magazine* (Jan. 1925, Dec. 1925); *Photoplay* (Apr. 1926); *Classic Images* (Dec. 1988, Feb. 1989) (filmography).

OBSCURE PUBLISHED SOURCES

CAA (Pat O'Malley Collection): *The Cast* (v. 1).

ARCHIVAL MATERIALS

• *Clipping File* – AZSU (Jimmy Starr Collection): Article (1930). CAA: Article (1921-23); film appearance (1922); obituary (1958). Periodical article: *Films in Review* (Jan. 1979?). CAUT: Obituary (1958). NYPL: Career (1927, 1929-30); newsphotos; stage appearance (1933); article (1925-26, undated); Australian film (1930s); film reviews (1920s, 1930s); obituary (1958). Periodical articles: *Picture Play* (Jan. 1926); *Motion Picture Magazine* (Mar. 1930). • *Other Clipping File* – AZSU (Jimmy Starr Collection), GBBF, MIDL, NYMA (Photoplay Collection), PAPL, WICF. • *Filmography* – CAA, NYMA. • *Legal File* – CAUW: Loanout (1924); letter (1926);

payroll record (1925, 1928); contract (1925, 1928); talent agreement (1924, 1926, 1928, 1930). • *Photograph/Still* – CAA (also in Hollywood Studio Museum Collection) (also in MGM Collection), CAFA, CAH, CASU, CAUT (Portrait File), CAUU, DCG (Quigley Photographic Archives), GBBF, MIDL, NJPT, NYB (Bettmann/UPI Collection) (Underwood Collection), NYCU (Dramatic Museum Portraits) (Palmer Collection), NYEH, NYPL, NYSU, OHCL, PAPL, TXU (A. Davis Collection), WICF. • *Scrapbook* – NYPL (also in R. Locke Collection). • *Studio Biography* – NYMA: Photoplay.

HULETTE, Gladys, New York, NY.

Gladys Hulette, pretty co-star of the classics *Tol'able David* (1921) and the *Iron Horse* (1924), began her career about 1909 and appeared in films for Edison, Thanhouser and Vitagraph, making over 130 films in all. Other roles were in *Unknown Treasures*, *Life's Crossroads*, *The Skyrocket* and *A Bowery Cinderella*. She did not make her talkie debut until 1933.

PUBLISHED SOURCES

• *Books* – **General:** *The Big V*. **Credits:** *Filmarama* (v. I and II); *Twenty Years of Silents*. **Encyclopedic Works:** *Filmlexicon degli Autori e delle Opere*. **Pictorial:** *Silent Portraits*.

• *Periodicals* – The following periodical articles are in addition to those included in the library listings below: *Photoplay* (Oct. 1918, Mar. 1929); *Motion Picture Classic* (Jan. 1922).

ARCHIVAL MATERIALS

• *Clipping File* – NYPL (Locke Collection): Stage appearance (1910); newsphotos; article (1914-15, 1917, undated); film appearance (1910s, 1912, 1914); film review (1910s); most popular juvenile star (1917); signs with Thanhouser (1915). Periodical articles: *Green Book Magazine* (Feb. 1911); *Photoplay* (Nov. 1916); *Motion Picture Magazine* (Jan. 1917). • *Other Clipping File* – GBBF, MAH, NYMA (Photoplay Collection),

WICF. • *Filmography* – CAA. • *Photograph/Still* – CAA (Hollywood Studio Museum Collection), CAUU, DCG (Quigley Photographic Archives), NYPL, NYSU, OHCL, TXU, WICF. • *Press Kit* – OHCL. • *Publicity Release* – NYPL: Pathé. • *Scrapbook* – NYPL (R. Locke Collection). • *Studio Biography* – CAA: Paramount (1933).

HURLOCK, Madeline, 1900/05-1988.

Among the more famous of Mack Sennett's bathing beauties was dark-haired Madeline Hurlock. Unlike most of the performers who got their start with Sennett, she remained with the master of mirth and appeared in a series of comedies during the 1920s with Ben Turpin, Harry Langdon and others. Among these efforts were *Don Juan's Three Nights*, *The Marriage Circus*, *The Wild Goose Chaser* and *When a Man's a Prince*. She departed Hollywood in 1928.

PUBLISHED SOURCES
• *Books* – General: *Famous Film Folk*. Credits: *Filmarama* (v. II); *Twenty Years of Silents*. Encyclopedic Works: *Film Encyclopedia*; *Who's Who in Hollywood*. Pictorial: *Silent Portraits*.
• *Periodicals* – *Photoplay* (Jan. 1921, Jan. 1925, June 1925); *Films in Review* (Feb. 1970) (Wampas Baby Stars).

ARCHIVAL MATERIALS
• *Clipping File* – CAA: Newsphotos; obituary (1989). NYPL: Marriage/divorce (1930, 1935); obituary (1989). • *Other Clipping File* – MIDL, NYSU, OHCL. • *Legal File* – CAA (Sennett Collection): Contract (1926); option (1926); talent agreement (1927); letter (1927). • *Photograph/Still* – CAA (also in Hollywood Studio Museum Collection) (also in MGM Collection), CAUU, DCG (Quigley Photographic Archives), GBBF, NYB (Underwood Collection), NYPL, OHCL, TXU, WICF. • *Publicity Release* – CAA (Mack Sennett Collection) (1924, undated). • *Scrapbook* –

NYPL. • *Studio Biography* – AZSU (Jimmy Starr Collection).

HYAMS, Leila, New York, NY, 1905-1977.

Blonde and beauteous Leila Hyams (she was called the "Golden Girl") appeared in over 40 films in a career which spanned the years 1924 to 1936. Although she made many silent films (including *Summer Bachelors* and *A Girl in Every Port*), her best roles generally came later. In the sound period she appeared with John Gilbert and was Bing Crosby's co-star in his first feature, *The Big Broadcast*. Among her more notable films were *Island of Lost Souls*, *Ruggles of Red Gap* and *Freaks*.

PUBLISHED SOURCES
• *Books* – Credits: *Filmarama* (v. II); *Forty Years of Screen Credits*; *Twenty Years of Silents*. Encyclopedic Works: *Film Encyclopedia*; *Filmlexicon degli Autori e delle Opere*; *Halliwell's Filmgoer's Companion*; *The Movie Makers*; *The Picturegoer's Who's Who and Encyclopedia of the Screen To-day*; *Quinlan's Illustrated Registry of Film Stars*; *Who's Who in Hollywood*; *Who's Who of the Horrors and Other Fantasy Films*; *The World Almananc Who's Who of Film*; *The World Film Encyclopedia*. Nostalgia: *Whatever Became of...* (9th). Pictorial: *They Had Faces Then*.
• *Periodicals* – *Motion Picture Classic* (Aug. 1927); *Motion Picture Magazine* (June 1930); *Photoplay* (Aug. 1930, Nov. 1931); *Movie Classic* (Sept. 1931); *Silver Screen* (Apr. 1932); *Cinema Digest* (July 25, 1932).

ARCHIVAL MATERIALS
• *Clipping File* – CAA: Nostalgia (1969); article (1975); newsphotos; obituary (1977). CAUT: Newsphotos. CAUU: Obituary (1977). NYMA (also in Photoplay Collection): Obituary (1977). NYMN: Newsphotos (numerous); article (1930). Periodical article: *Silver Screen* (Dec. 1931). NYPL: Newsphoto (numerous); career; leaves MGM (1932); article

(1933-34); film appearance (1932-33); obituary (1977). • *Other Clipping File*— AZSU (Jimmy Starr Collection), GBBF, MAH, MIDL, OHCL, WICF. • *Correspondence*—NYPL (C. & L. Brown Collection): 1919? • *Interview*— CAUU (R. Lamparski Collection). • *Legal File*—CAUT (Twentieth Century-Fox Collection): Loanout (1929-31); letters (1929-31). CAUW: Loanout (1927); talent agreement (1927-29); letter, memo (1927); agreement (1927); option (1927). • *Photograph/Still*—CAA (also in Hollywood Studio Museum Collection) (also in MGM Collection), CAFA, CASF, CAUT (Jessen Collection), CAUU (also in Frances Marion Collection), CNDA, DCG (Quigley Photographic Archives), GBBF, MIDL, NJPT, NYAM, NYB (Bettmann/UPI Collection), NYCU (Dramatic Museum Collection) (Palmer Collection), NYEH, NYMN, NYPL, NYSU, OHCL, TNUT (Clarence Brown Collection), TXU, WICF. • *Program*—CAUU: Film (1929?). • *Publicity Release*—CAA: Paramount (1935?). • *Scrapbook*— CAUU (C. Higham Collection), NJPT (Yeandle Collection), NYMA, NYPL. • *Studio Biography*—CAA: Paramount (1935). NYMA: Photoplay.

JOHNSON, Arthur (sometimes Arthur V. Johnson), Cincinnati, Ohio, 1876-1916.

Arthur Johnson was a former stage actor, an early matinee idol and one of D.W. Griffith's pioneer leading men, beginning in 1908. In his relatively brief career he appeared in many one- and two-reel melodramas, often with Florence Lawrence (q.v.). Later, he starred at the Lubin studio, ending his career shortly before his death.

PUBLISHED SOURCES

• *Books*—Credits: *Filmarama* (v. I); *Twenty Years of Silents*; *Who Was Who on Screen*. Encyclopedic Works: *Film Encyclopedia*; *Filmlexicon degli Autori e delle Opere*; *Who's Who in Hollywood*. Pictorial: *Silent Portraits*. Biography/

Autobiography: *When the Movies Were Young*.

• *Periodicals*—The following periodical articles are in addition to those included in the library listings below: *Photoplay* (July 1924, Mar. 1936); *Films in Review* (Oct. 1975).

ARCHIVAL MATERIALS

• *Clipping File*—NYMA: Periodical article: *Photoplay* (July 1915). NYPL (also in Locke Collection): Periodical article: *Theatre Magazine* (July 1914). • *Other Clipping File*—MAH, NYSU, PAPL, WICF. • *Filmography*—GBBF. • *Photograph/Still*—CAA, DCG (Quigley Photographic Archives), GBBF, NYEH, NYPL, OHCL, TXU, WICF. • *Scrapbook*—NYPL (R. Locke Collection).

JOHNSON, Edith, 1895-1969.

One of the leading serial queens at Vitagraph and Universal was vivacious Edith Johnson. With her leading man, and later husband, William Duncan, she appeared in several popular serials from about 1918 to the mid-1920s. These chapterplays included *Wolves of the North, The Steel Trail, Fighting Fate* and *Smashing Barriers*. They also co-starred in some features before her retirement in 1924.

PUBLISHED SOURCES

• *Books*—General: *Sweethearts of the Sage*; *Those Fabulous Serial Heroines*; *The Truth About the Movies*; *Who's Who in the Film World*; *Who's Who on the Screen*. Credits: *Filmarama* (v. I and II); *Twenty Years of Silents*; *Who Was Who on Screen*. Encyclopedic Works: *Film Encyclopedia*; *Filmlexicon degli Autori e delle Opere*; *Who's Who in Hollywood*.

• *Periodicals*—Feature Movie (Mar. 1916); *Motion Picture Classic* (Feb. 1920); *Photoplay* (Mar. 1921); *Filmplay Journal* (June 1922).

ARCHIVAL MATERIALS

• *Clipping File*—CAA: Newsphoto; film appearance (1920s). NYPL: Most beautiful actress (1916); newsphotos; film review (1910s); film appearance (1916); article (1915, 1919). • *Other Clipping File*—GBBF, MAH, WICF. • *Photograph/Still*—CAA (also in Hollywood Studio Museum Collection), CAUT (Jessen Collection), DCG (Quigley Photographic Archives), NYPL, NYSU, OHCL, TXU, WICF. • *Scrapbook*— NYPL (R. Locke collection).

JOHNSTON, Julanne, Indianapolis, IN, 1900/06–1988.

Julanne Johnston had her one memorable role as Douglas Fairbanks's co-star in *The Thief of Bagdad*. She was, however, a beautiful actress who appeared in many other popular silent films including *Venus of Venice*, *Oh Kay!* and *Aloma of the South Seas*. She essayed a few talkies, including John Barrymore's sound debut, *General Crack*, and DeMille's *Madam Satan*, before her film career ended about 1934.

PUBLISHED SOURCES
• *Books*—General: *Famous Film Folk*. Credits: *Filmarama* (v. I and II); *Forty Years of Film Credits*; *Twenty Years of Silents*. Encyclopedic Works: *Film Encyclopedia*; *Filmlexicon degli Autori e delle Opere*; *Who's Who in Hollywood*. Pictorial: *Silent Portraits*.
• *Periodicals*—*Films in Review* (Feb. 1970) (Wampas Baby Stars).

ARCHIVAL MATERIALS
• *Clipping File*—CAA: Film appearance (1923); marriage (1935); obituary (1989). NYMN: Newsphotos; marriage (1935). NYPL: Newsphotos; marriage. • *Other Clipping File*—AZSU (Jimmy Starr Collection), GBBF, MIDL, OHCL, PAPL, WICF. • *Correspondence*—CAA (Hedda Hopper Collection): 1947, 1955. • *Legal File*—CAUW: Talent agreement (1926-29). • *Photograph/Still*—CAA, CAUU, DCG (Quigley Photographic Archives), GBBF, NJPT, NYEH, NYPL, OHCL, TXU, WICF. • *Scrapbook*—NYPL. • *Studio Biography*—CAA: Goldwyn (1920s).

JOY, Leatrice (Leatrice J. Zeidler), New Orleans, LA, 1892/96–1985.

Leatrice Joy appeared in DeMille's *Manslaughter* and *The Ten Commandments* as well as numerous other films from 1916. Among these were *Java Head*, *Hell's Highroad*, *The Dressmaker from Paris*, and *For Alimony Only*. Her métier was the elegant socialite with expensive clothes and a severely bobbed, almost mannish, hairstyle. Her pronounced Southern accent precluded a successful sound career in leading roles but she appeared in character parts very sporadically until 1951. She was married to John Gilbert (q.v.).

PUBLISHED SOURCES
• *Books*—General: *Alice in Movieland*; *Blue Book of the Screen*; *Classics of the Silent Screen*; *Famous Film Folk*; *How I Broke Into the Movies*; *Ladies in Distress*; *Return Engagement*; *Speaking of Silents*; *The Truth About the Movies*. Credits: *Filmarama* (v. I and II); *Forty Years of Film Credits*; *Twenty Years of Silents*. Encyclopedic Works: *Film Encyclopedia*; *Filmlexicon degli Autori e delle Opere*; *Halliwell's Filmgoer's Companion*; *The Illustrated Who's Who of the Cinema*; *The Movie Makers*; *The Picturegoer's Who's Who and Encyclopedia of the Screen To-day*; *Variety Who's Who in Show Business*; *Who's Who in Hollywood*; *The World Almanac Who's Who of Film*; *The World Film Encyclopedia*. Nostalgia: *Whatever Became of...* (1st). Pictorial: *The Image Makers*; *Silent Portraits*; *They Had Faces Then*.
• *Periodicals*—The following periodical articles are in addition to those included in the library listings below: *Motion Picture Classic* (Apr.-May 1920, Sept. 1921, Aug. 1922, Feb. 1923); *Photoplay* (Apr. 1922, Aug. 1922, Jan. 1923, Nov. 1925, May 1926, July 1929); *Motion Picture Magazine* (Aug. 1922, Aug. 1924, July 1925, Nov. 1929); *Filmograph* (nos. 3-4, 1973); *Films in Review* (Apr. 1977, Feb. 1978); *Time*

(May 27, 1985); *Cine Revue* (June 6, 1985); *Classic Images* (Feb. 1991).

OBSCURE PUBLISHED SOURCES
CAA: *Leatrice Joy.*

ARCHIVAL MATERIALS
• *Clipping File* – CAA: Newsphotos; marriage/divorce (1925–26, 1931, 1943, 1945, 1952, 1954); film appearance (1920, 1928–29, 1948); nostalgia (1960, 1968, 1979, 1981); stage appearance (1928–30, 1952); legal problem (1930–31, 1946); home (1930); article (1929–30, 1951, 1965); TV appearance (1954); leaves First National (1929); obituary (1985). CAFI: Obituary (1985). CAUT: Stage appearance (1939); divorce (1920s, 1954). LANO: Obituary (1985). NYMA: 90th birthday (1982); article (1956); nostalgia (1977); obituary (1985). Periodical articles: *Motion Picture Classic* (undated); *Classic Images* (July 1986). NYMN: Divorce; newsphotos; obituary (1985). NYPL: Newsphotos (numerous); daughter; returns to films (1930s?, 1948); challenges Gilbert's will (1936); divorce; current life (1960); obituary (1985). • *Other Clipping File* – AZSU (Jimmy Starr Collection), CAH, CAUB, CNDA, GBBF, MIDL, OHCL, PAPL, WICF. • *Correspondence* – NYPL: Letters (C. & L. Brown Collection) (1948, undated); 6 letters (Herman Weinberg Collection) (1975–82); other (1973). • *Filmography* – NYMA (incomplete). • *Interview* – CAUU (R. Lamparski Collection). GBBF (Hollywood Collection): Transcript of interview for *Hollywood* (TV series). NYAM. • *Legal File* – CAUW: Personnel, payroll record (1929); letter, memo (1929); release (1929); contract (1929); agreement (1929). • *Photograph/Still* – AZSU (Jimmy Starr Collection), CAA (also in Hollywood Studio Museum Collection), CAUT (Jessen Collection), CAUU, DCG (Quigley Photographic Archives), GBBF, MIDL, NJPT, NYAM, NYB (Underwood Collection), NYCU (Bulliet Collection) (Dramatic Museum Portraits), NYEH, NYMN, NYPL, NYSU, OHCL, TXU, WICF. • *Scrapbook* – NYMA, UTBY (DeMille Archives).

• *Studio Biography* – CAA: Goldwyn (1920s); DeMille (1926).

JOYCE, Alice, Kansas City, MO, 1889/1890–1955.

Endowed with Madonna-like beauty, sloe-eyed Alice Joyce was one of the most popular stars of silent film's early days. From about 1910 she worked for pioneer companies such as Kalem and Vitagraph. During the 1920s she was absent from the screen for long periods of time but her career continued (sometimes in mother roles) in worthy films such as *Stella Dallas*, *The Green Goddess*, *Beau Geste*, *Sorrell and Son* and *Dancing Mothers*. She made the transition to talkies but appeared in only a few in 1929 and 1930, including a remake of *The Green Goddess*. She was married to Tom Moore (q.v.) and the director Clarence Brown.

PUBLISHED SOURCES
• *Books* – **Bibliography:** *The Idols of Silence.* **General:** *Classics of the Silent Screen; First One Hundred Noted Men and Women of the Screen; Ladies in Distress; Life Stories of the Movie Stars; Who's Who on the Screen.* **Credits:** *Filmarama* (v. I and II); *Forty Years of Screen Credits; Twenty Years of Silents; Who Was Who on Screen.* **Encyclopedic Works:** *Film Encyclopedia; Filmlexicon degli Autori e delle Opere; Halliwell's Filmgoer's Companion; The Movie Makers; The Picturegoer's Who's Who and Encyclopedia of the Screen To-day; Who's Who in Hollywood; The World Almanac Who's Who of Film; The World Film Encyclopedia.* **Pictorial:** *The Image Makers; Silent Portraits.*
• *Periodicals* – The following periodical articles are in addition to that included in the library listings below: *Theatre* (May 1913); *Cosmopolitan* (Nov. 1913); *Photoplay* (July 1914, May 1915, July 1916, Oct. 1917, Dec. 1918, Feb.-Mar. 1920, May 1924, Oct. 1926, Mar. 1927, Sept. 1930); *Motion Picture Magazine* (Jan. 1915, Apr. 1917, July 1919, Apr.-May 1920, July 1920, May

1925); *Motion Picture Classic* (Aug. 1916, Dec. 1918, Mar. 1926, Feb. 1930); *Picture Play Magazine* (Sept. 1916, July 1920); *Time* (Oct. 17, 1955); *Films in Review* (Dec. 1976).

ARCHIVAL MATERIALS
• *Clipping File* — AZSU (Jimmy Starr Collection): Obituary. CAA: Marriage/divorce (1932-33, 1945); legal problem (1946-47); illness (1954); article (1924); newsphotos; film appearance (1923); obituary (1955). NYMA (also in Photoplay Collection): Periodical article: *Photo-play World* (Apr. 1918). NYMN: Newsphotos; obituary (1955). NYPL (also in Locke Collection): Marriage/divorce (1932-33); newsphotos (numerous); film synopses; film review (1920s); bankruptcy (1932); article (undated); illness; obituary (1955). • *Other Clipping File* — GBBF, MAH, MIDL, MOSL, OHCL, PAPL, TXU, WICF. • *Correspondence* — CAA (Hedda Hopper Collection): Notes (1950, 1952). CAOC (B. Henry Collection): 3 letters (1948, 1951). NYPL: 1932. • *Filmography* — NYPL (incomplete). • *Legal File* — CAUW: Talent agreement (1928- 30). • *Photograph/Still* — CAA (also in Hollywood Studio Museum Collection) (also in MGM Collection), CASF, CASU, CAUU, CNDA, DCG (Quigley Photographic Archives), GBBF, NJFL, NJPT, NYAM, NYB (Bettmann/UPI Collection), NYEH, NYMN, NYPL, NYSU, OHCL, PAPL, TXSM, TXU (A. Davis Collection), WICF. • *Publicity* — CAHL: Exhibitors publicity and advertising book for *Within The Law* (undated). • *Scrapbook* — NYPL (R. Locke Collection). • *Studio Biography* — NYMA: Photoplay. *NOTE*: It does not appear that materials relating to AJ are among Clarence Brown's papers at TNUT.

KEATON, Buster (Joseph Keaton, Jr.), Piqua, KS, 1895-1966.

Buster Keaton's reputation has grown over the years and he is considered one of the comic geniuses of the silents. Known for his trademark unsmiling countenance, he made numerous two-reelers beginning in 1917 and several features, one of which was the classic *The General* (1927). Other notable films included *Our Hospitality*, *The Navigator*, *Steamboat Bill, Jr.* and *Sherlock Jr.* He began to decline after he was placed under the strict supervision of MGM in the late 1920s and his subsequent teaming with Jimmy Durante overwhelmed his own comic style. Beginning in the mid-1930s he appeared in a series of generally inferior shorts and played some small roles in features. His last films were released after his death.

PUBLISHED SOURCES
• *Books* — Bibliography: *The Idols of Silence*. General: *Agee on Film*; *The American Cinema*; *American Film Directors*; *American Vaudeville As Seen By Its Contemporaries*; *The Best of Buster*; *Blue Book of the Screen*; *Buster Keaton* (Coursodon); *Buster Keaton* (Lebel); *Buster Keaton* (Prinzler); *Buster Keaton* (Turconi/Savio); *Buster Keaton: Eine Dokumentation*; *Buster Keaton mit Selbstzeugnissen und Bilddokumenten*; *Buster, the Early Years*; *Le Cinéma Burlesque Américain au Temps du Muet*; *Classic Movie Comedians*; *Classics of the Silent Screen*; *Close-Ups*; *Comedy Films, 1894-1954*; *The Comic Mind*; *The Crazy Mirror*; *Do You Sleep in the Nude?*; *Famous Film Folk*; *Fifty Super Stars*; *Film: an Anthology*; *The Film Career of Buster Keaton*; *The Film Handbook*; *Film 70/71*; *Four Great Comedians*; *Funny Men of the Movies*; *The Funsters*; *The Golden Age of Sound Comedy*; *Great Film Directors*; *The Great Funnies*; *The Great Movie Comedians*; *The Great Movie Stars*; *Here Come the Clowns*; *L'Histoire de l'Art Cinématographique*; *The History of Motion Pictures*; *History of the American Cinema* (v. 3); *Hollywood Album*; *Hollywood and the Great Stars*; *Hollywood Directors, 1914-1940*; *Hollywood Hall of Fame*; *The Hollywood Reporter Star Profiles*; *How I Broke Into the*

Movies; *"Image" on the Art and Evolution of the Film*; *Interviews with Film Directors*; *Keaton et Cie*; *Mark Twain and Buster Keaton*; *Movie Comedians*; *The Movie Stars Story*; *The National Society of Film Critics on Movie Comedy*; *The National Society of Film Critics on the Movie Star*; *The Parade's Gone By*; *The Primal Screen*; *The Silent Clowns*; *The Stars* (Schickel); *Starstruck*; *Stunt*; *The Truth About the Movies*; *Twinkle, Twinkle, Movie Star*; *Unholy Fools*; *Who's Who on the Screen*; *The World of Comedy*; *World of Laughter*; *Yesterday's Clowns*. **Credits:** *Filmarama* (v. I and II); *Forty Years of Screen Credits*; *Twenty Years of Silents*; *Who Was Who on Screen*. **Encyclopedic Works:** *A Biographical Dictionary of Film*; *Cinema, a Critical Dictionary*; *A Companion to the Movies*; *Dictionary of Film Makers*; *A Dictionary of the Cinema*; *Film Encyclopedia*; *Filmlexicon degli Autori e delle Opere*; *The Illustrated Encyclopedia of the World's Great Movie Stars and Their Films*; *The Illustrated Who's Who of the Cinema*; *International Dictionary of Films and Filmmakers* (v. 2); *The International Encyclopedia of Film*; *Joe Franklin's Encyclopedia of Comedians*; *Halliwell's Filmgoer's Companion*; *The Movie Makers*; *The Oxford Companion to Film*; *The Picturegoer's Who's Who and Encyclopedia of the Screen To-day*; *Quinlan's Illustrated Directory of Film Comedy Actors*; *Quinlan's Illustrated Registry of Film Stars*; *Who's Who in Hollywood*; *The World Almanac Who's Who of Film*; *The World Encyclopedia of the Film*; *World Film Directors*; *The World Film Encyclopedia*. **Biography/ Autobiography:** *Buster Keaton* (Fernandez Cuenca); *Buster Keaton* (Robinson); *Keaton* (Blesh); *Keaton* (Dardis); *The Look of Buster Keaton*; *My Wonderful World of Slapstick*. **Films:** *Filmguide to The General*; *The Films of Buster Keaton*; *The Great Movie Shorts*; *Keaton: the Silent Features Close-Up*; *Selected Short Subjects*. **Thesis:** *Buster Keaton: a Rhetoric of Silents*; *Buster Keaton and His Role of Comedy in Silent Films*; *Buster Keaton and the Dynamics of Visual Wit*; *Buster Keaton's Comic Vision*; *An In-Depth Analysis of Buster Keaton's The General*; *Spatial Orientation and Dream in the Feature Films of Buster Keaton*. **Pictorial:** *The Image Makers*; *Silent Portraits*. **Recordings:** *Hollywood on Record*. **Factoids:** *Star Stats*.

• **Periodicals** – The following periodical articles are in addition to those included in the library listings below: *Motion Picture Classic* (Mar. 1921, Oct. 1921, June 1926); *Photoplay* (Sept. 1921, Oct. 1922, Jan. 1934); *Motion Picture Magazine* (Oct. 1921); *Pantomine* (Oct. 5, 1921); *Ladies' Home Journal* (June 1926); *Close-Up* (Apr. 1930); *Silver Screen* (Apr. 1932); *Cinema Digest* (Aug. 8, 1932); *Cinéma* (Italy) (1938); *Cue* (Jan. 3, 1953); *Life* (Jan. 23, 1956, May 6, 1957, Sept. 7, 1959, Oct. 10, 1960, Aug. 14, 1964); *Films and Filming* (Aug. 1958, Feb. 1984); *Film Quarterly* (Fall 1958); *Cinéma* (France) (Sept.-Oct. 1958, Aug.-Sept. 1960, Sept.-Oct. 1962, Mar. 1966, Oct. 1981); *Film* (Nov.-Dec. 1958, Winter 1964, no. 42, 1965, Oct. 1983); *Coronet* (Aug. 1959); *Newsweek* (Jan. 25, 1960, Feb. 14, 1966); *Cahiers du Cinéma* (Sept. 1960, Apr. 1962, Feb. 1966, Jan. 1979, July-Aug. 1982, Mar. 1987, Dec. 1989); *Cine Cubano* (no. 7, 1962); *Telecine* (Oct.-Nov. 1962); *New Yorker* (Apr. 27, 1963, Aug. 8, 1964); *Cinema Nuovo* (Sept.-Oct. 1963, Oct.-Nov. 1965, Mar.-Apr. 1966, May-June 1972, Sept.-Oct. 1977, June 1983); *Bianco e Nero* (Sept.-Oct. 1963, Mar.-Apr. 1973); *Image et Son* (June 1964, Dec. 1969, Nov. 1972); *Cineforum* (June 1964, Jan. 1966); *Filmcritica* (Feb. 1966, Mar. 1988); *Time* (Feb. 11, 1966, Nov. 2, 1970, Sept. 3, 1979); *National Review* (Feb. 22, 1966); *Chaplin* (Apr. 1966); *Positif* (Summer 1966, Sept. 1991); *Cinema Journal* (1966-67); *Kino* (no. 4, 1967, Feb. 1976); *Encounter* (Dec. 1967); *Sight and Sound* (Spring 1968, Winter 1970/71, Autumn 1975, Spring 1985); *Kosmorama* (July-Aug. 1969, Apr. 1972, no. 132, 1976, no. 138, 1978, Summer 1988); *Films in Review* (Jan. 1971, Dec. 1976); *Film News* (Apr.-May 1971); *Film Comment* (Sept.-Oct. 1972); *Ecran* (Jan. 1973); *Journal of*

Modern Literature (no. 2, 1973); *Cinema Societa* (Mar. 1973); *Skrien* (Aug. 1973, Winter 1978/79, Feb.-Mar. 1989); *Revue du Cinéma* (no. 269, 1973, Feb. 1980, Sept. 1980, Jan. 1983); *Jugend Film Fernsehen* (no. 3, 1973); *Cinéma* (Switzerland) (no.3, 1974); *Amis du Film et de la Télévision* (Mar. 1974); *Cine Revue* (Sept. 19, 1974, July 11, 1985); *Image* (Dec. 1974); *Avant-Scène du Cinéma* (Feb. 1975); *Literature/Film Quarterly* (Spring 1975); *Cinématographe* (Aug.-Sept. 1975, Nov. 1980); *Biography News* (Nov. 1975); *Film und Ton* (Apr. 1976); *Classic Film Collector* (Fall 1976-Spring 1977, Winter 1977-Spring 1978, Winter 1978, Mar. 1979); *American Film* (July-Aug. 1977, June 1979); *Lumiére du Cinéma* (Nov. 1977); *Focus on Film* (no. 26, 1977); *Metro* (Winter 1979); *Georgia Review* (no. 2, 1979); *Cahiers Cinématheque* (Summer/Autumn 1980); *Hudson Review* (Autumn 1981); *Quarterly Review of Film Studies* (Fall 1981); *Film Reader* (no. 5, 1982); *Casablanca* (May 1982, July-Aug. 1982); *Celuloide* (June 1983); *Western Humanities Review* (no. 4, 1983); *Film Dope* (Mar. 1984, Sept. 1984); *Classic Images* (Dec. 1984-Jan. 1985, July 1986, June 1990); *Cine Revue* (July 11, 1985); *Segnocinema* (Nov. 1985); *Filmvilag* (nos. 2-5, 1986); *Andere Sinema* (Jan.-Feb. 1987).

MEDIA

Buster Keaton (video); *Comedy, a Serious Business* (video); *The Great Stone Face* (video); *Keaton Special* (film); *Keaton, the Great Stone Face* (video); *TV Variety* (video); *Wm. S. Hart and the Sad Clowns* (video).

ARCHIVAL MATERIALS

• *Caricature*—NYPL, WICF. • *Clipping File*—CAA: Review of *Keaton* (Dardis) (1979); review of *Look of Buster Keaton* (1984); TV documentary (1986); article (1920, 1928, 1955, 1957, 1959, 1960, 1962-65, 1971, 1973, 1981); home (1926); legal problem (1927); assaulted by Kathleen Key (1930); marriage/divorce (1921, 1932-33); MGM contract ends (1933); TV appearance (1949, 1954, 1964); illness (1955); newsphotos; biographical film

(1957); stage appearance (1957); review of *My Wonderful World of Slapstick* (1960); donates films (1960); film appearance (1920, 1962, 1964-65); injury (1921); film festival (1963, 1971, 1976, 1978, 1981); review of *Keaton* (Blesh) (1966); program for Tribute to Buster Keaton (1967); obituary (1966). Periodical articles: *Photoplay* (June 1925-Apr. 1929) (numerous); *Collier's* (June 10, 1944); *Life* (Sept. 5, 1949, Mar. 13, 1950, Dec. 12, 1955, Feb. 11, 1966); *Harper's Bazaar* (May 1952); *MD* (1960s); *Columbia Forum* (Winter 1969); *Film Collector's World* (Feb. 1, 1970); *New Yorker* (Sept. 16, 1970); *Newsweek* (Oct. 5, 1970); *Hollywood Studio Magazine* (Sept. 1978); *Comedy* (Summer 1980); *New Orleans Review* (Winter 1981); *Architectural Digest* (Apr. 1990). CAFI: Article (1944, 1965, 1970-71, 1979, 1981, 1987, 1991); AFI tribute (1970); *Film* (name of BK film) (1984); film festival (1977, 1979, 1981); illness (1955); review of *Keaton* (Dardis) (1979); review of *Look of Buster Keaton* (1984); film appearance (1979); TV documentary (1987); biography; obituary (1966). Periodical article: *Newsweek* (Oct. 5, 1970). CAUT: Newsphotos; biographical film; sale of films (1963); review of *My Wonderful World of Slapstick*; article (1945, 1971); TV documentary (1987); combined review of *Keaton: the Man Who Wouldn't Lie Down, Keaton: the Silent Features Close Up, Buster Keaton* (Robinson), *Keaton* (Blesh) (1980); tribute. Periodical articles: *Sight and Sound* (Apr./June 1953; Winter 1959/60; Winter 1965/66; *Cahiers du Cinéma* (Aug. 1958); *Films and Filming* (Sept. 1961); *Film Quarterly* (Summer 1966); *Newsweek* (Oct. 5, 1970). CAUU: Film festival (1967, 1970-71, 1975, 1981); newsphotos; article (1964, 1966, 1971, 1981); review of *Keaton* (Dardis) (1979); *Films of Buster Keaton* (booklet) (1969); *Buster Keaton* (booklet) (M. Dennis) (1971); *Buster Keaton* (booklet) (National Film Theatre Folio Series no. 2); obituary (1966). Periodical articles: *Massachusetts Review* (Winter 1963): *New Yorker* (undated); *Premiere* (Mar. 1991). NYPL: PARTIAL CONTENTS:

Review of *The Look of Buster Keaton* (1984); TV documentary (1987); career (1991); article (1992); obituary (1966). • *Other Clipping File* — AZSU (Jimmy Starr Collection), CASF, CNDA, GBBF, MAH, MIDL, NYMA, OHCL, WICF. • *Discussion* — MISU: Marcel Marceau discusses the art of silent comedy, including BK, C. Chaplin and others (recording). • *Filmography* — CAA. CAUT: 1917–33. NYEH. • *Interview* — CAA (Hedda Hopper Collection): 1963, 1965. CAUB (housed in UC, Berkeley Bancroft Library): 1961. CAUS. CAUU (Hollywood Studio Museum Collection): 1964. GBBF (Hollywood Collection): Transcript of interview for *Hollywood* (TV series). MISU: BK talks about vaudeville and his early career (recording) (1965). • *Legal File* — CAUT (Twentieth Century–Fox Collection): Memo (1938–39, 1967); release (1948). CAUW: Release (1922, 1948); production agreement (1921–22); contract (1921); agreement (1926, 1929); letter (1922); distribution agreement (1929). NYPL: Contract (1941). • *Manuscript* — CAUT: *An Index to the Films of Buster Keaton* (George Geltzer) (1959). • *Oral History* — NYCO: Interviewed in 1958. Also mentioned in the following interviews: Robert Drew, Jay Leyda, James Mason, Elliot Nugent, Albert (Eddie) Sutherland, Bert Wheeler. • *Photograph/Still* — CAA (also in Hollywood Studio Museum Collection) (also in Jules White Collection) (also in MGM Collection), CAFA, CALM, CAUT (Jessen Collection) (Portrait File), CAUU, CNDA, DCG (Quigley Photographic Archives) (Terry Ramsaye Papers), IAU (Junkin Collection), NYB (Bettmann/UPI Collection) (Penguin Collection) (Springer Collection) (Underwood Collection), NYCU (Dramatic Museum Portraits) (Palmer Collection), NYEH, NYPL, NYSU, OHCL, OHSU, TXSM, TXU, WICF. • *Play Program* — CAHL: 1960. • *Press Kit* — OHCL. • *Scrapbook* — NYPL (also in R. Locke collection). • *Studio Biography* — CAA: Universal (1945); Paramount (1956–57); United Artists (1966). CAFI: Paramount (1950s?); United Artists (1960s).

KEITH, Ian (Keith Macauley Ross), Boston, MA, 1899–1961.

Well-known stage actor Ian Keith arrived in Hollywood in 1924 and co-starred with several top silent actresses, including Gloria Swanson, Corinne Griffith (q.v.) and Alla Nazimova. He went on to a long career as a supporting player in talkies in a variety of genres including westerns, costume dramas (*Queen Christina, The Spanish Main*) and mysteries. His last film was *The Ten Commandments* in 1956. He was married to Ethel Clayton (q.v.).

PUBLISHED SOURCES

• *Books* — **General:** *Character People; Famous Film Folk; Heroes, Heavies and Sagebrush; Screen Album.* **Credits:** *Filmarama* (v. II); *Forty Years of Screen Credits; Twenty Years of Silents; Who Was Who on Screen.* **Encyclopedic Works:** *Film Encyclopedia; Filmlexicon degli Autori e delle Opere; Halliwell's Filmgoer's Companion; The Movie Makers; The Picturegoer's Who's Who and Encyclopedia of the Screen To-day; Who Was Who in the Theatre; Who's Who in Hollywood; The World Almanac; Who's Who of Film; The World Film Encyclopedia.*
• *Periodicals* — *Motion Picture Magazine* (Dec. 1929); *Movie Classic* (Oct. 1931); *Newsweek* (Apr. 4, 1960); *American Cinematographer* (Dec. 1982); *Filmfax* (May 1990); *Classic Images* (July 1991).

ARCHIVAL MATERIALS

• *Caricature* — NYMN. • *Clipping File* — CAA: Marriage/divorce (1932–34, 1936–37, 1948); film appearance (1939); stage appearance (1941); legal problem (1953); obituary (1960). NYMN: Article (1937); newsphotos; disciplined for unprofessional behavior (1953); stage appearance (1924); engagement/marriage/divorce/separation (1932–36); injury (1936, 1938); obituary (1960). NYPL: Marriage/divorce (1922, 1924–27, 1932–36); bankruptcy (1932–33); play review (1920s, 1930s, 1940s, 1950s); newsphotos; disciplined by AFTRA: 1953; film appearance (1932, 1940s); article (undated); radio appearance; injury (1928); slashes wrists (1936). • *Other Clipping File* — CNDA, GBBF, MAH, MIDL, OHCL, PAPL, WICF. • *Correspondence* — NYPL: Letters (C. & L. Brown Collection) (1932, 1948-50); others (1927, 1960, undated). • *Legal File* — CAUW: Personnel, payroll record (1938-40); talent agreement (1926, 1928-29, 1938); document (1924). • *Photograph/Still* — CAA (also in Hollywood Studio Museum Collection), CAUS, CAUU, CNDA, DCG (Quigley Photographic Archives), GBBF, MIDL, NJPT, NYEH, NYMN, NYPL, NYSU, OHCL, TXSM, TXU, WICF. • *Play Program* — CAHL: 1931, 1933-34. • *Publicity Release* — CAA: RKO (1930s); Paramount (1930s). NYPL: National Broadcasting Company (1937); Columbia Broadcasting System (1937). • *Scrapbook* — NJPT (Yeandle Collection), NYPL. • *Studio Biography* — CAA: Paramount (1932, 1935).

KENT, Barbara (Barbara Klowtman), Gadsby, Alberta, Canada, 1906/09-

Brunette Barbara Kent's first film was *Prowlers of the Night* (1926). She made several silent films (the best of which was probably *The Drop Kick* with Richard Barthlemess) and was selected by Harold Lloyd to appear in his first two talkies, *Welcome Danger* and *Feet First*. She made other films in the 1930s, including *Vanity Fair* and *Oliver Twist*, before leaving the screen in mid-decade. One final film came in 1941.

PUBLISHED SOURCES

• *Books* — General: *Harold Lloyd* (Reilly). Credits: *Filmarama* (v. II); *Forty Years of Screen Credits*; *Twenty Years of Silents*. Encyclopedic Works: *Film Encyclopedia*; *Filmlexicon degli Autori e delle Opere*; *The Picturegoer's Who's Who and Encyclopedia of the Screen To-day*; *Who's Who in Hollywood*; *The World Film Encyclopedia*. Pictorial: *They Had Faces Then*.

• *Periodicals* — *Films in Review* (Feb. 1970) (Wampas Baby Stars).

ARCHIVAL MATERIALS

• *Clipping File* — CAA: Marriage (1932, 1934). CAUT: Film appearance (1929). NYPL: Comeback; film appearance (1930s); pilots plane; marriage (1932); article (undated). • *Other Clipping File* — GBBF, NYMA (Photoplay Collection), PAPL, WICF. • *Legal File* — CAUW: Document (1927); talent agreement (1927, 1930). • *Photograph/Still* — CAA (also in Hollywood Studio Museum Collection) (also in MGM Collection), CAUT (Jessen Collection), CAUU, CNDA, DCG (Quigley Photographic Archives), GBBF, MIDL, NJPT, NYAM, NYCU (Dramatic Museum Portraits), NYEH, NYPL, OHCL, TXU, WICF. • *Reminiscence* — MISU. • *Scrapbook* — NJPT (Yeandle Collection), NYMA. • *Studio Biography* — CAA: MGM (1920s); Harold Lloyd Corp. (1929-30); Universal (1930s). NYMA: Photoplay.

KENYON, Doris (Margaret D. Kenyon), Syracuse, NY, 1897/98-1979.

Beginning with *The Rack* (1915), Doris Kenyon made a succession of mostly minor but popular silent films with an occasionally more prestigious vehicle like Valentino's *Monsieur Beaucaire*. She appeared in Paramount's first all-talking drama *Interference* and in 1930s films such as *Alexander Hamilton*, *Voltaire* and *Counsellor-at-Law*. Her fine singing voice was used to good effect in several. By the mid-1930s her career began to wane; her last film was *The Man in the Iron Mask* (1939). She was married to Milton Sills (q.v.).

PUBLISHED SOURCES

• *Books* — Wrote *Doris Kenyon's Monologues* (1929), a revision of the 1921 publication: *Humorous Monologues*. General: *Famous Film Folk*; *Who's Who on the Screen*. Credits: *Filmarama* (v. I and II); *Forty Years of Screen Credits*; *Twenty Years of Silents*. Encyclopedic Works: *Film Encyclopedia*; *Filmlexicon degli Autori e delle Opere*; *Halliwell's*

Filmgoer's Companion; *The Movie Makers*; *The Picturegoer's Who's Who and Encyclopedia of the Screen To-day*; *Who Was Who in the Theatre*; *Who's Who in Hollywood*; *The World Almanac Who's Who of Film*; *The World Film Encyclopedia*. **Nostalgia:** *Whatever Became of...* (4th). **Pictorial:** *Silent Portraits*; *They Had Faces Then*.

• *Periodicals*—The following periodical articles are in addition to those included in the library listings below: *Photoplay* (Oct. 1916, July 1918, Oct. 1920, Aug. 1926, Dec. 1927, Feb. 1930); *Motion Picture Classic* (June 1917, Sept. 1921, Mar. 1924, July 1925); *Motion Picture Magazine* (Dec. 1918, Aug. 1922, Sept. 1924, Apr. 1925, Sept. 1925, Aug. 1926, Apr. 1927, Nov. 1928); *Picture Show* (Mar. 27, 1920); *Filmplay Journal* (June 1922, Aug. 1922); *Woman's Home Companion* (Apr. 1923); *Cine Revue* (Sept. 27, 1979); *Cinematographe* (Oct. 1979).

ARCHIVAL MATERIALS
• *Clipping File*—CAA: Film appearance (1921, 1924, 1932); legal problem (1932-33); marriage/divorce (1927, 1930, 1933-34, 1938-39); illness (1926-27); robbery (1935); stage appearance (1930?); article (late 1920s?); nostalgia (1967, 1976); obituary (1979). Periodical article: *Films in Review* (April 1980). CAFI: Periodical article: *Films in Review* (April 1980). CAUT: Newsphoto; legal problem (1933); obituary (1979). CAUU: Nostalgia (1969). NYMA: Article (1918, 1925, 1932); marriage/divorce (1926, 1933-34); concert appearance (1929, 1932-33); opera role (1934); husband's death (1930); film appearance (1910s, 1920s); illness (1925-26); stage appearance (1919, 1934); signs with Burr (1923). Periodical articles: *Modern Screen* (Nov. 1931); *Screen Play* (Jan. 1932). NYMN: Newsphotos (numerous); divorce (1933). NYPL (also in Locke Collection): Article (1925, 1933); newsphotos; film review (1910s, 1920s); marriage/divorce (1926, 1933-34); film appearance (1920s, 1930s); concert appearance (1933); obituary (1979). • *Other Clipping File*—AZSU (Jimmy Starr Collection), GBBF, MAH, MIDL,

OHCL, PAPL, TXU, WICF. • *Correspondence*—CAA: 3 notes (Hedda Hopper Collection) (1946, 1962, undated). • *Filmography*—NJFL. • *Interview*—CAUU (R. Lamparski Collection). • *Legal File*—CAUW: Talent agreement (1924-29, 1931, 1933); loanout (1926); agreement (1927); payroll record (1924-28); document (1928); contract (1924-28, 1931); letter, memo (1925-1931). • *Photograph/Still*—CAA (also in Hollywood Studio Museum Collection), CASU, CAUT (Jessen Collection), CAUU, DCG (Quigley Photographic Archives), GBBF, MIDL, NJFL, NJPT, NYAM, NYB (Bettmann/UPI Collection), NYCU (Dramatic Museum Portraits) (Palmer Collection), NYCZ (Ithaca Movie Industry Photograph Collection), NYEH, NYMN, NYPL, OHCL, PAPL, TXSM, TXU (A. Davis Collection), WICF. • *PublicityRelease*—CAA. NYMA: First National (1924). • *Recital Program*—AZSU, CAA. • *Scrapbook*—NYPL (also in R. Locke Collection) (also in C. & L. Brown Collection). • *Studio Biography*—CAA: Paramount (1930, 1936); RKO (1930s?); Photoplay (undated). NYMA: Photoplay.

KERRIGAN, J. Warren (Jack or George W. Kerrigan), Louisville, KY, 1883/89-1947.

J. Warren Kerrigan was an enormously popular leading man after his debut in 1909 and remained so throughout his entire career. Prior to that he had been a star on Broadway. His films were generally routine melodramas and westerns, but in the final year of his career he starred in *The Covered Wagon*, considered the first epic western, and a version of *Captain Blood*, his last work. Then he departed at the top.

PUBLISHED SOURCES
• *Books*—**Bibliography:** *The Idols of Silence*. **General:** *Blue Book of the Screen*; *Eighty Silent Film Stars*; *Famous Film Folk*; *The Hall Of Fame of Western Film Stars*; *Life Stories of the Movie Stars*; *Who's Who in the Film World*;

Winners of the West. **Credits:** *Filmarama* (v. I and II); *Twenty Years of Silents*; *Who Was Who on Screen*. **Encyclopedic Works:** *Film Encyclopedia*; *Filmlexicon degli Autori e delle Opere*; *Halliwell's Filmgoer's Companion*; *Who's Who in Hollywood*. **Pictorial:** *Silent Portraits*.
• *Periodicals* – The following periodical articles are in addition to those included in the library listings below: *Universal Weekly* (Jan. 17, 1914, July 27, 1914); *Photoplay* (June 1914, Aug. 1915, Feb. 1916, July 1923, Jan. 1931); *Motion Picture Magazine* (May 1915, Sept. 1916, May 1918, Oct. 1919, Oct. 1923, Sept. 1928); *Feature Movie* (June 25, 1915); *Green Book Magazine* (Sept. 1915); *Film Players Herald & Movie Pictorial* (Feb. 1916); *Motion Picture Classic* (Dec. 1916, Oct. 1917); *Picture Show* (Dec. 13, 1919); *Time* (June 23, 1947); *Classic Images* (Sept.-Oct. 1989) (filmography).

OBSCURE PUBLISHED SOURCES
CAA: *How I Became a Successful Moving Picture Star*.

ARCHIVAL MATERIALS
• *Clipping File* – CAA: Article (1914); obituary (1947). NYMA (also in Photoplay collection): Article (1918). Periodical articles: *Classic Film Collector* (Winter 1977); *Classic Images* (Sept. 1982). NYMN: Newsphotos; obituary (1947). NYPL (also in Locke Collection): Newsphotos; article (1923). • *Other Clipping File* – GBBF, MAH, NYSU, OHCL, PAPL, WICF. • *Correspondence* – CAA: Fan letter. • *Filmography* – CAA. • *Oral History* – NYCO: Mentioned in: Harold Lloyd interview. • *Photograph/Still* – CAA (also in Hollywood Studio Museum Collection), CAHL, CAUT (Jessen Collection), DCG (Quigley Photographic Archives), GBBF, IAU (Junkin Collection), NYB (Bettmann/UPI Collection) (Underwood Collection), NYCU (Dramatic Museum Portraits), NYPL, OHCL, TXU, WICF. • *Press Kit* – CAFA. • *Scrapbook* – NYPL (R. Locke Collection), WICF. • *Studio Biography* – NYMA: Photoplay.

KERRY, Norman (Norman or Arnold Kaiser), Rochester, NY, 1889/95-1956.
From *Manhattan Madness* (1916) to the early talkie period, tall (6'2") Norman Kerry and his finely waxed moustache appeared in numerous romantic roles. Best known for *The Phantom of the Opera* (1925), he did not make his first talkie until 1930 and made only a few after that, including a final "B" film at the beginning of World War Two.

PUBLISHED SOURCES
• *Books* – **General:** *Blue Book of the Screen*; *Classics of the Silent Screen*; *Eighty Silent Film Stars*; *Famous Film Folk*; *The Truth About the Movies*; *Who's Who on the Screen*. **Credits:** *Filmarama* (v. I and II); *Forty Years of Screen Credits*; *Twenty Years of Silents*; *Who Was Who on Screen*. **Encyclopedic Works:** *Film Encyclopedia*; *Filmlexicon degli Autori e delle Opere*; *Halliwell's Filmgoer's Companion*; *The Movie Makers*; *The Picturegoer's Who's Who and Encyclopedia of the Screen To-day*; *Who's Who in Hollywood*. **Pictorial:** *Silent Portraits*. **Factoids:** *Star Stats*.
• *Periodicals* – The following periodical articles are in addition to those included in the library listings below: *Motion Picture Magazine* (Aug. 1919, Aug. 1920, July 1926); *Motion Picture Classic* (Mar. 1920, Mar. 1929); *Newsweek* (Jan. 23, 1956); *Time* (Jan. 23, 1956).

ARCHIVAL MATERIALS
• *Clipping File* – CAA: Marriage/divorce (1932-34, 1945); illness (1954); article (1941); nostalgia (1951). CAUT: Divorce (1929); obituary (1956). NYMA (also in Photoplay Collection): Obituary (1956). Periodical articles: *Classic Images* (Feb. 1986, Sept. 1987). NYPL (also in Locke Collection): Article (undated); newsphotos; career (1940s?); marriage/divorce (1933-34); stows away (1930s); Army service; film appearance (1920s); film reviews (1920s); joins Foreign Legion (1940); obituary (1956). Periodical article: *Photoplay* (Aug.[?] 1927).

172   Kingston, N.; Kingston, W.; Kirkwood

• *Other Clipping File*–GBBF, MAH, MIDL, OHCL, PAPL, TXU, WICF. • *Legal File*–CAUW: Talent agreement (1929). • *Oral History*–NYCO: Mentioned in: Joseph Mankiewicz interview. • *Photograph/Still*–CAA (also in Hollywood Studio Museum Collection), CAFA, CAH, CASU, CAUT (Jessen Collection), CAUU, DCG (Quigley Photographic Archives), GBBF, NJPT, NYCU (Dramatic Museum Portraits), NYEH, NYPL, NYSU, OHCL, PAPL, TNUT (Clarence Brown Collection), TXU (A. Davis Collection), WICF. • *Press Kit*–OHCL. • *Scrapbook*–NYPL (also in R. Locke Collection), TNUT (Clarence Brown Collection). • *Studio Biography*–CAA: Paramount (1920s); Goldwyn (1925).

KINGSTON, Natalie, Vallejo or Sonoma, CA, 1904/05–19?1

Natalie Kingston played Jane in a couple of silent *Tarzan* serials and was the female foil in comedies with Harry Langdon and Ben Turpin. She also appeared in features, including an occasional prestigious one like *Street Angel*, before making a handful of talkies and fading from view in the early '30s.

PUBLISHED SOURCES
• *Books*–General: *Those Fabulous Serial Heroines*. Credits: *Filmarama* (v. II); *Forty Years of Screen Credits*; *Twenty Years of Silents*. Encyclopedic Works: *Film Encyclopedia*; *The Picturegoer's Who's Who and Encyclopedia of the Screen To-day*; *Who's Who in Hollywood*. Pictorial: *Silent Portraits*. • *Periodicals*–Motion Picture Classic (Nov. 1925); *Films in Review* (Feb. 1970) (Wampas Baby Stars).

ARCHIVAL MATERIALS
• *Clipping File*–NYPL: Newsphotos; article (1920). • *Other Clipping File*–CASP, GBBF, NYMA (Photoplay Collection), PAPL. • *Legal File*–CAA (Mack Sennett Collection): Contract (1924); option (1925). CAUW: Agreement (1926–27); payroll record (1926–27); letter, memo (1926–27); contract

(1926); talent agreement (1926–27). • *Photograph/Still*–AZSU (Jimmy Starr Collection), CAA (also in Hollywood Studio Museum Collection), CAHL, DCG (Quigley Photographic Archives), GBBF, NJPT, NYAM, NYB (Underwood Collection), NYEH, NYPL, OHCL, TXSM, TXU. • *Publicity Release*–CAA (Sennett Collection). • *Scrapbook*–NJPT (Yeandle Collection). • *Studio Biography*–CAA: Paramount (1929); Sennett (Sennett Collection). NYMA: Photoplay.

KINGSTON, Winifred, 1895–1967.

During a career which began about 1914 and lasted until the early 1920s, Winifred Kingston appeared in several classic adventure tales and westerns such as *The Squaw Man*, *The Virginian*, *The Scarlet Pimpernel* and *The Corsican Brothers*. Some of these costarred her husband Dustin Farnum (q.v.).

PUBLISHED SOURCES
• *Books*–General: *Sweethearts of the Sage*. Credits: *Filmarama* (v. I and II); *Twenty Years of Silents*; *Who Was Who on Screen*. Encyclopedic Works: *Film Encyclopedia*; *Who's Who in Hollywood*. • *Periodicals*–Photoplay (Jan. 1915, June 1916).

ARCHIVAL MATERIALS
• *Clipping File*–CAA: Marriage (1931); obituary (1967). NYPL (also in Locke Collection): Newsphotos; obituary (1967). • *Other Clipping File*–MAH, NYMA (Photoplay Collection), PAPL, WICF. • *Filmography*–GBBF. • *Photograph/Still*–CAA (Hollywood Studio Museum Collection), DCG (Quigley Photographic Archives), GBBF, NYEH, NYPL, OHCL, WICF.

KIRKWOOD, James, Grand Rapids, MI, 1883–1963.

Stage actor James Kirkwood entered films about 1909 and became a popular leading man to Mary Pickford, Florence Lawrence, Blanche Sweet and other leading actresses. He also directed many films. Among his better-known films were *Human Wreckage, Circe the Enchantress, That Royle Girl* and *The Great Impersonation.* He assumed supporting roles in sound films, including some westerns, and was sporadically active up through the 1950s. He was married to Lila Lee (q.v.).

PUBLISHED SOURCES

• *Books* — General: *Famous Film Folk.* Credits: *Filmarama* (v. I and II); *Forty Years of Screen Credits; Twenty Years of Silents; Who Was Who on Screen.* Encyclopedic Works: *Film Encyclopedia; Filmlexicon degli Autori e delle Opere; Halliwell's Filmgoer's Companion; The Picturegoer's Who's Who and Encyclopedia of the Screen To-day; Who's Who in Hollywood; The World Film Encyclopedia.* Biography/Autobiography: *When the Movies Were Young.* Pictorial: *Silent Portraits.*

• *Periodicals* — The following periodical articles are in addition to that included in the library listings below: *Motion Picture Magazine* (Apr. 1915, Nov. 1915, Oct.1921); *Picture Play* (Apr. 1920); *Motion Picture Classic* (Apr. 1921); *Photoplay* (May 1921, Jan. 1923, Oct. 1923); *Newsweek* (Sept. 9, 1963); *Classic Images* (Sept. 1981).

ARCHIVAL MATERIALS

• *Clipping File* — CAA: Film appearance (1921, 1923-24, 1962); article (1953); marriage/divorce/children (1922-24, 1930-31, 1933-34); obituary (1963). CAUT: Obituary (1963). CAUU: Obituary (1963). NYMA (also in Photoplay Collection): Obituary (1963). NYMN: Newsphotos; divorce (1933-34); romance with Mary Miles Minter (1937); obituary (1963). NYPL (also in Locke Collection): Injury (1928, 1934); stage appearance (1930s, undated); marriage/divorce/children (1923, 1933-34); newsphotos; article (1921); nostalgia (1936); film appearance (1923); comeback (1941). Periodical article: *Photoplay* (Apr.

1920). • *Other Clipping File* — AZSU (Jimmy Starr Collection), CNDA, GBBF, MAH, MIDL, OHSU, PAPL, WICF. • *Legal File* — CAUT (Twentieth Century-Fox Collection): Letter, memo (1931-32); contract (1931); loanout (1932). CAUW: Talent agreement (1926, 1928-29); letter (undated); contract (1926). • *Oral History* — NYCO: Mentioned in: Lila Lee interview. • *Photograph/Still* — AZSU (Jimmy Starr Collection), CAA (also in Hollywood Studio Museum Collection), CAUT (Jessen Collection), CAUU, DCG (Quigley Photographic Archives), GBBF, IAU (Junkin Collection), NJFL, NJPT, NYAM, NYCU (Dramatic Museum Portraits), NYEH, NYMN, NYPL, NYSU, OHCL, TXU, WICF. • *Play Program* — NYPL. • *Scrapbook* — NYPL (also in Players Collection). • *Studio Biography* — CAA: Goldwyn (1923); Paramount (1928, 1941).

KOSLOFF, Theodore, Moscow, Russia, 1882-1956.

Theodore Kosloff was a ballet dancer before he entered films and he ran a ballet school after his acting career was over. He appeared in numerous DeMille productions, including *The Woman God Forgot, Why Change Your Wife?, Adam's Rib* and *Feet of Clay* and was usually typecast in foreign roles. He appeared in bits in a couple of 1930s talkies and also did some film choreography.

PUBLISHED SOURCES

• *Books* — General: *Blue Book of the Screen; Dancing in the Sun; Famous Film Folk; First One Hundred Noted Men and Women of the Screen; The Truth About the Movies.* Credits: *Filmarama* (v. I and II); *Twenty Years of Silents; Who Was Who on Screen.* Encyclopedic Works: *Film Encyclopedia; Filmlexicon degli Autori e delle Opere; Who's Who in Hollywood.* Pictorial: *Silent Portraits.*

• *Periodicals* — *Picture Play Magazine* (Apr. 1920); *Motion Picture Magazine* (May 1922); *Motion Picture Classic* (Dec. 1922); *Photoplay* (Feb. 1923).

ARCHIVAL MATERIALS
• *Clipping File*—CAA: Divorce (1934); film appearance (1923); obituary (1956). • *Other Clipping File*—GBBF, MAH, MIDL, NYMA (Photoplay Collection), NYSU, PAPL, WICF. • *Photograph/Still*—CAA (also in Hollywood Studio Museum Collection), CAOC (Kiesling Collection), CAUT (Jessen Collection), GBBF, NYSU, OHCL, TXU, WICF. • *Program*—CAHL: Vaudeville (1919); ballet at Hollywood Bowl (1938). • *Scrapbook*—NYPL (R. Locke Collection), UTBY (DeMille Archives). • *Studio Biography*—CAA: Paramount (1922).

LABADIE, Florence, Canada?, 1893-1917.

The early death of Florence LaBadie ended a promising career. She appeared in films from 1909 which included *Man Without a Country*, *The Woman in White*, *The Merchant of Venice* and *Enoch Arden*. Her most popular film was not adapted from a literary classic but it was a classic of its own kind: the serial *The Million Dollar Mystery*. Her final film was *War and the Woman* (1917).

PUBLISHED SOURCES
• *Books*—General: *Life Stories of the Movie Stars*. **Credits:** *Filmarama* (v. I); *Twenty Years of Silents*; *Who Was Who on Screen*. **Encyclopedic Works:** *Film Encyclopedia*; *Who's Who in Hollywood*. **Pictorial:** *Silent Portraits*.
• *Periodicals*—*Photoplay* (Oct. 1912, Aug. 1914, Dec. 1916); *Blue Book Magazine* (May 1914, Sept. 1914); *Motion Picture Magazine* (Jan. 1915); *Motion Picture Classic* (July 1916); *Films in Review* (Dec. 1955); *Classic Film Collector* (Summer 1978).

ARCHIVAL MATERIALS
• *Clipping File*—CAA: Newsphotos. NYMA (also in Photoplay Collection): Newsphotos; biography (1916). NYPL (also in Locke Collection): Newsphotos; obituary (1918). • *Other Clipping File*—MAH, PAPL, WICF. • *Filmography*—

CAA. • *Photograph/Still*—CAA, NYPL, WICF. • *Program*—OHSU. • *Scrapbook*—NYPL (R. Locke Collection).

LAKE, Alice, Brooklyn, NY, 1896-1967.

Tiny "Sweet Alice" Lake was a Metro star. Before that, she paid her dues by appearances with Roscoe Arbuckle (q.v.), Buster Keaton (q.v.) and Ben Turpin (q.v.) at the Sennett studio. Among the features in which she had roles were *Lombardi Ltd.*, *Body and Soul*, *Souls for Sale* and *The Virgin*. Although she could be seen onscreen through the mid-1930s, her roles were by then in support and she played bits in the 1940s.

PUBLISHED SOURCES
• *Books*—General: *Blue Book of the Screen*; *Famous Film Folk*; *Who's Who on the Screen*. **Credits:** *Filmarama* (v. I and II); *Forty Years of Screen Credits*; *Twenty Years of Silents*; *Who Was Who on Screen*. **Encyclopedic Works:** *Film Encyclopedia*; *Filmlexicon degli Autori e delle Opere*; *The Picturegoer's Who's Who and Encyclopedia of the Screen To-day*; *Who's Who in Hollywood*. **Pictorial:** *Silent Portraits*.
• *Periodicals*—The following periodical articles are in addition to that included in the library listings below: *Photoplay* (Dec. 1918, May 1920); *Motion Picture Classic* (Dec. 1919, Apr. 1921, Feb. 1922, Apr. 1925); *Picture Play Magazine* (Apr. 1920); *Motion Picture Magazine* (June 1920, Feb. 1922).

ARCHIVAL MATERIALS
• *Clipping File*—CAA: Film appearance (1920-22, undated); newsphotos; illness (1953); article (1957); obituary (1967). Periodical article: *Films in Review* (June-July 1961). NYPL (also in Locke Collection): Marriage (1924); drunk driving (1936-37); financial situation; works as extra (1930s, 1937); newsphotos; film appearance (1922). • *Other Clipping File*—GBBF, MAH, NYMA (Photoplay Collection), OHCL, PAPL,

WICF. • *Legal File* – CAUW: Communication (1928). • *Photograph/Still* – CAA (also in Hollywood Studio Museum Collection), CALM, CAUT (Jessen Collection) (Portrait File), DCG (Quigley Photographic Archive), NYCU (Dramatic Museum Portraits), NYPL, NYSU, TXSM, TXU, OHCL, WICF. • *Scrapbook* – NYPL (also in R. Locke Collection).

LA MARR, Barbara (Reatha Watson), Richmond, VA, 1896–1926.

None of the melodramas in which Barbara La Marr appeared could match her own brief, tempestuous life. Her remarkable beauty (she was "The Girl Who Was Too Beautiful") was seen onscreen for six years; *The Three Musketeers* (1921) was her first major role. Others, in which she was sometimes cast as a villainess, included *The Prisoner of Zenda*, *Trifling Women*, *The Eternal City*, *Thy Name Is Woman* and *The Heart of a Siren*.

PUBLISHED SOURCES

• *Books* – **Bibliography:** *The Idols of Silence*. **General:** *Blue Book of the Screen*; *Famous Film Folk*; *Ladies in Distress*; *Love, Laughter and Tears*; *Sex Goddesses of the Silent Screen*. **Credits:** *Filmarama* (v. II); *Twenty Years of Silents*; *Who Was Who on Screen*. **Encyclopedic Works:** *Film Encyclopedia*; *Filmlexicon degli Autori e delle Opere*; *Halliwell's Filmgoer's Companion*; *The Illustrated Who's Who of the Cinema*; *The Movie Makers*; *Who's Who in Hollywood*; *The World Almanac Who's Who of Film*. **Pictorial:** *The Image Makers*; *Silent Portraits*. **Factoids:** *Star Stats*.

• *Periodicals* – The following periodical articles are in addition to those included in the library listings below: *Photoplay* (June 1922, May 1923, Aug. 1923, Nov.-Dec. 1923; June 1924, Oct. 1924, Feb. 1925, Jan. 1926, Apr. 1926, Jan. 1934); *Motion Picture Magazine* (July 1922, Nov. 1922, Jan. 1925, Mar. 1925, Aug. 1925, Feb. 1926, Feb. 1929,

Dec. 1930, June 1933); *Motion Picture Classic* (May 1924, Dec. 1924); *Metropolitan Magazine* (Aug. 1924); *Good Housekeeping* (July 1932); *Films in Review* (June-July 1964, Nov. 1972); *American Classic Screen* (Fall 1979); *Hollywood Then and Now* (Oct. 1990).

OBSCURE PUBLISHED SOURCES
CAA: *Barbara La Marr*.

ARCHIVAL MATERIALS
• *Clipping File* – CAA: Illness (1925); article (1923, 1951); adopts baby (1920s); newsphotos. Periodical article: *Hollywood Studio Magazine* (Feb. 1977). NYMA (also in Photoplay Collection): Outline for an article (*Look Magazine?*); newsphotos; article (1926, 1951, undated). Periodical articles: *Movie Weekly* (Jan. 24, 1925); *Classic Film Collector* (Summer 1972). NYPL: Funeral (1926); newsphotos; illness (1925); film review (1925); film synopses (1920s); article (1926, undated); marriage/divorce (1923–24); biography (1951). Periodical article: *Films in Review* (?) (undated). • *Other Clipping File* – AZSU (Jimmy Starr Collection), GBBF, MAH, MIDL, OHCL, PAPL, WICF. • *Filmography* – NYMA. • *Legal File* – CAUW: Contract (1923–29). • *Manuscript* – GBBF: *The Woman Who Was Too Beautiful* (Marsha McLaughlin). • *Photograph/Still* – CAA (also in Hollywood Studio Museum Collection) (also in MGM Collection), CALM, CAUT (Jessen Collection), DCG (Quigley Photographic Archives), NJFL, NYB (Bettmann/UPI Collection), NYEH, NYPL, NYSU, OHCL, TXSM, TXU, WICF. • *Scrapbook* – NYPL.

LANDIS, Cullen, Nashville, TN, 1895/98–1975.

Cullen Landis was a popular leading man in the 1920s. His career started about 1917 and he was active through the end of the silent era, appearing in many films including serials. His claim to fame (and just about the end of his career) was his starring role in the first all-talkie, Warner Bros.' *The Lights of New York*. He had been a director prior to his acting career and he eventually returned to directing as a maker of industrial films and documentaries in the 1940s.

PUBLISHED SOURCES

• *Books*—**General:** *Blue Book of the Screen; Famous Film Folk; Who's Who on the Screen.* **Credits:** *Filmarama* (v. I and II); *Twenty Years of Silents; Who Was Who on Screen.* **Encyclopedic Works:** *Film Encylopedia; Filmlexicon degli Autori e delle Opere; Halliwell's Filmgoer's Companion; Who's Who in Hollywood.* **Pictorial:** *Silent Portraits.*

• *Periodicals*—The following periodical articles are in addition to those included in the library listings below: *Photoplay* (Nov. 1919, Apr. 1921); *Picture Play Magazine* (Jan. 1920); *Motion Picture Classic* (July 1920); *Classic Images* (Nov. 1983, May 1988).

ARCHIVAL MATERIALS

• *Clipping File*—CAA: Film appearance (undated); United States Information Agency (1954); nostalgia (1969); newsphoto; obituary (1975). Periodical article: *Classic Film Collector* (Spring/ Summer 1970). CAUU: Obituary (1975). Periodical article: *Classic Film Collector* (Spring/ Summer 1970). NYMA (also in Photoplay Collection): Periodical articles: *Classic Film Collector* (Summer 1967, Spring/Summer 1970). NYPL (also in Locke Collection): Newsphotos; film appearance (1920s); article (1927, undated); marriage/divorce (1925, 1927); stage appearance (1929); career (1929); nostalgia (1936); obituary (1976). Periodical article: *Quirk's Review* (Oct. 1973). • *Other Clipping File*—GBBF, MIDL, PAPL, WICF. • *Filmography*—CAA (incomplete). • *Legal File*—CAUW: Talent agreement (1924). • *Photograph/Still*—CAA (also in Hollywood Studio Museum Collection), CAUU, DCG (Quigley Photographic Archives), NJFL, NYAM, NYPL, NYSU, OHCL, TXU, WICF. • *Scrapbook*—NYPL (also in C. & L. Brown Collection). • *Studio Biography*—NYMA: Photoplay.

LANGDON, Harry, Council Bluffs, IA, 1884-1944.

Harry Langdon is now considered to have been one of the great comic actors of silent films. His time at the top was brief, however, with three successful features to his credit: *The Strong Man, Tramp Tramp Tramp* and *Long Pants.* He had made over 20 two- and three-reelers prior to that and he continued making films afterwards but he was no longer a major star by the end of the silent era. In the 1930s and '40s he played small and featured parts, made a series of shorts and did some gag-writing.

PUBLISHED SOURCES

• *Books*—Written by (or ghostwritten for) HL: a chapter of *Breaking into the Movies.* **Bibliography:** *The Idols of Silence.* **General:** *Agee on Film; Alice in Movieland; Awake in the Dark; Le Cinéma Burlesque Américain au Temps du Muet; Classic Movie Comedians; Classics of the Silent Screen; Clown Princes and Court Jesters; The Comic Mind; The Crazy Mirror; Famous Film Folk; Film: an Anthology; Four Great Comedians; Funny Men of the Movies; The Funsters; The Golden Age of Sound Comedy; The Great Funnies; Great Movie Comedians; The Great Movie Stars; Harry Langdon* (Taibo); *Here Come the Clowns; Hollywood Album; Hollywood Directors, 1914-1940; Keaton et Cie; Lotte Reiniger, David W. Griffith, Harry Langdon; Motion Picture News Booking Guide and Studio Directory* (1927); *The Movie Stars Story; The National Society of Film Critics on Movie Comedy; The Parade's Gone By; The Silent Clowns; The Stars* (Schickel); *Starstruck; Unholy Fools; World of Laughter; Yesterday's Clowns.* **Credits:** *Filmarama* (v. II); *Forty Years of Screen Credits; Twenty Years of Silents; Who Was Who on Screen.* **Encyclopedic Works:** *A Biographical Dictionary of Film; Cinema, a Critical Dictionary; A Companion to the Movies; Dictionary of Film Makers; A Dictionary of the Cinema; Film Encyclopedia; Filmlexicon* degli Autori e delle Opere; Halliwell's Filmgoer's Companion; The Illustrated Encyclopedia of the World's Great Movie Stars and Their Films; The Illustrated Who's Who of the Cinema; International Dictionary of Films and Filmmakers (v. 3); The International Encyclopedia of Film; Joe Franklin's Encyclopedia of Comedians; The Movie Makers; The Oxford Companion to Film; Quinlan's Illustrated Directory of Film Comedy Actors; Quinlan's Illustrated Registry of Film Stars; Who's Who in Hollywood; The World Almanac Who's Who of Film; The World Encyclopedia of the Film. **Biography/Autobiography:** Harry Langdon (Rheuban); Harry Langdon (Schelly). **Films:** Selected Short Subjects. **Thesis:** Harry Langdon (Edmondson). **Pictorial:** The Image Makers; Silent Portraits.

• *Periodicals*—The following periodical articles are in addition to those included in the library listings below: Photoplay (June 1925, June 1959); Motion Picture Classic (July 1925); Cinema Art (Oct. 1926); Motion Picture Magazine (Dec. 1926, Oct. 1927, Jan. 1933); Theatre (Dec. 1927); Films in Review (Oct.-Dec. 1967 (filmography), Aug.-Sept. 1981, Jan. 1984, Mar.-Apr. 1992); Classic Film Collector (Fall/Winter 1967, Summer 1977, May 1979); Positif (Dec. 1971, July-Sept. 1978); Film Critica (Apr.-May 1972); Film Comment (Nov.-Dec. 1972); Revue du Cinéma (no. 269, 1973, no. 274, 1973); Kosmorama (Feb. 1974); Cinématographe (Aug.-Sept. 1975); Film und Ton (Apr. 1978); Cine Forum (Dec. 1980); Casablanca (May 1983); Video Movies (June 1984); Literature/Film Quarterly (no. 1, 1989); Cinema 91 (Nov. 1991).

MEDIA

Comedy—a Serious Business (video); Midwest Roots, Hollywood Dreams (video); Wm. S. Hart and the Sad Clowns (video).

ARCHIVAL MATERIALS

• *Clipping File*—CAA: First National contract (1925); film appearance (1925-26, 1932); marriage/divorce (1928-29, 1932-34); Roach contract (1928); legal

problem (1929-31, 1934, 1941); accident (1929); article (1959); award (1967); film festival (1967); obituary (1944). Periodical articles: Life (Sept. 5, 1949); New Yorker (Apr. 24, 1971); Classic Film Collector (Fall 1977). CAFI: Film festival (1971); article (undated). CAUT: Stage appearance (undated); article (1959, 1967, 1976). CAUU: Film festival (1971, 1976); booklet (1967). Periodical articles: New Yorker (Apr. 24, 1971); Classic Film Collector (Fall 1977). NYMA: Booklet by R. Rohauer; signs with First National (1925); marriage/separation/divorce/children (1925, 1928-32, 1934, 1938); article (1925, 1927, 1930, 1938); comeback (1930, 1934); bankruptcy (1931); legal problem (1930); signs with Roach (1928); signs for films (1923); obituary (1944). Periodical articles: Film Mercury (Apr. 10, 1928); Photoplay (June 1929, Feb. 1932); New Yorker (Apr. 24, 1971); Classic Film Collector (Summer 1974, Winter 1974, Summer 1975, Fall-Winter 1976); American Film (Nov. 1975); Classic Film/Video Images (May 1979, Summer 1980); Big Reel (Nov. 1981, Nov. 1984); Classic Images (Nov. 1983, Jan. 1988); Film Dope (Nov. 1985). NYMN: Newsphotos; divorce (1934); obituary (1944). NYPL (also in Locke Collection): Booklet Harry Langdon (Rohauer); newsphotos (numerous); comeback (1938, undated); stage appearance (1920, 1943); marriage/divorce (1932, 1934, 1938); bankruptcy (1931); article (1926, 1979); film appearance (1930s); review of Harry Langdon (Schelly) (1986); obituary (1944). Periodical articles: Films and Filming (Aug. 1966); New Yorker (Apr. 24, 1971); Silent Picture (Winter-Spring 1972); American Film (Nov. 1975); Big Reel (Nov. 1981). • *Other Clipping File*—AZSU (Jimmy Starr Collection), CAUB, CNDA, GBBF, MAH, MIDL, OHCL, PAPL, WICF. • *Filmography*—NYMA. • *Legal File*—CAA (Sennett Collection): Agreement (1923-25). CAUW: Contract (1925-47); agreement (1925-66); letter, memo (1925-66); personnel, payroll record (1927-47); document (1925-29); talent agreement (1930); rights transfer (1925-66); checklist (1926-27). • *Oral History*—

NYCO: Mentioned in the following interviews: Buster Keaton, Albert (Eddie) Sutherland. • *Photograph/Still* — CAA (also in Hollywood Studio Museum Collection) (also in Jules White Collection) (also in MGM Collection), CALM, CASF, CAUT (Jessen Collection) (Portrait File), CAUU, CNDA, DCG (Quigley Photographic Archives), NYB (Bettmann/UPI Collection) (Penguin Collection) (Springer Collection) (Underwood Collection), NYCU (Bulliet Collection) (Dramatic Museum Portraits), NYEH, NYMN, NYPL, NYSU, OHCL, TXSM, TXU, WICF. • *Publicity Release* — CAA (Mack Sennett Collection). NYMA: Unknown studio (1920s). • *Scrapbook* — NYPL. • *Studio Biography* — CAA: Roach (1939). NYMA: Roach.

LA PLANTE, Laura, St. Louis, MO, 1904– ₁ ९९ ७

Blonde Laura La Plante's career began in Christie comedy shorts; her role in the 1921 feature *The Old Swimmin' Hole* gave her a boost toward stardom. She was dubbed a Wampas Baby Star in 1923 and late in the decade two of her best-remembered films, *The Cat and the Canary* and the part-talkie *Showboat*, were made. Her career went into decline in the early 1930s but she returned to make one film each in the 1940s and '50s.

PUBLISHED SOURCES

• *Books* — Written by (or ghostwritten for) LLP: a chapter of *Breaking into the Movies*. **Bibliography:** *The Idols of Silence*. **General:** *Classics of the Silent Screen*; *Famous Film Folk*; *How I Broke Into the Movies*; *Let Me Entertain You*; *The Movie Stars Story*; *Return Engagement*; *Scream Queens*; *Speaking of Silents*; *Sweethearts of the Sage*; *The Truth About the Movies*. **Credits:** *Filmarama* (v. II); *Forty Years of Screen Credits*; *Twenty Years of Silents*. **Encyclopedic Works:** *Film Encyclopedia*; *Filmlexicon degli Autori e delle Opere*; *Halliwell's Filmgoer's Companion*; *The Illustrated Who's Who of the Cinema*; *The Picturegoer's Who's Who and Encyclopedia of the Screen To-day*; *Quinlan's Illustrated Registry of Film Stars*; *Variety Who's Who in Show Business*; *Who Was Who in the Theatre*; *Who's Who in Hollywood*; *Who's Who of the Horrors and Other Fantasy Films*; *The World Almanac Who's Who of the Film*; *The World Film Encyclopedia*. **Nostalgia:** *Whatever Became of...* (2nd, 8th). **Pictorial:** *Silent Portraits*; *They Had Faces Then*. **Factoids:** *Star Stats*.

• *Periodicals* — The following periodical articles are in addition to those included in the library listings below: *Photoplay* (July 1924, May 1927); *Motion Picture Classic* (Apr. 1926, Oct. 1928); *Motion Picture Magazine* (Nov. 1927, Aug. 1929, Apr. 1930); *Films in Review* (Feb. 1970 [Wampas Baby Stars], Oct. 1980); *Filmograph* (nos. 2-3 - 2-4, 1971, no. 3-1, 1972); *Classic Images* (Dec. 1989).

ARCHIVAL MATERIALS

• *Caricature* — NYPL (Sardi Collection). • *Clipping File* — CAA: Newsphotos; divorce (1934); film appearance (1956); rescue from fire (1935); TV appearance (1955); stage appearance (1956); nostalgia (1954, 1968, 1971, 1980–81). Periodical article: *Life* (February 1980). CAFI: Article (1980, 1983). CAUT: Article (1980). CAUU: Manuscript biography; article (1980). MOSL: Article (1929, 1935, 1941). NYMA: Excerpt from *Whatever Became of...* (2nd); film review (1934); film appearance (1956); newsphotos. Periodical articles: *Filmograph* (no. 4, 1972); *Classic Images* (Oct. 1982). NYMN: Newsphotos; returns from Europe (1930s); rescued from fire (1935). NYPL: Newsphotos; marriage/divorce/children (1934, undated); comeback (1950s); rescued from fire (1935); film review (1920s, 1956); article (1990). Periodical article: *Vanity Fair* (Jan. 1928). • *Other Clipping File* — AZSU (Jimmy Starr Collection), CAFI, CAUT, CAUU, GBBF, MIDL, OHCL, PAPL, TXU, WICF. • *Correspondence* — NYPL (C. & L. Brown Collection): 1956. • *Filmography* — NYMA (two-reelers only). • *Interview* — CAUU

(A. Slide Collection) (R. Lamparski Collection). • *Legal File* – CAUW: Talent agreement (undated, 1930); letter, document, memo (1933-34). • *Oral History* – NYCO: Mentioned in: Albert Delacorte interview. • *Photograph/ Still* – CAA (also in Hollywood Studio Museum Collection) (also in MGM Collection), CAFA, CAH, CAHL, CASF, CASU, CAUT (Jessen Collection), CAUU, DCG (Quigley Photographic Archives), GBBF, NJPT, NYB (Bettmann/UPI Collection), NYCU (Dramatic Museum Portraits) (Palmer Collection), NYEH, NYMN, NYPL, NYSU, OHCL, PAPL, TNUT (Clarence Brown Collection), TXSM, WICF. • *Play program* – CAA. CAHL: 1956, 1958. NYPL: 1956. • *Scrapbook* – NYMA, NYPL, TNUT (Clarence Brown Collection).

LA ROCQUE, Rod (Roderick or Rodrique La Rocque), Chicago, IL, 1896/98-1969.

Dashing 6'3" Rod La Rocque started out as an extra in Fort Lee, New Jersey, in 1914. He appeared in several DeMille films, including *The Ten Commandments*, before reaching stardom in *The Coming of Amos*. He appeared in talkies through 1930 whereupon he made no more films until 1933 and a final starring appearance in *SOS Iceberg*. His roles from 1935 until 1941's *Meet John Doe* were all in support. He was married to Vilma Banky (q.v.).

PUBLISHED RESOURCES

• *Books* – General: *Alice in Movieland*; *Eighty Silent Film Stars*; *Famous Film Folk*; *Gentlemen to the Rescue*; *The Movie Stars Story*; *The Real Tinsel*; *The Truth About the Movies*; *Who's Who on the Screen*. Credits: *Filmarama* (v. I and II); *Forty Years of Screen Credits*; *Twenty Years of Silents*; *Who Was Who on Screen*. Encyclopedic Works: *Film Encyclopedia*; *Filmlexicon degli Autori e delle Opere*; *Halliwell's Filmgoer's Companion*; *The Illustrated Who's Who of the Cinema*; *The Movie Makers*; *Quin-*

lan's Illustrated Registry of Film Stars; *Who's Who in Hollywood*; *The World Almanac Who's Who of Film*; *The World Film Encyclopedia*. Pictorial: *The Image Makers*; *Silent Portraits*. Factoids: *Star Stats*.

• *Periodicals* – The following periodical articles are in addition to those included in the library listings below: *Photoplay* (Nov. 1918, Nov. 1919, May-June 1924, Feb. 1925, Apr. 1927); *Motion Picture Classic* (Aug. 1919, Mar. 1921, May 1928); *Motion Picture Magazine* (July 1920, May 1924, June 1925, Mar. 1927); *Classic Film Collector* (Fall 1969); *Time* (Oct. 24, 1969); *Newsweek* (Oct. 27, 1969); *Films in Review* (Mar. 1974, Aug.-Sept. 1977).

ARCHIVAL MATERIALS

• *Clipping File* – AZSU (Jimmy Starr Collection): Obituary (1969). CAA: Film appearance (1927, 1933); stage appearance (1921); legal problem (1927, 1929); illness (1928); marriage (1927); article (1928, late 1920s?, 1931); interview (1950); obituary (1969). CAFI: Obituary (1969). CAUT: Obituary (1969). CAUU: Obituary (1969). NYMA (also in Photoplay Collection): Stage appearance (1932); film appearance (1910s, 1920s, 1930); comeback (1933, 1940); illness (1928); obituary (1969). Periodical articles: *Photoplay* (Mar. 1928, July 1932); *Classic Images* (Apr. 1986, June 1986, June 1987). NYMN: Newsphotos; returns to films (1933?); marriage (1936). • *Other Clipping File* – GBBF, MIDL, NYPL (also in Locke Collection), PAPL, TXU, WICF. • *Correspondence* – NYPL (C. & L. Brown Collection): 1933. • *Filmography* – CAA, NYMA. • *Legal File* – CAUW: Talent agreement (1928). • *Oral History* – NYCO: Mentioned in: Conrad Nagel interview. • *Photograph/Still* – CAA (also in Hollywood Studio Museum Collection) (also in MGM Collection), CAH, CAHL, CAPH, CAUU, DCG (Quigley Photographic Archives), GBBF, NJPT, NYAM, NYB (Bettmann/UPI Collection) (Underwood Collection), NYCU (Palmer Collection), NYEH, NYMN, NYPL, NYSU, OHCL, PAPL, TXSM,

TXU (A. Davis Collection), WICF. • *Publicity Release* — NYMA: Republic (1935); Burroughs. • *Scrapbook* — NYPL (also in R. Locke Collection), UTBY (DeMille Archives). • *Studio Biography* — NYMA: DeMille (1926); Photoplay.

LAWRENCE, Florence (Florence Bridgewood?), Hamilton, Ontario, Canada, 1886/90–1938.

A true film pioneer, Florence Lawrence was one of the most famous of the early players and one of the first to be billed by name. Initially known as "The Biograph Girl" and "The Imp Girl," she was a favorite of fans by 1907 and she appeared in numerous one- and two-reelers until about 1914 when an injury took her out of the public eye for two years. This ended her starring career and after some failed comeback attempts she played bits in the years before her death.

Published Sources

• *Books* — Bibliography: *The Idols of Silence*. General: *Early American Cinema*; *Movie Star*; *Stardom*; *The Truth About the Movies*. Credits: *Filmarama* (v. I and II); *Twenty Years of Silents*; *Who Was Who on Screen*. Encyclopedic Works: *Film Encyclopedia*; *Halliwell's Filmgoer's Companion*; *The Illustrated Encyclopedia of the World's Great Movie Stars and Their Films*; *The Illustrated Who's Who of the Cinema*; *International Dictionary of Films and Filmmakers* (v. 3); *Notable American Women, 1607–1950*; *The Oxford Companion to Film*; *Who's Who in Hollywood*; *The World Almanac Who's Who of Film*. Filmography: *Hollywood on the Palisades*. Pictorial: *Silent Portraits*. Factoids: *Star Stats*.

• *Periodicals* — The following periodical articles are in addition to those included in the library listings below: *Moving Picture World* (May 18, 1912); *Photoplay* (Sept. 1913, Jan. 1914, Nov. 1914–Mar. 1915, May 1921, July 1924); *Pictures and Picturegoer* (Apr. 18, 1914); *Green Book Magazine* (May 1914); *Blue Book Magazine* (Sept. 1914); *Motion Picture Magazine* (Mar. 1916); *Picture Play Magazine* (May 1916); *Cinema Digest* (June 13, 1932); *Newsweek* (Jan. 9, 1939); *Films in Review* (Nov. 1953, Aug.-Sept. 1980).

Archival Materials

• *Clipping File* — CAA: Divorce (1934); article (1990); newsphoto; obituary (1938). Periodical article: *Box-office* (Feb. 1982). NYMA (also in Photoplay Collection): Obituary (1938). Periodical article: *Classic Film/Video Images* (Sept. 1981). NYPL (also in Locke Collection): Newsphotos; article (1914); obituary (1938). • *Other Clipping File* — AZSU (Jimmy Starr Collection), CALM (see Collection), MAH, MIDL, PAPL, WICF. • *Collection* — CALM: Correspondence (1904–30, undated); legal papers; financial records; poems; film scenarios; clippings (1907–30, undated); play programs; ephemera (tickets, flyers, etc.). • *Correspondence* — CALM (see Collection). • *Filmography* — NJFL. • *Legal File* — CALM (see Collection). • *Oral History* — NYCO: Mentioned in: Blanche Sweet interview. • *Photograph/Still* — CAA (also in Hollywood Studio Museum Collection) (also in MGM Collection), CALM, CAUT (Jessen Collection), DCG (Quigley Photographic Archives), NJFL, NYB (Bettmann/UPI Collection) (Penguin Collection), NYPL, NYSU, OHCL, WICF. • *Play Program* — CALM (see Collection). • *Scrapbook* — NYPL (R. Locke Collection).

LEE, Gwen (Gwendolyn Le Pinski or Lepinski), Hastings, NE, 1905–1961.

A Wampas Baby Star of 1928, tall blonde Gwen Lee had been appearing in MGM films since 1925. Her height and somewhat strong features relegated her to wisecracking best friend and "other woman" roles in which she supported many of MGM's major stars, including Shearer, Garbo (q.v.) and Crawford. After her 1930 release from MGM, she was relegated to low-budget films for various studios until the late 1930s.

PUBLISHED SOURCES

• *Books*—Credits: *Filmarama* (v. II); *Forty Years of Screen Credits*; *Twenty Years of Silents*; *Who Was Who on Screen*. Encyclopedic Works: *The Picturegoer's Who's Who and Encyclopedia of the Screen To-day*; *Who's Who in Hollywood*. Pictorial: *Silent Portraits*; *They Had Faces Then*. • *Periodicals*—*Motion Picture Magazine* (Dec. 1927); *Motion Picture Classic* (Feb. 1928); *Films in Review* (Feb. 1970) (Wampas Baby Stars).

ARCHIVAL MATERIALS

• *Clipping File*—CAA: Engagement (1928–29); film appearance (1928); illness (1927); release from MGM (1930); legal problem (1932). CAUT: Newsphotos. NYPL: Newsphotos; article (1927, undated). • *Other Clipping File*—GBBF, MIDL, NYMA (Photoplay Collection), PAPL, WICF. • *Legal File*—CAUW: Payroll record (1926); talent agreement (1926–28). • *Photograph/Still*—CAA (also in Hollywood Studio Museum Collection), CAH, CAUT (Jessen Collection), CAUU, DCG (Quigley Photographic Archives), GBBF, MIDL, NJPT, NYB (Bettmann/UPI Collection) (Underwood Collection), NYCU (Dramatic Museum Portraits), NYEH, NYPL, NYSU, OHCL, PAPL, TNUT (Clarence Brown Collection), TXU (A. Davis Collection), WICF. • *Scrapbook*—NYPL.

LEE, Lila (Augusta Appel), New York City, 1901/05–1973.

Discovered as a child by vaudeville entrepreneur Gus Edwards, Lila Lee (known as Cuddles) toured with his troupe and made her film debut in 1917's *Cruise of the Make-Believe*. This was the first in a long string of films which included *Blood and Sand* and the talkie version of *The Unholy Three*. Her talkie debut was deemed to be successful but after the first year or two she did not receive leading roles in

major studio films and her career ended in 1937.

PUBLISHED SOURCES

• *Books*—General: *Blue Book of the Screen*; *Famous Film Folk*; *Ladies in Distress*; *Who's Who on the Screen*. Credits: *Filmarama* (v. I and II); *Forty Years of Screen Credits*; *Twenty Years of Silents*; *Who Was Who on Screen*. Encyclopedic Works: *Film Encyclopedia*; *Filmlexicon degli Autori e delle Opere*; *Halliwell's Filmgoer's Companion*; *The Movie Makers*; *The Picturegoer's Who's Who and Encyclopedia of the Screen To-day*; *Who's Who in Hollywood*; *The World Almanac Who's Who of Film*; *The World Film Encyclopedia*. Nostalgia: *Whatever Became of . . .* (1st). Pictorial: *Silent Portraits*; *They Had Faces Then*. • *Periodicals*—The following periodical articles are in addition to those included in the library listings below: *Picture Play Magazine* (Aug. 1918); *Motion Picture Classic* (Sept. 1918, Oct. 1920, Aug. 1921, July 1922, Nov. 1923, Sept. 1930, Aug. 1931); *Photoplay* (Sept. 1918, Aug. 1920, Nov. 1921–Jan. 1922, Oct. 1923, Sept. 1929); *Motion Picture Magazine* (Dec. 1918, Apr. 1921, Feb. 1922, Mar. 1923, Feb. 1929); *Silver Screen* (Dec. 1931); *Movie Classic* (Feb. 1932, Mar. 1933); *Films in Review* (Feb. 1970 (Wampas Baby Stars), Apr. 1972); *Classic Film Collector* (Winter 1973); *Newsweek* (Nov. 26, 1973).

ARCHIVAL MATERIALS

• *Clipping File*—AZSU: Marriage; legal problem. CAA: Engagement/marriage/divorce/children (1928, 1930–35, 1944); film appearance (1923, 1928); illness (1930–31, 1958); robbery (1934); legal problem (1936); nostalgia (1949, 1969, 1971); obituary (1973). CAFI: Newsphotos; article (undated); obituary (1973). Periodical article: *Films in Review* (Nov. 1984). CAUT: Obituary (1973). CAUU: Obituary (1973). NYMA: Obituary (1973). NYMN: Career (1936, 1940); newsphotos; investigation of murder (1936); marriage/divorce/children (1934–35); legal problem (1936). Periodical article: *New Movie Magazine* (1930).

NYPL (also in Locke Collection): News-photos; article (1949, 1954, 1956-57, un-dated); play review (1943); marriage/divorce (1923, 1931-35); investigation of murder (1936); signs with Paramount (1913); film review (1920s, 1930s); stage appearance (1930s); comeback (1932); obituary (1973). Periodical article: *New Movie Magazine* (undated). TXU: Obit-uary (1971). • *Other Clipping File* — CAFI, CAUT, CAUU, CNDA, GBBF, MAH, MIDL, OHCL, OHKS, PAPL, WICF. • *Correspondence* — NYPL: Let-ter(s) (C. & L. Brown Collection) (1951); others (1966, undated). OHKS. • *Filmog-raphy* — CAA, NYPL. • *Legal File* — CAUT (Twentieth Century-Fox Collec-tion): Loanout (1929). CAUW: Talent agreement (1928-30, undated); docu-ment (1929); payroll record (1930); memo, letter (1929-31); contract sum-mary (1930); contract (1929). • *Oral History* — NYCO: Interviewed in 1959. Also mentioned in the following inter-views: Sidney Blackmer, Glenda Farrell, Nita Naldi, Elliot Nugent. • *Paper Dolls* — CAH: 1920s. • *Photograph/Still* — CAA (also in Hollywood Studio Museum Collection) (also in MGM Col-lection), CAFA, CASF, CAUT (Jessen Collection), CAUU, CNDA, DCG (Quigley Photographic Archives), GBBF, MIDL, NJPT, NYAM, NYB (Bettmann/UPI Collection) (Underwood Collection), NYCU (Dramatic Museum Portraits), NYEH, NYMN, NYPL, NYSU, OHCL, PAPL, TXU (A. Davis Collection), WICF. • *Play Program* — NYPL: 1942, undated. • *Reminis-cence* — MISU. • *Scrapbook* — NYPL (also in R. Locke Collection), UTBY (DeMille Archives). • *Studio Biog-raphy* — CAA: Paramount (1932-33, mid-1930s).

LEWIS, Mitchell, Syracuse, NY, 1880-1956.

Big and burly Mitchell Lewis played both leads and character parts (often villains) in a long career that stretched from about 1914 to the mid-1950s. Among the early studios for which he appeared were Reliance and Than-

houser. His films included *The Docks of New York, Beau Sabreur, The Bar-rier, The Spoilers* (1923 version) and the serial *The Million Dollar Mystery*.

PUBLISHED SOURCES
• *Books* — General: *More Character People*; *The Versatiles*; *Who's Who on the Screen*. Credits: *Filmarama* (v. I and II); *Forty Years of Screen Credits*; *Twenty Years of Silents*; *Who Was Who on Screen*. Encyclopedic Works: *Film-lexicon degli Autori e delle Opere*; *The Picturegoer's Who's Who and Encyclo-pedia of the Screen To-day*; *Who's Who in Hollywood*.
• *Periodicals* — *Motion Picture Classic* (Mar. 1919); *Photoplay* (June 1919); *Pic-ture Show* (Dec. 13, 1919).

ARCHIVAL MATERIALS
• *Clipping File* — CAA: Obituary (1956). NYPL (also in Locke Collection): Newsphotos; stage appearance; career (1933); film appearance (1927, 1933); obituary (1956). • *Other Clipping File* — GBBF, NYMA (Photoplay Collection), OHCL, WICF. • *Legal File* — CAUW: Contract (1927); pay record (1927); con-tract (1928); talent agreement (1927-29); agreement (1926). • *Photograph/Still* — CAA (also in Hollywood Studio Museum Collection) (also in MGM Collection), CAFA, DCG (Quigley Photographic Ar-chives), NYCU (Dramatic Museum Por-traits), NYPL, NYSU, OHCL, TXU, WICF. • *Press Kit* — OHCL. • *Publicity Release* — NYMA: Unknown studio. • *Scrapbook* — NYPL (R. Locke Collec-tion). • *Studio Biography* — CAA: Para-mount (1932); MGM (1935). NYMA: Photoplay.

LINCOLN, Elmo (Otto E. Linkenhelt), Rochester, IN, 1889-1952.

Massive Elmo Lincoln played small parts in two D.W. Griffith master-pieces, *Birth of a Nation* and *Intol-erance*. His most famous roles came as the first screen Tarzan in *Tarzan of the Apes* and *The Romance of Tarzan*. He was also seen in serials like *Elmo the*

Mighty and *Elmo the Fearless*. He was gone from the screen by the mid-1920s and his return in the 1930s was as a supporting and bit player. (Not to be confused with actor E.K. Lincoln.)

PUBLISHED SOURCES

• *Books* – **General:** *Classics of the Silent Screen; Gentlemen to the Rescue; Hollywood Album 2; A Pictorial History of the Tarzan Movies; Tarzan of the Movies.* **Credits:** *Filmarama* (v. I and II); *Twenty Years of Silents; Who's Who on Screen.* **Encyclopedic Works:** *A Companion to the Movies; Film Encyclopedia; Filmlexicon degli Autori e delle Opere; Halliwell's Filmgoer's Companion; The Illustrated Who's Who of the Cinema; The Movie Makers; Who's Who in Hollywood; Who's Who of the Horrors and Other Fantasy Films; The World Almanac Who's Who of Film.* **Filmography:** *Hollywood on the Palisades.*

• *Periodicals* – The following periodical articles are in addition to those included in the library listings below: *Photoplay* (July 1919); *Life* (May 16, 1949).

ARCHIVAL MATERIALS

• *Clipping File* – CAA: Legal problem (1938); film appearance (1944, 1949); article (1951); divorce (1928, 1938); obituary (1952). NYMA (also in Photoplay Collection): Periodical articles: *Classic Film Collector* (Spring-Winter 1968, Fall 1974). NYPL (also in Locke Collection): Newsphotos; article (1947); joins circus; film review (1910s); obituary (1952). Periodical article: *Pic* (Sept. 5, 1939). • *Other Clipping File* – MIDL, WICF. • *Photograph/Still* – CAA, CAFA, CNDA, DCG (Quigley Photographic Archives), GBBF, NYEH, NYPL, NYSU, OHCL, WICF. • *Publicity Release* – CAA: Unknown studio (1939?). • *Scrapbook* – NYPL.

LITTLEFIELD, Lucien, San Antonio, TX, 1895/96-1960.

Lucien Littlefield was one of the premiere character actors of both silent and sound films, beginning in 1913. He was known for his mastery of makeup and, even when relatively young he convincingly played old men (e.g., his Caligari-like appearance in *The Cat and the Canary*). He was in hundreds of films through the 1950s, among them *Charley's Aunt, The Torrent, To Have and to Hold, Everywoman* and *Uncle Tom's Cabin.*

PUBLISHED SOURCES

• *Books* – **General:** *More Character People; The Real Stars* (v. 2); *The Truth About the Movies; The Versatiles.* **Credits:** *Filmarama* (v. I and II); *Forty Years of Screen Credits; Twenty Years of Silents; Who Was Who on Screen.* **Encyclopedic Works:** *Film Encyclopedia; Halliwell's Filmgoer's Companion; Hollywood Character Actors; The Movie Makers; The Picturegoer's Who's Who and Encyclopedia of the Screen To-day; Who's Who in Hollywood; The World Almanac Who's Who of Film; The World Film Encyclopedia.* **Pictorial:** *Silent Portraits.*

• *Periodicals* – The following periodical articles are in addition to that included in the library listings below: *Pantomime* (Sept. 28, 1921); *Motion Picture Magazine* (June 1929); *Popular Science* (Mar. 1938).

OBSCURE PUBLISHED SOURCES
CAA (Pat O'Malley Collection): *The Cast* (v. 1).

ARCHIVAL MATERIALS

• *Clipping File* – CAA: Obituary (1960). Periodical article: *Films in Review* (Aug.-Sept. 1960). CAUT: Film appearance (1957). NYMA (also in Photoplay Collection): Obituary (1960). NYPL: Film review (1920s, 1930s); film appearance (1930); injury (1937); career (1930s?); newsphotos. • *Other Clipping File* – CAUU (McCormick Collection), GBBF, MAH, MIDL, PAPL. • *Correspondence* – CAUU: Letter from daughter. • *Legal File* – CAA (Sennett Collection): Contract (1932). CAUW: Talent agreement (1924, 1928-30); contract (1928, 1933); document (1926). • *Photograph/Still* – CAA (also in Hollywood Studio Museum Collection),

CAUU, DCG (Quigley Photographic Archives), NYPL, NYSU, OHCL, TXU, WICF. • *Publicity Release* — CAA: Paramount (mid-1930s, 1939, 1941); RKO (1930s). • *Studio Biography* — CAA: Goldwyn (1923); Paramount (1953).

LIVINGSTON, Margaret, Salt Lake City, UT, 1896/1900–1985.

One of the silent screen's women you "loved to hate" was redhaired Margaret Livingston. Her somewhat leering eyes made her a natural for villainess and "other woman" roles, and the film for which she is remembered is undoubtedly Murnau's *Sunrise* (1927). She appeared in no fewer than 12 films in a 14-month period in 1928 and '29 but her career slowed after 1931 and she was soon gone from the screen.

PUBLISHED SOURCES

• *Books* — General: *Famous Film Folk*; *The Truth About the Movies*. **Credits:** *Filmarama* (v. I and II); *Forty Years of Screen Credits*; *Twenty Years of Silents*. **Encyclopedic Works:** *Film Encyclopedia*; *Filmlexicon degli Autori e delle Opere*; *The Movie Makers*; *The Picturegoer's Who's Who and Encyclopedia of the Screen To-day*; *Who's Who in Hollywood*. **Pictorial:** *They Had Faces Then*.

• *Periodicals* — The following periodical articles are in addition to that included in the library listings below: *Motion Picture Classic* (June 1921); *Photoplay* (Feb. 1926, Apr. 1930); *Cinema Art* (May 1926); *Motion Picture Magazine* (Mar. 1928, June 1929); *Movie Classic* (Nov. 1935); *Today's Health* (Feb. 1958); *Films in Review* (Jan. 1985).

ARCHIVAL MATERIALS

• *Clipping File* — CAA: Obituary (1989). CAUT: Vacation (1929). NYMA (also in Photoplay Collection): Obituary (1985). NYPL: Newsphotos; article (undated); film appearance (1932); nostalgia (1936); wife of Paul Whiteman (1938); marriage (1931); obituary (1985). Periodical article: *Hollywood* (Dec. 1,

1928). • *Other Clipping File* — CAUT, GBBF, MIDL, PAPL, TXU, WICF. • *Correspondence* — NYPL (Lamparski Collection): 1972. • *Legal File* — CAUT (Twentieth Century-Fox Collection): Letter (1926); talent agreement (1925). CAUW: Talent agreement (1924, 1928, 1931); document (1927). • *Photograph/Still* — CAA (also in Hollywood Studio Museum Collection), CAUT (Jessen Collection), CAUU (also Paul Whiteman Collection), DCG (Quigley Photographic Archives), GBBF, NJPT, NYB (Penguin Collection) (Underwood Collection), NYEH, NYPL, NYSU, OHCL, TXU (A. Davis Collection), WICF. • *Play Program* — OHSU. • *Studio Biography* — CAA: Paramount (1929). NYMA: Photoplay. *NOTE*: ML was married to Paul Whiteman whose collection is housed at CAUU. There is very little in it about ML except for some photographs as noted above.

LLOYD, Harold, Burchard, NE, 1893–1971.

After working as an extra and appearing in one- and two-reelers as Willie Work and the somewhat more popular Lonesome Luke, Harold Lloyd found lasting fame with the All-American boy "glasses" persona. In the 1920s he had enormous success with features like *Grandma's Boy*, *Girl Shy*, *The Freshman*, *The Kid Brother* and *Speedy*. He also made the memorable *Safety Last* which established his latter-day reputation as a "thrill" comedian. His gradual decline after talkies came has not tarnished his reputation as one of the great silent comic actors.

PUBLISHED SOURCES

• *Books* — HL was credited as author of a book of his photographs: *3-D Hollywood* (1992). **Bibliography:** *The Idols of Silence*. **General:** *Agee on Film*; *American Cinema*; *Behind the Screen*; *Blue Book of the Screen*; *Le Cinema Burlesque Américain au Temps du Muet*; *Cinema Stylists*; *Classic Movie Comedians*; *Classics of the Silent Screen*; *Close Ups*; *Comedy Films, 1894-1954*; *The*

Comic Mind; Famous Film Folk; Film: An Anthology; Four Great Comedians; Funny Men of the Movies; The Funsters; The Golden Age of Sound Comedy; The Great Funnies; The Great Movie Comedians; The Great Movie Stars; Harold Lloyd (American Film Institute); Harold Lloyd (D'Agostino); Harold Lloyd (Miller); Here Come the Clowns; L'Histoire de l'Art Cinématographique; The History of Motion Pictures; History of the American Cinema (v. 3); Hollywood Album; Hollywood and the Great Stars; Hollywood Directors, 1914-1940; Hollywood Hall of Fame; The Hollywood Style; How I Broke Into the Movies; "Image" on the Art and Evolution of the Film; Keaton et Cie; The Laugh Makers; Motion Picture News Booking Guide and Studio Directory; Movie Comedians; The Movie Stars Story; The National Society of Film Critics on Movie Comedy; The Parade's Gone By; Personal Glimpses of Famous Folks; The Primal Screen; The Saturday Evening Post Movie Book; Schickel on Film; Screen Personalities; The Silent Clowns; Special People, Special Times; The Stars; Starstruck; Stunt; Tres Comicos del Cine; The Truth About the Movies; Who's Who on the Screen; The World of Comedy; World of Laughter; Yesterday's Clowns. **Credits:** Filmarama (v. I and II); Forty Years of Screen Credits; Twenty Years of Silents. **Encyclopedic Works:** A Biographical Dictionary of Film; Cinema, a Critical Dictionary; A Companion to the Movies; Current Biography (1950, 1972); Dictionary of Film Makers; A Dictionary of the Cinema; Film Encyclopedia; Filmlexicon degli Autori e delle Opere; Halliwell's Filmgoer's Companion; The Illustrated Encyclopedia of the World's Great Movie Stars and Their Films; The Illustrated Who's Who of the Cinema; International Dictionary of Films and Filmmakers (v. 3); The International Encyclopedia of Film; Joe Franklin's Encyclopedia of Comedians; The Movie Makers; The Oxford Companion to Film; The Picturegoer's Who's Who and Encyclopedia of the Screen To-day; Quinlan's Illustrated Directory of Film

Comedy Actors; Quinlan's Illustrated Registry of Film Stars; Who's Who in Hollywood; The World Almanac Who's Who of Film; The World Encyclopedia of the Film; The World Film Encyclopedia. **Biography/Autobiography:** An American Comedy; Harold Lloyd (Borde); Harold Lloyd (Dardis); Harold Lloyd (Lacourbe); Harold Lloyd (Schickel); Harold Lloyd (Tichy). **Legal Material:** Harold Lloyd Corporation.... **Films:** Harold Lloyd (Reilly); Harold Lloyd's World of Comedy; Three Classic Silent Screen Comedies Starring Harold Lloyd. **Nostalgia:** Whatever Became of... (2nd). **Pictorial:** Harold Lloyd Estate Pictorial; Silent Portraits. **Recordings:** Hollywood on Record. **Factoids:** Star Stats.

• Periodicals—The following periodical articles are in addition to those included in the library listings below: Photo-play World (Dec. 1918); Motion Picture Magazine (June 1919, Apr.-May 1920, Aug. 1921, July 1922, Nov. 1922, July 1923, Feb. 1925, May 1925, Dec. 1925, May 1927, Sept. 1927, Feb. 1928, Oct. 1930, Sept. 1933, Nov. 1934, Feb. 1936, Dec. 1937); Photoplay (July 1919, Jan. 1920, July-Aug. 1922, July 1923, Apr.-Aug. 1924, Feb. 1925, Sept. 1925, Mar. 1927, May 1930, Sept. 1932, Aug. 1938); Motion Picture Classic (Oct. 1919, Jan. 1922, Oct. 1922, Feb. 1923, Oct. 1923, Nov. 1927, Mar. 1929, May 1931); Filmplay Journal (Apr. 1922); American Magazine (July 1922); Picturegoer (June 1923, Jan.-Feb. 1927, Oct. 1932); Literary Digest (July 14, 1923); Sunset (Aug. 1923); Motion Picture Director (Nov. 1925); New Yorker (Jan. 30, 1926, July 2, 1949); Ladies' Home Journal (May 1926, Feb. 1928); Graphic (Mar. 5, 1927); Theatre (May 1927); Collier's (June 11, 1927, June 1, 1946); Saturday Evening Post (Mar. 24-Apr. 28, 1928); National Magazine (Aug. 1928); Screen Mirror (Oct. 1930); Close Up (Mar. 1933); Motion Picture Story (Nov. 1934); Movie Classic (Jan. 1935, Feb. 1936); Cue (July 16, 1938, Feb. 3, 1945, Jan. 25, 1949, Nov. 18, 1950); Screen Book (Sept. 1938); Movies and the People Who Make Them (no. 2, 1940); Newsweek (Mar. 17,

1941, Aug. 16, 1943, June 4, 1962); *Movieland* (Oct. 1946); *Silver Screen* (Apr. 1946); *Saturday Review* (Nov. 4, 1950); *Popular Photography* (Aug. 1951, Aug. 1971); *Time* (Jan. 19, 1953, Mar. 22, 1971); *Life* (Jan. 23, 1956); *Film Quarterly* (Fall 1958, Summer 1962); *Sight and Sound* (Winter 1958/59); *Films in Review* (Aug.-Sept. 1962, May 1974); *Cineforum* (June 1964); *Sound Stage* (May 1965); *8mm Collector* (Spring 1966); *Positif* (Summer 1966, Dec. 1979); *Cinema Journal* (1966-67); *Classic Film Collector* (Winter/Spring 1967, Summer 1968, Spring 1971, Summer 1973, Summer-Fall 1974); *Cinéma* (France) (Mar.-May 1968, Feb. 1979); *Premier Plan* (Nov. 1968); *Film Comment* (Fall 1969); *Film Fan Monthly* (Apr. 1971); *Silent Picture* (Summer-Autumn 1971, Autumn 1972); *The Velvet Light Trap* (Winter 1971/72); *Box Office* (Feb. 11, 1974, June 24, 1974); *Image et Son* (June 1974); *Ecran* (June 1974); *Film (series 2)* (London) (June 1974); *Cine Revue* (Sept. 19, 1974); *American Film* (Sept. 1977, May 1978, June 1988); *Film und Ton* (Sept.-Oct. 1978); *Film News* (Nov.-Dec. 1978); *Cahiers du Cinéma* (Jan. 1979); *Metro* (Winter 1979); *Avant-Scène* (May 1, 1979, Oct. 15, 1980); *Chaplin* (no. 6, 1979); *Cinématographique* (Oct. 1979); *Classic Film/Video Images* (Jan. 1980, Sept. 1981); *Classic Images* (Mar. 1983, July 1983, May 1984, Apr. 1988, Aug. 1988-Feb. 1989); *New Republic* (Aug. 8-15, 1983); *Segnocinema* (Nov. 1985); *Film Dope* (Sept. 1986); *Stars* (biofilmography) (Dec. 1988); *Listener* (Feb. 15, 1990).

MEDIA

Comedy—A Serious Business (video); *Harold Lloyd* (video); *Midwest Roots, Hollywood Dreams* (video); *Wm. S. Hart and the Sad Clowns* (video).

ARCHIVAL MATERIALS

• *Clipping File*—CAA: Wife burned (1925); legal problem (1930, 1933, 1945, 1952-53, 1962); newsphotos; children (1931); surgery (1931, 1949, 1968, 1970); film appearance (1920-21, 1924, 1933, 1962); trip to Denver (1940); comeback (1945-46); illness (1948); Shriner (1949-

50); article (1949, 1953, 1962-63, 1975, 1978, 1980); painter (1953); taxes (1953, 1965); films revived (1960, 1971, 1973-74, 1976); review of Harold Lloyd's *World of Comedy* (film) (1962, 1974); film festival (1962, 1973, 1976); honor (1963); nostalgia (1970); AFI endowment (1988); home (1971-76, 1981, 1984); obituary (1971). Periodical articles: *Literary Digest* (Oct. 6, 1928); *Life* (Aug. 1, 1938, Sept. 5, 1949); *Time* (July 25, 1949); *Good Housekeeping* (May 1955); *Show Business Illustrated* (Apr. 1962); *New Yorker* (May 26, 1962); *Cue* (June 2, 1962); *Films and Filming* (Jan. 1964); *MD* (Dec. 1967); *Newsweek* (Mar. 22, 1971); *Entertainment Magazine* (Fall 1973); *Hollywood Studio Magazine* (Oct. 1974); *Quarterly Review of Film Studies* (Spring 1978); *Blackhawk Film Digest* (Mar. 1979, Winter 1980/81); *World of Yesterday* (June 1979); *Architectural Digest* (Apr. 1990). CAFI: Article (1971, 1975, 1978, 1988); film festival (1975-76); home (1971, 1975, 1977); sale of effects (1975); films (1971, 1974); Foundation (1988); synopses of films; review of *Harold Lloyd* (Dardis) (1984); obituary (1971). Periodical article: *Newsweek* (Mar. 22, 1971). CAUT: Distribution of films (1973); home (1971-76, 1985); article (1963, 1978); review of *Harold Lloyd* (Schickel); sale of effects (1975); estate (1976); review of *Harold Lloyd* (Dardis); newsphotos; injury (1928); honor (1963); obituary (1971). CAUU: TV documentary (1989); film festival (1976-77); sale of effects (1975); comeback (1950); home (1974-75, 1984); films made available (1949, 1973); interview (1965); review of *Harold Lloyd* (Schickel); obituary (1971). Periodical articles: *Image* (Sept. 1976); *Blackhawk Film Digest* (May 1979, July 1980). NYPL (also in Locke Collection): PARTIAL CONTENTS: TV documentary (1989); review of *Harold Lloyd* (Dardis) (1983); home (1984); obituary (1971). Periodical article: *Newsweek* (Mar. 22, 1971). • *Other Clipping File*—AZSU (Jimmy Starr Collection), CNDA, DCLC (see Collection), GBBF, MAH, MIDL, NYMA, OHCL, WICF. • *Collection*—DCLC (George Kleine Collection): May contain clipping files, correspondence and legal files about Harold Lloyd Corporation (1923). WYU: Not processed as of 1993. • *Correspondence* — CAUS (Preston Sturges Collection), DCLC (see Collection). • *Filmography* — CAA. CAUT: 1915-20. NYEH. • *Interview* — CAUU (A. Slide Collection): 1970. GBBF (Hollywood Collection): Transcript of interview for *Hollywood* (TV series). • *Legal File* — DCLC (see Collection). • *Oral History* — CAFI: Mentioned in: Harry Oliver interview. NYCO: Interviewed in 1959. Also mentioned in the following interviews: Frances Marion, Elliot Nugent, Otto Preminger, Charles Ruggles, George Seaton, Albert (Eddie) Sutherland, Blanche Sweet, Jerry Wald, Bert Wheeler, Adolph Zukor. • *Photograph/ Still* — CAA (also in Hollywood Studio Museum Collection), CALM, CAUS (Eddie Cantor Collection), CAUT (Jessen Collection) (Portrait File), CNDA, DCG (Quigley Photographic Archives), NYB (Bettmann/UPI Collection) (Penguin Collection) (Springer Collection) (Underwood Collection), NYCU (Dramatic Museum Portraits), NYEH, NYMN, NYPL, NYSU, OHCL, OHSU, TXSM, TXU, WICF. • *Press Kit* — OHCL. • *Program* — NYCU (Dramatic Museum Collection). • *Scrapbook* — NYMA, NYPL (also in R. Locke Collection). • *Studio Biography* — CAA: Famous Players-Lasky (1927); Paramount (1936); RKO (1946, 1949). CAFI: RKO (1940s). CAUU: RKO (1940s).

LOCKWOOD, Harold, Newark, NJ, 1887-1918.

At studios including Selig, Famous and Metro, Harold Lockwood was a major leading man with co-stars like Mary Pickford (q.v.) and May Allison (q.v.) with whom he teamed in a succession of popular romances. These films included *River of Romance*, *The Comeback* and *Big Tremaine*. Among his other films were *Tess of the Storm Country*, *Wildflower*, *Hearts Adrift* and *David Harum*. Several of his films

were released posthumously, confirming his great popularity.

PUBLISHED SOURCES

• *Books* — **General:** *From Hollywood*; *Life Stories of the Movie Stars*. **Credits:** *Filmarama* (V. I); *Twenty Years of Silents*; *Who Was Who on Screen*. **Encyclopedic Works:** *Film Encyclopedia*; *Who's Who in Hollywood*. **Pictorial:** *Silent Portraits*.
• *Periodicals* — The following periodical articles are in addition to those included in the library listings below: *Photoplay* (Oct. 1914, Dec. 1915, Feb. 1918, Jan. 1919, Mar. 1926); *Motion Picture Magazine* (Feb. 1915, Apr.-May 1915, Sept. 1915, Nov. 1915, Mar. 1917, Sept. 1917, June 1918, Jan. 1919); *Picture Play Magazine* (July 1916); *Motion Picture Classic* (May 1917); *Films in Review* (May 1971); *Classic Film Collector* (Fall 1976).

ARCHIVAL MATERIALS

• *Clipping File* — CAA: Newsphotos. Periodical article: *Motion Picture Magazine* (1918). NYMA (also in Photoplay Collection). Periodical articles: *Photoplay World* (Mar. 1918, Dec. 1918); *Classic Film Collector* (Spring 1977). NYPL (also in Locke Collection): Newsphotos; obituary (1918). • *Other Clipping File* — GBBF, MIDL, OHCL, PAPL, WICF. • *Filmography* — CAA, NYMA. • *Photograph/Still* — CAA (also in Hollywood Studio Museum Collection), CALM, CAUB, CAUT (Jessen Collection), CAUU, DCG (Quigley Photographic Archives), IAU (Junkin Collection), MIDL, NJFL, NYAM, NYPL, NYSU, OHCL, TXU, WICF. • *Scrapbook* — NYAM, NYPL (also in R. Locke Collection).

LOGAN, Jacqueline, Corsicana or San Antonio, TX, 1901/04-1983.

A popular and beautiful actress who appeared in more than 50 silent films, Jacqueline Logan's career sank almost without trace at the dawn of the talkies. She made her first film, *The Perfect Crime*, in 1921 and went on to appear in mostly lightweight fare for the rest of the decade. Her portrayal of Mary Magdalene in DeMille's *The King of Kings* (1927) is her best-remembered today. One of John Barrymore's co-stars in his talkie debut *General Crack*, she went to England to attempt a career revival and even co-directed a film, but to no avail.

PUBLISHED SOURCES

• *Books* — General: *Blue Book of the Screen*; *Famous Film Folk*; *How I Broke Into the Movies*; *The Truth About the Movies*. Credits: *Filmarama* (v. II); *Forty Years of Screen Credits*; *Twenty Years of Silents*. Encyclopedic Works: *Film Encyclopedia*; *Filmlexicon degli Autori e delle Opere*; *The Movie Makers*; *The Picturegoer's Who's Who and Encyclopedia of the Screen To-day*; *Who's Who in Hollywood*; *The World Film Encyclopedia*. Nostalgia: *Whatever Became of...* (2nd). Pictorial: *Silent Portraits*; *They Had Faces Then*.

• *Periodicals* — The following periodical articles are in addition to those included in the library listings below: *Motion Picture Classic* (June 1921, Oct. 1921, Feb. 1927); *Photoplay* (June 1924, May 1930); *Cinema Art* (Jan. 1926); *Motion Picture Magazine* (June 1928, June 1929); *Films in Review* (Feb. 1970 (Wampas Baby Stars), Apr. 1972, Apr. 1976).

ARCHIVAL MATERIALS

• *Clipping File* — AZSU (Jimmy Starr Collection): Obituary (1983). CAA: Film appearance (1921); divorce (1937); nostalgia (1970); obituary (1983). CAUT: Film appearance (1929); marriage (1929); illness (1928). NYMA (also in Photoplay Collection): Obituary (1983). Periodical articles: *Classic Film Collector* (Winter 1976, July 1979). NYMN: Newsphotos; divorce (1957); bankruptcy. NYPL: Stage appearance (1931–34); newsphotos; article (1921); obituary (1983). • *Other Clipping File* — GBBF, MAH, MIDL, OHCL, PAPL, TXU, WICF. • *Filmography* — CAA. • *Interview* — CAUU (R. Lamparski Collection). • *Legal File* — CAUT (Twentieth Century-Fox Collection): Memo (1925–26); statement (1926);

talent agreement (1925). CAUW: Contract (1928); talent agreement (1929). • *Photograph/Still* — CAA (also in Hollywood Studio Museum Collection), CAH, CASU, CAUT (Jessen Collection), DCG (Quigley Photographic Archives), GBBF, NJPT, NYAM, NYEH, NYMN, NYPL, NYSU, OHCL, PAPL, TXU (A. Davis Collection), WICF. • *Scrapbook* — UTBY (DeMille Archives). • *Studio Biography* — CAA: Goldwyn (1921, 1929). NYMA: Photoplay.

LOVE, Bessie (Juanita Horton), Midland, TX, 1898-1986.

Sometimes dubbed "The Little Brown Wren" (later to be blonde), pert Bessie Love made more than 120 films in an up-and-down career which dated from 1915. She appeared in films like *Intolerance*, *The Lost World* and *The Aryan* and in numerous romantic melodramas. Her star rose again with 1929's Academy Award–winning musical *The Broadway Melody* but in the thirties she moved to England where she appeared in many supporting roles in films and on television and the stage until the 1980s.

PUBLISHED SOURCES

• *Books* — Bibliography: *The Idols of Silence*. General: *Blue Book of the Screen*; *Classics of the Silent Screen*; *Famous Film Folk*; *Folks Ushud Know*; *The Kindergarten of the Movies*; *Ladies in Distress*; *The MGM Years*; *The Movie Musical from Vitaphone to 42nd Street*; *The Movie Stars Story*. Credits: *British Film Actors' Credits*; *Filmarama* (v. I and II); *Forty Years of Screen Credits*; *Twenty Years of Silents*. Encyclopedic Works: *The Biographical Encyclopaedia and Who's Who of the American Theatre*; *Film Encyclopedia*; *Filmlexicon degli Autori e delle Opere*; *Halliwell's Filmgoer's Companion*; *The Illustrated Encyclopedia of the World's Great Movie Stars and Their Films*; *The Illustrated Who's Who in British Films*; *The Illustrated Who's Who of the Cinema*; *International Dictionary of Films* and *Filmmakers* (v. 3); *The International Encyclopedia of Film*; *International Motion Picture Almanac* (1975–80); *The Movie Makers*; *Notable Names in the American Theatre*; *The Oxford Companion to Film*; *The Picturegoer's Who's Who and Encyclopedia of the Screen To-day*; *Quinlan's Illustrated Registry of Film Stars*; *Variety Who's Who in Show Business*; *Who's Who in Hollywood*; *Who's Who in the Theatre*; *The World Almanac Who's Who in Film*; *The World Film Encyclopedia.* **Pictorial:** *Silent Portraits*; *They Had Faces Then.* **Nostalgia:** *Is That Who I Think It Is?* (v. 1); *Whatever Became of...* (10th). **Biography/Autobiography:** *From Hollywood with Love.* **Recordings:** *Hollywood on Record.*

• *Periodicals* – The following periodical articles are in addition to those included in the library listings below: *Picture Play Magazine* (June 1916); *Photoplay* (Aug. 1916, Aug. 1917, Dec. 1919, Jan. 1925, Oct. 1925, May 1929); *Motion Picture Magazine* (Oct. 1916, Oct. 1917, Jan. 1918, Apr. 1918, Sept. 1920, May 1922, Aug. 1923, Mar. 1925); *Motion Picture Classic* (Sept. 1917, May 1918, Sept. 1920, Aug. 1922, May 1925, June 1929); *Filmplay Journal* (Sept. 1921); *Films in Review* (Feb. 1959 filmography), June–July 1959, Feb. 1970 (Wampas Baby Stars), Feb. 1982); *Films and Filming* (July 1962); *Monthly Film Bulletin* (Feb. 1972) (filmography); *Classic Film Collector* (Fall 1972, Summer 1976); *Cine Revue* (May 5, 1986); *Revue du Cinéma* (July–Aug. 1986); *Film Dope* (Feb. 1987).

ARCHIVAL MATERIALS
• *Caricature* – NYPL (Sardi Collection). • *Clipping File* – CAA: Newsphotos; film appearance (1921, 1926, 1953–54, 1960–61, 1967–68, 1982); playwright (1958); marriage/divorce (1929, 1936, 1939, 1947–48, 1953); article (1972, 1974); nostalgia (1970, 1976, 1980–82); stage appearance (1968, 1981); obituary (1986). Periodical articles: *Films and Filming* (Aug. 1966); *Cine Revue* (July 1978). CAFI: Newsphotos; article (1975); obituary (1986). CAUT: Injury (1929);

engagement (1929); newsphotos; article (1970s). CAUU: TV appearance (1982); obituary (1986). NYMA: Obituary (1986). Periodical article: *Classic Images* (Apr. 1985). NYMN: Newsphotos; obituary (1986). NYPL (also in Locke Collection): Newsphotos (numerous); article (1920s, 1929, undated); playwright (1958); marriage/divorce (1935–36); film review (1920s); *Broadway Melody* (film) (1969); first film job (1962); obituary (1986). Periodical articles: *Vanity Fair* (Oct. 1927); *Films and Filming* (Aug. 1966). • *Other Clipping File* – AZSU (Jimmy Starr Collection), CAH, CAUB, GBBF, MIDL, OHCL, PAPL, WICF. • *Correspondence* – GBBF (Balcon Collection): 1934–35. NYMA: 1972. • *Filmography* – NYPL (incomplete). • *Interview* – CAUU (A. Slide Collection): 1971. GBBF (Hollywood Collection): Transcript of interview for *Hollywood* (TV series). • *Oral History* – NYCO: Mentioned in: Jack Yellen interview. • *Photograph/Still* – AZSU (Jimmy Starr Collection), CAA (also in Hollywood Studio Museum Collection) (also in MGM Collection), CAFA, CASF, CAUT (Jessen Collection), CAUU, CNDA, DCG (Quigley Photographic Archives), GBBF, MIDL, NJPT, NYAM, NYB (Bettmann/UPI Collection) (Springer Collection), NYCU (Bulliet Collection) (Dramatic Museum Portraits) (Palmer Collection), NYEH, NYMN, NYPL, NYSU, OHCL, TXU, WICF. • *Press Kit* – CAFA. • *Program* – CAUU (A. Slide Collection): An evening with Bessie Love (1950s?). • *Publicity Release* – CAA: MGM (1982). • *Scrapbook* – NJPT (Yeandle Collection), NYPL (also in Locke Collection). • *Studio Biography* – CAA: Goldwyn (1923).

LOVE, Montague (sometimes Montagu), Portsmouth, England, 1877/80–1943.

A villain in dozens of films, Montague Love's career lasted far longer than those of many of the handsome heroes he menaced. From 1914 he played an occasional lead but seemed more at home in contemporary or costume melodramas as a memorable "baddie." Among his noteworthy silent films were *Don Juan, King of Kings, The Son of the Sheik, The Wind* and *The Eternal City.* His talkie roles continued up to the time of his death and one of his final films, *Devotion,* was actually released some three years after he died.

PUBLISHED SOURCES

• *Books – General: More Character People; The Versatiles.* **Credits:** *British Film Actors' Credits; Filmarama* (v. I and II); *Forty Years of Screen Credits; Twenty Years of Silents; Who Was Who on Screen.* **Encyclopedic Works:** *Film Encyclopedia; Filmlexicon degli Autori e delle Opere; Halliwell's Filmgoer's Companion; Hollywood Character Actors; The Illustrated Encyclopedia of Movie Character Actors; The Illustrated History of the Cinema; The Movie Makers; The Picturegoer's Who's Who and Encyclopedia of the Screen To-day; Who Was Who in the Theatre; Who's Who in Hollywood; The World Almanac Who's Who of Film; The World Film Encyclopedia.* **Pictorial:** *Silent Portraits.*
• *Periodicals –* The following periodical articles are in addition to those included in the library listings below: *Photoplay* (July 1917, Jan. 1919); *Motion Picture Classic* (Dec. 1918, Sept. 1920); *Cinefantastique* (Fall 1970); *Midnight Marquee* (Fall 1983).

ARCHIVAL MATERIALS

• *Clipping File –* CAA: Obituary. NYMA: Stage appearance (1920s, 1933, undated); film appearance (1910s, 1920s); bankruptcy (1933); career; marriage (1929); article (1918, 1921). Periodical articles: *Classic Images* (Aug. 1987, July-Aug. 1988). NYMN: Newsphotos; career; obituary (1943). NYPL (also in Locke Collection): Legal problem (1933); career (1933); stage appearance (1920s, 1930s); obituary (1943). • *Other Clipping File –* GBBF, MAH, MIDL, OHCL, PAPL, WICF. • *Correspondence –* MABU: Letter(s) (Myrna Loy Collection) (1938); letter(s) (Kate Smith Collection) (1933, undated). NYPL (C. & L.

Brown Collection): 1933. • *Filmography –* CAA. • *Legal File –* CAUW: Talent agreement (1926-31, 1936, 1938-40, 1942); personnel, payroll record (1927, 1936-42); letter (1940, 1942); document (1925, 1929, 1942); contract (1928, 1940). • *Photograph/Still –* CAA (also in Hollywood Studio Museum Collection), CAFA, CAUT (Jessen Collection), CAUU, CNDA, DCG (Quigley Photographic Archives), MABU (Basil Rathbone Collection), NJFL, NYAM, NYEH, NYMN, NYPL, NYSU, OHCL, TXU, WICF. • *Program –* OHSU. • *Scrapbook –* NYPL (R. Locke Collection). • *Studio Biography –* CAA: Fox (1930s); Paramount (1930s).

LOVELY, Louise (Louise Carbasse or Nellie Cowen), Sydney, Australia, 1896/97–1980.

Louise Lovely worked at Fox and Universal when she made her American films, including some westerns, from about 1916 to 1922. She had previously been one of Australia's first film stars. She co-starred with such leading men as Jack Mulhall (q.v.), Lon Chaney (q.v.) and William Farnum (q.v.), and among her films were *The Last of the Duanes, The Third Woman, The Skywayman* and *Life's Greatest Question,* her last.

PUBLISHED SOURCES

• *Books – General: Sweethearts of the Sage; Who's Who on the Screen.* **Credits:** *Filmarama* (v. I and II); *Twenty Years of Silents.* **Encyclopedic Works:** *Who's Who in Hollywood.* **Pictorial:** *Silent Portraits.*
• *Periodicals –* Photoplay (July 1917); *Motion Picture Classic* (Mar. 1918, Oct. 1919); *Cinema Papers* (June-July 1976); *Classic Images* (Feb. 1990).

ARCHIVAL MATERIALS

• *Clipping File –* CAA: Obituary (1980). CAFI: Newsphotos. NYMA (also in Photoplay Collection): Obituary (1980). NYPL (also in Locke Collection): Newsphotos; article (1924); obituary (1980). • *Other Clipping File –* GBBF,

WICF. • *Collection*—WYU: 12 photographs (1919–42); obituaries (1980); miscellany. • *Correspondence*—NYMA (Photoplay Collection). • *Filmography*—CAFI. • *Legal File*—CAUT (Twentieth Century-Fox Collection): Agreement (1920). • *Photograph/Still*—CAA (also in Hollywood Studio Museum Collection), CALM, CAPH, CAUT (Jessen Collection), CAUU, DCG (Quigley Photographic Archives), NYAM, NYPL, NYSU, OHCL, WICF, WYU (see Collection). • *Scrapbook*—NYPL (R. Locke Collection). • *Studio Biography*—CAA: Edison (1910s); Goldwyn (1920s). NYMA: Photoplay.

LOWE, Edmund, San Jose, CA, 1890/93–1971.

Dubbed "The Perfect Bachelor" for his onscreen elegance, Edmund Lowe essayed a large variety of roles and played against type opposite Victor McLaglen in a series of films which included *What Price Glory?*, *The Cockeyed World* and *Hot Pepper*. He appeared in almost 100 films beginning about 1916 and was onscreen regularly until the late 1940s, returning for some character parts a decade later. He was married to Lilyan Tashman (q.v.).

PUBLISHED SOURCES

• *Books*—**General:** *Famous Film Folk*; *Hollywood Album 2*; *Screen Personalities*; *Star Quality*. **Credits:** *Filmarama* (v. I and II); *Forty Years of Screen Credits*; *Twenty Years of Silents*; *Who Was Who on Screen*. **Encyclopedic Works:** *Film Encyclopedia*; *Filmlexicon degli Autori e delle Opere*; *Halliwell's Filmgoer's Companion*; *The Illustrated Who's Who of the Cinema*; *The Movie Makers*; *The Picturegoer's Who's Who and Encyclopedia of the Screen To-day*; *Quinlan's Illustrated Registry of Film Stars*; *Who Was Who in the Theatre*; *Who's Who in Hollywood*; *The World Almanac Who's Who of Film*; *The World Film Encyclopedia*. **Pictorial:** *Silent Portraits*.

• *Periodicals*—The following periodical articles are in addition to those included in the library listings below: *Motion Picture Magazine* (Mar.-Apr. 1920, Feb. 1929, May 1930); *Motion Picture Classic* (Aug. 1920, Nov. 1927, Feb. 1928, Apr. 1929); *Photoplay* (Aug. 1925, June 1929, July 1930, Mar. 1933, Mar. 1935); *Movies and the People Who Make Them* (no. 2, 1940); *Newsweek* (May 3, 1971); *Classic Film Collector* (Summer 1971); *World of Yesterday* (June 1982); *Classic Images* (Dec. 1986).

ARCHIVAL MATERIALS

• *Caricature*—NYMN. • *Clipping File*—CAA: Illness (1953, 1959, 1965); divorce (1940, 1942); TV appearance (1950–51); film appearance (1956); article (undated); obituary (1971). CAUT: Newsphotos; conservatorship (1959); obituary (1971). Periodical article: *Motion Picture Magazine* (June 1929). CAUU: Obituary (1971). NYMA: Newsphotos; obituary (1971). Periodical articles: *Classic Images* (Sept. 1982, Nov.-Dec. 1985). NYMN: Newsphotos (numerous); career; marriage (1936); article (1931). NYPL (also in Locke Collection): PARTIAL CONTENTS: Film appearance (1926, 1932); film review (1942, undated); newsphotos; obituary (1971). • *Other Clipping File*—CASP, CNDA, MAH, OHCL, WICF. • *Correspondence*—NYPL (C. & L. Brown Collection). • *Legal File*—CAUT (Twentieth Century-Fox Collection): Assignment (1923); loanout (1928–29); memo, letter (1926, 1928–29, 1931–35); agreement (1923, 1929, 1932–35). CAUW: Personnel, pay record (1957); talent agreement (1928–29, 1935, 1937); loanout (1928). NYPL (C. & L. Brown Collection): Contract (1920). • *Photograph/Still*—CAA (also in Hollywood Studio Museum Collection) (also in MGM Collection), CAFA, CALM, CAPH, CASP, CAUT (Jessen Collection) (Portrait File), CAUU, CNDA, DCG (Quigley Photographic Archives), NJFL, NYAM, NYB (Bettmann/UPI Collection) (Springer Collection) (Underwood Collection), NYCU (Dramatic Museum Portraits), NYMN, NYPL, OHCL, TXU, WICF. • *Press Kit*—OHCL. • *Publicity Release*—CAA: Columbia (1958).

192   Lucas; Lyon

• *Scrapbook* — NYMA, NYPL (also in C. & L. Brown Collection) (also in R. Locke Collection). • *Studio Biography* — CAA: Goldwyn (1920s); Fox (1931); Paramount (1932-33, 1960?); C.B. Rogers (1933); Columbia (1934, 1958); RKO (1941).

LUCAS, Wilfred (James Bruce), Ontario, Canada, 1871-1940.

Another of the very busy supporting players in both silent and sound films was Wilfred Lucas. Both as an actor and sometime screenwriter and director, his work was seen onscreen from 1908 to the year of his death. At the beginning of his career he played numerous leads, one of his most acclaimed performances coming in 1916's *Acquitted*. Some of his talkie character roles were in Laurel and Hardy features.

PUBLISHED SOURCES

• *Books* — General: *The Kindergarten of the Movies*; *Who's Who in the Film World*. Credits: *Filmarama* (v. I and II); *Forty Years of Screen Credits*; *Twenty Years of Silents*; *Who Was Who on Screen*. Encyclopedic Works: *Film Encyclopedia*; *Filmlexicon degli Autori e delle Opere*; *Halliwell's Filmgoer's Companion*; *Hollywood Character Actors*; *The Picturegoer's Who's Who and Encyclopedia of the Screen To-day*; *Who's Who in Hollywood*. Pictorial: *Silent Portraits*.

• *Periodicals* — The following periodical articles are in addition to that included in the library listings below: *Motion Picture Magazine* (Mar. 1915); *Photoplay* (June 1916).

ARCHIVAL MATERIALS

• *Clipping File* — CAA: Obituary (1940). NYMA (also in Photoplay Collection): Periodical article: *Classic Images* (Sept. 1981). NYPL (also in Locke Collection): Film appearance (1930s); film review (1940). • *Other Clipping File* — GBBF, MAH, PAPL. • *Legal File* — CAUW: Talent agreement (1924-25, 1929, 1932, 1936-37). • *Photograph/ Still* — CAA (also in Hollywood Studio Museum Collection), CALM, CAUT (Jessen Collection), DCG (Quigley Photographic Archives), NJFL, NYCU (Dramatic Museum Portraits), NYEH, NYPL, NYSU, WICF. • *Program* — OHSU.

LYON, Ben, Atlanta, GA, 1901-1979.

Probably best known as the caddish brother in *Hell's Angels* (1930), Ben Lyon appeared as a leading man in over 70 American films from the early 1920s to 1939. Among his silent roles were those in *Bluebeard's Seven Wives*, *The Pace That Thrills*, *So Big* and *High Hat*. His talkie appearances included *I Cover the Waterfront*, *Night Nurse*, *The Morning After* and *The Crooked Circle*. He and his wife Bebe Daniels (q.v.) went to England before World War Two where they eventually appeared in popular radio and television series as well as a few films. In the 1940s he was a talent director for Fox. He was later married to Marion Nixon (q.v.).

PUBLISHED SOURCES

• *Books* — Bibliography: *The Idols of Silence*. General: *Famous Film Folk*; *How I Broke Into the Movies*; *Screen Personalities*; *The Stars Appear*; *Stunt*; *The Truth About the Movies*. Credits: *British Film Actors' Credits*; *Filmarama* (v. I and II); *Forty Years of Film Credits*; *Twenty Years of Silents*. Encyclopedic Works: *Film Encyclopedia*; *Filmlexicon degli Autori e delle Opere*; *Halliwell's Filmgoer's Companion*; *The Illustrated Who's Who in British Films*; *The Illustrated Who's Who of the Cinema*; *The Movie Makers*; *The Oxford Companion to Film*; *The Picturegoer's Who's Who and Encyclopedia of the Screen To-day*; *Quinlan's Illustrated Registry of Film Stars*; *Who Was Who in the Theatre*; *Who's Who in Hollywood*; *The World Almanac Who's Who of Film*; *The World Film Encyclopedia*. Nostalgia: *Whatever Became of...* (4th). Biography/Autobiography: *Bebe and Ben*; *Life with the Lyons*. Pictorial:

Silent Portraits. **Recordings:** *Hollywood on Record.*

• *Periodicals* – The following periodical articles are in addition to those included in the library listings below: *Motion Picture Magazine* (Dec. 1924, Mar. 1925, Sept. 1928); *Photoplay* (Jan.-Feb. 1925, Feb. 1926, July 1930, Sept. 1930); *Motion Picture Classic* (Jan. 1926, Feb. 1927, May 1930, Sept. 1930); *Silver Screen* (Jan. 1932); *Time* (Dec. 28, 1942); *Show* (Aug. 1962); *Silent Picture* (Spring 1971) (filmography); *Cine Revue* (Apr. 5, 1979); *Cinématographique* (May 1979).

ARCHIVAL MATERIALS

• *Clipping File* – CAA: Extortion threat (1932); threatened by fan (1930); legal problem (1929, 1931-32); film appearance (1927, 1954); romance (1927); stage appearance (1929, 1951); marriage/children (1931, 1972); nostalgia (1971); TV appearance (1953, 1956); article (1945-46, 1954, 1962, 1967, 1972, 1977, 1984); honor (1946, 1977, 1979); newsphotos; obituary (1979). Periodical article: *Hollywood Studio Magazine* (Sept. 1972). CAFI: Article (1977, 1984); obituary (1979). CAUT: Article (1977); obituary (1979). CAUU: Article (1977); obituary (1979). NYMA (also in Photoplay Collection): Article (1977); head of 20th Century-Fox talent office in England (1945); obituary (1979). NYMN: Newsphotos; obituary (1979). NYPL: Newsphotos (numerous); Air Force major (1940s); wartime service (1940s, 1959); film reviews; returns to U.S. (1941); film appearance (1920s, 1930s); article (1925, 1927-28, 1930-31, undated); engagement/marriage/children (1926, 1928, 1930, 1932); romances (1920s?, 1929); illness (1932); stage appearance (1929); life in England (1954); relationship with Bebe Daniels (1967); assaulted by Helen Ferguson (1926); obituary (1979). Periodical articles: *Picture Play* (Oct. 1928); *Hollywood* (Apr. 1930); *New Movie* (Aug. 1930); *Motion Picture Magazine* (May 1931); *Screen Romances* (June 1931); *Hollywood Studio Magazine* (Dec. 1979). • *Other Clipping File* – AZSU (Jimmy Starr Collection), CNDA, GBBF, MAH, MIDL, OHCL, PAPL, WICF. • *Corre-*

spondence – CAUS (Preston Sturges Collection), NYMA (Photoplay Collection). NYPL: Letters (C. & L. Brown Collection) (various dates and 1928-36); others (1923, 1920s, undated). • *Interview* – CAUU (R. Lamparski Collection) (A. Slide Collection): Joint interview with Bebe Daniels (Slide) (1970). GBBF (Hollywood Collection): Transcript of interview for *Hollywood* (TV series). • *Legal File* – CAUT (Twentieth Century-Fox Collection): Letter, memo, telegram (1945-52); contract (1945); option (1946, 1948-49). CAUW: Personnel, payroll record (1921-32); contract (1930); letter, memo (1921-32); contract summary (1921-32); talent agreement (1926, 1930-32); loanout (1927, 1931); document (1923, 1928, 1931-32); option (1921-32). • *Oral History* – NYCO: Mentioned in the following interviews: Harold Lloyd, Mrs. John Williams. • *Photograph/Still* – AZSU (Jimmy Starr Collection), CAA (also in MGM Collection), CAHL, CAUT (Jessen Collection) (Portrait File), CAUU, DCG (Quigley Photographic Archives), GBBF, MIDL, NJFL, NJPT, NYAM, NYB (Bettmann/UPI Collection), NYCU (Dramatic Museum Portraits) (Palmer Collection), NYEH, NYMN, NYPL, NYSU, OHCL, TXU, WICF. • *Play Program* – NYPL. • *Scrapbook* – NJPT (Yeandle Collection), NYPL. • *Studio Biography* – CAA: Goldwyn (1920s); RKO (1930s); Columbia (1932); Fox (1935, 1940s?); First National (1936). NYMA: Photoplay.

LYTELL, Bert (Bertram Lytell), New York City, 1884/85– 1954.

Stage-trained Bert Lytell became a popular matinee idol after his first film, *The Lone Wolf*, in 1917. He made a series of films based on this character on into the talkie era. His first big hit, *The Right of Way* (1920), made him a major leading man through the rest of the decade. He appeared in only five talking pictures, *On Trial* (1928) being his first, before returning to Broadway.

He was married to Claire Windsor (q.v.).

PUBLISHED SOURCES

• *Books*—General: *Blue Book of the Screen*; *Famous Film Folk*; *Famous Movie Detectives*; *First One Hundred Noted Men and Women of the Screen*; *Who's Who on the Screen*. **Credits:** *Filmarama* (v. I and II); *Forty Years of Film Credits*; *Twenty Years of Silents*; *Who Was Who on Screen*. **Encyclopedic Works:** *Dictionary of National Biography* (v. 43); *Film Encyclopedia*; *Filmlexicon degli Autori e delle Opere*; *Halliwell's Filmgoer's Companion*; *The Movie Makers*; *National Cyclopedia of American Biography* (1961); *Who Was Who in the Theatre*; *Who's Who in Hollywood*; *The World Almanac Who's Who of Film*; *The World Film Encyclopedia*. **Pictorial:** *Silent Portraits*.

• *Periodicals*—The following periodical articles are in addition to those included in the library listings below: *Picture Play Magazine* (Feb. 1918); *Photoplay* (Oct. 1918, Feb. 1920, Feb.-Mar. 1922, July 1922, Nov. 1924); *Motion Picture Magazine* (Nov. 1918, Aug. 1920, July 1922, Dec. 1924); *Motion Picture Classic* (Nov. 1919, Oct. 1920, Jan. 1922); *Newsweek* (Oct. 11, 1954); *Time* (Oct. 11, 1954); *Films in Review* (Aug.-Sept. 1983); *Classic Images* (Dec. 1983, July 1989, Sept. 1989) (filmography).

OBSCURE PUBLISHED SOURCES
CAA, NYMA: *Bert Lytell*.

ARCHIVAL MATERIALS

• *Caricature*—NYPL (Sardi Collection). • *Clipping File*—CAA: Newsphotos; marriage (1930, 1932); film appearance (1922); TV appearance (1949); Lambs Club (1952); obituary (1954). CAUT: Newsphotos; obituary (1954). NYMA: Periodical article: *Photo-play World* (Apr. 1918). NYMN: President of Actors' Equity; newsphotos; President of Lamb's Club (1952); marriage (1930); article (1933); obituary (1954). NYPL (also in Locke Collection): Article (undated); Actors' Equity honor (1946); play appearance (1930s, 1940s); newsphotos; play review (1930s); wife

dies (1978); elected president of Actors' Equity (1940s); in charge of WWII camp shows (1940s); obituary (1954). Periodical article: *Films in Review* (Apr. 1973). TXU: Obituary (1954). • *Other Clipping File*—CASF, CAUB, CAUT, GBBF, MIDL, OHCL, PAPL, WICF. • *Correspondence*—CAUU (see Collection under entry for Claire Windsor). NYPL: Letters (C. & L. Brown Collection) (1930s, 1940s); others (1943, 1946-48, 1950-51). OHCL: Few items. • *Legal File*—CAUW: Contract (1928); letter, memo (1928-29); talent agreement (1923-25). • *Memorabilia*—NYMN: Awards, plaques, medals. • *Photograph/Still*—CAA (also in Hollywood Studio Museum Collection), CAFA, CAH, CAOC (Kiesling Collection), CASF, CASU, CAUT (Jessen Collection), CAUU, CNDA, DCG (Quigley Photographic Archives), GBBF, MIDL, NJFL, NJPT, NYAM, NYB (Bettmann/UPI Collection) (Underwood Collection), NYCU (Palmer Collection), NYEH, NYMN, NYPL, NYSU, OHCL, PAPL, TXU (A. Davis Collection), WICF. • *Play Program*—CAHL: 1912, 1916, 1925. • *Publicity Release*—NYPL: CBS (1940-42); WHN. • *Scrapbook*—NYPL (also in R. Locke Collection). • *Studio Biography*—CAA: Paramount (1936).

McAVOY, May, New York City, NY, 1901-1984.

Best known today as Al Jolson's leading lady in the epochal part-talkie *The Jazz Singer* (1927), May McAvoy began her career as an extra about 1916 and made *Hate*, her first major film, the following year. She continued on with a long string of popular films like *Lady Windermere's Fan*, *The Enchanted Cottage*, *Sentimental Tommy*, *Ben Hur* and Howard Hawks's first film, *The Road to Glory*. She made a few more part-talkies and only one full talkie and was doing bits and extra work in the 1940s.

PUBLISHED SOURCES

• *Books*—Bibliography: *The Idols of Silence*. **General:** *Blue Book of the*

Screen; *Famous Film Folk*; *How I Broke Into the Movies*; *More from Hollywood*; *The Movie Stars Story*; *Scream Queens*; *Speaking of Silents*; *Stars of the Silents*. **Credits:** *Filmarama* (v. I and II); *Forty Years of Screen Credits*; *Twenty Years of Silents*. **Encyclopedic Works:** *Film Encyclopedia*; *Filmlexicon degli Autori e delle Opere*; *Halliwell's Filmgoer's Companion*; *The Movie Makers*; *Who's Who in Hollywood*; *The World Almanac Who's Who of Film*; *The World Film Encyclopedia*. **Nostalgia:** *Whatever Became of...* (3rd). **Pictorial:** *Silent Portraits*; *They Had Faces Then*.
• *Periodicals—Photoplay* (Feb. 1921, Nov. 1921, Apr. 1924, July 1924, Apr. 1927); *Motion Picture Magazine* (June 1921, Aug. 1921, Jan. 1922, Jan. 1923, Nov. 1925); *Motion Picture Classic* (Aug. 1921, June 1922, Jan. 1923, Dec. 1926, Feb. 1928, Dec. 1928); *Filmplay Journal* (Sept. 1921); *Films in Review* (Oct. 1968) (filmography), Dec. 1968, Apr. 1969); *Classic Film Collector* (Winter 1972); *Newsweek* (May 14, 1984); *Cinématographique* (July 1984).

ARCHIVAL MATERIALS
• *Clipping File—AZSU* (Jimmy Starr Collection): Marriage; reminiscences; obituary (1984). CAA: Honor (1947, 1959); Rose Queen (1959, 1967, 1978, 1980–81); newsphotos; film appearance (1922–24); article (1984); nostalgia (1956, 1968, 1981); engagement/divorce (1923, 1940); obituary (1984). CAFI: Article (1976, 1983); newsphotos; obituary (1984). CAUT: Marriage (1929); illness (1961); home (postcard). NYMA (also in Photoplay Collection): Newsphotos; obituary (1984). NYPL (also in Locke Collection): Newsphotos (numerous); Rose Queen (1983); article (1921, 1941, undated); engagement/divorce/children (1921, undated); film review (1922); obituary (1984). • *Other Clipping File—* MAH, MIDL, OHCL, PAPL, WICF.
• *Correspondence—OHKS.* • *Filmography—NYMA.* • *Interview—CAUU* (Hollywood Studio Museum Collection) (R. Lamparski Collection). • *Photograph/Still—CAA* (also in Hollywood Studio Museum Collection) (also in

MGM Collection), CAH, CAOC (Kiesling Collection), CASU, CAUB, CAUT (Jessen Collection) (Portrait File), CAUU, DCG (Quigley Photographic Archives), GBBF, MIDL, NJFL, NJPT, NYAM, NYB (Underwood Collection), NYCU (Dramatic Museum Portraits) (Palmer Collection), NYEH, NYPL, NYSU, OHCL, PAPL, TXU (A. Davis Collection) (Robbins Collection), WICF.
• *Scrapbook—NYPL.*

McCOY, Tim, Saginaw, MI, 1891–1978.

Gimlet-eyed Colonel Tim McCoy starred in a series of westerns and other historical dramas for MGM in the 1920s. In all he made almost 90 films for various studios including a long string of "B" westerns and the early sound serial *The Indians Are Coming*. He had a strong affinity for Native Americans and in 1933 produced two film documentaries about them. Although his starring career ended in the early 1940s, he played supporting roles in a few films as late as 1965.

PUBLISHED SOURCES
• *Books*—There were some juvenile books written between 1935 and 1937 about TMcC's fictional adventures including *Tim McCoy in the Prescott Kid*, *Tim McCoy in The Westerner*, *Tim McCoy on the Tomahawk Trail*. Some of these appear to be novelizations of his films. **General:** *The BFI Companion to the Western*; *The Filming of the West*; *The Great Cowboy Stars of Movies & Television*; *Great Western Stars*; *The Hall of Fame of Western Film Stars*; *Heroes, Heavies and Sagebrush*; *Heroes of the Range*; *Hollywood Album 2*; *Hollywood Corral*; *A Pictorial History of Westerns*; *They Went Thataway*; *Tim McCoy's Real Wild West and Rough Riders of the World*; *The Western* (Eyles); *Winners of the West*. **Credits:** *Filmarama* (v. II); *Forty Years of Screen Credits*; *Twenty Years of Silents*. **Encyclopedic Works:** *Film Encyclopedia*; *Filmlexicon degli Autori e delle Opere*; *Halliwell's Filmgoer's Companion*; *The*

Illustrated Who's Who of the Cinema; *International Motion Picture Almanac* (1975–78); *The Picturegoer's Who's Who and Encyclopedia of the Screen To-day*; *Who's Who in Hollywood*; *The World Almanac Who's Who of Film*; *The World Film Encyclopedia*. Nostalgia: *Is That Who I Think It Is?* (v. 1); *Whatever Became of...* (7th). Biography/Autobiography: *Col. Tim McCoy*; *Tim McCoy Remembers the West*. Factoids: *Star Stats*.

• *Periodicals*—The following periodical articles are in addition to those included in the library listings below: *Motion Picture Classic* (Oct. 1927, May 1928); *Motion Picture Magazine* (Feb. 1928, June 1928); *Films in Review* (Apr. 1968 (filmography), June-July 1968); *Views & Reviews* (Summer 1970–Spring 1971); *Those Enduring Matinee Idols* (no. 8, 1974); *American Heritage* (June 1977); *Time* (Feb. 13, 1978); *Classic Images* (Jan. 1984, Aug. 1987).

OBSCURE PUBLISHED SOURCES
CAA: *Injun Talk*.

MEDIA
The Silent Language of the Plains (video).

ARCHIVAL MATERIALS
• *Clipping File*—CAA: Film appearance (1964); nostalgia (1966, 1970); National Cowboy Hall of Fame (1974); review of *Tim McCoy Remembers the West* (1977); children (1947); article (1978). Periodical articles: *TV-Radio Life* (Nov. 16, 1951); *TV and Movie Western* (Aug. 1959); *Filmograph* (no. 1-1, 1970). CAFI: Article (1978); obituary (1978). CAUT: Article (1976); obituary (1978). CAUU: Review of *Tim McCoy Remembers the West* (1977); article (1978); obituary (1978). NYMA: Article (1977); obituary (1978). Periodical articles: *Classic Film/Video Images* (May 1980); *Big Reel* (Sept. 1986, Sept. 1988); *Classic Images* (Apr. 1989). NYMN: Article (undated). NYPL: Article (1974, 1978–79); newsphotos; film review (1940s); separation (1931); film appearance (1930s); Wild West show (1937–38, undated); obituary (1978). • *Other Clip-*

ping File—AZSU (Jimmy Starr Collection), CNDA, GBBF, MAH, WYU (see Collection). • *Collection*—WYU: Legal papers, including deeds, abstracts, contracts (1918–40); biographical data (1928–78); miscellany; correspondence (1919–78); financial records (1938, 1958); manuscripts (1922–77); clippings (including periodicals) (1917–78); programs (1945–77); press releases (1925); scrapbooks (1905–57, 1977). • *Correspondence*—NYMN: 1956. WYU (see Collection). • *Filmography*—NYMA. • *Interview*—GBBF: Transcript of interview for *Hollywood* (TV series). • *Legal File*—WYU (see Collection). • *Oral History*—NYCO: Mentioned in the following interviews: Walter Brennan, Bosley Crowther, David Selznick. • *Photograph/Still*—CAA (also in Hollywood Studio Museum Collection) (also in MGM Collection), CAUT (Jessen Collection), DCG (Quigley Photographic Archives), NYCU (Dramatic Museum Portraits), NYEH, NYMN, NYPL, NYSU, TXU, WYU (see Collection). • *Program*—WYU (see Collection). • *Publicity Release*—CAFI: Columbia (1930s). WYU (see Collection). • *Scrapbook*—WYU (see Collection).

MacDERMOTT (sometimes McDermott), Marc, Gouldbourne or Sydney, Australia, or London, England, 1880/81-1929.

A busy leading man at the Edison studios from about 1911, and also a Biograph player, Marc MacDermott was in the prototype serial *What Happened to Mary* as well as a host of other films. Later in his career, for Fox and MGM, he was seen in both lead and support in films such as *He Who Gets Slapped*, *The Lights of New York*, *Kiki*, *The Sea Hawk* and *Dorothy Vernon of Haddon Hall*.

PUBLISHED SOURCES
• *Books*—General: *Life Stories of the Movie Stars*; *The Truth About the Movies*. Credits: *Filmarama* (v. I and II); *Twenty Years of Silents*; *Who Was*

Who on Screen. **Encyclopedic Works:** *Filmlexicon degli Autori e delle Opere*; *Who's Who in Hollywood.* **Pictorial:** *Silent Portraits.*
• *Periodicals*—The following periodical articles are in addition to those included in the library listings below: *Photoplay* (Oct. 1914); *Motion Picture Magazine* (Mar. 1915, May 1917, July 1919, Jan. 1921).

ARCHIVAL MATERIALS
• *Clipping File*—CAUT: Obituary (1929). NYMA (also in Photoplay Collection): Personal data summary. Periodical articles: *Photo-play World* (Mar. 1918); *Classic Film Collector* (Winter 1975). NYPL (also in Locke Collection): Legal problem (1922). Periodical article: *Photoplay* (Oct. 1917). • *Other Clipping File*—MAH. • *Correspondence*—NYPL (C. & L. Brown Collection): 1918. • *Filmography*—CAA. • *Photograph/Still*—CAA (also in Hollywood Studio Museum Collection) (also in MGM Collection), DCG (Quigley Photographic Archives), NYPL, NYSU, OHCL, TXU. • *Studio Biography*—CAA: MGM (1920s?).

MacDONALD, Katherine, Pittsburgh, PA, 1891-1956.
Dubbed "The American Beauty" and publicized as the most beautiful woman in the world, Katherine MacDonald was onscreen for about eight years (1918-1926). Although she was not considered an outstanding actress, among her costars were William S. Hart, Tommy Meighan and Douglas Fairbanks. Her films included *The Woman Thou Gavest Me, Riddle Gawne, The Squaw Man* and *The Beautiful Liar.* Her sister was Mary MacLaren (q.v.).

PUBLISHED SOURCES
• *Books*—**General:** *Blue Book of the Screen*; *Who's Who on the Screen.* **Credits:** *Filmarama* (v. I and II); *Twenty Years of Silents*; *Who Was Who on Screen.* **Encyclopedic Works:** *Filmlexicon degli Autori e delle Opere*; *Who's*

Who in Hollywood. **Pictorial:** *Silent Portraits.*
• *Periodicals*—*Motion Picture Classic* (Nov. 1918, July 1920); *Photoplay* (Nov. 1918, Aug. 1919, June 1920, Oct. 1921); *Theatre* (Apr. 1919); *Motion Picture Magazine* (Oct. 1919, Mar. 1921); *Movie Classic* (Oct. 1931); *Films in Review* (Apr. 1985).

ARCHIVAL MATERIALS
• *Clipping File*—CAA: Newsphotos; film appearance (1922); illness (1956); obituary (1956). CAUT: Obituary (1956). NYMA (also in Photoplay collection): Article (1937). NYPL (also in Locke Collection): Legal problem; marriage (1923, undated); newsphotos; film appearance (1923); article (1922); obituary (1956). • *Other Clipping File*—GBBF, OHCL, PAPL, PAPT, WICF. • *Legal File*—CAUW: Talent agreement (1923); literary property (1921-22); production agreement (1919, 1921); document (1922, 1927); letter (1920, 1927). • *Photograph/Still*—CAA (also in Hollywood Studio Museum Collection), CALM, CAUT (Jessen Collection), DCG (Quigley Photographic Archives), NYCU (Dramatic Museum Portraits), NYPL, NYSU, OHCL, TXSM, TXU, WICF. • *Scrapbook*—NYPL (R. Locke Collection).

McDOWELL, Claire, New York, NY, 1877-1966.
Handsome Claire McDowell was a leading actress in D.W. Griffith two-reelers before she matured into the maternal roles for which she became greatly popular. She was perhaps the archetypal screen mother in prestigious silent films like *The Big Parade, Ben Hur, Ponjola* and *Black Oxen.* She continued on in such talkies as *An American Tragedy, Rebecca of Sunnybrook Farm* and *Imitation of Life* before ending her "nurturing" career in the mid-1940s.

PUBLISHED SOURCES
• *Books*—**Credits:** *Filmarama* (v. I and II); *Forty Years of Screen Credits*;

Twenty Years of Silents; Who Was Who on Screen. **Encyclopedic Works:** Film Encyclopedia; Filmlexicon degli Autori e delle Opere; The Picturegoer's Who's Who and Encyclopedia of the Screen To-day; Who's Who in Hollywood. **Pictorial:** Silent Portraits.
• Periodicals—The following periodical article is in addition to those included in the library listings below: Motion Picture Stories (Aug. 7, 1914).

ARCHIVAL MATERIALS
• Clipping File—CAA: Article (1957, 1962); obituary (1966). Periodical article: Classic Film Collector (Winter 1970). NYMA: Periodical articles: Classic Film Collector (Winter 1970); Classic Images (Nov.-Dec. 1985, Apr. 1992). NYPL (also in Locke Collection): Newsphotos; film review (1920s); film appearance (1940s?); obituary (1966). Periodical article: Motion Picture Classic (July 1916). • Other Clipping File—GBBF. • Legal File— CAUW: Talent agreement (1927, 1929–30). • Photograph/Still—CAA (also in Hollywood Studio Museum Collection), CAUT (Jessen Collection) (Portrait File), DCG (Quigley Photographic Archives), NYB (Underwood Collection), NYPL, NYSU, WICF. • Studio Biography—CAA: MGM (1920s).

McGREGOR, Malcolm, Newark, NJ, 1892–1945.
Dark-haired, clean-cut Malcolm McGregor had a successful career as a leading man through the 1920s. He began with a role in The Prisoner of Zenda (1922) and then appeared in at least 30 more, including All the Brothers Were Valiant and The Vanishing American. At the advent of talkies his starring career came to a virtual halt and he was seen in only a few, the last one about 1937.

PUBLISHED SOURCES
• Books—General: Famous Film Folk. **Credits:** Filmarama (v. II); Forty Years of Screen Credits; Twenty Years of Silents; Who Was Who on Screen. **Encyclopedic Works:** Filmlexicon degli

Autori e delle Opere; Who's Who in Hollywood. **Pictorial:** Silent Portraits.
• Periodicals—The following periodical articles are in addition to those included in the library listings below: Motion Picture Magazine (July 1922); Photoplay (Dec. 1922, Jan. 1924, July 1924).

ARCHIVAL MATERIALS
• Clipping File—CAA: Marriage (1938); legal problem (1943); obituary (1945). NYPL: Newsphotos (numerous); film review (1920s); article (undated); obituary (1945). Periodical articles: Picture Show (May 24, 1924, May 22, 1926); Picture Play (Nov. 1925). • Other Clipping File—GBBF, NYMA (Photoplay Collection), PAPL, WICF. • Legal File—CAUW: Talent agreement (1926–27, 1929). • Photograph/Still—CAA (also in Hollywood Studio Museum Collection), CAH, CAUT (Jessen Collection) (Portrait File), CAUU, DCG (Quigley Photographic Archives), GBBF, NJPT, NYB (Underwood Collection), NYCU (Dramatic Museum Portraits), NYEH, NYPL, NYSU, OHCL, PAPL, TNUT (Clarence Brown Collection), TXU (A. Davis Collection), WICF. • Scrapbook—NYPL, TNUT (Clarence Brown Collection). • Studio Biography— CAA: Goldwyn (1920s?). NYMA: Photoplay.

McGUIRE, Kathryn, Peoria, IL, 1897–1978.
Kathryn McGuire made films in all genres, including westerns with Tom Mix, but is best known as Buster Keaton's unhelpful costar in The Navigator and Sherlock, Jr. She was a Sennett alumna and also worked at Metro, Fox and First National. Among her films were Naughty But Nice, Woman of Bronze, Crossroads of New York and Lilac Time. Her career virtually ended when sound came in with apparently only two talkies to her credit.

PUBLISHED SOURCES
• Books—General: Blue Book of the

Screen; *Famous Film Folk*; *The Truth About the Movies*. **Credits:** *Filmarama* (v. II); *Forty Years of Screen Credits*; *Twenty Years of Silents*. **Encyclopedic Works:** *Film Encyclopedia*; *Filmlexicon degli Autori e delle Opere*; *Who's Who in Hollywood*.
• *Periodicals* — *Motion Picture Classic* (Oct. 1928); *Films in Review* (Feb. 1970 [Wampas Baby Stars]).

ARCHIVAL MATERIALS
• *Clipping File* — CAA: Obituary (1978). NYPL: Newsphotos; career; obituary (1978). • *Other Clipping File* — GBBF, MAH, NYMA (Photoplay Collection). • *Photograph/Still* — CAA (also in Hollywood Studio Museum Collection), CALM, CAUT (Jessen Collection), DCG (Quigley Photographic Archives), NYB (Underwood Collection), NYPL, NYSU, OHCL, TXU. • *Scrapbook* — NYPL. • *Studio Biography* — NYMA: Photoplay.

MACKAILL, Dorothy, Hull, England, 1903/04–1990.

From her initial American film, *The Lotus Eater*, blonde Dorothy Mackaill portrayed self-sufficient ladies in a string of '20s films, mainly light fare which included the popular two-reel *Torchy* series with Johnny Hines (q.v.) and efforts like *Subway Sadie* and *Chickie*. She made the transition to talkies with the part-talkie *The Barker* and continued making films (mostly of the "B" variety) until 1937. One of her more prestigious efforts in the '30s was *No Man of Her Own* with Carole Lombard and Clark Gable.

PUBLISHED SOURCES
• *Books* — **Bibliography:** *The Idols of Silence*. **General:** *Famous Film Folk*. **Credits:** *British Film Actors' Credits*; *Filmarama* (v. II); *Forty Years of Screen Credits*; *Twenty Years of Silents*. **Encyclopedic Works:** *Film Encyclopedia*; *Filmlexicon degli Autori e delle Opere*; *Halliwell's Filmgoer's Companion*; *The Movie Makers*; *The Picturegoer's Who's Who and Encyclopedia of the Screen*

To-day; *Who's Who in Hollywood*; *The World Film Encyclopedia*. **Nostalgia:** *Whatever Became of...* (11th). **Pictorial:** *Silent Portraits*; *They Had Faces Then*.
• *Periodicals* — The following periodical articles are in addition to that included in the library listings below: *Photoplay* (Aug. 1923, Nov. 1924, July 1926, Mar. 1930, Jan. 1932); *Motion Picture Classic* (Dec. 1924, Dec. 1929, Feb. 1931, June 1931, Aug. 1931); *Motion Picture Magazine* (May 1925, Apr.-May 1929, Feb. 1932); *Silver Screen* (Oct. 1931); *Films in Review* (Mar. 1960, Feb. 1970 (Wampas Baby Stars), Dec. 1977); *Classic Film Collector* (Fall 1969); *Filmograph* (no. 1–2, 1970); *Classic Images* (Oct. 1990); *Skoop* (Oct. 1990).

ARCHIVAL MATERIALS
• *Caricature* — NYPL (Sardi Collection). • *Clipping File* — CAA: Engagement/marriage/divorce (1924, 1926–28, 1931, 1934, 1947); film appearance (1927, 1930–32); newsphotos; legal problem (1923, 1927, 1929–30); robbery (1932); contract expires (1930); article (1931, 1949); TV appearance (1976); nostalgia (1969, 1972, 1980–81); obituary (1990). NYMA: Article (1969); career (1928); obituary (1990). Periodical article: *Classic Images* (July 1983). NYMN: Marriage/divorce (1931, 1934); newsphotos; article (undated). NYPL: Stage appearance (1934, 1939); divorce (1934); newsphotos (numerous); film appearance (1932); article (1936, 1959); obituary (1990). • *Other Clipping File* — AZSU (Jimmy Starr Collection), CAUB, CAUU (A. Slide Collection), GBBF, MIDL, OHCL, PAPL, WICF. • *Correspondence* — CAUU (A. Slide Collection): 1970. NYPL: 1940. • *Legal File* — CAUW: Letter, memo, document (1925–32); contract summary (1925); contract (1925, 1930); payroll record (1926–32); talent agreement (1925–31). • *Photograph/Still* — CAA (also in Hollywood Studio Museum Collection) (also in MGM Collection), CAH, CAUU, CNDA, DCG (Quigley Photographic Archives), GBBF, MIDL, NJFL, NJPT, NYAM, NYB (Bettmann/UPI Collection), NYCU (Dramatic Museum Por-

traits) (Palmer Collection), NYEH, NYMN, NYPL, NYSU, OHCL, PAPL, WICF. • *Scrapbook* — NYPL. • *Studio Biography* — CAA: Paramount (1932).

MacKENNA, Kenneth (Leo Mielziner, Jr.), Canterbury, NH, 1899-1962.

The offspring of a well-known theatrical family, Kenneth MacKenna came from Broadway about 1925 and soon was a popular leading man. Although his fame was relatively brief and virtually over by 1929, he continued in films through 1931 when he returned to the stage. He eventually went back to Hollywood as a story editor, producer and director for MGM, and in the early 1960s he had small parts in such films as *Judgement at Nuremberg*.

PUBLISHED SOURCES

• *Books* — Credits: *Filmarama* (v. II); *Forty Years of Screen Credits*; *Who Was Who on Screen*. Encyclopedic Works: *Film Encyclopedia*; *Filmlexicon degli Autori e delle Opere*; *Halliwell's Filmgoer's Companion*; *National Cyclopedia of American Biography* (1965); *The Picturegoer's Who's Who and Encyclopedia of the Screen To-day*; *Who Was Who in the Theatre*; *Who's Who in Hollywood*; *The World Film Encyclopedia*.
• *Periodicals* — *Motion Picture Classic* (Apr. 1930).

ARCHIVAL MATERIALS

• *Clipping File* — CAA: Producer (1945); head of MGM Story Department (1953); returns to acting (1959); obituary (1962). CAUT: Obituary (1962). NYMA (also in Photoplay Collection): Obituary (1962). NYMN: Newsphotos; divorce (1934); stage appearance (1935); obituary (1962). NYPL: Returns to Broadway (1952); biography; play review (1936); stage appearance (1930s, 1959); MGM producer (1946); divorce (1934); newsphotos; obituary (1962). • *Other Clipping File* — GBBF, MIDL, OHCL, PAPL, WICF. • *Correspondence* —

CAUS: 2 letters (Preston Sturges Collection); 1 letter (Paul J. Smith Collection). MABU: 12 letters (1938-50). NYPL: Letters (C. & L. Brown Collection) (1927-37); letters (Richard Rodgers Collection) (1959-60); others (1931, 1941-42, 1953-54, 1956, 1958, undated). • *Genealogy* — NYMN. • *Legal File* — CAUT (Twentieth Century-Fox Collection): Letter, memo, telegram (1929-32); loanout (1930); agreement (1929, 1931). • *Oral History* — NYCO: Interviewed in 1958. Also mentioned in the following interviews: Edward McCabe, Dore Schary. • *Photograph/Still* — CAA, CAUT (Jessen Collection) (Portrait File), CNDA, GBBF, NJPT, NYAM, NYEH, NYMN, NYPL, OHCL, PAPL, TXU (A. Davis Collection), WICF. • *Privately Printed Material* — MAH: *Words Spoken by Kenneth MacKenna at the Memorial Service (for Osgood Perkins) Held at the Church of the Transfiguration in the City of New York on October 15, 1937.* • *Scrapbook* — NYPL (also in C. & L. Brown Collection). • *Studio Biography* — CAA: MGM (1950s?). NYMA: Photoplay.

MacLAREN, Mary (Mary MacDonald), Pittsburgh, PA, 1900-1985.

Beautiful Mary MacLaren's career began about 1916, somewhat before that of her sister Katherine MacDonald (q.v.). Probably her best-remembered role was opposite Douglas Fairbanks in *The Three Musketeers* but she also starred in *Shoes*, one of the silent era's biggest moneymakers. Other films included *Under the Red Robe*, *The Courageous Coward*, *The Dark Swan* and *The Face in the Fog*. Her starring career ended in 1923. In the late 1970s, now an eccentric and elderly woman, she was once again in the spotlight when she had a series of highly publicized legal problems.

PUBLISHED SOURCES

• *Books* — General: *Let Me Entertain You*; *Who's Who on the Screen*. Credits: *Filmarama* (v. I and II); *Forty Years of*

Screen Credits; *Twenty Years of Silents.* **Encyclopedic Works:** *Filmlexicon degli Autori e delle Opere*; *Who's Who in Hollywood.* **Nostalgia:** *Whatever Became of...* (7th). **Pictorial:** *Silent Portraits.*
• *Periodicals—Moving Picture Weekly* (June 26, 1916); *Photoplay* (Feb. 1917, Oct. 1919, Dec. 1919, Dec. 1920, June 1928, Feb. 1933); *Green Book Magazine* (Mar. 1917); *Motion Picture Classic* (Sept. 1917, Apr.-May 1920); *Motion Picture Magazine* (Mar. 1919, May 1922); *Picture Show* (Jan. 17, 1920); *Films in Review* (May 1966, Apr. 1985); *Classic Film Collector* (Winter 1970); *Cine Revue* (Nov. 28, 1985); *Griffithiana* (Oct. 1991).

ARCHIVAL MATERIALS
• *Clipping File*—CAA: Nostalgia (1973-74, 1981); article (1973); marriage (1965); legal problem (1952, 1979-82); author (1950, 1961); newsphotos; accident (1961); obituary (1985). CAFI: Legal problem (1979-83); fire (1981); newsphotos; article (1975, 1984); obituary (1985). CAUT: Legal problem (1980, 1982-83). CAUU: Legal problem (1979-80). NYMA (also in Photoplay Collection): Article (1970, 1974, 1979, 1981); legal problem (1979); obituary (1985). NYPL (also in Locke Collection): Legal problem (1979, 1983); film appearance (1930s); newsphotos; loses home (1983); article (1920, 1974); marriage (1965); writes novel (1952); obituary (1985).
• *Other Clipping File*—CAUB, GBBF, MAH, MIDL, OHCL, PAPL, PAPT, WICF. • *Legal File*—CAUW: Talent agreement (1924). • *Photograph/Still*—CAA (also in Hollywood Studio Museum Collection), CAUT (Jessen Collection), CNDA, DCG (Quigley Photographic Archives), NYPL, NYSU, OHCL, TXU, WICF. • *Press Kit*—OHCL. • *Scrapbook*—NYPL (R. Locke Collection).

MacLEAN, Douglas, Philadelphia, PA, 1897?-1967.
A popular actor in light comedies, Douglas MacLean first appeared onscreen in the mid-1910s and starred

in such films as *Captain Kidd, Jr.*, *23 1/2 Hours Leave, Going Up* and *The Hottentot.* He remained a leading performer until 1929 and thereafter he became an important Hollywood producer for many years.

PUBLISHED SOURCES
• *Books—General:* *Blue Book of the Screen*; *Famous Film Folk*; *Motion Picture News Booking Guide and Studio Directory* (1927); *The Truth About the Movies*; *Who's Who on the Screen.* **Credits:** *Filmarama* (v. I and II); *Forty Years of Screen Credits*; *Twenty Years of Silents*; *Who Was Who on Screen.* **Encyclopedic Works:** *Film Encyclopedia*; *Filmlexicon degli Autori e delle Opere*; *Halliwell's Filmgoer's Companion*; *The Movie Makers*; *The Picturegoer's Who's Who and Encyclopedia of the Screen To-day*; *Who's Who in Hollywood.* **Pictorial:** *Silent Portraits.*
• *Periodicals—*The following periodical articles are in addition to those included in the library listings below: *Motion Picture Classic* (Sept. 1919, Sept. 1925, Nov. 1926); *Picture Play Magazine* (Dec. 1919); *Photoplay* (Jan. 1920, Aug. 1920, Mar. 1922, Jan. 1925, Jan. 1926, June 1926, Sept. 1926, Nov. 1926); *Motion Picture Magazine* (Nov. 1920, July 1921, Jan. 1935).

ARCHIVAL MATERIALS
• *Clipping File*—CAA: Newsphotos; divorce (1935-36, 1948); draft article by DM (1930s); obituary (1967). Periodical article: *Science of Mind* (Nov. 1961). CAFI: Film appearance (1967); article (1967). CAUT: Separation (1935); obituary (1967). Article: *Motion Picture Classic* (Nov. 1927). NYMA (also in Photoplay Collection): Obituary (1967). NYPL (also in Locke Collection): TV appearance; obituary (1967). • *Other Clipping File*—GBBF, MAH, MIDL, OHCL, PAPL, WICF. • *Correspondence*—NYPL (C. & L. Brown Collection): 1917-18, 1936. • *Photograph/Still*—CAA (also in Hollywood Studio Museum Collection), CAUT (Jessen Collection), CAUU, DCG (Quigley Photographic Archives), NJFL, NYEH,

NYPL, NYSU, OHCL, TXSM, TXU, WICF. • *Press Kit*—OHCL. • *Scrapbook*—NYPL (also in R. Locke Collection). • *Studio Biography*—NYMA: Photoplay.

MARLOWE, June (Gisela Goetten), St. Cloud, MN, 1903/07–1984.

Best remembered today as the teacher Miss Crabtree in the talkie *Our Gang* series, June Marlowe's career began in silents about 1923. She was yet another of Rin-Tin-Tin's "leading ladies" and also was seen in *Don Juan*, *The Old Soak*, *A Lost Lady* and *Alias the Deacon*. Her sound features were few in number and included Laurel and Hardy's first starring feature, *Pardon Us*.

PUBLISHED SOURCES

• *Books*—General: *Famous Film Folk*. Credits: *Filmarama* (v. II); *Forty Years of Screen Credits*; *Twenty Years of Silents*. Encyclopedic Works: *Film Encyclopedia*; *Filmlexicon degli Autori e delle Opere*; *The Picturegoer's Who's Who and Encyclopedia of the Screen To-day*; *Who's Who in Hollywood*. Pictorial: *Silent Portraits*.
• *Periodicals*—The following periodical articles are in addition to those included in the library listings below: *Films in Review* (Dec. 1969, Feb. 1970) (Wampas Baby Stars); *Escape to the Minnesota Good Times* (Aug.–Oct. 1986).

ARCHIVAL MATERIALS

• *Clipping File*—CAA: Obituary (1984). CAFI: Newsphotos; obituary (1984). NYMA (also in Photoplay Collection): Obituary (1984). Periodical articles: *Classic Images* (Mar.–May 1986). NYPL: Newsphotos; obituary (1984).
• *Other Clipping File*—GBBF, MIDL, PAPL. • *Legal File*—CAUW: Talent agreement (1927). • *Photograph/Still*—CAA (Hollywood Studio Museum Collection), CAUT (Jessen Collection), CAUU, DCG (Quigley Photographic Archives), NYB (Underwood Collection), NYPL, NYSU, OHCL, TXU.

MARMONT, Percy, London, England, 1883/86–1977.

Percy Marmont entered American films about 1918 and for many years was a popular, if mature, leading man. One memorable role was opposite Clara Bow in *Mantrap*; others included *The Light That Failed*, *The Shooting of Dan McGrew*, *Aloma of the South Seas*, *Love's Penalty* and *The Vengeance of Durand*. His biggest personal triumph was probably 1923's *If Winter Comes*. He returned to England at the end of the silent era and was seen in numerous supporting roles until the 1950s.

PUBLISHED SOURCES

• *Books*—General: *Famous Film Folk*. Credits: *British Film Actors' Credits*; *Filmarama* (v. I and II); *Forty Years of Screen Credits*; *Twenty Years of Silents*. Bibliography: *The Idols of Silence*. Encyclopedic Works: *Film Encyclopedia*; *Filmlexicon degli Autori e delle Opere*; *Halliwell's Filmgoer's Companion*; *The Illustrated Encyclopedia of Movie Character Actors*; *The Illustrated Who's Who in British Films*; *The Movie Makers*; *The Picturegoer's Who's Who and Encyclopedia of the Screen To-day*; *Universal Filmlexikon*; *Who Was Who in the Theatre*; *Who's Who in Hollywood*; *The World Film Encyclopedia*. Pictorial: *Silent Portraits*.
• *Periodicals*—The following periodical articles are in addition to that included in the library listings below: *Motion Picture Classic* (May 1919); *Picture Play Magazine* (Oct. 1919); *Photoplay* (Nov. 1919, May 1926); *Motion Picture Magazine* (June 1920, Sept. 1922, Apr. 1924); *Cinema Art* (Dec. 1927).

ARCHIVAL MATERIALS

• *Clipping File*—CAA: Film appearance (1920, 1922); newsphotos. CAUT: Film appearance (1929); legal problem (1929). NYPL (also in Locke Collection): Article (1923); newsphotos; film review (1940s, 1950s); nostalgia (1936); obituary (1977). Periodical article: *Silent Picture* (Summer 1970).

• *Other Clipping File*—GBBF, MAH, NYMA (Photoplay Collection), OHCL, PAPL, WICF. • *Correspondence*—CAUU (A. Slide Collection): 1969, 1971. • *Interview*—CAUU (A. Slide Collection): 1969. • *Photograph/Still*—CAA (also in Hollywood Studio Museum Collection), CAUT (Jessen Collection), DCG (Quigley Photographic Archives), NJFL, NYAM, NYB (Underwood Collection), NYCU (Dramatic Museum Portraits), NYPL, NYSU, OHCL, TXU, WICF. • *Scrapbook*—NYPL (also in R. Locke Collection). • *Studio Biography*—CAA: Goldwyn (1920s).

MARSH, Mae (Mary Marsh), New Madrid, NM, 1895–1968.

One of D.W. Griffith's most luminous actresses, Mae Marsh had leading roles in *Birth of a Nation, Intolerance* and *The White Rose* as well as many of his earlier one- and two-reelers. In the 1920s she also appeared in British and German films. Her career was inactive during the latter 1920s and her 1931 comeback film, a remake of *Over the Hill*, did little to revive her screen fortunes. Sporadic character roles followed, most notably in nearly all of John Ford's films.

PUBLISHED SOURCES

• *Books*—Wrote *Screen Acting* (1921) and a book of verses for children, *When They Ask Me My Name* (1932). **Bibliography:** *The Idols of Silence.* **General:** *Classics of the Silent Screen; The Griffith Actresses; The Kindergarten of the Movies; Ladies in Distress; Life Stories of the Movie Stars; The Movie Stars Story; The National Society of Film Critics on the Movie Star; The Real Tinsel; Return Engagement; Who's Who in the Film World; Who's Who on the Screen.* **Credits:** *British Film Actors' Credits; Filmarama* (v. I and II); *Forty Years of Screen Credits; Twenty Years of Silents; Who Was Who on Screen.* **Encyclopedic Works:** *A Biographical Dictionary of Film; Film Encyclopedia; Filmlexicon degli Autori e delle Opere; Halliwell's Filmgoer's Companion; The*

Illustrated Encyclopedia of the World's Great Movie Stars and Their Films; The Illustrated Who's Who of the Cinema; International Dictionary of Films and Filmmakers (v. 3); *The International Encyclopedia of Film; The Movie Makers; Notable American Women: The Modern Period; The Oxford Companion to Film; Quinlan's Illustrated Registry of Film Stars; Who's Who in Hollywood; The World Almanac Who's Who of Film; The World Encyclopedia of the Film; The World Film Encyclopedia.* **Nostalgia:** *Whatever Became of...* (1st, 8th). **Pictorial:** *Silent Portraits; They Had Faces Then.* **Factoids:** *Star Stats.* **Filmography:** *Hollywood on the Palisades.*

• *Periodicals*—The following periodical articles are in addition to those included in the library listings below: *Photoplay* (Dec. 1914, July 1915, Mar. 1917, June 1917, July 1919, Oct. 1919, Mar. 1920, Sept. 1920, Mar. 1923, Mar. 1932); *Green Book Magazine* (Mar. 1915); *Motion Picture Magazine* (Mar. 1915, Feb. 1919, Feb. 1921, May 1923, Mar. 1924); *Film Players Herald & Movie Pictorial* (Feb. 1916); *Motion Picture Classic* (Oct. 1916, June 1918, Mar. 1920, July 1931); *Picture Play Magazine* (Sept. 1920); *Movie Weekly* (Dec. 23, 1922); *Life* (Jan. 23, 1956); *Films in Review* (Aug.-Sept. 1958, Mar. 1959, Oct. 1968); *Saturday Review* (Aug. 26, 1961); *Show* (Dec. 1962); *Film Culture* (Spring/Summer 1965); *Time* (Feb. 23, 1968); *New Yorker* (Feb. 24, 1968); *Newsweek* (Feb. 26, 1968); *Silent Picture* (Autumn 1969); *Filmkritik* (Jan. 1972); *Classic Images* (Apr. 1983).

ARCHIVAL MATERIALS

• *Clipping File*—CAA: Bankruptcy (1939); film appearance (1922, 1948, 1953, 1956); award (1955); newsphotos; nostalgia (1959, 1964, 1968); artist (1947); obituary (1968). Periodical article: *Films in Review* (July 1958). CAUT: Film appearance (1956, 1962); article (1968); obituary (1968). CAUU: Article (1968). NYMA: Article (1916, 1948); obituary (1968). Periodical articles: *Photo-play World* (Mar. 1918); *Films in Review* (June–July 1958) (filmography); *Classic*

Film Collector (Spring 1968). NYMN: Newsphotos. NYPL (also in Locke Collection): Newsphotos (numerous); marriage (1940); illness (1935); article (1936, 1953, undated); bankruptcy; film appearance (1930s); nostalgia (1962); obituary (1968). Periodical articles: *Motion Picture Magazine* (Aug. 1915); *Silent Picture* (Spring 1973). • *Other Clipping File*—AZSU (Jimmy Starr Collection), CAUB, CNDA, GBBF, MAH, MIDL, PAPL, WICF. • *Correspondence*—CAA (Hedda Hopper Collection): 1929, 1941, 1948, 1953, 1955, 1961, 1964. CAOC (B. Henry Collection): 1954. CAUS (Preston Sturges Collection). • *Filmography*—NYMA. • *Interview*—CAUT: 1967. • *Legal File*—CAUT (Twentieth Century-Fox Collection): Letter, memo (1931-32); contract summary (1931); contract (1931). CAUW: Personnel, payroll record (1934, 1959); talent agreement (1924, 1934). • *Oral History*—NYCO: Interviewed in 1950s. Also mentioned in: Blanche Sweet interview. • *Photograph/ Still*—CAA (also in Hollywood Studio Museum Collection), CALM, CAUT (Jessen Collection), CAUU, CNDA, DCG (Quigley Photographic Archives), NJFL, NYB (Bettmann/UPI Collection) (Underwood Collection), NYCU (Dramatic Museum Portraits) (Palmer Collection), NYEH, NYMN, NYPL, NYSU, OHCL, TXU, WICF. • *Scrapbook*—NYPL (also in R. Locke Collection). • *Studio Biography*—CAA: Fox (1950s). CAUU: Fox. NYPL: Warner (1960).

MARSHALL, Tully (William Phillips), Nevada City, CA, 1864-1943.

Tully Marshall played a variety of roles in his hundreds of film appearances (going back to *Intolerance*) but in his villainous roles he could leer better than any of the other screen badmen of his day. Among his more memorable silent films were *The Merry Widow*, *The Trail of '98*, *The Covered Wagon*, *Alias Jimmy Valentine* and *He Who Gets Slapped*. Sound did nothing

to slow his career; he was onscreen up to the time of his death.

PUBLISHED SOURCES
• *Books*—General: *Character People*; *Eighty Silent Film Stars*; *Famous Film Folk*; *First One Hundred Noted Men and Women of the Screen*; *The Kindergarten of the Movies*; *The Truth About the Movies*; *Who's Who on the Screen*. **Credits:** *Filmarama* (v. I and II); *Forty Years of Screen Credits*; *Twenty Years of Silents*; *Who Was Who on Screen*. **Encyclopedic Works:** *Film Encyclopedia*; *Filmlexicon degli Autori e delle Opere*; *Halliwell's Filmgoer's Companion*; *Hollywood Character Actors*; *The Illustrated Who's Who of the Cinema*; *The Movie Makers*; *The Picturegoer's Who's Who and Encyclopedia of the Screen To-day*; *Who Was Who in the Theatre*; *Who's Who in Hollywood*; *The World Almanac Who's Who of Film*. **Pictorial:** *Silent Portraits*.
• *Periodicals*—The following periodical articles are in addition to those included in the library listings below: *Theatre* (Mar. 1910); *Motion Picture Classic* (Feb. 1917, Feb. 1923); *Photoplay* (Dec. 1918, Aug. 1919, June 1924); *Architecture & Buildings* (Apr. 1923); *Time* (Mar. 22, 1943); *Films in Review* (Nov. 1966, Jan. 1967); *Classic Images* (July 1987, May 1991).

ARCHIVAL MATERIALS
• *Clipping File*—CAA: Obituary (1943). Periodical article: *Picture Show* (May 1920). NYMA (also in Photoplay Collection): Obituary (1943). Periodical articles: *Classic Images* (June 1987, Jan.-Feb. 1991) (filmography). NYPL (also in Locke Collection): PARTIAL CONTENTS: Newsphotos; film review (1920s); film synopses (1920s); 25th year in films; obituary (1943). • *Other Clipping File*—GBBF, MAH, MIDL, OHCL, PAPL, WICF. • *Correspondence*—CAA (Marion Fairfax Collection): 1922, 1930, undated. *NOTE*: Fairfax was TM's wife. CAHL: 1908. NYPL: Letters (C. & L. Brown Collection) (1910, 1941); other (1918). • *Filmography*—NYMA (silents only). • *Legal File*—CAUT (Twentieth Century-Fox

Collection): Letter, memo (1930); loanout (1930). CAUW: Document (1930-32); agreement (1929); letter, memo (1929-30); option (1929-30); contract (1929); loanout (1930); talent agreement (1928-34). • *Photograph/Still*— CAA (also in Hollywood Studio Museum Collection) (also in Marion Fairfax Collection), CASF, CAUT (Jessen Collection) (Portrait File), DCG (Quigley Photographic Archives), NYB (Underwood Collection), NYCU (Bulliet Collection) (Dramatic Museum Portraits), NYEH, NYPL, NYSU, OHCL, TNUT (Clarence Brown Collection), TXU, WICF. • *Program*—OHSU. • *Scrapbook*—NYPL (also in R. Locke Collection), TNUT (Clarence Brown Collection). • *Studio Biography*—CAA: Goldwyn (1920s). NYMA: Photoplay.

MASON, Shirley (Leonie Flugrath), Brooklyn, NY, 1900/01-1979.

Like her sister Viola Dana (q.v.), the career of petite Shirley Mason began when she was a child and continued right through the silent era. She was a very pretty and popular leading lady in numerous programmers like *Ever Since Eve*, *Shirley of the Circus*, *My Husband's Wives* and *The Great Diamond Mystery*. Despite her stage training, she did not survive the coming of sound.

PUBLISHED SOURCES
• *Books*—**General:** *Blue Book of the Screen*; *Famous Film Folk*; *First One Hundred Noted Men and Women of the Screen*; *Who's Who on the Screen*. **Credits:** *Filmarama* (v. I and II); *Twenty Years of Silents*. **Encyclopedic Works:** *Film Encyclopedia*; *Filmlexicon degli Autori e delle Opere*; *Halliwell's Filmgoer's Companion*; *The Picturegoer's Who's Who and Encyclopedia of the Screen To-day*; *Who's Who in Hollywood*; *The World Film Encyclopedia*. **Pictorial:** *Silent Portraits*.
• *Periodicals*—*Motion Picture Magazine* (Nov. 1916, Sept. 1917, Jan. 1921, Apr. 1922); *Photoplay* (Mar. 1917, Nov.

1918, June 1919, July 1920, Feb. 1922, Jan. 1926, June 1926); *Motion Picture Classic* (June 1917, Sept. 1918, Apr.-May 1920, Oct. 1921); *Films in Review* (Mar. 1976, June-July 1976); *Cine Revue* (Aug. 16, 1979).

ARCHIVAL MATERIALS
• *Clipping File*—CAA: Obituary (1979). CAFI: Newsphotos (numerous); obituary (1979). CAUT: Article (1916); obituary (1979). CAUU: Obituary (1979). NYMA (also in Photoplay Collection): Obituary (1979). NYPL (also in Locke Collection): Marriage (1927); newsphotos (numerous); article (1918, undated); obituary (1979). • *Other Clipping File*—CAUB, GBBF, MIDL, OHCL, PAPL, WICF. • *Legal File*—CAUT (Twentieth Century-Fox Collection): Letter (1924); talent agreement (1919, 1921-22, 1924). CAUW: Talent agreement (1926); agreement (1929). • *Photograph/Still*—CAA (also in Hollywood Studio Museum Collection), CAPH, CAUT (Jessen Collection), CAUU, CNDA, DCG (Quigley Photographic Archives), NYAM, NYB (Bettmann/UPI Collection) (Underwood Collection), NYCU (Dramatic Museum Portraits), NYPL, NYSU, OHCL, TXU, WICF. • *Scrapbook*—NYPL (also in R. Locke Collection).

MEHAFFEY, Blanche (also known as Janet Morgan), Cincinnati, Ohio, 1905/07-1968.

A Wampas Baby Star of 1924, Blanche Mehaffey made films in various genres including melodramas, mysteries and westerns. Among her films were *A Woman of the World*, *Princess from Hoboken*, *Take It from Me* and *The White Sheep*. In the talkies she used at least one new name in an attempt to prolong her career but without much success. She made several "B" westerns in the '30s; her final film was *Held for Ransom* (1938).

PUBLISHED SOURCES
• *Books*—**General:** *Sweethearts of the Sage*. **Credits:** *Filmarama* (v. II); *Who*

Was Who on Screen. **Encylopedic Works:** B Western Actors Encyclopedia; Filmlexicon degli Autori e delle Opere; The Picturegoer's Who's Who and Encyclopedia of the Screen To-day; Who's Who in Hollywood; The World Film Encyclopedia.
• Periodicals—Films in Review (Feb. 1970 [Wampas Baby Stars]).

ARCHIVAL MATERIALS
• Clipping File—NYPL (also in Locke Collection): Article (1926); newsphotos; divorce; signs with Roach (1923); sues Paramount; leaves Universal. • Other Clipping File—GBBF, MAH, NYMA (Photoplay Collection), OHCL. • Photograph/Still—CAA (also in Hollywood Studio Museum Collection), DCG (Quigley Photographic Archives), NYB (Underwood Collection), NYPL, NYSU, OHCL, TXSM, TXU.

MEIGHAN, Thomas, Pittsburgh, PA, 1879–1936.
Thomas Meighan (pronounced Meehan) stood near the top of the pantheon of silent film male stars. The rugged Paramount star came to films in 1915, after stage experience, and eventually costarred with most of the era's major actresses. The year 1919 saw him propel to the top with appearances in The Miracle Man and DeMille's Male and Female. He remained a major star through the silent period in more than 70 films, many of them outdoor melodramas. His first talkie, The Argyle Case, came in 1929 and only five more followed.

PUBLISHED SOURCES
• Books—General: Blue Book of the Screen; Classics of the Silent Screen; Eighty Silent Film Stars; Famous Film Folk; Gentlemen to the Rescue; The Truth About the Movies; Who's Who on the Screen. **Credits:** Filmarama (v. I and II); Forty Years of Screen Credits; Twenty Years of Silents; Who Was Who on Screen. **Encyclopedic Works:** Film Encyclopedia; Filmlexicon degli Autori e delle Opere; Halliwell's Filmgoer's Com-

panion; The Illustrated Who's Who of the Cinema; The Movie Makers; The Picturegoer's Who's Who and Encyclopedia of the Screen To-day; Who Was Who in the Theatre; Who's Who in Hollywood; The World Almanac Who's Who of Film; The World Film Encyclopedia. **Pictorial:** The Revealing Eye; Silent Portraits.
• Periodicals—The following periodical articles are in addition to those included in the library listings below: Motion Picture Magazine (Feb. 1917, Nov. 1919, Aug. 1920, Apr. 1922, Nov. 1922, Jan. 1924, Jan. 1925); Photoplay (Aug. 1917, Nov. 1918, Oct. 1919, Sept. 1920, Sept. 1921, Nov. 1921, Mar. 1922, Sept. 1922, July 1923, Sept. 1923, Mar. 1924, June–Aug. 1924, Oct. 1927, Jan. 1935, Sept. 1936); Motion Picture Classic (Mar. 1920, Mar. 1922, May 1925, Dec. 1926); American Magazine (Apr. 1925); Collier's (Aug. 22, 1925); Cinema Art (Nov. 1927); Movie Mirror (Oct. 1931).

ARCHIVAL MATERIALS
• Clipping File—CAA: Newsphotos; film appearance (1921–24, 1934); home (1920s); article (1922, undated); estate (1937); obituary (1936). CAUT: Obituary (1936). NYMA (also in Photoplay Collection): Newsphotos; personal data summary. Periodical articles: Films in Review (Apr. 1974); Classic Images (Apr. 1985, May 1991). NYMN: Estate (1936–37); article (1931); illness; newsphotos; obituary (1936). NYPL (also in Locke Collection): Surgery (1935); career (1936); article (1924, 1926–27, 1936); illness (1936); newsphotos (numerous); article (1924, undated); film appearance (1932, 1934); marriage (1934); film review (1910s, 1920s). PAPT: Article (1922, 1931); estate (1936); burial (1937); obituary (1936). • Other Clipping File—MIDL, OHCL, PAPL, WICF. • Correspondence—CAA (Adolph Zukor Collection): 1924–26. Includes letters from film locations, invitations to Lambs' Club functions, etc. NYMA (Wilk Collection) (Photoplay Collection). NYPL: Letter (C. & L. Brown Collection) (1927); other (1929). • Filmography—NYMA.
• Legal File—CAUT (Twentieth Cen-

tury-Fox Collection): Letter, memo (1930-31); agreement (1930). CAUW: Contract (1928). • *Oral History* — NYCO: Mentioned in the following interviews: James Wong Howe, Nita Naldi, Blanche Ring. • *Photograph/ Still* — CAA (also in Hollywood Studio Museum Collection), CAH, CASF, CASU, CAUB, CAUS (Eddie Cantor Collection), CAUT (Jessen Collection), CAUU, DCG (Quigley Photographic Archives), GBBF, MIDL, NJFL, NJPT, NYAM, NYB (Bettmann/UPI Collection) (Underwood Collection), NYCU (Dramatic Museum Portraits), NYEH, NYMA, NYMN, NYPL, NYSU, OHCL, PAPL, TXU (A. Davis Collection), WICF. • *Play Program* — OHSU. • *Scrapbook* — NYPL (also in Locke Collection), UTBY (DeMille Archives). • *Studio Biography* — CAA: Fox (1930s).

MERSEREAU, Violet, 1897–?.

Called "The Child Wonder," Violet Mersereau made her film debut at the age of ten and appeared in almost 90 films, mostly one- and two-reelers between 1908 and 1919. Her career declined in the 1920s and she made about ten more films (including two in Italy) before leaving the screen in 1926. Among her films were *The Shepherd King*, *The Midnight Flyer*, *Broken Fetters*, *Luck*, *The Boy-Girl* and her last, *Wives of the Prophet*.

PUBLISHED SOURCES

• *Books* — Credits: *Filmarama* (v. I and II); *Twenty Years of Silents.* Encyclopedic Works: *Filmlexicon degli Autori e delle Opere.* Pictorial: *Silent Portraits.*
• *Periodicals* — *Universal Weekly* (Nov. 7, 1914); *Moving Picture World* (Dec. 26, 1914); *Motion Picture Supplement* (Sept. 1915); *Motion Picture Magazine* (Nov. 1915, Mar. 1917, Feb. 1919); *Photoplay* (Dec. 1917).

ARCHIVAL MATERIALS

• *Clipping File* — CAA: Article (1921); film appearance (1922). NYPL (also in Locke Collection): Stage appearance

(1913); article (1913, undated); newsphotos. • *Other Clipping File* — GBBF, NYMA (Photoplay Collection), OHCL, WICF. • *Filmography* — CAA. • *Photograph/Still* — CAA (also in Hollywood Studio Museum Collection), DCG (Quigley Photographic Archives), NYAM, NYCU (Dramatic Museum Portraits), NYPL, NYSU, OHCL, WICF. • *Scrapbook* — NYPL (R. Locke Collection), WICF. • *Studio Biography* — NYMA: Photoplay.

MILJAN, John, Lead, SD, 1892/93-1960.

Another dependable villain in both silents and talkies was saturnine John Miljan. In his hundreds of films he was said to have had the "distinction" of being killed more often than any other featured player. He also had some leads earlier in his career, which started in 1923, and managed some sympathetic character portrayals as well. He remained active until the latter part of the 1950s.

PUBLISHED SOURCES

• *Books* — General: *Heroes, Heavies and Sagebrush*; *The Versatiles.* Credits: *Filmarama* (v. II); *Forty Years of Screen Credits*; *Twenty Years of Silents*; *Who Was Who on Screen.* Encyclopedic Works: *Film Encyclopedia*; *Filmlexicon degli Autori e degli Opere*; *Halliwell's Filmgoer's Companion*; *Hollywood Character Actors*; *The Illustrated Encyclopedia of Movie Character Actors*; *The Movie Makers*; *The Picturegoer's Who's Who and Encyclopedia of the Screen To-day*; *Who's Who in Hollywood*; *The World Almanac Who's Who of Film*; *The World Film Encyclopedia.*
• *Periodicals* — *Motion Picture Magazine* (Aug. 1932); *Midnight Marquee* (Fall 1981).

ARCHIVAL MATERIALS

• *Clipping File* — CAA: Film appearance (1954); obituary (1960). CAUT: Obituary (1960). NYMA (also in Photoplay Collection): Obituary (1960). NYMN: Newsphotos; obituary (1960).

NYPL: Newsphotos; film appearance (1933-34); career (1933); obituary (1960). • *Other Clipping File*—GBBF, MIDL, OHCL, PAPL, WICF. • *Filmography*— NYMA. • *Legal File*—CAUW: Personnel, payroll record (1932-39); agreement (1938); letter, memo (1927, 1938-39); option (1938-39); contract (1938); talent agreement (1926-28, 1932); loan out (1932). • *Photograph/Still*—CAA (also in Hollywood Studio Museum Collection) (also in MGM Collection), CALM, CAUT (Jessen Collection), CAUU, DCG (Quigley Photographic Archives), NYB (Bettmann/UPI Collection), NYCU (Palmer Collection), NYMN, NYPL, OHCL, TXU, WICF. • *Press Kit*—OHCL. • *Publicity Release*— CAA: Unknown studio (1930s). NYMA: Universal (1944). • *Studio Biography*— CAA: RKO (1930s); Fox (1935).

MILLER, Patsy Ruth (Patricia Ruth Miller), St. Louis, MO, 1904/05-1995.

Patsy Ruth Miller had a respectable silent career after her debut in a small role in *Camille* (1921). In ten years she made more than 70 films of which perhaps only one was memorable: Lon Chaney's *The Hunchback of Notre Dame* (1923). Another worthy role was in Ernst Lubitsch's *So This Is Paris* (1927). Her first talkie, *The Fall of Eve*, was followed by several others which did little to prolong her career, and in 1931 she made her final film.

PUBLISHED SOURCES

• *Books*—Wrote a play, *Windy Hill*; several short stories, two of which appeared in *Best Short Stories of 1935* and one in *Vanity Fair* (June 1934), and a novel, *That Flannigan Girl* (1939). General: *Blue Book of the Screen*; *Broken Silence*; *Famous Film Folk*; *Speaking of Silents*. Credits: *Filmarama* (v. I and II); *Forty Years of Screen Credits*; *Twenty Years of Silents*. Encyclopedic Works: *Film Encyclopedia*; *Filmlexicon degli Autori e delle Opere*; *Halliwell's Filmgoer's Companion*; *The Movie Makers*; *The Picturegoer's Who's*

Who and Encyclopedia of the Screen To-day; *Who's Who in Hollywood*; *Who's Who of the Horrors and Other Fantasy Films*; *The World Almanac Who's Who of Film*; *The World Film Encyclopedia*. Bibliography: *The Idols of Silence*. Biography/Autobiography: *My Hollywood*. Nostalgia: *Whatever Became of...* (1st). Pictorial: *Silent Portraits*; *They Had Faces Then*.

• *Periodicals*—The following periodical articles are in addition to those included in the library listings below: *Motion Picture Classic* (Feb. 1922, Aug. 1923, June 1928); *Photoplay* (Oct. 1922, Dec. 1926); *Motion Picture Magazine* (Feb. 1924, Nov. 1926); *Vanity Fair* (May 1934); *Films in Review* (Feb. 1970 [Wampas Baby Stars], Apr. 1972, Apr. 1989); *Filmograph* (no. 2-4, 1972); *Classic Images* (Jan.-Feb. 1989).

ARCHIVAL MATERIALS

• *Caricature*—NYPL (Sardi Collection). • *Clipping File*—CAA: Film appearance (1922, 1925?, 1950); divorce (1933, 1937, 1946); playwright (1944); nostalgia (1969, 1971, 1981); legal problem (1980s). CAUT: Marriage (1929); newsphoto. MOSL: Article (1933); divorce (1933). NYMA (also in Photoplay Collection): Libel suit (1992); entry from *Whatever Became of...*; film review (1920s); article (1989); party for *My Hollywood*. Periodical articles: *Filmograph* (nos. 1-2, 1971); *Classic Film Collector* (Winter 1973); *Classic Images* (May 1988, Mar. 1989, Feb. 1992). NYMN: Newsphotos. NYPL: Article (1923, 1936, 1952, 1985, 1988, undated); newsphotos (numerous); divorce; stage appearance (1933, undated); review of *That Flannigan Girl* (1939); legal problem (1982). Periodical articles: *Classic Film Collector* (Winter 1973); *Connecticut's Finest* (Autumn 1989). • *Other Clipping File*—CNDA, GBBF, MIDL, OHCL, OHSU, PAPL, TXU, WICF, WYU (see Collection). • *Collection*— NYPL: Photographs (1922-86); fan letters (1930-83); draft autobiography (1974); personal correspondence (1926-38, 1956-75); business correspondence (1934, 1938-40). WYU: Correspondence

(1971); manuscript (1930s); newspaper clippings (1926, 1931, 1936, 1939, 1944–45, 1947, 1954, 1974, 1976, 1979, undated); periodical articles (1925, 1928, 1931, 1934, 1936, 1939, 1971, 1973, 1975, undated); posters (1931, 1935); photographs and stills (1921–41); play programs (1930–45); scrapbooks (1921–34). • *Correspondence* – NYPL (see Collection), WYU (see Collection). • *Filmography* – NYMA, WYU (see Collection). • *Interview* – CAUU (R. Lamparski Collection). MISU: Recorded from a telephone interview. • *Legal File* – CAUW: Talent agreement (1926, 1929); agreement (1928); memo (1926). • *Photograph/Still* – CAA (also in Hollywood Studio Museum Collection) (also in MGM Collection), CAFA, CAHL, CAUT (Jessen Collection), CAUU, DCG (Quigley Photographic Archives), GBBF, NJPT, NYB (Underwood Collection), NYCU (Dramatic Museum Portraits), NYEH, NYMN, NYPL (also in Collection), NYSU, OHCL, OHSU, PAPL, TXU (Robbins Collection), WICF, WYU (see Collection). • *Play Program* – WYU (see Collection). • *Scrapbook* – NYPL, WYU (see Collection). • *Studio Biography* – CAA: Goldwyn (1921). NYMA: Photoplay.

MINTER, Mary Miles (also known as Juliet Shelby) (Juliet Reilly), Shreveport, LA, 1899/1902–1984 (some sources suggest she may have been older).

Blonde beauty Mary Miles Minter was considerably more sophisticated than her demure onscreen persona revealed. Her career was destroyed by the scandal following the murder of director William Desmond Taylor in 1922. Before that, however, she was a most popular star in over 50 films, beginning in 1912, including *Anne of Green Gables*, *Tillie*, *A Cumberland Romance*, *Barbara Frietchie* and *Dimples*. A few of her films were released after the scandal broke but

they did nothing to restore her to screen favor.

PUBLISHED SOURCES
• *Books* – **Bibliography:** *The Idols of Silence*. **General:** *Blue Book of the Screen*; *A Cast of Killers*; *Celebrity Circus*; *A Deed of Death*; *Fallen Angels*; *First One Hundred Noted Men and Women of the Screen*; *Hollywood Heartbreak*; *Hollywood Kids*; *Hollywood Lolitas*; *The Hollywood Murder Casebook*; *Hollywood Tragedy*; *Hollywood's Unsolved Mysteries*; *Ladies in Distress*; *Whodunit? Hollywood Style*; *Who's Who on the Screen*. **Credits:** *Filmarama* (v. I and II); *Twenty Years of Silents*. **Encyclopedic Works:** *Film Encyclopedia*; *Filmlexicon degli Autori e delle Opere*; *Halliwell's Filmgoer's Companion*; *The Illustrated Who's Who of the Cinema*; *The Movie Makers*; *Variety Who's Who in Show Business*; *Who Was Who in the Theatre*; *Who's Who in Hollywood*; *The World Almanac Who's Who of Film*. **Pictorial:** *The Image Makers*; *Silent Portraits*.
• *Periodicals* – The following periodical articles are in addition to those included in the library listings below: *Photoplay* (Nov. 1915, Jan. 1917, Feb. 1918, Jan. 1919, June 1920, Feb. 1923, Feb. 1928); *Green Book Magazine* (Feb. 1916); *Delineator* (July 1916); *Motion Picture Magazine* (May 1917, Jan. 1918, Mar. 1918, Mar. 1920, May 1921); *Motion Picture Classic* (Aug. 1918, June 1919, Aug. 1920, Aug. 1921); *Literary Digest* (Feb. 13, 1937); *After Dark* (Nov. 1974); *Cine Revue* (Aug. 23, 1984); *Films and Filming* (Mar. 1985); *Films in Review* (May 1985, Nov. 1986); *American Film* (June 1986).

ARCHIVAL MATERIALS
• *Clipping File* – CAA: Newsphotos; article (1981, 1987); estate (1988); W.D. Taylor murder (1929–30, 1937, 1940, 1956, 1990); review of *Cast of Killers* (1986); legal problem (1928, 1930, 1932–34, 1973); romance (1928); home (1932); robbery (1981); obituary (1984). Periodical article: *Films in Review* (Oct. 1969) (filmography). CAFI: Article (1972); robbery (1981); estate (1988); obituary

(1984). Periodical article: *Films in Review* (Oct. 1969). CAUT: Legal problem (1956, 1973, undated); marriage (undated); obituary (1984). CAUU: Obituary (1984). NYMA (also in Photoplay Collection): Robbery (1981); newsphotos; W.D. Taylor scandal (1923?); obituary (1984). Periodical articles: *Classic Images* (July-Aug. 1991). NYMN: W.D. Taylor murder (1936-37); newsphotos; article (undated); obituary (1984). Periodical article: *Photoplay* (1920). NYPL (also in Locke Collection): Engagement/marriage (1921, 1923, undated); newsphotos; W.D. Taylor murder (1922-23, 1936-37, 1951, 1958, 1990, undated); article (1951, undated); sues for funds (1956, undated); nostalgia (1933); film review (1920s); injury (1922-23); legal problem (1936, 1956, undated); film review (1920s); review of *A Cast of Killers* (1986); family problem (1923); biography (1910s?); film appearance (1920); obituary (1984). Periodical articles: *Theatre Magazine* (Mar. 1912); *Motion Picture Magazine* (May 1916). • *Other Clipping File* — AZSU (Jimmy Starr Collection), CAUB, GBBF, MAH, MIDL, OHCL, PAPL, WICF. • *Correspondence* — CAA (Adolph Zukor Collection): 1920. CAUS (Paul J. Smith Collection). • *Filmography* — NYMA. • *Interview* — CAUU (R. Lamparski Collection). • *Oral History* — CAUS: Mentioned in: James Wong Howe interview. NYCO: Mentioned in the following interviews: Roddy McDowall, Conrad Nagel. • *Photograph/Still* — CAA (also in Hollywood Studio Museum Collection), CALM, CAOC (Kiesling Collection), CASF, CAUB, CAUC (Motion Picture Photograph Collection), CAUT (Jessen Collection), CAUU, CNDA, DCG (Quigley Photographic Archive), NYB (Penguin Collection) (Underwood Collection), NYCU (Palmer Collection), NYEH, NYMN, NYPL, NYSU, OHCL, TXU, WICF. • *Scrapbook* — NYMA (also in R. Locke Collection).

MIX, Tom, Mix Run, PA, 1880-1940.

Tom Mix was probably the most popular cowboy star ever, combining glitz and action in just the right proportions. He was with Selig as early as 1910 but made his greatest success as a Fox star in the 1920s. His films included *The Heart of Texas Ryan*, *The Riders of the Purple Sage*, *Three Jumps Ahead* and *The Yankee Señor*. He also appeared in non-westerns such as *Dick Turpin*. His voice was not too well-suited to talkies but he made several, concluding his career in 1935 with the serial *The Miracle Rider*.

PUBLISHED SOURCES

• *Books* — The following are among the adventure stories for children, using TM's name, which were written in the 1930s and '40s: *Tom Mix and His Circus on the Barbary Coast* (1940), *Tom Mix and the Hoard of Montezuma* (1937), *Tom Mix and the Range War* (1937), *Tom Mix and the Mystery of the Flaming Warrior* (1940), *Tom Mix and the Stranger from the South* (1936), *Tom Mix Plays a Lone Hand* (1935) and *Tom Mix Avenges the Dry-Gulched Range King* (1939). At least two works of adult fiction were written about TM: *Tom Mix and Pancho Villa* (Clifford Irving, 1984) and *Tom Mix Died for Your Sins* (Darryl Ponicsan, 1976). Tom Mix was credited as the compiler of *Western Songs* (1935). Written by (or ghostwritten for) TM: *Cinema* (one part); *The Trail of the Terrible Six* (1935); *The West of Yesterday, and Tony's Story* (1923). **Bibliography:** *The Idols of Silence*. **General:** *The BFI Companion to the Western*; *Classics of the Silent Screen*; *The Cowboy*; *Famous Film Folk*; *Famous Stars of Filmdom (Men)*; *The Filming of the West*; *Gentlemen to the Rescue*; *The Great Cowboy Stars of Movies & Television*; *The Great Movie Serials*; *Great Western Stars*; *The Hall of Fame of Western Film Stars*; *Heroes, Heavies and Sagebrush*; *History of the American Cinema* (v. 3); *Hollywood Album*; *Hollywood Corral*; *Hollywood Hall of Fame*; *How I Broke Into the Movies*; *"Image" on the Art and Evolution of the Film*; *Immortals of the Screen*; *Love, Laughter and Tears*; *The Matinee Idols*;

The Movie Stars Story; A Pictorial History of Westerns; Saddle Aces of the Cinema; Screen Personalities; Six Gun Heroes; Star Babies; The Stars (Schickel); Stunt; They Went Thataway; Tom Mix (Nicholas); Tom Mix and Tony; The Tom Mix Book; Tom Mix Highlights; The Truth About the Movies; The War, the West and the Wilderness; The Western (Eyles); The Western (Fenin); What the Stars Told Me; Who's Who in the Film World; Who's Who on the Screen; Wild West Characters; Winners of the West. **Credits:** Filmarama (v. I and II); Forty Years of Screen Credits; Twenty Years of Silents; Who Was Who on Screen. **Encyclopedic Works:** B Western Actors Encyclopedia; A Companion to the Movies; Dictionary of American Biography (Supplement 2); Film Encyclopedia; Filmlexicon degli Autori e delle Opere; Halliwell's Filmgoer's Companion; The Illustrated Encyclopedia of the World's Great Movie Stars and Their Films; The Illustrated Who's Who of the Cinema; International Dictionary of Films and Filmmaking (v. 3); The International Encyclopedia of Film; The Movie Makers; The Oxford Companion to Film; The Picturegoer's Who's Who and Encyclopedia of the Screen To-day; Quinlan's Illustrated Registry of Film Stars; Who's Who in Hollywood; The World Almanac Who's Who of Film; The World Encyclopedia of the Film; The World Film Encyclopedia. **Pictorial:** Photostory of the World's Greatest Cowboy Star; Silent Portraits. **Biography/Autobiography:** The Fabulous Tom Mix; The Life and Legend of Tom Mix; Tom Mix, Portrait of a Superstar. **Films:** King Cowboy. **Comic Book:** Tom Mix Holiday Album (1990-); Tom Mix Western (1948-53, 1988-). **Factoids:** Star Stats.

• Periodicals — The following periodical articles are in addition to those included in the library listings below: Moving Picture World (May 28, 1910); Feature Movie Magazine (Apr. 15, 1915, Aug. 25, 1915, Mar. 1916); Photoplay (Sept. 1916, Dec. 1919, June 1923, Apr. 1924, Feb.-Apr. 1925, July 1925, Sept. 1926, Jan. 1927, Apr. 1927, June 1927, Sept. 1927, Dec. 1927-July 1928, Mar. 1929, Feb. 1931, Mar. 1932, Jan. 1933); Motion Picture Magazine (Nov. 1918, Feb. 1919, Oct. 1921, Mar. 1923, Apr. 1925, Nov. 1926, Mar. 1932); Photo-play World (May 1919); Motion Picture Classic (Oct. 1919, July 1922, July 1926, Feb. 1929, Feb. 1932); Pictures and Picturegoer (Jan. 1921, Sept. 1923, Apr. 30, 1932, Nov. 26, 1932, Nov. 2, 1940); Sunset (Nov. 1926); Ladies' Home Journal (Mar. 1927); Cinema Digest (Aug. 22, 1932); Movie Classic (Sept. 1932, Jan. 1933); Time (Oct. 21, 1940); Newsweek (Oct. 21, 1940); Films in Review (Oct. 1954, Jan. 1955, Oct. 1957, Jan. 1970); Show (Sept. 1962); 8mm Collector (Aug. 1963); Classic Film Collector (Spring 1968, Summer 1969, Fall 1975); Views & Reviews (no. 3-4, 1972); Western Horseman (Nov. 1973); Nostalgia Illustrated (Nov. 1974); Journal of the West (Dec. 1977, Oct. 1983); Boxoffice (Oct. 16, 1978); Classic Images (Nov. 1981, May 1982, July 1982, May-June 1983, Dec. 1983, Mar. 1984, May 1984, July 1984, Nov. 1984, Nov. 1985, Apr. 1987, July 1987, Mar. 1988, Oct. 1988, Apr. 1989, Aug. 1989, Oct. 1989, July-Aug. 1990, Nov. 1990); Hobbies (Sept. 1983); Hollywood Studio Magazine (Jan.-Feb. 1984); Listener (Mar. 8, 1984); Griffithiana (Sept. 1988); Film Dope (Mar. 1990); American Heritage (May-June 1992).

MEDIA

Saddle Up (video).

ARCHIVAL MATERIALS

• Caricature — NYMN. • Clipping File — CAA: Marriage/divorce/children (1922, 1927-30, 1932); memorial (1989); injury (1927, 1932); legal problem (1928-33); FBO contract (1928); fistfight (1928); home (1929, 1954, 1962, 1981); illness (1930-31); article (1932, 1961, 1963, 1968, 1975, 1979-80, 1984); ends career (1932); excerpt from Tony and His Pals (1934); estate (1955, 1960); film biography (1974-75); review of Tom Mix Died for Your Sins (1976); obituary (1940). Periodical articles: Roxy Theatre Weekly Review (Oct. 8, 1927); Classic Film Collector (Winter 1970); Movie Classics (Aug.

1973); *American Legion Magazine* (Sept. 1976); *Collectibles Monthly* (Apr. 1977); *Nostalgia Monthly* (Apr. 1978); *Real West Yearbook* (Summer 1978); *American Cinematographer* (June 1987); *New Yorker* (June 3, 1991). CAFI: Hometown (1980, 1984); home (1981); article (1979). CAUT: Home (1984–85); legal problem (1929); film rights (1955); review of *Tom Mix Died for Your Sins* (1976); article (1940, 1980); obituary (1940). CAUU (also in McCormick Collection): Monument (1986); article (1969, 1983); review of *Tom Mix Died for Your Sins* (1976); biographical film (1974); radio program (1985). NYMA (also in Photoplay Collection): Article (1969, 1971); film synopses (1920); Tom Mix Festival (1980–81, 1984–85, 1988); newsphotos; subject of film (1974); personal data summary; birthplace to be park (1987–88); review of *Tom Mix Died for Your Sins*; obituary (1940). Periodical articles: *Photoplay* (undated); *8mm Collector* (Sept. 1964); *Tom Mix Museum* (May 27, 1968); *Classic Film Collector* (Winter 1974, Summer 1975); *American Legion Magazine* (Sept. 1976); *Classic Images* (Jan. 1980, July 1981, Oct. 1983, June 1984, Oct. 1984, Aug. 1985, Feb. 1986, Aug. 1987, Nov. 1987–Jan. 1988, Aug. 1988, Sept. 1989); *Big Reel* (Nov. 1984, Oct. 1985, Jan. 1987); *New Yorker* (June 3, 1991). NYPL (also in Locke Collection) (also in C. & L. Brown Collection): Film appearance (1920s); shot by wife; film review (1920s, 1930s); producer (1940); newsphotos; legal problem (1932–34); sale of effects (1941); retires (1932); estate (1940); marriage/divorce (1932); stunt (1933); article (1940, undated); funeral (1940); biography (1940, 1950); circus; film publicity (1920s); review of *The Life and Legend of Tom Mix* (1972); subject of film (1974); TM festival (1980–81, 1983, 1990–91); obituary (1940). Periodical articles: *Signature* (Mar. 1967); *Blackhawk Film Digest* (Mar. 1979); *American Cinematographer* (June 1987). • *Other Clipping File* — AZSU (Jimmy Starr Collection), CNDA, GBBF, MAH, MIDL, OHCL, WICF. • *Collection* — OKTM: Memorabilia; thousands of photographs; personal articles including saddles, boots, whips and firearms. OKU (Miller Brothers 101 Ranch Collection): Testimony and correspondence between Zack Miller and his attorney: 1927–34, relating to a lawsuit against TM for failure to appear in the Miller Brothers Wild West Show. Also some social correspondence to and from TM. • *Correspondence* — CAA (Selig Collection): 1910, 1914. CAUS (Rob Wagner Collection): Letter(s) relating to *Rob Wagner's Script* (periodical). OHCL. OKU (see Collection). • *Filmography* — NYEH, NYPL. • *Legal File* — CAUT (Twentieth Century–Fox Collection): Letter, memo, telegram (1916, 1918, 1920, 1925, 1927, 1938, 1940, 1955, 1968, 1970, 1980–81); assignment (1925); talent agreement (1917–19, 1923, 1925). OKU (see Collection). • *Manuscript* — CAA: *My Million Memories Out West* (John H. Nicholas). • *Oral History* — NYCO: Mentioned in the following interviews: Andy Devine, Conrad Nagel, Adela R. St. Johns, John Wayne. • *Photograph/Still* — CAA (also in Hollywood Studio Museum Collection), CAFA, CALM, CAPH, CASF, CAUS, CAUT (Portrait File), CAUU, CNDA, DCG (Quigley Photographic Archives), NYB (Bettmann/UPI Collection) (Penguin Collection) (Springer Collection) (Underwood Collection), NYCU (Dramatic Museum Portraits), NYEH, NYMN, NYPL, NYSU, OHCL, OKTM (see Collection), TXU, WICF. • *Press Kit* — OHCL. • *Program* — NYPL: TM Circus (1937). • *Publicity Release* — AZSU. • *Reminiscence* — MISU. • *Scrapbook* — NYPL (also in R. Locke Collection). • *Studio Biography* — CAA: Universal (1936).

MOORE, Colleen (Kathleen Morrison), Port Huron, MI, 1900/03–1988.

After appearing in Tom Mix westerns and other programmers for several years beginning in 1917, Colleen Moore became one of the silents' biggest stars with *Flaming Youth* (1923). She was the personification of the "flapper" in films such as *Orchids and*

Ermine, Oh Kay!, *The Perfect Flapper* and *Naughty But Nice*. She also could be a sensitive actress in dramas such as *Lilac Time*. She made few talkies but had worthy roles in *The Power and the Glory*, *The Scarlet Letter* and *Success at Any Price*.

PUBLISHED SOURCES

• *Books* – Wrote *How Women Can Make Money in the Stock Market* (1969); wrote (or ghostwritten for) CM: a chapter of *Breaking into the Movies*. **Bibliography:** *The Idols of Silence*. **Doll House:** *Colleen Moore's Doll House: The Story of the Most Exquisite Toy in the World*; *Colleen Moore's Doll House*; *Colleen Moore's Fairy Castle*; *The Doll House of Colleen Moore*. **General:** *Blue Book of the Screen*; *Classics of the Silent Screen*; *The Faces of Hollywood*; *Famous Film Folk*; *Hollywood: The Golden Era*; *Hollywood Hall of Fame*; *Hollywood Lolitas*; *How I Broke into the Movies*; *Love, Laughter and Tears*; *Motion Picture News Booking Guide and Studio Directory* (1927); *Movie Star*; *The Movie Stars Story*; *People Will Talk*; *Personal Glimpses of Famous Folks*; *Return Engagement*; *Some Are Born Great*; *Speaking of Silents*; *The Stars Appear*; *The Truth About the Movies*; *Who's Who on the Screen*. **Credits:** *Filmarama* (v. I and II); *Forty Years of Screen Credits*; *Twenty Years of Silents*. **Encyclopedic Works:** *Film Encyclopedia*; *Filmlexicon degli Autori e delle Opere*; *Halliwell's Filmgoer's Companion*; *The Illustrated Encyclopedia of the World's Great Movie Stars and Their Films*; *The Illustrated Who's Who of the Cinema*; *International Dictionary of Films and Filmmakers* (v. 3); *The Movie Makers*; *The Picturegoer's Who's Who and Encyclopedia of the Screen To-day*; *Quinlan's Illustrated Registry of Film Stars*; *Variety Who's Who in Show Business*; *Who's Who in Hollywood*; *The World Almanac Who's Who of Film*; *The World Film Encyclopedia*. **Nostalgia:** *Whatever Became of...* (2nd). **Pictorial:** *The Image Makers*; *Leading Ladies*; *The Revealing Eye*; *Silent Portraits*; *They Had Faces Then*. **Biography/**

Autobiography: *Silent Star*. • **Oral History:** *Colleen Moore: the Jazz Age's Movie Flapper at San Simeon*. **Factoids:** *Star Stats*.

• *Periodicals* – The following periodical articles are in addition to those included in the library listings below: *Photoplay* (Feb. 1919, June 1920, Mar. 1921, Aug. 1922, Nov.–Dec. 1924, Aug. 1926, Apr. 1930, Dec. 1930, May 1935); *Picture Play Magazine* (Jan. 1920); *Motion Picture Classic* (Jan. 1921, July 1922, Nov. 1928, Aug. 1931); *Motion Picture Magazine* (June 1921, June 1922, Sept. 1924, May 1925, Oct. 1925, Dec. 1925, Feb. 1927, June 1928, Feb. 1930, Sept. 1932, June 1935); *National Magazine* (July/Aug. 1921); *American Magazine* (Jan. 1927); *Ladies' Home Journal* (Aug. 1927); *Pictorial Review* (Dec. 1927); *Movie Classic* (May 1932, Sept. 1933); *Silver Screen* (Oct. 1932); *Newsweek* (Apr. 13, 1935, Feb. 8, 1988); *Good Housekeeping* (June 1968); *Films in Review* (Feb. 1970) (Wampas Baby Stars); *Filmograph* (no. 3–4, 1973); *Films* (Feb. 1982); *Classic Images* (Aug. 1983, Feb. 1988); *Time* (Feb. 8, 1988); *Cine Revue* (Feb. 11, 1988); *EPD Film* (Mar. 1988); *Film en Televisie + Video* (Mar. 1988); *Film Dope* (Mar. 1990).

MEDIA

Colleen Moore Discusses Silent Star with Columnist Robert Cromie (recording); *Colleen Moore's Incredible Jewelled Castle* (video).

OBSCURE PUBLISHED SOURCES
NYMA: *Colleen Moore*.

ARCHIVAL MATERIALS
• *Clipping File* – AZSU (Jimmy Starr Collection): Dollhouse. (Other CM materials are also in the Jimmy Starr Collection). CAA (also in Collection): Marriage/divorce (1930–32, 1935, 1937); MGM contract (1932); legal problem (1927, 1932–33); dollhouse (1935, 1937, 1948, 1971); stage appearance (1930, 1932); film appearance (1921, 1933); illness (1930, 1936); threatened (1935); First National contract (1927–28); injury (1925); newsphotos; review of *Colleen Moore's Doll House* (1971); nostalgia

214   Moore

(1963, 1974, 1981); review of *Silent Star* (1968); article (1950, undated); obituary (1988). Periodical articles: *After Dark* (Oct. 1968); *Films and Filming* (Apr. 1970). CAFI: Review of *Silent Star* (1968); tribute (1977); obituary (1988). CAUT: Article (1975). Periodical article: *After Dark* (Oct. 1968). CAUU: Review of *Silent Star* (1968). NYMA: News-photos (numerous); marriage (1983); article (1955, 1968, 1971). Periodical articles: *Classic Film Collector* (Winter-Spring 1967, Fall 1967–Spring 1968); *Classic Images* (Nov. 1982, July 1986). NYMN: Newsphotos. NYPL (also in Locke Collection): PARTIAL CONTENTS: Newsphotos; injury (1935); divorce (1935); film appearance (1934); biography (1950); article (1968, 1971, 1975); money management (1969); obituary (1988). Periodical articles: *Films in Review* (Aug.–Sept. 1963); *After Dark* (Oct. 1968); *Hollywood Studio Magazine* (Oct. 1974). • *Other Clipping File*— CAUB, CNDA, GBBF, MAH, MIDL, PAPL, WICF. • *Collection*—CAA: 36 scrapbooks containing clippings about CM's First National films (1925–29); personal clippings (1922–29); doll house (1935–36). • *Correspondence*—CAA: Several letters, notes, telegrams (Hedda Hopper Collection) (1940, 1952, 1954, 1959, 1964); 2 letters (W. Selig Collection) (1918, 1926). CAUS (Preston Sturges Collection), NYCU (Palmer Papers). • *Interview*—CAUU (Hollywood Studio Museum Collection) (1964); (R. Lamparski Collection). GBBF (Hollywood Collection): Transcript of interview for *Hollywood* (TV series). NYAM. • *Legal File*—CAUT (Twentieth Century-Fox Collection): Letter, telegram (1933); loanout (1933). CAUW: Letter, memo (1925–29, 1948); tax problem (1931); personnel, payroll record (1923–31); communication (1923–29); contract (1924–28, 1928–29); agreement (1926–29); document (1925, 1929, undated); talent agreement (1927); budget (1928–29). • *Manuscript*—NYMA: *Colleen Moore von Colleen Moore.* Deutsche Bearbeitung von Hans Lefebre. A mimeographed work in German (possibly a translation of previously published English-language articles?). • *Oral History*—NYCO: Mentioned in: Adela St. Johns interview. • *Paper Dolls*— NYMA: Xeroxed from originals. • *Photograph/Still*—CAA (also in Hollywood Studio Museum Collection) (also in MGM Collection), CALM, CASF, CAUS, CAUT (Jessen Collection), CAUU, CNDA, DCG (Quigley Photographic Archives), NYAM, NYB (Bettmann/UPI Collection) (Underwood Collection), NYCU (Dramatic Museum Portraits) (Palmer Collection), NYEH, NYMN, NYPL, NYSU, OHCL, TXU, WICF. • *Scrapbook*—CAA (see Collection), NYPL (also in R. Locke Collection). • *Studio Biography*—CAA: Goldwyn (1921); RKO (1930s). NYMA: Doubleday (1968).

MOORE, Matt, County Meath, Ireland, 1888–1960.

The next to youngest of the famous Moore brothers (Owen [q.v.], Tom [q.v.] and Joe were the others), Matt Moore had a longer but somewhat less significant career. He played romantic and action leads from about 1913 and supporting roles from the early 1930s to the 1950s. His films included *Side Street* (with two of his brothers), *His Majesty, Bunker Bean, The Unholy Three* (1925 version) and *Tillie the Toiler*; later pictures were *Seven Brides for Seven Brothers, Neptune's Daughter* and *Executive Suite.*

PUBLISHED SOURCES

• *Books*—Credits: *Filmarama* (v. I and II); *Forty Years of Screen Credits; Twenty Years of Silents; Who Was Who on Screen.* **Encyclopedic Works:** *Film Encyclopedia; Filmlexicon degli Autori e delle Opere; Halliwell's Filmgoer's Companion; The Picturegoer's Who's Who and Encyclopedia of the Screen To-day; Who's Who in Hollywood; The World Film Encyclopedia.* **Pictorial:** *Silent Portraits.*

• *Periodicals*—*Photoplay* (Aug. 1915, Apr. 1916, Dec. 1918, Oct. 1925); *Motion Picture Classic* (Apr. 1917); *Motion Pic-*

ture Magazine (June 1919); Classic Images (May 1988).

ARCHIVAL MATERIALS

• Clipping File—CAA: Robbery (1932); obituary (1960). CAUT: Obituary (1960). NYPL: Obituary (1960). • Other Clipping File—GBBF, MIDL, NYMA (Photoplay Collection), PAPL, WICF. • Correspondence—NYMA (Photoplay Collection). • Legal File—CAUW: Loanout (1926); release (1926); letter, memo (1925-26); talent agreement (1924, 1931). • Photograph/Still—CAA (also in Hollywood Studio Museum Collection) (also in MGM Collection), CAUT (Jessen Collection), DCG (Quigley Photographic Archives), GBBF, NJFL, NJPT, NYAM, NYEH, NYPL, OHCL, TXU, WICF. • Scrapbook—NJPT (Yeandle Collection), NYPL (also in Locke Collection). • Studio Biography—CAA: MGM (1920s). NYMA: Photoplay.

MOORE, Owen, County Meath, Ireland, 1886-1939.

One of four actor brothers, Owen Moore was a pioneer in silent films, beginning his career about 1908 and costarring with most of the prominent actresses of the silents. His career continued apace throughout the 1920s and he appeared in an early talkie, Side Street (1929), with his brothers Tom (q.v.) and Matt (q.v.). His speaking voice was not well-suited to the talkies, however, and he was in only 7 sound films in the 1930s, including She Done Him Wrong and his last role in 1937's A Star Is Born. He was married to Mary Pickford (q.v.).

PUBLISHED SOURCES

• Books—General: Blue Book of the Screen; Famous Film Folk; Life Stories of the Movie Stars; Who's Who on the Screen. Credits: Filmarama (v. I and II); Forty Years of Screen Credits; Twenty Years of Silents; Who Was Who on Screen. Encyclopedic Works: Film Encyclopedia; Filmlexicon degli Autori e delle Opere; Halliwell's Filmgoer's Com-

panion; The Picturegoer's Who's Who and Encyclopedia of the Screen To-day; Who's Who in Hollywood; The World Film Encyclopedia. Pictorial: Silent Portraits.

• Periodicals—The following periodical articles are in addition to those included in the library listings below: Photoplay (Mar. 1915, Aug. 1915, Apr. 1916, Dec. 1918, Dec. 1919, June 1924, Oct. 1925); Picture Play Magazine (May 1916); Motion Picture Magazine (Sept. 1916, July 1917); Motion Picture Classic (Dec. 1921); Classic Images (May 1988).

ARCHIVAL RESOURCES

• Clipping File—AZSU (Jimmy Starr Collection): Obituary (1939). CAA: Film appearance (1921-23); illness (1924); obituary (1939). NYMA (also in Photoplay Collection): Film appearance (1921); personal data summary; obituary (1939). Periodical article: Classic Images (Apr. 1988). NYPL (also in Locke Collection): Article (1923, 1928, 1937?, undated); marriage (1921); confined to psychiatric ward (1935?); injury (1924); legal problem (1923); newsphotos; film review (1920s, 1933); stage appearance (1932, undated); film appearance (1923); obituary (1937). Periodical article: Motion Picture Magazine (Aug. 1915); Dramatic Mirror (July 14, 1920); Picture Show (Sept. 10, 1921). • Other Clipping File— GBBF, MAH, OHCL, PAPL, WICF. • Legal File—CAUW: Document (1927). • Oral History—NYCO: Mentioned in the following interviews: Nita Naldi, Albert (Eddie) Sutherland, Blanche Sweet. • Photograph/Still—CAA (also in Hollywood Studio Museum Collection) (also in MGM Collection), CAFI, CAUT (Jessen Collection), GBBF, MIDL, NJFL, NJPT, NYB (Underwood Collection), NYCU (Dramatic Museum Portraits), NYEH, NYPL, OHCL, PAPL, TXU (A. Davis Collection), WICF. • Program—NYMN: Film. • Scrapbook—NYPL (also in R. Locke Collection).

MOORE, Tom, County Meath, Ireland, 1884/85-1955.

Tom Moore began his screen career about 1912, working at several studios including Kalem, Lubin, Selznick and Goldwyn. He specialized in the rugged but romantic hero and starred in numerous films of the '20s. He did not make a strong transition to talkies and left the screen in the mid-1930s but returned about ten years later to appear in several supporting roles. In the interim his talents were put to use as a drama coach with 20th Century–Fox. He was the brother of Owen Moore (q.v.) and Matt Moore (q.v.).

PUBLISHED SOURCES
• *Books – General: Famous Film Folk; Who's Who on the Screen.* **Credits:** *Filmarama* (v. I and II); *Forty Years of Screen Credits; Twenty Years of Silents; Who Was Who on Screen.* **Encyclopedic Works:** *Film Encyclopedia; Filmlexicon degli Autori e delle Opere; Halliwell's Filmgoer's Companion; The Movie Makers; The Picturegoer's Who's Who and Encyclopedia of the Screen To-day; Who's Who in Hollywood; The World Film Encyclopedia.* **Pictorial:** *Silent Portraits.*
• *Periodicals* – The following periodical articles are in addiiton to those included in the library listings below: *Photoplay* (May 1915, Aug. 1915, Apr. 1916, Dec. 1918, May 1921, Oct. 1925); *Motion Picture Supplement* (Oct. 1915); *Motion Picture Classic* (Feb. 1920); *Motion Picture Magazine* (Dec. 1920, July 1922); *Newsweek* (Feb. 21, 1955); *Classic Images* (May 1988).

ARCHIVAL MATERIALS
• *Clipping File* – CAA: Film appearance (1952); marriage (1921); obituary (1955). NYMA (also in Photoplay Collection): Periodical article: *Classic Film Collector* (July 1978); *Classic Images* (Mar. 1988). NYPL (also in Locke Collection) (also in C. &. L. Brown Collection): Newsphotos; comeback (1933); film review (1910s, 1920s); stage appearance (1923); injury; article (1930); obituary (1955). TXU: Obituary (1955).
• *Other Clipping File* – CAFI, CAUT, GBBF, MAH, MIDL, OHCL, PAPL,

WICF. • *Correspondence* – NYPL: Letters (C. & L. Brown Collection) (1930s–40s); other (1952). • *Legal File* – CAA (Sennett Collection): Contract (1933). CAUW: Talent agreement (1920s). • *Photograph/Still* – CAA (also in Hollywood Studio Museum Collection) (also in MGM Collection), CAUT (Jessen Collection), CAUU, DCG (Quigley Photographic Archives), GBBF, MIDL, NJFL, NJPT, NYAM, NYB (Bettmann/UPI Collection), NYCU (Dramatic Museum Portraits), NYEH, NYPL, NYSU, OHCL, PAPL, TXSM, TXU (A. Davis Collection), WICF. • *Press Kit* – OHCL. • *Scrapbook* – NYPL (also in R. Locke Collection) (also in C. & L. Brown Collection). • *Studio Biography* – CAA: Goldwyn (1920s?). NYMA: Photoplay.

MORAN, Lois (Lois Darlington Dowling), Pittsburgh, PA, 1908/09–1990.
Lois Moran appeared in two French films before being signed by Sam Goldwyn for his prestigious production of *Stella Dallas* in 1925. It was a major success but, although she made more than 30 films, it proved to be the only memorable one. The remainder of her career was spent in minor efforts through 1931 but she found success in the hit Broadway musical *Of Thee I Sing* and its sequel, *Let 'Em Eat Cake.*

PUBLISHED SOURCES
• *Books – General: Broken Silence.* **Credits:** *Filmarama* (v. II); *Forty Years of Screen Credits; Twenty Years of Silents.* **Encyclopedic Works:** *Film Encyclopedia; Filmlexicon degli Autori e delle Opere; The Picturegoer's Who's Who and Encyclopedia of the Screen To-day; Who Was Who in the Theatre; Who's Who in Hollywood; The World Film Encyclopedia.* **Nostalgia:** *Whatever Became of...* (10th). **Pictorial:** *Silent Portraits; They Had Faces Then.* **Factoids:** *Star Stats.*
• *Periodicals* – The following periodical articles are in addition to those included in the library listings below:

Photoplay (June 1926, Aug. 1927); Theatre (Jan. 1927); Motion Picture Magazine (Nov. 1927, Sept. 1929, Aug. 1930, Mar. 1931, Mar. 1932); Motion Picture Classic (Jan. 1928, Mar. 1929); Screen Mirror (Nov. 1930); Collier's (Dec. 24, 1932); Harper's Magazine (Sept. 1952); Hollywood Studio Magazine (Sept. 1989); Classic Images (Sept. 1990); Skoop (Sept. 1990).

ARCHIVAL MATERIALS
• Clipping File—CAA: Newsphotos; film appearance (1925); stage appearance (1931); marriage (1935); nostalgia (1969, 1971, 1976, 1980-81). Periodical article: Collier's (Dec. 24, 1932). CAFI: Periodical article: Screenland (1926 or 1927). CAUT: Periodical article: Motion Picture Magazine (1929). NYMA (also in Photoplay Collection): Obituary (1990). Periodical article: Classic Images (Dec. 1988). NYMN: Newsphotos; marriage (1935); article (1931, undated); obituary (1990). NYPL: Article (1926, 1930-32, 1952, undated); newsphotos; marriage (1935); film appearance (1926); stage appearance (1933); obituary (1990). PAPT: Article (1931). • Other Clipping File— CAUB, GBBF, MAH, MIDL, OHCL, PAPL, WICF. • Correspondence— CAA (Hedda Hopper Collection): 2 letters (not from LM) about LM's volunteer work (1950, 1963). • Filmography— CAA. • Legal File—CAUW: Talent agreement (1929). • Photograph/Still— CAA (also in Hollywood Studio Museum Collection) (also in MGM Collection), CAH, CAUT (Jessen Collection) (Portrait File), CAUU, CNDA, DCG (Quigley Photographic Archives), GBBF, NJPT, NYAM, NYB (Underwood Collection), NYCU (Dramatic Museum Portraits), NYEH, NYMN, NYPL, NYSU, OHCL, PAPL, TXU (A. Davis Collection), WICF. • Reminiscence—MISU. • Scrapbook—NYMA, NYPL.

MORENO, Antonio (Antonio Garido or Garrido Montea-gudo), Madrid, Spain, 1887/88-1967.
Long before he became another of

the "Latin lovers" in the wake of Rudolph Valentino, Antonio Moreno appeared in numerous serials and features, including those of D.W. Griffith. Onscreen since 1912, the 1920s found him at the peak of his career, costarring with such actresses as Greta Garbo, Alice Terry, Gloria Swanson, Pola Negri and Marion Davies. In the 1930s, limited by his accent, he made Spanish versions of American talkies and then played supporting roles until the 1950s.

PUBLISHED SOURCES
• Books—General: The Big V; Eighty Silent Film Stars; Famous Film Folk; Gentlemen to the Rescue; More from Hollywood; The Truth About the Movies; Who's Who on the Screen. Credits: Filmarama (v. I and II); Forty Years of Screen Credits; Twenty Years of Silents; Who Was Who on Screen. Encyclopedic Works: Film Encyclopedia; Filmlexicon degli Autori e delle Opere; Halliwell's Filmgoer's Companion; The Illustrated Who's Who of the Cinema; The Movie Makers; The Picturegoer's Who's Who and Encyclopedia of the Screen To-day; Quinlan's Illustrated Registry of Film Stars; Who's Who in Hollywood; The World Almanac Who's Who of Film; The World Film Encyclopedia. Pictorial: Silent Portraits. Factoids: Star Stats.
• Periodicals—The following periodical articles are in addition to those included in the library listings below: Motion Picture Magazine (Oct. 1916, July 1917, Dec. 1917, Dec. 1919, Feb. 1921, June 1922, Nov. 1922, July 1923, Nov. 1924, Apr. 1925); Photoplay (Aug. 1917, May 1921, Mar. 1922, Mar. 1924, July 1926, Sept. 1926, Nov. 1926); Motion Picture Classic (Apr. 1918, Oct. 1918, Aug. 1921, Nov. 1922, May 1923, May 1924, May 1930); Picture Play Magazine (Jan. 1920, Sept. 1920); Theatre (Sept. 1925, Nov. 1926); Classic Film Collector (Winter/Spring 1967); Films in Review (Aug.-Nov. 1967).

ARCHIVAL MATERIALS
• Clipping File—CAA: Estate (1933-

34, 1964–65, 1967); home (1953, 1955); film appearance (1921–24); wife's death (1933); legal problem (1936); marriage (1922–23); illness (1965); article (1941, 1947, 1949); obituary (1967). CAUT: Estate (1967); obituary (1967). NYMA (also in Photoplay Collection): Obituary (1967). Periodical articles: *Classic Images* (Jan. 1982, May–June 1990). NYMN: Death of wife (1933); newsphotos. NYPL (also in Locke Collection): Newsphotos (numerous); article (1923, 1926, undated); film review (1920s, 1930s, 1940s); death of wife (1933); separation (1933); comeback (1938, 1941); obituary (1967). Periodical articles: *Movie Weekly* (Nov. 1, 1924, undated); *Cine-Mundial* (July 1930); *Films in Review* (June–July 1967) (filmography). • *Other Clipping File* — AZSU (Jimmy Starr Collection), CNDA, GBBF, MAH, MIDL, OHCL, PAPL, WICF. • *Correspondence* — NYMA (Photoplay Collection). NYPL (C. & L. Brown Collection): 1936. • *Filmography* — CAA, NYMA. • *Legal File* — CAA (Vertical File Collection): Contract (Vitagraph, Goldwyn, Famous Players-Lasky, MGM, Monogram) (1916–1938). CAUW: Personnel, payroll record (1932–50); talent agreement (1928, 1930); contract (1929, 1932); agreement (1932–33). • *Photograph/ Still* — AZSU (Jimmy Starr Collection), CAA (also in Hollywood Studio Museum Collection) (also in MGM Collection), CAUT (Jessen Collection), CAUU, CNDA, DCG (Quigley Photographic Archives), GBBF, NJPT, NYAM, NYB (Underwood Collection), NYCU (Dramatic Museum Portraits), NYEH, NYMN, NYPL, OHCL, TXU, WICF. • *Publicity Release* — CAA: Universal (1950s). • *Scrapbook* — NYPL (also in C. & L. Brown Collection) (also in Locke Collection). • *Studio Biography* — CAA: MGM (late 1920s). NYMA: Photoplay.

MULHALL, Jack, Wappingers Falls, NY, 1887/90–1977.

The breezy hero of many silents, Jack Mulhall appeared in well over 100 films, many with Dorothy Mackaill (q.v.). His career began in the mid-1910s and continued well into the 1950s. Before segueing into character roles in the 1930s, he was seen in such films as *Within the Law*, *The Call of the Wild*, *Orchids and Ermine* and *The Mad Whirl*. An interesting early talkie was *Dark Streets*; others included *Mississippi*, *Beloved Enemy* and *Cheers for Miss Bishop*. He also appeared in many sound serials.

PUBLISHED SOURCES

• *Books* — Bibliography: *The Idols of Silence*. General: *Blue Book of the Screen*; *Eighty Silent Film Stars*; *Famous Film Folk*; *How I Broke Into the Movies*; *Who's Who on the Screen*. Credits: *Filmarama* (v. I and II); *Forty Years of Screen Credits*; *Twenty Years of Silents*. Encyclopedic Works: *Film Encyclopedia*; *Filmlexicon degli Autori e delle Opere*; *Halliwell's Filmgoer's Companion*; *The Movie Makers*; *The Picturegoer's Who's Who and Encyclopedia of the Screen To-day*; *Who's Who in Hollywood*; *The World Almanac Who's Who of Film*; *The World Film Encyclopedia*. Nostalgia: *Whatever Became of...* (4th). Pictorial: *Silent Portraits*.
• *Periodicals* — The following periodical articles are in addition to those included in the library listings below: *Moving Picture Weekly* (Apr. 7, 1915); *Picture Show* (Jan. 10, 1920); *Photoplay* (Feb. 1920, Nov. 1928, Nov. 1930); *Motion Picture Magazine* (July 1920, June 1921, Apr. 1922, Dec. 1927, Aug. 1928); *Architecture & Buildings* (June 1928); *Motion Picture Classic* (Nov. 1930); *Classic Film Collector* (Winter 1977).

ARCHIVAL MATERIALS

• *Clipping File* — CAA: Newsphotos; article (1926, 1937, 1950, 1971); nostalgia (1961, 1968); illness (1965); obituary (1979). CAFI: Obituary (1979). CAUT: Property (1929); First National contract (1929); legal problem (1929); illness (1960); obituary (1979). CAUU: Obituary (1979). NYMA (also in Photoplay Collection): 90th birthday (1977); obituary (1979). Periodical articles: *Classic Images* (Mar. 1985, Oct.–Nov. 1991). NYMN: Newsphotos. NYPL (also in

Locke Collection): Film appearance (1920s); newsphotos; legal problem (1933); film appearance (1920s, 1930s); bankruptcy (1935); article (1939, 1959, undated); nostalgia (1948?); obituary (1979). Periodical article: *Screenland* (undated). • *Other Clipping File* – AZSU (Jimmy Starr Collection), GBBF, MAH, MIDL, OHCL, PAPL, WICF. • *Correspondence* – CAUU (A. Slide Collection). NYPL (C. & L. Brown Collection): 1954. • *Filmography* – CAA. • *Interview* – CAUU (Hollywood Studio Museum Collection): 1964. NYAM. • *Legal File* – CAA (Sennett Collection): Contract (1921). CAUW: Loanout (1926–30); payroll record (1926–30); option (1926–30); agreement (1928); letter (1926, 1930); talent agreement (1926–29); communication (1926–30). • *Oral History* – NYCO: Mentioned in: Albert Hackett interview. • *Photograph/Still* – AZSU (Jimmy Starr Collection), CAA (also in Hollywood Studio Museum Collection), CAUT (Jessen Collection) (Portrait File), CAUU (also in A. Slide Collection), CNDA, DCG (Quigley Photographic Archives), GBBF, NJPT, NYAM, NYB (Underwood Collection), NYCU (Palmer Collection), NYEH, NYMN, NYPL, NYSU, OHCL, TXU, WICF. • *Scrapbook* – NJPT (Yeandle Collection), NYPL. • *Studio Biography* – CAA: RKO (1936, 1938). NYMA: Photoplay.

MURRAY, Charlie, Laurel, IN, 1872–1941.

Charlie Murray had the "map of Ireland" on his face and thus convincingly played Kelly in the long-running *Cohens and Kellys* series, as well as other Irish characters. Originally part of the popular Murray and Mack vaudeville team, he began at Biograph, went to Keystone with Sennett and eventually became a character comedian in features while continuing his work in shorts. Among his films were *Irene*, *The Gorilla*, *Lilies of the Field*, *The Girl in the Limousine* and *The Life of Riley*. His appearances continued during the 1930s.

PUBLISHED SOURCES

• *Books* – General: *Character People*; *Clown Princes and Court Jesters*; *Kops and Custards*; *Life Stories of the Movie Stars*; *Mack Sennett's Keystone*; *The Truth About the Movies*; *Who's Who in the Film World*. Credits: *Filmarama* (v. I and II); *Forty Years of Screen Credits*; *Twenty Years of Silents*; *Who Was Who on Screen*. Encyclopedic Works: *Film Encyclopedia*; *Halliwell's Filmgoer's Companion*; *The Picturegoer's Who's Who and Encyclopedia of the Screen To-day*; *Quinlan's Illustrated Directory of Film Comedy Actors* (with George Sidney); *Who's Who in Hollywood*. Pictorial: *Silent Portraits*. Factoids: *Star Stats*.

• *Periodicals* – The following periodical articles are in addition to those included in the library listings below: *Photoplay* (Feb. 1915, Oct. 1917, Oct. 1927); *Motion Picture Magazine* (Feb. 1928); *Classic Film/Video Images* (May 1981).

ARCHIVAL MATERIALS

• *Clipping File* – CAA: Obituary (1941). CASF: Hats (1928). NYMA (also in Photoplay Collection): Obituary (1941). Periodical articles: *Classic Images* (Aug.–Sept. 1989). NYPL (also in Locke Collection) (also under Murray and Mack): Newsphotos; biography (1932); film review (1920s); obituary (1941). • *Other Clipping File* – GBBF, MAH, MIDL, OHCL, PAPL, WICF. • *Legal File* – CAA (Sennett Collection): Talent agreement (1917); option (1918); contract (1919–20). CAUW: Letter, memo (1925–28); contract (1925–26); contract summary (1925–28); payroll record (1925–28); option (1926–27); agreement (1927); loanout (1926); talent agreement (1925–27). • *Oral History* – NYCO: Mentioned in the following interviews: Albert Hackett, Harold Lloyd. • *Photograph/Still* – CAA (also in Hollywood Studio Museum Collection) (also in Jules White Collection), CAUT (Jessen Collection), CAUU, DCG (Quigley Photographic Archives), NYB (Underwood Collection), NYPL, NYSU, OHCL, TXU, WICF. • *Program* – CAHL: Vaudeville appearance (as part of Murray and Mack) (1899, 1902, undated). • *Scrapbook* – NYPL (under Murray and Mack). • *Studio Biography* – CAA (also in Mack Sennett Collection): Goldwyn (1920s?).

MURRAY, James, The Bronx, NY, 1901-1936.

If it were not for his performance in King Vidor's MGM classic *The Crowd* (1928), James Murray would be as anonymous today as was his character in that film. His later movies were undistinguished, except possibly for *Rose Marie*, and his prior career was largely as an extra. He was the leading man in several low-grade melodramas (e.g., *High Gear*) in the early 1930s but his career had sputtered out by 1935.

PUBLISHED SOURCES

• *Books* – **General:** *Hollywood Heaven.* **Credits:** *Filmarama* (v. II); *Forty Years of Screen Credits*; *Twenty Years of Silents*; *Who Was Who on Screen.* **Encyclopedic Works:** *Film Encyclopedia*; *Filmlexicon degli Autori e delle Opere*; *Halliwell's Filmgoer's Companion*; *The Movie Makers*; *The Picturegoer's Who's Who and Encyclopedia of the Screen To-day*; *Who's Who in Hollywood.* • *Periodicals* – *Photoplay* (Mar. 1927); *Motion Picture Classic* (Apr. 1927, Dec. 1929); *Motion Picture Magazine* (Jan. 1928); *Movie Classic* (Feb. 1933); *Films in Review* (Dec. 1968, Mar. 1969); *Positif* (Dec. 1977–Jan. 1978).

ARCHIVAL MATERIALS

• *Clipping File* – CAA: Film appearance (1927). NYMA (also in Photoplay Collection): Personal data summary. • *Other Clipping File* – CNDA, GBBF, MIDL, PAPL, WICF. • *Correspondence* – NYPL (C. & L. Brown Collection): 1936. • *Filmography* – NYMA. • *Legal File* – CAUW: Contract (1929); talent agreement (1928, 1932). • *Photograph/Still* – CAA (also in Hollywood Studio Museum Collection) (also in MGM Collection), DCG (Quigley Photographic Archives), GBBF, NJPT, NYB (Underwood Collection), NYEH,

NYPL, NYSU, OHCL, TXU, WICF. • *Scrapbook* – NJPT (Yeandle Collection), NYPL.

MURRAY, Mae (Adrienne Koenig), Portsmouth, VA, 1886/90-1965.

In some ways a stereotypical silent star, Mae Murray projected an eccentric image which eventually finished her career. A former dancer and Follies showgirl, she entered films in 1916 and made a modest success in her early roles in such films as *Sweet Kitty Bellairs*, *The Mormon Maid*, *Virtuous Sinners* and *Idols of Clay*. She gained further popularity in the 1920s with *Peacock Alley*, *Circe the Enchantress* and especially *The Merry Widow* (1925). This was the apex of her career, however, and after a trio of unsuccessful talkies (1930-31), she was gone from the screen.

PUBLISHED SOURCES

• *Books* – **Bibliography:** *The Idols of Silence.* **General:** *Behind the Screen*; *Blue Book of the Screen*; *Classics of the Silent Screen*; *Famous Film Folk*; *Hollywood Album 2*; *Hollywood Hall of Fame*; *Immortals of the Screen*; *Intimate Talks with Movie Stars*; *Ladies in Distress*; *The MGM Girls*; *Movie Star*; *The Movie Stars Story*; *Sex Goddesses of the Silent Screen*; *The Stars* (Schickel); *The Truth About the Movies*; *Who's Who on the Screen.* **Credits:** *Filmarama* (v. I and II); *Forty Years of Screen Credits*; *Twenty Years of Silents*; *Who Was Who on Screen.* **Encyclopedic Works:** *The Complete Encyclopedia of Popular Music and Jazz*; *Film Encyclopedia*; *Filmlexicon degli Autori e delle Opere*; *Halliwell's Filmgoer's Companion*; *The Illustrated Encyclopedia of the World's Great Movie Stars and Their Films*; *The Illustrated Who's Who of the Cinema*; *The Movie Makers*; *The Oxford Companion to Film*; *The Picturegoer's Who's Who and Encyclopedia of the Screen To-day*; *Who's Who in Hollywood*; *The World Almanac Who's Who of Film*; *The*

World Film Encyclopedia. **Nostalgia:** *Whatever Became of...* (9th). **Biography/Autobiography:** *The Self-Enchanted.* **Pictorial:** *The Image Makers*; *Leading Ladies*; *Silent Portraits*; *They Had Faces Then.*
• *Periodicals* – The following periodical articles are in addition to those included in the library listings below: *Photoplay* (Oct. 1916, Mar. 1917, Aug. 1920, Aug. 1921, Jan. 1922, Sept. 1923, July 1924, Oct. 1924, Sept. 1925, Nov. 1925, Nov. 1926); *Motion Picture Magazine* (Mar. 1917, Aug. 1917, Jan. 1918, Sept. 1922, July 1923, Oct. 1924, Sept.-Oct. 1925); *Motion Picture Classic* (June 1917, Feb. 1919, Nov. 1921); *Moving Picture Weekly* (Sept. 8, 1917); *Theatre* (June 1919); *Shadowland* (Mar. 1921); *8mm Collector* (May 1964); *Time* (Apr. 2, 1965); *Newsweek* (Apr. 5, 1965); *Filmograph* (no. 1-3, 1970); *Films in Review* (Dec. 1975, Jan. 1976, Mar. 1976); *Cine Revue* (Sept. 8, 1977); *American Film* (July–Aug. 1981).

ARCHIVAL MATERIALS
• *Clipping File* – CAA: Film appearance (1922-23, 1929); newsphotos; marriage/divorce/children (1925-28, 1931, 1933, 1961); article (1922, 1924-25, 1938, 1956, 1964, undated); bankruptcy (1924, 1946); legal problem (1926-30, 1932-33); home (1928, 1931); robbery (1931); stage appearance (1935, 1941, 1950); lecture brochure (1945); illness (1960, 1964); biography (1959-60); obituary (1965). Periodical articles: *Picture Play* (1923); *Movie Weekly* (1923); *Liberty* (Sept. 1938); *Films in Review* (Feb. 1979). CAFI: Lecture brochure (1945/46). CAUT: Newsphotos; comeback (1947); marriage (1961). Periodical article: *Motion Picture Magazine* (Dec. 1928). CAUU: Film festival (undated). NYMA: Illness (1960); article (1924, 1964); newsphotos; obituary (1965). NYMN: Newsphotos; taken into shelter (1964); article (1934, 1941, 1956); illness (1960); nostalgia; legal problem (1934); bankruptcy (1934); divorce/children (1933, 1940); home (1920s?); obituary (1965). NYPL (also in Locke Collection): PARTIAL CONTENTS: Marriage (1977); biog-

raphy (1942); newsphotos; taken into shelter (1964); obituary (1965). Periodical articles: *Movie Album* (no. 14, 1964); *Quirk's Review* (Dec. 1989). • *Other Clipping File* – AZSU (Jimmy Starr Collection), CNDA, GBBF, MAH, MIDL, OHCL, PAPL, WICF. • *Correspondence* – CAA: Few letters (Hedda Hopper Collection) (1947, undated); letters (Vertical File Collection) (1929-64). NYPL (C. & L. Brown Collection). • *Filmography* – NYMA. • *Oral History* – NYCO: Interviewed 1959. Also mentioned in the following interviews: William K. Everson, Otto Harbach. • *Photograph/Still* – CAA (also in Hollywood Studio Museum Collection) (also in MGM Collection), CALM, CAUT (Jessen Collection), CAUU, CNDA, DCG (Quigley Photographic Archives), GBBF, NJPT, NYAM, NYB (Bettmann/UPI Collection) (Springer Collection) (Underwood Collection), NYCU (Dramatic Museum Portraits), NYEH, NYMN, NYPL, NYSU, OHCL, TXU, WICF. • *Scrapbook* – NJPT (Yeandle Collection), NYPL (also in Locke Collection). • *Studio Biography* – CAA: MGM (1927).

MYERS, Carmel, San Francisco, CA, 1899/1901-1980.
Carmel Myers's first films were made in 1916 and she progressed to a steady stream of programmers for Fox and Universal with occasional nuggets like *Ben Hur, Sorrell and Son* and *Beau Brummell.* She is perhaps best remembered for donning a blonde wig and portraying the vamp in *Ben Hur.* *The Ghost Talks* in 1929 marked Carmel Myers's talkie debut and after about seven or eight more (including 1931's *Svengali*) her career virtually ended, except for a couple of supporting roles in the 1940s. In the 1970s she did a few television and film cameo roles.

PUBLISHED SOURCES
• *Books* – Wrote a book of pop psychology, *Don't Think About It* (1952). **General:** *Blue Book of the Screen*;

Famous Film Folk; The Kindergarten of the Movies; Return Engagement; Tribute to Mary Pickford; Who's Who on the Screen. **Credits:** Filmarama (v. I and II); Forty Years of Screen Credits; Twenty Years of Silents. **Encyclopedic Works:** Film Encyclopedia; Filmlexicon degli Autori e delle Opere; Halliwell's Filmgoer's Companion; The Movie Makers; The Picturegoer's Who's Who and Encyclopedia of the Screen To-day; Who's Who in Hollywood; The World Film Encyclopedia. **Nostalgia:** Whatever Became of... (11th). **Pictorial:** Silent Portraits; They Had Faces Then.

• Periodicals – The following periodical articles are in addition to those included in the library listings below: Motion Picture Magazine (Jan. 1918, Mar. 1921, Feb. 1922, July 1924, June 1925); Photoplay (June 1918, July 1920); Motion Picture Classic (Oct. 1918); Movie Classic (Apr. 1932); Show (Oct. 1962); Harper's Bazaar (July 1971); Cinématographique (Jan. 1981).

ARCHIVAL MATERIALS

• Clipping File – CAA: Film debut (1917); article (1916, 1925, 1951–52, 1958, 1968, 1971, 1974–76, 1990); TV appearance (1975); invention (1951); marriage (1951); newsphotos; film festival (1976); interviews (1976–77); introduces perfume (1978); nostalgia (1968, 1971); obituary (1980). Article: Films in Review (March 1980). CAUT: Article (1968, 1970s, 1974, 1976, 1980); marriage (1929); film appearance (1929?); obituary (1980). CAUU: Interview (1976); introduces perfume (1978); article (1974–76); obituary (1980). NYMA (also in Photoplay Collection): Interview (1977?); obituary (1980). Periodical articles: Photo-play World (Mar. 1918). NYPL (also in Locke Collection): Engagement/marriage/divorce (1921–23, 1933); film appearance; stage appearance (1933); robbery (1932); TV role (1951); earns patent; legal problem (1926); perfume business (1959); newsphotos (numerous); article (1946, 1950s, 1960s); nostalgia (1961–62); obituary (1980). Periodical articles: Theatre Magazine (Feb. 1929); Hollywood Reporter Anniversary Issue (1976). • Other

Clipping File – CASP, CAUT, CNDA, GBBF, MAH, MIDL, OHCL, PAPL, TXU, WICF. • Correspondence – CAA (Hedda Hopper Collection): 1960. NYMA (Photoplay Collection). NYPL: 1955, 1971. • Filmography – NYMA. • Interview – CAUU (Hollywood Studio Museum Collection) (R. Lamparski Collection). • Legal File – CAUW: Talent agreement (1929–30); personnel, payroll record (1944). • Oral History – NYCO: Mentioned in: Irving Rapper interview. • Photograph/Still – CAA (also in Hollywood Studio Museum Collection), CAH, CAHL, CASP, CASU, CAUT (Jessen Collection), CNDA, DCG (Quigley Photographic Archives), GBBF, NJPT, NYB (Underwood Collection), NYCU (Bulliet Collection), NYEH, NYMN, NYPL, NYSU, OHCL, PAPL, TXU (A. Davis Collection), WICF. • Play Program – CAA: 1929. CAHL: 1933. • Privately Printed Material – CAA: The Silent Stars Speak. AMPAS, 1979. • Press Kit – AZSU (Jimmy Starr Collection): Republic Pictures. • Publicity Release – NYPL: MGM (1975). • Scrapbook – NYPL (also in R. Locke Collection). • Studio Biography – CAA: Goldwyn. NYMA: Photoplay.

NAGEL, Conrad, Keokuk, IA, 1897–1970.

Stage-trained Conrad Nagel was one of the busiest silent film actors during the transition to sound. Capitalizing on his sonorous voice, he made more than 30 films in just two years. Prior to the arrival of the talkies, he was a romantic leading man in numerous films from 1919, among them Three Weeks, Tess of the D'Urbervilles, Bella Donna, Pretty Ladies and two with Greta Garbo. Although his starring career was over by the mid-1930s he continued to appear in films and television through the 1950s. He was also a founder of the Academy of Motion Picture Arts and Sciences.

PUBLISHED SOURCES

• Books – A lecture given by CN in 1929 was included as part of Introduction to the Photoplay, 1929. **Bibliography:** The Idols of Silence. **General:** Blue Book of the Screen; Eighty Silent Film Stars; Famous Film Folk; First One Hundred Noted Men and Women of the Screen; Hollywood Album; How I Broke Into the Movies; Popular Men of the Screen; The Real Tinsel; What the Stars Told Me; Who's Who on the Screen. **Credits:** Filmarama (v. I and II); Forty Years of Screen Credits; Twenty Years of Silents; Who Was Who on Screen. **Encyclopedic Works:** The Biographical Encyclopaedia and Who's Who of the American Theatre; Film Encyclopedia; Filmlexicon degli Autori e delle Opere; Halliwell's Filmgoer's Companion; The Illustrated History of the Cinema; The Movie Makers; The Picturegoer's Who's Who and Encyclopedia of the Screen To-day; Quinlan's Illustrated Registry of Film Stars; Who Was Who in the Theatre; Who's Who in Hollywood; The World Almanac Who's Who of Film; The World Film Encyclopedia. **Pictorial:** Silent Portraits. **Recordings:** Hollywood on Record. **Factoids:** Star Stats.

• Periodicals — The following periodical articles are in addition to those included in the library listings below: Motion Picture Classic (Mar. 1919, Oct. 1920, Nov. 1921, June 1922); Motion Picture Magazine (Aug. 1919, Mar. 1921, Mar. 1922, Jan. 1926, Mar. 1927, Mar. 1928, Nov. 1928, Mar.-Apr. 1930, Feb. 1931, Mar. 1933); Picture Play (Aug. 1920); Photoplay (Feb. 1921, June 1924, Feb. 1927, Jan. 1929, Feb. 1933); Filmplay Journal (Sept. 1921); Silver Screen (Dec. 1930); Movie Classic (Feb. 1932); Ladies' Home Journal (Sept. 1932); Cue (July 9, 1949); Classic Film Collector (Winter 1970); Newsweek (Mar. 9, 1970); Time (Mar. 9, 1970).

OBSCURE PUBLISHED SOURCES
CAA: Life Story of Conrad Nagel.

ARCHIVAL MATERIALS
• Caricature — NYMN. • Clipping File — CAA: Nostalgia (1970); film appearance (1918, 1955, 1959); newsphotos; Equity meeting (1929); marriage/divorce (1934, 1945, 1947-48, 1955-56); stage appearance (1946, 1960); TV appearance (1949); honor (1990); obituary (1970). Periodical article: Films in Review (May 1979). CAUT: Obituary (1970). CAUU: Obituary (1970). NYMA: Obituary (1970). Periodical articles: Photoplay (June 1919); Reel 2 (Spring 1970); Classic Images (Nov. 1986). NYMN: Newsphotos; divorce (1934); stage appearance (1943); Actors' Equity (1929); obituary (1970). Periodical article: Photoplay (Sept. 1930). NYPL (also in Locke Collection): PARTIAL CONTENTS: Obituary (1970). • Other Clipping File — AZSU (Jimmy Starr Collection), CNDA, GBBF, MAH, MIDL, OHCL, PAPL, WICF. • Correspondence — CAA (Adolph Zukor Collection): 1933. CAHL: 1931-33. MABU (Kate Smith Collection): 1933. NYPL: Letters (C. & L. Brown Collection) (1922-48); others (1953, undated.) OHCL. • Filmography — CAA, CNDA. • Interview — CAUU (R. Lamparski Collection). • Legal File — CAUT (Twentieth Century-Fox Collection). Letter, memo (1928, 1930); loanout (1928, 1930). CAUW: Letter, memo (1927-31, 1936-39); payroll record (undated); contract (1931, 1936-37); agreement (1927); loanout (1929-30); document (1927); talent agreement (1927, 1931). NYPL (C. & L. Brown Collection): Contract (1944, 1948). • Oral History — NYCO: Interviewed in 1958. Also mentioned in the following interviews: Lila Lee, Myrna Loy, Blanche Sweet. • Photograph/Still — CAA (also in Hollywood Studio Museum Collection) (also in MGM Collection), CAFA, CALM, CASF, CAUS, CAUT (Jessen Collection), CAUU, CNDA, DCG (Quigley Photographic Archives), GBBF, MIDL, NJPT, NYB (Bettmann/UPI Collection) (Springer Collection), NYCU (Dramatic Museum Portraits) (Palmer Collection), NYEH, NYMN, NYPL, NYSU, OHCL, TXU, WICF. • Play Program — CAHL: 1946. • Scrapbook — NJPT (Yeandle Collection), NYMA, NYPL (also in Locke Collection), UTBY (DeMille Archives). • Studio Biography — CAA: MGM (1931); RKO (1933); Paramount (1940).

NALDI, Nita (Anita Dooley), New York, NY, 1899-1961.

One of the 1920s' greatest exponents of the "vamp," feline-ish Nita Naldi smoldered her way through films like *Blood and Sand, A Sainted Devil, Cobra,* and *Doctor Jekyll and Mr. Hyde* (her first film). She was rarely allowed to deviate from her unsympathetic screen persona and her career had dwindled away by the end of the decade. She later appeared on the stage.

PUBLISHED SOURCES

• *Books*—General: *Blue Book of the Screen; Famous Film Folk; Ladies in Distress.* Credits: *Filmarama* (v. I and II); *Twenty Years of Silents; Who Was Who on Screen.* Encyclopedic Works: *Film Encyclopedia; Filmlexicon degli Autori e delle Opere; Halliwell's Filmgoer's Companion; The Illustrated Who's Who of the Cinema; The Picturegoer's Who's Who and Encyclopedia of the Screen To-day; Who's Who in Hollywood; The World Almanac Who's Who of Film.* Pictorial: *Silent Portraits.* Factoids: *Star Stats.*

• *Periodicals*—The following periodical articles are in addition to that included in the library listings below: *Motion Picture Classic* (July 1921, Jan. 1923); *Photoplay* (July 1922, Apr. 1924, June 1924, Nov. 1924, Nov. 1925); *Metropolitan Magazine* (Nov. 1922); *Motion Picture Magazine* (Jan. 1923, Oct. 1924, Mar. 1925, Oct. 1925); *Theatre Arts* (Oct. 1952); *Time* (Feb. 24, 1961); *Newsweek* (Feb. 27, 1961).

ARCHIVAL MATERIALS

• *Caricature*—NYMN. • *Clipping File*—CAA: Newsphoto; Paramount contract (1922); article (1941, 1955); obituary (1961). NYMA: Career (1952); biography; obituary (1961). Periodical article: *Classic Images* (Dec. 1982). NYMN: Newsphotos (numerous); marriage; bankruptcy (1933); article (1937, 1940-41, 1952, 1959, undated); vamp image (1941, 1955); career (1941); stage appearance (1941, 1945, 1950); nostalgia (1936). NYPL (also in Locke Collection):

PARTIAL CONTENTS: Article; newsphotos; obituary (1961). • *Other Clipping File*—CNDA, GBBF, MAH, MIDL, OHCL, PAPL, WICF. • *Correspondence*—NYPL: 1931, 1945. • *Legal File*—NYMN: Business records, including tax returns and tax notices (1940s); contract (1933, 1950). • *Oral History*—NYCO: Interviewed in 1958. Also mentioned in: Lila Lee interview. • *Photograph/Still*—CAA (also in Hollywood Studio Museum Collection), CAOC (Kiesling Collection), CAUT (Jessen Collection) (Portrait File), CNDA, DCG (Quigley Photographic Archives), NJFL, NYAM, NYB (Bettmann/UPI Collection), NYCU (Dramatic Museum Portraits), NYEH, NYMN, NYPL, OHCL, WICF. • *Scrapbook*—NYPL, UTBY (DeMille Archive).

NAZIMOVA, Alla (Adelaide Leventon), Yalta, Russia, 1878/79-1945.

A famous stage actress by the time films beckoned, Alla Nazimova (sometimes billed as Nazimova) made a smashing debut with *War Brides* (1916). There were several more through the mid-1920s, including *The Red Lantern, Madame Peacock* and *The Redeeming Sin.* She is best known for the self-produced (and stylized to the point of being bizarre) film versions of *Salome* and *Camille.* Talkie roles came with *Escape* (1940) and then she played several more character parts up to the time of her death.

PUBLISHED SOURCES

• *Books*—Bibliography: *The Idols of Silence.* General: *The Civil War on the Screen and Other Essays; Classics of the Silent Screen; The Entertainers; Famous Film Folk; First One Hundred Noted Men and Women of the Screen; The Garden of Allah; Intimate Talks with Movie Stars; More from Hollywood; Movie Star; Who's Who on the Screen.* Credits: *Filmarama* (v. I and II); *Forty Years of Screen Credits; Twenty Years of Silents; Who Was Who on Screen.* Encyclopedic Works: *A Concise Encyclo-*

pedia of the Theatre; The Encyclopedia of World Theater; Famous Actors and Actresses on the American Stage; Film Encyclopedia; Filmlexicon degli Autori e delle Opere; Halliwell's Filmgoer's Companion; The Illustrated Encyclopedia of the World's Great Film Stars and Their Films; The Illustrated Who's Who of the Cinema; International Dictionary of Films and Filmmakers (v. 3); The International Encyclopedia of Film; The Movie Makers; National Cyclopaedia of American Biography (1950); Notable American Women, 1607–1950; Notable Women in the American Theatre; The Oxford Companion to Film; The Oxford Companion to the Theatre; The Picturegoer's Who's Who and Encyclopedia of the Screen To-day; Who Was Who in the Theatre; Who's Who in Hollywood; Who's Who on the Stage (1908); Women Who Make Movies; The World Almanac Who's Who of Film; The World Encyclopedia of the Film. **Filmography:** Hollywood on the Palisades. **Pictorial:** Great Stars of the American Stage; The Image Makers; The Revealing Eye; Silent Portraits. **Thesis:** A Descriptive Study of the Acting of Alla Nazimova. **Factoids:** Star Stats.

• *Periodicals* — The following periodical articles are in addition to those included in the library listings below: Critic (Apr. 1906); Current Literature (Jan. 1907, Dec. 1907); Theatre (Jan. 1907, Mar. 1907, Sept. 1907, May 1910, Dec. 1912, Mar. 1915, Mar. 1917, Nov. 1918, Apr. 1929); Harper's Weekly (Feb. 16, 1907, Apr. 20, 1907); Cosmopolitan (Apr. 1907, Nov. 1912); Nation (Apr. 18, 1907, Nov. 22, 1933, Nov. 28, 1936); Putnam's Magazine (Jan. 1908); Canadian Magazine (Mar. 1909); Collier's (May 7, 1910, Dec. 10, 1932); Munsey's Magazine (June 1910); Green Book Album (Mar. 1912); Green Book Magazine (Feb. 1916); Motion Picture Classic (July 1917, Sept. 1922, Nov. 1922, Nov. 1923); Photoplay (Mar. 1918, July 1918, Feb. 1920, Aug. 1921, Dec. 1921, Apr. 1922, Mar. 1923, Oct. 1926); New Republic (Apr. 20, 1918); Theatre Arts Magazine (May 1918); Motion Picture Magazine (July 1918, Oct. 1920, Jan. 1922); Picture Play

Magazine (Sept. 1920); American Magazine (Apr. 1922); New Republic (Jan. 24, 1923); National Magazine (July 1923); Pictures and Picturegoer (Jan. 1925); Theatre Guild Magazine (June 1930); Bookman (June/July 1932); Delineator (Apr. 1936); Commonweal (Nov. 27, 1936, Aug. 3, 1945); Newsweek (July 23, 1945); Catholic World (Oct. 1945); Equity (May 1959); Sight and Sound (Summer 1960); Film Comment (Nov.–Dec. 1972); Kino (Feb. 1979); Films in Review (June-Sept. 1985); Architectural Digest (Apr. 1990); Film Dope (Mar. 1991).

ARCHIVAL MATERIALS
• *Caricature* — NYMN, NYPL. • *Clipping File* — CAA: Biographical play (1982); Garden of Allah (1959); radio appearance (1941); film appearance (1921); newsphotos; obituary (1945). Periodical articles: Century Magazine (June 1907); Green Book Magazine (Mar. 1913); Sketch (June 22, 1927); Rob Wagner's Script (May 10, 1941); Quarterly Journal of Speech (Apr. 1959), MS (1981). CASF: Film appearance (1925). CAUT: Film appearance (1929); newsphotos; stage appearance (undated). Periodical articles: MS (Feb. 1974); Rob Wagner's Script (July 28, 1945). NYMA: Signs with Vitagraph; film appearance (1910s, 1920s, 1940); stage appearance (1920s, 1930, 1935–36); marriage/divorce (1925); career (1920, 1925, 1936); article (1923, 1925); signs with United Artists (1921); legal problem (1936); play review (1939); newsphotos. Periodical articles: Green Book Magazine (May 1915, undated); Motion Picture Magazine (1918?); Collier's (Dec. 10, 1932); Theatre Arts Magazine (Dec. 1936, Dec. 1949); Playbill (Nov. 1982); LC Information Bulletin (Apr. 6, 1992). NYMN: Legal problem (1936–37); article (1935, undated); returns to films (1940); newsphotos (numerous); stage appearance (1936). Periodical articles: Century Magazine (undated); Putnam's Monthly (Aug. 1907). NYPL (also in Locke Collection): PARTIAL CONTENTS: Article (undated); newsphotos; obituary (1945). Periodical article: Films in Review (Dec.

1972). • *Other Clipping File* – AZSU (Jimmy Starr Collection), DCLC (see Collection), GBBF, MAH, MIDL, OHCL, OHSU, PAPL, WICF. • *Collection* – DCLC: 175 letters exchanged between AN, her sister and niece (1906-43); numerous letters to and from Leona Scott, a friend (1930s-40s); audiotape interviews with family members and AN's secretary; playbills; photographs; rare published materials; clippings and other materials for Lucy Lewton's privately printed biography (see below); materials for a proposed biography by Harry Vineyard, including correspondence and materials covering AN's American career (1907-44); sketches; scrapbooks. • *Correspondence* – DCLC (see also Collection) (George Middleton Papers). MABU (Kate Smith Collection): Telegram (1933). NYCU (Belmont Collection): 1919, undated. NYPL: Letters (C. & L. Brown Collection) (1926-44); others (1917, undated). • *Filmography* – NYMA: Silents only, and stageography (incomplete). • *Interview* – DCLC (see Collection). • *Legal File* – CAUW: Personnel, payroll record (1943); contract (1924, 1943); document (1924); talent agreement (1924). • *Oral History* – NYCO: Mentioned in: Rouben Mamoulian interview. • *Photograph/Still* – CAA (also in Hollywood Studio Museum Collection) (also in MGM Collection), CALM, CAUS, CNDA, DCG (Quigley Photographic Archives), DCLC (see Collection), NJFL, NYAM, NYB (Bettmann/UPI Collection) (Springer Collection), NYCU (Bulliet Collection), NYEH, NYMN, NYPL, NYSU, OHCL, TXU, WICF. • *Play Program* – CAHL: 1909-10. CASF, DCLC (see Collection), NYCU (Dramatic Museum Portraits). NYPL: 1932, 1937. • *Privately Printed Material* – CAA: *Alla Nazimova, My Aunt: A Personal Memoir* (Lucy O. Lewton) (1988). (See Collection for research materials for this work.) • *Publicity Release* – CAA: Paramount (1938). NYMA: Unknown studio (1920s). • *Scrapbook* – CASU (Stark Collection), DCLC (see Collection), NYPL (also R. Locke Collection) (also Players Collection). • *Studio Biography* – CAA: Fox (1941).

NEGRI, Pola (Barbara Apollonia Chalupec or Chalupiec), Yanowa, Poland, 1894/99-1987.

Tempestuous was the word for Pola Negri, both off and onscreen. She played the role of star to the hilt; this contributed both to her great popularity and her ultimate decline. After a European film career she came to Hollywood in a blaze of publicity and appeared in a string of Paramount films including *Bella Donna, Passion, The Spanish Dancer, A Woman of the World* and *Hotel Imperial*. The appeal of her persona faded by the late 1920s and the coming of sound effectively finished her career. After one unsuccessful talkie, she returned to European films and, thereafter, had only two supporting roles in American films.

PUBLISHED SOURCES

• *Books* – **Bibliography:** *The Idols of Silence.* **General:** *Alice in Movieland; Behind the Screen; Blue Book of the Screen; Classics of the Silent Screen; Las Estrellas* (v. 8); *Famous Film Folk; The Great Movie Stars; History of the American Cinema* (v. 3); *The Hollywood Exiles; The Movie Stars Story; Popcorn Venus; Return Engagement; Sex Goddesses of the Silent Screen; Stardom; The Stars* (Schickel); *The Stars Appear; The Truth About the Movies; Venus in Hollywood; What the Stars Told Me; Wicked Women of the Screen.* **Credits:** *Filmarama* (v. I and II); *Forty Years of Screen Credits; Twenty Years of Silents.* **Encyclopedic Works:** *A Biographical Dictionary of Film; A Dictionary of the Cinema; Film Actors Guide: Western Europe; Film Encyclopedia; Filmlexicon degli Autori e delle Opere; Halliwell's Filmgoer's Companion; The Illustrated Encyclopedia of the World's Great Movie Stars and Their Films; The Illustrated Who's Who of the Cinema; International Dictionary of Films and Filmmakers* (v. 3); *The International Encyclopedia of Film; The Movie Makers; The Oxford Companion to Film; The*

Picturegoer's Who's Who and Encyclopedia of the Screen To-day; *Quinlan's Illustrated Registry of Film Stars*; *Who's Who in Hollywood*; *The World Almanac Who's Who of Film*; *The World Encyclopedia of the Film*; *The World Film Encyclopedia*. **Nostalgia:** *Whatever Became of . . .* (1st). **Pictorial:** *The Image Makers*; *Leading Ladies*; *Silent Portraits*; *They Had Faces Then*. **Biography/Autobiography:** *Memoirs of a Star*; *Polita*. **Thesis:** *The Film Career of Pola Negri, 1914-1964*. **Recordings:** *Hollywood on Record*. **Factoids:** *Star Stats*.

• *Periodicals* — The following periodical articles are in addition to those included in the library listings below: *Motion Picture Classic* (Feb. 1921, Oct. 1922); *Shadowland* (Feb. 1922); *Photoplay* (May 1922, Nov. 1922, Jan. 1923, Mar. 1923, Nov. 1923, Jan.-Apr. 1924, June-July 1924, Nov. 1924, Feb. 1925, Jan. 1926, Apr.-May 1926, July 1926, Dec. 1928, Jan. 1932); *Filmplay Journal* (June 1922); *Exceptional Photoplays* (Apr. 1923); *Motion Picture Director* (Mar. 1926); *Vanity Fair* (Aug. 1926); *Pictures and Picturegoer* (Mar. 1931); *Motion Picture Magazine* (Aug. 1931); *True Story Magazine* (Apr. 1934); *Delineator* (May 1936); *American Magazine* (June 1944); *Films in Review* (Mar. 1964); *Players Showcase* (Fall 1965); *Screen Facts* (no. 15, 1967); *Newsweek* (Apr. 20, 1970, Aug. 17, 1987); *Cine Revue* (Aug. 29, 1974, Aug. 13, 1987); *Take One* (Sept. 1978); *Classic Film/Video Images* (Nov. 1981); *Film* (Poland) (Sept. 9, 1984); *Hollywood Studio Magazine* (Nov. 1984); *Classic Images* (May 1986, Sept. 1987, Aug. 1989); *Time* (Aug. 17, 1987); *EPD Film* (Sept. 1987); *Films and Filming* (Sept. 1987); *Revue du Cinéma* (Oct. 1987); *Griffithiana* (Oct. 1990).

ARCHIVAL MATERIALS
• *Caricature* — NYPL. • *Clipping File* — CAA: Article (1920-21, 1927, 1941-43, 1949, 1954, 1966, 1970, 1976, 1984); newsphotos; draft article by PN (1923, 1925); film appearance (1924, 1932-33, 1935, 1943, 1959, 1963-64); review of

Memoirs of a Star (1970); honor (1972, 1975, 1977); extortion plot (1925); legal problem (1925-30, 1932, 1944, 1951-52); interview (1924, 1926); romance with Valentino (1926-27); marriage/divorce (1927-32); illness (1927, 1931-32); injury (1928); draft autobiography (1920s); comeback (1931); citizenship (1941, 1951); nostalgia (1959, 1963, 1969-70, 1972); obituary (1987). Periodical articles: *Motion Picture Magazine* (1922); *Time* (July 26, 1943); *Town and Country* (Nov. 1950); *Films in Review* (Dec. 1961); *New Yorker* (Jan. 11, 1964); *Hollywood Studio Magazine* (May 1973). CAFI: Newsphotos; article (1967, 1976, 1985, undated); nostalgia (1970); obituary (1987). Periodical articles: *MD* (Feb. 1966); *Take One* (Sept. 1978). CAUT: Article (1973-74, 1976); film appearance (1964); honor (1977). Periodical article: *Picture Play* (Mar. 1923). CAUU: Obituary (1987). NYMA: Article (1970); newsphotos; review of *Memoirs of a Star* (1970); obituary (1987). Periodical articles: *Theatre Magazine* (June 1927); *Time* (July 26, 1943); *Town and Country* (Nov. 1950). NYMN: Debt (1940s?); article (1937, 1970); relationship with Hitler (1937); newsphotos; marriage (1935); stage appearance (1936); film appearance (1935, 1959). NYPL: PARTIAL CONTENTS: Article (1970, 1974, 1977, 1987); newsphotos; obituary (1987). • *Other Clipping File* — AZSU (Jimmy Starr Collection), CAUB, CNDA, GBBF, MAH, MIDL, OHCL, PAPL, WICF. • *Correspondence* — CAA (Adolph Zukor Collection): 1922-23. NYPL: Letters (C. & L. Brown Collection) (1940s-1950s); letters (Herman Weinberg Collection) (1970, 1977). • *Filmography* — CAA: 1914-43. • *Legal File* — CAUW: Advertisement (1923-24). • *Manuscript* — NYMA: *Pola Negri: Bromberg-Hollywood* (Douglas Howard). Deutsche Bearbeitung von Hans Lefebre. A mimeographed work in German (possibly a translation of English-language articles about PN?). • *Oral History* — NYCO: Mentioned in the following interviews: David Selznick, Carl Van Vechten. • *Photograph/Still* — CAA (also in Hollywood Studio Museum Collection),

CALM, CAUB, CAUT (Jessen Collection), CAUU, CNDA, DCG (Quigley Photographic Archives), NYAM, NYB (Bettmann/UPI Collection) (Penguin Collection) (Springer Collection), NYCU (Dramatic Museum Portraits) (Palmer Collection), NYEH, NYMN, NYPL, NYSU, OHCL, TXSM, TXU, WICF. • *Press Kit*—OHCL. • *Publicity Release*—AZSU (Jimmy Starr Collection). CAA: Paramount (1920s, 1927); Disney (1963–64). • *Recording*—MISU: Pola Negri sings "Paradise," a song from her film *A Woman Commands* (1932). • *Scrapbook*—NYPL. • *Studio Biography*—CAA: Paramount (1926); unknown studio (1943).

NILSSON, Anna Q(uerentia), Ystad, Sweden, 1888/90–1974.

Fated to be remembered as one of the "Waxworks" in Billy Wilder's *Sunset Boulevard*, lovely blonde Anna Q. Nilsson was a popular actress from the time of her debut in 1911. She made many films through the late 1920s, including *Ponjola*, *Sorrell and Son*, *The Lotus Eaters*, *The Whip*, *Adam's Rib* and *Souls for Sale*. An accident ended her silent career and the advent of talkies limited her to supporting roles thereafter.

PUBLISHED SOURCES

• *Books*—Bibliography: *The Idols of Silence*. General: *Blue Book of the Screen*; *Famous Film Folk*; *Strangers in Hollywood*; *The Truth About the Movies*; *Who's Who on the Screen*. Credits: *Filmarama* (v. I and II); *Forty Years of Screen Credits*; *Twenty Years of Silents*; *Who Was Who on Screen*. Encyclopedic Works: *Film Encyclopedia*; *Filmlexicon degli Autori e delle Opere*; *Halliwell's Filmgoer's Companion*; *The Illustrated Who's Who of the Cinema*; *The Movie Makers*; *The Picturegoer's Who's Who and Encyclopedia of the Screen To-day*; *Who's Who in Hollywood*; *The World Almanac Who's Who of Film*. Nostalgia: *Whatever Became*

of... (3rd). Pictorial: *The Image Makers*; *Silent Portraits*.

• *Periodicals*—The following periodical articles are in addition to those included in the library listings below: *Motion Picture Magazine* (May 1915, Sept. 1919, June 1920, Nov. 1920, Aug. 1921, Oct. 1922, May 1923, Mar. 1925, May 1925, Jan. 1927, Nov. 1927); *Motion Picture Supplement* (Nov. 1915); *Motion Picture Classic* (Apr. 1917, Mar. 1929); *Photoplay* (Aug. 1919, Nov. 1920, July 1924, Mar. 1925, July 1926, May 1930, Oct. 1930); *Filmplay Journal* (Sept. 1921); *Movie Classic* (Nov. 1931); *Classic Film Collector* (Spring 1974); *Films in Review* (Feb. 1976, Apr.–May 1976), *Classic Images* (Nov. 1981).

ARCHIVAL MATERIALS

• *Clipping File*—CAA: Joins Kalem (1910s?); nostalgia (1968, 1971); film appearance (1924, 1941, 1947); newsphotos; legal problem (1949); interview (1953); obituary (1974). CAUT: Obituary (1974). CAUU: Obituary (1974). NYMA (also in Photoplay Collection): Obituary (1974). NYPL: Newsphotos (numerous); article (1913, 1930s?); comeback (1930s); stage appearance (1933); film review (1920s); film appearance (1910s, 1920s); obituary (1974). Periodical articles: *Photoplay* (Mar. 1915); *Vanity Fair* (Sept. 1926). • *Other Clipping File*—AZSU (Jimmy Starr Collection), GBBF, MAH, MIDL, OHCL, PAPL, WICF. • *Correspondence*—NYMA (Photoplay Collection), NYCU (Palmer Collection). • *Filmography*—NYPL (incomplete). • *Interview*—CAUU (R. Lamparski Collection). • *Legal File*—CAUW: Letter, memo (1927); contract (1925); agreement (1925–27); payroll record (1927); talent agreement (1925, 1927–28, 1933). • *Photograph/Still*—CAA (also in Hollywood Studio Museum Collection), CALM, CASF, CAUT (Jessen Collection), CAUU, DCG (Quigley Photographic Archives), IAU (Junkin Collection), NYAM, NYB (Bettmann/UPI Collection), NYCU (Bulliet Collection) (Dramatic Museum Portraits), NYEH, NYPL, NYSU, OHCL, TXU, WICF. • *Scrapbook*—NYPL (also in R. Locke Collection). • *Studio Biography* — CAA: Goldwyn (1920s). NYMA: Photoplay.

NIXON, Marion (sometimes Marian), Superior, WI, 1904/06–1983.

Elfin Marion Nixon did bits and appeared in two-reelers from about 1922 and had her first lead in Tom Mix's *Riders of the Purple Sage* in 1925. From there on it was a series of generally unremarkable pictures. When sound arrived, she made the transition with *Geraldine* (1929) and then made more than 40 more films, many in supporting roles. After *Captain Calamity* in 1936 she left the screen. She was married to Ben Lyon (q.v.).

PUBLISHED SOURCES

• *Books* — **General:** *Sweethearts of the Sage.* **Credits:** *Filmarama* (v. II); *Forty Years of Screen Credits*; *Twenty Years of Silents.* **Encyclopedic Works:** *Film Encyclopedia*; *Filmlexicon degli Autori e delle Opere*; *Halliwell's Filmgoer's Companion*; *The Picturegoer's Who's Who and Encyclopedia of the Screen To-day*; *Who's Who in Hollywood*; *The World Film Encyclopedia.* **Nostalgia:** *Is That Who I Think It Is?* (v. 3); *Whatever Became of...* (11th). **Pictorial:** *Silent Portraits*; *They Had Faces Then.*
• *Periodicals* — The following periodical articles are in addition to those included in the library listings below: *Motion Picture Classic* (Mar. 1928, Feb. 1930); *Motion Picture Magazine* (Apr. 1928); *Photoplay* (July 1932); *Films in Review* (Feb. 1970) (Wampas Baby Stars); *Filmograph* (no. 3, 1971, no. 1, 1976); *Cine Revue* (Mar. 24, 1983); *Classic Images* (July 1990).

ARCHIVAL MATERIALS

• *Clipping File* — AZSU (Jimmy Starr Collection): Obituary (1983). CAA: Marriage/divorce (1926, 1929, 1932–34, 1972); robbery (1930, 1932); film appearance (1929, 1932); freelances (1933); article (1920s); obituary (1983). CAFI: Newsphotos; obituary (1983). CAUT:

Marriage/divorce (1929); obituary (1983). Periodical article: *Motion Picture Magazine* (July 1932). CAUU: Obituary (1983). NYMA: Newsphotos. Periodical articles: *Classic Images* (Jan.–Feb. 1986) (filmography). NYMN: Obituary (1983). NYPL: Nostalgia; obituary (1983). • *Other Clipping File* — GBBF, MIDL, OHCL, PAPL, WICF. • *Filmography* — NYMA. • *Legal File* — CAUT (Twentieth Century–Fox Collection): Memo, letter, telegram (1931–33); option (1932); contract summary (1932); contract (1931–32); talent agreement (1923). CAUW: Talent agreement (1928–30); contract (1929, 1932); personnel record (1932); loanout (1930); letter, memo (1929–32); authorization (1932). • *Photograph/Still* — CAA (also in Hollywood Studio Museum Collection), CAH, CAPH, CASU, CAUT (Jessen Collection) (Portrait File), DCG (Quigley Photographic Archives), GBBF, MIDL, NJPT, NYB (Bettmann/UPI Collection), NYCU (Dramatic Museum Portraits), NYEH, NYMN, NYPL, OHCL, PAPL, TXU (A. Davis Collection), WICF. • *Studio Biography* — CAA: RKO (1933). NYMA: Warner (undated).

NOLAN, Mary (Mary Robertson), Louisville, KY, 1905–1948.

Scarcely anything was written about blonde Mary Nolan which did not refer to her as "The Hard Luck Girl." After a stint in the Ziegfeld Follies, where she was known as Imogene "Bubbles" Wilson, she appeared in German films in 1925 through 1927 and made her Hollywood debut in 1927 with *Sorrell and Son.* After that promising beginning the hard luck came in the form of numerous personal problems, including drug abuse. The remainder of her career was undistinguished, ending with *The Midnight Patrol* in 1932.

PUBLISHED SOURCES

• *Books* — **General:** *Hollywood R.I.P*; *Twinkle, Twinkle, Movie Star.* **Credits:** *Filmarama* (v. I and II); *Forty Years of Screen Credits*; *Twenty Years of Silents*;

Who Was Who on Screen. **Encyclopedic Works:** *Film Encyclopedia; Filmlexicon degli Autori e delle Opere; Halliwell's Filmgoer's Companion; The Picturegoer's Who's Who and Encyclopedia of the Screen To-day; Who's Who in Hollywood; The World Film Encyclopedia.*
• *Periodicals*—The following periodical articles are in addition to those included in the library listings below: *Motion Picture Classic* (Sept. 1928); *Motion Picture Magazine* (Apr. 1929, Dec. 1931).

ARCHIVAL MATERIALS
• *Clipping File*—CAA: Illness (1929); article (1927, 1930, 1932, 1937, 1948–49); Universal contract (1929–31); film appearance (1927–30); newsphoto; illness (1929, 1948); legal problem (1930–32, 1934); marriage/divorce (1931–33); stage appearance (1932); bankruptcy (1931); obituary (1948). Periodical article: *Films in Review* (May 1980). CAFI: Newsphotos (numerous); article (1949); obituary (1948). Periodical article: *Films in Review* (May 1980). CAUU: Obituary (1948). NYMA: Legal problem (1930–32, 1935, 1937, undated); film appearance (1929–31); drug addiction (1930); leaves Universal (1930); article (1930, undated); radio appearance; injury (1929); marriage/divorce (1930–32); film contract (1927); biography (1932–33); husband sentenced (1930); stage appearance (1932); surgery (1933); comeback (1934). Periodical articles: *Photoplay* (Feb. 1930); *Liberty* (Mar. 15, 1930); *Motion Picture Magazine* (May 1931); *Hollywood* (June 1931); *Motion Picture Classic* (Aug. 1931); *Classic Images* (Dec. 1984). NYMN: Newsphotos; legal problem (1932, undated); "bad luck" girl (1936); night club appearance; marriage/divorce; illness; Follies (1937); comeback (1937); obituary (1948). NYPL: Newsphotos; biography (1941, 1946, 1949, 1963); legal problem (1937, undated); comeback; article (1944, undated); returns from Germany (1927); husband sentenced; marriage (1931); romance (1937); obituary (1948). • *Other Clipping File*—AZSU (Jimmy Starr Collection), GBBF, MAH, MIDL, OHCL,

PAPL, WICF. • *Correspondence*—AZSU (Jimmy Starr Collection): Letter from MN's landlord asking for help in publishing her biography. • *Photograph/Still*—AZSU (Jimmy Starr Collection), CAA (also in Hollywood Studio Museum Collection) (also in MGM Collection), CAUT (Portrait File), CNDA, DCG (Quigley Photographic Archives), GBBF, NJPT, NYB (Bettmann/UPI Collection), NYCU (Dramatic Museum Portraits), NYEH, NYMN, NYPL, NYSU, OHCL, TXU, WICF. • *Scrapbook*—NYPL (R. Locke Collection). • *Studio Biography*—NYMA: Universal (1928); Photoplay.

NORMAND, Mabel, Boston, MA, 1894–1930.
Vivacious Mabel Normand brought much more to silent comedy than an ability to take pratfalls. She was immensely popular from the time of her debut around 1910 and at Keystone she appeared in numerous one-reelers with Charlie Chaplin and Roscoe Arbuckle. As a testament to her popularity, many of them bore her name in the title (e.g., *Mabel's New Job, Mabel at the Wheel*). She could also be a sensitive actress as was apparent from her features like *Mickey, The Extra Girl* and *Molly O.* Her involvement with slain director William Desmond Taylor effectively ended her career after 1922 although she continued to appear in a few short films. She was married to Lew Cody (q.v.).

PUBLISHED SOURCES
• *Books*—**Bibliography:** *The Idols of Silence.* **General:** *Behind the Screen; Blue Book of the Screen; A Cast of Killers; Classics of the Silent Screen; Clown Princes and Court Jesters; A Deed of Death; Early American Cinema; Fallen Angels; Famous Film Folk; Father Goose; First One Hundred Noted Men and Women of the Screen; Funny Women; The Funsters; The Great Movie Comedians; Hollywood Album; Hollywood Hall of Fame; Hollywood Heartbreak; Hollywood Lolitas; The Holly-*

wood Murder Casebook; Hollywood R.I.P.; Hollywood's Unsolved Mysteries; Immortals of the Screen; Keaton et Cie; Kops and Custards; Love, Laughter and Tears; Mack Sennett's Keystone; The Movie Stars Story; Reel Women; Whodunit? Hollywood Style; Who's Who in the Film World; Who's Who on the Screen; Women in Comedy; World of Laughter. **Credits:** Filmarama (v. I and II); Twenty Years of Silents; Who Was Who on Screen. **Encyclopedic Works:** A Biographical Dictionary of Film; Film Encyclopedia; Filmlexicon degli Autori e delle Opere; Halliwell's Filmgoer's Companion; The Illustrated Encyclopedia of the World's Great Movie Stars and Their Films; The Illustrated Who's Who of the Cinema; International Dictionary of Films and Filmmaking (v. 3); The International Encyclopedia of Film; Joe Franklin's Encyclopedia of Comedians; The Movie Makers; Notable American Women, 1607-1950; The Oxford Companion to Film; Quinlan's Illustrated Directory of Film Comedy Actors; Quinlan's Illustrated Registry of Film Stars; Who's Who in Hollywood; Women Who Make Movies; The World Almanac Who's Who of Film; The World Encyclopedia of the Film. **Filmography:** Hollywood on the Palisades. **Biography/Autobiography:** King of Comedy; Mabel; My Autobiography (Chaplin). **Pictorial:** The Image Makers; Silent Portraits. **Factoids:** Star Stats.

• Periodicals — The following periodical articles are in addition to those included in the library listings below: Blue Book Magazine (July 1914); Moving Picture World (July 11, 1914); Photoplay (Aug. 1915, Apr. 1916, July 1916, Aug. 1918, Nov. 1920, Aug. 1921, Dec. 1922, July 1929, May 1930, Aug. 1933); Picture Play Magazine (Apr. 1916, Feb. 1918); Green Book Magazine (Dec. 1916); Motion Picture Classic (Dec. 1916, Jan. 1923); Motion Picture Magazine (Dec. 1916, Nov. 1918, Sept. 1921, June 1933); Out West (Apr. 1917); New York Dramatic Mirror (Mar. 20, 1920); Pantomime (Oct. 12, 1921); Metropolitan Magazine (Apr. 1923); Shadowland (May 1923); Good Housekeeping (July 1932); Films in Review (Dec. 1968–Jan. 1969 (about M. Sennett), Mar. 1974); Classic Film Collector (Fall 1970, Fall 1973); Film Comment (Nov.–Dec. 1972); After Dark (Nov. 1974); Classic Film/Video Images (July 1980); Classic Images (Nov. 1988, Dec. 1990–Feb. 1991) (filmography); Film History (Nov./Dec. 1988) (filmography).

ARCHIVAL MATERIALS

• Clipping File — CAA: Film appearance (1921-22); W.D. Taylor murder (1922, 1990); review of Cast of Killers (1986); article (1924). Periodical article: Liberty (Sept.–Oct. 1930). CAA (Sennett Collection): Legal problem (1924); illness (1924); vacation (1924); film appearance (1925); article (1925). CAFI: Newsphotos; review of Mabel (1982). Periodical article: Films in Review (Aug.–Sept. 1974). CAUT: Article (1929); newsphotos; illness (1929). Periodical article: Classic Images (Nov. 1990). CAUU: Periodical article: Classic Film Collector (Spring/Summer 1970, Winter 1970). NYMA (also in Photoplay Collection): Article (1941, 1970, 1989); newsphotos; review of Mack and Mabel (musical); review of Mabel (1982). Periodical articles: Photo-play World (Mar. 1918); Motion Picture Classic (May 1930); Classic Film Collector (Spring-Winter 1970, Fall 1973). NYMN: Periodical article: Films in Review (Aug.–Sept. 1974). NYPL (also in Locke Collection): Newsphotos (numerous); review of Mabel (1982); murder of W.D. Taylor (1922, 1963, 1990); illness (1927, 1929); article (1941, 1956, undated); excerpt from King of Comedy (1953); marriage (1926); shooting (1924); Mack and Mabel (musical) (1974); obituary (1930). • Other Clipping File — AZSU (Jimmy Starr Collection), CAUB, CNDA, GBBF, MAH, MIDL, OHCL, PAPL, WICF. • Correspondence — CAA (Adolph Zukor Collection): 1922. NYPL. • Filmography — CAA. • Legal File — CAA (Sennett Collection): Telegram (1917); talent agreement (1921). • Oral History — NYCO: Mentioned in the following interviews: Mildred Gilman, Albert Hackett, Buster

Keaton, Gloria Swanson. • *Photograph/ Still* – CAA (also in Hollywood Studio Museum Collection) (also in MGM Collection), CALM, CAUB, CAUT (Jessen Collection) (Portrait File), CAUU, CNDA, DCG (Quigley Photographic Archives), NJFL, NYAM, NYB (Bettmann/UPI Collection) (Penguin Collection), NYEH, NYMN, NYPL, OHCL, TXU, WICF. • *Press Kit* – OHCL. • *Publicity Release* – CAA (Sennett Collection). • *Scrapbook* – NYPL (also in R. Locke Collection).

NORTON, Barry (Alfredo Biraben or de Biraben), Buenos Aires, Argentina, 1905-1959.

Handsome Barry Norton played sensitive youths in late silent films like *The Lily* (his first film), *What Price Glory?*, *Sins of the Fathers* and *Legion of the Condemned*. His brief popularity lasted into the early sound era but he found most of his work in Spanish language versions of American films and later in Mexican movies. He continued to make sporadic appearances in American films and television through the 1950s.

PUBLISHED SOURCES

• *Books* – General: *Popular Men of the Screen*. Credits: *Filmarama* (v. II); *Forty Years of Screen Credits*; *Twenty Years of Silents*; *Who Was Who on Screen*. Encyclopedic Works: *Film Encyclopedia*; *Filmlexicon degli Autori e delle Opere*; *The Picturegoer's Who's Who and Encyclopedia of the Screen To-day*; *Who's Who in Hollywood*; *The World Film Encyclopedia*. Pictorial: *Silent Portraits*.

• *Periodicals* – The following periodical articles are in addition to those included in the library listings below: *Motion Picture Classic* (May 1927); *Motion Picture Magazine* (May 1929).

ARCHIVAL MATERIALS

• *Clipping File* – CAA: Legal problem (1933); obituary (1959). NYMA: Immigration problem (1933); article (1927).

Periodical articles: *Photoplay* (Jan. 1929, Aug. 1930); *Screen Play Secrets* (Oct. 1930); *Movie Classic* (Apr. 1932). NYPL (also in C. & L. Brown Collection): Newsphotos; film appearance (1933); film reviews; article (undated); obituary (1959). Periodical articles: *Photoplay* (Feb. 1927, Jan. 1929). • *Other Clipping File* – GBBF, PAPL, WICF. • *Legal File* – CAUT (Twentieth Century-Fox Collection): Contract summary (1927); letter, telegram (1926-29); contract (1928); loanout (1928); talent agreement (1926, 1928). CAUW: Contract (1945); document (1945); talent agreement (1937). • *Photograph/Still* – CAA (also in Hollywood Studio Museum Collection), CASF, CAUT (Jessen Collection), CAUU, DCG (Quigley Photographic Archives), GBBF, NJPT, NYCU (Dramatic Museum Portraits), NYEH, NYPL, NYSU, OHCL, WICF. • *Scrapbook* – NJPT (Yeandle Collection). • *Studio Biography* – CAA: Paramount (1932). NYMA: Fox, Paramount, Photoplay.

NOVAK, Eva, St. Louis, MO, 1898-1988.

Eva Novak had a varied career which included a stint as a Mack Sennett bathing beauty, American westerns with Tom Mix and William S. Hart, Australian "westerns" and leading roles in melodramas in the 1920s. She was as beautiful as her sister Jane (q.v.) but less successful, and her starring career was not sustained very long. After talkies arrived, she was seen in many small parts, including some John Ford films.

PUBLISHED SOURCES

• *Books* – General: *Sweethearts of the Sage*; *The Truth About the Movies*. Credits: *Filmarama* (v. I and II); *Forty Years of Screen Credits*; *Twenty Years of Silents*. Encyclopedic Works: *Filmlexicon degli Autori e delle Opere*; *Halliwell's Filmgoer's Companion*; *Who's Who in Hollywood*. Nostalgia: *Whatever Became of...* (1st). Pictorial: *Silent Portraits*.

• *Periodicals* — The following periodical articles are in addition to those included in the library listings below:
Motion Picture Classic (July 1920);
Classic Images (Nov. 1981, June 1988).

ARCHIVAL MATERIALS
• *Clipping File* — CAA: Article (1982);
film appearance (1921-22, 1956); obituary
(1988). CAFI: Newsphotos; article
(1982); obituary (1988). NYMA (also in
Photoplay Collection): Obituary (1988).
Periodical articles: *Classic Images* (Mar.-
Apr. 1983, Jan. 1985, July 1987). NYPL:
Newsphotos; article (1922, undated); film
appearance (1922); obituary (1988).
• *Other Clipping File* — GBBF, MIDL,
OHCL, WICF. • *Photograph/Still* —
CAA (also in Hollywood Studio Museum
Collection), CAUU, DCG (Quigley
Photographic Archives), NYPL, NYSU,
OHCL, TXU, WICF. • *Press Kit* —
OHCL. • *Publicity Release* — CAA: Fox
(1946?). • *Studio Biography* — NYMA:
Photoplay.

NOVAK, Jane, St. Louis, MO,
1896-1990.
The more successful of the beautiful
Novak sisters (the other being Eva
[q.v.]), Jane Novak made almost 110
films for various studios including
Ince, Vitagraph, Selig and Goldwyn.
One of her most successful films was
Thelma; others included *The Lullaby*,
The Tiger Man, *Colleen of the Pines*
and *What Price Love?* She was leading
lady to William S. Hart in several films
and went to Germany for three in the
mid-1920s. Her starring career ended
with the silent era but she returned for
some small parts about 1936 and was
seen onscreen to the mid-1950s.

PUBLISHED SOURCES
• *Books* — **Bibliography:** *The Idols of
Silence.* **General:** *Blue Book of the
Screen*; *Famous Film Folk*; *Ladies in
Distress*; *Sweethearts of the Sage*; *The
Truth About the Movies*; *Who's Who on
the Screen.* **Credits:** *Filmarama* (v. I and
II); *Forty Years of Screen Credits*;
Twenty Years of Silents. **Encyclopedic**

Works: *Filmlexicon degli Autori e delle
Opere*; *Halliwell's Filmgoer's Compan-
ion*; *Who's Who in Hollywood.* **Nos-
talgia:** *Whatever Became of... (1st).*
Pictorial: *Silent Portraits.*
• *Periodicals* — The following period-
ical articles are in addition to those in-
cluded in the library listings below:
Motion Picture Magazine (Oct. 1918);
Motion Picture Classic (Apr.-May 1920,
July 1920, Apr. 1924); *Photoplay* (Jan.
1922, Nov. 1924); *Picture Play Magazine*
(Apr. 1922); *Filmograph* (no. 1-1, 1970);
Classic Images (Nov. 1981, July 1987,
Apr. 1990); *Skoop* (Apr. 1990); *Film en
Televisie + Video* (July-Aug. 1990).

ARCHIVAL MATERIALS
• *Clipping File* — CAA: Legal problem
(1937-38); article (1974, 1982); film appearance (1920, 1922, 1956); newsphotos.
Periodical articles: *Pic* (Oct. 3, 1939);
Hollywood Studio Magazine (Mar.
1972); *Classic Images* (Apr. 1983). CAFI:
Newsphotos; nostalgia; article (1982);
obituary (1990). NYMA (also in Photo-
play Collection): Obituary (1990).
Periodical articles: *Classic Film Collec-
tor* (Spring 1968-Spring 1969). NYPL
(also in Locke Collection): Newsphotos;
article (undated); stage appearance;
nostalgia (1939, 1982); obituary (1990).
Periodical articles: *Picture Play
Magazine* (Apr. 1920); *Silent Picture*
(Spring 1972). • *Other Clipping File* —
GBBF, WICF. • *Interview* — CAUU (A.
Slide Collection): 1971. • *Oral History* —
NYCO: Mentioned in: Harold Lloyd in-
terview. • *Photograph/Still* — CAA,
CALM, CAUT (Jessen Collection),
CAUU (also in A. Slide Collection),
CNDA, DCG (Quigley Photographic Ar-
chives), NYEH, NYPL, NYSU, OHCL,
TXSM, TXU, WICF. • *Press Kit* —
OHCL. • *Publicity Release* — CAUU (A.
Slide Collection): Goldwyn (1920s?).
• *Studio Biography* — NYMA: Photo-
play.

**NOVARRO, Ramon (Jose Ra-
mon Gil Samaniegos),** Du-
rango, Mexico, 1899-1968.
A very popular romantic lead in the

1920s, handsome Ramon Novarro was more than a second-string Valentino. He appeared in such major successes as *The Prisoner of Zenda*, *The Student Prince* and the title role of *Ben Hur*, as well as some obligatory "Latin lover" roles. He continued to receive good roles in early sound films like *Mata Hari* (with Garbo [q.v.]). Eventually his star waned and he turned to quickies in the latter 1930s, as well as Mexican and French films. He reappeared in 1949 for some character parts.

PUBLISHED SOURCES

• *Books* — Written by (or ghostwritten for) RN: a chapter of *Breaking into the Movies*. **Bibliography:** *The Idols of Silence*. **General:** *Bloody Wednesday*; *Blue Book of the Screen*; *Classics of the Silent Screen*; *Famous Film Folk*; *Folks Ushud Know*; *Gentlemen to the Rescue*; *Great Lovers of the Movies*; *The Great Movie Stars*; *Hollywood Album*; *Hollywood Hall of Fame*; *Hollywood Heartbreak*; *The Hollywood Murder Casebook*; *How I Broke into the Movies*; *"Image" on the Art and Evolution of the Film*; *The Matinee Idols*; *The MGM Years*; *More from Hollywood*; *The Movie Musical from Vitaphone to 42nd Street*; *The Movie Stars Story*; *Popular Men of the Screen*; *Ramon Novarro*; *Screen Personalities*; *Those Scandalous Sheets of Hollywood*. **Credits:** *Filmarama* (v. I and II); *Forty Years of Screen Credits*; *Twenty Years of Silents*; *Who Was Who on Screen*. **Encyclopedic Works:** *A Biographical Dictionary of Film*; *The Complete Encyclopedia of Popular Music and Jazz*; *A Dictionary of the Cinema*; *Film Encyclopedia*; *Filmlexicon degli Autori e delle Opere*; *Halliwell's Filmgoer's Companion*; *The Illustrated Encyclopedia of the World's Great Movie Stars and Their Films*; *The Illustrated Who's Who of the Cinema*; *International Dictionary of Films and Filmmakers* (v. 3); *The International Encyclopedia of Film*; *Mexican American Biographies*; *The Movie Makers*; *The Oxford Companion to Film*; *The Picturegoer's Who's Who and Encyclo-*pedia of the Screen To-day; *Quinlan's Illustrated Registry of Film Stars*; *Who's Who in Hollywood*; *The World Almanac Who's Who of Film*; *The World Encyclopedia of the Film*; *The World Film Encyclopedia*. **Nostalgia:** *Whatever Became of...* (1st). **Biography/Autobiography:** *Ramon Novarro*. **Pictorial:** *Leading Men*; *Silent Portraits*. **Recordings:** *Hollywood on Record*. **Factoids:** *Star Stats*.

• *Periodicals* — The following periodical articles are in addition to those included in the library listings below: *Photoplay* (Jan. 1923, Apr. 1923, Feb. 1924, May–July 1924, Apr. 1925, Oct. 1925, Oct. 1927, Oct. 1928, Apr. 1930, Feb. 1932, Nov. 1932, Apr. 1933); *Motion Picture Magazine* (Aug. 1924, June 1925, Oct. 1925, June 1926, Sept. 1926, Feb. 1927, Feb. 1929, Jan. 1930, June 1930, Jan. 1931, Mar. 1932, Apr. 1933); *Motion Picture Classic* (Oct. 1925, May 1927, Feb. 1930, July 1931); *Silver Screen* (June 1931, Dec. 1931, Mar. 1932, May 1934); *Movie Classic* (Feb. 1932); *Vanity Fair* (Oct. 1932); *Cinema Digest* (Jan. 9, 1933); *Pictures and Picturegoer* (July 1, 1933); *Saturday Evening Post* (Jan. 15, 1944); *Players Showcase* (Summer 1965); *Newsweek* (Nov. 6, 1967, Nov. 11, 1968); *Films in Review* (Nov. 1967 [filmography]); *Time* (Nov. 15, 1968); *Films and Filming* (Feb. 1970); *Classic Film Collector* (Summer 1973); *Cine Revue* (July 11, 1974); *Hollywood Studio Magazine* (May 1985, Mar. 1991).

MEDIA
Why Ever Did They? (CD recording).

ARCHIVAL MATERIALS
• *Clipping File* — CAA: Legal problem (1931, 1934, 1946, 1959–60, 1962); home (1930, 1934, 1945, 1955, 1988); stage appearance (1933–34, 1962–63); army service (1942); film appearance (1922–23, 1942, 1949, 1956, 1959); estate (1968); newsphotos; illness (1926, 1960); nostalgia (1944, 1967, 1990); article (1930, 1933–34, 1949, 1953, 1962, 1964–65); TV appearance (1964–65); MGM contract (1928, 1931–32, 1935); honor (1931); director (1931); murder (1968–69); obituary (1968). Periodical articles: *RNFC* (Ra-

mon Novarro Fan Club) *News* (1954, 1963–64, 1966). CAFI: Article (1943, 1967); obituary (1968). CAUT: Stage appearance (1959); nostalgia (1965); murder (1968); ranch (undated); film appearance (1929, 1956, 1959); legal problem (1962); estate (1968); obituary (1968). CAUU: Article (1964); trial of murderers (1969). NYMA: Article (undated); obituary (1968). Periodical articles: *Theatre Magazine* (Jan. 1928); *Classic Film Collector* (Fall/Winter 1968); *Silent Picture* (Summer 1969); *Ramon Novarro Club* (newsletter) (Autumn/Winter 1972/73, Summer 1973, Autumn/Winter 1973/74). NYMN: Newsphotos; article (1950s?, 1964). NYPL: PARTIAL CONTENTS: Murder suspects (1968); murder trial (1969); article (1923, 1958–59, 1962, 1964–65, undated); drunk driving (1941–42, 1959–60, 1962, 1967); estate (1968); murderers sentenced (1969); newsphotos (numerous); stage appearance (1940, 1962); TV appearance (1958, 1964); Mexican career (1943); sues U.S. government (1966); movie romances (1950); film appearance (1959); lives in Mexico (1962); obituary (1968). Periodical articles: *Movie Weekly* (undated); *Silent Picture* (Summer 1969); *Classic Film Collector* (Summer 1973). • *Other Clipping File* — AZSU (Jimmy Starr Collection), CAUB, GBBF, MAH, MIDL, OHCL, PAPL, WICF. • *Correspondence* — NYPL (C. & L. Brown Collection): 1940. • *Filmography* — NYMA. • *Interview* — CAUU (Hollywood Studio Museum Collection): 1964. • *Photograph/Still* — AZSU (Jimmy Starr Collection), CAA (also in Hollywood Studio Museum Collection) (also in MGM Collection), CAHL, CALM, CAOC (Kiesling Collection), CAUS, CAUT (Jessen Collection), CNDA, DCG (Quigley Photographic Archives), GBBF, IAU (Junkin Collection), MIDL, NJPT, NYAM, NYB (Bettmann/UPI Collection) (Penguin Collection) (Springer Collection), NYCU (Dramatic Museum Portraits) (Palmer Collection), NYEH, NYMN, NYPL, NYSU, OHCL, TNUT (Clarence Brown Collection), TXU, WICF. • *Program* — CAHL: Film (1926). • *Scrapbook* — NJPT (Yeandle Collection), NYMA,

NYPL. • *Studio Biography* — CAA: RKO (1949); MGM (1950s); Disney (1958). CAFI: Disney (1958). NYMA: Paramount (1959).

O'BRIEN, Eugene, Boulder, CO, 1882–1966.

Handsome Eugene O'Brien had been a stage actor and was a leading matinee idol during the 12 or so years of his silent film career. He partnered most of the leading actresses including Mary Pickford, Gloria Swanson and especially Norma Talmadge, with whom he frequently costarred. Among his films were *The Voice from the Minaret*, *The Scarlet Woman*, *Souls for Sale*, *Graustark* and *Gilded Lies*. He made his last film in 1928.

PUBLISHED SOURCES

• *Books* — **General:** *Blue Book of the Screen*; *Famous Film Folk*; *Who's Who on the Screen*. **Credits:** *Filmarama* (v. I and II); *Twenty Years of Silents*; *Who Was Who on Screen*. **Encyclopedic Works:** *Film Encyclopedia*; *Filmlexicon degli Autori e delle Opere*; *Who's Who in Hollywood*. **Pictorial:** *Silent Portraits*.

• *Periodicals* — The following periodical articles are in addition to those included in the library listings below: *Motion Picture Magazine* (Nov. 1916, Nov. 1918, July 1921, June 1925); *Photoplay* (Aug. 1917, Nov. 1918, Mar. 1922, June–July 1924); *Motion Picture Classic* (July 1919, July 1922); *Films in Review* (Aug.–Sept. 1966, Oct. 1986).

OBSCURE PUBLISHED SOURCES
CAA: *Life Story of Eugene O'Brien.*

ARCHIVAL MATERIALS
• *Clipping File* — CAA: Illness (1954); inheritance (1954); newsphotos; obituary (1966). Periodical articles: *Films in Review* (June–July 1961). CAUT: Obituary (1966). CODL: Obituary (1966). NYMA (also in Photoplay Collection): Obituary (1966). NYMN: Newsphotos; poem by EO'B. NYPL (also in Locke Collection): Stage appearance (1910s, 1920s, 1930); article (1923, undated); film appearance; career (1923); legal problem

(1922); newsphotos; film review (1910s); obituary (1966). Periodical articles: *Motion Picture Magazine* (July ?); *Movie Weekly* (Sept. 16, ?); *Photoplay* (July ?). • *Other Clipping File* – ASZU (Jimmy Starr Collection), GBBF, MAH, MIDL, OHCL, PAPL, WICF. • *Correspondence* – NYMA (Photoplay Collection). NYPL: Letters (C. & L. Brown Collection) (1911–12, 1928–30); other (1922). • *Photograph/Still* – CAA (also in Hollywood Studio Museum Collection), CAUU, CNDA, DCG (Quigley Photographic Archives), NYAM, NYB (Underwood Collection), NYCU (Dramatic Museum Portraits), NYMN, NYPL, NYSU, OHCL, TXU, WICF. • *Scrapbook* – NYAM, NYPL (also in R. Locke Collection). • *Studio Biography* – NYMA: Photoplay.

O'BRIEN, George, San Francisco, CA, 1900–1985.

Although he was dubbed "The Torso" and "The Chest" for his athletic build, George O'Brien proved himself a sensitive actor in such silent films as *The Iron Horse, Three Bad Men* and, most notably, *Sunrise* (1927). He found himself largely relegated to westerns in the sound period, and after about 75 films, he played his last starring role in 1940. He returned later in the decade for some worthy character roles.

PUBLISHED SOURCES

• *Books* – **General:** *The BFI Companion to the Western; Famous Film Folk; The Filming of the West; The Great Cowboy Stars of Movies & Television; Great Western Stars; The Hall of Fame of Western Film Stars; Heroes, Heavies and Sagebrush; Heroes of the Range; Hollywood Corral; A Pictorial History of Westerns; Popular Men of the Screen; Riders of the Range; Twinkle, Twinkle, Movie Star; The Western* (Eyles). **Credits:** *Filmarama* (v. II); *Forty Years of Screen Credits; Twenty Years of Silents.* **Encyclopedic Works:** *B Western Actors Encyclopedia; A Companion to the Movies; Film Encyclopedia; Filmlex-*

icon degli Autori e delle Opere; Halliwell's Filmgoer's Companion; The Illustrated Who's Who of the Cinema; International Motion Picture Almanac (1975-80); *The Movie Makers; The Picturegoer's Who's Who and Encyclopedia of the Screen To-day; Quinlan's Illustrated Registry of Film Stars; Who's Who in Hollywood; The World Almanac Who's Who of Film; The World Encyclopedia of the Film; The World Film Encyclopedia.* **Nostalgia:** *Whatever Became of...* (4th). **Pictorial:** *Silent Portraits.*

• *Periodicals* – The following periodical articles are in addition to those included in the library listings below: *Photoplay* (Feb.–Mar. 1925); *Motion Picture Classic* (Aug. 1925, Aug. 1926, Oct. 1927, May 1930); *Movie Classic* (Dec. 1933); *Silver Screen* (Sept. 1934); *Film Fan Monthly* (May 1971); *Filmkritik* (Jan. 1972); *Cine Revue* (Sept. 26, 1985); *Revue du Cinema* (Dec. 1985); *Classic Images* (Aug. 1987).

ARCHIVAL MATERIALS

• *Clipping File* – CAA: Film appearance (1924, 1928, 1933); nostalgia (1972–73, 1976, 1979, 1981, 1984); marriage/divorce/children (1933–34, 1948); injury (1930); Fox contract (1932); article (1927, 1968, 1978); leaves navy (1945); obituary (1985). Periodical article: *Films in Review* (Nov. 1962) (filmography). CAFI: Obituary (1985). CAUT: Nostalgia; film appearance (1929, 1963); obituary (1985). CAUU: Obituary (1985). NYMA: Obituary (1985). Periodical articles: *Modern Screen* (Mar. 1936); *Classic Film Collector* (Mar. 1979); *Classic Images* (Oct. 1985); *Big Reel* (Oct. 1982, Sept. 1985). NYPL: Newsphotos; film review (1930s, 1940s); film synopses (1920s); article (undated); film appearance (1920s, 1930s); marriage/divorce/children (1933–34, 1948); dropped by Fox (1933); vaudeville tour (1933); obituary (1985). Periodical articles: *Cinema Art* (Apr. 1926); *Picture Show* (Aug. 7, 1926); *Film Fan Monthly* (May 1972). • *Other Clipping File* – ASZU (Jimmy Starr Collection), CASP, GBBF, MAH, MIDL, PAPL, WICF.

• *Correspondence* — CAHL: 1933–42. NYPL: Letters (C. & L. Brown Collection) (1925, 1935); other (1929). • *Filmography* — NYPL. • *Interview* — CAUU (R. Lamparski Collection). GBBF (Hollywood Collection): Transcript of interview for *Hollywood* (TV series). • *Legal File* — CAUT (Twentieth Century-Fox Collection): Contract summary (1927); letter, telegram (1927–33); contract (1933); option (1929); talent agreement (1923, 1925, 1928, 1930, 1932–33). CAUW: Document (1928); talent agreement (1928, 1946). • *Photograph/Still* — CAA (also in Hollywood Studio Museum Collection), CASP, CAUC (Motion Picture Photograph Collection), CAUT (Jessen Collection) (Portrait File), DCG (Quigley Photographic Archives), GBBF, NJPT, NYAM, NYB (Springer Collection) (Underwood Collection), NYCU (Dramatic Museum Portraits) (Palmer Collection), NYEH, NYPL, NYSU, OHCL, TXU, WICF. • *Scrapbook* — NJPT (Yeandle Collection), NYPL (also in C. & L. Brown Collection). • *Studio Biography* — CAA: Unknown studio (1929, 1930s). NYMA: Warner.

O'DAY, Molly (sometimes Mollie) (also known as Sue O'Neil) (Susan or Suzanne Noonan), Bayonne, NJ, 1911/ 12–. 1998

Known early in her career as Sue O'Neil (she was the younger sister of Sally O'Neil [q.v.]), Molly O'Day appeared in such late 1920s films as *The Patent Leather Kid* (with Richard Barthelmess), *The Lovelorn* and *Shepherd of the Hills*. She soon made news by developing a persistent weight problem which resulted in lost roles and ill-advised surgery. She made a comeback of sorts in the early '30s and, usually playing brash young women (e.g. *Gigolettes of Paris*), continued sporadically in films until 1935.

PUBLISHED SOURCES

• *Books* — Credits: *Filmarama* (v. II); *Forty Years of Screen Credits*; *Twenty*

Years of Silents. **Encyclopedic Works:** *Film Encyclopedia*; *Filmlexicon degli Autori e delle Opere*; *The Picturegoer's Who's Who and Encyclopedia of the Screen To-day*; *Who's Who in Hollywood.* **Pictorial:** *Silent Portraits.* • *Periodicals* — *Motion Picture Classic* (Oct. 1927); *Photoplay* (Aug. 1928); *Films in Review* (Feb. 1970) (Wampas Baby Stars); *American Classic Screen* (May–June 1983).

ARCHIVAL MATERIALS

• *Clipping File* — CAA: Marriage, divorce (1934, 1951–52, 1956); surgery (1928); illness (1927); vaudeville appearance (1930); stage appearance (1929); legal problem (1929–30); comeback (1934); weight problem (1927–30); escapes shooting (1930); rescues son (1956). NYPL: Newsphotos; film appearance (1933). • *Other Clipping File* — GBBF, MIDL, NYMA (Photoplay Collection), OHCL, PAPL, WICF. • *Legal File* — CAUW: Payroll record (1927–28); loan-out (1927); contract (1927); option exercise (1927); letter (1929); talent agreement (1927). • *Photograph/Still* — CAA (also in Hollywood Studio Museum Collection), CAFI, DCG (Quigley Photographic Archives), GBBF, NJPT, NYB (Underwood Collection), NYCU (Dramatic Museum Portraits), NYEH, NYPL, NYSU, OHCL, TXU (A. Davis Collection), WICF. • *Scrapbook* — NYPL (also in Glenda Farrell Collection). • *Studio Biography* — NYMA: Photoplay.

OLAND, Warner (Werner [some sources say Johan or Johann] Ohlund), Umea, Sweden, 1880–1938.

Only in Hollywood could a Swedish stage actor find his niche as a Chinese detective, but Warner Oland did just that. In silent films he appeared often in villain roles in features such as *East Is West*, *Don Juan* and *When a Man Loves*; his serials included *The Fatal Ring*, *Patria* and *The Phantom Foe*. He also did more straightforward character parts in films such as *The*

Jazz Singer. It is for his portrayal of Charlie Chan in the 1930s that he will undoubtedly be remembered.

PUBLISHED SOURCES

• *Books*—With his wife, actress Edith Shearn, WO translated several plays by August Strindberg in 1912 and 1914. **General:** *Charlie Chan at the Movies; Eighty Silent Film Stars; Famous Movie Detectives; The Great Movie Series; Hollywood Album; The Movie Stars Story; Saturday Afternoon at the Bijou; Strangers in Hollywood; Who's Who on the Screen.* **Credits:** *Filmarama* (v. I and II); *Forty Years of Screen Credits; Twenty Years of Silents; Who Was Who on Screen.* **Encyclopedic Works:** *A Companion to the Movies; Film Encyclopedia; Filmlexicon degli Autori e delle Opere; Halliwell's Filmgoer's Companion; The International Who's Who of the Cinema; The Movie Makers; The Picturegoer's Who's Who and Encyclopedia of the Screen To-day; Quinlan's Illustrated Registry of Film Stars; Who Was Who in the Theatre; Who's Who in Hollywood; Who's Who of the Horrors and Other Fantasy Films; The World Almanac Who's Who of Film; The World Film Encyclopedia.* **Pictorial:** *Silent Portraits.* **Factoids:** *Star Stats.*
• *Periodicals*—The following periodical articles are in addition to that included in the library listings below: *Photoplay* (Feb. 1918, Jan. 1923, Jan. 1936); *Motion Picture Classic* (Feb. 1919, June 1920); *Picture Play Magazine* (Sept. 1920); *Silver Screen* (July 1937); *Newsweek* (Aug. 15, 1938); *Films in Review* (Jan. 1955 [performers who played Charlie Chan], June–July 1985).

ARCHIVAL MATERIALS

• *Clipping File*—CAA: Newsphotos; divorce (1938); Charlie Chan (1968); obituary (1938). NYMA (also in Photoplay Collection): Personal data summary. Periodical article: *Classic Images* (Dec. 1986). NYMN: Newsphotos; career (early 1930s); obituary (1938). NYPL (also in Locke Collection): Film appearance (1910s, 1920s, 1930s); film review (1930s); will (1938); article (un-

dated); newsphotos; suspended by Fox (1938); career; Charlie Chan (1936); sued by wife (1937); illness (1938); obituary (1938). • *Other Clipping File*—AZSU (Jimmy Starr Collection), GBBF, MAH, MIDL, OHCL, WICF. • *Correspondence*—NYMN: 1909. NYPL (E. Goodman Collection): 1912–13. • *Filmography*—NYPL. • *Legal File*—CAUT (Twentieth Century–Fox Collection): Letter, memo, telegram (1931–38); option (1933–36); suspension (1938); contract (1934, 1938); talent agreement (1934, 1936); lawsuit (1931–32). Some matters of interest in this collection are WO's intoxication during filming and failure to appear for filming. CAUW: Personnel, payroll record (1933); letter, memo (1927–28, 1933); affidavit (1927); talent agreement (1926–28, 1933). • *Photograph/Still*—CAA (also in Hollywood Studio Museum Collection), CAFA, CAUT (Portrait File), CAUU, CNDA, DCG (Quigley Photographic Archives), IAU (Blees Collection), NJFL, NYAM, NYB (Underwood Collection), NYCU (Dramatic Museum Portraits), NYEH, NYMN, NYPL, NYSU, OHCL, OHSU, TXU, WICF. • *Play Program*—NYPL. • *Press Kit*—CAFA, OHCL. • *Publicity Release*—AZSU (Jimmy Starr Collection). • *Reminiscence*—MISU: Recording. • *Scrapbook*—NYPL (R. Locke Collection). • *Studio Biography*—CAA: Goldwyn.

OLMSTED (sometimes **Olmstead**), **Gertrude,** Chicago, IL, 1897/1904–1975.

Pretty Gertrude Olmsted was one of the few actresses who had a substantial film career as the result of winning a beauty contest. From 1920 to the end of the silent period she made numerous films, including several with cowboy star Hoot Gibson. She also appeared with Rudolph Valentino, John Gilbert and Lon Chaney. Her more memorable films included *Cameo Kirby, Ben Hur, The Torrent, California Straight Ahead* and *Babbitt.*

PUBLISHED SOURCES

• *Books* — **General:** *Blue Book of the Screen*; *Famous Film Folk*; *Sweethearts of the Sage*; *The Truth About the Movies.* **Credits:** *Filmarama* (v. II); *Forty Years of Screen Credits*; *Twenty Years of Silents*; *Who Was Who on Screen.* **Encyclopedic Works:** *Film Encyclopedia*; *Filmlexicon degli Autori e delle Opere*; *The Picturegoer's Who's Who and Encyclopedia of the Screen To-day*; *Who's Who in Hollywood.* **Pictorial:** *Silent Portraits.*

• *Periodicals* — *Films in Review* (May 1975); *Classic Images* (July 1990) (filmography).

ARCHIVAL MATERIALS

• *Clipping File* — CAA (also in Collection): Newsphotos; obituary (1975). CAFI: Obituary (1975). NYPL: Newsphotos; career; obituary (1975). • *Other Clipping File* — GBBF, NYMA (Photoplay Collection), WICF. • *Collection* — CAA (Gertrude Olmstead Collection): 8 scrapbooks, including correspondence, photographs (some from childhood), clippings (marriage, film career) (1920-36). Films represented by clippings include *Cameo Kirby, Cobra, Trilby, Ben Hur, Girl of the Limberlost* and *Shadows of Conscience. NOTE*: There may also be a bit of material in the Robert Z. Leonard Collection (GO's husband). • *Interview* — CAUU (A. Slide Collection). • *Legal File* — CAUT (Twentieth Century-Fox Collection): Talent agreement (1923). CAUW: Talent agreement (1924, 1928). • *Photograph/Still* — CAA (also in Collection) (also in Hollywood Studio Museum Collection) (also in MGM Collection), CASF, DCG (Quigley Photographic Archives), NYB (Underwood Collection), NYCU (Dramatic Museum Portraits), NYEH, NYPL, NYSU, OHCL, TXU, WICF. • *Scrapbook* — CAA (see Collection), NYPL. • *Studio Biography* — CAA: MGM (1920s?). NYMA: Photoplay.

O'MALLEY, Pat, Forest City, PA, 1890/92-1966.

One of the contenders for the actor with the longest career would be Pat O'Malley. For Universal, Essanay, Kalem, Edison and other studios he appeared in hundreds of films over a 55 year period (1907-62). He was a popular leading man in the teens and twenties in films such as *The Man From Brodney's, The Fighting American, My Wild Irish Rose* and the *White Desert.* He also made films in Ireland. After his starring days ended he played character parts both in films and on television. (Not to be confused with character actor J. Pat O'Malley.)

PUBLISHED SOURCES

• *Books* — **General:** *Character People*; *Famous Film Folk*; *The Truth About the Movies.* **Credits:** *Filmarama* (v. I and II); *Forty Years of Screen Credits*; *Twenty Years of Silents*; *Who Was Who on Screen.* **Encyclopedic Works:** *Film Encyclopedia*; *The Picturegoer's Who's Who and Encyclopedia of the Screen To-day*; *Who's Who in Hollywood*; *The World Film Encyclopedia.* **Pictorial:** *Silent Portraits.*

• *Periodicals* — *Movie Pictorial* (July 1915); *Photoplay* (Feb. 1916, Mar. 1921); *Motion Picture Classic* (Jan. 1921, Oct. 1926); *Motion Picture Magazine* (Aug. 1921, Feb. 1925).

OBSCURE PUBLISHED SOURCES

CAA (Pat O'Malley Collection): *The Cast* (v. 1).

ARCHIVAL MATERIALS

• *Clipping File* — CAA (also in Collection): Film appearance (1924, 1953); obituary (1966). NYPL (also in Locke Collection): Article (1922, 1927, undated); film appearance (1930s, 1940s); newsphotos; film review (1920s, 1930s); comeback (1929); obituary (1966). • *Other Clipping File* — AZSU (Jimmy Starr Collection), CAUB, GBBF, MAH, MIDL, NYMA (Photoplay Collection), OHCL, PAPL, WICF. • *Collection* — CAA: Photographs; reviews; clippings (1913-1940s); correspondence (1911-53); newsphotos; scripts; legal files, including talent agreements (1918-51); personnel record (1920); contracts (1930-40); scrapbook. • *Correspondence* — CAA (see

Collection), NYMA (Photoplay Collection). • *Legal File*—CAA (Sennett Collection) (also in Collection): Contract (1930). • *Photograph/Still*—CAA (also in Collection) (also in Hollywood Studio Museum Collection), CAH, CAUT (Jessen Collection), DCG (Quigley Photographic Archives), NYCU (Dramatic Museum Portraits), NYPL, NYSU, OHCL, TXU, WICF. • *Program*—CAA (see Collection). • *Publicity Release*—AZSU (Jimmy Starr Collection). • *Scrapbook*—CAA (see Collection), NYPL. • *Studio Biography*—CAA: Goldwyn (1922). NYMA: Photoplay.

O'NEIL (sometimes O'Neill), Sally (Virginia Louise Noonan), Bayonne, NJ, 1908/12–1968.

After one of her earliest roles in *Sally, Irene and Mary*, perky Sally O'Neil became a star portraying the "gamine." She continued playing variations of that role until the public (and MGM who released her) apparently tired of her persona. By 1930 her career was on the decline although she recreated her stage role in John Ford's *The Brat* (1930). After a few more insubstantial efforts (ending in 1935 with *Too Tough to Kill*), her career was over in Hollywood. She attempted an unsuccessful comeback in 1937 with *Kathleen*, a film made in Ireland. Her sister was Mollie O'Day (q.v.).

PUBLISHED SOURCES
• *Books*—Credits: *Filmarama* (v. II); *Forty Years of Screen Credits*; *Twenty Years of Silents*; *Who Was Who on Screen*. Encyclopedic Works: *Film Encyclopedia*; *Filmlexicon degli Autori e delle Opere*; *Halliwell's Filmgoer's Companion*; *The Movie Makers*; *The Picturegoer's Who's Who and Encyclopedia of the Screen To-day*; *Who's Who in Hollywood*; *The World Almanac Who's Who of Film*; *The World Film Encyclopedia*. Pictorial: *They Had Faces Then*.

• *Periodicals*—The following periodical articles are in addition to that included in the library listings below: *Motion Picture Classic* (Sept. 1925, Apr. 1931); *Motion Picture Magazine* (Sept. 1927, Oct. 1929, Oct. 1931); *Photoplay* (Nov. 1931); *Movie Mirror* (Nov. 1931); *Films in Review* (Feb. 1970) (Wampas Baby Stars); *American Classic Screen* (May–June 1983).

OBSCURE PUBLISHED SOURCES
CAA: *Follywood* [sic]—*And How!*

ARCHIVAL MATERIALS
• *Clipping File*—CAA: Film appearance (1929, 1933); legal problem (1928–31, 1933); MGM option (1927); marriage (1932); escapes shooting (1930). CAUT: Obituary (1968). NYMA (also in Photoplay Collection): Obituary (1968). NYPL: Newsphotos; article (1940, undated); stage appearance (1932, 1940); nightclub fight (1933); film review; comeback (1935); film appearance (1933); obituary (1968). Periodical article: *Films in Review* (Feb. 1972). • *Other Clipping File*—CNDA, GBBF, MAH, MIDL, OHCL, WICF. • *Correspondence*—NYPL (C. & L. Brown Collection): 1937–44. • *Legal File*—CAUT (Twentieth Century-Fox Collection): Memo, letter (1931–32); option (1931); contract (1931); agreement (1931). • *Oral History*—NYCO: Mentioned in: George K. Arthur interview. • *Photograph/Still*—CAA (also in Hollywood Studio Museum Collection) (also in MGM Collection), CAH, CASU, CAUT (Jessen Collection), DCG (Quigley Photographic Archives), GBBF, NJPT, NYAM, NYCU (Dramatic Museum Portraits), NYEH, NYPL, NYSU, OHCL, TXU (A. Davis Collection), WICF. • *Scrapbook*—NYPL. • *Studio Biography*—NYMA: Photoplay.

OWEN, Seena (Signe Auen), Spokane, WA, 1894/96–1966.

Two images of Seena Owen, from opposite ends of her career, come readily to mind: The Princess Beloved of D.W. Griffith's *Intolerance* reclining among the towering pillars of Babylon and the mad Queen whipping Gloria Swanson through the palace halls in *Queen Kelly*. In between, for Fox, DeMille and other studios, she appeared in films such as *Branding Broadway*, *The Face in the Fog*, *The Hunted Woman* and *Faint Perfume*. Her talkies were few but she became a successful screenwriter in the 1930s and '40s. She was married to George Walsh (q.v.).

PUBLISHED SOURCES

• *Books* – General: *Famous Film Folk*; *The Kindergarten of the Movies*; *Life Stories of the Movie Stars*; *Strangers in Hollywood*. **Credits:** *Filmarama* (v. I and II); *Twenty Years of Silents*; *Who Was Who on Screen*. **Encyclopedic Works:** *Film Encyclopedia*; *Filmlexicon degli Autori e delle Opere*; *Halliwell's Filmgoer's Companion*; *The Illustrated Who's Who of Film*; *The Picturegoer's Who's Who and Encyclopedia of the Screen To-day*; *Who's Who in Hollywood*. **Pictorial:** *Silent Portraits*.
• *Periodicals* – *Photoplay* (Mar. 1916, May 1920, June 1921); *Motion Picture Classic* (June 1920, Aug. 1921); *Motion Picture Magazine* (Aug. 1923); *Offbeat* (no. 4, 1959).

ARCHIVAL MATERIALS

• *Clipping File* – CAA: Obituary (1966). NYMA (also in Photoplay Collection): Obituary (1966). NYPL (also in Locke Collection): Newsphotos; legal problem (1922); article (1923); film review (1920s); film appearance (1920s); obituary (1966). • *Other Clipping File* – CNDA, GBBF, MAH, PAPL, WICF. • *Photograph/Still* – CAA (also in Hollywood Studio Museum Collection), CALM, CAUT (Jessen Collection), CAUU, CNDA, DCG (Quigley Photographic Archives), NYCU (Dramatic Museum Portraits), NYEH, NYPL, NYSU, OHCL, WICF. • *Scrapbook* – NYPL (also in R. Locke Collection). • *Studio Biography* – CAA: MGM (1926). NYMA: Photoplay.

PAGE, Anita (Anita Pomares), Flushing, NY, 1910-.

Having begun her career as an extra in *A Kiss for Cinderella*, blonde and pretty Anita Page made several silents for MGM, including *Our Dancing Daughters* which brought her to the public's attention. Her talkie appearances began in 1929, the same year she was named a Wampas Baby Star. The highlight of her career also came that year with *The Broadway Melody*. Although she continued appearing in films through 1933, and made one more a few years later, her films were bottom-of-the-bill fare after 1930.

PUBLISHED SOURCES

• *Books* – Credits: *Filmarama* (v. II); *Forty Years of Screen Credits*; *Twenty Years of Silents*. **Encyclopedic Works:** *Film Encyclopedia*; *Filmlexicon degli Autori e delle Opere*; *The Picturegoer's Who's Who and Encyclopedia of the Screen To-day*; *Who's Who in Hollywood*; *The World Film Encyclopedia*. **Nostalgia:** *Whatever Became of...* (5th). **Pictorial:** *They Had Faces Then*.
• *Periodicals* – The following periodical articles are in addition to those included in the library listings below: *Photoplay* (May 1928, Feb. 1930); *Motion Picture Classic* (May 1928, Sept. 1928, June 1929, June 1930); *Movie Classic* (Sept. 1932, Oct. 1934); *Films in Review* (Feb. 1970 [Wampas Baby Stars], Jan. 1972).

ARCHIVAL MATERIALS

• *Clipping File* – CAA: Marriage (1934, 1937); article (1977); nostalgia (1974, 1981); illness (1988, 1992); honor (1991). Article: *San Diego Magazine* (May 1970). CAFI: Newsphotos (numerous); article (undated, 1974). CAUT: Article (1929); newsphoto; MGM contract (1929). CAUU: Nostalgia (1975). NYMN: Newsphotos; marriage (1937). NYPL: Marriage (1927); newsphotos; film appearance (1930s); stage appearance (1935); article (1930s). Periodical article: *Vanity Fair* (Apr. 1930). • *Other Clipping File* – CAUT, GBBF, MIDL, NYMA (Photoplay Collection), PAPL, TXU, WICF. • *Filmography* – NYPL. • *Interview* – CAUU (R. Lamparski Collection). • *Photograph/Still*—CAA (also in Hollywood Studio Museum Collection) (also in MGM Collection), CAH, CAOC (Kiesling Collection), CASU, CAUT (Jessen Collection) (Portrait File), CAUU, DCG (Quigley Photographic Archives), GBBF, MIDL, NJPT, NYAM, NYB (Bettmann/UPI Collection) (Springer Collection) (Underwood Collection), NYCU (Dramatic Museum Portraits), NYEH, NYMN, NYPL, OHCL, PAPL, TNUT (Clarence Brown Collection), TXU (A. Davis Collection), WICF. • *Scrapbook*—NYMA, NYPL. • *Studio Biography*—NYMA: Photoplay.

PEARSON, Virginia, Louisville, KY, 1879/88–1958.

Virginia Pearson was one of the actresses who followed in Theda Bara's vamping footsteps, and closely resembled her, in films like *The Kiss of a Vampire*, *Blazing Love* and *The Bishop's Emeralds*. In the 1920s, when the "vamp" vogue had ended, she was seen in supporting roles in *The Phantom of the Opera*, *The Wizard of Oz*, *What Price Beauty?* and many others. She made a very few talkie appearances as well.

PUBLISHED SOURCES

• *Books*—General: *First One Hundred Noted Men and Women of the Screen*. Credits: *Filmarama* (v. I and II); *Forty Years of Screen Credits*; *Twenty Years of Silents*; *Who Was Who on Screen*. Encyclopedic Works: *The Picturegoer's Who's Who and Encyclopedia of the Screen To-day*; *Who's Who in Hollywood*. Pictorial: *Silent Portraits*.

• *Periodicals*—The following periodical articles are in addition to that included in the library listings below: *Motion Picture Classic* (Dec. 1917); *Photoplay* (Mar. 1918); *Motion Picture Magazine* (Nov. 1918).

ARCHIVAL MATERIALS

• *Clipping File*—CAA: "Perfect back" (1922); bankruptcy (1924); obituary (1958). NYMN: Newsphotos; obituary

(1958). NYPL (also in Locke Collection): Stage appearance (1910–11, 1915, undated); article (1913); newsphotos; disfigurement; obituary (1958). Periodical article: *Green Book Magazine* (Mar. 1914). • *Other Clipping File*—GBBF, WICF. • *Photograph/Still*—CAA (also in Hollywood Studio Museum Collection), DCG (Quigley Photographic Archives), NJFL, NYB (Bettmann/UPI Collection) (Underwood Collection), NYCU (Bulliet Collection), NYMN, NYPL, NYSU, OHCL, TXU, WICF. • *Scrapbook*—NYPL (R. Locke Collection), WICF.

PERCY, Eileen, Belfast, Ireland, 1899/1901–1973.

The highlights of Eileen Percy's career were her co-starring roles with Douglas Fairbanks in several of his pre-swashbuckler films including *Wild and Woolly* and *The Americano*. Most of her other efforts were programmers like *The Blushing Bride*, *Pardon My Nerve*, *The Unchastened Woman* and *Burnt Fingers*. Her career barely outlasted the silent period with a sprinkling of minor talkies.

PUBLISHED SOURCES

• *Books*—General: *Famous Film Folk*. Credits: *Filmarama* (v. I and II); *Twenty Years of Silents*; *Who Was Who on Screen*. Encyclopedic Works: *Film Encylopedia*; *Filmlexicon degli Autori e delle Opere*; *The Picturegoer's Who's Who and Encyclopedia of the Screen To-day*; *Who's Who in Hollywood*. Nostalgia: *Whatever Became of...* (4th). Pictorial: *Silent Portraits*.

• *Periodicals*—*Photoplay* (Feb. 1918); *Motion Picture Classic* (Apr. 1918, Dec. 1920); *Classic Film Collector* (Fall 1973).

ARCHIVAL MATERIALS

• *Clipping File*—CAA: Obituary (1973). NYPL: Newsphotos; obituary (1973). • *Other Clipping File*—GBBF, NYMA (Photoplay Collection), OHCL, PAPL, WICF. • *Legal File*—CAUT (Twentieth Century–Fox Collection): Agreement (1920). • *Photograph/Still*—

CAA (also in Hollywood Studio Museum Collection), CAH, CAUT (Jessen Collection), CNDA, DCG (Quigley Photographic Archives), GBBF, IAU (Junkin Collection), NJFL, NJPT, NYAM, NYEH, NYPL, OHCL, TXU, WICF. • *Scrapbook* – NYPL.

PERDUE, Derelys, Kansas City, MO.

A Wampas Baby Star of 1923, Derelys Perdue worked at several studios during the 1920s and '30s, including Chadwick, Fox, Truart and FBO. She made relatively few films, among which were *Untamed Youth*, *A Dangerous Adventure*, *The Gingham Girl*, *The Smiling Terror* and the serial *The Mystery Rider* (1928).

PUBLISHED SOURCES
• *Books* – General: *Blue Book of the Screen*. Credits: *Filmarama* (v. II); *Twenty Years of Silents*. Encyclopedic Works: *Who's Who in Hollywood*.
• *Periodicals* – *Films in Review* (Feb. 1970 [Wampas Baby Stars]); *Classic Images* (June 1990) (filmography).

ARCHIVAL MATERIALS
• *Clipping File* – GBBF, MAH.
• *Photograph/Still* – CAA (also in Hollywood Studio Museum Collection), DCG (Quigley Photographic Archives), NYPL, WICF.

PETROVA, Olga (Muriel Harding), Liverpool(?), England, 1886-1977.

Stage actress Olga Petrova starred in films for only four years (1915-1918) and made about 20. They were melodramas with titles like *The Vampire* (her first), *The Black Butterfly*, *The Soul of a Magdalen*, *The Eternal Question* and *Tempered Steel*. Her films were popular and she had her own production company, but she apparently preferred the stage, to which she returned.

PUBLISHED SOURCES
• *Books* – Wrote several stories and plays, including *The Black Virgin* (1926), *Hurricane* (1924), *What Do We Know?* (1930), *The White Peacock* (1922) and *The Ghoul* (1925). General: *The Idols of Silence*; *Ladies in Distress*. Credits: *Filmarama* (v. I); *Twenty Years of Silents*. Encyclopedic Works: *Film Encyclopedia*; *Halliwell's Filmgoer's Companion*; *Who Was Who in the Theatre*; *Who's Who in Hollywood*; *The World Almanac Who's Who of Film*. Biography/Autobiography: *Butter with My Bread*. Filmography: *Hollywood on the Palisades*. Pictorial: *Silent Portraits*.
• *Periodicals* – The following periodical articles are in addition to those included in the library listings below: *Green Book Magazine* (Aug. 1912, Apr. 1916); *Cosmopolitan* (Aug. 1914); *Moving Picture World* (Dec. 12, 1914); *Photoplay* (Oct. 1916, June 1917, Dec. 1917, Nov. 1920, Jan. 1921, Mar. 1921, Mar. 1922, May 1922); *Motion Picture Classic* (Feb. 1917, Feb. 1918, Sept. 1918); *Motion Picture Magazine* (Oct. 1917, Mar. 1919); *American Magazine* (Dec. 1924).

ARCHIVAL MATERIALS
• *Clipping File* – CAA: Film appearance (1922); article (1970); nostalgia (1977); obituary (1977). CAUU: Obituary (1977). CASF: Pet mongoose (undated); interview (1924). NYMA (also in Photoplay Collection): Obituary (1977). Periodical articles: *Classic Film Collector* (Fall 1966–Spring 1967, Spring 1978). NYMN: Newsphotos; article (1933); marriage; playwright (1922). NYPL (also in Locke Collection): Review of *Butter with My Bread* (1942); article (1922, 1933, 1942, 1971, undated); newsphotos; stage appearance (1920s); accident; legal problem (1923, 1927); marriage (1923, 1932); cornea transplant (1976–77); nostalgia (1936); death of husband; obituary (1977). Periodical articles: *American Magazine* (undated); *Silent Picture* (Summer[?] 1973, Winter[?] 1974).
• *Other Clipping File* – GBBF, MAH, MIDL, PAPL, WICF, WYU (see Collection). • *Biography* – CAUU (A. Slide

Collection). • *Collection* — WYU: Correspondence (1919–76); manuscripts of OP's plays and poems; clippings (1918–74); periodical issues; photostats of programs; columns by OP; advertisements; drawings; photographs. • *Correspondence* — CAHL: 1918. CAUU (A. Slide Collection): 1972–76. DCLC (Janet Flanner/Solita Solano Papers): 1931–75. NYMA (Photoplay Collection): NYPL: Letters (C. & L. Brown Collection) (1948–50); others (1912, undated). WYU (see Collection). • *Photograph/Still* — CAA (also in Hollywood Studio Museum Collection), CAUU (A. Slide Collection), DCG (Quigley Photographic Archives), NJFL, NYAM, NYB (Underwood Collection), NYEH, NYMN, NYPL, NYSU, OHCL, WICF, WYU (see Collection). • *Play Program* — CASF, WYU (see Collection). • *Scrapbook* — NYPL (also in R. Locke Collection).

PHILBIN, Mary, Chicago, IL, 1903–. 1993

One of the enduring images of silent cinema is undoubtedly the unmasking scene in *The Phantom of the Opera*. The heroine in peril was Mary Philbin; the "Phantom" was, of course, Lon Chaney. Her other films, beginning with *The Blazing Trail* in 1921, were not comparably prestigious. They included *Drums of Love, The Gaiety Girl, The Temple of Venus* and *Girl Overboard*. She appeared in only four talking films.

PUBLISHED SOURCES

• *Books* — Credits: *Filmarama* (v. II); *Twenty Years of Silents*. **Bibliography:** *The Idols of Silence.* **General:** *Blue Book of the Screen; Famous Film Folk; How I Broke Into the Movies; Scream Queens; The Truth About the Movies.* **Encylopedic Works:** *Film Encyclopedia; Filmlexicon degli Autori e delle Opere; Halliwell's Filmgoer's Companion; Who's Who in Hollywood; Who's Who of the Horrors and Other Fantasy Films; The World Almanac Who's Who of*

Film. **Nostalgia:** *Whatever Became of . . .* (11th). **Pictorial:** *Silent Portraits.*
• *Periodicals* — *Motion Picture Magazine* (Feb. 1923, Feb. 1925); *Photoplay* (Oct. 1924, Nov. 1926); *Motion Picture Classic* (Oct. 1925, Dec. 1926, Apr. 1928); *Theatre* (Oct. 1926); *Films in Review* (Feb. 1970 (Wampas Baby Stars), June–July 1970); *American Cinematographer* (Apr. 1990).

ARCHIVAL MATERIALS

• *Clipping File* — CAA: Legal problem (1948); film appearance (1920s, 1922, 1927); newsphotos; nostalgia (1975). NYMA (also in Photoplay collection): Film appearance (1923). NYPL: Film appearance (1923); article (1923, 1926, undated); newsphotos (numerous); film reviews. • *Other Clipping File* — GBBF, MIDL, OHCL, PAPL, WICF. • *Photograph/Still* — CAA (also in Hollywood Studio Museum Collection), CAFA, CASF, CAUS, CAUT (Jessen Collection) (Portrait File), CNDA, DCG (Quigley Photographic Archives), GBBF, NJPT, NYB (Bettmann/UPI Collection), NYCU (Dramatic Museum Portraits) (Palmer Collection), NYEH, NYPL, NYSU, OHCL, TXU, WICF. • *Scrapbook* — NJPT (Yeandle Collection). • *Studio Biography* — NYMA: Photoplay.

PICKFORD, Jack (Jack Smith), Toronto, Canada, 1896–1933.

Given the enormous Hollywood presence of Mary Pickford (q.v.), it was perhaps inevitable that her younger brother Jack would have a film career. He was an appealing actor in his own right, however, especially when playing youthful heroes in films such as *Tom Sawyer, The Little Shepherd of Kingdom Come, His Majesty, Bunker Bean* and *Seventeen*. His career began to peter out in the late 1920s, his final film coming in 1928. He was married to Olive Thomas (q.v.).

PUBLISHED SOURCES

• *Books* — General: *Blue Book of the*

Screen; *Famous Film Folk*; *Hollywood Kids*; *Life Stories of the Movie Stars*; *The Truth About the Movies*; *Who's Who on the Screen*. **Credits:** *Filmarama* (v. I and II); *Twenty Years of Silents*; *Who Was Who on Screen*. **Encyclopedic Works:** *Film Encyclopedia*; *Filmlexicon degli Autori e delle Opere*; *Halliwell's Filmgoer's Companion*; *The Picturegoer's Who's Who and Encyclopedia of the Screen To-day*; *Who's Who in Hollywood*; *The World Almanac Who's Who of Film*; *The World Film Encyclopedia*. **Pictorial:** *Silent Portraits*.

• *Periodicals*—The following periodical articles are in addition to those included in the library listings below: *Motion Picture Supplement* (Nov. 1915); *Photoplay* (Sept. 1917, Mar. 1933); *Motion Picture Magazine* (Apr. 1919, Sept. 1920, July 1922, Oct. 1923, Oct. 1924, Apr. 1925); *Motion Picture Classic* (Sept. 1920); *Movie Classic* (May 1932); *Films in Review* (Mar. 1986).

ARCHIVAL MATERIALS

• *Clipping File*—CAA (see also Collection under entry for Mary Pickford): Marriage/divorce (1922, 1926–27, 1930, 1932); legal problem (1928); illness (1928–29, 1931–32); obituary (1933). NYMA (also in Photoplay Collection): Personal data summary. Periodical article: *Classic Film Collector* (Spring 1978). NYMN: Obituary (1933). NYPL: Engagement/marriage/separation/divorce (1922, 1925–26, 1928, 1932); newsphotos; film review (1920s); film appearance (1910s, 1926); joins Navy (1918); injury; debts (1930); illness (1928); article (1930, undated); obituary (1933). Periodical articles: *Photoplay* (Oct. 1917); *Movie Weekly* (undated); *Motion Picture Magazine* (undated). • *Other Clipping File*—GBBF, MAH, MIDL, WICF. • *Oral History*—NYCO: Mentioned in: Joseph Mankiewicz interview. • *Photograph/Still*—CAA (also in Hollywood Studio Museum Collection) (also in Mary Pickford Collection), CAUT (Jessen Collection), CAUU, CNDA, DCG (Quigley Photographic Archives), IAU (Junkin Collection), MABU (Douglas Fairbanks Jr. Collection), NJFL,

NYAM, NYB (Underwood Collection), NYEH, NYPL, NYSU, OHCL, TNUT (Clarence Brown Collection), TXSM, WICF. • *Scrapbook*—NYPL (also in R. Locke Collection), TNUT (Clarence Brown Collection).

PICKFORD, Mary (Gladys Smith), Toronto, Canada, 1893–1979.

Indisputably the most famous screen actress of the 1910s and '20s, Mary Pickford was indeed America's—and the world's—"sweetheart." As well as being an accomplished actress, she was a prodigious businesswoman, a founder of United Artists and, with her second husband Douglas Fairbanks (q.v.), a cultural icon. Her nearly 200 films included popular roles in *Pollyanna*, *Tess of the Storm Country* (two versions), *The Poor Little Rich Girl*, *Rebecca of Sunnybrook Farm*, *Daddy Long Legs* and *Little Annie Rooney*. Her popularity faded after the arrival of sound films and there were only four talkies, although she won the second Academy Award for Best Actress in *Coquette* (1929). She was also married to Owen Moore (q.v.) and Buddy Rogers (q.v.).

PUBLISHED SOURCES

• *Books*—Written by (or ghostwritten for) MP: *Cinema* (one part). She wrote *The Demi-Widow* (novel, 1935) and *Why Not Try God?* **Bibliography:** *The Idols of Silence*. **General:** *Alice in Movieland*; *The American Film Heritage*; *Behind the Screen*; *Blue Book of the Screen*; *Celebrity Homes*; *The Celluloid Sacrifice*; *The Civil War on the Screen and Other Essays*; *Classics of the Silent Screen*; *Close Ups*; *Come to Judgment*; *Co-Starring Famous Women and Alcohol*; *Doug and Mary and Others*; *Famous Film Folk*; *Famous Stars of Filmdom (Women)*; *Fifty Super Stars*; *The Film Answers Back*; *First One Hundred Noted Men and Women of the Screen*; *The Great Movie Stars*; *The Griffith Actresses*; *History of the American Cinema*

(v. 3); *History of the American Film Industry*; *Hollywood: The Golden Era*; *Hollywood Album 2*; *Hollywood and the Great Stars*; *Hollywood Be Thy Name*; *Hollywood Exiles*; *Hollywood Hall of Fame*; *Hollywood Kids*; *Hollywood Lolitas*; *Hollywood Love Stories*; *The Hollywood Reporter Star Profiles*; *The Hollywood Style*; *Hollywood's Children*; *How I Broke Into the Movies*; *"Image" on the Art and Evolution of the Film*; *Intimate Talks with Movie Stars*; *Ladies in Distress*; *Life Stories of the Movie Stars*; *Love Goddesses of the Movies*; *Love, Laughter and Tears*; *Mary Pickfordova*; *A Million and One Nights*; *Movie Star*; *The Movie Stars*; *The Movie Stars Story*; *The Movies Come from America*; *The Movies in the Age of Innocence*; *The National Society of Film Critics on the Movie Star*; *The Oscar People*; *The Parade's Gone By*; *Pickfair*; *Popcorn Venus*; *The Public is Never Wrong*; *Reel Women*; *Rolling Breaks and Other Movie Business*; *The Saturday Evening Post Movie Book*; *Screen Personalities*; *Screening Out the Past*; *Spellbound in Darkness*; *Stardom*; *The Stars* (Schickel); *Stars!*; *The Stars Appear*; *Stars of the Silents*; *Take Them Up Tenderly*; *Tribute to Mary Pickford* (1970); *A Tribute to Mary Pickford* (1981); *The Truth About the Movies*; *Two Reels and a Crank*; *United Artists*; *Venus in Hollywood*; *Virgins, Vamps and Flappers*; *Who's Who in the Film World*; *Who's Who on the Screen*; *With Eisenstein in Hollywood*; *You Must Remember This*. **Credits:** *Filmarama* (v. I and II); *Twenty Years of Silents*. **Encyclopedic Works:** *A Biographical Dictionary of Film*; *Cinema, a Critical Dictionary*; *Current Biography* (1945, 1980); *A Dictionary of the Cinema*; *Film Encyclopedia*; *Filmlexicon degli Autori e delle Opere*; *Halliwell's Filmgoer's Companion*; *The Illustrated Encyclopedia of the World's Great Movie Stars and Their Films*; *The Illustrated Who's Who of the Cinema*; *International Dictionary of Films and Filmmakers* (v. 3); *The International Encyclopedia of Film*; *International Motion Picture Almanac* (1975– 79); *The Movie Makers*; *The Oxford Companion to Film*; *The Picturegoer's Who's Who and Encyclopedia of the Screen To-day*; *Quinlan's Illustrated Registry of Film Stars*; *Who Was Who in the Theatre*; *Who's Who in Hollywood*; *Women Who Make Movies*; *The World Almanac Who's Who of Film*; *The World Encyclopedia of the Film*; *The World Film Encyclopedia*. • *Filmography—Hollywood on the Palisades*. **Pictorial:** *The Fairbanks Album*; *Leading Ladies*; *Life and Death in Hollywood*; *The Revealing Eye*; *Silent Portraits*; *They Had Faces Then*; *Wallace Neff*. **Biography/Autobiography:** *Autobiography of Cecil B. DeMille*; *Doug & Mary*; *Mary Pickford, America's Sweetheart*; *Mary Pickford and Douglas Fairbanks*; *My Autobiography* (Chaplin); *My Rendezvous with Life*; *Sunshine and Shadow*; *Sweetheart*; *When the Movies Were Young*. **Films:** *The Films of Mary Pickford*; *Mary Pickford, Comedienne*. **Recordings:** *Hollywood on Record*. **Catalog:** *The J. M. Goodman Auction Gallery ... presents the Auction of the Mary Pickford Estate*. **Factoids:** *Star Stats*.

MEDIA

The Birth of a Legend (video).

• *Periodicals*—The following periodical articles are in addition to those included in the library listings below: *Munsey's Magazine* (May 1913); *Theatre* (June 1913, Apr. 1919); *Green Book Magazine* (July 1913); *Cosmopolitan* (July 1913, Oct. 1956); *Photoplay* (Aug. 1913, Sept. 1914, Mar. 1915, Nov. 1915–Feb. 1916, Apr. 1916, Mar. 1917, Oct. 1917, July 1918, Oct. 1918, Dec. 1919, Mar.–Apr. 1920, June 1920, Dec. 1921, July 1923, Sept. 1923, Jan. 1924, May–June 1924, Sept. 1924, Nov. 1924, Feb. 1925, June 1925, Sept.–Nov. 1925, Feb. 1927, Mar. 1928, Sept. 1928, May 1929, Aug. 1930, Jan. 1931, May 1931, Apr. 1932, Mar. 1933, Sept. 1933, Feb. 1934, Feb. 1935, May 1936, Aug. 1936, Sept. 1971); *American Magazine* (Apr. 1914, May 1918, May 1923); *Moving Picture World* (July 11–18, 1914); *Blue Book Magazine* (Aug. 1914); *Motion Picture Magazine* (Jan.–Feb. 1915, Jan. 1916,

Mar. 1916, July 1916, Sept.-Nov. 1916, Aug. 1917, Nov. 1917, Apr. 1918, June 1919, Sept. 1919, Mar. 1920, Oct.-Nov. 1920, June 1922, Dec. 1922, Aug. 1924, Jan. 1925, Aug. 1926, June 1928, Oct. 1928, July 1929, Sept. 1929, May 1930, Sept. 1930, Dec. 1930, Mar. 1931, Apr.-May 1932, July 1932, Feb. 1933, Oct. 1933, Mar. 1934, Feb. 1936); *Ladies' Home Journal* (Jan. 1915, Oct. 1919, July-Aug. 1923); *Nash's & Pall Mall* (Apr. 1915); *Everybody's Magazine* (June 1915, June 1916, Nov. 1920, May 1926); *Feature Movie Magazine* (Oct. 10, 1915); *Motion Picture Classic* (Feb.-Mar. 1917, Sept. 1917, July 1918, Jan. 1922, Aug. 1922, Aug. 1923, July 1925, Mar. 1931, Aug. 1931, Feb. 1936); *Harper's Bazaar* (Apr. 1917); *New Republic* (July 7, 1917, Feb. 15, 1919, June 6, 1955, June 23, 1979); *Woman's Home Companion* (Aug. 1919, Feb. 1929); *National Magazine* (Oct. 1919, July 1924, Mar. 1929); *Filmplay Journal* (Sept. 1921); *Collier's* (June 10, 1922); *Pictorial Review* (Apr. 1927, Mar. 1931, Jan. 1934); *Overland Monthly* (Mar. 1928); *Literary Digest* (Nov. 3, 1928); *World Today* (Dec. 1928); *Everygirl's* (Oct. 1929); *Vanity Fair* (June 1930); *Saturday Evening Post* (Aug. 23, 1930); *Good Housekeeping* (Oct. 1930, Apr. 1933); *National Board of Review Magazine* (Feb. 1931, Feb. 1940); *Time* (May 11, 1931, May 13, 1974, June 11, 1979); *Outlook* (May 13, 1931); *Cinema Digest* (Nov. 14, 1932, Apr. 3, 1933, Apr. 24, 1933); *Movie Classic* (Mar. 1933, Sept. 1933, Nov.-Dec. 1934, Nov. 1935); *Silver Screen* (May 1933, Nov. 1933, Feb. 1934); *Forum* (Aug. 1933); *Newsweek* (Nov. 10, 1934, May 16, 1936, Nov. 6, 1967, Nov. 28, 1977, June 11, 1979); *Rob Wagner's Script* (June 25, 1938); *Movieland* (Aug. 1945); *Life* (Nov. 17, 1947, Apr. 13, 1953, Jan. 23, 1956, Apr. 16, 1956); *Saturday Review* (June 11, 1955); *Films in Review* (Aug.-Sept. 1959, Feb. 1966, May 1978, Mar. 1986, Dec. 1987); *8mm Collector* (May 1964, Summer 1965); *Cahiers du Cinéma* (Sept. 1966); *Classic Film Collector* (Fall 1966, Fall/Winter 1967, Fall 1970, Summer 1971, Winter 1971); *Players Showcase* (Winter 1966); *Premiere*

(v. 11, no 5); *Filmograph* (no. 1-4, 1970); *Look* (Nov. 3, 1970); *Film Fan Monthly* (Dec. 1970); *Film* (Spring 1971); *Silent Picture* (Spring 1971); *Screen Greats* (Summer 1971); *American Heritage* (Dec. 1971); *Biography News* (Nov. 1975); *Box-office* (Apr. 17, 1978, June 4-11, 1979); *Wide Angle* (no. 1, 1979); *Classic Film/Video Images* (July 1979, Jan. 1980, Nov. 1981); *Ecran* (July 1979); *Cinéma* (France) (July-Aug. 1979); *Cinématographique* (July 1979); *Cinema 2002* (July-Aug. 1979); *Cinema Nuovo* (Aug. 1979); *Film a Doba* (Sept. 1979); *Bianco e Nero* (Sept.-Dec. 1979); *Imagenes* (Oct. 1979); *Cinéaste* (Fall 1979); *Film en Televisie* (Oct. 1979); *Film und Ton* (Nov. 1979); *Kinoizkustvo* (Nov. 1979); *Avant-Scène du Cinema* (Nov. 1, 1980); *Esquire* (Nov. 1983); *Classic Images* (July 1984, Apr. 1985, June 1991); *Filmfaust* (Aug.-Sept. 1985); *Film Fax* (Mar. 1990); *Architectural Digest* (Apr. 1990).

ARCHIVAL MATERIALS
• *Caricature*—NYPL.   • *Clipping File*—CAA (also in Collection). Film appearance (1920, 1951-52); trip to New York (1921); article by MP (1927, 1931, undated); legal problem (1927-28, 1930-31, 1945, 1947-51, 1956-57, 1959, 1961, 1963); mother's death (1928); travels (1928, 1933); cuts hair (1928); robbery (1920s, 1954, 1961); marriage/divorce/children (1931, 1933-34, 1944); injury (1932, 1956, 1965); stage appearance (1933); kidnap plot (1934); honor (1935, 1951, 1960-61, 1963); bond tour (1953); article (1915, 1924, 1933, 1947, 1950, 1954, 1963, 1965, 1971-72, 1974, 1978-79, 1988, undated); illness (1954-55); United Artists (1954-56); party (1956, 1968, 1978); film festival (1966, 1970-73, 1976, 1979-80); nostalgia (1967); donates films to Library of Congress (1970); Academy Award (1976); review of *Mary Pickford and Douglas Fairbanks* (1977); documentary (1978); donates memorabilia to Academy of Motion Picture Arts and Sciences (1979); Pickfair (1947, 1952-53, 1961, 1978-81, 1986); will; excerpt from *Hollywood Be Thy Name*; auction (1981); gift to Library of Congress (1978); ranch

(1990); review of *Mary Pickford* (1990); newsphotos; obituary (1979). Periodical articles: *Liberty* (June 1928, Nov. 1929, Aug. 1933, Feb. 1934, Jan. 1935, Dec. 1935, 1936); *Vanity Fair* (Aug. 1932); *New Yorker* (Apr. 7, 1934); *McCall's* (Mar.-June 1954); *Films and Filming* (Dec. 1973); *Celebrity Pictorial* (Apr. 1974); *National Aeronautics* (July-Aug. 1974); *Hollywood Studio Magazine* (June 1976); *American Classic Screen* (Nov.-Dec. 1976); *Collectibles Illustrated* (May-June 1984); *Life* (Spring 1989). CAFI: Film festival (1976); article (1965, 1976, 1979); biographical TV film (1977); Oscar (1976); divorce (undated). Periodical articles: *Image* (Dec. 1959); *Hollywood Studio Magazine* (June 1976); *American Classic Screen* (Sept.-Oct. 1976). CASF: Pickfair; career retrospective; obituary (1979). CAUT: Article (1960, 1971-72, 1974, 1976, 1979); United Artists (1954-55; buys radio station (1958); newsphotos; injury (1965); legal problem (1947, 1959, 1961); review of *Mary Pickford and Douglas Fairbanks* (1977); special Academy Award (1976); program for Bicentennial Salute to Mary Pickford (1976); donates films to Library of Congress (1949); Pickfair (1978-80); documentary (1978); film festival (1971, 1976, 1980); tribute (1979); review of *Doug and Mary* (1977); memorabilia (1981); program for Tribute to Mary Pickford (1970); estate (1979); obituary (1979). Periodical article: *Theatre Magazine* (1910s). CAUU (also in McCormick Collection): Legal problem (1947, 1950, 1955, 1957, 1959, 1961); honor (1955, 1960, 1963, 1976, 1979); robbery (1962); Pickfair (1961, 1979-81, 1986); buys studio (1949, 1954-55); newsphotos; politics (1952); illness (1954); film appearance (1951); film festival (1971, 1976, 1979); article (1971-72, 1974, 1976-78); memorabilia (1979); program from Tribute to Mary Pickford (1979); photo exhibit (1978); tribute (1976); obituary (1979). Periodical articles: *Liberty* (Nov. 9, 1929); *McCall's* (June 1954); *National Aeronautics* (July-Aug. 1974). NYMA: Newsphotos; booklet: AFI *Tribute to Mary Pickford* (1970); article (1947, 1958, 1965, 1970-71, 1974, 1976, 1978-80); alco-

holism (1959); release of films (1972); radio appearance (1934); donates films (1970); Academy Award (1976); sale of Pickfair (1980); excerpt from *The Griffith Actresses*; program for *Bicentennial Salute to Mary Pickford*; separation (1934); Pickfair razed (1990); memorabilia (1981); estate (1979); film retrospective (1979); excerpt from *Current Biography* (1945); obituary (1979). Periodical articles: *Everybody's Magazine* (undated); *Photo-play World* (Mar. 1918); *New Yorker* (Apr. 7, 1934); *8mm Collector* (Fall/Winter 1965); *Films and Filming* (Dec. 1973); *American Classic Screen* (Nov.-Dec. 1976); *Classic Film Collector* (Fall/Winter ?, Winter 1976, Summer 1977); *Classic Images* (Oct. 1983); *Hollywood Studio Magazine* (undated). NYMN: Newsphotos (numerous); article (1929, 1930s, 1937, 1955); Pickfair; marriage (1937); film appearance (1951); engagement/marriage/children (1930s, 1933-36); stage appearance (1935); legal problem (1936-37); obituary (1979). NYPL: PARTIAL CONTENTS: Filmmaking (1958); program for a Tribute to Mary Pickford (1979); review of *Mary Pickford, Comedienne* (1970); review of *Mary Pickford and Douglas Fairbanks* (1978); will (1979); Pickfair (1979-80, 1990); sale of effects (1981); newsphotos; TV documentary; film festival (1979); article (1970); appreciation by AFI (and other sponsors) film festival; review of *Mary Pickford* (1991); Mary Pickford Theatre (Library of Congess). Periodical articles: *Classic Film Collector* (Winter 1970, Spring 1973); *Liberty* (Spring 1972); *Hollywood Studio Magazine* (Aug. 1979). • *Other Clipping File*—AZSU (Jimmy Starr Collection), CAUB, CNDA, GBBF, MABU (Douglas Fairbanks Jr. Collection), MAH, MASC (Sophia Smith Collection), MIDL, OHSU, PAPL, WICF. • *Collection*—CAA: Includes clippings (1920s-1960s); legal files; photographs; correspondence (1920s-1970s); scripts; financial records; scrapbooks; miscellaneous memorabilia. *NOTE:* Unprocessed and unavailable to researchers as of 1993. • *Correspondence*—CAA (also in Collection): Notes (Hedda Hopper Collection) (1940, 1943–44, 1960); 6 letters (Adolph Zukor Collection) (1919, 1925, 1933, 1970–71). CAHL: 1933, 1935. CAOC (Kiesling Collection): Note about Motion Picture Relief Fund (1930). CAUS (Rob Wagner Collection) (Eddie Cantor Collection) (Preston Sturges Collection), DCG (Terry Ramsaye Papers), DCLC (Thomas J. Geraghty Papers). MABU: Letter(s), telegram (Robert H. Andrews Collection) (1963–64); letters (Malcolm Boyd Collection) (1949–75). MASC (Sophia Smith Collection): 4 letters to Elliott Carter re administration of the Pickford Cosmetic Co. (1937–41). NYCU: Letter(s) (Spewack Papers); 4 letters (Erskine Collection) (1933, undated); 1 letter (Strong Collection) (1935); 2 letters (Salisbury Collection) (1945); 1 letter (Steegmuller Collection) (1953). NYPL (see also under entry for Buddy Rogers): 41 letters (Mary Pickford and Buddy Rogers Correspondence Collection) (1943–76); letters (C. & L. Brown Collection) (1943, 1947); letters (Richard Rodgers Collection) (1962); others (1934, 1939–45, 1948, 1954, 1959–60, 1968). • *Filmography* – CAA, CAUT, CAUU. • *Interview* – CAUU (Hollywood Studio Museum Collection). • *Legal File* – CAA (see Collection). CAUT (Twentieth Century-Fox Collection): Letter, memo, telegram (1935); contract (1935). CAUW: Periodical (1932); letter (1914, 1927–29, 1939, 1946); document (1918). • *Manuscript* – CAA (Searle Dawley Collection): Biographical notes by SD about directing MP. • *Oral History* – CAUS: Mentioned in the following interviews: Ben Carre, Karl Struss. NYCO: Interviewed in 1959. Mentioned in the following interviews: Sidney Blackmer, Louis A. Bonn, Johnny Mack Brown, Marc Connelly, Jackie Cooper, George Cukor, Jessica Dragonette, Lillian Gish, Sessue Hayakawa, Leo Hurwitz, Jay Leyda, Lila Lee, Harold Lloyd, Charles McAdam, Joel McCrea, Frances Marion, Chester Morris, Conrad Nagel, Elliot Nugent, Louella Parsons, Adela St. Johns, Gloria Swanson, Blanche Sweet, R.G. White, Max Youngstein, Jerome Zerbe, Adolph Zukor. • *Photograph/Still* – CAA (also in Collection) (also in

Hollywood Studio Museum Collection) (also in MGM Collection), CAHL, CALM, CAPH, CASF, CAUB, CAUC (Motion Picture Photograph Collection), CAUT (Jessen Collection) (Portrait File), CAUU (also in A. Slide Collection), CNDA, DCG (Quigley Photographic Archives), IAU (Junkin Collection), MABU (Douglas Fairbanks Jr. Collection), MASC (Sophia Smith Collection), NJFL, NYAM, NYB (Bettmann/UPI Collection) (Penguin Collection) (Springer Collection) (Underwood Collection), NYCU (Dramatic Museum Portraits) (Palmer Collection), NYEH, NYMN, NYPL, NYSU, OHCL, TXSM, TXU, WICF. • *Press Kit* – OHCL. • *Program* – CASF: Tribute at the California Palace of the Legion of Honor. OHSU. • *Reminiscence* – MISU: MP describes the Academy Award for *Wings*, and *Buddy Rogers meets MP* (recording). • *Scrapbook* – CAA (see Collection), CASU (Stark Collection), NYAM, NYMA, NYPL (also in R. Locke Collection).

POLO, Eddie, San Francisco, CA, 1875/76–1961.

Athletic daredevil Eddie Polo was one of the preeminent serial kings in such 1917–23 Universal chapterplays as *The Lure of the Circus*, *Captain Kidd*, *Do or Die*, *The Circus King* and *The Secret Four*. He also appeared in the *Cyclone Smith* series. His career faltered in the mid-1920s but he returned in the 1940s to play a few supporting roles.

PUBLISHED SOURCES

• *Books* – **General:** *Bound and Gagged*; *Early American Cinema*; *Eighty Silent Film Stars*; *Stunt*; *Who's Who on the Screen*. **Credits:** *Filmarama* (v. I and II); *Twenty Years of Silents*; *Who Was Who on Screen*. **Encyclopedic Works:** *Film Encyclopedia*; *Filmlexicon degli Autori e delle Opere*; *Who's Who in Hollywood*.

• *Periodicals* – The following periodical articles are in addition to those included in the library listings below: *Life*

250   Prevost

(Apr. 12, 1948); *Films in Review* (Aug.-Sept. 1961); *Classic Film/Video Images* (Sept. 1979).

ARCHIVAL MATERIALS

• *Clipping File* — CAA: Mistaken identity (1949); comeback (1961); obituary (1961). NYMA (also in Photoplay Collection): Obituary (1961). Periodical articles: *Classic Film Collector* (Summer 1966, Fall 1973); *Classic Images* (Mar. 1984). NYPL: Career (1918); article (1918–19, 1940s?); newsphotos; stage appearance (1923); obituary (1961). Periodical articles: *Motion Picture Magazine* (Feb. 1918); *Picture Play Magazine* (Oct. 1919). • *Other Clipping File* — CASP, CNDA, GBBF, MIDL, OHCL, WICF. • *Photograph/Still* — CAA (also in Hollywood Studio Museum Collection), CASP, CAUT (Jessen Collection), DCG (Quigley Photographic Archives), NYB (Underwood Collection), NYPL, NYSU, WICF. • *Publicity Release* — CAA: Paramount (1939); Fox (1940). • *Scrapbook* — NYPL. • *Studio Biography* — CAA: MGM (1933). NYMA: Photoplay.

PREVOST, Marie (Mary Bickford Dunn or Gunn), Sarnia, Canada, 1898/1901–1937.

Marie Prevost debuted in 1917 as a Mack Sennett bathing beauty and by the mid-1920s had starred in three Ernst Lubitsch films. Her later '20s films tended to be ultra-lightweight fare such as *Getting Gertie's Garter* and *Up in Mabel's Room*. Because of excess weight and other problems, she made the transition to sound films as a supporting player. At the time of her death she had made something of a comeback. She was married to Kenneth Harlan (q.v.).

PUBLISHED SOURCES

• *Books* — **General:** *Blue Book of the Screen*; *Famous Film Folk*; *How I Broke Into the Movies*; *The Truth About the Movies*; *Who's Who on the Screen.* **Credits:** *Filmarama* (v. I and II); *Forty Years of Screen Credits*; *Twenty Years of*

Silents; *Who Was Who on Screen.* **Encyclopedic Works:** *Film Encyclopedia*; *Filmlexicon degli Autori e delle Opere*; *Halliwell's Filmgoer's Companion*; *The Illustrated Who's Who of the Cinema*; *The Movie Makers*; *The Picturegoer's Who's Who and Encyclopedia of the Screen To-day*; *Who's Who in Hollywood*; *The World Almanac Who's Who of Film*; *The World Film Encyclopedia.* **Pictorial:** *Silent Portraits*; *They Had Faces Then.*

• *Periodicals* — *Motion Picture Magazine* (May 1919, Dec. 1921, Feb. 1929, Mar. 1931); *Photoplay* (July 1921, Sept. 1922, Sept. 1925); *Motion Picture Classic* (Mar. 1922, Mar. 1925, Nov. 1927, Oct. 1928); *Focus on Film* (Autumn 1974); *Classic Film/Video Images* (Sept. 1979); *Hollywood Studio Magazine* (May 1986).

ARCHIVAL MATERIALS

• *Clipping File* — CAA: Article (1927); marriage/reconciliation/divorce (1924, 1927–29); legal problem (1920s, 1929–30, 1932–33); film appearance (1922–23, 1927, 1933); weight problem (1932, 1934); illness (1930); nostalgia (1970); obituary (1937). CAUT: Film appearance (1928); divorce (1929); obituary (1937). NYMA (also in Photoplay Collection): Newsphotos; personal data summary; obituary (1937). NYPL (also in Locke Collection): Career (1937); newsphotos (numerous); article (undated); death investigated (1937); divorce (1927); estate (1937); film appearance (1930s); Sennett bathing beauty (1917, 1919–20); obituary (1937). • *Other Clipping File* — GBBF, MIDL, OHCL, PAPL, TXU, WICF. • *Correspondence* — CAHL: 1924. • *Filmography* — NYMA. • *Legal File* — CAA (Sennett Collection): Contract (1919); option (1920–21); letter (1921). CAUW: Letter (1924–25); personnel, payroll record (1923, 1935–36); contract (1924). • *Photograph/Still* — CAA (also in Hollywood Studio Museum Collection) (also in MGM Collection), CAH, CAHL, CASU, CAUB, CAUT (Jessen Collection), CAUU, CNDA, DCG (Quigley Photographic Archives), GBBF, MIDL, NJPT, NYB (Bettmann/UPI Collection), NYCU (Dramatic

Museum Portraits) (Palmer Collection), NYEH, NYMN (Mack Sennett file), NYPL, NYSU, OHCL, PAPL, TXU (A. Davis Collection), WICF. • *Scrapbook* – UTBY (DeMille Archives). • *Studio Biography* – CAA: Metropolitan (1926); DeMille (1927).

PRINGLE, Aileen (Aileen Bisbee), San Francisco, CA, 1895–1989.

Aileen Pringle was a regal-looking brunette and an MGM star throughout the 1920s, her forte being the "vamp" and "other woman" roles. She was especially popular after her roles in two Elinor Glyn vehicles, Madame Glyn having proclaimed that she had "It." Her career declined after her talkie debut in *Night Parade*, and although she made film appearances into the early 1940s, her roles had diminished into bit parts.

PUBLISHED SOURCES

• *Books* – • *Oral History* – *Aileen Pringle, Silent Movie Actress and Frequent Guest*. **General:** *Famous Film Folk*; *Ladies in Distress*; *The Truth About the Movies*. **Credits:** *Filmarama* (v. I and II); *Forty Years of Screen Credits*; *Twenty Years of Silents*. **Encyclopedic Works:** *Film Encyclopedia*; *Filmlexicon degli Autori e delle Opere*; *Halliwell's Filmgoer's Companion*; *The Movie Makers*; *The Picturegoer's Who's Who and Encyclopedia of the Screen To-day*; *Who's Who in Hollywood*; *The World Almanac Who's Who of Film*; *The World Film Encyclopedia*. **Nostalgia:** *Whatever Became of...* (2nd). **Pictorial:** *Silent Portraits*; *They Had Faces Then*.

• *Periodicals* – The following periodical articles are in addition to that included in the library listings below: *Photoplay* (Jan. 1924, Nov. 1925, Dec. 1926, Feb. 1928, Jan. 1929); *Motion Picture Magazine* (June 1925, May 1926, Nov. 1928); *Motion Picture Classic* (June 1925, Jan. 1926, Feb. 1929); *Movie Classic* (June 1932); *Hollywood Studio Magazine* (Dec. 1971); *Classic Images* (Jan. 1990); *Skoop* (Feb. 1990); *Films in Review* (Mar. 1990).

ARCHIVAL MATERIALS

• *Clipping File* – AZSU (Jimmy Starr Collection): Obituary (1989). CAA: Marriage/divorce (1930, 1933, 1935, 1944, 1947); film appearance (1924); article (1927); nostalgia (1969, 1971); obituary (1989). Article: *Films in Review* (October 1979). CAFI: Obituary (1985). CAUT: Divorce; newsphotos. NYMA (also in Photoplay collection): Obituary (1989). NYPL: Newsphotos; engagement/divorce (1926, 1933); film appearance (1926); article (undated); robbery (1933); obituary (1989). Periodical article: *Films in Review* (Oct. 1979). • *Other Clipping File* – CASP, CAUB, GBBF, MIDL, OHCL, OHSU, PAPL, TXU, WICF. • *Correspondence* – CAA (Hedda Hopper Collection): Letter about AP's reaction to *Citizen Kane*; note (1941, 1953). • *Legal File* – CAUW: Personnel record (1941). • *Oral History* – NYCO: Mentioned in: Arthur Hornblow Jr. interview. • *Photograph/Still* – CAA (also in Hollywood Studio Museum Collection) (also in MGM Collection), CASP, CAUT (Portrait File), CAUU, CNDA, DCG (Quigley Photographic Archives), GBBF, NJPT, NYAM, NYB (Bettmann/UPI Collection) (Underwood Collection), NYCU (Dramatic Museum Portraits), NYEH, NYMN, NYPL, NYSU, OHCL, PAPL, TNUT (Clarence Brown Collection), TXSM, TXU (A. Davis Collection), WICF. • *Scrapbook* – NYPL. • *Studio Biography* – NYMA: Photoplay.

QUIRK, William ("Billy"), Jersey City, NJ, 1873/83–1926.

For some years after his debut (about 1908), Billy Quirk was a popular Biograph comic actor who costarred with Mary Pickford and Constance Talmadge in a series of one- and two-reelers. He also worked at Gem and Solax. Many of the films bore his name in the title (e.g., *Billy's Troubles*, *Billy's Wager*) and he appeared in the *Muggsie* series as well. In the mid-

1910s his career began to decline and after a hiatus of several years he came back in the '20s for some supporting roles.

PUBLISHED SOURCES

• *Books* — **General:** *Clown Princes and Court Jesters.* **Credits:** *Filmarama* (v. I and II); *Twenty Years of Silents; Who Was Who on Screen.* **Encyclopedic Works:** *Film Encyclopedia; Filmlexicon degli Autori e delle Opere; Who's Who in Hollywood.* **Pictorial:** *Silent Portraits.*

• *Periodicals* — The following periodical article is in addition to those included in the library listings below: *Moving Picture Stories* (Oct. 1, 1915).

ARCHIVAL MATERIALS

• *Clipping File* — NYMA: Periodical articles: *Green Book Magazine* (May 1915); *Classic Images* (Oct. 1988). • *Other Clipping File* — PAPL, WICF. • *Photograph/Still* — DCG (Quigley Photographic Archives), NJFL, NYAM, NYPL, WICF.

RALSTON, Esther, Bar Harbor, ME, 1902–1994.

After beginning as an extra about 1916, beautiful blonde Esther Ralston hit her screen stride in *Peter Pan*, a Paramount film of 1924. Dubbed "The American Venus" after the title of her 1926 film, she had leading roles in such films as *A Kiss for Cinderella*, *Old Ironsides* and *The Case of Lena Smith.* She made more than 20 sound films through 1941 but her starring career in major films was over in the early 1930s.

PUBLISHED SOURCES

• *Books* — **Bibliography:** *The Idols of Silence.* **General:** *Broken Silence; Classics of the Silent Screen; How I Broke Into the Movies; Return Engagement; Speaking of Silents; The Stars Appear; Sweethearts of the Sage; Twinkle, Twinkle Movie Star.* **Credits:** *Filmarama* (v. II); *Forty Years of Screen Credits; Twenty Years of Silents.* **Encyclopedic Works:** *Film Encyclopedia; Filmlexicon degli Autori e delle Opere; Halliwell's*

Filmgoer's Companion; The Illustrated Who's Who of the Cinema; The Movie Makers; The Picturegoer's Who's Who and Encyclopedia of the Screen To-day; Who's Who in Hollywood; Women Who Make Movies; The World Film Encyclopedia. **Biography/Autobiography:** *Someday We'll Laugh.* **Nostalgia:** *Whatever Became Of...* (2nd, 8th). **Pictorial:** *Silent Portraits; They Had Faces Then.*

• *Periodicals* — The following periodical articles are in addition to those included in the library listings below: *Photoplay* (Nov. 1923, Apr. 1925, Oct. 1925, Oct. 1926, Sept. 1927, Apr. 1928, Jan. 1931); *Motion Picture Magazine* (July 1925, Apr. 1928, Sept. 1929); *Motion Picture Classic* (Dec. 1925); *Pictorial Review* (July 1928); *Movie Classic* (Dec. 1931, June 1934); *Films in Review* (Feb. 1970); *Movie Digest* (Jan. 1973); *Classic Images* (Nov. 1981, Oct. 1984).

ARCHIVAL MATERIALS

• *Clipping File* — CAA: Marriage, divorce (1934, 1938–39); film appearance (1940); articles by ER (1920s, 1962); article (1962, 1979); biography (1962, 1987); nostalgia (1972, 1976, 1979, 1981, undated); stage appearance (1975); newsphotos; obituary (1994). Periodical articles: *TV Guide* (Aug. 18, 1962); *Hollywood Studio Magazine* (Dec. 1972, Aug. 1974); *Films in Review* (March 1980); *American Classic Screen* (July-Aug. 1981). CAUT: Home (postcard). Periodical articles: *Motion Picture Magazine* (1920s, Dec. 1925, Apr. 1931); *TV Guide* (Aug. 18, 1962). NYMA (also in Photoplay Collection): Newsphotos. Periodical articles: *TV Guide* (Aug. 18, 1962); *Classic Film Collector* (Spring 1974); *Classic Images* (Sept. 1984, Nov. 1988). NYMN: Career (1930s?). NYPL: Marriage/divorce (1933, 1939, undated); newsphotos (numerous); stage appearance (1939, undated); film appearance (1920s); film review (1933); MGM contract (1933); article (1954, 1961–62). Periodical articles: *TV Guide* (Aug. 18, 1962); *Films in Review* (Dec. 1969). • *Other Clipping File* — CNDA, GBBF, MAH, MIDL, OHCL, PAPL, TXU,

WICF, WYU (see Collection). • *Collection* — WYU: Scrapbooks containing newspaper clippings and periodical articles (1925–29). • *Correspondence* — CAA: Letter (Adolph Zukor Collection) (1925); letter (Hedda Hopper Collection). NYPL (C. & L. Brown Collection): 1939. • *Filmography* — NYPL. • *Legal File* — CAUT (Twentieth Century–Fox Collection): Memo, letter (1940); agreement (1940). • *Photograph/Still* — CAA (also in Hollywood Studio Museum Collection) (also in MGM Collection), CAH, CASU, CAUB, CAUU, DCG (Quigley Photographic Archives), GBBF, MIDL, NJPT, NYAM, NYB (Bettmann/UPI Collection) (Springer Collection), NYCU (Dramatic Museum Portraits) (Palmer Collection), NYEH, NYMN, NYPL, NYSU, OHCL, TNUT (Clarence Brown Collection), TXU (A. Davis Collection) (Robbins Collection), WICF. • *Play Program* — NYPL: 1938, 1952, undated. • *Press Kit* — OHCL. • *Privately Printed Material* — CAA: *The Silent Stars Speak.* AMPAS, 1979. • *Publicity Release* — CAA: Paramount (numerous) (1920s). NYPL: CBS (1940). • *Scrapbook* — WYU (see Collection). • *Studio Biography* — CAA: Paramount; MGM (1930s). NYMA: Paramount; Photoplay.

RALSTON, Jobyna, South Pittsburgh, TN, 1900/04– 1967.

After Harold Lloyd (q.v.) married his former leading lady, pert Jobyna Ralston appeared in many of his remaining (and best) silent films, including *The Freshman, Girl Shy,* and *The Kid Brother.* She made several other films, such as *Wings,* but sound was not kind to her and there were only three talkies, the last being *Sheer Luck* (1931). She was married to Richard Arlen (q.v.).

PUBLISHED SOURCES
• *Books* — General: *Harold Lloyd* (Reilly). **Credits:** *Filmarama* (v. II); *Twenty Years of Silents; Who Was Who on Screen.* **Encyclopedic Works:** *Film Encyclopedia; Filmlexicon degli Autori e*

delle Opere; Halliwell's Filmgoer's Companion; The Movie Makers; The Picturegoer's Who's Who and Encyclopedia of the Screen To-day; Who's Who in Hollywood. **Pictorial:** *Silent Portraits.* • *Periodicals* — *Photoplay* (Nov. 1923, Aug. 1924, Apr. 1928, Apr. 1929, Oct. 1929); *Motion Picture Classic* (May 1926, Apr. 1927, Sept. 1928); *Motion Picture Magazine* (Aug. 1927, May 1931); *Movie Classic* (Apr. 1933); *Films in Review* (Feb. 1970) (Wampas Baby Stars); *Classic Images* (Aug.–Sept. 1983).

ARCHIVAL MATERIALS
• *Clipping File* — CAA: Stage appearance (1929); injury (1926); film appearance (1928); marriage/divorce/children (1927, 1933, 1945); legal problem (1926, 1929); obituary (1967). NYPL: Newsphotos; article (undated); saves son; marriage/separation/divorce/children (1927, 1933, undated); obituary (1967). • *Other Clipping File* — AZSU (Jimmy Starr Collection), GBBF, MAH, MIDL, NYMA (Photoplay Collection), OHCL, PAPL, WICF. • *Legal File* — CAUW: Talent agreement (1929). • *Photograph/ Still* — AZSU (Jimmy Starr Collection), CAA (also in Hollywood Studio Museum Collection), CAUT (Portrait File), DCG (Quigley Photographic Archives), GBBF, NJPT, NYB (Bettmann/UPI Collection), NYEH, NYPL, NYSU, OHCL, TXU, WICF. • *Studio Biography* — NYMA: Photoplay.

RAWLINSON, Herbert, Brighton, England, 1885/86– 1953.

One of Universal's top silent stars, Herbert Rawlinson was seen in innumerable serials and dramas from 1911. Busy throughout much of the 1920s, latterly in support, he temporarily left the screen for stage work in the late '20s. From 1935 he was back to play mature and dignified character parts, including many western roles, until his final film in 1951. Among his films were *The Millionaire, The Prisoner, Damon and Pythias, Seven*

Sinners, Bullets or Ballots and Mary of the Movies.

PUBLISHED SOURCES

• Books—General: Blue Book of the Screen; Character People; Eighty Silent Film Stars; Famous Film Folk; Gentlemen to the Rescue; The Truth About the Movies; Who's Who in the Film World. Credits: British Film Actors' Credits; Filmarama (v. I and II); Forty Years of Screen Credits; Twenty Years of Silents; Who Was Who on Screen. Encyclopedic Works: Film Encyclopedia; Filmlexicon degli Autori e delle Opere; The Movie Makers; Who's Who in Hollywood. Pictorial: Silent Portraits.
• Periodicals—The following periodical articles are in addition to those included in the library listings below: Photoplay (Jan. 1914, May 1917, Aug. 1918, May 1920, Mar. 1924); Moving Picture World (May 30, 1914); Motion Picture Magazine (June 1918, Jan. 1921, Jan. 1922); Motion Picture Classic (Nov. 1918, Sept. 1920); Films in Review (Apr. 1972).

ARCHIVAL MATERIALS

• Caricature—NYPL (Sardi Collection). • Clipping File—CAA: Divorce (1922); obituary (1953). NYMA (also in Photoplay Collection): Periodical articles: Classic Images (May 1984, Jan.-Mar. 1985, June 1986). NYMN: Newsphotos; career. NYPL (also in Locke Collection): Stage appearance (1929, 1930s); legal problem (1922-23); newsphotos; obituary (1953). • Other Clipping File—AZSU (Jimmy Starr Collection), GBBF, MAH, MIDL, OHCL, PAPL, WICF. • Correspondence—CAA (Hedda Hopper Collection): 1940. NYPL: Letters (C. & L. Brown Collection) (1930-31); other (1933). • Filmography—CAA. • Legal File—CAHL: Affidavit (1913). CAUW: Talent agreement (1937); contract (1937).
• Photograph/Still—CAA (also in Hollywood Studio Museum Collection), CAUT (Jessen Collection), CAUU, DCG (Quigley Photographic Archives), IAU (Junkin Collection), NJFL, NYAM, NYCU (Palmer Collection), NYMN, NYPL, NYSU, OHCL, TXU,

WICF. • Scrapbook—NYAM, NYPL (also in Locke Collection). • Studio Biography—NYMA: Photoplay.

RAY, Allene (Allene Burch), San Antonio, TX, 1901-1978.
The most famous serial queen of the 1920s was blonde Allene Ray. A Pathé star, she was eventually teamed with rugged Walter Miller in many popular chapterplays including Hawk of the Hills, The Green Archer, The Man Without a Face, The House Without a Key and Sunken Silver. She also appeared with Tim McCoy (q.v.) in the pioneering sound serial The Indians Are Coming. After a few indifferent sound westerns, including Overland Bound, she left the screen.

PUBLISHED SOURCES

• Books—General: Bound and Gagged; Continued Next Week; Famous Film Folk; Ladies in Distress, Motion Picture News Booking Guide and Studio Directory (1927); Sweethearts of the Sage; Those Fabulous Serial Heroines. Credits: Filmarama (v. II); Twenty Years of Silents. Encyclopedic Works: Film Encyclopedia; Filmlexicon degli Autori e delle Opere; Who's Who in Hollywood.
• Periodicals—The following periodical articles are in addition to those included in the library listings below: Photoplay (Feb. 1921); Motion Picture Classic (Apr. 1921); Films in Review (Aug.-Sept. 1955); Classic Images (July 1990) (filmography).

ARCHIVAL MATERIALS

• Clipping File—CAA: Newsphotos; excerpts from the following books: Ladies in Distress, Motion Picture News Blue Book (1930), Motion Picture News Studio Directory (1921) and Motion Picture Almanac (1936-37). NYMA: Periodical articles: Big Reel (Oct. 1985); Classic Images (May 1989). NYPL: Newsphotos; excerpt from Motion Picture News Studio Directory (late 1920s?).
• Other Clipping File—AZSU (Jimmy Starr Collection), GBBF, PAPL.
• Photograph/Still—CAA (also in

Hollywood Studio Museum Collection), CALM, CAUT (Jessen Collection) (Portrait File), CAUU, DCG (Quigley Photographic Archives), NYCU (Bulliet Collection), NYPL, NYSU, TXU, WICF. • *Publicity Release* – AZSU (Jimmy Starr Collection).

RAY, Charles, Jacksonville, IL, 1891-1943.

Charles Ray gained huge popularity playing country boys and other naifs in scores of films from 1912. These included *The Clodhopper, Homer Come Home, The Old Swimmin' Hole* and *The Coward.* In the 1920s he began producing his films as well; it was the expensive 1924 failure *Miles Standish* which effectively ended his starring career. His attempt to return with a more sophisticated persona was not successful. Starting in the mid-1930s, he had a minor comeback playing bits and a few larger roles.

PUBLISHED SOURCES

• *Books* – Wrote *Seven Faces West* and *Writer's Cramp* in the 1920s. **Bibliography:** *The Idols of Silence.* **Credits:** *Filmarama* (v. I and II); *Twenty Years of Silents; Who Was Who on Screen.* **General:** *Blue Book of the Screen; Classics of the Silent Screen; Famous Film Folk; Gentlemen to the Rescue; More from Hollywood; The Movie Stars Story; The Truth About the Movies; Who's Who in the Film World; Who's Who on the Screen.* **Encyclopedic Works:** *Film Encyclopedia; Filmlexicon degli Autori e delle Opere; Halliwell's Filmgoer's Companion; The Movie Makers; Who's Who in Hollywood.* **Pictorial:** *The Image Makers; Silent Portraits.*

• *Periodicals* – The following periodical articles are in addition to those included in the library listings below: *Photoplay* (Oct. 1914, Jan. 1916, May 1919, Dec. 1919, Mar. 1922, June 1922, Nov. 1924, June 1926, Sept. 1927); *Motion Picture Magazine* (Apr. 1915, Sept. 1917, Sept. 1918, Jan. 1920, Oct. 1920, Mar. 1922, Apr. 1923, Nov. 1924, May

1926); *Feature Movie* (July 10, 1915); *New York Dramatic Mirror* (Mar. 13, 1920); *Motion Picture Classic* (July 1921, Mar. 1922, June 1924, Oct. 1925); *Theatre* (May 1926); *Newsweek* (Dec. 6, 1943); *Time* (Dec. 6, 1943); *National Board of Review Magazine* (Jan. 1944); *Films in Review* (Nov. 1968 (filmography), Dec. 1968-Jan. 1969, Mar.-Apr. 1969, Apr. 1973); *Classic Film Collector* (Spring 1969-Fall 1969); *Silent Picture* (Spring 1972); *Classic Film/Video Images* (July-Sept. 1980); *Classic Images* (Nov. 1984, Apr. 1988).

ARCHIVAL MATERIALS

• *Caricature* – NYPL (Sardi Collection). • *Clipping File* – CAA: Film appearance (1921-23, 1941); comeback (1934); legal problem (1934, 1941); divorce/marriage (1935, 1941); illness (1943); former studio (1979); obituary (1943). Periodical article: *Newman Theatres Magazine* (Sept. 1920). CAUT: Article (1924); nostalgia (1936); film appearance (1920s); legal problem (1929). Periodical article: *Picture Play Magazine* (Apr. 1927). CAUU: Bankruptcy (1940s); film company (post card). NYMN: Separation/divorce (1934-35); newsphotos; obituary (1943). Periodical article: *Motion Picture Magazine* (1920s). NYPL (also in Locke Collection): PARTIAL CONTENTS: Stage appearance (1927-28); playwright (1928); film appearance (1926); comeback (1928); obituary (1943). Periodical article: *Films and Filming* (May 1972). • *Other Clipping File* – GBBF, MAH, MIDL, NYMA (Photoplay Collection), OHCL, PAPL, WICF. • *Correspondence* – CAA: Letter (Adolph Zukor Collection) (1922); letters relating to the film *The Girl I Loved* (Vertical File Collection) (1921-1922); letter (Hedda Hopper Collection) (1940). CAUS (Theodore Gerson Collection), NYMA (Photoplay Collection). NYPL (C. & L. Brown Collection): 1920s, 1930s, 1940s. • *Filmography* – CAA. • *Legal File* – CAUW: Contract (1920-23); payroll record (1923-26); communication (1920). • *Manuscript* – CAA: *Sixty Years of Studio.* Manes, 1971. The history of a Hollywood studio which CR owned at one time. • *Oral History* — NYCO: Mentioned in: Reginald Denny interview. • *Photograph/Still* — AZSU (Jimmy Starr Collection), CAA (also in Hollywood Studio Museum Collection) (also in MGM Collection), CASF, CAUB, CAUC (Motion Picture Photograph Collection), CAUT (Jessen Collection) (Portrait File), CAUU, DCG (Quigley Photographic Archives), GBBF, IAU (Junkin Collection), MIDL, NJPT, NYAM, NYCU (Palmer Collection), NYEH, NYMN, NYPL, NYSU, OHCL, TXSM, TXU, WICF. • *Publicity Release* — CAA: Fox (1941-42). • *Scrapbook* — NJPT (Yeandle Collection), NYAM, NYPL (also in R. Locke Collection). • *Studio Biography* — CAA: Metropolitan (1926); Fox (1935). NYMA: Photoplay.

REED, Donald (Ernest Guillen or Gillen), Mexico City, Mexico, 1902/05-1973.

Making his debut about 1927, Donald Reed was a serviceable leading man to stars such as Colleen Moore, Billie Dove and Alice White in films such as *Naughty But Nice*, *The Mad Hour*, *Show Girl*, *A Most Immoral Lady* and *Hardboiled*. He also appeared in a couple of serials. His career continued in generally lesser efforts, with an occasional better film like *The Devil Is a Woman*, until 1937.

PUBLISHED SOURCES
• *Books* — Credits: *Filmarama* (v. II); *Who Was Who in Hollywood*. **Encyclopedic Works:** *Film Encyclopedia*; *Filmlexicon degli Autori e delle Opere*; *The Picturegoer's Who's Who and Encyclopedia of the Screen To-day*; *Who's Who in Hollywood*.
• *Periodicals* — *Photoplay* (Dec. 1927); *Motion Picture Magazine* (Oct. 1928).

ARCHIVAL MATERIALS
• *Clipping File* — NYPL: Film appearance (1933); newsphotos. • *Other Clipping File* — GBBF, OHCL, WICF.
• *Legal File* — CAUW: Talent agreement (1926-29). • *Photograph/Still* — CAA

(also in Hollywood Studio Museum Collection), NYEH, NYPL, TXU, WICF.

REID, Wallace (William W. Reid), St. Louis, MO, 1890/ 92-1923.

Wallace Reid's early death ended a career which had taken him to the heights of Hollywood stardom. He had been in films since 1910 but it was a small role in *Birth of a Nation* which led to his breakthrough. Appearing opposite Geraldine Farrar and numerous other actresses in the course of almost 180 films through 1922, his films included *Double Speed*, *Across the Continent*, *Valley of the Giants*, *The Love Mask* and *Joan the Woman*. He was married to Dorothy Davenport (q.v.).

PUBLISHED SOURCES
• *Books* — Bibliography: *The Idols of Silence*. **General:** *The Big V*; *Blue Book of the Screen*; *Classics of the Silent Screen*; *First One Hundred Noted Men and Women of the Screen*; *From Hollywood*; *Gentlemen to the Rescue*; *History of the American Cinema* (v. 3); *Hollywood Album 2*; *Hollywood Heartbreak*; *Hollywood Heaven*; *Hollywood R. I. P.*; *Immortals of the Screen*; *Love, Laughter and Tears*; *The Matinee Idols*; *The Movie Stars Story*; *The Stars* (Schickel); *Who's Who in the Film World*; *Who's Who on the Screen*. **Credits:** *Filmarama* (v. I and II); *Twenty Years of Silents*; *Who Was Who on Screen*. **Encyclopedic Works:** *Film Encyclopedia*; *Filmlexicon degli Autori e delle Opere*; *Halliwell's Filmgoer's Companion*; *The Illustrated Who's Who of the Cinema*; *International Dictionary of Films and Filmmakers* (v. 3); *The Movie Makers*; *Who Was Who in the Theatre*; *Who's Who in Hollywood*; *The World Almanac Who's Who of Film*. **Biography/Autobiography:** *Wallace Reid* (Reid). **Pictorial:** *The Image Makers*; *Leading Men*; *Life and Death in Hollywood*; *Silent Portraits*. **Factoids:** *Star Stats*.
• *Periodicals* — The following periodical articles are in addition to those included in the library listings below: *Uni-*

versal Weekly (Sept. 27, 1913); *Motion Picture Magazine* (Jan. 1915, May 1915, Sept. 1916, Nov. 1916, Feb. 1917, Jan. 1918, July 1918, May 1919, Sept. 1919, Oct. 1920, June 1921, Sept. 1921, Feb. 1922, Aug.–Sept. 1922, Jan. 1924, Jan. 1929, Dec. 1930, June 1933); *Feature Movie* (July 10, 1915); *Photoplay* (Mar. 1916, Nov. 1919, Jan. 1921, Oct.–Nov. 1921, Mar. 1922, Nov. 1922, Mar. 1923, Sept. 1924, Mar. 1925, Mar. 1926, Jan. 1934); *Picture Play Magazine* (July 1916, Aug. 1918, Feb. 1921, Jan.–Apr. 1922, Nov. 1922); *Motion Picture Classic* (July 1916, Dec. 1916, Apr. 1918, Mar. 1921, Feb. 1922, May 1922, Aug. 1922); *Pictures and Picturegoer* (Feb. 1921, Oct. 1922); *Filmplay Journal* (Sept. 1921); *Saturday Review* (Oct. 13, 1956); *Films in Review* (May–Sept. 1966, June–July 1967); *Hollywood Studio Magazine* (Feb. 1988).

OBSCURE PUBLISHED SOURCES
CAA (both), NYMA (first title), NYMN (first title): *Wallace Reid: As He Is to Those Who Know Him*; *Wallace Reid Memorial Bay in St. John the Divine.*

ARCHIVAL MATERIALS
• *Clipping File*—CAA: Film appearance (1922); review of *Human Wreckage* (film) (1923); newsphotos; article (1950); nostalgia (1957). Periodical articles: *Photoplay* (Nov. 1916, June 1918, Jan. 1925); *Picture Play Magazine* (Apr. 1919); *Picture Show* (Jan. 7, 1922); *Pictures and Picturegoer* (Feb. 1923); *Liberty* (June 30–July 14, 1928); *Bulletin of the Wallace Reid Memorial Club* (May 1926, 1929); *Classic Film Collector* (Winter 1970). CAUU: Periodical article: *Classic Film Collector* (Winter 1970). NYMA (also in Photoplay Collection): Article (undated); comments on the *Wallace Reid Memorial Bay in St. John the Divine. Periodical articles: Classic Film Collector* (Fall 1969–Winter 1970). NYMN: Newsphotos; article (1950). Periodical article: *Liberty* (June 23, 1928). NYPL: Newsphotos (numerous); film appearance (1920s); article (1918); illness (1922); estate (1923); separation (1921); biography (1923); addiction (1970); in-

jury (1922); obituary (1923). Periodical article: *Photoplay* (June 1925); *Films in Review* (Apr. 1966). • *Other Clipping File*—AZSU (Jimmy Starr Collection), GBBF, MAH, MIDL, OHCL, PAPL, WICF. • *Correspondence*—CAA (Wallace Reid Jr. Collection): 1918. • *Film Program*—CAHL: 1917. • *Filmography*—NYMA, NYPL. • *Legal File*—CAUW: Story digest (1911); rights (1911). • *Oral History*—NYCO: Mentioned in the following interviews: Sidney Blackmer, Sessue Hayakawa, Lila Lee, Conrad Nagel, Gloria Swanson. • *Photograph/Still*—CAA (also in Hollywood Studio Museum Collection) (also in MGM Collection), CAHL, CALM, CAUC (Motion Picture Photograph Collection), CAUT (Jessen Collection) (Portrait File), CAUU, IAU (Junkin Collection), NYB (Bettmann/UPI Collection) (Springer Collection) (Underwood Collection), NYEH, NYMN, NYPL, NYSU, OHCL, TXU, WICF. • *Scrapbook*—CAA (Wallace Reid Jr. Collection), NYAM, NYPL (also in Locke Collection).

REVIER, Dorothy (Doris Velarga or Velagra), San Francisco, CA, 1904–1993.

A Wampas Baby Star of 1925, Dorothy Revier was one of the premier "vamps" of the silent era. She began appearing in films in 1922, some of her early efforts being directed by then-husband Harry Revier. In 1929 she was in Douglas Fairbanks's *The Iron Mask* and that year also made her talkie debut in *The Donovan Affair*. Although she continued to appear in a lengthy list of films through 1936 they were largely westerns and other quickies; she was no longer the star she had been before sound came.

PUBLISHED SOURCES
• *Books*—**General:** *Broken Silence*; *Let Me Entertain You*; *Return Engagement*; *Sweethearts of the Sage.* **Credits:** *Filmarama* (v. II); *Forty Years of Screen Credits*; *Twenty Years of Silents.* **Encyclopedic Works:** *B Western Actors En-*

cyclopedia; *Film Encyclopedia; Filmlexicon degli Autori e delle Opere; The Picturegoer's Who's Who and Encyclopedia of the Screen To-day; Who's Who in Hollywood; The World Film Encyclopedia.* **Nostalgia:** *Whatever Happened to . . .* (7th). **Pictorial:** *They Had Faces Then.*
• *Periodicals—Motion Picture Magazine* (May 1928); *Films in Review* (Feb. 1970 [Wampas Baby Stars]); *Classic Images* (Nov. 1981, Oct.–Nov. 1989) (filmography); *International Collector* (Aug. 1983).

ARCHIVAL MATERIALS
• *Clipping File*—CAA: Marriage (1930); nostalgia (1980–81, 1983). NYMN: Newsphotos. NYPL: Film appearance (1933–34); newsphotos. • *Other Clipping File*—GBBF, NYMA (Photoplay Collection), PAPL, WICF.
• *Collection*—WYU: 8 photographs.
• *Filmography*—NYPL (incomplete).
• *Legal File*—CAUT (Twentieth Century-Fox Collection): Talent agreement (1927). CAUW: Letter, memo (1927); talent agreement (1927, 1929–30).
• *Photograph/Still*—CAA (also in Hollywood Studio Museum Collection), CAFA, CASP, DCG (Quigley Photographic Archives), GBBF, NJPT, NYEH, NYPL, NYSU, OHCL, TXU (A. Davis Collection), WICF, WYU (see Collection).

REYNOLDS, Vera (Norma ?), Richmond, VA, 1900/05–1962.
After a start in two-reel comedies, petite Vera Reynolds was seen in several DeMille productions, including *Feet of Clay* and *The Golden Bed.* With few exceptions, her silent films were undistinguished and the coming of sound nearly finished her career. She appeared in fewer than a dozen quickies from 1929 to 1932 and then the pretty ex-dancer disappeared from the screen.

PUBLISHED SOURCES
• *Books—General: Famous Film*

Folk. **Credits:** *Filmarama* (v. II); *Forty Years of Screen Credits; Twenty Years of Silents; Who Was Who on Screen.* **Encyclopedic Works:** *Film Encyclopedia; Filmlexicon degli Autori e delle Opere; The Picturegoer's Who's Who and Encyclopedia of the Screen To-day; Who's Who in Hollywood; The World Film Encyclopedia.* **Pictorial:** *Silent Portraits.*
• *Periodicals—Photoplay* (Apr. 1923, Sept. 1924); *Films in Review* (Feb. 1970 [Wampas Baby Stars]).

ARCHIVAL MATERIALS
• *Clipping File*—CAA: Film appearance (1924); divorce (1936, 1938); obituary (1962). CAUT: Marriage/divorce (1928, 1936). NYPL: Newsphotos; breach of promise suit (1937); legal problem. • *Other Clipping File*—GBBF, NYMA (Photoplay Collection), OHCL, WICF. • *Correspondence*—NYPL (C. & L. Brown Collection): 1936. • *Legal File*—CAA (Sennett Collection): Contract (1917). • *Photograph/Still*—CAA (also in Hollywood Studio Museum Collection), CAH, CAUT (Jessen Collection), CNDA, DCG (Quigley Photographic Archives), GBBF, NJPT, NYAM, NYB (Bettmann/UPI Collection), NYEH, NYPL, NYSU, OHCL, PAPL, TXU (A. Davis Collection), WICF. • *Studio Biography*—CAA: DeMille (1926). • *Scrapbook*—UTBY (DeMille Archives).

RHODES, Billie (Levita Axelrod), San Francisco, CA, 1894–1988.
A popular comedienne in 200 films including numerous Christie comedies, Billie Rhodes worked for several studios, among them Kalem and Nestor, and was known as "The Nestor Girl." She turned to features in the 1920s but left the screen in mid-decade to return to nightclub performing. Among her films were *His Pajama Girl, Girl of My Dreams, The Love Call* and *Fires of Youth.*

PUBLISHED SOURCES
• *Books—Bibliography: The Idols of*

Silence. **General:** *Clown Princes and Court Jesters*; *Early American Cinema.* **Credits:** *Filmarama* (v. I and II); *Twenty Years of Silents.* **Encyclopedic Works:** *Film Encyclopedia*; *Filmlexicon degli Autori e delle Opere*; *Who's Who in Hollywood.* **Pictorial:** *Silent Portraits.*

• *Periodicals* — The following periodical articles are in addition to those included in the library listings below: *Photoplay* (July 1917); *Motion Picture Classic* (Jan. 1919); *Picture Show* (Mar. 13, 1920); *Films in Review* (Dec. 1988).

ARCHIVAL MATERIALS
• *Clipping File* — CAA: Divorce (1922); film appearance (1917). CAFI: Obituary (1988). NYMA (also in Photoplay Collection): Obituary (1988). Periodical articles: *Classic Film Collector* (Winter 1976–Spring 1977). NYPL (also in Locke Collection): Newsphotos; obituary (1988). • *Other Clipping File* — CASP, CAUB, CNDA, GBBF, MAH, WICF. • *Correspondence* — CAUU (A. Slide Collection): 1970. • *Photograph/Still* — CAA (also in Hollywood Studio Museum Collection), CASP, CAUT (Jessen Collection), CAUU (A. Slide Collection), DCG (Quigley Photographic Archives), NYEH, NYPL, NYSU, OHCL, WICF. • *Scrapbook* — NYPL (R. Locke Collection). • *Studio Biography* — NYMA: Photoplay.

RICH, Irene (Irene Luther), Buffalo, NY, 1890/97–1988.
A respected actress in several mediums, including radio and the stage, Irene Rich was probably best known as Will Rogers's wife in early talkies. She also played sophisticated women in silents like *Lady Windermere's Fan*, *Beau Brummell*, *Eve's Lover*, *Women They Talk About* and *Don't Tell the Wife.* By the 1930s she was playing mature supporting roles which she continued sporadically until the late 1940s.

PUBLISHED SOURCES
• *Books* — **General:** *Blue Book of the Screen*; *Famous Film Folk*; *Folks Ushud*

Know; *How I Broke Into the Movies*; *Sweethearts of the Sage*; *Who's Who on the Screen.* **Credits:** *Filmarama* (v. I and II); *Forty Years of Screen Credits*; *Twenty Years of Silents.* **Encyclopedic Works:** *Film Encyclopedia*; *Filmlexicon degli Autori e delle Opere*; *Halliwell's Filmgoer's Companion*; *International Motion Picture Almanac* (1975–80); *The Movie Makers*; *The Picturegoer's Who's Who and Encyclopedia of the Screen To-day*; *Variety Who's Who in Show Business*; *Who's Who in Hollywood*; *The World Almanac Who's Who of Film*; *The World Film Encyclopedia.* **Nostalgia:** *Whatever Became of . . .* (1st). **Pictorial:** *Silent Portraits*; *They Had Faces Then.*

• *Periodicals* — The following periodical articles are in addition to those included in the library listings below: *Motion Picture Classic* (Aug. 1920, Jan. 1922, Mar. 1924, Sept. 1925, Apr. 1928); *Photoplay* (Dec. 1920, June 1924); *Motion Picture Magazine* (Jan. 1921, Oct. 1930); *Theatre* (Aug. 1928); *Pictorial Review* (Dec. 1937); *Classic Images* (Jan. 1984); *Films and Filming* (Jan. 1986); *Time* (May 9, 1988); *EPD Film* (June 1988); *Classic Images* (June–July 1988).

ARCHIVAL MATERIALS
• *Clipping File* — CAA (also in Collection): Legal problem (1929); marriage/divorce (1927, 1931, 1950); film appearance (1924, 1927–28); home (1927, 1944); Warner contract (1928); newsphotos; article (early 1930s); nostalgia (1969, 1971, 1981–82); obituary (1988). CAFI: Newsphotos (numerous); obituary (1988). CAUT: Periodical article: *Motion Picture Classic* (1920s). NYMN: Article (undated); marriage/divorce/children (1931–32, 1950); career. Periodical article: *New Movie Magazine* (undated). NYPL (also in Locke Collection): PARTIAL CONTENTS: Film appearance (1930s); newsphotos; retirement; stage appearance (1930s, 1949); marriage (1935, 1950); biography (1927); article (1930, 1932, 1934, 1940, undated); nostalgia (1936); friend killed (1949); obituary (1988). • *Other Clipping File* — AZSU (Jimmy Starr Collection), CAUB,

GBBF, MAH, MIDL, OHCL, PAPL, WICF. • *Collection* — CAA: Hundreds of clippings (1920–44, 1948–50, 1975–76); 10 scrapbooks; periodicals; sheet music; programs. • *Correspondence* — CAA (also in Collection): Letter, telegram (Hedda Hopper Collection) (1940, 1954). CAOC (B. Henry Collection): 1949. NYPL: Letters (C. & L. Brown Collection) (1930s–40s); others (1940, undated). • *Legal File* — CAUW: Personnel, payroll record (1939–41); letter, memo (1927–28); talent agreement (1924, 1927–28, 1930, 1939, 1941); option (1925–26). • *Oral History* — NYCO: Mentioned in the following interviews: Douglass Montgomery, Beth C. Short. • *Photograph/Still* — AZSU (Jimmy Starr Collection), CAA (also in Hollywood Studio Museum Collection) (also in MGM Collection), CASF, CAUU, CNDA, DCG (Quigley Photographic Archives), GBBF, NJPT, NYB (Bettmann/UPI Collection) (Springer Collection), NYCU (Bulliet Collection), NYEH, NYMN, NYPL, NYSU, OHCL, TXU, WICF. • *Program* — CAA (see Collection). • *Scrapbook* — CAA (see Collection), NJPT (Yeandle Collection), NYAM, NYPL. • *Studio Biography* — NYPL: CBS (1943).

RICH, Lillian, London, England, 1900–1954.

Lillian Rich's face was her fortune and she starred in silent films with leading men such as Tom Mix and Bert Lytell. Her movies were usually programmers like *Never Say Die, Cheap Kisses, Web of Fate* and *The Love Master* but she did appear in DeMille's *The Golden Bed* and a few other worthwhile efforts. Although her career declined after 1929 she still could be seen in small parts in the 1930s.

PUBLISHED SOURCES
• *Books* — General: *The Truth About the Movies.* Credits: *British Film Actors' Credits; Filmarama* (v. I and II); *Forty Years of Screen Credits; Twenty Years of Silents; Who Was Who on Screen.* Encyclopedic Works: *Film Encyclopedia;*

Filmlexicon degli Autori e delle Opere; Who's Who in Hollywood; The World Film Encyclopedia.
• *Periodicals* — *Photoplay* (Nov. 1924); *Classic Images* (July 1990) (filmography).

ARCHIVAL MATERIALS
• *Clipping File* — CAA: Divorce (1932); film appearance (1921); obituary (1954). NYPL: Newsphotos; stage appearance; divorce (1932); obituary (1954). • *Other Clipping File* — AZSU (Jimmy Starr Collection), GBBF, NYMA (Photoplay Collection), PAPL. • *Photograph/Still* — CAA (also in Hollywood Studio Museum Collection) (also in MGM Collection), DCG (Quigley Photographic Archives), GBBF, NJPT, NYEH, NYPL, OHCL, TXU. • *Scrapbook* — UTBY (DeMille Archives).

ROBERTS, Edith, New York, NY, 1899–1935.

A popular actress from her debut in 1917, stage actress Edith Roberts was in many films during the 1920s including *Saturday Night, The Dangerous Age, Thy Name Is Woman* and *Seven Keys to Baldpate.* She costarred with such actors as Tom Moore, Lon Chaney and George Arliss. Despite her theater training, her career did not survive the coming of sound.

PUBLISHED SOURCES
• *Books* — General: *Blue Book of the Screen; Famous Film Folk; Who's Who on the Screen.* Credits: *Filmarama* (v. I and II); *Twenty Years of Silents; Who Was Who on Screen.* Encyclopedic Works: *Film Encyclopedia; Filmlexicon degli Autori e delle Opere; The Picturegoer's Who's Who and Encyclopedia of the Screen To-day; Who's Who in Hollywood.* Pictorial: *Silent Portraits.*
• *Periodicals* — The following periodical articles are in addition to that included in the library listings below: *Green Book Magazine* (Aug. 1916); *Picture Play* (July 1920); *Motion Picture Magazine* (Jan. 1921, Apr. 1922); *Motion Picture Classic* (Dec. 1921, Nov. 1922).

ARCHIVAL MATERIALS
• *Clipping File*—CAA: Film appearance (1921–22). CAUT: Obituary (1935). NYMA (also in Photoplay Collection): Personal data summary. NYPL (also in Locke Collection): Newsphotos; article (1923); obituary (1935). Periodical article: *Photoplay* (June 1920). • *Other Clipping File*—CASP, GBBF, OHCL, PAPL, WICF. • *Legal File*—CAUW: Talent agreement (1924). • *Photograph/Still*—CAA (also in Hollywood Studio Museum Collection), CASP, CAUT (Jessen Collection), CAUU, DCG (Quigley Photographic Archives), NYPL, NYSU, OHCL, WICF. • *Scrapbook*—NYPL.

ROBERTS, Theodore, San Francisco, CA, 1861–1928.

Veteran stage actor Theodore Roberts came to Hollywood about 1914 and was generally cast in patriarchal roles, the culmination of which was his appearance as Moses in DeMille's first version of *The Ten Commandments* (1923). Known as "The Grand Old Man of the Screen" and "The Grand Duke of Hollywood," his films included *Grumpy*, *Peg o' My Heart*, *The Old Homestead* and *Our Leading Citizen*.

PUBLISHED SOURCES
• *Books*—General: *Blue Book of the Screen*; *Las Estrellas*; *Famous Film Folk*; *The Truth About the Movies*; *Who's Who on the Screen*. Credits: *Filmarama* (v. I and II); *Twenty Years of Silents*; *Who Was Who on Screen*. Encyclopedic Works: *Film Encyclopedia*; *Filmlexicon degli Autori e delle Opere*; *Halliwell's Filmgoer's Companion*; *Who Was Who in the Theatre*; *Who's Who in Hollywood*; *Who's Who on the Stage* (1908). Pictorial: *Silent Portraits*.
• *Periodicals*—Theatre (Feb. 1908); *Photoplay* (Sept. 1915, July 1917, Jan. 1923, Apr. 1924, May 1925); *Motion Picture Magazine* (Nov. 1918, Feb. 1921, June 1933); *Picture Show* (Jan. 10, 1920); *Motion Picture Classic* (Feb. 1920, Dec. 1921, Dec. 1922–Jan. 1923, Oct. 1928); *Collier's* (Sept. 15, 1928); *Good House-*

keeping (Aug. 1932); *Films in Review* (Apr. 1972).

ARCHIVAL MATERIALS
• *Clipping File*—CAA: Illness (1921); excerpt from *Las Estrellas*; article (1930s?); obituary (1928). CASF: Obituary (1928). CAUT: Estate (1929); obituary (1928). NYMA (also in Photoplay Collection): Obituary (1928). NYMN: Estate; newsphotos; obituary (1928). NYPL (also in Locke Collection): Stage appearance (1920s); newsphotos; will; article (1924, 1926, 1928); legal problem (1927); illness (1923); career (1918); biography; obituary (1928). • *Other Clipping File*—AZSU (Jimmy Starr Collection), CNDA, GBBF, MAH, MIDL, OHSU, PAPL, WICF. • *Correspondence*—NYPL. • *Filmography*—CASF. • *Oral History*—NYCO: Mentioned in the following interviews: Cecil B. DeMille, Carl Haverlin, Conrad Nagel. • *Photograph/Still*—CAA (also in Hollywood Studio Museum Collection), CAHL, CALM, CAOC (Kiesling Collection), CASF, CAUT (Jessen Collection), CAUU, DCG (Quigley Photographic Archives), IAU (Junkin Collection), NYAM, NYB (Bettmann/UPI Collection) (Underwood Collection), NYCU (Dramatic Museum Portraits), NYEH, NYMN, NYPL, NYSU, OHCL, TXSM, TXU, WICF. • *Play Program*—CAHL: 1902. NYPL, OHSU. • *Scrapbook*—NYPL (also in R. Locke Collection), UTBY (DeMille Archives).

ROGERS, Charles ("Buddy"), Olathe, KS, 1904–.

Handsome Buddy Rogers made his debut in 1926's *Fascinating Youth* and had his best roles within a year or so in *My Best Girl*, with his future wife Mary Pickford (q.v.), and in the classic *Wings*. He appeared in several early sound musicals (e.g., *Close Harmony*, *Paramount on Parade*, *Safety in Numbers*) and, sporadically, in some "B" films of the 1930s and early '40s.

PUBLISHED SOURCES
• *Books*—General: *How I Broke Into*

the Movies; Popular Men of the Screen; Tribute to Mary Pickford; Twinkle, Twinkle, Movie Star; What the Stars Told Me. Credits: Filmarama (v. II); Forty Years of Screen Credits; Twenty Years of Silents. Encyclopedic Works: The Complete Encyclopedia of Popular Music and Jazz; Film Encyclopedia; Filmlexicon degli Autori e delle Opere; Halliwell's Filmgoer's Companion; The International Motion Picture Encyclopedia (1975-80); The Movie Makers; The Picturegoer's Who's Who and Encyclopedia of the Screen To-day; Variety Who's Who in Show Business; Who's Who in Hollywood; The World Almanac Who's Who of Film; The World Film Encyclopedia. Nostalgia: Whatever Became of... (3rd). Pictorial: The Image Makers; Silent Portraits. Recordings: Hollywood on Record.

• Periodicals – The following periodical articles are in addition to that included in the library listings below: Motion Picture Magazine (May 1926, Aug. 1927, Dec. 1928, May 1929, Sept. 1930, Mar. 1933); Cinema Art (Aug. 1927); Photoplay (Oct. 1927, July 1928, July 1929, Nov. 1929, June 1930, June 1931, Mar. 1932); Motion Picture Classic (Aug. 1928, Nov. 1928, June 1929, Apr. 1931); Silver Screen (Nov. 1930); Movie Classic (Oct. 1931); Life (Nov. 17, 1947); Silent Picture (Summer–Autumn 1971); American Classic Screen (Jan.-Feb. 1979); Classic Images (Jan. 1982); Films in Review (Dec. 1987); Kansas History (Summer 1990).

OBSCURE PUBLISHED SOURCES
CAA: Graduating Exercises of the Paramount Pictures School Class of 1926.

ARCHIVAL MATERIALS
• Caricature – NYPL. • Clipping File – CAA (also in Collection under entry for Mary Pickford): Band (1931-32); producer (1946, 1949); legal problem (1932-33, 1956); stage appearance (1929, 1954); film appearance (1930, 1936, 1956); rescue (1930, 1937); article (1932, 1948, 1952, 1961, 1963); radio appearance (1931); Paramount contract (1929, 1931);

draft article by CR; joins navy (1946); injury (1938); newsphotos; anniversary (1962); honor (1966, 1983, 1986-87, 1990-91); film revival (1965); TV appearance (1951, 1962, 1964); personal appearance (1970, 1979); Mary Pickford estate (1979-80); Pickfair (1978-80, 1983, 1986); nostalgia (1987-88); marriage (1981); charity work (1985). Periodical article: Film Fan Monthly (Dec. 1970). CAFI: Article (1976, 1987); honor (1986); marriage (1981); Pickfair (1980). CAPS: Newsphotos; first Academy Award ceremony (1992); tribute (1989-90); article (1968, 1987, 1989); Pickfair (1980); honor (1987). CAUU: Christmas card (1948); honor (1986). NYMN: Newsphotos (numerous); home (1930); article (1930); injury (1938). NYPL: Biography (1931, 1933); article (1980, undated); newsphotos; Pickfair (1979-1980); injury (1938); TV appearance (1979, undated); engagement/marriage (1936, 1940s?, 1981); comeback (1935, 1940, 1948); film appearance (1926, 1956, undated); stage appearance (1933-34); Jean Hersholt Award (1986); Wings (film) (1987); radio appearance; band (1930s). • Other Clipping File – AZSU (Jimmy Starr Collection), CNDA, GBBF, MIDL, OHCL, PAPL, WICF. • Correspondence – CAA (Mary Pickford Collection), DCLC (Lillian Gish Collection). MABU: Letter (Kate Smith Collection) (1933); postcard (Leonard Sillman Collection) (1964); card (restricted collection; needs donor approval) (1975). NYPL: 30 letters (Mary Pickford and Buddy Rogers Correspondence Collection) (1965-76); letter (C. & L. Brown Collection) (1936); others (1940, 1967). • Interview – CAUU (R. Lamparski Collection) (A. Slide Collection): 1971 (Slide). NYAM. • Legal File – CAUT (Twentieth Century-Fox Collection): Letter, memo, telegram (1933, 1940); talent agreement (1933, 1940). • Oral History – NYCO: Mentioned in: Jerome Zerbe interview. • Photograph/Still – AZSU (Jimmy Starr Collection), CAA (also in Hollywood Studio Museum Collection) (also in Mary Pickford Collection) (also in MGM Collection), CAPH, CASF, CAUB, CAUT (Jessen

Collection) (Portrait File), CAUU (also in A. Slide Collection), DCG (Quigley Photographic Archives), GBBF, IAU (Junkin Collection), MABU, MIDL, NJPT, NYAM, NYB (Bettmann/UPI Collection) (Springer Collection) (Underwood Collection), NYCU (Dramatic Museum Portraits) (Palmer Collection), NYEH, NYMN, NYPL, NYSU, OHCL, TXU, WICF. • *Publicity Release*—CAA: Fox; Paramount (1930s). • *Reminiscence*—MISU: BR meets Mary Pickford (recording); BR reminisces with Mike Douglas (recording). • *Scrapbook*—NJPT (Yeandle Collection), NYMA, NYPL. • *Studio Biography*—CAA: Fox (1930s–40s); unknown studio (1935?, 1950s?). • *Testimonial*—DCG (Quigley Collection): From BR to Martin Quigley on the 50th anniversary of the *Motion Picture Herald*.

ROLAND, Ruth, San Francisco, CA, 1892–1937.

Ruth Roland made over 200 films in her career but it was in her serial appearances that she became a major star and the closest rival to Pearl White (q.v.). Some of the serials bore her name (*Ruth of the Range, Ruth of the Rockies, The Adventures of Ruth*). Others included *The Tiger's Trail, The Avenging Arrow, Hands Up!* and the *Timber Queen*. She made only two sound films, the last in Canada shortly before her death.

PUBLISHED SOURCES

• *Books*—Bibliography: *The Idols of Silence*. General: *Blue Book of the Screen; Bound and Gagged; Continued Next Week; Eighty Silent Film Stars; Famous Film Folk; First One Hundred Noted Men and Women of the Screen; The Serials; Sweethearts of the Sage; Those Fabulous Serial Heroines; The Truth About the Movies; Who's Who in the Film World; Who's Who on the Screen*. Credits: *Filmarama* (v. I and II); *Twenty Years of Silents; Who Was Who on Screen*. Encyclopedic Works: *Film Encyclopedia; Filmlexicon degli Autori e delle Opere; Halliwell's Filmgoer's Companion; The International Who's Who of the Cinema; Who's Who in Hollywood; The World Almanac Who's Who of Film*. Pictorial: *Silent Portraits*.
• *Periodicals*—The following periodical articles are in addition to those included in the library listings below: *Kalem Kalendar* (Dec. 22, 1911); *Moving Picture World* (Mar. 7, 1914, July 11, 1914); *Cosmopolitan* (Jan. 1915); *Motion Picture Magazine* (Apr. 1915, Nov. 1915, May 1916, Sept. 1916, Dec. 1921, Feb. 1925, Oct. 1928, June 1929); *Photoplay* (June 1915, Apr. 1916, Apr. 1919, Aug. 1922); *Filmplay Journal* (Oct. 1915); *Green Book Magazine* (Apr. 1916); *Motion Picture Classic* (Sept. 1916, Apr. 1917, Aug. 1918, July 1919, Nov. 1921); *Pantomime* (Dec. 10, 1921); *Classic Images* (Jan. 1992).

OBSCURE PUBLISHED SOURCES
CAA: *Ruth Rolland* (sic).

ARCHIVAL MATERIALS
• *Caricature*—NYPL (Sardi Collection). • *Clipping File*—CAA: Accident (1921); newsphoto; films acquired by UCLA (1980); film appearance (1924). Periodical article: *Films in Review* (Nov.–Dec. 1960). NYMA: Newsphotos; obituary (1937). Periodical articles: *Classic Film Collector* (Spring 1974, Winter 1975); *Classic Images* (Oct. 1985). NYMN: Marriage (1937); will (1937); bigamy (1936); estate (1937); newsphotos; obituary (1937). NYPL (also in Locke Collection): Estate (1937); newsphotos (numerous); engagement (1923); article (undated); attacked by dog (1934); obituary (1937). • *Other Clipping File*—AZSU (Jimmy Starr Collection), CASP, GBBF, MAH, MIDL, OHCL, WICF. • *Legal File*—CAUW: Agreement (1926). • *Filmography*—CAA, NYMA. • *Oral History*—NYCO: Mentioned in the following interviews: Carl Foreman, Joel McCrea. • *Photograph/Still*—CAA (also in Hollywood Studio Museum Collection), CAHL, CALM, CAUB, CAUT (Jessen Collection), CAUU, CNDA, DCG (Quigley Photographic Archives), NYB (Bettmann/UPI Collection), NYMN, NYPL, NYSU, OHCL, TXSM,

TXU, WICF. • *Publicity Release* —
NYPL: Unknown studio (1930s).
• *Scrapbook* — NYPL (R. Locke Collection).

RUBENS, Alma (Alma Smith), San Francisco, CA, 1897–1931.

Debuting in 1916, sultry Alma
Rubens became a major star in such
films as *Cytherea, Humoresque, Under
the Red Robe* and *The World and His
Wife*. During the latter part of the
1920s, her career declined, probably as
a result of drug addiction, and she
played supporting roles in her final
films, the last being the part-talkie *She
Goes to War*. She was married to
Ricardo Cortez (q.v.).

PUBLISHED SOURCES

• *Books* — Bibliography: *The Idols of
Silence*. General: *Famous Film Folk*;
Hollywood's Unsolved Mysteries; *The
Kindergarten of the Movies*; *Who's Who
on the Screen*. Credits: *Filmarama* (v. I
and II); *Twenty Years of Silents*; *Who
Was Who on Screen*. Encyclopedic
Works: *Film Encyclopedia*; *Filmlexicon
degli Autori e delle Opere*; *Halliwell's
Filmgoer's Companion*; *The Illustrated
Who's Who of the Cinema*; *The Movie
Makers*; *Who's Who in Hollywood*; *The
World Film Encyclopedia*. Pictorial:
Silent Portraits.
• *Periodicals* — The following period-
ical articles are in addition to that included in the library listings below:
Photoplay (Apr. 1917, Feb. 1918, July
1923, June 1924, Apr. 1930); *Motion Pic-
ture Classic* (Aug. 1918, July 1919, Oct.
1923); *Motion Picture Magazine* (Mar.
1920, Aug. 1920, Sept. 1925, May 1931,
June 1933); *Good Housekeeping* (July
1932); *Classic Film Collector* (Spring
1968).

ARCHIVAL MATERIALS

• *Clipping File* — CAA: Newsphoto;
article (1924). NYMA (also in Photoplay
Collection): Placed in asylum (1929); personal data summary. Periodical article:
Classic Film Collector (Winter 1972).

NYMN: Newsphotos; funeral (1931);
obituary (1931). NYPL (also in Locke
Collection): Newsphotos (numerous);
surgery (1929); obituary (1931). • *Other
Clipping File* — CASP, GBBF, MAH,
OHCL, PAPL, WICF. • *Legal File* —
CAUT (Twentieth Century-Fox Collec-
tion): Letter, memo, telegram (1926);
talent agreement (1917, 1924–25).
• *Photograph/Still* — CAA (also in
Hollywood Studio Museum Collection),
CALM, CAUT (Jessen Collection),
CAUU, DCG (Quigley Photographic Ar-
chives), NYAM, NYCU (Dramatic Mu-
seum Portraits), NYEH, NYPL, NYSU,
OHCL, TXSM, TXU, WICF. • *Press
Kit* — OHCL. • *Scrapbook* — NYPL (also
in Locke Collection).

RUSSELL, William (William Lerche or Leach), The Bronx, NY, 1884/86–1929.

For studios like Thanhouser, American, Fox and Warner Bros., William
Russell starred in numerous films and
serials, including the legendary *Diamond from the Sky* and its sequel. His
films, in which he was generally cast as
a man of action, included *Bare
Knuckles, A Self-Made Man, The
Beloved Brute* and *Big Pal*. The leading
roles continued until the time of his
death. He was married to Helen
Ferguson (q.v.).

PUBLISHED SOURCES

• *Books* — General: *Eighty Silent Film
Stars; First One Hundred Noted Men and
Women of the Screen; The Hall of Fame
of Western Film Stars*. Credits:
Filmarama (v. I and II); *Twenty Years of
Silents; Who Was Who on Screen*. En-
cyclopedic Works: *Film Encyclopedia*;
Filmlexicon degli Autori e delle Opere;
Who's Who in Hollywood. Pictorial:
Silent Portraits.
• *Periodicals* — The following period-
ical articles are in addition to those in-
cluded in the library listings below:
Photoplay (Mar. 1915, Apr. 1917); *Mo-
tion Picture Magazine* (May 1917); *Mo-
tion Picture Classic* (Jan. 1920, June
1921); *Picture Show* (Feb. 21, 1920);

Classic Images (July 1990) (filmography).

ARCHIVAL MATERIALS

• *Clipping File* – CAA: Newsphoto; film appearance (1919). NYMA (also in Photoplay Collection): Personal data summary. Periodical articles: *Classic Images* (Aug. 1983, June 1987). NYPL (also in Locke Collection): Legal problem (1921); newsphotos. • *Other Clipping File* – CAUB, GBBF, MIDL, PAPL, WICF. • *Correspondence* – NYPL (C. & L. Brown Collection): 1924. • *Legal File* – CAUT (Twentieth Century-Fox Collection): Talent agreement (1919, 1921-22); letter, telegram (1919, 1921). CAUW: Talent agreement (1924, 1927, 1928). • *Photograph/Still* – CAA (also in Hollywood Studio Museum Collection) (also in MGM Collection), CAUT (Jessen Collection), CNDA, DCG (Quigley Photographic Archives), NYAM, NYPL, NYSU, OHCL, TXU, WICF. • *Scrapbook* – NYPL (also in C. & L. Brown Collection) (also in R. Locke Collection).

SAIS, Marin (May Smith?), San Rafael, CA, 1888/90-1971.
Marin Sais was one of the premier female action stars of westerns and serials after her debut with Kalem about 1910; she could hold her own with any villain. Among her serials were *The Social Pirates*, *The Girl from Frisco* and *Stingaree*. Her career as a leading lady continued through the 1920s in action films and she was seen in character roles until 1949.

PUBLISHED SOURCES

• *Books* – **General:** *The BFI Companion to the Western*; *Ladies in Distress*; *Sweethearts of the Sage*; *Those Fabulous Serial Heroines*; *Who's Who in the Film World*. **Credits:** *Filmarama* (v. I and II); *Forty Years of Screen Credits*; *Twenty Years of Silents*. **Encyclopedic Works:** *B Western Actors Encyclopedia*; *Film Encyclopedia*; *Who's Who in Hollywood*. **Pictorial:** *Silent Portraits*.

• *Periodicals* – The following period-

ical articles are in addition to that included in the library listings below: *Photoplay* (Aug. 1916, Mar. 1917); *Motion Picture Magazine* (Sept. 1916); *Motion Picture Classic* (Sept. 1916, June 1917); *Classic Film Collector* (Spring 1978); *Classic Images* (Nov. 1981, July 1988, Feb. 1991).

ARCHIVAL MATERIALS

• *Clipping File* – CAA: Article (1916); newsphotos (numerous); synopses of serial appearances in 1916-17. Article: *Picture Play* (June 1917). NYPL (also in Locke Collection): Newsphotos. • *Other Clipping File* – NYMA (Photoplay Collection), WICF. • *Collection* – CAA (Vertical File Collection): Poetry by MS; drawings; real estate deeds (1924-25); miscellany. • *Legal File* – CAA (see Collection). CAUU (Universal Pictures Collection): Personnel record (1949). • *Photograph/Still* – CAA, CAUT (Jessen Collection), DCG (Quigley Photographic Archives), NYPL. • *Scrapbook* – NYPL (R. Locke Collection). • *Studio Biography* – NYMA: Photoplay.

SANTSCHI, Tom (Paul Santschi), Kokomo, IN or Lucerne, Switzerland, 1876/79-1931.
Although he made many features and serials from 1909 until his death, rugged Tom Santschi's fame rests on that famous fistfight in the 1914 version of *The Spoilers*, and perhaps his co-starring role in the early serial *The Adventures of Kathlyn*. His films included numerous westerns and adventure melodramas like *The Plunderer*, *The Cradle of Courage* and *Jim the Conqueror*.

PUBLISHED SOURCES

• *Books* – **General:** *Blue Book of the Screen*; *Eighty Silent Film Stars*; *Famous Film Folk*; *The Hall of Fame of Western Film Stars*; *Life Stories of the Movie Stars*; *Who's Who in the Film World*. **Credits:** *Filmarama* (v. I and II); *Forty Years of Screen Credits*; *Twenty Years of*

Silents; *Who Was Who on Screen.* **Encyclopedic Works:** *Film Encyclopedia*; *Filmlexicon degli Autori e delle Opere*; *Halliwell's Filmgoer's Companion*; *Who's Who in Hollywood*; *The World Almanac Who's Who of Film.* **Pictorial:** *Silent Portraits.*

• *Periodicals* — The following periodical articles are in addition to those included in the library listings below: *Photoplay* (Aug. 1916); *Picture Show* (Feb. 7, 1920); *Films in Review* (Oct. 1963); *Cinema Trails* (no. 2); *Classic Images* (Jan.-Feb. 1990 (filmography), Mar. 1991).

ARCHIVAL MATERIALS

• *Clipping File* — NYMA (also in Photoplay Collection): Personal data summary. Periodical article: *Classic Images* (July 1980). NYPL (also in Locke Collection). Newsphotos; obituary (1931). Periodical article: *Motion Picture Magazine* (Sept. 1919). • *Other Clipping File* — GBBF, OHCL, PAPL, WICF. • *Legal File* — CAUW: Talent agreement (1926-28, 1930); letter (1926). • *Filmography* — CAA. • *Photograph/Still* — CAA (also in Hollywood Studio Museum Collection), CAUT (Jessen Collection), DCG (Quigley Photographic Archives), NYB (Penguin Collection), NYEH, NYPL, NYSU, OHCL, TXU, WICF. • *Scrapbook* — NYPL.

SEBASTIAN, Dorothy, Birmingham, AL, 1903/06-1957. *Sackcloth and Scarlet* (1924) was Dorothy Sebastian's first film, then it was mainly programmers until 1928's *Our Dancing Daughters* gave her the first of several better roles. She went on to costar with Buster Keaton (q.v.) and also appeared with Garbo (q.v.) in two films before being released by MGM. As a freelancer she had roles in a serial, comedy shorts and some westerns that marked the decline of her career until it ended in the early 1940s.

PUBLISHED SOURCES

• *Books* — Credits: *Filmarama* (v. II); *Forty Years of Screen Credits*; *Twenty!*

Years of Silents; *Who Was Who on Screen.* **Encyclopedic Works:** *Film Encyclopedia*; *Filmlexicon degli Autori e delle Opere*; *The Picturegoer's Who's Who and Encyclopedia of the Screen To-day*; *Who's Who in Hollywood*; *The World Film Encyclopedia.* **Pictorial:** *They Had Faces Then.*

• *Periodicals* — *Motion Picture Magazine* (July 1925, June 1928); *Photoplay* (Sept. 1925, July 1929, Mar. 1931, Oct. 1932, Mar. 1934); *Motion Picture Classic* (July 1926); *Time* (Apr. 22, 1957); *Classic Images* (Nov. 1981).

ARCHIVAL MATERIALS

• *Clipping File* — CAA: Marriage (1927, 1930, 1936, 1947); legal problem (1929, 1935, 1937-38); illness (1928-29); release from MGM (1930); obituary (1957). NYPL: Newsphotos; marriage/ divorce (1930, 1936, undated); legal problem; film appearance (1934); obituary (1957). • *Other Clipping File* — CTY, GBBF, MIDL, OHCL, PAPL, WICF. • *Correspondence* — CAA: Letter (Adolph Zukor Collection) (1925); letter (Hedda Hopper Collection) (1955). • *Legal File* — CAUW: Talent agreement (1933). • *Photograph/Still* — CAA (also in Hollywood Studio Museum Collection) (also in MGM Collection), CAH, CASU, CAUT (Portrait File), DCG (Quigley Photographic Archives), GBBF, NJFL, NJPT, NYAM, NYB (Springer Collection), NYCU (Dramatic Museum Portraits) (Palmer Collection), NYEH, NYPL, NYSU, OHCL, PAPL, TXU (A. Davis Collection), WICF. • *Scrapbook* — NYPL.

SEDGWICK, Eileen (later known as Greta Yoltz), Galveston, TX, 1895/97-1991. From 1915 Eileen Sedgwick was a popular leading actress in about 12 serials (e.g., *Lure of the Circus*, *The Great Radium Mystery*, *The Diamond Queen*, *Terror Trail*) and many features, including westerns. Her career ended in 1928 but not before she had changed her screen image (and name) to that of a comic actress with appearances in films like *A Girl in Every Port* and *Beautiful But Dumb*.

PUBLISHED SOURCES

• *Books*—General: *Sweethearts of the Sage*; *Those Fabulous Serial Heroines*; *The Truth About the Movies*. Credits: *Filmarama* (v. I and II); *Twenty Years of Silents*. Encyclopedic Works: *Film Encyclopedia*; *Filmlexicon degli Autori e delle Opere*; *Who's Who in Hollywood*.

• *Periodicals*—The following periodical articles are in addition to that included in the library listings below: *Motion Picture Classic* (Jan. 1922); *Films in Review* (Oct. 1963); *Film en Televisie + Video* (July–Aug. 1991).

ARCHIVAL MATERIALS

• *Clipping File*—CAA: Injury (1923); obituary (1991). NYMA (also in Photoplay Collection): Obituary (1991). Periodical article: *Classic Images* (Mar. 1986). • *Other Clipping File*—GBBF. • *Photograph/Still*—CAA (also in Hollywood Studio Museum Collection), CAUT (Jessen Collection), CAUU, DCG (Quigley Photographic Archives), NYPL, NYSU, OHCL, TXU. • *Studio Biography*—NYMA: Photoplay.

SEMON, Larry, West Point, MS, 1889–1928.

In films from 1916 to 1928, Larry Semon was a very popular comic actor for much of that time. The hallmarks of his unsubtle two-reelers, in which he generally appeared in whiteface, were speed and mayhem. Eventually his career declined and his features like the *Wizard of Oz*, *The Girl in the Limousine* and *Spuds* were not successful. A switch to character parts came shortly before his death. He was married to Dorothy Dwan (q.v.).

PUBLISHED SOURCES

• *Books*—Bibliography: *The Idols of Silence*. General: *Blue Book of the Screen*; *Clown Princes and Court Jesters*; *Comedy Films, 1894-1954*; *Famous Film Folk*; *Keaton et Cie*; *The Silent Clowns*; *Who's Who on the Screen*; *World of Laughter*. Credits: *Filmarama* (v. I and II); *Twenty Years of Silents*; *Who Was Who on Screen*. Encyclopedic Works: *Film Encyclopedia*; *Filmlexicon degli Autori e delle Opere*; *Halliwell's Filmgoer's Companion*; *The Illustrated Who's Who of the Cinema*; *The International Encyclopedia of Film*; *Joe Franklin's Encyclopedia of Comedians*; *The Oxford Companion to Film*; *Quinlan's Illustrated Directory of Film Comedy Actors*; *Who's Who in Hollywood*; *The World Encyclopedia of the Film*. Screenplay: *Ridolini e la Collana della Suocera e Ridolini Esploratore, di Larry Semon*. Pictorial: *Silent Portraits*.

• *Periodicals*—The following periodical articles are in addition to those included in the library listings below: *Motion Picture Magazine* (Nov. 1920); *Motion Picture Classic* (Dec. 1920, Apr. 1922, Feb. 1924); *Classic Images* (June 1985, Mar. 1989); *Cineforum* (Dec. 1989); *Cinéma* (France) (Jan. 1990).

ARCHIVAL MATERIALS

• *Clipping File*—CAA: Newsphotos; Vitagraph contract (1922, 1924); legal problem (1922); marriage (1922). NYMA (also in Photoplay Collection): Obituary (1928). Periodical articles: *8mm Collector* (Winter 1964); *Classic Film/Video Images* (Sept. 1980); *Classic Images* (Apr. 1989). NYPL: Newsphotos; film appearance (1920); signs with Vitagraph (1919); legal problem (1920). • *Other Clipping File*—AZSU (Jimmy Starr Collection), CNDA, GBBF, MAH, MIDL, PAPL, WICF. • *Legal File*—CAA (Sennett Collection): Talent agreement (as director) (1926). CAUW: Document (1922); rights (1913, 1916, 1922-23, undated); story digest (1913, 1916, 1922, 1937, undated); agreement (1922); letter (1922, 1944-48); film synopsis (undated); copyright (1922-23); payroll record (1913, 1916). • *Oral History*—NYCO: Mentioned in: Joseph Mankiewicz interview. • *Photograph/Still*—CAA (also in Hollywood Studio Museum Collection), CALM, CAUB, CAUU, CNDA, DCG (Quigley Photographic Archives), NYEH, NYPL, NYSU, OHCL, TXU, WICF. • *Scrap-*

book—NYPL (also in R. Locke Collection).

SHERMAN, Lowell, San Francisco, CA, 1885–1934.

A stage actor since childhood, Lowell Sherman made his mark in films as the scoundrel who wronged Lillian Gish (q.v.) in D.W. Griffith's *Way Down East* (1920). He played similar (albeit sometimes more likeable) roles in a host of other films. With the advent of talkies he became a director and acted in many of his own films, generally playing sophisticated world-weary men. One notable role came in *What Price Hollywood*? Among the films he directed were *She Done Him Wrong* and *Morning Glory*. He was married to Pauline Garon (q.v.) and Helene Costello (q.v.).

PUBLISHED SOURCES

• *Books*—General: *The American Cinema*. **Credits:** *Filmarama* (v. I and II); *Forty Years of Screen Credits*; *Twenty Years of Silents*; *Who Was Who on Screen*. **Encyclopedic Works:** *A Biographical Dictionary of Film*; *Film Encyclopedia*; *Filmlexicon degli Autori e delle Opere*; *Halliwell's Filmgoer's Companion*; *The Illustrated Who's Who of the Cinema*; *The Picturegoer's Who's Who and Encyclopedia of the Screen To-day*; *Who Was Who in the Theatre*; *Who's Who in Hollywood*; *The World Encyclopedia of the Film*; *The World Film Encyclopedia*. **Pictorial:** *Silent Portraits*.

• *Periodicals*—*Theatre* (June 1920, Jan. 1927); *Photoplay* (Feb. 1921, July 1923); *Motion Picture Magazine* (June 1930, Feb. 1932); *Motion Picture Classic* (Dec. 1930); *Film Comment* (May–June 1973); *Film Fan Monthly* (June 1974); *Focus on Film* (Winter 1975-76).

ARCHIVAL MATERIALS

• *Caricature*—NYPL. • *Clipping File*—CAA: Film appearance (1929). NYMA (also in Photoplay Collection): Personal data summary. NYMN: Newsphotos; divorce (early 1930s); obituary (1934).

NYPL (also in Locke Collection): Article (1924, undated); director (1933–34); marriage (1934); play review (1910s, 1921); witness in Arbuckle scandal (1921); bankruptcy (1922); film review (1920s); film appearance (1920s, 1930s); newsphotos; obituary (1934). • *Other Clipping File*—CASP, CAUB, GBBF, MIDL, NYPL, PAPL, WICF. • *Filmography*—NYMA. • *Legal File*—CAUW: Talent agreement (1928). • *Oral History*—NYCO: Mentioned in the following interviews: George Cukor, Albert Hackett, Joel McCrea, Mae Murray, Adela R. St. Johns. • *Photograph/Still*—CAA (also in Hollywood Studio Museum Collection), CASP, CASU, CAUU, CNDA, DCG (Quigley Photographic Archives), GBBF, NJPT, NYAM, NYB (Bettmann/UPI Collection), NYCU (Dramatic Museum Portraits), NYEH, NYMN, NYPL, NYSU, OHCL, PAPL, TXU (A. Davis Collection), WICF. • *Play Program*—OHSU. • *Scrapbook*—NYPL (also in C. & L. Brown Collection).

SHORT, Antrim, Cincinnati, Ohio, 1900–1972.

Antrim Short began as a popular juvenile lead about 1914 and worked at American Biograph. His films included *Tom Sawyer*, *Black Beauty*, *O'Malley of the Mounted*, *Classmates and Wildfire*. His major onscreen career lasted through the mid-1920s but he had bit parts in the '30s; later he became a casting director at several studios.

PUBLISHED SOURCES

• *Books*—Credits: *Filmarama* (v. I and II); *Forty Years of Screen Credits*; *Twenty Years of Silents*; *Who Was Who on Screen*. **Encyclopedic Works:** *Who's Who in Hollywood*.

• *Periodical*—*Motion Picture Classic* (July 1920).

ARCHIVAL MATERIALS

• *Clipping File*—CAA: Obituary (1972). CAUT: Obituary (1972). NYPL: Newsphotos; obituary (1973). • *Other Clipping File*—MIDL, NYMA (Photoplay Collection). • *Photograph/Still* — CAA (Hollywood Studio Museum Collection), DCG (Quigley Photographic Archives), NJFL, NYPL, NYSU, WICF.

SILLS, Milton, Chicago, IL, 1882–1930.

After a stage career, Milton Sills went to Hollywood in 1914 and became a highly popular leading man. He appeared in over 70 films, including *Miss Lulu Bett, Adams Rib, The Sea Hawk, The Spoilers* (1923 version) and the part-talkie *The Barker*. Many of his films were adventures or romantic melodramas in which he could display his rugged good looks. He made a promising transition to talkies, his final film being the well-received *The Sea Wolf*.

Published Sources

• *Books* — Wrote (i.e., was transcribed posthumously from his conversations) *Values, a Philosophy of Human Needs*. A lecture given by MS in 1927 appeared in the book *The Story of the Films*. **General:** *Blue Book of the Screen; Classics of the Silent Screen; Eighty Silent Film Stars; Famous Film Folk; First One Hundred Noted Men and Women of the Screen; Gentlemen to the Rescue; How I Broke Into the Movies; The Truth About the Movies.* **Credits:** *Filmarama* (v. I and II); *Forty Years of Screen Credits; Twenty Years of Silents; Who Was Who on Screen.* **Encyclopedic Works:** *Film Encyclopedia; Filmlexicon degli Autori e delle Opere; Halliwell's Filmgoer's Companion; The Movie Makers; Who's who in Hollywood; The World Almanac Who's Who of Film.* **Pictorial:** *Silent Portraits.*
• *Periodicals* — *Theatre* (Apr. 1909); *Green Book Album* (Jan. 1910); *Photoplay* (June 1918, June 1926, Mar. 1930, Jan. 1934); *Motion Picture Magazine* (Sept. 1918, Nov. 1921, Mar.–Apr. 1925); *Motion Picture Classic* (June 1921, Jan. 1923, June 1930); *Architecture & Buildings* (May 1928); *Films in Review* (Dec. 1971–Jan. 1972, Jan. 1973); *Classic Images* (Mar. 1986).

Archival Materials

• *Clipping File* — CAA: Film appearance (1922, 1930); home (1951); article (1924, 1926, 1920s, 1970, undated); newsphotos; marriage (1926); illness (1929); Fox contract (1930); obituary (1930). NYMN: Newsphotos; article (1930); obituary (1930). NYPL (also in Locke Collection): Newsphotos; play review; film review (1920s); publication of *Values...* (1932); obituary (1930). • *Other Clipping File* — CNDA, GBBF, MAH, NYMA (Photoplay Collection), PAPL, WICF. • *Correspondence* — CAHL: 1927–30. • *Filmography* — CAA, NYMA, NYPL. • *Legal File* — CAUW: Contract (1923–25, 1928); contract summary (1925–29); payroll record (1925–29); agreement (1928); memo, letter (1928–29); talent agreement (1923–25, 1927–29). • *Oral History* — NYCO: Mentioned in the following interviews: Cecil B. DeMille, Carey Wilson. • *Photograph/Still* — CAA (also in Hollywood Studio Museum Collection), CALM, CAUS, CAUT (Jessen Collection), CAUU, DCG (Quigley Photographic Archives), GBBF, MIDL, NJPT, NYAM, NYB (Bettmann/UPI Collection) (Springer Collection) (Underwood Collection), NYCU (Bulliet Collection) (Dramatic Museum Portraits), NYEH, NYMN, NYPL, NYSU, OHCL, TXU, WICF. • *Play Program* — NYPL: 1914. • *Scrapbook* — NJPT (Yeandle Collection), NYMA, NYPL (also in C. & L. Brown Collection) (also in Locke Collection).

SNOW, Marguerite, Denver, CO, 1889–1958.

Marguerite Snow may have been the most beautiful of serial stars. She did not appear in many chapterplays but among them were two of the most famous: *The Million Dollar Mystery* and *Zudora* (also known as *The Twenty Million Dollar Mystery*). Other films in a career which spanned the years 1911 to 1925 were *The Silent Voice, Broadway Jones, Daughter of Kings* and *The Woman in Room 13*.

PUBLISHED SOURCES
• *Books—General:* *Life Stories of the Movie Stars*; *Those Fabulous Serial Heroines.* **Credits:** *Filmarama* (v. I and II); *Twenty Years of Silents*; *Who Was Who on Screen.* **Encyclopedic Works:** *Film Encyclopedia*; *Filmlexicon degli Autori e delle Opere*; *Who's Who in Hollywood.* **Pictorial:** *Silent Portraits.* • *Periodicals—Blue Book Magazine* (Sept. 1914); *Photoplay* (Nov. 1914, July 1915, Oct. 1915, Sept. 1918, July 1924); *Cosmopolitan* (Dec. 1914); *Motion Picture Classic* (May 1916, Dec. 1916); *Motion Picture Magazine* (Apr. 1917, Aug. 1917); *Films in Review* (June/July 1958).

ARCHIVAL MATERIALS
• *Clipping File—CAA:* Obituary (1958). NYMA (also in Photoplay Collection): Article (1916). NYPL (also in Locke Collection): Newsphotos; film review (1915); obituary (1957). • *Other Clipping File—MAH, MIDL, OHSU, PAPL, WICF.* • *Correspondence—NYMA* (Photoplay Collection). • *Photograph/Still—CAA* (also in Hollywood Studio Museum Collection), CAUT (Jessen Collection), CNDA, DCG (Quigley Photographic Archives), NYAM, NYEH, NYPL, NYSU, OHCL, TXU, WICF. • *Scrapbook—NYPL* (also in R. Locke Collection). • *Studio Biography—NYMA:* Photoplay.

SOUTHERN, Eve, Texas, 1898–?.

In a career that lasted from the late teens to the late 1930s, pretty Eve Southern had one notable film appearance, *The Gaucho*, opposite Douglas Fairbanks (q.v.). Other roles included *Resurrection*, *Stormy Waters*, *Clothes Make the Woman* and *Law of the Sea.* She worked at several studios including Paramount, First National, Tiffany and finally Monogram.

PUBLISHED SOURCES
• *Books—Credits:* *Filmarama* (v. II); *Twenty Years of Silents.* **Encyclopedic Works:** *Filmlexicon degli Autori e delle*

Opere; *The Picturegoer's Who's Who and Encyclopedia of the Screen To-day*; *Who's Who in Hollywood.* • *Periodicals—Photoplay* (Sept. 1927); *Motion Picture Classic* (Sept. 1927); *Motion Picture Magazine* (Sept. 1929).

ARCHIVAL MATERIALS
• *Clipping File—NYPL:* Newsphotos; article (undated). • *Other Clipping File—GBBF*, NYMA (Photoplay Collection), WICF. • *Legal File—CAUW:* Talent agreement (1929). • *Photograph/Still—CAA* (Hollywood Studio Museum Collection), DCG (Quigley Photographic Archives), NYCU (Dramatic Museum Portraits), NYPL, NYSU, OHCL, TXU, WICF.

STARKE, Pauline (Pauline Stark?), Joplin, MO, 1900/01–1977.

Pretty Pauline Starke began her film career lost among the "cast of thousands" in Griffiths's *Intolerance* (1916). She soon emerged from the crowd, however, and had a creditable career of 53 films, almost all of them silents. They included *Man Without a Country*, *Dante's Inferno* and *Sun Up.* She made very few talking pictures; the last came in 1935 after a lengthy hiatus.

PUBLISHED SOURCES
• *Books—General:* *Famous Film Folk*; *The Kindergarten of the Movies.* **Credits:** *Filmarama* (v. I and II); *Forty Years of Screen Credits*; *Twenty Years of Silents.* **Encyclopedic Works:** *Film Encyclopedia*; *Filmlexicon degli Autori e delle Opere*; *Halliwell's Filmgoer's Companion*; *The Picturegoer's Who's Who and Encyclopedia of the Screen To-day*; *Who's Who in Hollywood.* **Nostalgia:** *Whatever Became of...* (1st). **Pictorial:** *Silent Portraits.* • *Periodicals—Motion Picture Classic* (Sept. 1917, Jan 1922, Feb. 1926); *Photoplay* (July 1918, Nov. 1919, July 1921, Aug. 1925, July 1926, June 1930); *Motion Picture Magazine* (Nov. 1921, Oct. 1923); *Cinema Art* (Apr. 1926);

Movie Classic (Jan. 1933); *Films in Review* (Feb. 1970 (Wampas Baby Stars), May 1977); *Classic Images* (June 1991).

ARCHIVAL MATERIALS
• *Clipping File*—CAA: Film appearance (1922); engagement (1922); illness (1948); legal problem (1938); nostalgia (1961, 1975); obituary (1977). CAUU: Nostalgia (1975); obituary (1977). NYMN: Newsphotos. NYPL (also in Locke Collection): Newsphotos; film appearance (1923); obituary (1977). • *Other Clipping File*—GBBF, MIDL, NYMA (Photoplay Collection), OHCL, PAPL, WICF. • *Collection*—WYU: 7 photographs. • *Filmography*—NYPL (incomplete). • *Interview*—CAUU (A. Slide Collection): 1975. • *Legal File*—CAUT (Twentieth Century-Fox Collection): Agreement (1920). CAUW: Letter, memo (1926); payroll record (1926); loanout (1928); talent agreement (1926). • *Photograph/Still*—CAA (also in Hollywood Studio Museum Collection), CAH, CAHL, CASU, DCG (Quigley Photographic Archives), GBBF, NJPT, NYAM, NYB (Bettmann/UPI Collection) (Underwood Collection), NYCU (Dramatic Museum Portraits), NYEH, NYMN, NYPL, NYSU, OHCL, PAPL, TXU (A. Davis Collection), WICF, WYU (see Collection). • *Scrapbook*—NYPL (also in R. Locke Collection). • *Studio Biography*—NYMA: Photoplay.

STERLING, Ford (George Stitch), La Crosse, WI, 1880/83-1939.

From 1912, Ford Sterling was a Keystone regular, often portraying the befuddled chief of the Keystone Kops. He was very popular for a time, starring with Mabel Normand (q.v.), Roscoe Arbuckle (q.v.), Charlie Chaplin (q.v.) and others in numerous one- and two-reelers. He never gained stardom but his career continued through the early 1930s in character parts. Among his features were *So Big*, *He Who Gets Slapped*, *Oh Kay!* and *Alice in Wonderland*.

PUBLISHED SOURCES
• *Books*—**General:** *Clown Princes and Court Jesters*; *Mack Sennett's Keystone*; *The Truth About the Movies*; *Who's Who in the Film World*; *Who's Who on the Screen*. **Credits:** *Filmarama* (v. I and II); *Forty Years of Screen Credits*; *Twenty Years of Silents*; *Who Was Who on Screen*. **Encyclopedic Works:** *Film Encyclopedia*; *Filmlexicon degli Autori e delle Opere*; *Halliwell's Filmgoer's Companion*; *The Illustrated Who's Who of the Cinema*; *The Movie Makers*; *The Picturegoer's Who's Who and Encyclopedia of the Screen To-day*; *Quinlan's Illustrated Directory of Film Comedy Actors*; *Who's Who in Hollywood*; *The World Almanac Who's Who of Film*; *The World Film Encyclopedia*. **Pictorial:** *Silent Portraits*.
• *Periodicals*—*Moving Picture World* (Mar. 14, 1914); *Motion Picture Classic* (Apr. 1921, Jan. 1926).

ARCHIVAL MATERIALS
• *Clipping File*—CAA: Leg amputated; newsphotos. NYMA (also in Photoplay Collection): Obituary (1939). NYPL (also in Locke Collection): Newsphotos; film review; article (undated); illness; obituary (1939). • *Other Clipping File*—CNDA, GBBF, MAH, MIDL, OHCL, PAPL, WICF. • *Legal File*—CAUW: Personnel, payroll record (1935); contract (1929); talent agreement (1928-29, 1931). • *Oral History*—NYCO: Mentioned in the following interviews: Albert Hackett, Buster Keaton, Harold Lloyd. • *Photograph/Still*—CAA (also in Hollywood Studio Museum Collection), CAUT (Jessen Collection), CAUU, NYAM, NYB (Penguin Collection), NYEH, NYPL, NYSU, OHCL, TXU, WICF. • *Press Kit*—OHCL. • *Publicity Release*—CAA (numerous).

STEWART, Anita (Anna Stewart), Brooklyn, NY, 1895/96-1961.

Redhaired Anita Stewart was a star almost from the time of her debut at Vitagraph in 1912. Later she became Louis B. Mayer's first major star.

Among her popular films (many with Earle Williams [q.v.]) were *The Goddess, The Mind-the-Paint Girl, The Girl Philippa, In Old Kentucky, A Million Bid* and *Playthings of Destiny*. When she left the screen after *Sisters of Eve* (1928), she was still near the top.

PUBLISHED SOURCES

• *Books*—Wrote a mystery, *The Devil's Toy* (1935). **Bibliography:** *The Idols of Silence*. **General:** *The Big V; Blue Book of the Screen; Early American Cinema; Famous Film Folk; First One Hundred Noted Men and Women of the Screen; From Hollywood; Life Stories of the Movie Stars; Who's Who on the Screen*. **Credits:** *Filmarama* (v. I and II); *Twenty Years of Silents; Who Was Who on Screen*. **Encyclopedic Works:** *Film Encyclopedia; Filmlexicon degli Autori e delle Opere; Halliwell's Filmgoer's Companion; The Illustrated Who's Who of the Cinema; The Picturegoer's Who's Who and Encyclopedia of the Screen To-day; Who's Who in Hollywood*. **Pictorial:** *Silent Portraits*. **Factoids:** *Star Stats*.

• *Periodicals*—The following periodical articles are in addition to that included in the library listings below: *Green Book Magazine* (Oct. 1914, May 1916); *Cosmopolitan* (Mar. 1915); *Photoplay* (Apr. 1915, Sept. 1915, May 1917, Oct. 1918, Sept. 1919, Mar. 1920, Oct. 1933); *Theatre* (July 1915); *Motion Picture Classic* (May–June 1916, July 1919, July 1921); *Motion Picture Magazine* (July–Aug. 1916, Apr. 1917, Oct.–Nov. 1917, Aug. 1918, Apr.–May 1920, Oct.–Nov. 1921, June 1922, Dec. 1924, June 1925); *Motography* (Sept. 22, 1917, Nov. 3, 1917); *Picture Show* (Feb. 28, 1920); *New York Dramatic Mirror* (Apr. 24, 1920); *Time* (May 12, 1961); *Films in Review* (Mar. 1968 (filmography), June–July 1968).

ARCHIVAL MATERIALS

• *Clipping File*—CAA: Film appearance (1920–22); Mayer contract (1922); newsphotos; article (1920s); Vitagraph contract (1917); estate (1961); obituary (1961). CAUT: Newsphotos; marriage (1929); obituary (1961). NYMA (also in Photoplay Collection): Article (1916); obituary (1961). Periodical article: *Photo-play World* (Dec. 1918). NYMN: Newsphotos; obituary (1961). • *Other Clipping File*—AZSU (Jimmy Starr Collection), CNDA, GBBF, MAH, MIDL, OHCL, NYPL, PAPL, WICF. • *Filmography*—CAA. • *Legal File*—CAUW: Agreement (1918). NYMA (Joel Swensen Collection): Contract (1918); agreement (1920). • *Photograph/Still*—CAA (also in Hollywood Studio Museum Collection), CAHL, CALM, CASF, CAUT (Jessen Collection), CAUU, DCG (Quigley Photographic Archives), NYB (Bettmann/UPI Collection) (Underwood Collection), NYCU (Dramatic Museum Portraits), NYEH, NYMA, NYMN, NYPL, NYSU, OHCL, TXU, WICF. • *Press Kit*—OHCL. • *Scrapbook*—CASU (Stark Collection). • *Studio Biography*—NYMA: Photoplay.

STEWART, Roy, San Diego, CA, 1884/89–1933.

Burly Roy Stewart alternated with seeming ease between social drama, western films and the occasional serial in a starring career which began about 1916 and ran through the end of the silent era. Among his films were *The Heart of the North, The Love Brand, Sparrows, The Viking* and *The Sagebrush Trail*. He was still going strong in supporting roles at the time of his death.

PUBLISHED SOURCES

• *Books*—**General:** *Blue Book of the Screen; The Hall of Fame of Western Film Stars; Saddle Aces of the Cinema; The Truth About the Movies; Winners of the West*. **Credits:** *Filmarama* (v. I and II); *Forty Years of Screen Credits; Twenty Years of Silents; Who Was Who on Screen*. **Encyclopedic Works:** *Filmlexicon degli Autori e delle Opere; The Picturegoer's Who's Who and Encyclopedia of the Screen To-day; Who's Who in Hollywood*. **Pictorial:** *Silent Portraits*.

• *Periodicals*—The following periodical articles are in addition to that included in the library listings below: *Photoplay* (Sept. 1918, Dec. 1919); *Motion Picture Classic* (July 1921); *Classic Images* (Nov. 1981).

ARCHIVAL MATERIALS
• *Clipping File* – CAA: Newsphotos. NYMA (also in Photoplay Collection): Personal data summary. Periodical article: *Classic Film Collector* (Fall 1977). NYPL (also in Locke Collection): Newsphotos; stage appearance (1927); obituary (1933). • *Other Clipping File* – GBBF, OHCL, WICF. • *Legal File* – CAUW: Talent agreement (1929). • *Oral History* – NYCO: Mentioned in: Harold Lloyd interview. • *Photograph/Still* – CAA (also in Hollywood Studio Museum Collection), CAUT (Jessen Collection), CAUU, DCG (Quigley Photographic Archives), NYPL, NYSU, OHCL. TXU, WICF. • *Scrapbook* – NYAM, NYPL (also in R. Locke Collection).

STONEHOUSE, Ruth, Victor or Denver, CO or Chicago, IL, 1893/94–1941.

Ex-dancer Ruth Stonehouse appeared in numerous films for Essanay and Universal, among them the successful serials *The Adventures of Peg o' the Ring* and *The Master Mystery*. She also co-starred with matinee idol Francis X. Bushman (q.v.) in several films. Among her features were *Flames of Passion*, *Broken Barriers*, *Girl of the Limberlost* and *I Am Guilty*. By the late 1920s, she was being seen in supporting roles.

PUBLISHED SOURCES
• *Books* – General: *Life Stories of the Movie Stars*; *Reel Women*; *Those Fabulous Serial Heroines*; *Who's Who on the Screen*. Credits: *Filmarama* (v. I and II); *Twenty Years of Silents*; *Who Was Who on Screen*. Encyclopedic Works: *Film Encyclopedia*; *Filmlexicon degli Autori e delle Opere*; *Who's Who in Hollywood*; *Women Who Make Movies*. Pictorial: *Silent Portraits*.
• *Periodicals* – *Photoplay* (Feb. 1915,

Sept. 1917); *Feature Movie* (Sept. 10, 1915); *Motion Picture Classic* (Apr. 1916); *Motion Picture Magazine* (Apr. 1916, Feb. 1919, Feb. 1920); *Film Comment* (Nov.–Dec. 1972); *Classic Images* (Apr. 1990).

ARCHIVAL MATERIALS
• *Clipping File* – CAA: Film appearance (1922, 1924); obituary (1941). NYMA (also in Photoplay collection): Article (1916); newsphotos. NYPL (also in Locke Collection): Newsphotos; obituary (1941). • *Other Clipping File* – GBBF, PAPL, WICF. • *Correspondence* – CAHL: 1917. • *Photograph/Still* – CAA, CAUT (Jessen Collection), DCG (Quigley Photographic Archives), NYPL, NYSU, OHCL, TXU, WICF. • *Scrapbook* – NYPL (also in R. Locke Collection). • *Studio Biography* – NYMA: Photoplay.

STOREY, Edith, New York, NY, 1892–1955.

Known for her onscreen athleticism, pretty Edith Storey was one of the silent screen's earlier leading women. Her screen appearances began about 1908 and for Vitagraph and Metro she made such films as *The Ruling Power*, *Queen Louise*, *Eyes of Mystery*, *The Christian* and *Legion of Death*. Her career ended in 1921.

PUBLISHED SOURCES
• *Books* – General: *The Big V*; *First One Hundred Noted Men and Women of the Screen*; *Who's Who on the Screen*. Credits: *Filmarama* (v. I and II); *Twenty Years of Silents*. Encyclopedic Works: *Film Encyclopedia*; *Who's Who in Hollywood*. Pictorial: *Silent Portraits*.
• *Periodicals* – The following periodical articles are in addition to those included in the library listings below: *Blue Book Magazine* (May 1914); *Motion Picture Magazine* (Apr. 1915, Jan. 1917, May 1918); *Photoplay* (May 1916, Sept. 1917, Nov. 1918, July 1919, July 1924); *Motion Picture Classic* (Aug. 1916, June 1919, Jan. 1920); *Picture Play Magazine* (Apr. 1920); *Classic Images* (Feb. 1990).

ARCHIVAL MATERIALS

• *Clipping File* — CAA: Newsphotos. Periodical article: *Green Book Magazine* (Dec. 1914). NYMA (also in Photoplay Collection): Periodical article: *Photoplay World* (Apr. 1918). NYPL (also in Locke Collection): Newsphotos; poem dedicated to ES. • *Other Clipping File* — WICF. • *Photograph/Still* — CAA (also in Hollywood Studio Museum Collection), CASF, DCG (Quigley Photographic Archives), IAU (Junkin Collection), NYCU (Bulliet Collection), NYPL, NYSU, OHCL, TXU, WICF. • *Scrapbook* — NYPL (R. Locke Collection). • *Studio Biography* — NYMA: Photoplay.

STUART, Nick (Nicholas Prata, Pratza, Bratza and other versions of the name), Romania, 1904–1973.

After first working behind the scenes in Hollywood, wavy-haired Nick Stuart played a collegian in his first film at Fox about 1927 and continued the role through a popular series of films into the early sound period. He continued on in melodramas, westerns and other roles which became increasingly less important until 1936 when he formed his own band. He returned for a few small film roles in the '50s and '60s. He was married to Sue Carol (q.v.).

PUBLISHED SOURCES

• *Books* — Credits: *Filmarama* (v. II); *Forty Years of Screen Credits*; *Twenty Years of Silents*; *Who Was Who on Screen*. Encyclopedic Works: *Film Encyclopedia*; *Filmlexicon degli Autori e delle Opere*; *The Picturegoer's Who's Who and Encyclopedia of the Screen To-day*; *Who's Who in Hollywood*; *The World Film Encyclopedia*.
• *Periodicals* — The following periodical articles are in addition to that included in the library listings below: *Motion Picture Classic* (Mar. 1928); *Motion Picture Magazine* (Sept. 1928, Feb. 1930); *Photoplay* (Oct. 1928).

ARCHIVAL MATERIALS

• *Clipping File* — CAA: Divorce (1934, 1937); film appearance (1953, 1965); obituary (1973). CAUT: Obituary (1973). CAUU: Obituary (1973). NYMA (also in Photoplay Collection): Obituary (1973). NYPL: Newsphotos; divorce (1934); film review (1920s, 1933); article (1929); obituary (1933). Periodical article: *Hollywood* (Nov. 15, 1928). TXU: Obituary (1973). • *Other Clipping File* — GBBF, MIDL, WICF, WYU (see Collection). • *Collection* — WYU: Materials relating to NS orchestra: over 15 telegrams from various celebrities (1935); 34 newspaper clippings (1935); 4 photographs; sheet music; advertisements; program. • *Correspondence* — NYPL (C. & L. Brown Collection): 1934–44. WYU (see Collection). • *Legal File* — CAA (Sennett Collection): Talent agreement (1930); contract (1930). CAUT (Twentieth Century-Fox Collection): Option (1928); agreement (1927–28); memo, letter (1927–29). • *Photograph/Still* — CAA (also in Hollywood Studio Museum Collection), CASU, CNDA, DCG (Quigley Photographic Archives), GBBF, MIDL, NJPT, NYB (Underwood Collection), NYCU (Dramatic Museum Portraits), NYEH, NYPL, NYSU, OHCL, PAPL, WICF, WYU (see Collection). • *Studio Biography* — NYMA: Photoplay.

SURATT, Valeska, Terre Haute, IN, 1882–1962.

Among the "vamps" following in Theda Bara's footsteps was stage actress Valeska Suratt. She presumably was Fox's back-up in case of temperament problems with their star. Her film career was brief, lasting from 1915 to 1917, during which time she appeared in such films as *Jealousy*, *She*, *The Slave*, *The Immigrant* and *Soul of Broadway*.

PUBLISHED SOURCES

• *Books* — Credits: *Filmarama* (v. I); *Twenty Years of Silents*; *Who Was Who on Screen*. Filmography: *Hollywood on* the Palisades. **Encyclopedic Works:** Who's Who in Hollywood.

• Periodicals — The following periodical articles are in addition to those included in the library listings below: Picture Play Magazine (Aug. 1916); Motion Picture Magazine (Dec. 1916).

ARCHIVAL MATERIALS

• Clipping File — NYMN: Newsphotos (numerous); valuables (1934); writes screenplay for King of Kings. NYPL (also in Locke Collection): Newsphotos; stage appearance (1923-24); legal problem (1925, 1927-28); marriage/divorce (1911). Periodical articles: Photoplay (Mar. 1916?); Modern Screen (Apr. 1917). • Other Clipping File — MAH, NYMA (Photoplay Collection), OHCL, WICF. • Correspondence — NYPL (C. & L. Brown Collection). • Photograph/ Still — CAA (also in Hollywood Studio Museum Collection), CAUT (Jessen Collection), DCG (Quigley Photographic Archives), NJFL, NYCU (Bulliet Collection), NYMN, NYPL, NYSU, OHCL, WICF. • Scrapbook — NYAM, NYPL (also in Culver Collection) (also in R. Locke Collection).

SWAIN, Mack, Tacoma, WA, 1876-1935.

Mack Swain's screen immortality derives from his portrayal of the prospector Big Jim in Chaplin's classic The Gold Rush (1925). He had been in films since 1914 and was a Keystone staple, most notably as Ambrose in a series of two-reelers. In the 1920s he played a string of supporting roles, and even a couple of leads, in films such as Hands Up, Tillie's Punctured Romance (1928 version) and Finnegan's Ball. He continued on in both shorts and features until 1933.

PUBLISHED SOURCES

• Books — General: Clown Princes and Court Jesters; Immortals of the Screen; Kops and Custards; Mack Sennett's Keystone. Credits: Filmarama (v. I and II); Forty Years of Screen Credits; Twenty Years of Silents; Who Was Who

on Screen. **Encyclopedic Works:** Film Encyclopedia; Filmlexicon degli Autori e delle Opere; Halliwell's Filmgoer's Companion; The Illustrated Who's Who of the Cinema; Joe Franklin's Encyclopedia of Comedians; The Movie Makers; The Picturegoer's Who's Who and Encyclopedia of the Screen To-day; Quinlan's Illustrated Directory of Film Comedy Actors; Who's Who in Hollywood; The World Film Encyclopedia.

• Periodicals — The following periodical article is in addition to those included in the library listings below: Photoplay (Sept. 1926).

ARCHIVAL MATERIALS

• Clipping File — CAA: Newsphotos. NYMA (also in Photoplay Collection): Article (1917, 1928, undated); signs with Frohman (1919); returns to Sennett (1923); obituary (1935). Periodical articles: 8mm Film Collector (Fall-Winter 1965); Classic Film Collector (Fall 1978). NYPL: Returns to Sennett (1923); newsphotos; article (1917, undated); film review (1916); obituary (1935). • Other Clipping File — CAUB, GBBF, MAH, PAPL. • Legal File — CAA (Sennett Collection): Talent agreement (1927). CAUW: Talent agreement (1927-28). • Oral History — NYCO: Mentioned in: Gloria Swanson interview. • Photograph/Still — CAA (Hollywood Studio Museum Collection), CALM, CAUT (Jessen Collection), DCG (Quigley Photographic Archives), NYB (Penguin Collection), NYEH, NYPL, OHCL, WICF. • Publicity Release — CAA (Mack Sennett Collection). • Scrapbook — NYPL. • Studio Biography — NYMA: Photoplay.

SWANSON, Gloria (some sources say Swenson or Svenssen), Chicago, IL, 1898/99-1983.

In the 1920s Gloria Swanson was at the very top of the Hollywood pantheon. She began modestly enough as a Mack Sennett leading lady in 1915; it was her C.B. DeMille films (Male and Female, Why Change Your Wife?, etc.) which made her a star. Paramount superstardom came in the 1920s where she was equally at home in comedy (*Manhandled, Wages of Virtue*) and melodrama (*Beyond the Rocks, Madame Sans Gene, Sadie Thompson*). Although she made a successful transition to talkies in *The Trespasser*, subsequent vehicles were weak and her career had faltered by 1934. She made a triumphant Academy Award–nominated return with *Sunset Boulevard* but appeared in only a few more films subsequently.

PUBLISHED SOURCES

• *Books*—**Bibliography:** *The Idols of Silence.* **General:** *Alice in Movieland; America; Blue Book of the Screen; Classics of the Silent Screen; Close Ups; Debrett Goes to Hollywood; Doug and Mary and Others; The Faces of Hollywood; Famous Film Folk; Famous Stars of Filmdom (Women); Fifty Super Stars; Folks Ushud Know; The Great Movie Stars; History of the American Cinema* (v. 3); *Hollywood Greats of the Golden Years; Hollywood Hall of Fame; The Hollywood Reporter Star Profiles; How I Broke Into the Movies; Intimate Talks with Movie Stars; Ladies in Distress; Love Goddesses of the Movies; Love, Laughter and Tears; Mack Sennett's Keystone; Mike Wallace Asks; Movie Star; The Movie Stars; The Movie Stars Story; The National Society of Film Critics on the Movie Star; The Parade's Gone By; The Paramount Pretties; People Will Talk; Return Engagement; The Saturday Evening Post Movie Book; Screen Album; Screen Personalities; Spellbound in Darkness; Stardom; The Stars* (Schickel); *Stars!; The Stars Appear; The Truth About the Movies; What the Stars Told Me; Who's Who on the Screen.* **Credits:** *Filmarama* (v. I and II); *Forty Years of Screen Credits; Twenty Years of Silents.* **Encyclopedic Works:** *A Biographical Dictionary of Film; The Biographical Encyclopaedia and Who's Who of the American Theatre; Current Biography* (1950, 1984); *A Dictionary of the Cinema; Film Encyclopedia; Filmlexicon degli Autori e delle Opere; Halli-*

well's Filmgoer's Companion; The Illustrated Encyclopedia of the World's Great Movie Stars and Their Films; The Illustrated Who's Who of the Cinema; International Dictionary of Films and Filmmakers (v. 3); *The International Encyclopedia of Film; International Motion Picture Almanac* (1975-80); *The Movie Makers; The Oxford Companion to Film; The Picturegoer's Who's Who and Encyclopedia of the Screen To-day; Quinlan's Illustrated Registry of Film Stars; Variety Who's Who in Show Business; Who Was Who in the Theatre; Who's Who in Hollywood; The World Almanac Who's Who of Film; The World Encyclopedia of the Film; The World Film Encyclopedia.* **Biography/Autobiography:** *Autobiography of Cecil B. DeMille; Gloria and Joe; Swanson on Swanson.* **Pictorial:** *Four Fabulous Faces; Gloria Swanson; The Image Makers; Leading Ladies; The Revealing Eye; Silent Portraits; They Had Faces Then.* **Films:** *The Films of Gloria Swanson.* **Thesis:** *Gloria Swanson at United Artists, 1925-1933.* **Recordings:** *Hollywood on Record.* **Catalog:** *Property from the Estate of Gloria Swanson.* **Factoids:** *Star Stats.*

• *Periodicals*—The following periodical articles are in addition to those included in the library listings below: *Photoplay* (Aug. 1918, Aug. 1919, July 1920, Sept. 1920, June 1921, Nov. 1921, Feb. 1922, Sept. 1922, Nov. 1922, Mar. 1923, Sept. 1923, June 1924, Oct.-Nov. 1924, Feb. 1925, Apr. 1925, June-July 1925, Oct.-Dec. 1925, Apr.-May 1926, Aug. 1926, Nov. 1926, May 1927, Nov. 1928, July 1929, Aug.-Sept. 1930, Jan. 1931, June-July 1931, Jan.-Feb. 1932, Mar. 1933, June 1933, Oct. 1933, Feb. 1935, May 1937, Feb. 1951, Jan. 1961, Mar. 1975, June 1983); *Motion Picture Magazine* (Dec. 1918, Aug. 1919, Dec. 1919, Apr. 1921, Dec. 1921, June 1922, Oct. 1923, June 1925, Sept. 1925, Dec. 1925, Oct. 1926, Apr. 1927, July 1928, Nov. 1928, Mar. 1930, Nov. 1930, Feb. 1931, June 1933, Oct. 1937); *Motion Picture Classic* (July 1919, Feb. 1920, June 1921, Oct. 1921, Aug. 1922, Oct. 1922, June 1923, Dec. 1924, May 1925, Nov.

1925, Feb. 1926, July 1926, Jan. 1927, May 1931); *Red Book* (June 1920); *Picture Play Magazine* (July 1920); *Woman Citizen* (Mar. 22, 1924); *Bookman* (July 1925); *Vanity Fair* (May 1926, Dec. 1926, Mar. 1930, Apr. 1934); *Theatre* (Nov. 1926); *Collier's* (June 8, 1929); *New Yorker* (Jan. 18, 1930, Mar. 30, 1940); *Movie Classic* (Nov. 1931, Jan.–Feb. 1932, June 1932, Nov. 1932, May 1934); *Movie Mirror* (Dec. 1931); *Pictures and Picturegoer* (Mar. 26–Apr. 16, 1932); *Cinema Digest* (Oct. 3, 1932, Apr. 3, 1933); *Silver Screen* (Sept. 1934, Aug. 1941, Nov. 1949); *Time* (Dec. 10, 1934, Sept. 29, 1941, Aug. 14, 1950, Aug. 5, 1974, Feb. 16, 1976, Apr. 18, 1983, Dec. 26, 1983); *International Photographer* (July 1941); *Vogue* (Aug. 15, 1941); *Ladies' Home Journal* (Nov. 1941); *Cue* (Oct. 22, 1949); *Liberty* (Dec. 1949); *Life* (June 5, 1950, Feb. 19, 1951, Jan. 23, 1956, Sept. 17, 1971); *Newsweek* (Oct. 30, 1950, Feb. 16, 1976); *Reader's Digest* (Jan. 1951, Jan. 1955); *Harper's Weekly* (Feb. 1951); *Saturday Review* (Mar. 24, 1951); *Theatre Arts* (July 1951); *TV Guide* (May 22, 1953); *Theatre* (June 1961); *8mm Collector* (Sept. 1964, Spring 1966); *Film* (Autumn 1964, Summer 1966, Nov. 1979); *Films in Review* (Apr. 1965 (filmography), Aug.–Oct. 1965, Dec. 1967, Mar. 1988); *Classic Film Collector* (Fall/Winter 1967); *Sight and Sound* (Autumn 1968, Spring 1969); *New Woman* (Feb. 1972); *Inter/View* (Sept. 1972); *Cinéma* (France) (May 1974, Sept. 1983); *Films Illustrated* (Dec. 1974); *Films and Filming* (Mar. 1975); *Cine Revue* (Aug. 31, 1978, Sept. 21, 1978, Apr. 7–14, 1983); *Interview* (Feb. 1981); *Films* (June 1981); *Celuloide* (June 1983); *Film & Kino* (no. 3, 1983); *Filmrutan* (no. 2, 1983); *Macleans* (Apr. 18, 1983, Jan. 2, 1984); *National Review* (Apr. 29, 1983); *Cinématographique* (May 1983); *Revue du Cinéma* (May–June 1983); *Film a Doba* (Sept. 1983); *Hollywood Studio Magazine* (Oct. 1983, June 1984); *Film en Televisie* (Feb. 1984); *American Film* (Mar. 1985); *Filmvilag* (no. 10, 1985); *Cinema Nuovo* (Jan.–Feb. 1987); *Grand Angle* (Feb. 1988); *Classic Images* (Mar. 1989).

MEDIA

Gloria Swanson/Laurel and Hardy (video); *Swanson & Valentino* (video); *Why Ever Did They?* (CD recording).

ARCHIVAL MATERIALS

• *Caricature* – NYMN, NYPL. • *Clipping File* – CAA: Article (1941, 1946, 1949, 1950–51, 1953, 1958, 1961–62, 1966–67, 1971–74, 1976, 1980–81, 1983); marriage/divorce/children (1920, 1934, 1945–46, 1948, 1976); comeback (1947); film appearance (1949, 1975); nutrition (1950, 1971); TV appearance (1950, 1952, 1962–63, 1965–66, 1973–74); award (1951); legal problem (1951–53, 1974, 1976); stage appearance (1951, 1955, 1959); age (1960); honor (1966, 1973, 1978); interview (1972, 1980–81); review of *Swanson on Swanson* (1980); papers to University of Texas (1983); film festival (1984); romance with Joe Kennedy (1987); reviews of *Gloria and Joe* (1988); obituary (1983). Periodical articles: *Photoplay* (July 1934); *Rob Wagner's Script* (May 24, 1941); *Cue* (July 10 or 20, 1948, Aug. 5, 1950); *Pageant* (Nov. 1949); *Flair* (Mar. 1950); *Newsweek* (June 26, 1950); *People Today* (July 4, 1950); *Saturday Evening Post* (July 22–29, 1950); *Vogue* (July 1950, Dec. 1980); *Quick* (Nov. 6, 1950); *Look* (Jan. 30, 1951, Mar. 27, 1951); *MD* (1960s); *Esquire* (Aug. 1966); *Screen Greats* (Summer 1971); *TV Guide* (Feb. 23, 1974); *Hollywood Studio Magazine* (July 1974, Mar. 1975); *Film Fan Monthly* (Feb. 1975); *Reader's Digest* (July 1975); *People* (Feb. 16, 1976); *Films and Filming* (Feb. 1979); *Liberty* (Mar. 20, 1979); *Ladies' Home Journal* (Nov. 1980); *Architectural Digest* (Apr. 1990). CAFI: Article (1950, 1971–72, 1974, 1980, undated); newsphotos (numerous); film appearance (1974, 1981); review of *Swanson on Swanson* (1980); birthday (1979); nostalgia (1970); romance (1981); marriage (1976); film festival (1985); University of Texas documentary (1983). Periodical articles: *Newsweek* (June 26, 1950); *MD* (Dec. 1965); *Girl Talk* (Nov. 1971); *Film Fan Monthly* (Feb. 1975); *People* (Feb. 1976). CAPS: Article (1974); marriage (1976). CASF: Marriage (1931); obituary (1983).

CAUT: Article (undated, 1971, 1974, 1976, 1980-81, 1983); Joe Kennedy (1983); marriage/children (1976, 1983); papers to University of Texas (1982); review of *Swanson on Swanson* (1980); newsphotos; 80th birthday (1979); legal problem (1976); interview (1984); obituary (1983). Periodical article: *TV Guide* (Feb. 23, 1974). CAUU (Also in McCormick Collection): Film appearance (1950); article (1949, 1951, 1964-65, 1967, 1971, 1974, 1980); interview (undated); film festival (1985); review of *Swanson on Swanson* (1981); 80th birthday (1979); marriage (1976); obituary (1983). Periodical articles: *Esquire* (Aug. 1966); *TV Guide* (Feb. 23, 1974); *Show* (Nov. 1971). NYMN: Papers to University of Texas (1982); newsphotos; *Sunset Boulevard* (1949?); article (1937, 1950, 1965, 1981, undated); play review (1951); film review (1952); marriage (1945); stage appearance (1971). Periodical article: *Photoplay* (Apr. 1937). NYPL (also in C. & L. Brown Collection): PARTIAL CONTENTS: Archive at University of Texas (1987); article (1982-83, undated); newsphotos; program for film festival; illness (1983); obituary (1983). • *Other Clipping File* — AZSU (Jimmy Starr Collection), CAUB, CNDA, GBBF, MAH, MIDL, NYMA, OHCL, OHSU, PAPL, TXU (see Collection), WICF. • *Collection* — TXU: Over 100,000 items, covering the years 1913-83, including photographs, notes for her autobiography, videotapes and audiotapes, scrapbooks, diaries, financial records, clippings. (Correspondence with Joe Kennedy closed until 2000.) • *Correspondence* — CAA: Few notes, telegram (Hedda Hopper Collection) (1941, 1950); 8 letters (Adolph Zukor Collection) (1922-25, 1967). CAUS (Rob Wagner Collection) (Preston Sturges Collection) (Hugo Ballin Collection), DCG (Terry Ramsaye Papers). NYCU: Letter (R. Flaherty Collection); 6 letters (Curtis Brown Collection) (1963-64). NYMN: 1951. OHCL. NYPL: Letters (C. & L. Brown Collection) (1930s-1950s); 3 letters (Herman Weinberg Collection) (1950-66); others (1943, 1951, undated). TXU (see Collection). • *Interview* —

GBBF (Hollywood Collection): Transcript of interview for *Hollywood* (TV series). • *Legal File* — CAUT (Twentieth Century-Fox Collection): Letter, memo (1934); loanout (1934). CAUW: Letter (1925-50); document (1936); telegram (1936); option (1936); rights (1925-50); agreement (1925). NYPL: Contract (C. & L. Brown Collection) (1942, 1947); contract (1943). • *Manuscript* — CAFI, NYMN, TXU: *A Visit from Gloria Swanson* by Raymond Daum (1984). The shooting script of the film documentary. • *Oral History* — NYCO: Interviewed in 1958. Mentioned in the following interviews: G.M. Anderson, Melvyn Douglas, Lila Lee, Roddy McDowall, Joel McCrea, Douglass Montgomery, Louella Parsons, Frederick Sommer, Carey Wilson. • *Photograph/Still* — CAA (also in Hollywood Studio Museum Collection) (also in MGM Collection), CAHL, CALM, CAPH, CASU, CAUB, CAUT (Jessen Collection), CAUU, CNDA, DCG (Quigley Photographic Archives), NJFL, NYAM, NYB (Bettmann/UPI Collection) (Penguin Collection) (Springer Collection) (Underwood Collection), NYCU (Dramatic Museum Portraits), NYEH, NYMN, NYPL, NYSU, OHCL, TXSM, TXU (see also Collection), WICF. • *Press Kit* — AZSU, NYMA, OHCL. • *Publicity Release* — CAA: Paramount (1949). CAFI: Universal (1975?). CAUU: Universal (1974). • *Reminiscence* — MISU: GS talks about her various careers and her interest in world hunger (recording), GS talks about health foods and theatrical erotica (recording). • *Scrapbook* — CASU (Stark Collection), NYMA, NYPL (also in Locke Collection), TXU (see Collection), UTBY (DeMille Archives). • *Studio Biography* — CAA: Fox (1934); RKO (1941); Paramount (1949). CAUU: Paramount (1949).

SWEET, Blanche (Sarah B. Sweet), Chicago, IL, 1895/96–1986.

One of D.W. Griffith's talented stars was Blanche Sweet ("The Biograph Blonde"). She was in many of his early films, from 1908, such as *A Corner in Wheat*, *The Goddess of Sagebrush Gulch*, *The Lonedale Operator* and, notably, *Judith of Bethulia*. During the 1920s, her career faltered a bit although there were noteworthy roles in the first version of *Anna Christie* (1923) and *Tess of the D'Urbervilles*. She had substantial roles in three 1930 sound films and possibly made a last, brief appearance in 1959. She was married to Raymond Hackett (q.v.).

PUBLISHED SOURCES

• *Books*—**Bibliography:** *The Idols of Silence*. **General:** *Blue Book of the Screen*; *Classics of the Silent Screen*; *Famous Film Folk*; *First One Hundred Noted Men and Women of the Screen*; *The Griffith Actresses*; *"Image" on the Art and Evolution of the Film*; *Ladies in Distress*; *More from Hollywood*; *The Movie Stars Story*; *The Real Tinsel*; *Return Engagement*; *Speaking of Silents*; *Sweethearts of the Sage*; *Tribute to Mary Pickford*; *The Truth About the Movies*; *Who's Who in the Film World*. **Credits:** *Filmarama* (v. I and II); *Forty Years of Screen Credits*; *Twenty Years of Silents*. **Encyclopedic Works:** *The Biographical Encyclopaedia and Who's Who of the American Theatre*; *Film Encyclopedia*; *Filmlexicon degli Autori e delle Opere*; *Halliwell's Filmgoer's Companion*; *The Illustrated Who's Who of the Cinema*; *International Dictionary of Films and Filmmakers* (v. 3); *The Movie Makers*; *The Oxford Companion to Film*; *The Picturegoer's Who's Who and Encyclopedia of the Screen To-day*; *Variety Who's Who in Show Business*; *Who's Who in Hollywood*; *The World Almanac Who's Who of Film*; *The World Film Encyclopedia*. **Nostalgia:** *Whatever Became of...* (1st). **Pictorial:** *Silent Portraits*.

• *Periodicals*—The following periodical articles are in addition to those included in the library listings below: *Motion Picture Story Magazine* (Jan. 1914); *Cosmpolitan* (Feb. 1915); *Photoplay* (Apr. 1915, May 1918, Aug. 1922, June 1924, Sept. 1924); *Filmplay Journal* (May 17, 1915); *Motion Picture Magazine* (Aug. 1915, Apr. 1916, Nov. 1916, Aug.

1923, Jan. 1925, Feb. 1930); *Movie Pictorial* (Aug. 1915); *Feature Movie* (Aug. 25, 1915); *Picture Play* (Aug. 1916, Sept. 1918); *Motion Picture Classic* (Nov. 1918, Feb. 1924, Oct. 1928); *Picture Show* (Nov. 1, 1919); *Motion Picture Director* (Aug. 1926); *Cue* (July 10, 1943); *Films in Review* (Feb. 1966, June–July 1967, Oct.–Nov. 1967, Mar. 1986); *Silent Picture* (Spring 1972); *Griffithiana* (Mar.–July 1980, Jan. 1982); *Newsweek* (Sept. 22, 1986); *Cine Revue* (Oct. 2, 1986); *Cinématographique* (Oct. 1986); *Classic Images* (Oct.–Nov. 1986, May 1989); *Segnocinema* (Nov. 1986).

MEDIA

Portrait of Blanche Sweet (film).

ARCHIVAL MATERIALS

• *Clipping File*—CAA: Article (1983, 1986); tribute (1984, 1986); nostalgia (1968, 1972, 1979, 1981); TV appearance (1958); public appearance (1979); program of tribute to Mary Pickford. Periodical articles: *Filmplay Journal* (1920s); *Cinema* (no. 35, 1976). CAFI: Article (1967, 1975, 1980s, 1983); newsphotos (numerous); nostalgia; obituary (1988). Periodical article: *Films in Review* (June/July 1981). CAUT: Nostalgia (1975). CAUU: Film review (A. Slide Collection); obituary (1986). Periodical articles: *Motion Picture Magazine* (Dec. 1920, Nov. 1923, Nov.–Dec. 1925); *Films in Review* (Nov.–Dec. 1965 (filmography), June/July 1981); *Classic Film Collector* (Summer 1975). NYMA (also in Photoplay Collection): Article (1975, 1977, 1981, 1983); film review (1920s, 1930); biography; Vachel Lindsay poem dedicated to BS; homage to BS (1981); obituary (1986). Periodical articles: *Image* (Mar. 1975); *Classic Film Collector* (Summer 1975, Summer 1977); *Films in Review* (undated); *Classic Images* (Oct. 1984, June 1989). NYMN: Newsphotos; marriage (1935); TV appearance (1958); obituary (1986). • *Other Clipping File*—AZSU (Jimmy Starr Collection), CAUB, GBBF, MAH, MIDL, NYPL (also in Locke Collection), OHCL, PAPL, WICF. • *Correspondence*—CAHL: 1930. NJPT (S. Enright Papers): 1941–42, 1944, 1947 (some written with Raymond Hackett). NYPL (C. & L. Brown Collection): 1916, 1935, 1944. • *Filmography*—CAA (incomplete), NYMA. • *Interview*—CAUU (A. Slide Collection): 1970–71. GBBF (Hollywood Collection): Transcript of an interview for *Hollywood* (TV series). MISU: Recorded from a telephone interview. • *Legal File*—CAUW: Contract (1919, 1925, 1929); letter (1925); talent agreement (1925, 1929). • *Oral History*—NYCO: Interviewed in 1981. Also mentioned in the following interviews: Louella Parsons, Sidney Blackmer. • *Photograph/Still*—AZSU (Jimmy Starr Collection), CAA (also in Hollywood Studio Museum Collection) (also in MGM Collection), CALM, CAUT (Jessen Collection), CAUU (also in A. Slide Collection), DCG (Quigley Photographic Archives), GBBF, NJFL, NJPT, NYB (Bettmann/UPI Collection) (Springer Collection) (Underwood Collection), NYCU (Bulliet Collection) (Palmer Collection), NYEH, NYMN, NYPL, NYSU, OHCL, TXU, WICF. • *Program*—CAFI: Film (1983). NYMA: Toronto Film Society festival (1983); an evening with BS. • *Scrapbook*—NYPL (also in R. Locke Collection). • *Studio Biography*—NYMA: Photoplay.

TALIAFERRO, Mabel, New York, NY, 1887/89–1979.

A well-known stage actress, Mabel Taliaferro did not appear in many films but was a popular performer. Known as "The Sweetheart of American Movies," her first role was in *Cinderella* (1911). Among her other films for Selig and Metro were *Snowbird*, *Sunbeam*, *Sentimental Tommy* and *A Magdelene of the Hills*. She returned to the stage in 1921 and appeared in only one further film, *My Love Came Back*, in 1940. Her sister Edith Taliaferro was also a screen actress.

PUBLISHED SOURCES
• *Books*—Credits: *Filmarama* (v. I and II); *Twenty Years of Silents*. Encyclopedic Works: *The Biographical Encyclopaedia and Who's Who of the American Theatre*; *Film Encyclopedia*; *Who Was Who in the Theatre*; *Who's Who in Hollywood*; *Who's Who on the Stage* (1908). Pictorial: *Silent Portraits*.
• *Periodicals*—The following periodical articles are in addition to those included in the library listings below: *Theatre* (June 1908, Feb. 1914); *Green Book Album* (Aug. 1909); *Harper's Weekly* (Oct. 9, 1909); *Bookman* (Dec. 1909); *Moving Picture World* (Dec. 23, 1911); *Munsey's Magazine* (Dec. 1913); *Green Book Magazine* (June 1914).

ARCHIVAL MATERIALS
• *Clipping File*—CAA: Obituary (1979). NYMA (also in Photoplay collection): Obituary (1979). Periodical article: *Classic Images* (Nov. 1988). NYMN: Newsphotos; stage appearance. NYPL (also in Locke Collection): Newsphotos (numerous); career (1930s?, 1949); article (1908, 1944, 1948); play review (1900s, 1920s, 1930s); divorce (1929); obituary (1979). Periodical article: *Success Magazine* (April(?) 1908). • *Other Clipping File*—GBBF, MAH, MIDL, OHCL, OHSU, PAPL, WICF. • *Correspondence*—NYMA (Photoplay Collection). NYPL: Note (C. & L. Brown Collection) (1934); other (1944). • *Photograph/Still*—CAA (also in Hollywood Studio Museum Collection), CAUS, DCG (Quigley Photographic Archives), NYCU (Bulliet Collection), NYMN, NYPL, NYSU, OHCL, TXU, WICF. • *Play Program*—NYPL, OHSU. • *Print*—CAHL. • *Scrapbook*—NYPL (also in C. & L. Brown Collection) (also in Locke Collection).

TALMADGE, Constance, Brooklyn, NY, 1898/1900–1973.

Pretty blonde Constance Talmadge appeared in numerous two-reelers from 1914 but her role as the Mountain Girl in *Intolerance* was a career-maker. She eventually had her own production company and was a premier comic actress of the 1920s in films like *Dulcy* (her biggest hit), *Her Sister from Paris*, *Polly of the Follies*, *The Duchess of*

Buffalo and *Venus of Venice*. After a 1929 silent made in France, she retired without appearing in a sound film. She was the sister of Norma Talmadge (q.v.).

PUBLISHED SOURCES

• *Books* – **Bibliography:** *The Idols of Silence*. **General:** *Alice in Movieland; Behind the Screen; Blue Book of the Screen; Classics of the Silent Screen; Co-Starring Famous Women and Alcohol; Doug and Mary and Others; Famous Film Folk; From Hollywood; The Funsters; Hollywood Album; Intimate Talks with Movie Stars; The Kindergarten of the Movies; Lillian Gish: The Movies, Mr. Griffith and Me; The Truth About the Movies*. **Credits:** *Filmarama* (v. I and II); *Twenty Years of Silents; Who Was Who on Screen*. **Encyclopedic Works:** *Film Encyclopedia; Filmlexicon degli Autori e delle Opere; Halliwell's Filmgoer's Companion; The Illustrated Who's Who of the Cinema; The Movie Makers; The Oxford Companion to Film; Quinlan's Illustrated Directory of Film Comedy Actors; Who's Who in Hollywood; The World Almanac Who's Who of Film; The World Encyclopedia of the Film; The World Film Encyclopedia*. **Nostalgia:** *Whatever Became of...* (1st). **Biography/Autobiography:** *The Talmadge Girls; The Talmadge Sisters*. **Pictorial:** *The Image Makers; The Revealing Eye; Silent Portraits*. **Factoids:** *Star Stats*.

• *Periodicals* – The following periodical articles are in addition to that included in the library listings below: *Motion Picture Magazine* (May 1915, Jan. 1917, Aug. 1918, Oct. 1918, Apr. 1919, Sept. 1920, May 1922, Sept. 1924, Nov. 1925, Dec. 1926, Apr. 1928); *Photoplay* (May 1917, Apr. 1918, July 1919, Sept. 1920, Oct. 1923, Oct.-Nov. 1924, Feb. 1925, Aug. 1927); *Motion Picture Classic* (July 1918, July 1919, Feb. 1922, Sept 1922, Dec. 1922, Apr. 1925, July 1925, Nov.-Dec. 1928); *Picture Show* (Mar. 6, 1920); *National Magazine* (July 1920); *Pantomime* (Oct. 5, 1921); *Cinema Art* (Nov. 1926); *Theatre* (Dec. 1926); *Movie Classic* (Dec. 1932); *Films in Review* (Apr. 1967, Dec. 1967 (filmography), Jan. 1968, Dec. 1968, Aug.-Sept. 1972); *Time* (Dec. 10, 1973); *Classic Film Collector* (Spring 1974); *Classic Images* (Nov. 1989).

ARCHIVAL MATERIALS

• *Clipping File* – CAA: Newsphotos; writes song (1922); United Artists contract (1926); marriage/divorce (1926-29, 1938-39); article (1920s, 1950); robbery (1932); review of *The Talmadge Girls* (1978); obituary (1973). Periodical article: *Select Pictures Magazine* (1918). CAUT: Review of *The Talmadge Girls* (1978); obituary (1973). CAUU: Obituary (1973). NYMA: Newsphotos; will (1973); obituary (1973). NYPL (also in Locke Collection): Will (1973); signs with Schenck (1919); newsphotos (numerous); death of mother (1933); review of *The Talmadge Girls* (1978); marriage/divorce (1921-22, 1927, 1932, 1939); stock swindle (1934); kidnapping (1936); film appearance (1910s); film review (1920s); article (1923, undated); obituary (1923). • *Other Clipping File* – AZSU (Jimmy Starr Collection), CAUB, GBBF, MAH, MIDL, OHCL, PAPL, WICF. • *Correspondence* – CAA (Adolph Zukor Collection): 1919. DCG (Terry Ramsaye Papers). • *Filmography* – NYMA, NYPL (incomplete). • *Legal File* – CAUW: Letter, memo (1926-29); agreement (1919-20, 1922-25, 1929); document (1919-21, 1927-28); rights (1926-29); talent agreement (1922, 1926-27, undated). • *Oral History* – NYCO: Mentioned in the following interviews: Reginald Denny, Arthur Hornblow, Jr., Anita Loos, Albert (Eddie) Sutherland, Gloria Swanson. • *Photograph/Still* – CAA (also in Hollywood Studio Museum Collection), CAH, CALM, CAPH, CASF, CAUB, CAUT (Jessen Collection), CNDA, DCG (Quigley Photographic Archives), NYAM, NYB (Bettmann/UPI Collection) (Springer Collection) (Underwood Collection), NYCU (Dramatic Museum Portraits), NYEH, NYMN, NYPL, NYSU, OHCL, TXU, WICF. • *Scrapbook* – CASU (Stark Collection), NYPL (also in R. Locke Collection).

TALMADGE, Norma, Jersey City, NJ (older sources say Niagara Falls, NY), 1893/97–1957.

Norma Talmadge, the queen of the "weepies," began her career with Vitagraph in 1910. Early successes included *A Tale of Two Cities* (1911 version) and *The Battle Cry of Peace*. After she had appeared in more than 200 short films, her persona as the long-suffering heroine was established and it made her a greatly popular feature star. In the 1920s her films included *The Voice from the Minaret*, *Smilin' Through*, *Kiki* (1926 version), *Ashes of Vengeance* and *Camille*. She was a casualty of the talkies, making only two, both of which were poorly received. Her sister was Constance Talmadge (q.v.).

PUBLISHED SOURCES

• **Books—Bibliography:** *The Idols of Silence*. **General:** *Alice in Movieland*; *Behind the Screen*; *The Big V*; *Blue Book of the Screen*; *Classics of the Silent Screen*; *Doug and Mary and Others*; *Early American Cinema*; *Famous Film Folk*; *First One Hundred Noted Men and Women of the Screen*; *History of the American Cinema* (v. 3); *Hollywood: The Golden Era*; *Hollywood Album*; *Hollywood Hall of Fame*; *How I Broke Into the Movies*; *Immortals of the Screen*; *Intimate Talks with Movie Stars*; *The Kindergarten of the Movies*; *Ladies in Distress*; *The Movie Stars*; *The Movie Stars Story*; *Norma Talmadge*; *The Stars* (Schickel); *The Stars Appear*; *The Truth About the Movies*. **Credits:** *Filmarama* (v. I and II); *Forty Years of Screen Credits*; *Twenty Years of Silents*; *Who Was Who on Screen*. **Encyclopedic Works:** *A Biographical Dictionary of Film*; *Film Encyclopedia*; *Filmlexicon degli Autori e delle Opere*; *Halliwell's Filmgoer's Companion*; *The Illustrated Encyclopedia of the World's Great Movie Stars and Their Films*; *The Illustrated Who's Who of the Cinema*; *International Dictionary of Films and Filmmakers* (v. 3); *The Movie Makers*;

National Cyclopedia of American Biography (1965); *The Oxford Companion to Film*; *Quinlan's Illustrated Registry of Film Stars*; *Who's Who in Hollywood*; *The World Almanac Who's Who of Film*; *The World Encyclopedia of the Film*; *The World Film Encyclopedia*. **Biography/Autobiography:** *The Talmadge Girls*; *The Talmadge Sisters*. **Pictorial:** *The Image Makers*; *The Revealing Eye*; *Silent Portraits*; *They Had Faces Then*. **Films:** *Norma Talmadge in Her Most Successful.* . . . **Factoids:** *Star Stats*.

• *Periodicals*—The following periodical articles are in addition to those included in the library listings below: *Photoplay* (Feb. 1915, Aug. 1915, Feb. 1917, Oct. 1917, Jan. 1920, June 1920, Feb. 1921, May 1923, Aug.–Sept. 1923, June–July 1924, Feb. 1926); *Motion Picture Magazine* (May 1915, Jan. 1917, Oct. 1917, Apr. 1918, Oct. 1918, Mar. 1921, Aug. 1923, Nov. 1923, Sept. 1924, Mar. 1925, July 1926, Nov. 1926, Jan. 1928, May 1928, May 1932, Dec. 1932); *Motion Picture Classic* (Sept. 1916, Jan.–Feb. 1920, Dec. 1920, Dec. 1921, July 1923, Oct. 1926, Dec. 1928, Feb. 1931); *Moving Picture World* (July 21, 1917); *Photoplay Journal* (Mar. 1919); *Everybody's Magazine* (May 1919); *Picture Show* (Mar. 20, 1920); *New York Dramatic Mirror* (Apr. 17, 1920); *National Magazine* (Sept. 1920); *American Magazine* (June 1922); *Shadowland* (Sept. 1922); *Ladies' Home Journal* (Mar. 1925); *Theatre* (Nov. 1926); *Saturday Evening Post* (Mar. 26, 1927, Apr. 9, 1927, May 7, 1927, May 21, 1927, June 25, 1927); *Pictures and Picturegoer* (July 1928); *Movie Classic* (Dec. 1932); *Cinema Digest* (May 29, 1933); *Life* (Jan. 23, 1956); *Time* (Jan. 6, 1958); *Newsweek* (Jan. 6, 1958); *Films in Review* (Jan.–Mar. 1967 (filmography), Feb. 1972, Dec. 1987).

ARCHIVAL MATERIALS

• *Clipping File*—CAA: Film appearance (1922–23); newsphotos; article (1927–28, 1947); stage appearance (1930); marriage/divorce (1930, 1932, 1934, 1939, 1946); legal problem (1928, 1931);

romance with George Jessel (1932); estate (1958); home (1971, 1974); obituary (1957). Periodical articles: *Motion Picture Classic* (Dec. 1922); *Cine Revue* (May 1979). CAUU: Obituary (1957). NYMA: Newsphotos; divorce (1934). Periodical articles: *Photo-play World* (Apr. 1918); *Saturday Evening Post* (Mar. 12, 1927). NYMN: Newsphotos; estate (1958); marriage/divorce (1934); obituary (1957). NYPL (also in Locke Collection): PARTIAL CONTENTS: Will (1958); film appearance (1922, 1920s); article (1918, undated); newsphotos (numerous); funeral (1957); story editor (1937); leading men (1924); review of *The Talmadge Girls* (1978); romance with George Jessel (1934); biography; sale of effects; robbery (1935); marriage/divorce (1939, 1947); radio appearance (1936); obituary (1957). Periodical articles: *American Magazine* (undated); *Films and Filming* (May 1973). • *Other Clipping File*—AZSU (Jimmy Starr Collection), CAUB, GBBF, MAH, MIDL, OHCL, PAPL, WICF. • *Filmography*—NYMA. • *Legal File*—CAUW: Talent agreement (various dates); agreement (1919-20, 1925); contract (1919-25). • *Oral History*—NYCO: Mentioned in the following interviews: Bennett Cerf, Ben Hecht, Arthur Hornblow Jr., Lila Lee, Anita Loos, Geraldine Page, Blanche Sweet. • *Photograph/Still*—CAA (also in Hollywood Studio Museum Collection) (also in MGM Collection), CALM, CAUS, CAUT (Jessen Collection), CAUU, DCG (Quigley Photographic Archives), NJFL, NYAM, NYB (Bettmann/UPI Collection) (Penguin Collection) (Springer Collection) (Underwood Collection), NYCU (Dramatic Museum Portraits), NYEH, NYMN, NYPL, NYSU, OHCL, TNUT (Clarence Brown Collection), TXSM, TXU, WICF. • *Press Kit*—OHCL. • *Scrapbook*—CASU (Stark Collection), NYPL (also in R. Locke Collection), TNUT (Clarence Brown Collection).

TALMADGE, Richard (Ricardo Metezzeti or Sylvester Metzetti), Munich, Germany or Switzerland, 1892/96-1981.

After a career as a stuntman for Douglas Fairbanks and other stars, Richard Talmadge migrated to acting himself in 1922. He was a modestly popular action star in adventure stories whose titles told it all: *Danger Ahead, Tearing Through, Laughing at Danger, The Prince of Pep, Doubling with Danger*. His accent curtailed his career in talkies but he continued onscreen until 1936 and also became a second unit director. A final role came in 1948 with some unbilled bits in the 1960s.

PUBLISHED SOURCES
• *Books*—**General:** *Eighty Silent Film Stars*; *Stunt*. **Credits:** *Filmarama* (v. I and II); *Forty Years of Screen Credits*; *Twenty Years of Silents*. **Encyclopedic Works:** *Film Encyclopedia*; *Filmlexicon degli Autori e delle Opere*; *Halliwell's Filmgoer's Companion*; *The Illustrated Who's Who of the Cinema*; *Who's Who in Hollywood*; *The World Film Encyclopedia*. **Pictorial:** *Silent Portraits*.
• *Periodicals*—*Cine Revue* (Apr. 16, 1981); *Cinématographique* (May 1981); *Classic Film/Video Images* (May 1981); *Classic Images* (Dec. 1982, Nov. 1983).

ARCHIVAL MATERIALS
• *Clipping File*—CAA: Stunt man (1969); obituary (1981). CAFI: Obituary (1981). CAUT: Obituary (1981). CAUU: Obituary (1981). NYPL: Stunt man (1939); biography (1941, 1944); honor (1974); obituary (1981). • *Other Clipping File*—GBBF, MAH, MIDL, NYMA (Photoplay Collection), WICF. • *Correspondence*—NYMA (Photoplay Collection). • *Filmography*—CAA. • *Legal File*—CAUT (Twentieth Century-Fox Collection): Letter, memo (1953, 1964); payroll record (1950, 1953-55, 1957, 1959-60, 1963-64); agreement (1953, 1964). • *Photograph/Still*—CAA (also in Hollywood Studio Museum Collection), CNDA, DCG (Quigley Photographic Archives), NYPL, NYSU, OHCL, TXU, WICF.

TASHMAN, Lilyan (Lillian Tashman), Brooklyn, NY, 1899-1934.

Follies girl Lilyan Tashman made her first film in 1921 but it was with *Garden of Weeds* (1924) that her career began in earnest. Her usual persona was the woman who had seen it all: the best friend of the heroine or the "other woman." Known for her stylish clothes, she appeared in numerous films throughout the 1920s and proceeded on in supporting roles until her death. She was married to Edmund Lowe (q.v.).

PUBLISHED SOURCES

• *Books — General:* *Screen Personalities*; *Some Are Born Great.* **Credits:** *Filmarama* (v. II); *Forty Years of Screen Credits*; *Twenty Years of Silents*; *Who Was Who on Screen.* **Encyclopedic Works:** *Film Encyclopedia*; *Filmlexicon degli Autori e delle Opere*; *Halliwell's Filmgoer's Companion*; *The Movie Makers*; *The Picturegoer's Who's Who and Encyclopedia of the Screen To-day*; *Who Was Who in the Theatre*; *Who's Who in Hollywood*; *World Almanac Who's Who of Film*; *The World Film Encyclopedia.* **Pictorial:** *They Had Faces Then.*

• *Periodicals* — The following periodical articles are in addition to those included in the library listings below: *Photoplay* (Aug. 1925, Mar. 1926, June 1929, May 1931, Mar. 1933, June 1934); *Motion Picture Magazine* (Feb. 1928, Mar. 1930, Nov. 1930, Mar. 1931, July 1933, June 1934); *Motion Picture Classic* (Dec. 1929); *Silver Screen* (Jan. 1931, Dec. 1931, Sept. 1932); *Movie Classic* (Nov. 1931, July 1934); *Fashion & Society* (Jan. 1932); *Collier's* (Nov. 19, 1932); *Shadowland* (Mar. 1934).

ARCHIVAL MATERIALS

• *Clipping File* — CAA: Newsphotos; obituary (1934). Periodical article: *Films and Filming* (Nov. 1970). NYMA (also in Photoplay Collection): Personal data summary. Periodical article: *Screen Book Magazine* (undated). NYMN: Career (1934); newsphotos (numerous); estate (1934); funeral (1934); obituary (1934). Periodical articles: *Vanity Fair* (Oct. 1930); *New Movie Magazine* (1932). NYPL: Film appearance (1930s); estate (1934); funeral (1934); newsphotos; surgery (1932); obituary (1934). Periodical articles: *Pictorial Review* (Dec. 1931); *Vogue* (Jan. 1, 1933). • *Other Clipping File* — GBBF, MAH, MIDL, NYMN, OHCL, PAPL, WICF. • *Correspondence* — NYPL (C. & L. Brown): 1933. • *Filmography* — NYMA, NYPL. • *Legal File* — CAUW: Talent agreement (1924, 1926, 1928-30); contract (1927, 1932); agreement (1926); personnel record (1932); loanout (1926). • *Oral History* — NYCO: Mentioned in the following interviews: Joel McCrea, Nita Naldi. • *Photograph/Still* — CAA (also in Hollywood Studio Museum Collection) (also in MGM Collection), CAPH, DCG (Quigley Photographic Archives), NJPT, NYAM, NYB (Bettmann/UPI Collection) (Underwood Collection), NYCU (Dramatic Museum Portraits), NYEH, NYMN, NYPL, NYSU, OHCL, PAPL, TXU (A. Davis Collection), WICF. • *Publicity Release* — CAA: Paramount (several). • *Scrapbook* — NYPL (also in C. & L. Brown Collection). • *Studio Biography* — NYMA: Photoplay.

TAYLOR, Estelle (Ida Estelle or Estella Boylan), Wilmington, DE, 1899/1903-1958.

Sultry Estelle Taylor made her first film in 1920 but the role that first caught the public's eye was her remake of *A Fool There Was* (1922). Some of her better-known silents were *Dorothy Vernon of Haddon Hall*, *The Ten Commandments* and *Don Juan*. Her talkie career did not endure but she did have some good moments in two 1931 films, *Street Scene* and *Cimarron*, and she made a respectable departure in her only 1940s — and last — film, *The Southerner*.

PUBLISHED SOURCES

• *Books — General:* *Doug and Mary and Others*; *Famous Film Folk*; *The*

Truth About the Movies. **Credits:** *Filmarama* (v. II); *Forty Years of Screen Credits*; *Twenty Years of Silents*; *Who Was Who on Screen.* **Encyclopedic Works:** *Film Encyclopedia*; *Filmlexicon degli Autori e delle Opere*; *Halliwell's Filmgoer's Companion*; *The Picturegoer's Who's Who and Encyclopedia of the Screen To-day*; *Who's Who in Hollywood*; *The World Film Encyclopedia.* **Pictorial:** *Silent Portraits*; *They Had Faces Then.*

• *Periodicals* — The following periodical articles are in addition to those included in the library listings below: *Motion Picture Classic* (Aug. 1920, June 1922, Oct. 1927, Feb. 1928, Sept. 1928, June 1931); *Photoplay* (Jan. 1921, July 1924, Apr. 1925, Mar. 1927, Sept.–Oct. 1930); *Photo Drama* (Sept. 1921); *Motion Picture Magazine* (Mar. 1923, Jan. 1927, July 1927, Mar. 1929, July 1930, July 1931); *Collier's* (Oct. 12, 1929); *Movie Classic* (Nov. 1931, Apr. 1932, July 1932); *Newsweek* (Apr. 28, 1958); *Time* (Apr. 28, 1958).

ARCHIVAL MATERIALS

• *Caricature* — NYPL. • *Clipping File* — AZSU (Jimmy Starr Collection): Relationship with Jack Dempsey (1920s?). CAA: Marriage/divorce (1924– 25, 1931, 1943–45); relationship with Jack Dempsey (1927, 1929); legal problem (1932–33); illness (1927, 1929, 1932, undated); film appearance (1922–23, 1927–28, 1931); injury (1931–32); stage appearance (1928, 1930); leaves RKO (1927); vaudeville tour (1929); home (1932); draft article by ET (1932); romance (1932); appointed to city commission (1953); obituary (1958). Periodical article: *Modern Screen* (July 1931). NYMA (also in Photoplay Collection): Obituary (1958). NYMN: Injury (1936); newsphotos; article (1921, undated); obituary (1958). Periodical articles: *Screen Secrets Magazine* (1920s?); *Modern Screen* (undated). NYPL: Stage appearance (1933, 1939, undated); newsphotos; comeback (1942); article (1936, undated); singer (1935); play review (1928); marriage/divorce (1926, 1931, 1934, undated); injury (1932); film appearance (1920s); obituary

(1958). • *Other Clipping File* — GBBF, MAH, MIDL, OHCL, PAPL, WICF. • *Correspondence* — CAA (Hedda Hopper Collection): Letter about ET from a theater manager (1947). • *Legal File* — CAUT (Twentieth Century–Fox Collection): Agreement (1922); letter (1922). • *Oral History* — NYCO: Mentioned in: James Wong Howe interview. • *Photograph/Still* — CAA (also in Hollywood Studio Museum Collection) (also in MGM Collection), CAH, CASU, CAUT (Jessen Collection), DCG (Quigley Photographic Archives), GBBF, MIDL, NJPT, NYAM, NYB (Bettmann/UPI Collection), NYCU (Dramatic Museum Portraits), NYEH, NYPL, NYSU, OHCL, PAPL, TXU (A. Davis Collection), WICF. • *Scrapbook* — NYPL, UTBY (DeMille Archives).

TEARLE, Conway (Frederick Levy), New York, NY, 1878– 1938.

An experienced stage actor, Conway Tearle was a distinguished leading man in many silent films from the early 1910s. His forte was the sophisticated man of the world in such films as *Black Oxen, Stella Maris, Dancing Mothers, Bella Donna* and *The Rustle of Silk.* His career in talkies was in supporting roles, including westerns, a serial and some crime dramas. He did exit on a high note: 1936's *Romeo and Juliet.*

PUBLISHED SOURCES

• *Books* — **General:** *Blue Book of the Screen*; *Eighty Silent Film Stars*; *Famous Film Folk*; *The Movie Stars Story*; *The Truth About the Movies.* **Credits:** *Filmarama* (v. I and II); *Forty Years of Screen Credits*; *Twenty Years of Silents*; *Who Was Who on Screen.* **Encyclopedic Works:** *B Western Actors Encyclopedia*; *Film Encyclopedia*; *Filmlexicon degli Autori e delle Opere*; *Halliwell's Filmgoer's Companion*; *The Movie Makers*; *The Picturegoer's Who's Who and Encyclopedia of the Screen To-day*; *Who Was Who in the Theatre*; *Who's Who in Hollywood*; *The World Almanac Who's*

Who of Film; *The World Film Encyclopedia*. **Pictorial:** *Silent Portraits*.

• *Periodicals*—The following periodical articles are in addition to that included in the library listings below: *Photoplay* (Sept. 1918, Oct. 1920, Aug. 1921, June–Aug. 1924, Feb. 1925); *Motion Picture Classic* (May 1919, Oct. 1920, Apr. 1923); *Motion Picture Magazine* (Jan. 1920, Apr. 1922, Sept. 1924); *Picture Play* (July 1920); *Newsweek* (Oct. 10, 1938).

ARCHIVAL MATERIALS

• *Clipping File*—CAA: Contract (1920s); obituary (1938). NYMA (also in Photoplay Collection): Personal data summary; obituary (1938). Periodical article: *Classic Images* (Jan. 1988). NYMN: Newsphotos; bankruptcy; alimony (1926, 1935–36); estate; obituary (1938). NYPL: PARTIAL CONTENTS: Newsphotos; stage appearance (1908, 1910s, 1930s); injury (1923); film appearance (1910s, 1930s); nostalgia (1936); divorce (1908, 1912, 1916); radio appearance (1933); article (1916–18, 1923, 1932); alimony (1913–14); legal problem (1921–22); career (1916); obituary (1938). • *Other Clipping File*—GBBF, MAH, MIDL, OHCL, OHSU, PAPL, WICF. • *Correspondence*—NYPL: Letters (C. & L. Brown Collection) (1931–37); other (1922). • *Legal File*—CAUW: Talent agreement (1926, 1929–30); letter (1930). • *Filmography*—NYMA. • *Oral History*—NYCO: Mentioned in: Nita Naldi interview. • *Photograph/Still*—CAA (also in Hollywood Studio Museum Collection) (also in MGM Collection), CAHL, CASF, CAUT (Jessen Collection) (Portrait File), CAUU, DCG (Quigley Photographic Archives), NJFL, NYAM, NYCU (Dramatic Museum Portraits), NYMN, NYPL, NYSU, OHCL, TXU, WICF. • *Play Program*—CAHL: 1928. NYPL. • *Publicity Release*—NYPL: CBS (1937). • *Scrapbook*—NYAM, NYPL (also in R. Locke Collection) (also in Players Collection).

TELL, Alma, 1894/98–1937.

The less successful of the Tell sisters (Olive [q.v.] was the other), Alma Tell had leads in programmers and an occasional better film during the 1920s. Among them were *A Broadway Rose*, *The Iron Trail*, *On with the Dance* and *Paying the Piper*. She also appeared on the stage during the early part of the decade.

PUBLISHED SOURCES

• *Books*—**General:** *Who's Who on the Screen*. **Credits:** *Filmarama* (v. I and II); *Twenty Years of Silents*; *Who Was Who on Screen*. **Encyclopedic Works:** *Who Was Who in the Theatre*; *Who's Who in Hollywood*.

ARCHIVAL MATERIALS

• *Clipping File*—CAA: Marriage (1932). NYMN: Newsphotos; article (undated); marriage (1933). NYPL (also in Locke Collection): Newsphotos; article (1926); stage appearance (1920s); marriage (1932); obituary (1938). Periodical article: *Shadowland* (Sept. 1920?). • *Other Clipping File*—MAH, MIDL, NYMA (Photoplay Collection), OHCL, WICF. • *Correspondence*—NYPL: 1929. • *Legal File*—CAUW: Talent agreement (1928). • *Photograph/Still*—CAA (also in Hollywood Studio Museum Collection), NYMN, NYPL, OHCL, TXU, WICF. • *Play Program*—CAHL: 1926. • *Scrapbook*—NYPL (C. & L. Brown Collection) (R. Locke Collection).

TELL, Olive, New York, NY, 1894–1951.

Mutual star Olive Tell's screen debut came about 1916 and she appeared in many pictures, sometimes as second lead, throughout the 1920s. Her films included *The Unforeseen*, *Chickie*, *Summer Bachelors*, *Worlds Apart*, *Slaves of Beauty* and *Sailors' Wives*. In the talkies, she was seen in supporting roles in such films as *The Scarlet Empress* and *Zaza* (1939), possibly her last. Alma Tell (q.v.) was her sister.

PUBLISHED SOURCES

• *Books*—**General:** *Who's Who on the Screen*. **Credits:** *Filmarama* (v. I and II);

Forty Years of Screen Credits; *Twenty Years of Silents*; *Who Was Who on Screen*. **Encyclopedic Works:** *Filmlexicon degli Autori e delle Opere*; *The Picturegoer's Who's Who and Encyclopedia of the Screen To-day*; *Who Was Who in the Theatre*; *Who's Who in Hollywood*.
• *Periodicals*—*Photoplay* (Feb. 1918); *Motion Picture Classic* (Nov. 1918).

ARCHIVAL MATERIALS
• *Clipping File*—NYMN: Marriage (1926); newsphotos; obituary (1951). NYPL (also in Locke Collection): Newsphotos; stage appearance (1920s); career (1916, 1918); marriage (1923, 1926); film appearance (1933); film review (1920s); obituary (1951). • *Other Clipping File*—MAH, MIDL, NYMA (Photoplay Collection), WICF. • *Filmography*—NYPL (incomplete). • *Legal File*—CAUW: Talent agreement (1929–30, 1936). • *Photograph/Still*—CAA (also in Hollywood Studio Museum Collection), DCG (Quigley Photographic Archives), NJFL, NYMN, NYPL, NYSU, OHCL, TXU, WICF. • *Scrapbook*—NYPL (also in R. Locke Collection).

TELLEGEN, Lou (Isidor Van Dameler or Von Dammeler), Holland, 1881-1934.
Lou Tellegen's great good looks caught the eye of Sarah Bernhardt and he became her leading man on and offstage. He became a leading man in American films as well from 1915, sometimes appearing with his then-wife Geraldine Farrar (*Maria Rosa, The World and Its Woman*, etc). Among the other films in which he starred were *Single Wives*, *The Redeeming Sin*, *Womanpower* and *A Breath of Scandal*. His popularity waned in the latter '20s and he made single talkies in 1931 and 1934.

PUBLISHED SOURCES
• *Books*—General: *The Matinee Idols*. Credits: *Filmarama* (v. I and II); *Twenty Years of Silents*; *Who Was Who on Screen*. **Encyclopedic Works:** *Film Encyclopedia*; *Filmlexicon degli Autori e delle Opere*; *Halliwell's Filmgoer's Companion*; *Who Was Who in the Theatre*; *Who's Who in Hollywood*. **Biography/Autobiography:** *Women Have Been Kind*. **Pictorial:** *Silent Portraits*.
• *Periodicals*—The following periodical articles are in addition to that included in the library listings below: *Theatre* (Aug. 1913, Sept. 1915); *Strand Magazine* (NY) (July 1915); *Photoplay* (May 1916, Dec. 1917, Jan. 1921); *Everybody's Magazine* (Sept. 1919); *Films in Review* (Apr. 1988).

ARCHIVAL MATERIALS
• *Clipping File*—CAA: Marriage (1930); excerpts from newspaper serialization of *Women Have Been Kind* (1934); obituary (1934). NYMA (also in Photoplay Collection): Article (1977); personal data summary. NYMN: Article (1932); newsphotos; stage appearance (1920s, 1932, undated); marriage (1930, 1934); bankruptcy (1928); review of *Women Have Been Kind* (1931); alimony; estate (1935); funeral (1934); obituary (1934). NYPL (also in C. & L. Brown Collection) (also in Locke Collection): Article (1912, 1914–16, 1929, undated); newsphotos; estate (1935); marriage/separation/divorce (1916, 1921, 1923); play review (1910s); returns to films (1919); returns to stage (1916); obituary (1934). Periodical article: *Stage* (Apr. 24, 1920). • *Other Clipping File*—GBBF, MAH, MIDL, OHCL, OHSU, PAPL, WICF. • *Correspondence*—NYPL: Letters (C. & L. Brown Collection) (1929–34); other (1923). • *Filmography*—NYMA. • *Legal File*—CAUT (Twentieth Century-Fox Collection): Talent agreement (1925-26). NYPL: Contract. • *Photograph/Still*—CAA (also in Hollywood Studio Museum Collection), CAHL, CALM, CAUS, CAUT (Jessen Collection), DCG (Quigley Photographic Archives), NYB (Bettmann/UPI Collection) (Underwood Collection), NYEH, NYMN, NYPL, NYSU, OHCL, TXU, WICF. • *Play Program*—NYPL. • *Reminiscence*—MISU. • *Scrapbook*—NYPL (also in Locke Collection).

TERRY, Alice (Alice Taafe), Vincennes, IN, 1899-1987.

Alice Terry was a beautiful actress of cool demeanor whose film ouevre was small but significant. Among her films, some directed by her husband Rex Ingram, were *Mare Nostrum, The Prisoner of Zenda* and *The Four Horsemen of the Apocalypse.* Although she had made her debut in 1916, it was the latter film which propelled both her and Rudolph Valentino (q.v.) to stardom in 1921. Later films included *The Arab, The Garden of Allah* and *Sackcloth and Scarlet*; she also made some films in Europe before leaving the screen in 1929.

PUBLISHED SOURCES

• *Books—General: Alisa Terri* (i.e., Alice Terry); *Blue Book of the Screen*; *Classics of the Silent Screen*; *Famous Film Folk*; *The Idols of Silence*; "*Image*" *on the Art and Evolution of the Film*; *Ladies in Distress*; *The Movie Stars Story.* **Credits:** *Filmarama* (v. I and II); *Twenty Years of Silents.* **Encyclopedic Works:** *Film Encyclopedia*; *Filmlexicon degli Autori e delle Opere*; *Halliwell's Filmgoer's Companion*; *The Illustrated Who's Who of the Cinema*; *The Movie Makers*; *The Picturegoer's Who's Who and Encyclopedia of the Screen To-day*; *Variety Who's Who in Show Business*; *Who's Who in Hollywood.* **Pictorial:** *Silent Portraits.*

• *Periodicals—*The following periodical articles are in addition to those included in the library listings below: *Motion Picture Classic* (July 1921, Nov. 1922); *Photoplay* (Oct. 1921, Dec. 1922, Sept. 1923, Jan. 1924, June–July 1924, Nov. 1924, Feb. 1925); *Motion Picture Magazine* (Jan. 1922, Nov. 1924, Feb. 1926, Jan. 1927); *Films in Review* (Feb.-Mar. 1975); *Cine Revue* (Jan. 7, 1988); *Classic Images* (Feb. 1988).

ARCHIVAL MATERIALS

• *Clipping File—*CAA: Marriage (1921); libel suit (1951–53); nostalgia (1972, 1979); obituary (1987). CAFI: Newsphotos (numerous); obituary (1987). NYMA (also in Photoplay Collection): Obituary (1987). Periodical articles: *Motion Picture Classic* (Mar. 1922); *Image* (Mar. 1937). NYPL (also in Locke Collection): Newsphotos (numerous); article (undated); obituary (1987). • *Other Clipping File—*CAUB, GBBF, MIDL, OHCL, PAPL, WICF. • *Oral History—*NYCO: Mentioned in: Albert Hackett interview. • *Photograph/Still—*CAA (also in Hollywood Studio Museum Collection) (also in MGM Collection), CAUT (Jessen Collection), CAUU, DCG (Quigley Photographic Archives), NYB (Underwood Collection), NYCU (Dramatic Museum Portraits) (Palmer Collection), NYEH, NYMN, NYPL, OHCL, TXU, WICF. • *Scrapbook—*NYPL.

THEBY, Rosemary (Rose Masing), St. Louis, MO, 1885-?.

Rosemary Theby probably made her screen debut in Vitagraph's *The Wager* in 1910. She was seen in leading and supporting roles in a variety of genres including serials and dramas such as *So Big, Woman Against the World, Fifth Avenue Models, The Red Lily* and *A Connecticut Yankee in King Arthur's Court.* Other studios for which she worked included Bluebird and Metro. In sound films she appeared in small parts through 1940's *One Million B.C.*

PUBLISHED SOURCES

• *Books—General: Who's Who on the Screen.* **Credits:** *Filmarama* (v. I and II); *Twenty Years of Silents.* **Encyclopedic Works:** *Filmlexicon degli Autori e delle Opere*; *The Picturegoer's Who's Who and Encyclopedia of the Screen To-day*; *Who's Who in Hollywood.*

• *Periodicals—Photoplay* (Nov. 1913, June 1914, Dec. 1916, Oct. 1920); *Motion Picture Magazine* (Apr. 1915, Nov. 1919, Oct. 1920, Feb. 1922); *Motion Picture Classic* (May 1916, Nov. 1916, Aug. 1921); *Classic Images* (Nov. 1981, Aug. 1989).

ARCHIVAL MATERIALS

• *Clipping File—*NYPL (also in Locke Collection): Newsphotos; death of husband; article (1915); nostalgia (1936).

• *Other Clipping File* – GBBF, NYMA (Photoplay Collection), OHCL, WICF. • *Correspondence* – NYMA (Photoplay Collection). • *Photograph/Still* – CAA (also in Hollywood Studio Museum Collection) (also in MGM Collection), CAUT (Jessen Collection), DCG (Quigley Photographic Archives), IAU (Junkin Collection), NYPL, NYSU, OHCL, TXU, WICF. • *Scrapbook* – NYPL (also in R. Locke Collection).

THOMAS, Olive (Oliveretta Duffy?), Charleroi, PA, 1895?–1920.

A former Follies girl, Olive Thomas was considered one of the world's great beauties. During a career which lasted less than five years she was seen in films such as *Limousine Life*, *The Flapper* (1920, her last), *An Heiress for a Day*, *The Glorious Lady* and *The Follies Girl*. She was married to Jack Pickford (q.v.).

PUBLISHED SOURCES

• *Books* – Credits: *Filmarama* (v. I and II); *Twenty Years of Silents*; *Who Was Who on Screen*. **Encyclopedic Works:** *Film Encyclopedia*; *Filmlexicon degli Autori e delle Opere*; *Halliwell's Filmgoer's Companion*; *Who's Who in Hollywood*. **Pictorial:** *Silent Portraits*.

• *Periodicals* – The following periodical articles are in addition to that included in the library listings below: *Motion Picture Classic* (July 1917, Feb. 1918, Apr. 1919, June 1919, Mar. 1920); *Photoplay* (Sept. 1917, Dec. 1917, Oct. 1918, Feb. 1920, Mar. 1926); *Motion Picture Magazine* (July 1919); *The Era* (Sept. 15, 1920); *Good Housekeeping* (July 1932).

ARCHIVAL MATERIALS

• *Clipping File* – CAA: Newsphotos; engagement (1916?). NYMA (also in Photoplay Collection): Personal data summary; obituary (1920). Periodical article: *Photo-play World* (Dec. 1918). NYPL (also in Locke Collection): Reunion of Follies girls (1936); newsphotos (numerous); estate (1923); funeral (1920).

• *Other Clipping File* – GBBF, MAH, OHSU, PAPL, WICF. • *Photograph/Still* – CAA (also in Hollywood Studio Museum Collection), CAUT (Jessen Collection), NYB (Bettmann/UPI Collection), NYCU (Dramatic Museum Portraits), NYPL, NYSU, OHCL, TXU, WICF. • *Scrapbook* – NYPL (also in Locke Collection).

THOMSON, Fred (Alfred[?] Thomson), Pasadena, CA, 1890/91–1928.

At the height of his fame as a western star, Fred Thomson rivalled Tom Mix as the screen's most popular cowboy. Formerly a minister, he began his career in 1921 dramas (*The Love Light*, *Just Around the Corner*) but hit his stride in Paramount, FBO and Universal westerns like *Thundering Hoofs*, *Lone Hand Saunders*, *The Bandit's Baby*, *The Tough Guy* and *North of Nevada*. His films were heavy in the action sequences and stunts beloved by juvenile audiences. After his death his horse Silver King was featured in its own series.

PUBLISHED SOURCES

• *Books* – General: *The BFI Companion to the Western*; *Classics of the Silent Screen*; *The Cowboy*; *Eighty Silent Film Stars*; *The Filming of the West*; *The Hall of Fame of Western Film Stars*; *Saddle Aces of the Cinema*; *The Western* (Eyles); *The Western* (Fenin); *Winners of the West*. **Credits:** *Filmarama* (v. II); *Twenty Years of Silents*; *Who Was Who on Screen*. **Encyclopedic Works:** *Film Encyclopedia*; *Filmlexicon degli Autori e delle Opere*; *Who's Who in Hollywood*. **Biography/Autobiography:** *More Than a Cowboy*. **Pictorial:** *Silent Portraits*; *Wallace Neff*.

• *Periodicals* – The following periodical articles are in addition to those included in the library listings below: *Photoplay* (Jan. 1924, Aug. 1927, Oct. 1927, Jan. 1934); *Films in Review* (June–July 1960); *Show* (Sept. 1962); *Films in Review* (Jan.–Feb. 1966); *Classic Images* (May 1989, Dec. 1990).

ARCHIVAL MATERIALS
• *Clipping File* — CAA: Article (1970s?); film appearance (1923, 1928); Silver King (horse) in films (1930); home (1976); obituary (1928). Periodical articles: *World of Yesterday* (Apr. 1977); *Under Western Skies* (Jan. 1978); *American Classic Screen* (Mar.-Apr. 1982). CAUU (Frances Marion Collection): Career (various dates). *NOTE*: Frances Marion was FT's wife. NYMA (also in Photoplay Collection): Personal data summary. Periodical articles: *Classic Film Collector* (Winter 1970-Spring 1971); *Classic Images* (Aug. 1984); *Big Reel* (Sept. 1988, May 1989). • *Other Clipping File* — AZSU (Jimmy Starr Collection), CAUB, GBBF, MIDL, OHCL, PAPL, WICF. • *Filmography* — CAA. • *Oral History* — NYCO: Mentioned in: Frances Marion interview. • *Photograph/Still* — CAA (also in Hollywood Studio Museum Collection), CALM, CAUU (Frances Marion Collection), DCG (Quigley Photographic Archives), NYB (Underwood Collection), NYCU (Dramatic Museum Portraits), NYEH, NYPL, NYSU, OHCL, TXU, WICF. • *Studio Biography* — CAA: Paramount (1927).

THOMSON, Kenneth, Pittsburgh, PA, 1899-1967.
One of the founders of the Screen Actors' Guild and its longtime executive secretary, handsome Kenneth Thomson was a leading man in the late silent and early sound days. He came to Hollywood after appearances in many Broadway plays and was seen in several DeMille films. His roles turned to supporting ones in the early '30s and he was often cast as a villain. The year 1935 was the last one in which he made a full complement of films; by 1937 he was no longer on the screen.

PUBLISHED SOURCES
• *Books* — Credits: *Filmarama* (v. II); *Forty Years of Screen Credits*; *Twenty Years of Silents*; *Who Was Who on Screen*. Encyclopedic Works: *Filmlexicon degli Autori e delle Opere*; *Interna-*

tional Motion Picture Almanac (1975-76); *The Picturegoer's Who's Who and Encyclopedia of the Screen To-day*; *Who's Who in Hollywood*.
• *Periodicals* — *Theatre Arts* (Dec. 1939).

OBSCURE PUBLISHED SOURCES
CAA (Pat O'Malley Collection): *The Cast* (v. 1).

ARCHIVAL MATERIALS
• *Clipping File* — CAA: Quits SAG (1943); named head of Composer and Lyricists Guild (1965); obituary (1967). CAUU: Obituary (1967). NYPL: Screen Actors' Guild (1930s); film appearance (1920s, 1934); career (1927-28); newsphotos. PAPT: Article (1926, 1931). NYMN: Marriage (1928, undated); newsphotos. • *Other Clipping File* — GBBF, NYMA (Photoplay Collection), PAPL, WICF. • *Correspondence* — NYPL (C. & L. Brown Collection): 1929, 1931. • *Legal File* — CAUW: Talent agreement (1929-31, 1933); contract (1929, 1932-33); authorization (1932). NYPL (C. & L. Brown Collection): Contract (1926). • *Photograph/Still* — CAA (also in Hollywood Studio Museum Collection), DCG (Quigley Photographic Archives), GBBF, NJPT, NYCU (Dramatic Museum Portraits), NYEH, NYPL, PAPL, TXU (A. Davis Collection), WICF. • *Studio Biography* — CAA: DeMille (1926).

TORRENCE, Ernest (Ernest Tayson or Thoyson), Edinburgh, Scotland, 1878-1933.
Although he was actually a person of great culture, indeed an opera singer, Ernest Torrence had the face of a fearsome villain. His memorable first role as Luke Hatburn in the 1921 classic *Tol'able David* foreshadowed much of his career. He was a versatile character actor, however, who also appeared in sympathetic roles. Among his better-known films were *Peter Pan* (another villain, Captain Hook), *The Covered Wagon*, *The Hunchback of Notre Dame*, *The King of Kings*, *Steamboat*

Bill, Jr. and *Mantrap.* He made a smooth transition to talkies and was active until his death.

PUBLISHED SOURCES
• *Books – General: Character People; Eighty Silent Film Stars; Ernest Torrens* (i.e., Torrence); *Famous Film Folk; The Truth About the Movies.* **Encyclopedic Works:** *Film Encyclopedia; Filmlexicon degli Autori e delle Opere; Halliwell's Filmgoer's Companion; Hollywood Character Actors; The Movie Makers; The Picturegoer's Who's Who and Encyclopedia of the Screen To-day; Who Was Who in the Theatre; Who's Who in Hollywood; The World Almanac Who's Who of Film; The World Film Encyclopedia.* **Credits:** *British Film Actors' Credits; Filmarama* (v. II); *Forty Years of Screen Credits; Twenty Years of Silents; Who Was Who on Screen.* **Pictorial:** *Silent Portraits.*
• *Periodicals* – The following periodical articles are in addition to that included in the library listings below: *Motion Picture Classic* (June 1923, July 1924, June 1927); *Photoplay* (June 1923, May 1925, July 1925); *Motion Picture Magazine* (June 1924, Mar. 1925, Nov. 1927); *National Magazine* (Jan. 1926); *Collier's* (Aug. 24, 1929); *Musical Courier* (May 27, 1933); *The Etude* (Aug. 1933); *Classic Images* (May 1992) (filmography).

ARCHIVAL MATERIALS
• *Clipping File* – CAA: Newsphotos; obituary (1933). NYMA (also in Photoplay Collection): Article (1923); personal data summary. Periodical article: *Classic Images* (Nov. 1985). NYMN: Career (1932); funeral (1933); obituary (1933). NYPL (also in Locke Collection): Newsphotos; film review (1933); illness (1933); film appearance (1920s, 1932); article (undated); estate (1933); obituary (1933). • *Other Clipping File* – AZSU (Jimmy Starr Collection), GBBF, MAH, MIDL, WICF. • *Correspondence* – NYPL (C. & L. Brown Collection): 1916. • *Legal File* – CAUW: Talent agreement (1930). • *Photograph/Still* – CAA (also in Hollywood Studio Museum Collection) (also in MGM Collection), CALM,

CAPH, CASF, CAUS, CAUT (Jessen Collection), DCG (Quigley Photographic Archives), NYB (Bettmann/UPI Collection) (Underwood Collection), NYCU (Dramatic Museum Portraits), NYEH, NYMN, NYPL, NYSU, OHCL, TXSM, TXU, WICF. • *Scrapbook* – NYPL, UTBY (DeMille Archives). • *Studio Biography* – CAA (Mack Sennett Collection): MGM; Sennett (1932).

TRYON, Glenn, Julietta, Idaho, 1894/99–1970.

Fresh-faced Glenn Tryon was a leading man, starting in 1924, in comedies like *The Poor Nut, Thanks for the Buggy Ride, The Gate Crasher, A Hero for a Night,* and *Hot Heels.* His appearances continued into the sound era in light fare like *Dames Ahoy, The Sky Spider* and *The Big Payoff.* When his career waned in the early 1930s, he turned to screenwriting, directing and producing although he still could be seen in a few small parts in the '40s.

PUBLISHED SOURCES
• *Books – General: The "B" Directors; Motion Picture News Booking Guide and Studio Directory* (1927). **Credits:** *Filmarama* (v. II); *Forty Years of Screen Credits; Twenty Years of Silents; Who Was Who on Screen.* **Encyclopedic Works:** *Film Encylopedia; Filmlexicon degli Autori e delle Opere; The Picturegoer's Who's Who and Encyclopedia of the Screen To-day; Who's Who in Hollywood; The World Film Encyclopedia.* **Pictorial:** *Silent Portraits.*
• *Periodicals* – *Photoplay* (Dec. 1928); *Classic Images* (June 1990) (filmography).

ARCHIVAL MATERIALS
• *Clipping File* – CAA: Newsphotos. NYPL: Director (1934, undated); article (undated); newsphotos. • *Other Clipping File* – AZSU (Jimmy Starr Collection), GBBF, MIDL, NYMA (Photoplay Collection), PAPL, WICF. • *Correspondence* – NYPL (C. & L. Brown Collection): 1931. • *Oral History* – Mentioned in: Paul Fejos interview. • *Photograph/*

Still—CAA (also in Hollywood Studio Museum Collection), CAUT (Jessen Collection), CAUU, DCG (Quigley Photographic Archives), GBBF, MIDL, NJPT, NYB (Underwood Collection), NYCU (Dramatic Museum Portraits), NYEH, NYPL, OHCL, WICF. • *Scrapbook*—NYAM, NYMA, NYPL. • *Studio Biography*—CAA: RKO (1930s). NYMA: Photoplay.

TURNER, Florence, New York, NY, 1885-1946.

Florence Turner was a pioneer of silent film (from 1907) and one of the most popular actresses of her day. She was known as "The Vitagraph Girl" at a time when performers did not receive billing. In 1913 she went to England for several years and upon returning found herself out of favor with the American public. She never regained her earlier fame although she continued to appear in both American and British films throughout the 1920s. In the '30s she played occasional bits.

PUBLISHED SOURCES

• *Books*—**General:** *The Big V*; *Early American Cinema.* **Credits:** *British Film Actors' Credits*; *Filmarama* (v. I and II); *Twenty Years of Silents*; *Who Was Who on Screen.* **Encyclopedic Works:** *Film Encyclopedia*; *Filmlexicon degli Autori e delle Opere*; *Halliwell's Filmgoer's Companion*; *The Illustrated Who's Who in British Films*; *The Illustrated Who's Who of the Cinema*; *The Movie Makers*; *Notable American Women, 1607-1950*; *The Picturegoer's Who's Who and Encyclopedia of the Screen To-day*; *Who's Who in Hollywood.* **Bibliography:** *The Idols of Silence.* **Pictorial:** *Silent Portraits.*

• *Periodicals*—The following periodical articles are in addition to that included in the library listings below: *Film Index* (Oct. 23, 1909); *Moving Picture World* (July 23, 1910, May 18, 1912, Mar. 22, 1913, July 18, 1914, Aug. 17, 1916); *Bioscope* (May 15, 1913); *Motion Picture Classic* (Feb. 1919, July 1920); *Motion Picture Studio* (Apr. 15, 1922); *Motion*

Picture News (May 24, 1924); *Photoplay* (July 1924); *Cinema Digest* (June 13, 1932); *Films in Review* (Nov. 1953, Mar. 1974).

ARCHIVAL MATERIALS

• *Clipping File*—CAA: Obituary (1946). CAUU (A. Slide Collection): Film reviews. NYMA (also in Photoplay Collection): Newsphotos; obituary (1946). Periodical article: *Classic Images* (Sept. 1981). NYPL (Locke Collection): Newsphotos; most popular film actress (1911); article (1912, 1914); film review (1910s); stars in Mutual films (1916); makes films in England (1910s, 1916); accuses English police (1921). • *Other Clipping File*—AZSU (Jimmy Starr Collection), CALM (see Collection), GBBF, MAH, MIDL, PAPL, WICF. • *Collection*—CALM: 2 scrapbooks (1910-28 and 1913-16); clippings; letters; photos; stills from four films (1915). • *Correspondence*—CAHL: 1940. CALM (see Collection). NYPL: Note (C. & L. Brown Collection) (1941); other (1943). • *Photograph/Still*—CAA (also in Hollywood Studio Museum Collection), CALM (also in Collection), CAUU (A. Slide Collection), CNDA, DCG (Quigley Photographic Archives), NYEH, NYPL, NYSU, TXU, WICF. • *Program*—CAUU (A. Slide Collection): Film. • *Scrapbook*—CALM (see Collection), NYPL (also in R. Locke Collection).

TURPIN, Ben (Bernard Turpin), New Orleans, LA, 1869/74-1940.

Although he joined Essanay in 1907, Ben Turpin did not hit his screen stride until about 1915. With his one crossed eye (which did not occur until adulthood), he attained modest success in countless slapstick two-reelers, but his real renown came after he began parodying hit films of the 1920s, among them *The Shriek of Araby* and *Three Foolish Weeks.* He continued appearing in both features and shorts during the 1920s and, to a much lesser extent, during the following decade as well.

PUBLISHED SOURCES

• *Books*—**General:** *Ben Tiurpin* (i.e., Turpin); *Blue Book of the Screen*; *Classics of the Silent Screen*; *Clown Princes and Court Jesters*; *Eighty Silent Film Stars*; *Famous Film Folk*; *The Funsters*; *Hollywood Album 2*; *Keaton et Cie*; *Twinkle, Twinkle, Movie Star*; *World of Laughter*. **Credits:** *Filmarama* (v. I and II); *Forty Years of Screen Credits*; *Twenty Years of Silents*; *Who Was Who on Screen*. **Encyclopedic Works:** *The Dictionary of American Biography* (Supplement 2); *Film Encyclopedia*; *Filmlexicon degli Autori e delle Opere*; *Halliwell's Filmgoer's Companion*; *The Illustrated Encyclopedia of the World's Great Movie Stars and Their Films*; *The Illustrated Who's Who of the Cinema*; *The International Encyclopedia of Film*; *Joe Franklin's Encyclopedia of Comedians*; *The Movie Makers*; *The Picturegoer's Who's Who and Encyclopedia of the Screen To-day*; *Quinlan's Illustrated Directory of Film Comedy Actors*; *Who's Who in Hollywood*; *The World Almanac Who's Who of Film*; *The World Encyclopedia of the Film*; *The World Film Encyclopedia*. **Pictorial:** *Silent Portraits*.

• *Periodicals*—The following periodical articles are in addition to those included in the library listings below: *Moving Picture World* (Apr. 3, 1909); *Motion Picture Classic* (Mar. 1918, July 1925); *Motion Picture Magazine* (Nov. 1921); *Motion Picture Classic* (Feb. 1922); *Photoplay* (Nov. 1923, Aug. 1924, Nov. 1933); *American Magazine* (Nov. 1924); *Life* (Sept. 5, 1949); *Films in Review* (Oct. 1977); *Classic Images* (Jan. 1982, Jan. 1989, June 1991).

OBSCURE PUBLISHED SOURCES
CAA, NYMA: *Ben Turpin*.

ARCHIVAL MATERIALS
• *Clipping File*—CAA: Stage appearance (1922); article (1924, 1950s?); obituary (1940). LANO: Obituary (1940). NYMA (also in Photoplay Collection): Newsphotos. Periodical articles: *8mm Collector* (Sept. 1964); *Classic Images* (Dec. 1982, July 1983, July 1986, Dec. 1988). NYPL (also in Locke Collection):

Article (1932, 1934, 1936, 1940, undated); newsphotos; film appearance (1932); obituary (1940). Periodical articles: *Motion Picture Classic* (Mar. 1918); *Photoplay* (Dec. 1918); *American Magazine* (undated); *New Yorker* (July 16, 1927). • *Other Clipping File*—AZSU (Jimmy Starr Collection), GBBF, MAH, MIDL, OHCL, PAPL, WICF. • *Correspondence*—DCG (Terry Ramsaye Papers). • *Legal File*—CAA (Sennett Collection): Contract (1917, 1919); option (1917–18, 1921–23); talent agreement (1920–24, 1926); letter, telegram (1925–26). • *Oral History*—NYCO: Mentioned in the following interviews: G.M. Anderson, Buster Keaton. • *Photograph/Still*—CAA (also in Hollywood Studio Museum Collection), CALM, CAUT (Jessen Collection) (Portrait File), CAUU, CNDA, DCG (Quigley Photographic Archives), NYB (Bettmann/UPI Collection) (Penguin Collection) (Springer Collection) (Underwood Collection), NYEH, NYPL, NYSU, OHCL, TXU, WICF. • *Publicity Release*—CAA (Sennett Collection): Numerous. • *Scrapbook*—NYPL. • *Studio Biography*—CAA (Sennett Collection).

VALENTINO, Rudolph (Rodolpho di Guglielmi Valentina d'Antonguolla), Castellaneta, Italy, 1895-1926.

After a most unpromising start in films (from 1917) playing gangsters and gigolos, ex-dancer Rudolph Valentino became the world-famous "Latin lover" in *The Four Horsemen of the Apocalypse* (1921). The success of *The Sheik* and *Blood and Sand* cemented his fabulous celebrity. Eventually poor films and poorer advice sent his career into a decline which was reversed by the success of *The Eagle* and *The Son of the Sheik*. The latter, however, was his final film.

PUBLISHED SOURCES
• *Books*—Written by (or ghostwritten for) RV: *Day Dreams* (poetry) (1923); *How You Can Keep Fit* (1923). **Bibliography:** *The Idols of Silence*. **General:**

Authors on Film; Babel and Babylon; Behind the Screen; The Big Book of Italian-American Culture; Blue Book of the Screen; Classics of the Silent Screen; Close Ups; Famous Film Folk; Fifty Super Stars; Final Placement; Gentlemen to the Rescue; Great Lovers of the Movies; The Great Movie Stars; Great Stars of Hollywood's Golden Age; History of the American Cinema (v. 3); Hollywood: The Pioneers; Hollywood Album; Hollywood and the Great Stars; Hollywood Hall of Fame; Hollywood Heaven; Hollywood Hunks; The Hollywood Reporter Star Profiles; I Love You, Clark Gable, Etc.; Immortals of the Screen; Les Immortels du Cinéma; The Intimate Sex Lives of Famous People; Kings of Tragedy; Love, Laughter and Tears; The Matinee Idols; The Movie Stars; The Movie Stars Story; The National Society of Film Critics on the Movie Star; The Public Is Never Wrong; The Return of Rudolph Valentino; The Rise and Fall of the Matinee Idol; Rudolfo Valentino; The Saturday Evening Post Movie Book; The Self-Enchanted; Stardom; Stars!; The Stars (Schickel); Starstruck; There Is a New Star in Heaven, Valentino; Those Scandalous Sheets of Hollywood; Those Who Died Young; Too Young to Die; The Truth About the Movies; Twinkle, Twinkle, Movie Star; Venus in Hollywood; The Voice of Valentino; What the Fans Think of Rudolph Valentino; What the Stars Told Me. **Credits:** Filmarama (v. I and II); Twenty Years of Silents; Who Was Who in Hollywood. **Biography/Autobiography:** The Intimate Journal of Rudolph Valentino; The Intimate Life of Rudolph Valentino; Madam Valentino; The Magic of Rudolph Valentino; Memoirs of a Star; My Private Diary; Remember Valentino; Rodolfo Valentino; Rudolph Valentino (Ben-Allah); Rudolph Valentino (de Recqueville); Rudolph Valentino (Oberfirst); Rudolph Valentino (Walker); Rudolph Valentino (Recollections); Rudy; Valentino (Arnold); Valentino (Botham/Donnelly); Valentino (Shulman); Valentino (Steiger/Mank); Valentino (Tajiri); Valentino As I Knew Him; Valentino the

Unforgotten. **Encyclopedic Works:** A Biographical Dictionary of Film; A Companion to the Movies; A Dictionary of the Cinema; Film Encyclopedia; Filmlexicon degli Autori e delle Opere; Halliwell's Filmgoer's Companion; The Illustrated Encyclopedia of the World's Great Movie Stars and Their Films; The Illustrated Who's Who of the Cinema; International Dictionary of Films and Filmmakers (v. 3); The International Encyclopedia of Film; The Movie Makers; The Oxford Companion to Film; Quinlan's Illustrated Registry of Film Stars; Who's Who in Hollywood; The World Almanac Who's Who of Film; The World Encyclopedia of the Film; The World Film Encyclopedia. **Catalog:** The Estate of Rudolph Valentino. **Paper Dolls:** Rudolph Valentino Paper Dolls. **Pictorial:** The Image Makers; Leading Men; Life and Death in Hollywood; Silent Portraits. **Recordings:** Hollywood on Record. **Factoids:** Star Stats.

• **Periodicals**—The following periodical articles are in addition to those included in the library listings below: Motion Picture Classic (Nov. 1920, Dec. 1921, Oct. 1922, Dec. 1923, June 1925, May 1926); Literary Digest (Mar. 26, 1921, Aug. 20, 1927, Feb. 7, 1931); Motion Picture Magazine (July 1921, May 1922, Feb. 1923, June 1923, Oct. 1924, Aug. 1925, Nov. 1925, Nov. 1928, Jan. 1929, Jan. 1930, Dec. 1930, Mar. 1931, July 1931, Sept. 1932, June 1933, Oct. 1933, Jan. 1935); Photoplay (Sept. 1921, Nov. 1921, Mar. 1922, May 1922, July 1922, Sept. 1922, Dec. 1922-Apr. 1923, May–June 1924, Oct.–Nov. 1924, Feb. 1925, May 1925, July 1926, Oct.–Nov. 1926, Feb. 1927, Jan. 1928, July–Aug. 1930, Sept. 1938); Metropolitan Magazine (Jan. 1923); Pictures and Picturegoer (July 1924–Oct. 1925); Cinema Art (Jan. 1926); Collier's (Jan. 16, 1926); The Nation (Sept. 8, 1926); Theatre (Oct. 1926); Vanity Fair (Oct. 1926); Liberty (Sept. 21–Oct. 12, 1929, Fall 1973); Cinema Digest (Jan. 9, 1933); True Story Magazine (Apr. 1934); Movie Classic (Sept. 1934); Cinema (Italy) (1938); Cue (June 18, 1939); Sequence (Summer 1949); Time (Aug. 1, 1949); Coronet

(Jan. 1951); *Newsweek* (Sept. 5, 1955, Apr. 10, 1961, Sept. 1, 1975, Aug. 8, 1977); *Films and Filming* (May 1956, Aug. 1976, Dec. 1983); *Cosmopolitan* (Oct. 1956); *Saturday Review* (Oct. 13, 1956); *Image* (May 1958); *American Heritage* (Aug. 1965); *Screen Legends* (Oct. 1965); *8mm Collector* (Spring 1966); *Classic Film Collector* (Summer 1966, Spring/Summer 1970); *Screen Facts* (no. 17, 1968); *Anthologie du Cinéma* (no. 5, 1969); *Cinema Journal* (Spring 1970, Summer 1986) *Screen Greats* (Summer 1971); *Filmihullu* (no. 2, 1976); *Travel* (May 1976); *Kino* (Sept. 1976); *Ecran* (Nov. 1976); *Vogue* (Aug. 1977); *Lumière du Cinéma* (Sept. 1977); *Kosmorama* (Winter 1977); *Classic Images* (Apr. 1982); *Frauen und Film* (Oct. 1982); *Skoop* (Apr. 1984); *Cine Revue* (Apr. 11, 1985); *American Cinematographer* (Aug. 1985); *Hollywood Studio Magazine* (Mar. 1986, July 1991); *Film Criticism* (Winter 1989).

MEDIA

Heroes (video); *Irving Berlin, John Barrymore, Rudolph Valentino* (video); *Rudolph Valentino* (video); *Swanson & Valentino* (video); *Valentino* (recording); *Why Ever Did They?* (CD recording).

ARCHIVAL MATERIALS

• *Clipping File*—CAA: Tribute (1976); film appearance (1921–22); memorial service (1938, 1940, 1949, 1950, 1952, 1954–55, 1959–61, 1963–64, 1966–67, 1976–78, 1981, 1983, 1988, 1990–91); statue (1930, 1950, 1952, 1988); legal problem (1921, 1925); separation/divorce (1925–26); illness (1925–26); funeral (1926, 1986); sale of effects (1926, 1945, 1972); estate (1926–28, 1930–31, 1933–34); spirit (1930, 1932, 1939, 1944, 1948); home (1938, 1949, 1951, 1953, 1961); excerpt from *Remember Valentino* (1938); review of *Valentino* (1967); article (1945, 1948–51, 1960–61, 1963, 1967, 1972, 1975, 1977, 1986); biographical film (1949, 1975, 1989); shrine (1956); home town (1975); film festival (1977, 1979, 1982); TV biography (1975); obituary (1926). Periodical articles: *Bookman* (Feb. 1923); *Literary Digest* (Sept. 11, 1926); *Liberty* (Sept.[?] 1929); *Collier's* (July 2, 1949); *Life* (Jan. 2,

1950); *Pageant* (Mar. 1951); *Films in Review* (Apr. 1952) (filmography); *Saturday Evening Post* (Jan. 20, 1962); *Players* (Fall 1964); *Movie Classics* (Aug. 1973); *TV Guide* (Nov. 22, 1975). CAFI: Memorial service (1976, 1983–84); film biography (1976); article (1976); newsphotos. CAUT: Review of *Rudolph Valentino* (Walker) (1977); memorial service (1951, 1972, 1976–77, 1983); article (1935, 1945); marriage (1977); estate (1926); newsphotos; biographical film (1976); bibliography of books and articles. Periodical articles: *Motion Picture Classic* (Mar. 1926); *Picture Play* (Apr. 1927); *Motion Picture Magazine* (Feb. 1928, Aug. 1930); *Life* (June 20, 1938); *Saturday Evening Post* (Jan. 10, 1962); *Ballroom Dance Magazine* (Feb. 1968). CAUU: Memorial service (1949, 1966, 1976, 1983); newsphotos; film festival; home town (1975). Periodical article: *Movie Classics* (undated). NYMN: Newsphotos (numerous); article (1945, undated). Periodical article: *Saturday Evening Post* (undated). NYPL: PARTIAL CONTENTS: Woman in black (1984); newsphotos; article (1988, 1991). Periodical articles: *Quirk's Reviews* (Aug. 1986); *Interview* (Aug. 1986). • *Other Clipping File*—AZSU (Jimmy Starr Collection), CAUB, CAUS (see Collection), CNDA, DCLC, GBBF, MAH, MIDL, NYMA, OHCL, OHSU, PAPL, WICF. • *Collection*—CAUS (Victor M. Shapiro Papers): Scrapbook, clippings, photographs. Shapiro was a Hollywood publicist. • *Correspondence*—CAA (Adolph Zukor Collection): 4 letters, one about his prosecution for bigamy (1922–24). DCG (Terry Ramsaye Papers). DCLC (George Kleine Collection): 1925–26 (may contain clippings or other materials). NYMA (Photoplay Collection). • *Filmography*—CAA. • *Oral History*—NYCO: Mentioned in the following interviews: Sidney Blackmer, G.H. Combs, W. Evans, Lila Lee, Frances Marion, Joel McCrea, A. Mencken, Mae Murray, Nita Naldi, Jack Poppele, Blanche Sweet. • *Photograph/Still*—CAA, CALM, CAOC (Kiesling Collection), CAPH, CAUT (Jessen Collection), CAUB, CAUS (see Collection),

CAUU, CNDA, DCG (Quigley Photographic Archives), MABU (Douglas Fairbanks Jr. Collection), NYAM, NYB (Bettmann/UPI Collection) (Springer Collection) (Underwood Collection), NYCU (Dramatic Museum Portraits) (Palmer Collection), NYEH, NYMN, NYPL, NYSU, OHCL, TNUT (Clarence Brown Collection), TXU, WICF. • *Press Kit* – OHCL. • *Publicity Release* – AZSU (Jimmy Starr Collection). CAA: 1950s. • *Reminiscence* – MISU. • *Scrapbook* – AZSU (Jimmy Starr Collection), CASU (Stark Collection), CAUS (see Collection), GBBF (Andersson Collection), NYAM, NYCU (Dramatic Museum Portraits), NYPL, TNUT (Clarence Brown Collection).

VALLI, Virginia (Virginia McSweeney), Chicago, IL, 1895/1900–1968.

Pretty brunette Virginia Valli first appeared in films for Chicago-based studios, beginning in 1915, and went to Hollywood in the early 1920s. She was seen throughout the decade in such films as *Sentimental Tommy*, *The Signal Tower*, *Wild Oranges*, *Flames* and *Street of Illusion*. Her sound film output was meager and she left the screen in 1931. She was married to Charles Farrell (q.v.).

PUBLISHED SOURCES

• *Books* – General: *Blue Book of the Screen*; *Famous Film Folk*; *The Truth About the Movies*. Credits: *Filmarama* (v. I and II); *Forty Years of Screen Credits*; *Twenty Years of Silents*; *Who Was Who on Screen*. Encyclopedic Works: *Film Encyclopedia*; *Filmlexicon degli Autori e delle Opere*; *Halliwell's Filmgoer's Companion*; *The Movie Makers*; *The Picturegoer's Who's Who and Encyclopedia of the Screen To-day*; *Who's Who in Hollywood*; *The World Film Encyclopedia*. Nostalgia: *Whatever Became of...* (11th). Pictorial: *Silent Portraits*.
• *Periodicals* – *Photoplay* (Feb. 1918, Sept. 1922, Dec. 1924, May 1927, Jan. 1931); *Motion Picture Classic* (Nov. 1921,

May 1925, Feb. 1928, May 1931); *Motion Picture Magazine* (Aug. 1922, July 1928, Sept. 1931); *Vanity Fair* (Mar. 1927).

ARCHIVAL MATERIALS

• *Clipping File* – CAA: Film appearance (1921–23); newsphotos; article (1924); obituary (1968). CAPH: Obituary (1968). CAPS: Obituary (1968). NYMA (also in Photoplay Collection): Newsphotos; obituary (1968). NYPL: Obituary (1968). • *Other Clipping File* – GBBF, MAH, MIDL, OHCL, PAPL, WICF. • *Correspondence* – NYPL (C. & L. Brown Collection): 1939. • *Legal File* – CAUT (Twentieth Century-Fox Collection): Letter (1926–27); talent agreement (1926–27). CAUW: Talent agreement (1929). • *Photograph/ Still* – AZSU (Jimmy Starr Collection), CAA (also in Hollywood Studio Museum Collection) (also in MGM Collection), CAH, CAPH, CAUB, CAUU, DCG (Quigley Photographic Archives), GBBF, NJFL, NJPT, NYCU (Dramatic Museum Portraits) (Palmer Collection), NYEH, NYPL, OHCL, TNUT (Clarence Brown Collection), TXU, WICF. • *Scrapbook* – NJPT (Yeandle Collection), NYPL (also in Locke Collection), TNUT (Clarence Brown Collection). • *Studio Biography* – NYMA: Photoplay.

VAUGHN, Alberta, Ashland, AL, 1905?–1992.

Beginning her movie career in 1923, Wampas Baby Star Alberta Vaughn appeared primarily in comedies (both shorts and features) but also in dramas and a few serials. Her silent films included *Ain't Love Funny?*, *Sinews of Steel*, *The Broadway Sap* and *Queen of Burlesque*. Among her talkies were *Midnight Morals*, *Love in High Gear* and the John Wayne "B" western *Randy Rides Alone* (1934). Her last films came in 1935.

PUBLISHED SOURCES

• *Books* – General: *Famous Film Folk*. Credits: *Filmarama* (v. II); *Forty Years of Screen Credits*; *Twenty Years of*

Silents. **Encyclopedic Works:** *Filmlexicon degli Autori e delle Opere*; *The Picturegoer's Who's Who and Encyclopedia of the Screen To-day*; *Who's Who in Hollywood*; *The World Film Encyclopedia.*
• *Periodicals* — *Motion Picture Classic* (Dec. 1924, Apr. 1927); *Motion Picture Magazine* (May 1926); *Films in Review* (Feb. 1970 [Wampas Baby Stars]).

ARCHIVAL MATERIALS
• *Clipping File* — CAA: Marriage (1934, 1948); legal problem (1948–49); film appearance (1927); obituary (1992). NYPL: Newsphotos (numerous); marriage/divorce (1934–35); signs with Famous Players-Lasky (1927); drunk driving. • *Other Clipping File* — AZSU (Jimmy Starr Collection), GBBF, NYMA (Photoplay Collection), OHCL, PAPL, WICF. • *Correspondence* — NYMA (Photoplay Collection). • *Legal File* — CAA (Sennett Collection): Contract (1923). CAUW: Talent agreement (1929–30); contract (1929). • *Photograph/Still* — CAA (also in Hollywood Studio Museum Collection), CAUT (Jessen Collection) (Portrait File), DCG (Quigley Photographic Archives), GBBF, NJPT, NYCU (Bulliet Collection), NYEH, NYPL, OHCL, TXU, WICF. • *Publicity Release* — CAA (Mack Sennett Collection): 1923. • *Studio Biography* — CAA (Mack Sennett Collection). NYMA: Photoplay.

VIDOR, Florence (Florence Cobb, later Arto), Houston, TX, 1895–1977.

Luminous Florence Vidor achieved her greatest popularity during what was to prove the last three years of her career. Her films during that period included *Are Parents People?*, *The Grand Duchess and the Waiter*, *The Popular Sin* and *One Woman to Another*. She had been in films since 1916, first attracting notice with *A Tale of Two Cities*. Her one talkie — *Chinatown Nights* — was not successful. She was married to director King Vidor.

PUBLISHED SOURCES
• *Books* — **Bibliography:** *The Idols of Silence.* **General:** *Blue Book of the Screen*; *Classics of the Silent Screen*; *Famous Film Folk*; *Ladies in Distress.* **Credits:** *Filmarama* (v. I and II); *Twenty Years of Silents.* **Encyclopedic Works:** *Film Encyclopedia*; *Filmlexicon degli Autori e delle Opere*; *Halliwell's Filmgoer's Companion*; *The Movie Makers*; *The Picturegoer's Who's Who and Encyclopedia of the Screen To-day*; *Who's Who in Hollywood*; *The World Almanac Who's Who of Film*; *The World Film Encyclopedia.* **Pictorial:** *Silent Portraits.*
• *Periodicals* — The following periodical articles are in addition to those included in the library listings below: *Photoplay* (Aug. 1917, Apr. 1921, Oct. 1922, Aug. 1923, Aug. 1924, Apr. 1926); *Motion Picture Magazine* (Nov. 1918, Mar. 1922, Jan. 1926, Jan. 1927, Aug. 1928); *Motion Picture Classic* (Feb. 1919, Apr. 1921, Sept. 1921, Apr. 1923, July 1926, Nov. 1928); *Films in Review* (Jan. 1970, Oct. 1970).

ARCHIVAL MATERIALS
• *Clipping File* — CAA: Illness (1947); article (1921); home (1927); Paramount contract (1927); legal problem (1928, 1953); draft articles by FV; film appearance (1923–24, 1927); newsphotos; marriage/divorce/children (1926, 1928, 1930, 1932, 1945–46); obituary (1977). CAFI: Obituary (1977). CAUT: Obituary (1977). CAUU: Obituary (1977). NYMA (also in Photoplay Collection): Obituary (1977). Periodical article: *Theatre Magazine* (Nov. 1927). NYPL (also in Locke Collection): Article (1920–21, 1946, 1953, undated); marriage (1921, 1934, 1946); newsphotos (numerous); film review (1920s); tax problem; Paramount stardom (1926); obituary (1977). Periodical article: *Vanity Fair* (July 1930). • *Other Clipping File* — GBBF, MAH, MIDL, OHCL, PAPL, WICF. • *Correspondence* — CAA: Fan letter (undated). • *Filmography* — NYMA. • *Oral History* — NYCO: Mentioned in the following interviews: Schuyler Chapin, King Vidor. • *Photograph/Still* — CAA (also in Hollywood Studio

Museum Collection), CAUU, DCG (Quigley Photographic Archives), GBBF, NJPT, NYAM, NYCU (Underwood Collection), NYCU (Bulliet Collection) (Dramatic Museum Portraits), NYEH, NYMN, NYPL, OHCL, TXU, WICF. • *Publicity Release* — CAA: Paramount. • *Scrapbook* — NJPT (Yeandle Collection), NYPL. • *Studio Biography* — NYPL: Paramount (1929?).

VON ELTZ, Theodore, New Haven, CT, 1894-1964.

Theodore Von Eltz was another of those dependable character men who could play any part well. He began as a leading man about 1920 in such films as the *Red Kimono, The Sea Wolf, Bardelys the Magnificent* and *The Way of the Strong*. With talkies he segued into a lengthy career in supporting roles, among which were *The Big Sleep, Topper, Sergeant York, Saratoga Trunk* and *Magnificent Obsession* (1936 version). His last film was made in 1950.

PUBLISHED SOURCES
• *Books* — General: *More Character People; The Versatiles.* Credits: *Filmarama* (v. I and II); *Forty Years of Screen Credits; Twenty Years of Silents; Who Was Who on Screen.* Encyclopedic Works: *Film Encyclopedia; Filmlexicon degli Autori e delle Opere; The Movie Makers; The Picturegoer's Who's Who and Encyclopedia of the Screen To-day; Who's Who in Hollywood; The World Film Encyclopedia.*

OBSCURE PUBLISHED SOURCES
CAA (Pat O'Malley Collection): *The Cast* (v. 1).

ARCHIVAL MATERIALS
• *Clipping File* — CAA: Marriage (1932); obituary (1964). NYPL: Career (1933, undated). • *Other Clipping File* — GBBF, NYMA (Photoplay Collection), OHCL. • *Legal File* — CAUW: Talent agreement (1924, 1939). • *Photograph/ Still* — CAA (also in Hollywood Studio Museum Collection), CAUU, CNDA,

DCG (Quigley Photographic Archives), NYEH, NYPL, NYSU, OHCL.

WALKER, Charlotte, Galveston, TX, 1878-1958.

Charlotte Walker was already a well-known stage actress and somewhat mature for a leading lady when she came to Hollywood about 1915. Among her films were *Kindling* (her first), *The Trail of the Lonesome Pine, Classmates, The Savage* and *The Lone Wolf.* She continued to make very sporadic appearances in sound films such as *Three Faces East* and *Lightnin'* until 1941.

PUBLISHED SOURCES
• *Books* — Credits: *Filmarama* (v. I and II); *Forty Years of Screen Credits; Twenty Years of Silents; Who Was Who on Screen.* Encyclopedic Works: *Film Encyclopedia; Filmlexicon degli Autori e delle Opere; Halliwell's Filmgoer's Companion; The Picturegoer's Who's Who and Encyclopedia of the Screen To-day; Who Was Who in the Theatre; Who's Who in Hollywood; Who's Who on the Stage* (1908).

ARCHIVAL MATERIALS
• *Clipping File* — CAA: Obituary (1958). NYMA (also in Photoplay Collection): Periodical article: *Classic Images* (Nov. 1988). NYMN: Newsphotos; stage appearance (1914); article (1913); obituary (1958). NYPL (also in Locke Collection) (also in C. & L. Brown Collection): Newsphotos (numerous); nostalgia (1936); career (1954); play review (1920s, 1932); horsewoman (1908); article (1909); obituary (1958). • *Other Clipping File* — MAH, OHSU, PAPL, WICF. • *Correspondence* — NYPL: Letter (C. & L. Brown Collection) (undated); others (1901-02, 1936, undated). • *Photograph/ Still* — CAA (also in Hollywood Studio Museum Collection), CAUT (Jessen Collection), DCG (Quigley Photographic Archives), NYAM, NYCU (Dramatic Museum Portraits), NYMN, NYPL, NYSU, OHCL, WICF. • *Publicity Release* — NYMN. • *Scrapbook* — NYPL (also in R. Locke Collection).

WALKER, Johnnie (sometimes Johnny), New York City, NY, 1894/98–1949.

Johnnie Walker appeared in 1920's *Over the Hill (To the Poorhouse)*, one of the most sentimental of silent films. Most of the time, however, he was battling the villains as a leading action hero of the screen in films such as *Fangs of Justice* and *Snarl of Hate*. His career did not long outlast the advent of sound. The year 1931 was his last before the camera but he directed a film, *Mr. Broadway*, two years later and still later tried his hand at screenwriting.

PUBLISHED SOURCES

• *Books* — General: *Blue Book of the Screen*; *Famous Film Folk*; *The Truth About the Movies*. Credits: *Filmarama* (v. I and II); *Forty Years of Screen Credits*; *Twenty Years of Silents*; *Who Was Who on Screen*. Encyclopedic Works: *Film Encyclopedia*; *Filmlexicon degli Autori e delle Opere*; *Who's Who in Hollywood*.
• *Periodical* — *Classic Images* (Nov. 1981).

ARCHIVAL MATERIALS

• *Clipping File* — CAA: Film appearance (1922); legal problem (1924). NYPL: Legal problem (1925); newsphotos; producer (1931); film review (1920s, 1931); divorce (1925); stage appearance (1929); article (1929, undated); obituary (1949).
• *Other Clipping File* — GBBF, NYMA (Photoplay Collection), PAPL, WICF.
• *Correspondence* — NYPL (C. & L. Brown Collection): Ca. 1938. • *Legal File* — CAUT (Twentieth Century-Fox Collection): Letter, memo (1944); agreement (1944). CAUW: Talent agreement (1930). • *Photograph/Still* — CAA (also in Hollywood Studio Museum Collection), CAH, CNDA, DCG (Quigley Photographic Archives), GBBF, NJPT, NYEH, NYPL, NYSU, PAPL, TXU (A. Davis Collection), WICF. • *Scrapbook* — NYPL.

WALSH, George, New York, NY, 1889–1981.

A rugged and athletic actor, George Walsh was, for a while, a most popular leading man. His screen persona was readily revealed in such titles as *The Yankee Way*, *Bold and Brave*, *Luck and Pluck*, *Never Say Quit* and *American Pluck*. He had a career decline in the late 1920s and ended by playing a few supporting roles in talkies, through 1936. He was married to Seena Owen (q.v.).

PUBLISHED SOURCES

• *Books* — Written by (or ghostwritten for) GW: a chapter of *Breaking into the Movies*. **Bibliography:** *The Idols of Silence*. **General:** *Blue Book of the Screen*; *Eighty Silent Film Stars*; *Famous Film Folk*; *The Truth About the Movies*. **Credits:** *Filmarama* (v. I and II); *Forty Years of Screen Credits*; *Twenty Years of Silents*. **Encyclopedic Works:** *Film Encyclopedia*; *Filmlexicon degli Autori e delle Opere*; *The Picturegoer's Who's Who and Encyclopedia of the Screen To-day*; *Who's Who in Hollywood*. **Pictorial:** *Silent Portraits*.
• *Periodicals* — The following periodical articles are in addition to those included in the library listings below: *Motion Picture Magazine* (Oct. 1918, Jan. 1921, Nov. 1921, Dec. 1923); *Motion Picture Classic* (Aug. 1919, May 1922); *Picture Show* (Nov. 22, 1919); *Photoplay* (Nov. 1924); *Silent Picture* (Summer-Autumn 1971); *Classic Images* (Nov. 1981, June 1990) (filmography); *Films in Review* (Apr. 1982).

ARCHIVAL MATERIALS

• *Clipping File* — CAA: Film appearance (1922, 1920s); marriage (1922); obituary (1981). CAFI: Obituary (1981). CAUT: Newsphotos; obituary (1981). CAUU: Obituary (1981). NYMA (also in Photoplay Collection): Obituary (1981). Periodical articles: *Theatre Magazine* (Apr. 1928); *Classic Images* (Apr. 1984). NYPL: Film review (1920s); newsphotos; article (1926, undated); film appearance (1925); obituary (1981). Periodical articles: *Films in Review* (Mar. 1970); *Silent*

Picture (Autumn 1972). • *Other Clipping File* — GBBF, MAH, MIDL, PAPL, WICF. • *Correspondence* — NYPL (C. & L. Brown Collection): 1938. • *Filmography* — CAA. • *Interview* — CAUU (A. Slide Collection): 1972. • *Photograph/Still* — CAA (also in Hollywood Studio Museum Collection), CAUS, CAUT (Jessen Collection), CAUU (also in A. Slide Collection), DCG (Quigley Photographic Archives), GBBF, NJFL, NJPT, NYB (Underwood Collection), NYEH, NYPL, OHCL, TXU, WICF. • *Scrapbook* — NYAM. • *Studio Biography* — NYMA: Photoplay.

WALTHALL, Henry B(razeal), Shelby City, AL, 1876/78–1936.

Henry B. Walthall's claim to screen greatness was his role as The Little Colonel in *Birth of a Nation*. However, he appeared with distinction in innumerable films before and after, beginning in 1909 as a D.W. Griffith stalwart. Although his slight stature probably limited his possibilities as a romantic leading man, his character roles were legion up to the time of his death.

PUBLISHED SOURCES

• *Books* — **General:** *Blue Book of the Screen*; *Classics of the Silent Screen*; *Famous Film Folk*; *Gentlemen to the Rescue*; *The Idols of Silence*; *Immortals of the Screen*; *Life Stories of the Movie Stars*; *The Truth About the Movies*; *The Versatiles*; *Who's Who in the Film World*. **Credits:** *Filmarama* (v. I and II); *Forty Years of Screen Credits*; *Twenty Years of Silents*; *Who Was Who on the Screen*. **Encyclopedic Works:** *The Dictionary of American Biography* (Supplement 2); *Film Encyclopedia*; *Filmlexicon degli Autori e delle Opere*; *Halliwell's Filmgoer's Companion*; *Hollywood Character Actors*; *The Illustrated Who's Who of the Cinema*; *International Dictionary of Films and Filmmakers* (v. 3); *The Movie Makers*; *The Oxford Companion to Film*; *The Picturegoer's Who's Who and Encyclopedia of the Screen*

To-day; *Who's Who in Hollywood*; *Who's Who of the Horrors and Other Fantasy Films*; *The World Almanac Who's Who of Film*. **Pictorial:** *Silent Portraits*.

• *Periodicals* — The following periodical articles are in addition to those included in the library listings below: *Moving Picture World* (Dec. 12, 1914); *Motography* (June 12, 1915); *Photoplay* (July 1915, Sept. 1917, Dec. 1917, June 1923, June 1934); *Movie Pictorial* (Sept. 1915); *Motion Picture Magazine* (Oct. 1915, Apr. 1916, Dec. 1917, May 1919, Sept. 1921, Jan. 1929); *McClure's Magazine* (Jan. 1916); *Feature Movie* (Jan. 1916); *Motion Picture Classic* (Feb. 1916, June 1916, Nov. 1918, Nov. 1922, Nov. 1925); *Picture Play Magazine* (Aug. 1916); *Silver Screen* (Oct. 1934); *Film Culture* (Spring/Summer 1965); *Griffithiana* (Mar./July 1980); *Classic Images* (Jan. 1989).

ARCHIVAL MATERIALS

• *Clipping File* — CAA: Article (1936); film appearance (1921); obituary (1936). Periodical article: *Films in Review* (Mar. 1952). NYMA (also in Photoplay Collection): Personal data summary; career (1936); article (1916); newsphotos; obituary (1936). NYMN: Newsphotos; article; obituary (1936). Periodical article: *Motion Picture Classic* (undated). NYPL (also in Locke Collection): Career (1934, 1936); newsphotos; article (1916); stage appearance (1918, 1922); film appearance (1910s, 1930s); funeral (1936); film review (1930s); obituary (1936). Periodical articles: *New Movie Magazine* (undated); *Photoplay* (Aug. 1915). NYPL (also in Locke Collection). • *Other Clipping File* — CNDA, GBBF, MAH, MIDL, PAPL, WICF. • *Correspondence* — NYPL: 1915. • *Legal File* — CAUW: Personnel, payroll record (1932–36); talent agreement (1928–29, 1932, 1936); document (1932). • *Photograph/Still* — CAA (also in Hollywood Studio Museum Collection), CAFA, CALM, CAUT (Jessen Collection), CNDA, DCG (Quigley Photographic Archives), NJFL, NYEH, NYPL, NYSU, NJFL, OHCL, TXU, WICF. • *Press Kit* — OHCL. • *Scrap-*

book—NYPL (also in R. Locke Collection), UTBY (DeMille Archives). • *Studio Biography*—CAA: Fox (1934).

WARD, Fannie (sometimes Fanny) (Fannie Buchanan), St. Louis, MO, 1868/72–1952.

Stage and screen star Fannie Ward's acting abilities were somewhat overshadowed by the constant publicity about her supposedly perennially youthful appearance. She was a competent actress who made a hit in melodramas like *The Cheat*, *Our Better Selves*, *The Yellow Ticket*, *The Marriage of Kitty* and *Common Clay*. Her film career was virtually over by the early 1920s.

PUBLISHED SOURCES

• *Books*—**General:** *Behind the Screen*; *Ladies in Distress.* **Credits:** *Filmarama* (v. I and II); *Twenty Years of Silents*; *Who Was Who on Screen.* **Encyclopedic Works:** *Filmlexicon degli Autori e delle Opere*; *Halliwell's Filmgoer's Companion*; *The Oxford Companion to the Theatre*; *The Picturegoer's Who's Who and Encyclopedia of the Screen To-day*; *Who Was Who in the Theatre*; *Who's Who in Hollywood*; *Who's Who on the Stage* (1908). **Pictorial:** *The Revealing Eye.* **Films:** *Fannie Ward.*

• *Periodicals*—The following periodical articles are in addition to those included in the library listings below: *Photoplay* (July 1916, Jan. 1919); *Picture Play Magazine* (July 1916); *Green Book Magazine* (Sept. 1916); *Motion Picture Classic* (Aug. 1917, June 1918); *Motion Picture Magazine* (May 1919, May 1927); *Picture Show* (Nov. 1, 1919); *Graphic* (July 14, 1928); *Harper's Bazaar* (Sept. 1948); *Newsweek* (Feb. 4, 1952); *Time* (Feb. 4, 1952); *Life* (Feb. 11, 1952); *Films in Review* (Dec. 1985).

ARCHIVAL MATERIALS

• *Clipping File*—CAA: Article (1949); illness (1952); estate (1952); obituary (1952). NYMA (also in Photoplay Collection): Newsphotos; obituary (1952). Periodical articles: *Classic Film Collector* (Summer 1976, Summer 1977). NYMN:

Newsphotos (numerous); estate (1952); article (1931, undated); death of daughter (1938); obituary (1952). NYPL (also in Locke Collection): Illness (1952); article (1922, undated); surgery (1923); estate; newsphotos; play review (1909); stage appearance (1920s, 1934, undated); marriage; sale of effects (1954); obituary (1952). • *Other Clipping File*—CASF, GBBF, MAH, MIDL, OHCL, WICF. • *Correspondence*—NYPL: Letter (C. & L. Brown Collection); other (1935). • *Oral History*—NYCO: Mentioned in the following interviews: Alan Parado, Vincent Sherman. • *Photograph/Still*—CAA (also in Hollywood Studio Museum Collection), CAUT (Jessen Collection), DCG (Quigley Photographic Archives), NYB (Bettmann/UPI Collection), NYCU (Bulliet Collection) (Dramatic Museum Portraits), NYMN, NYPL, OHCL, TXU, WICF. • *Play Program*—NYPL. • *Press Kit*—CAG (Motion Picture Industry ca. 1914–1930 Collection). • *Scrapbook*—NYPL (also in R. Locke Collection) (also in Players Collection).

WARNER, H(enry) B(yron) (one source says surname was Lickfold), London, England, 1876–1958.

H.B. Warner was a much-honored leading man and supporting player in 130 films from 1914 to 1956. He appeared in many prestigious films including *The King of Kings* (he played Jesus), *Lost Horizons* (he was nominated for the Best Supporting Actor Academy Award), *Sorrell and Son* (silent and sound versions), *A Tale of Two Cities*, *Mr. Smith Goes to Washington* and *It's a Wonderful Life.* One of his final roles was in the 1956 remake of *The Ten Commandments.*

PUBLISHED SOURCES

• *Books*—**General:** *Eighty Silent Film Stars*; *Hollywood Album 2*; *More Character People*; *The Versatiles.* **Credits:** *British Film Actors' Credits*; *Filmarama* (v. I and II); *Forty Years of Screen Credits*; *Twenty Years of Silents*; *Who Was Who on Screen.* **Encyclopedic**

302   Warwick

Works: *Film Encyclopedia; Filmlexicon degli Autori e delle Opere; Halliwell's Filmgoer's Companion; Hollywood Character Actors; The Illustrated Encyclopedia of Movie Character Actors; The Illustrated Who's Who of the Cinema; The Movie Makers; The Picturegoer's Who's Who and Encyclopedia of the Screen To-day; Who's Who in Hollywood; The World Almanac Who's Who of Film; The World Film Encyclopedia.* **Pictorial:** *Silent Portraits.* **Recordings:** *Hollywood on Record.*

• *Periodicals*—The following periodical articles are in addition to those included in the library listings below: *Green Book Album* (May 1910); *Motion Picture Classic* (Apr. 1919); *Photoplay* (Aug. 1919); *Motion Picture Magazine* (Nov. 1919, Apr. 1929); *Picture Show* (Nov. 15, 1919); *Theatre* (Aug. 1923, Feb. 1928); *American Magazine* (Oct. 1923); *Newsweek* (Jan. 5, 1959).

ARCHIVAL MATERIALS

• *Clipping File*—CAA: Divorce/children (1921, 1933); article (1943, 1987); bankruptcy (1943); film appearance (1951); obituary (1958). NYMA (also in Photoplay Collection): Signs with Liberty (1930); obituary (1958). Periodical article: *Classic Images* (Jan.–Feb. 1987). NYMN: Newsphotos; article (1937); divorce (1933); career. NYPL (also in Locke Collection): Newsphotos; career (1924-25, 1927-29); film review (1920s); film appearance (1920s); stage appearance (1924); article (1925, 1927); obituary (1959). Periodical article: *Picture Play* (Aug. 1929). • *Other Clipping File*—AZSU (Jimmy Starr Collection), CNDA, GBBF, MAH, MIDL, OHCL, PAPL, WICF. • *Correspondence*—CAA (Hedda Hopper Collection): 1948. CAHL: 2 letters (Jack London Collection) (1913); other (1913). NYMA (Photoplay Collection). NYPL: Letter (C. & L. Brown Collection) (1943); others (1907, 1934). • *Filmography*—CAA. • *Legal File*—CAUW: Letter, memo (1928-31, 1941); payroll record (1929); agreement (1929-30); contract (1928-29); talent agreement (1928, 1930). • *Photograph/Still*—CAA (also in Hollywood

Studio Museum Collection), CAFA, CASF, CAUT (Jessen Collection) (Portrait File), CAUU, CNDA, DCG (Quigley Photographic Archives), NYAM, NYB (Underwood Collection), NYCU (Bulliet Collection) (Dramatic Museum Portraits), NYEH, NYMN, NYPL, NYSU, OHCL, TNUT (Clarence Brown Collection), TXU, WICF. • *Press Kit*—OHCL. • *Play Program*—CAHL: 1911. OHSU. • *Publicity Release*—CAA: DeMille (1926). • *Scrapbook*—NYPL (also in Locke Collection) (also in Players Collection), UTBY (DeMille Archives). • *Studio Biography*—CAA: Paramount (1955). NYMA: Photoplay.

WARWICK, Robert (Robert Bien), Sacramento, CA, 1878–1964.

A popular stage actor, Robert Warwick was a matinee idol in silent films (one of the Famous Players) from about 1914 to 1920. Among his films were *Alias Jimmy Valentine, The Mad Lover, The Face in the Moonlight* and *Human Driftwood.* He was back in the theater for most of the '20s, returning to the screen for a long string of character roles beginning in 1931. He was seen onscreen until 1959 and also appeared on television.

PUBLISHED SOURCES

• *Books*—**Filmography:** *Hollywood on the Palisades.* **General:** *Heroes, Heavies and Sagebrush; More Character People; The Versatiles; Who's Who on the Screen.* **Credits:** *Filmarama* (v. I and II); *Forty Years of Film Credits; Twenty Years of Silents; Who Was Who on Screen.* **Encyclopedic Works:** *Film Encyclopedia; Filmlexicon degli Autori e delle Opere; Halliwell's Filmgoer's Companion; Hollywood Character Actors; The Movie Makers; National Cyclopedia of American Biography* (1970); *The Picturegoer's Who's Who and Encyclopedia of the Screen To-day; Who Was Who in the Theatre; Who's Who in Hollywood; The World Almanac Who's Who of Film.* **Pictorial:** *Silent Portraits.*

• *Periodicals*—The following periodical articles are in addition to those included in the library listings below: *Photoplay* (Oct. 1918); *Motion Picture Classic* (May 1919, Jan. 1921).

ARCHIVAL MATERIALS

• *Clipping File*—CAA: Newsphotos; article (1957); obituary (1964). CAUU: Obituary (1964). NYMA (also in Photoplay Collection): Obituary (1964). Periodical article: *Classic Images* (June 1988). NYMN: Newsphotos; career (1920s); obituary (1964). NYPL: Newsphotos; stage appearance (1900s, 1910s); article (1906, 1909, 1912-13, 1915-16, 1919); legal problem (1909); film review (1910s); divorce (1909); signs with World Film (1914); career (1914); sues Famous Players (1920); war service (1919). Periodical articles: *Moving Picture World* (Oct. 10, 1914); *Motion Picture Magazine* (Jan. 1917); *Photoplay* (Mar. 1917, Sept. 1919, Jan. 1920). • *Other Clipping File*—CASP, CNDA, GBBF, MAH, MIDL, WICF. • *Correspondence*—CAHL (Jack London Collection): 1915. NYPL: Letters (C. & L. Brown Collection) (1926, undated); other (1947). • *Legal File*—CAUW: Personnel, pay record (1932-60); talent agreement (1931-32, 1934, 1937-39, 1947); contract (1931-32); document (1931). • *Photograph/Still*—CAA (also in Hollywood Studio Museum Collection) (also in MGM Collection), CASP, DCG (Quigley Photographic Archives), NJFL, NYAM, NYCU (Palmer Collection), NYEH, NYPL, NYSU, OHCL, WICF. • *Scrapbook*—NYPL (also in R. Locke Collection). • *Studio Biography*—CAA: United Artists (1948).

WASHBURN, Bryant (Franklin B. Washburn), Chicago, IL, 1889-1963.

Although Bryant Washburn was frequently seen (often as a villain) in sound serials, melodramas and westerns from the 1930s to 1947, he began as a leading man about 1911. He appeared in the *Skinner* series and in films such as *Rupert of Hentzau*, *Passionate Youth*, *Too Much Johnson* and

Flames. His talkie efforts included the serials *The Clutching Hand*, *Jungle Jim* and *The Adventures of Captain Marvel*.

PUBLISHED SOURCES

• *Books*—**General:** *Blue Book of the Screen*; *Character People*; *Eighty Silent Film Stars*; *Famous Film Folk*; *First One Hundred Noted Men and Women of the Screen*; *Gentlemen to the Rescue*; *Life Stories of the Movie Stars*. **Credits:** *Filmarama* (v. I and II); *Forty Years of Screen Credits*; *Twenty Years of Silents*; *Who Was Who on Screen*. **Encyclopedic Works:** *Film Encyclopedia*; *Filmlexicon degli Autori e delle Opere*; *Halliwell's Filmgoer's Companion*; *Hollywood Character Actors*; *The Movie Makers*; *The Picturegoer's Who's Who and Encyclopedia of the Screen To-day*; *Who's Who in Hollywood*; *The World Film Encyclopedia*. **Pictorial:** *Silent Portraits*. • *Periodicals*—The following periodical articles are in addition to those included in the library listings below: *Photoplay* (Mar. 1915, May 1915, Aug. 1917); *Motion Picture Magazine* (May 1915, Dec. 1915, Sept. 1916, Sept. 1917, July 1918, Nov. 1920, July 1922); *Feature Movie* (May 5, 1915); *Motion Picture Classic* (Sept. 1916, Jan. 1918, Dec. 1918, Aug. 1920, May 1922); *Moving Picture World* (July 21, 1917); *Classic Images* (Feb. 1988).

ARCHIVAL MATERIALS

• *Clipping File*—CAA: Illness (1946); film appearance (1922); obituary (1963). CAUT: Obituary (1963). CAUU: Obituary (1963). NYMA (also in Photoplay Collection): Article (1916); obituary (1963). Periodical articles: *Classic Images* (Dec. 1987–Jan. 1988). NYMN: Newsphotos; obituary (1963). NYPL (also in Locke Collection): Article (1939); divorce; film appearance (1922); newsphotos; obituary (1963). • *Other Clipping File*—GBBF, MAH, MIDL, PAPL, WICF. • *Correspondence*—NYMA (Photoplay Collection). • *Filmography*—CAA (silents only). • *Legal File*—CAUW: Contract (1929, 1933); payroll record (1929). • *Photograph/Still*—CAA, CALM, CAUT (Jessen

304 White, A.; White, P.

Collection), CAUU, DCG (Quigley Photographic Archives), NJFL, NYPL, NYSU, OHCL, TXU, WICF. • *Scrapbook* – NYPL. • *Studio Biography* – CAA: RKO (1940s?). CAUU: RKO (1940s?). NYMA: Photoplay.

WHITE, Alice (Alva White), Paterson, NJ, 1906/08–1983.

"Jazz baby" Alice White's road to stardom, however brief, began behind the scenes as a studio script girl and secretary. Her first film appearance was in *The Sea Tiger* (1927); her first starring film was *Show Girl* the following year. She made approximately 15 silents (most of them as a "second string" Clara Bow) which were followed by about 20 talkies, mostly "B" films. By 1938 her career was essentially over except for some small roles in the '40s.

PUBLISHED SOURCES
• *Books* – **General:** *How I Broke Into the Movies*; *Screen Album*. **Credits:** *Filmarama* (v. II); *Forty Years of Screen Credits*; *Twenty Years of Silents*. **Encyclopedic Works:** *Film Encyclopedia*; *Filmlexicon degli Autori e delle Opere*; *The Picturegoer's Who's Who and Encyclopedia of the Screen To-day*; *Who's Who in Hollywood*; *The World Film Encyclopedia*. **Pictorial:** *Silent Portraits*; *They Had Faces Then*.
• *Periodicals* – The following periodical articles are in addition to those included in the library listings below: *Photoplay* (Apr. 1927, Dec. 1929, Dec. 1930, Jan. 1931, May 1932, Dec. 1932, May 1933); *Motion Picture Classic* (May 1927, Aug. 1929, Mar. 1930, May 1930); *Motion Picture Magazine* (Feb. 1928, June 1929, Mar. 1933, Mar. 1934); *Movie Classic* (Aug. 1933); *Films in Review* (May 1967); *Filmograph* (no. 1–2, 1970); *Cine Revue* (Mar. 17, 1983); *Hollywood Studio Magazine* (May 1983).

ARCHIVAL MATERIALS
• *Caricature* – NYMN. • *Clipping File* – CAA: Legal problem (1933, 1950); marriage/divorce (1933, 1935–39, 1946,

1948, 1955); film appearance (1950); obituary (1983). CAFI: Obituary (1983). CAUU: Obituary (1983). Periodical article: *American Dancer* (1930). NYMA (also in Photoplay Collection): Newsphotos; obituary (1983). NYPL: Newsphotos; article (1932, 1950, 1958); film appearance (1930s); assaulted (1933); marriage (1933, undated); career (1928); comeback (1937); obituary (1983). Periodical article: *Screenland* (July 1930). • *Other Clipping File* – CAUB, GBBF, MAH, MIDL, OHCL, PAPL, WICF, WYU (see Collection). • *Collection* – WYU: Artifacts; clippings (1927–83); personal documents; correspondence (1929–83); filmography; diaries; financial records (1930–83); sound recordings (1937–40); more than 1,000 photographs. • *Correspondence* – NYPL (C. & L. Brown Collection), WYU (see Collection). • *Filmography* – WYU (see Collection). • *Legal File* – CAUW: Talent agreement (1932, 1949); contract (1948); personnel, payroll record (1932–49); document (1926); letter, memo (1929–30); loanout (1927). • *Photograph/Still* – CAA (also in Hollywood Studio Museum Collection), CAH, CAUU, DCG (Quigley Photographic Archives), GBBF, MIDL, NJPT, NYB (Penguin Collection) (Springer Collection) (Underwood Collection), NYCU (Dramatic Museum Portraits), NYEH, NYPL, NYSU, OHCL, PAPL, TXU (A. Davis Collection), WICF, WYU (see Collection).

WHITE, Pearl, Green Ridge, MO, 1889/93–1938.

The most famous of all serial queens had been in films for at least four years when her epochal *The Perils of Pauline* appeared in 1914. Two-reelers like *The Gypsy Flirt*, *The Maid of Niagara* and *Pearl's Mistake* gave way to lengthy chapterplays like *The Exploits of Elaine*, *The Romance of Elaine*, *The House of Hate* and *Pearl of the Army*. The actress also appeared in several features from 1919 to 1922 before she made her final serial, *Plunder*. Her final film, the French-made feature *Terror* (also known as *The Perils of Paris*), was released in 1925.

PUBLISHED SOURCES

• *Books* — **Bibliography:** *The Idols of Silence.* **Encyclopedic Works:** *The Dictionary of American Biography* (Supplement 2); *Film Encyclopedia*; *Filmlexicon degli Autori e delle Opere*; *Halliwell's Filmgoer's Companion*; *The Illustrated Encyclopedia of the World's Great Movie Stars and Their Films*; *The Illustrated Who's Who of the Cinema*; *International Dictionary of Films and Filmmakers* (v. 3); *The International Encyclopedia of Film*; *The Movie Makers*; *Notable American Women, 1607-1950*; *The Oxford Companion to Film*; *The Picturegoer's Who's Who and Encyclopedia of the Screen To-day*; *Quinlan's Illustrated Registry of Film Stars*; *Who's Who in Hollywood*; *Who's Who of the Horrors and Other Fantasy Films*; *The World Almanac Who's Who of Film*; *The World Encyclopedia of the Film*. **General:** *Bound and Gagged*; *Classics of the Silent Screen*; *Continued Next Week*; *Early American Cinema*; *The Great Movie Serials*; *History of the American Cinema* (v. 3); *Hollywood Album*; *Hollywood Hall of Fame*; *Hollywood Heaven*; *Intimate Talks with Movie Stars*; *Life Stories of the Movie Stars*; *Pearl White* (Mitry); *Reel Women*; *The Serials*; *Stunt*; *Those Fabulous Serial Heroines*; *We All Went to Paris*. **Credits:** *Filmarama* (v. I and II); *Twenty Years of Silents*; *Who Was Who on Screen*. **Filmography:** *Hollywood on the Palisades*. **Biography/Autobiography:** *Just Me*; *Pearl White, the Peerless Fearless Girl*. **Pictorial:** *Silent Portraits*. **Factoids:** *Star Stats*.

• *Periodicals* — The following periodical articles are in addition to those included in the library listings below: *Photoplay* (Oct. 1913, Oct. 1914, Jan. 1916, Nov. 1916, Sept. 1917, Jan. 1920, Apr. 1920, Feb. 1921, June 1923, Apr. 1924, Mar. 1925); *Cosmopolitan* (July 1914); *Nash's & Pall Mall* (Mar. 1915); *Motion Picture Magazine* (Feb. 1916, June 1916, Jan.-Feb. 1917, Oct. 1917, May 1918, July 1919, Feb. 1921, Jan.

1923); *Motion Picture Classic* (May-June 1916, Jan. 1917, Oct. 1917, Mar. 1918, Aug. 1918, Jan.-Feb. 1919, Jan. 1922, Feb. 1925); *Theatre* (July 1916); *Pictures and Picturegoer* (Oct. 5, 1918); *Picture Show* (Nov. 8, 1919, Nov. 29, 1919-Mar. 6, 1920); *American Magazine* (Sept. 1921); *Newsweek* (Aug. 15, 1938, July 7, 1947); *Time* (Aug. 15, 1938); *Life* (July 1, 1946); *Films in Review* (May 1951, Dec. 1960, Aug.-Sept. 1967, Feb. 1988); *Cinema* (France) (no. 79, 1963); *8mm Collector* (Spring 1966); *Anthologie du Cinéma* (no. 5, 1969); *Classic Images* (Oct.-Nov. 1983, Dec. 1985).

ARCHIVAL MATERIALS

• *Clipping File* — CAA: Returns from Paris (1937); article (1949, 1964, 1969); last film shown (1970); review of *Pearl White, the Peerless Fearless Girl* (1970); obituary (1938). Periodical articles: *Life* (Apr. 5, 1937); *Collier's* (July 6, 1946); *Films in Review* (Nov.-Dec. 1959); *Classic Film Collector* (Winter 1970). CAUU (also in McCormick Collection): Periodical article: *Classic Film Collector* (Winter 1970). MOSL: Will (1940); obituary (1938). NYMA (also in Photoplay Collection): Personal data summary; article (1916, 1932); illness (1938?); review of *Pearl White, the Peerless Fearless Girl* (1970); serials (1936, 1938, 1966); career (1959); obituary (1938). Periodical articles: *Cue* (June 7, 1947); *Cornell Widow* (Oct. 1949); *Classic Film Collector* (Winter 1970, Summer 1977); *Classic Images* (May-June 1982). NYMN: Newsphotos; article (1933, 1937); estate; funeral (1938); obituary (1938). NYPL: PARTIAL CONTENTS: Film appearance (1922); illness (1938); funeral (1938); estate; article (1937, 1959, undated); biography (1946, undated); musical (1963); nostalgia (1936); marriage/divorce: (1921, 1934); newsphotos; obituary (1938). Periodical article: *American Magazine* (undated). • *Other Clipping File* — CNDA, GBBF, MAH, MIDL, OHCL, PAPL, WICF. • *Filmography* — NYMA (incomplete), NYPL. • *Manuscript* — CAA (Searle Dawley Collection): Notes by SD about directing PW. • *Oral History* — NYCO: Mentioned in the following interviews: Sidney Blackmer, Ross Browne, Carl Foreman, Albert Hackett, Sidney Swensrud. • *Photograph/Still*—CAA (also in Hollywood Studio Museum Collection), CALM, CAUB, CAUT (Portrait File), CAUU, CNDA, NJFL, NYAM, NYB (Bettmann/UPI Collection) (Penguin Collection) (Springer Collection) (Underwood Collection), NYCZ (Ithaca Movie Industry Photograph Collection), NYEH, NYMN, NYPL, NYSU, OHCL, TXU, WICF. • *Scrapbook*—NYPL (also in R. Locke Collection). • *Studio Biography*—CAA: Paramount (1946). CAUU: Paramount (1946).

WILBUR, Crane, Athens, NY, 1889-1973.

After stage training, Crane Wilbur entered films in 1912 and found fame as Pearl White's leading man in the legendary serial *The Perils of Pauline* (1914). During the 1920s, he divided his time between stage and screen before becoming a screenwriter and then a director in the 1930s. He directed over 20 films, wrote 50 screenplays and found time to direct 12 Broadway plays as well. His film appearances included *The Heart of Maryland*, *The Blood of His Fathers* and the serial *The Road o' Strife*.

PUBLISHED SOURCES

• *Books*—**General:** *The "B" Directors.* **Credits:** *Filmarama* (v. I and II); *Forty Years of Screen Credits*; *Twenty Years of Silents*; *Who Was Who on Screen.* **Encyclopedic Works:** *Film Encyclopedia*; *Filmlexicon degli Autori e delle Opere*; *Halliwell's Filmgoer's Companion*; *Who Was Who in the Theatre*; *Who's Who in Hollywood.*
• *Periodicals*—The following periodical articles are in addition to those included in the library listings below: *Moving Picture World* (Nov. 14, 1914); *Photoplay* (Dec. 1914); *Motion Picture Magazine* (Oct. 1915, May 1917, Dec. 1917); *Motion Picture Classic* (Sept. 1916); *Films in Review* (Jan. 1972); *Classic Film Collector* (Winter 1973).

ARCHIVAL MATERIALS

• *Clipping File*—CAA: Directs film (1950, 1957); producer (1941?); divorce (1933); film appearance (1916); obituary (1973). CAFI: Obituary (1973). CAUT: Directs film (1959); obituary (1973). CAUU: Obituary (1973). NYMA (also in Photoplay Collection): Periodical article: *Photo-play World* (Apr. 1918). NYPL (also in Locke Collection): Becomes producer; playwright (1920s, 1930s); legal problem (1933); marriage (1923); film appearance (1920); newsphotos; article (1925-26, 1929-31); career (1925); stage appearance (1920s). Periodical article: *Motion Picture Classic* (Dec. 1919). • *Other Clipping File*—GBBF, MAH, MIDL, OHCL, WICF. • *Collection*—CAUU: Correspondence, scrapbooks, photographs, diaries, scripts (film, TV, radio, Broadway). • *Correspondence*—CAUU (see Collection). NYPL (C. & L. Brown Collection): 1930. • *Legal File*—CAUW: Document (1937, 1944); personnel record (1944); contract (1944); letter (1938, 1944-45, undated); talent agreement (1936, 1950, 1963); rights transfer (1921, 1929, 1936-40, 1944, 1960); acquisition of rights (1944); film rights (1939); transfer of copyright (1922); release (1939); story digest (1936-39, 1944); agreement (1960). • *Oral History*—CAFI. • *Photograph/Still*—CAA, CASF, CAUT (Jessen Collection), CAUU (see Collection), DCG (Quigley Photographic Archives), NJFL, NYB (Bettmann/UPI Collection), NYPL, NYSU, OHCL, WICF. • *Publicity Release*—NYPL: CBS (1941). • *Scrapbook*—CAFI: Stills from several films, 1916-17. CAUU (see Collection). NYPL.

WILLIAMS, Earle, Sacramento, CA, 1880-1927.

Earle Williams was a major Vitagraph leading man from 1908 and he remained a star until nearly the time of his death. His teamings with Clara Kimball Young and Anita Stewart were especially popular. Among the films in which he appeared were *Arsene Lupin*, *The Fortune Hunter*, *The*

Ancient Mariner and *A Gentleman of Quality*.

PUBLISHED SOURCES
• *Books*–General: *The Big V*; *Famous Film Folk*; *First One Hundred Noted Men and Women of the Screen*; *Life Stories of the Movie Stars*. **Credits:** *Filmarama* (v. I and II); *Twenty Years of Silents*; *Who Was Who on Screen*. **Encyclopedic Works:** *Film Encyclopedia*; *Filmlexicon degli Autori e delle Opere*; *Who's Who in Hollywood*. **Pictorial:** *Silent Portraits*.
• *Periodicals*–The following periodical articles are in addition to that included in the library listings below: *Photoplay* (May 1915, Jan. 1916, Nov. 1926); *Motion Picture Magazine* (Nov. 1915, Nov. 1916, Aug. 1917, Oct. 1917, June 1918, Jan. 1919, Mar. 1920, June 1922); *Green Book Magazine* (Aug. 1916); *Motion Picture Classic* (Aug. 1917, May 1919); *Films in Review* (May 1978).

OBSCURE PUBLISHED SOURCES
CAA: *Life of Earle Williams*.

ARCHIVAL MATERIALS
• *Clipping File*–CAA: Film appearance (1922); obituary (1927). NYPL: Death of wife (1931); newsphotos; article (undated); divorce (1922); film review (1920s); obituary (1927). Periodical article: *Photoplay* (Jan. 1918). • *Other Clipping File*–AZSU (Jimmy Starr Collection), CASP, GBBF, NYMA (Photoplay Collection), PAPL, WICF.
• *Photograph/Still*–CAA (also in Hollywood Studio Museum Collection), CAUT (Jessen Collection), CAUU, DCG (Quigley Photographic Archives), NYPL, NYSU, OHCL, TXU, WICF.
• *Press Kit*–OHCL. • *Scrapbook*–NYPL (also in R. Locke Collection).

WILLIAMS, Kathlyn, Butte, MT, 1888?–1960 (some sources suggest she may have been considerably older).
Kathlyn Williams made her mark as the titular heroine of one of the earliest serials, *The Adventures of Kathlyn* (1913). She had been in films with Selig

since about 1908 as "The Selig Girl" and remained a popular leading actress until the early 1920s in films such as *The Spoilers*, *Just a Wife*, *Forbidden Fruit* and *The Whispering Chorus*. She played supporting roles during the remainder of the 1920s and appeared in a few talkie roles, the last of which was in 1947.

PUBLISHED SOURCES
• *Books*–General: *Blue Book of the Screen*; *The Idols of Silence*; *Ladies in Distress*; *Life Stories of the Movie Stars*; *Sweethearts of the Sage*; *Those Fabulous Serial Heroines*. **Credits:** *Filmarama* (v. I and II); *Forty Years of Screen Credits*; *Twenty Years of Silents*; *Who Was Who on Screen*. **Encyclopedic Works:** *Film Encyclopedia*; *Filmlexicon degli Autori e delle Opere*; *Halliwell's Filmgoer's Companion*; *The Illustrated Who's Who of the Cinema*; *The Picturegoer's Who's Who and Encyclopedia of the Screen To-day*; *Who's Who in Hollywood*. **Pictorial:** *Silent Portraits*.
• *Periodicals*–*Blue Book Magazine* (May 1914); *Sunset* (June 1914); *Feature Movie* (June 10, 1915); *Movie Pictorial* (Sept. 1915); *Motion Picture Classic* (Mar. 1916, Jan. 1917, Nov. 1921, May 1923); *Motion Picture Magazine* (July 1916, Nov. 1916, Feb. 1920, Aug. 1921); *Photoplay* (Jan. 1917, Nov. 1917, Sept. 1924); *8mm Collector* (Winter 1964); *Films in Review* (Mar. 1974, Feb. 1984).

ARCHIVAL MATERIALS
• *Clipping File*–CAA: Injury (1949); legal problem (1950–51); article (1957); estate (1960); obituary (1960). NYMA (also in Photoplay Collection): Obituary (1960). NYPL (also in Locke Collection): Injury; film review (1923); newsphotos; obituary (1960). • *Other Clipping File*–AZSU (Jimmy Starr Collection), GBBF, MAH, MIDL, OHCL, PAPL, WICF.
• *Legal File*–CAUW: Contract (1929–30). • *Photograph/Still*–CAA (also in Hollywood Studio Museum Collection), CALM, CAUT (Jessen Collection), DCG (Quigley Photographic Archives), IAU (Junkin Collection), NYEH, NYPL, NYSU, OHCL, TXU,

WICF. • *Scrapbook* — NYPL (R. Locke Collection). • *Studio Biography* — NYMA: Photoplay.

WILSON, Ben, Clinton, IA, 1876-1930.

Said to have been in over 250 films, Ben Wilson was the hero of numerous serials, most frequently teaming with serial queen Neva Gerber. Among these chapterplays from 1912 to the late 1920s were *The Mysterious Pearl*, *Trail of the Octopus*, *Officer 444*, *The Power God* and *What Happened to Mary*, considered to be the very first serial. He was also seen in action features and westerns, his last made in 1930.

PUBLISHED SOURCES
• *Books* — General: *Gentlemen to the Rescue*; *Who's Who on the Screen*. Credits: *Filmarama* (v. I and II); *Twenty Years of Silents*; *Who Was Who on Screen*. Encyclopedic Works: *Filmlexicon degli Autori e delle Opere*; *Who's Who in Hollywood*.
• *Periodicals* — The following periodical articles are in addition to those included in the library listings below: *Motion Picture Magazine* (Apr. 1915); *Classic Images* (Dec. 1987, June 1990).

ARCHIVAL MATERIALS
• *Clipping File* — NYMA (also in Photoplay Collection): Periodical article: *Classic Film/Video Images* (Nov. 1981). NYPL: Film review (1910s); newsphotos; career (1915); accident (1917); builds home (1915); stage appearance (1900s); article (1913–14). Periodical articles: *Moving Picture Weekly* (undated); *Moving Picture World* (Apr. 18, 1914); *Motography* (Aug. 15, 1914). • *Other Clipping File* — WICF. • *Filmography* — CAA. • *Photograph/Still* — CAA (Hollywood Studio Museum Collection), CAUT (Jessen Collection), NYPL, NYSU, WICF.

WILSON, Lois, Pittsburgh, PA, 1896/98-1988.

Lois Wilson appeared in many prestigious films during her 100+ film career, most notably *The Covered Wagon*, but also *Miss Lulu Bett*, *What Every Woman Knows*, *Bella Donna*, *The Great Gatsby* and *Monsieur Beaucaire*. She continued into sound films, eventually settling into supporting roles until about 1941. There was one final film in 1949. She also could be seen in television soap operas and on the stage.

PUBLISHED SOURCES
• *Books* — Written by (or ghostwritten for) LW: a chapter of *Breaking into the Movies*. Bibliography: *The Idols of Silence*. General: *Blue Book of the Screen*; *Famous Film Folk*; *How I Broke into the Movies*; *Speaking of Silents*; *Sweethearts of the Sage*; *The Truth About the Movies*. Credits: *Filmarama* (v. I and II); *Forty Years of Screen Credits*; *Twenty Years of Silents*. Encyclopedic Works: *The Biographical Encyclopaedia and Who's Who of the American Theatre*; *Film Encyclopedia*; *Filmlexicon degli Autori e delle Opere*; *Halliwell's Filmgoer's Companion*; *The Movie Makers*; *Notable Names in the American Theatre*; *The Picturegoer's Who's Who and Encyclopedia of the Screen To-day*; *Who's Who in Hollywood*; *The World Film Encyclopedia*. Nostalgia: *Whatever Became of...* (5th). Pictorial: *Silent Portraits*; *They Had Faces Then*.
• *Periodicals* — The following periodical articles are in addition to those included in the library listings below: *Moving Picture Weekly* (Dec. 4, 1915, Apr. 15, 1916); *Motion Picture Magazine* (May 1917, Aug. 1919, Jan. 1921, Dec. 1921, Apr. 1925, July 1926, Sept. 1931); *Photoplay* (Apr. 1921, July 1923, Dec. 1923, Mar. 1924, May 1924, Nov. 1924, Mar. 1927, Feb. 1938, Feb. 1940); *Motion Picture Classic* (Sept. 1921, Sept. 1922, May 1925, Apr. 1929); *Films in Review* (Mar. 1965, Feb. 1970 [Wampas Baby Stars], Dec. 1971, Jan. 1973, Mar.–Apr. 1973, Oct. 1973, Dec. 1973, May 1974); *Filmograph* (no. 1-4, 1970, no. 3-4, 1973); *Classic Film Collector* (Winter 1971, Summer 1973); *Classic Images* (Nov.

1981, Apr. 1988); *American Classic Screen* (Jan.-Feb. 1984).

ARCHIVAL MATERIALS
• *Caricature* — NYMN. • *Clipping File* — CAA: Newsphotos; film appearance (1922); nostalgia (1969, 1979, 1981); stage appearance (1934, 1946, 1973); honor (1975); obituary (1988). Periodical articles: *Classic Film Collector* (Winter 1970); *Films in Review* (Mar. 1980). CAFI: Obituary (1988). NYMA (also in Photoplay Collection): Article (1937, 1973); obituary (1988). Periodical article: *Classic Film Collector* (Winter 1970). NYPL: Stage appearance; newsphotos (numerous); film appearance (1930s); illness (1943); article (1926-27, 1939, 1944, 1964, 1973, undated); TV appearance (1951); Broadway debut (1937); *Great Gatsby* (film) (1973); obituary (1988). Periodical articles: *Classic Film Collector* (Winter 1970); *Films in Review* (May-July 1973). • *Other Clipping File* — CAUB, CNDA, GBBF, MAH, MIDL, OHCL, OHKS (see Collection), PAPL, PAPT, WICF. • *Collection* — OHKS: Scrapbooks; correspondence (1942-75); clippings; stills. Correspondents include Agnes DeMille, Douglas Fairbanks, Jr., Lillian Gish, Harold Lloyd and Gloria Swanson. • *Correspondence* — CAA (Hedda Hopper Collection): 1951-53. NYPL: Letters (C. & L. Brown Collection) (ca. 1939, undated); other (1952). OHKS (see Collection). • *Filmography* — CAA. • *Interview* — CAUU (R. Lamparski Collection) (A. Slide Collection): 1970 (Slide). GBBF (Hollywood Collection): Transcript of an interview for *Hollywood* (TV series). NYAM. • *Legal File* — CAUW: Contract (1928-29); letter, memo (1928-30); personnel, payroll record (1929-30, 1932-48); release (1930); agreement (1928); talent agreement (1928-30, 1933, 1948). • *Photograph/Still* — CAA (also in Hollywood Studio Museum Collection) (also in MGM Collection), CALM, CAUT (Jessen Collection), CNDA, DCG (Quigley Photographic Archives), GBBF, NJFL, NJPT, NYAM, NYCU (Dramatic Museum Portraits) (Palmer Collection), NYEH, NYPL, NYSU, OHCL, OHKS (see Collection), TXU, WICF. • *Privately Printed Material* — CAA: *The Silent Stars Speak.* AMPAS, 1979. • *Scrapbook* — NJPT (Yeandle Collection), OHKS (see Collection). • *Studio Biography* — CAA: Fox (1935). NYMA: Photoplay.

WINDSOR, Claire (Clara Viola [Ola] Cronk), Cawker City, KS, 1897/98-1972.

By the time Claire Windsor was named a Wampas Baby Star in 1922 she had already appeared in several films directed by pioneer woman director Lois Weber. A tall and striking blonde, she became a star in a series of romantic melodramas such as *Nellie the Beautiful Cloak Model* and *Souls for Sables.* She made few talkies and her final appearance, after many years out of the limelight, was in a 1945 "B" film. She was married to Bert Lytell (q.v.).

PUBLISHED SOURCES
• *Books* — **General:** *Blue Book of the Screen*; *Famous Film Folk*; *The Truth About the Movies*; *You Must Remember This.* **Credits:** *Filmarama* (v. I and II); *Forty Years of Screen Credits*; *Twenty Years of Silents*; *Who Was Who on Screen.* **Encyclopedic Works:** *Film Encyclopedia*; *Filmlexicon degli Autori e delle Opere*; *Halliwell's Filmgoer's Companion*; *The Movie Makers*; *The Picturegoer's Who's Who and Encyclopedia of the Screen To-day*; *Who's Who in Hollywood*; *The World Film Encyclopedia.* **Nostalgia:** *Whatever Became of...* (2nd). **Pictorial:** *Silent Portraits.* **Factoids:** *Star Stats.*
• *Periodicals* — The following periodical articles are in addition to that included in the library listings below: *Motion Picture Classic* (Apr. 1921, Apr. 1922); *Motion Picture Magazine* (Sept. 1921); *Photoplay* (Feb. 1922, June 1922, Nov. 1924); *Cinema Art* (Dec. 1926); *Movie Classic* (June 1932); *Films in Review* (Feb. 1970 [Wampas Baby Stars], Apr. 1972); *Classic Film Collector*

(Winter 1972); *Filmograph* (no. 3-2, 1972).

ARCHIVAL MATERIALS

• *Caricature* – NYMN. • *Clipping File* – CAA: Disappearance (1921); engagement/marriage/divorce/children (1925, 1927, 1929); freelances (1927); alienation of affection suit (1932-33); stage appearance (1928, 1932); artist (1928); article by CW (1929); accident (1930). CAUT: Obituary (1972). CAUU: Obituary (1972). NYMA (also in Photoplay Collection): Obituary (1972). Periodical article: *Classic Film/Video Images* (Nov. 1980). NYPL (also in Locke Collection): Newsphotos (numerous); stage appearance (1933, undated); legal problem (1933); alienation of affection suit (1932-34); film appearance (1926, 1933); article (1935); obituary (1972). • *Other Clipping File* – CNDA, GBBF, MAH, MIDL, OHCL, PAPL, WICF. • *Collection* – CAUU: Materials cover the years 1921-1972, including photographs and stills (1921-65); correspondence (much with Bert Lytell in the mid-1920s), scrapbooks (including stills from films directed by Lois Weber), film periodicals, taped interview (1968). • *Correspondence* – CAUU (see Collection). NYPL (C. & L. Brown Collection): 1942. • *Interview* – CAUU (see Collection) (R. Lamparski Collection). • *Photograph/Still* – CAA (also in Hollywood Studio Museum Collection) (also in MGM Collection), CAH, CAPH, CASU, CAUT (Jessen Collection), CAUU (also in Collection), DCG (Quigley Photographic Archives), GBBF, NJPT, NYB (Bettmann/UPI Collection) (Underwood Collection), NYCU (Dramatic Museum Portraits), NYEH, NYPL, NYSU, OHCL, PAPL, TNUT (Clarence Brown Collection), TXU (A. Davis Collection), WICF. • *Scrapbook* – CAUU (see Collection), NYPL, TNUT (Clarence Brown Collection). • *Studio Biography* – NYMA: Photoplay.

WINTON, Jane, New York City, NY, 1905/06-1959.

"The Green-Eyed Goddess of Holly-wood" is what Jane Winton was called – at least by the PR people of her studio. Starting in 1926, she worked her way up to "goddess" status by small roles in big films like *Sunrise, Don Juan* and *The Beloved Rogue* and bigger roles in "B" films such as *Bare Knees, Honeymoon Flats* and *Gay Old Bird*. She appeared in small parts in a few talkies, including *Hell's Angels* (1930), but was not seen onscreen after 1934's *Hired Wife*.

PUBLISHED SOURCES

• *Books* – Wrote novels *Park Avenue Doctor* (1951) and *Passion Is the Gate* (or *Gale*). **Credits:** *Filmarama* (v. II); *Forty Years of Screen Credits; Twenty Years of Silents.* **Encyclopedic Works:** *The Picturegoer's Who's Who and Encyclopedia of the Screen To-day; Who's Who in Hollywood; The World Film Encyclopedia.* **Pictorial:** *Silent Portraits.*
• *Periodicals* – The following periodical articles are in addition to that included in the library listings below: *Motion Picture Classic* (June 1926); *Motion Picture Magazine* (Aug. 1928, Mar. 1929).

ARCHIVAL MATERIALS

• *Clipping File* – CAA: Divorce (1934); obituary (1959). NYPL: Newsphotos; stage appearance (1933-34); article (1928, 1931, 1954); film appearance (1920s); marriage/divorce (1935, undated); obituary (1959). Periodical article: *Picture Play* (June 1930). • *Other Clipping File* – GBBF, MIDL, NYMA (Photoplay Collection), OHCL, PAPL. • *Correspondence* – NYPL (C. and L. Brown Collection). • *Legal File* – CAUW: Talent agreement (1926-27); contract (1929); document (1927). • *Photograph/Still* – CAA (also in Hollywood Studio Museum Collection), DCG (Quigley Photographic Archives), GBBF, NJPT, NYAM, NYEH, NYPL, NYSU, OHCL, TXU (A. Davis Collection), WICF.

WOLHEIM, Louis, New York, NY, 1880-1931.

Louis Wolheim's battered-looking

face was made for villainy and he was a memorable bad man in such films as *Doctor Jekyll and Mr. Hyde*, *America*, *Orphans of the Storm* and *The House of Hate*. He was also a distinguished stage actor who originated the role of *The Hairy Ape*. He could play sympathetic roles as well, the most famous of which was his portrayal of the gruff German sergeant in *All Quiet on the Western Front* (1930).

PUBLISHED SOURCES

• *Books*—General: *Actorviews*; *Character People*; *The Civil War on the Screen and Other Essays*. Credits: *Filmarama* (v. I and II); *Forty Years of Screen Credits*; *Twenty Years of Silents*; *Who Was Who on Screen*. Encyclopedic Works: *Film Encyclopedia*; *Filmlexicon degli Autori e delle Opere*; *Halliwell's Filmgoer's Companion*; *The Movie Makers*; *The Oxford Companion to the Theatre*; *Who's Who in Hollywood*; *The World Almanac Who's Who of Film*; *The World Film Encyclopedia*. Pictorial: *The Revealing Eye*; *Silent Portraits*.

• *Periodicals*—The following periodical articles are in addition to that included in the library listings below: *Theatre* (Aug. 1922, Sept. 1927); *Motion Picture Classic* (Dec. 1927, May 1930, May 1931); *Motion Picture Magazine* (Jan. 1931, June 1933); *Photoplay* (Jan. 1931, May 1931); *Good Housekeeping* (Aug. 1932); *Films in Review* (Mar. 1972, May 1973).

ARCHIVAL MATERIALS

• *Clipping File*—CAA: Article (1930s). Periodical article: *Shadowland* (June 1922). NYMA (also in Photoplay Collection): Personal data summary. NYMN: Career (1931?); newsphotos; obituary (1931). NYPL (also in Locke Collection): Newsphotos; play review (1924); surgery (1931); article (1922); obituary (1931). • *Other Clipping File*—GBBF, MAH, MIDL, WICF. • *Filmography*—CAA. • *Oral History*—NYCO: Mentioned in the following interviews: Lew Ayres, Sol Jacobson, Nita Naldi. • *Photograph/Still*—CAA (also in Hollywood Studio Museum Collection), CAFA, CALM,

MABU (Douglas Fairbanks Jr. Collection), NYAM, NYB (Bettmann/UPI Collection) (Underwood Collection), NYCU (Dramatic Museum Portraits) (Palmer Collection), NYPL, NYSU, OHCL, TXU, WICF. • *Press Kit*—OHCL.

WONG, Anna May (Wong Liu Tsong), Los Angeles, CA, 1902/07–1961.

In films since about 1919, Anna May Wong came to prominence with her supporting role in 1924's *The Thief of Bagdad*. Her other 1920s roles were largely undistinguished (e.g., *A Trip to Chinatown*, *Mr. Wu*, *Streets of Shanghai* and *The Devil Dancer*). She went to Europe later in the decade where she appeared in numerous British films and in what is thought to be the first European talkie. In later American roles she was generally cast as a villainess, and except for a few small roles in the 1950s and '60s, her film career was virtually over by 1942.

PUBLISHED SOURCES

• *Books*—General: *Hollywood Album*; *Hollywood Players: The Thirties*; *Immortals of the Screen*. Credits: *Filmarama* (v. I and II); *Forty Years of Screen Credits*; *Twenty Years of Silents*; *Who Was Who on Screen*. Encyclopedic Works: *Film Encyclopedia*; *Filmlexicon degli Autori e delle Opere*; *Halliwell's Filmgoer's Companion*; *The Illustrated Who's Who of the Cinema*; *International Dictionary of Films and Filmmakers* (v. 3); *The Movie Makers*; *Notable American Women: The Modern Period*; *The Picturegoer's Who's Who and Encyclopedia of the Screen To-day*; *Quinlan's Illustrated Registry of Film Stars*; *Who Was Who in the Theatre*; *Who's Who in Hollywood*; *The World Almanac Who's Who of Film*; *The World Film Encyclopedia*. Pictorial: *The Image Makers*; *Leading Ladies*; *Silent Portraits*; *They Had Faces Then*.

• *Periodicals*—The following periodical articles are in addition to those included in the library listings below:

Photoplay (June 1923, June 1924); *Motion Picture Magazine* (Mar. 1928, Oct. 1931); *The Era* (Feb. 27, 1929); *Movie Classic* (Nov. 1931); *Theatre World* (July 1944); *Time* (Feb. 10, 1961); *Newsweek* (Feb. 13, 1961); *Films in Review* (Dec. 1968-Jan. 1969, Mar. 1987, Nov. 1987, Jan.-Feb. 1988, Apr. 1988); *Gidra* (Jan. 1974); *Classic Images* (Apr. 1985); *China Doll* (an entire periodical devoted to AMW) (1991-).

ARCHIVAL MATERIALS

• *Clipping File* — CAA: Film appearance (1928, 1948, 1960); returns home (1931); article (1931, 1987); stage appearance (1943); TV appearance (1958); obituary (1961). Article: *Look* (Mar. 1, 1938); *Films and Filming* (June 1971). NYMA: Newsphotos; obituary (1961). NYMN: Poem by AMW; newsphotos (numerous); extortion threat (1937); stage appearance (1943); article (undated); visits China (1937); film appearance (1937); obituary (1961). NYPL: Film appearance (1934, 1937, 1957, 1959, 1987); extortion threat (1937); article (1932, 1937, 1939, 1960, undated); visits China (1930s); TV appearance (1951); comeback (1960); newsphotos; biography; stage appearance (1932, 1937, 1939, 1943, 1956); film review (1930s, 1940s); radio appearance; views about Hawaii (1936); obituary (1961). • *Other Clipping File* — AZSU (Jimmy Starr Collection), CAUB, GBBF, MAH, MIDL, OHCL, PAPL, WICF. • *Correspondence* — MABU (Robert Benchley Collection): 1932. NYPL: Letter (C. & L. Brown Collection) (1941); other (1960). • *Filmography* — CAA, NYMA. • *Legal File* — CAUW: Letter, memo (1937-38); contract summary (1937-38); talent agreement (1927, 1938); agreement (1938). • *Oral History* — NYCO: Mentioned in: Carl Van Vechten interview. • *Photograph/Still* — CAA (also in Hollywood Studio Museum Collection), CAFA, CASF, CAUB, CAUS, CAUU, CNDA, DCG (Quigley Photographic Archives), NYAM, NYB (Bettmann/UPI Collection) (Springer Collection) (Underwood Collection), NYCU (Dramatic Museum Portraits), NYEH, NYMN (also in Van Vechten Collection), NYPL, NYSU, OHCL, TXU, WICF. • *Play Program* — NYPL: 1920s, 1930s. • *Publicity Release* — AZSU (Jimmy Starr Collection). CAA: Paramount (1931, 1938). • *Scrapbook* — NYPL. • *Studio Biography* — CAA: Universal (1960).

YOUNG, Clara Kimball, Chicago, IL, 1890/91-1960.

One of Vitagraph's biggest stars, Clara Kimball Young had her own production company and appeared in popular films such as *My Official Wife*, *House of Glass*, *The Easiest Way*, *Eyes of Youth*, *The Deep Purple* and *The Common Law*. Among her frequent costars was Earle Williams (q.v.). In 1916 she was was named the foremost star in films but her decline in the 1920s was steep and she left the screen in 1925. When she returned in 1930 it was in bits and supporting roles in "B" melodramas, serials and even Three Stooges comedy shorts. Her final film came in 1941.

PUBLISHED SOURCES

• *Books* — **Bibliography:** *The Idols of Silence*. **General:** *The Big V*; *Blue Book of the Screen*; *Classics of the Silent Screen*; *Famous Film Folk*; *First One Hundred Noted Men and Women of the Screen*; *Intimate Talks with Movie Stars*; *Ladies in Distress*; *Life Stories of the Movie Stars*. **Credits:** *Filmarama* (v. I and II); *Forty Years of Screen Credits*; *Twenty Years of Silents*; *Who Was Who on Screen*. **Encyclopedic Works:** *Film Encyclopedia*; *Filmlexicon degli Autori e delle Opere*; *Halliwell's Filmgoer's Companion*; *The Illustrated Who's Who of the Cinema*; *The Movie Makers*; *The Oxford Companion to Film*; *The Picturegoer's Who's Who and Encyclopedia of the Screen To-day*; *Who's Who in Hollywood*; *Women Who Make Movies*; *The World Almanac Who's Who of Film*; *The World Film Encyclopedia*. **Filmography:** *Hollywood on the Palisades*. **Pictorial:** *Clara Kimball Young*; *Silent Portraits*.

• *Periodicals* — The following periodical articles are in addition to those included in the library listings below: *Moving Picture World* (Oct. 3, 1914, July 21, 1917); *Photoplay* (Oct. 1914, May 1915, Sept. 1917, Mar. 1920, Jan. 1931); *Motion Picture Classic* (June 1917, Dec. 1919, Mar. 1923); *Theatre* (Feb. 1918, Nov. 1918); *Motion Picture Magazine* (May 1918, Mar. 1919, Jan. 1921, Sept. 1935); *Filmplay Journal* (Jan. 1919, Apr. 1922); *Newsweek* (Oct. 24, 1960).

ARCHIVAL MATERIALS

• *Clipping File* — CAA: Production company (1917); comeback (1933, 1935); sale of effects (1932); TV appearance (1956); obituary (1960). Periodical article: *Films in Review* (Aug.-Oct. 1961). NYMA (also in Photoplay Collection): Article (1914, 1916-17); newsphotos; film appearance (1910s); builds New York studio (1916); legal problem (1916?); obituary (1960). Periodical articles: *Photo-play World* (Mar. 1918, Dec. 1918); *Classic Images* (Nov. 1988-Jan. 1989). NYMN: Article (1938); obituary (1960). NYPL (also in Locke Collection): Newsphotos; film review (1920s); comeback (1934); destitute (1933); marriage (1932); article (undated); film synopses; works as extra (1935); robbery; illness (1924); nostalgia (1936?); TV appearance (1950s?); obituary (1960). Periodical article: *Movie Weekly* (undated). • *Other Clipping File* — AZSU (Jimmy Starr Collection), CNDA, GBBF, MAH, MIDL, OHCL, PAPL, WICF. • *Correspondence* — NYPL (C. & L. Brown Collection): 1927. • *Filmography* — CAA (incomplete), NYMA, NYPL (incomplete). • *Oral History* — NYCO: Mentioned in: David Selznick interview. • *Photograph/Still* — CAA (also in Hollywood Studio Museum Collection) (also in MGM Collection), CALM, CAUS, CAUT (Jessen Collection) (Portrait File), CAUU, DCG (Quigley Photographic Archives), NJFL, NYB (Bettmann/UPI Collection), NYEH, NYMN, NYPL, NYSU, OHCL, TXSM, TXU, WICF. • *Program* — OHSU. • *Press Kit* — OHCL. • *Scrapbook* — NYPL (also in R. Locke Collection). • *Studio Biography* — NYMA: Photoplay.

Appendix: Directory of Collections Relating to Silent Film

It is likely that hours of availability, contact persons and other information may vary from time to time. Consult the particular institution for up-to-date information.

UNITED STATES

ARIZONA

Arizona State University
Special Collections, Hayden Library
Tempe, AZ 85287-0302
(602) 965-3950
 Contact: Marilyn Wurzburger. *Hours*: Monday–Friday. *Access*: Paged by staff. Materials available for copying (fee charged). *Restrictions*: Materials must remain in Special Collections.

CALIFORNIA

Academy of Motion Picture Arts and Sciences
Margaret Herrick Library
Center for Motion Picture Study
333 S. La Cienega Boulevard
Beverly Hills, CA 90211
(310) 247-3020; FAX: (310) 657-5193
 Hours: Monday–Tuesday, Thursday–Friday, 10:00–6:00. *Contact*: Linda Mehr, Director; Samuel A. Gill, Archivist (Special Collections/Manuscripts); Robert B. Cushman, Photograph Curator (Special Collections/Photographs). *Access*: Books on open shelves; other

materials including periodicals, pamphlets, scripts, photographs and files paged by staff. Mail and telephone reference service also available, the latter from 9:00 to 3:00 on the open days. *Restrictions*: Special collection materials are available by prior appointment to qualified students, scholars and researchers. No materials circulate.

Ackerman Fantasy Archives
2495 Glendower Avenue
Hollywood, CA 90027
(213) 666-6326
 Hours: Any day by appointment. *Contact*: Forrest Ackerman. *Access*: File drawers, wingmasters. *Restrictions*: On-site use only.

American Film Institute
Louis B. Mayer Library
2021 N. Western Avenue
Los Angeles, CA 90027
(213) 856-7660
 Hours: Monday–Thursday, 1:00–5:00. *Access*: Books on open shelves. Archival materials paged by staff. *Restrictions*: In-house use only.

315

California State Library
California Section
Library-Courts Building
914 Capitol Mall, P.O. Box 942837
Sacramento, CA 94237-0001
(916) 654-0176; FAX: (916) 654-0241
Hours: Monday–Friday, 8:00–5:00.
Contact: Reference Librarian. *Access*:
Paging by staff. *Restrictions*: Non-circulating; limited copying.

California State University, Fullerton
University Library, Special Collections
800 N. State College Boulevard
Fullerton, CA 92634
(714) 773-3444 or (714) 773-3445
Contact: Sharon Perry or Jane Olsen.
Relevant holdings: Contains the Fred
Guiol Script Collection with scripts
(some in various versions) from the 1920s
to 1957 and associated production
reports. Among the performers represented are C. Chase and G. Tryon.

Hollywood Studio Museum
2100 N. Highland Avenue
Los Angeles, CA 90068
(213) 874-2276
Hours: By appointment only; very limited use. *Access*: Paged by staff.

Huntington Library
1151 Oxford Road
San Marino, CA 91108
(818) 405-2205 (Manuscripts); (818)
405-2181 (Prints and Ephemera Dept.);
FAX: (818) 405-0225
Hours: (Manuscripts) Monday–Saturday, 8:30–5:00; (Theatre Collection)
Tuesday, Thursday–Friday, by appointment. *Contact*: Virginia Renner, Reader
Services Librarian (contact in advance.)
Sara Hodson is Curator of Literary
Manucripts; Cathy Cherbosque is Curator of the Theatre collection. *Access*:
Paged by staff. *Restrictions*: Open for
qualified researchers whose topics are directly related to materials in the collections.

Institute of the American Musical, Inc.
121 North Detroit Street
Los Angeles, CA 90036
(213) 934-1221

Contact: Miles Kreuger. *Relevant
holdings*: Contains the world's largest archives on the history of musical theater
and film, including sheet music, over
100,000 recordings dating back to the
1890s, photographs, biographies, files,
scripts, etc. Most probably contains information about some of the performers
in this *Guide* who made musical films.

Los Angeles Public Library
Frances Howard Goldwyn – Hollywood
Regional Branch
1623 Ivar Avenue
Los Angeles, CA 90028
(213) 467-1821; FAX: (213) 467-5707
Relevant holdings: Contains 10,000
stills, 2,000 motion picture and television
scripts, dance and theater programs, motion picture production files, lobby cards
and posters.

*Natural History Museum of Los Angeles
County*
900 Exposition Boulevard
Los Angeles, CA 90007
(213) 744-3388 (Research Library); (213)
744-3359 (Seaver); FAX: (213) 746-2999
Note: Two departments have materials:
1. Research Library
2. Seaver Center for Western History
Research
Contact: Donald W. McNamee (Research Library); Janet Evander (Seaver).
Hours: Monday–Friday, 10:00–5:00 (Research Library); Tuesday, Thursday,
1:00–4:00 (Seaver). *Access*: Paging by
staff; photocopies may be made at librarian's discretion.

Occidental College
Special Collections Department
Library
1600 Campus Road
Los Angeles, CA 90041
(213) 259-2852; FAX: (213) 341-4991
Hours: Monday–Friday, 1:00–4:30.
Contact: Michael C. Sutherland. *Access*:
Closed stacks; access through librarian.

Palm Springs Historical Society
221 S. Palm Canyon Drive
Palm Springs, CA 92262
or

P. O. Box 1498
Palm Springs, CA 92263
(619) 323-8297
Hours: By appointment only. Wednesday and Sunday, 9:00–Noon. *Contact*: Sally McManus, Director/Curator. *Access*: $25.00 per hour fee; additional fee for copying photographs. Celebrity photographs arranged by year, category and accession number. Paged by director. *Restrictions*: Director must be present while researcher examines materials.

Palm Springs Public Library
300 S. Sunrise Way
Palm Springs, CA 92262
(619) 323-8294
Contact: Suzanne Sutton, Reference Coordinator or Nancy Robinson, Local History. *Hours*: Monday–Saturday. *Access*: Clipping files paged by staff.

San Francisco Performing Arts Library and Museum
399 Grove Street
San Francisco, CA 94102
(415) 255-4800; FAX: (415) 255-1913
Hours: Tuesday–Saturday. *Contact*: Kirsten Tanaka. *Access*: Paging by staff. *Restrictions*: Non-circulating; subject to copyright restrictions.

San Francisco Public Library
San Francisco History Room
Civic Center
San Francisco, CA 94132
(415) 557-4567 (Reference questions not accepted by FAX)
Hours: Tuesday–Wednesday, Friday, 1:00–6:00, Thursday, Saturday, 10:00–12:00, 1:00–6:00. *Contact*: Faun McInnis, Manager or Stan Carroll, Librarian or Pat Akre, Photo Curator. *Access*: Some open shelf materials; some paging by staff; some materials are off-site and require 24 hours' retrieval time. Written inquiries should be accompanied by a self-addressed stamped envelope and will be handled as time permits. First priority is given to patrons who come to the Library. The room is sometimes closed for special events; it is advisable to call ahead. *Restrictions*: Photocopies made by staff only. No materials may be removed from the room.

Stanford University
Department of Special Collections
Stanford University Libraries
Stanford, CA 94305-6004
(415) 725-1022; FAX: (415) 723-8690
Hours: Monday–Friday, 9:00–5:00. *Contact*: Linda Long. *Access*: Paging by staff.

University of California at Berkeley
1) University Art Museum
Pacific Film Archive
Library and Film Study Center
2625 Durant Avenue
Berkeley, CA 94720
(415) 642-1437
2) Special Collections
Bancroft Library
Berkeley, CA 94720
(415) 642-3781
Contact: Nancy Goldman. *Hours*: Monday–Friday, 1:00–5:00. *Access*: All materials are non-circulating; duplication available. *Restrictions*: Phone reference available for questions that can be answered in 20 minutes or less. $3.00 per day use fee for all but UC Berkeley faculty and students and Archive members.

University of California, Los Angeles
Arts Library—Special Collections
22478 University Research Library
405 Hilgard Avenue
Los Angeles, CA 90024-1575
(310) 825-7253
Hours: By appointment, Monday–Friday, 9:00–5:00. *Contact*: Librarian. *Access*: For special collections, paging by staff 24 hours in advance; for clippings, paging by staff. *Restrictions*: No photocopying of archival and studio materials.

University of California, Los Angeles
Special Collections
A1713 University Research Library
405 Hilgard Avenue
Los Angeles, CA 90024-157511
(310) 825-4988; FAX: (310) 206-1864
Hours: Monday–Saturday, 9:00–5:00. *Contact*: Anne Caiger, Manuscripts Curator, James Davis, Rare Book Librarian or Charlotte Brown, University Archivist. *Access*: Daily paging by staff

for materials in the Research Library and the Southern Regional Library Facility. Fees charged for providing photocopying and for permission to publish. *Restrictions*: Materials do not circulate; room use only by registered users. Users involved with commercial projects may be limited in the number of items requested depending on the number of requests by UC users. Materials from some collections cannot be duplicated.

University of California, Santa Cruz
Special Collections – Motion Picture
  Photograph Collection
University Library
1156 High Street
Santa Cruz, CA 95064
(408) 459-2547; FAX: (408) 459-8206
  Hours: Monday–Friday, 10:00–12:00, 1:00–4:00; Summer: Monday–Friday, 10:00–12:00. *Contact*: Rita Bottoms, Head, Special Collections. *Access*: Paging by staff. Researchers should call and/or write in advance about their research needs. *Restrictions*: Photographic services are available but not on premises.

University of Southern California
Cinema-Television Library and Archives
  of the Performing Arts
Doheny Library
Los Angeles, CA 90089-0182
(213) 740-8906; FAX: (213) 747-3301
  Hours: Monday–Friday. *Contact*: Steven Hanson, Head Librarian or Ned Comstock, Archives Assistant. *Access*: Paging by staff. *Restrictions*: Archival materials for library use only.

University of Southern California
Warner Brothers Archives
Cinema-TV Library
University Park
Los Angeles, CA 90089-2211
(213) 748-7747; FAX: (213) 747-3301
  (Although materials are accessed via the Cinema-TV Library these numbers are for the Archives only).
  Hours: Monday–Friday: 9:00–5:00. *Contact*: Bill Whittington. *Access*: Paging by staff with minimum of two weeks' notice. *Restrictions*: Materials viewed in the Special Collections reading room only. Duplicating of some materials requires permission from copyright holder.

COLORADO

Denver Public Library
Western History Department
1357 Broadway
Denver, CO 80203-2165
(303) 640-8880; FAX: (303) 640-8887
  Hours: Monday–Wednesday, 10:00–9:00; Thursday–Saturday, 10:00–5:30; Sunday, 1:00–5:00. *Contact*: Eleanor Gehres, Manager. *Access*: Various methods. *Restrictions*: Research collection only.

Pikes Peak Library District
Penrose Library
Local History and Genealogy
20 North Cascade
Colorado Springs, CO 80903
  or
P.O. Box 1579
Colorado Springs, CO 80901-1579
(719) 531-6333; FAX: (719) 632-5744
  Hours: Monday–Thursday, 10:00–9:00, Friday–Saturday, 10:00–6:00. *Contact*: Ree Mobley, Local History and Genealogy Librarian. *Access*: Online catalog; open shelves. *Restrictions*: Collections are non-circulating in local history and genealogy.

CONNECTICUT

Wesleyan University
Wesleyan Cinema Archives
Middletown, CT 06459
(203) 347-9411, x2259; FAX: (203) 343-3940
  Contact: Leith G. Johnson, Assistant Curator. *Hours*: Monday–Friday, 9:15–4:30. *Access*: Paged by staff. *Restrictions*: Researchers must be working on bona fide projects and must submit written requests prior to using materials.

Yale University
Manuscripts and Archives
Sterling Memorial Library

120 High Street
New Haven, CT 06520
(203) 432-1744
Relevant holdings: The Crawford
Theatre Collection contains approximately forty-four linear feet of clipping
files with textual and pictorial materials
about stage and cinema performers.
There are ten linear feet of film stills
(alphabetically by film title), from the
1930s and 1940s. Also included are five
linear feet of portrait photographs
(alphabetically by performer's name) and
three linear feet of film programs, 1920s–
1970s, the earlier of which are from New
York area theaters.

DISTRICT OF COLUMBIA

Georgetown University
Special Collections, Library
37th and O Streets, NW
Washington, DC 20057-1006
(202) 994-6455
Contact: Person at front desk. *Hours*:
Monday–Friday, 9:00–5:30. *Access*:
Quigley Photographic Archives in open
filing cabinets; Terry Ramsaye Papers
paged by staff. *Restrictions*: Materials
available for copying (fee charged), no
more than 50 pages.

Library of Congress
Manuscript Division
James Madison Memorial Building
Room 101
Washington, DC 20450
(202) 707-5383
Hours: Monday–Friday, 8:30–5:00.
Restrictions: Only one folder of material
at a time for photocopying. Microfilm
editions of manuscripts are consulted
unless there is compelling reason to con-
sult the original.

ILLINOIS

Chicago Historical Society
Clark Street at North Avenue
Chicago, IL 60614
(312) 642-4600
Relevant holdings: Contains the John
Freuler Collection of photographs,

scripts, contracts, posters, etc. relating to
the history of the Mutual Film Company
and the American Film Company from
the 1900s to the late 1920s. Also contains
the Essanay Film Studio Collection of
photographs, business records and other
papers from the 1910s to the 1930s. Other
collections may also have some relevant
data.

Illinois State Historical Library
Old State Capitol
Springfield, IL 62701
(217) 524-6358

IOWA

University of Iowa
Special Collections, University of Iowa
Libraries
Iowa City, IA 52242
(319) 335-5867
Contact: Robert McCown, Special
Collections Librarian. *Hours*: Monday–
Friday, 9:00–5:00. *Access*: Paged by
staff.

KANSAS

Wichita State University
Ablah Library
Department of Special Collections
1845 Fairmount
Wichita, KS 67260-0068
(316) 689-3590; FAX: (316) 689-3048
Contact: Michael Kelly, Curator.
Hours: Monday–Friday, 8:00–5:00 and
by appointment. *Access*: Paging by staff;
photocopying available. *Restrictions*: No
restrictions on research, some on publication.

LOUISIANA

New Orleans Public Library
Louisiana Division
219 Loyola Avenue
New Orleans, LA 70140
(504) 596-2610; FAX: (504) 596-2609
Contact: Wayne Everard. *Hours*:
Monday–Thursday, Saturday. *Access*:

Open shelving for some materials; others paged by staff. Manuscripts and other rare materials by appointment.

MASSACHUSETTS

Boston University
Department of Special Collections
Mugar Memorial Library
771 Commonwealth Avenue
Boston, MA 02215
(617) 353-3710
Hours: Monday–Friday, 9:00–5:00. *Contact*: Margaret Goostray, Assistant Director or Karen Mix, Manuscript Technician. *Access*: Paged by staff. Advance appointments suggested. *Restrictions*: Some collections may have restrictions.

Harvard University
Harvard Theatre Collection
Harvard College Library
Cambridge, MA 02138
(617) 495-2445
Hours: Monday–Friday, 9:00–5:00. *Contact*: Jeanne T. Newlin, Curator. *Access*: Reading room available. Paging by staff. Advance consultation advised. *Restrictions*: Nothing circulates.

Smith College
Sophia Smith Collection
Smith College Libraries
Alumnae Gymnasium
Northampton, MA 01603
(413) 585-2970
Contact: Margery Sly, Acting Director or Amy Hague, Assistant Curator. *Hours*: Monday–Friday, 10:00–5:00, some Sundays, 1:00–4:00, when classes are in session. *Access*: Paged by staff. *Restrictions*: No collections are restricted. Limited photocopying available.

MICHIGAN

Detroit Public Library
Performing Arts Collection
Music and Performing Arts Department
5201 Woodward Avenue

Detroit, MI 48202
(313) 833-1000
Contact: Agatha Pfeiffer Kalkanis. *Hours*: Tuesday, Thursday, Friday, Saturday, 9:30–5:30, Wednesday, 1:00–9:00. *Access*: Open and closed shelves. No restrictions on in-house use.

Michigan State University
G. Robert Vincent Voice Library
Michigan State University Libraries
East Lansing, MI 48824-1048
(517) 355-5122
Contact: Maurice Crane or John Shaw. *Hours*: Monday–Friday, 8:00–4:30. *Access*: Paging by staff. *Restrictions*: Materials under copyright not duplicated by Library. Anyone planning to broadcast any materials must obtain copyright permission.

MINNESOTA

Blackwood Hall Memorial Library
Theatre Collection
205 Fourth Avenue
Albert Lea, MN 56007
Contact: William Studer.

MISSOURI

Kansas City (Mo.) Public Library
311 E. 12th Street
Kansas City, MO 64106
(816) 221-2685; FAX (816) 842-6839
Contact: Anna Horn, Associate Director of the Main Library or Sara Hallier, Acting Manager, Missouri Valley Special Collections. *Hours*: Monday–Thursday, 9:00–9:00, Friday–Saturday, 9:00–5:00, Sunday, 1:00–5:00. *Access*: Paging by staff. *Restrictions*: Nothing may be checked out; some items may not be photocopied.

St. Louis Public Library
1301 Olive Street
St. Louis, MO 63103
(314) 241-2288; FAX: (314) 241-4305
Hours: Monday, 10:00–9:00, Tuesday–Friday, 10:00–6:00, Saturday, 9:00–5:00. *Access*: "Tin Room" clipping col-

lection and Fine Arts Portrait files paged by staff.

NEBRASKA

Nebraska State Historical Society
Library Archives
1500 R Street
P. O. Box 82554
Lincoln, NE 68510
(402) 471-4771; FAX: (402) 471-3100
  Hours: Monday–Friday (Saturday and Sunday by special arrangement). *Contact*: Paul Eisloeffel. *Access*: Paging by staff.

NEW JERSEY

Edison National Historical Site
Main Street and Lakeside Avenue
West Orange, NJ 07052
(201) 736-0550; FAX: (201) 736-8496
  Contact: George Tselos, Archivist. *Relevant holdings*: Contains the Edison Archives with personal, laboratory and business records, including the Motion Picture Patents Company. The Document File contains motion picture material which is arranged by year.

Fort Lee Public Library
320 Main Street
Fort Lee, NJ 07024
(201) 592-3614
  Contact: Rita Altomara. *Hours*: Monday–Saturday. *Access*: Photographs consulted by appointment. *Restrictions*: Photographs do not circulate.

Princeton University
William Seymour Theatre Collection
Princeton, NJ 08544
(609) 258-3223
  Consult: Mary Ann Jensen, Curator. *Access*: Paged by staff.

NEW YORK

American Museum of the Moving Image
36-01 35th Avenue
Astoria, NY 11106
(718) 784-4520; FAX: (718) 784-4681

  Contact: Eleanor Mish. *Hours*: Monday–Friday, 9:30–5:30. *Access*: The collection is arranged primarily by film title. Researchers provide a filmography, with release dates, and a letter describing the project. A search will be conducted ($10.00 fee). Xerox copies are provided unless the materials are too fragile or there is too much material. An appointment to view materials can then be made. Copy prints of photographs in the collection can be made for $25.00 (plus $5.00 postage/handling) and must be returned after publication. Original photography of artifacts can be done for $50.00 per hour with the researcher's own equipment.

Bettmann
902 Broadway
New York, NY 10010
(212) 777-6200; FAX: (212) 533-4034
  Hours: Seven days a week by appointment only. *Contact*: Research Department. *Access*: Professionals may do research during normal business hours. Pictures may be rented for 30 or 90 days. Research and license fees charged. *Restrictions*: Not open to the public; for comunications professionals and researchers only. Fee charged according to use of photographs.

Columbia University
Oral History Research Office
Box 20
Butler Library
New York, NY 10027
(212) 854-2273; FAX: (212) 222-0331
  Hours: Monday–Friday, 9:00–5:00; call beforehand. *Contact*: Staff. *Access*: Paging by staff. Users register at Oral History Office; materials are available in the Rare Books and Manuscripts Library. Tapes are available for most interviews conducted after 1962. *Restrictions*: Restrictions on individual interviews. Some projects are closed until their completion and some require permission before consultation. Photocopying may be limited; sometimes permission of person interviewed or sponsoring institution is required.

Columbia University
Rare Book and Manuscript Library
Butler Library, Sixth Floor
535 West 114th Street
New York, NY 10027
(212) 854-3528; FAX: (212) 222-0331
  Hours: Monday–Friday, 9:00–4:45.
Contact: Bernard Crystal, Acting Director. *Access*: Paged by staff. Use of rare books and manuscripts is facilitated by writing well in advance of a visit. *Restrictions*: Books do not circulate. Permission to publish must be obtained in writing from the Librarian.

Cornell University
Division of Rare and Manuscript Collections, University Library
2B Carl A. Kroch Library
Ithaca, NY 14853-5302
(607) 255-3530; FAX: (607) 255-9524
  Hours: Monday–Friday, 9:00–5:00, Saturday, 9:00–1:00 during the regular University session. *Contact*: Mary-Beth B. Bunge, Head of Public Services, Elaine Engst, Curator of Manuscripts or H. Thomas Hickerson, Director. *Access*: Paging by staff. *Restrictions*: Materials must be used in the Division's supervised Reading Room. Individual collections may have specific donor restrictions. Photocopying provided by staff only.

George Eastman House, International Museum of Photography and Film
Film Collections
900 East Avenue
Rochester, NY 14607
(716) 271-3361; FAX: (716) 271-3970
  Contact: Dr. Jan-Christopher Horak. *Hours*: Tuesday–Friday. *Access*: Appointments made three weeks in advance by Film Study Center request forms, mail and FAX inquiries. *Restrictions*: Reproductions made only after copyright clearance, except for study purposes.

Museum of Modern Art
Celeste Bartos International Film Study
  Center
Department of Film
11 West 53rd Street
New York, NY 10019-5498

(212) 708-9613/708-9614; FAX: (212)
  708-9531
  Hours: Monday–Friday, 1:00–5:00 by appointment only. *Contact*: Charles Silver, Nancy Barnes or Ron Magliozzi. *Access*: Paged by staff. *Restrictions*: Qualified scholars only. Subject to restrictions based on condition of the material and the degree to which the collections have been processed. Two weeks' advance notice is required for access to special collections such as the Photoplay Collection.

Museum of Modern Art — Film Stills
  Archive
11 West 53rd Street
New York, NY 10019-5498
(212) 708-9400
  Contact: Mary Corliss, Assistant Curator. *Relevant holdings*: Contains one of the world's largest collections of film stills: approximately four million stills from more than 50,000 films. Special holdings include the D.W. Griffith Collection (contains the Biograph and feature productions, the Carol Dempster and Billy Bitzer collections); Essanay films from 1913 to 1917; the Ince Collection; the Richard Barthelmess Collection; the Douglas Fairbanks Sr. Collection, and the Georges Méliès Collection. There are also extensive collections of stills from foreign films (especially the Russian, French and Japanese cinema) and recent American films. Duplicates of stills are sold; the requester must obtain appropriate copyright clearances if material is to be published.

Museum of the City of New York
Theater Collection
1220 Fifth Avenue
New York, NY 10029
(212) 534-1672, Ext. 210; FAX: (212)
  534-5974
  Contact: Marty Jacobs. *Hours*: Monday–Friday, 9:00–3:30 by appointment only. *Access*: Researchers must mail or FAX their alphabetical list of inquiries prior to arrival. Fee per visit: $10.00 for full-time graduate students and university faculty; others $25.00.

New York Public Library for the Performing Arts
40 Lincoln Center Plaza
New York, NY 10023-7498
(212) 870-1639; FAX: (212) 787-3852
Hours: Monday, Thursday: 12:00–7:45; Wednesday, Friday, Saturday: 12:00–5:45. *Contact*: Bob Taylor, Curator. *Access*: Some books on open shelves; some books, all clippings, photographs, etc. paged by staff. *Restrictions*: Readers must be over 18 years of age unless approved for a special project.

State University of New York at Purchase
McDonald Collection
Library
735 Anderson Hill Road
Purchase, NY 10577
(914) 251-6435; FAX: (914) 251-6437
Hours: Monday–Friday, 9:00–5:00. *Contact*: Rosalind Smith. *Access*: In open files. *Restrictions*: Does not circulate.

University of Rochester
Department of Rare Books and Special Collections
Rush Rhees Library
Rochester, NY 14627
(716) 275-4477
Hours: Monday–Thursday, 9:00–12:00, 1:00–5:00. *Contact*: Mary Huth. *Access*: Paged by staff.

OHIO

Bowling Green State University
Popular Culture Library
Jerome Library, Fourth Floor
Bowling Green, OH 43403
(419) 372-2450
Relevant holdings: Contains the collection of Anthony Slide, film historian and writer on film. The collection has research materials, notes and correspondence relating to Slide's books, essays, reviews, lectures, and original motion picture production materials such as cast lists, synopses, scripts and shooting schedules. Printed materials include press releases and promotion materials, theater programs and playbills and

numerous periodicals. The Library also has collections of movie advertisements, press kits, posters, scripts, clippings and various film periodicals, including obscure fan magazines.

Cleveland Public Library
Theatre Collection, Literature Department
325 E. Superior
Cleveland, Ohio 44114
(216) 623-2881; FAX: (216) 269-2901
Contact: Evelyn M. Ward. *Hours*: Monday–Saturday, 9:00–6:00, Sunday, 1:00–5:00 (Sunday hours September–May only). *Access*: Varies according to type of material.

Kent State University
Department of Special Collections and Archives
Kent State University Libraries
Kent, Ohio 44242
(216) 672-2270
Contact: Alex Gildzen. *Hours*: Monday–Friday, 1:00–5:00. *Access*: Paging by staff. *Restrictions*: Three items at a time.

Ohio State University
Library of the Jerome Lawrence and Robert E. Lee Theatre Research Institute
1430 Lincoln Tower
1800 Cannon Drive
Columbus, Ohio 43210-1230
(614) 292-6614; FAX: (614) 292-3061
Contact: Nena Couch or Alan Woods. *Hours*: Monday–Friday. *Access*: Paging by staff. Some restrictions on use and duplication although most materials are unrestricted.

Public Library of Cincinnati and Hamilton County
Art and Music Department
800 Vine Street
Cincinnati, Ohio 45202
(513) 369-6955; FAX: (513) 369-6063
Contact: Anna J. Horton or Judy Inwood. *Hours*: Monday–Saturday, 9:00–6:00, Sunday, 1:00–5:00 (September–May only). *Access*: Some open shelves, some materials paged by staff.

OKLAHOMA

Tom Mix Museum
721 N. Delaware Avenue
Dewey, OK 74029
(918) 534-1555
  Hours: Tuesday–Friday, 9:00–5:00;
Saturday–Sunday, 2:00–5:00.

University of Oklahoma
University Libraries
Western History Collections
Room 452, Monnet Hall
Norman, OK 73019
(405) 325-3641; FAX: (405) 325-2943
  Hours: Monday–Friday, 8:00–5:00.
Contact: Donald L. DeWitt, Curator;
John R. Lovett, Librarian. *Access*:
Paged by staff. *Restrictions*: No camera
or sound recording allowed.

PENNSYLVANIA

Carnegie Library of Pittsburgh
Pennsylvania Department
4400 Forbes Avenue
Pittsburgh, PA 15213
(412) 622-3154; FAX: (412) 621-1267
  Hours: Monday–Wednesday, Friday,
9:00–9:00, Thursday, Saturday, 9:00–
5:30, Sunday, 1:00–5:00 (October–May).
Contact: Marilyn Holt, Department
Head. *Access*: Paging by staff. Photo-
copy machine available; photocopies
may be mailed to researcher at $.50 per
copy plus postage and applicable state
tax. *Restrictions*: Does not circulate.

Free Library of Philadelphia
Theatre Collection
Logan Square
19th and Vine Streets
Philadelphia, PA 19103-1157
(215) 686-5368
  Contact: Geraldine Duclow.

TENNESSEE

University of Tennessee
University Libraries
Special Collections
Hoskins Library

Knoxville, TN 37996-4000
(615) 974-4480; FAX: (615) 974-2708
  Contact: Dr. James B. Lloyd or Nick
Wyman. *Hours*: Monday–Friday, 9:00–
5:30. *Access*: Closed stacks. Paged by
staff. *Restrictions*: Non-circulating.

TEXAS

Amon Carter Museum
Mailing address: P. O. Box 2365
Fort Worth, TX 76113
Street address: 3501 Camp Bowie
  Boulevard
Fort Worth, TX 76107
(817) 738-1933; FAX: (817) 738-2034
  Hours: Monday–Friday, 10:00–4:30,
by appointment only. *Contact*: Photography Collection. *Access*: Paging by
staff. *Restrictions*: For scholarly research
and publication. Some materials may be
copyrighted or controlled by studios.

Southern Methodist University
SMU Oral History Collection on the Per-
  forming Arts
DeGolyer Library
Southern Methodist University
Dallas, TX 75275
(214) 768-3231
  Hours: Monday–Friday, 8:30–5:00.
Contact: Ronald L. Davis or Kay Bost.
Access: Paging by staff. *Restrictions*:
Each interview contains restrictions as
designated by interviewee.

Southern Methodist University
Southwest Film/Video Archives
6100 Hillcrest
Greer Garson Theatre, 3rd Floor
Dallas, TX 75275-4194
(214) 373-3665
  Contact: Rebecca Rice or Walid
Khaldi. *Hours*: Monday–Friday, 9:00–
5:00. *Access*: In files. Materials available
for copying (fee may be charged). *Restrictions*: Viewing on site only.

University of Texas at Austin
Harry Ransom Humanities Research
  Center
Austin, TX 78713
(512) 471-9119; FAX: (512) 471-9646
  Contact: Dr. Charles Bell.

UTAH

Brigham Young University
Cecil B. DeMille Archives
Special Collections and Manuscripts
Department
Harold B. Lee Library
Provo, UT 84602
(801) 378-3514; FAX: (801) 378-6347
Hours: Monday–Friday, 9:00–5:00.
Contact: James V. D'Arc, Curator. *Access*: Paging by staff. *Restrictions*: No photocopying of script materials. Portion of collection accessible via microfilm only.

WISCONSIN

State Historical Society of Wisconsin
816 State Street
Madison, WI 53706
(608) 264-6400; FAX: (608) 264-6404
Hours: Monday–Friday, 8:00–5:00,

Saturday, 9:00–4:00. *Contact*: Archives Reference. *Access*: Paged by staff.

Wisconsin Center for Film and Theatre Research
816 State Street
Madison, WI 53706
(608) 264-6466; FAX: (608) 264-6472
Contact: Crystal Hyde or Maxine Fleckner-Duccy. *Hours*: Monday–Friday, 1:00–5:00. *Access*: Card catalog. *Restrictions*: On site viewing only after 24 hour notice to retrieve materials.

WYOMING

University of Wyoming
American Heritage Center
PO Box 3924
Laramie, WY 82071
(307) 766-4114
Contact: Rick Ewig. *Hours*: Monday–Friday, 8:00–5:00, Saturday, 11:00–5:00. *Access*: Paged by staff.

CANADA

National Archives of Canada
Audio-Visual and Cartographic Archives
344 Wellington Street, Room 1016
Ottawa, Ontario, K1A ON3, Canada
(613) 995-1312; (613) 996-6890
Contact: Caroline Forcier Holloway or Sylvie Robitaille. *Hours*: Monday–Friday, 8:30–4:45, preferably by appointment. *Access*: Clipping (vertical) files accessible through card index. Stills accessible through card index by film title. All materials are paged by staff. *Restrictions*: Some stills must have copyright clearance from copyright holder prior to reproduction.

GREAT BRITAIN

British Film Institute
21 Stephen Street
London W1P 1PL, England
071 255 1444; FAX: 071 436 7950
Hours: Monday, Friday, 10:30–5:30; Tuesday, Thursday, 10:30–8:00; Wednesday: 1:00–8:00. *Access*: Most materials, including microfiched clippings, paged by staff. Some materials are housed in remote storage and are not available the day requested. *Restrictions*: Open to members only (day and annual membership available for a fee). Unpublished materials may not be photocopied without permission from the copyright holder or donor. Fragile materials may not be photocopied.

Bibliography

Film Credits

British Film Actors' Credits, 1895–1987 (Scott Palmer). Jefferson, NC: McFarland, 1988.
Contains separate sections on sound and silent films, the latter section including only those who never appeared in talkies. Also contains American actors who appeared in British films. This is a major updating and revision of the author's *A Who's Who of British Film Actors* (Scarecrow, 1981).

Filmarama (John Stewart, compiler). Vol. I: *The Formidable Years, 1893–1913*; Vol. II: *The Flaming Years: 1920–1929*. Metuchen, NJ: Scarecrow, 1975–77.
Film titles are alphabetical; no release years are given.

Forty Years of Screen Credits, 1929–1969 (John T. Weaver, compiler). 2 vols. Metuchen, NJ: Scarecrow, 1970.
Credits are arranged by year of release.

Motion Picture Players' Credits: Worldwide Performers of 1967 Through 1980 with Filmographies of Their Entire Careers, 1905–1983 (Jeffrey Oliviero). Jefferson, NC: McFarland, 1991.
Includes Lillian Gish.

Twenty Years of Silents, 1908–1928 (John Weaver, compiler). Metuchen, NJ: Scarecrow, 1971.
Films made later than 1928 are included for some performers.

Who Was Who on Screen (Evelyn M. Truitt). 3rd ed. New York: Bowker, 1983.
Although this contains very brief career data its major usefulness is the listing of credits for thousands of performers. The 1984 edition is a condensed (and hence less useful) version of this edition.

Other Books

Acting in the Cinema (James Naremore). Berkeley, CA: University of California Press, 1988.
Theoretical and historical analysis of film acting with major sections on Chaplin and L. Gish.

Actorviews: Intimate Portraits (Ashton Stevens). Chicago: Covici-McGee, 1923.
Interviews with actors and actresses, including G. Arliss, J. Barrymore, E. Ferguson and L. Wolheim.

L'Age d'Or du Comique: Semiologie de Charlot (Adolphe Nysenholc). Brussels: Editions de l'Université de Bruxelles, 1979.
About C. Chaplin's screen persona.

Agee on Film: Reviews and Comments (James Agee). New York: McDowell, Obolensky, 1958.
>   Among those discussed in these pieces are C. Chaplin, B. Keaton, H. Langdon and H. Lloyd. Reprinted by Beacon (1964) and Grosset & Dunlap (1969).

Aileen Pringle, Silent Movie Actress and Frequent Guest. San Simeon, CA: Hearst San Simeon Region, 1990.
>   An oral history interview about AP's visits to San Simeon.

Alice in Movieland (Alice M. Williamson). New York: Appleton, 1928.
>   Contains sections on M. Davies, D. Fairbanks, P. Negri, M. Pickford and G. Swanson. On microfiche in the Chadwyck-Healey *History of the Cinema* series (1987).

Alisa Terri (i.e., Alice Terry) (A. Gidoni). Moscow: Tea-Kino-Pechat, 1928.
>   A brief pamphlet in Russian.

All My Sins Remembered (Elaine Barrymore and Sandford Doody). New York: Appleton-Century, 1964.
>   J. Barrymore's last wife remembers her life with him.

America: An Illustrated Diary of Its Most Exciting Years. 3 vols. Valencia, CA: A.F.E. Press, 1973.
>   A compilation of previously published articles by, or about, performers including J. Barrymore, L. Chaney and G. Swanson.

The American Cinema: Directors and Directions, 1929–1968 (Andrew Sarris). Chicago, IL: University of Chicago Press, 1985.
>   Very brief career analyses and filmographies of filmmakers, including C. Chaplin, B. Keaton and L. Sherman. Reprint of the Dutton edition (1968).

An American Comedy (Harold Lloyd). New York: Blom, 1971.
>   An autobiography. A republication of the Longmans Green edition (1928). Also reprinted, with additional material, by Dover (1971).

American Directors (Jean-Pierre Coursodon with Pierre Sauvage). 2 vols. New York: McGraw-Hill, 1983.
>   Analytical essays and filmographies on numerous directors including C. Chaplin.

American Film Directors: With Filmographies and Index of Critics and Films (Stanley Hochman, compiler and editor) (A Library of Film Criticism). New York: Ungar, 1974.
>   A compilation of excerpts from previously published film reviews and books about directors including C. Chaplin and B. Keaton.

The American Film Heritage: Impressions from the American Film Institute Archives (Tom Shales and Kevin Brownlow). Washington, DC: Acropolis Books, 1972.
>   A lavishly illustrated glimpse at several famous films, filmmakers and performers, including M. Pickford.

The American Movie Goddess (Marsha McCreadie, editor). New York: Wiley, 1973.
>   A collection of short essays from the 1930s to '50s, many of which are about G. Garbo.

American Screenwriters. 2nd Series. (*Dictionary of Literary Biography*, v. 44). Detroit, MI: Gale Research, 1986.
>   Contains a lengthy section, with illustrations, on C. Chaplin.

American Vaudeville as Seen by Its Contemporaries (Charles W. Stein, editor). New York: Knopf, 1984.
>   One of the articles is by Buster Keaton.

American Visions: The Films of Chaplin, Ford, Capra and Welles, 1936–1941 (Charles Maland). New York: Arno, 1977.
>   Originally a 1975 Ph.D. thesis.

Analiz Igry Kino-aktera: Masterstvo Lilian (i.e., Lillian) *Gish* (Ippolit Sokolov). Leningrad: Tea-Kino-Pechat, 1929.
>   A brief pamphlet in Russian about L. Gish.

Arthur and Pat Lake: Dagwood Bumstead and Marion Davies' Niece (Metta Hake). San Simeon, CA: San Simeon Region, 1992.

Oral history of their memories of San Simeon and M. Davies.
Assuming Responsibilities (Douglas Fairbanks). New York: Britton, 1918.
One of a series of books by (or ghostwritten for) DF about life and success.
Authors on Film (Harry Geduld, editor). Bloomington, IN: Indiana University Press, 1972.
Generally brief essays by prominent American and foreign authors. A few of the essays are about C. Chaplin and R. Valentino.
The Autobiography of Cecil B. DeMille (Cecil B. DeMille). New York: Garland, 1985.
A reprint of the Prentice-Hall edition (1959). Among the stars mentioned in detail are M. Pickford and G. Swanson.
Awake in the Dark: An Anthology of American Film Criticism, 1915 to the Present (David Denby, editor). New York: Vintage, 1977.
A collection of previously published pieces, one of which is about H. Langdon.
The "B" Directors: A Biographical Directory (Wheeler W. Dixon). Metuchen, NJ: Scarecrow, 1985.
Brief narratives and filmographies for directors, some of whom were also performers, including R. Cortez, I. Cummings, G. Tryon and C. Wilbur.
B Western Actors Encyclopedia: Facts, Photos and Filmographies for More Than 250 Familiar Faces (Ted Holland). Jefferson, NC: McFarland, 1989.
Brief narratives about performers who appeared in at least a few Western films, including W. Beery, V.B. Faire, B. Mehaffey, T. Mix, G. O'Brien, D. Revier, M. Sais, C. Tearle. The filmographies are for their Western films only.
Babel and Babylon: Spectatorship in American Silent Film (Miriam Hansen). Cambridge, MA: Harvard University Press, 1991.
A scholarly study on the nature of spectatorship that includes a section on R. Valentino.
Barbara La Marr: Una Historia de Placer y de Dolor (Gabriel Navarro). San Antonio, TX: Lozano, 1926.
In Spanish.
The Barrymores (Hollis Alpert). New York: Dial, 1964.
Biography.
The Barrymores: The Royal Family in Hollywood (James Kotsilibas-Davis). New York: Crown, 1981.
Profusely illustrated.
Bebe and Ben (Jill Allgood). London: R. Hale, 1975.
A joint biography of Bebe Daniels and Ben Lyon, with much information about their lives in England.
Before My Eyes: Film Criticism and Comment (Stanley Kauffmann). New York: Harper & Row, 1980.
One of the pieces is about C. Chaplin.
Behind the Screen (Samuel Goldwyn). New York: G.H. Doran, 1923.
The famed producer discusses his experiences with numerous stars of the era.
Ben Tiurpin (i.e., Turpin) (L. Dombrovskii). Moscow: Tea-Kino-Pechat, 1928.
A brief pamphlet in Russian.
Ben Turpin: As He Is To Those Who Know Him (Charles D. Fox). (Little Movie Mirror Books). Ross, 1920.
A brief illustrated pamphlet-style "puff piece."
Bert Lytell: As He Is to Those Who Know Him (Little Movie Mirror Books). New York: Ross, 1920.
A brief illustrated pamphlet-style "puff piece."
The Best of Buster: The Classic Comedy Scenes Direct from the Films of Buster Keaton (Richard Anobile, editor). New York: Darien House, 1976.
Beverly Hills Is My Beat (Clinton Anderson). Englewood Cliffs, NJ: Prentice-Hall, 1960.

Included among these anecdotes by the chief of the Beverly Hills police department is one on C. Chaplin's 1943 paternity case.

Beyond the Image: Approaches to the Religious Dimension in the Cinema (Ronald Holloway). Geneva, SW: World Council of Churches, 1977.

A survey of certain aspects of the portrayal of religion in films, including a section about C. Chaplin.

The BFI Companion to the Western (Edward Buscombe, editor). New York: Da Capo, 1991.

A detailed survey of Western films and TV series which includes brief biographies and Western credits of performers such as A. Acord, G.M. Anderson, D. Farnum, R. Dix, W.S. Hart, J. Holt, T. McCoy, T. Mix, G. O'Brien, M. Sais and F. Thomson. Reprint of the Atheneum edition (1988).

The Big Book of Italian-American Culture (edited by Lawrence DiStasi). New York: Harper Perennial, 1990.

Includes a section on R. Valentino. A revised edition of *Dream Streets* (1988).

The Big V: A History of the Vitagraph Company (Anthony Slide). New rev. ed. Metuchen, NJ: Scarecrow, 1987.

Contains chapters about J. Bunny and F. Turner and a "Vitagraph Who's Who" with brief biographies on other Vitagraph stars, including A. Calhoun, L. Baird, M. Costello, H. Gardner, G. Hulette, A. Moreno, W. Reid, A. Stewart, E. Storey, N. Talmadge, E. Williams and C.K. Young.

A Biographical Dictionary of Film (David Thomson). 2nd ed., rev. New York: Morrow, 1981.

Most entries are brief and include filmographies. Some of the more important stars are treated at greater length.

The Biographical Encyclopaedia & Who's Who of the American Theatre (Walter Rigdon, editor). New York: Heinemann, 1966.

Each entry includes stageographies, filmographies and TV appearances as appropriate. The second edition was called *Notable Names in the American Theatre* (q.v.).

Bloody Wednesday (Joel L. Harrison). Canoga Park, CA: Major Books, 1978.

The story behind Ramon Novarro's murder.

The Blue Book of the Screen (Ruth Wing, editor). Hollywood, CA: The Blue Book of the Screen, 1923.

Full page portraits and very brief career summaries. Data on some of the performers included, although not always accurate, may be difficult to find elsewhere.

The Book of People: Photographs, Capsule Biographies and Vital Statistics of Over 500 Celebrities (Christopher P. Andersen). New York: Putnam, 1981.

One of the celebrities is G. Garbo.

Books on/by Chaplin (Lennart Ericson). Eriksson, 1981.

A mimeographed listing (no annotations) of thousands of books on Chaplin in numerous languages from Arabic to Yiddish. Some are translations. The second edition was published in *Classic Images*, November 1981–May 1982.

Bound and Gagged: The Story of the Silent Serials (Kalton C. Lahue). South Brunswick, NJ: Barnes, 1968.

Among the stars discussed in some detail are W. Desmond, E. Polo, A. Ray, R. Roland and P. White.

Breaking into the Movies (Charles R. Jones, editor). New York: Unicorn, 1927.

Each chapter is on a different aspect of filmmaking, e.g., "Up from the Extra Ranks," and is written by (or ghostwritten for) a film performer or other person in the industry.

Broken Silence: Conversations with 23 Silent Film Stars (Michael G. Ankerich). Jefferson, NC: McFarland, 1993.

Interviews which cover the performers' careers and personal lives. Includes W. Bakewell, L. Basquette, M. Bellamy, E. Boardman, D. Gulliver, P. Miller, L. Moran, E. Ralston and D. Revier.

Buster Crabbe: King of the Serial Aces and Western Action (Mario De Marco). DeMarco, 1983 or 1984(?).
  Contains a brief biography of W. Desmond.
Buster Keaton (Jean-Pierre Coursodon). New ed. Paris: Atlas; Lherminier, 1986.
  In French.
Buster Keaton (Carlos Cuenca Fernandez). Madrid: Filmoteca Nacional De España, 1967.
  In Spanish. Contains lengthy synopses and commentaries on the shorts and features.
Buster Keaton (J.P. Lebel) (International Film Guide Series). New York: Barnes, 1967.
  An analysis of Keaton's genius as director and actor.
Buster Keaton (David Robinson). 3rd ed. London: Secker & Warburg, 1973.
Buster Keaton (Davide Turconi and Francesco Savio). Venice: Edizioni M.I.A.C., 1963.
  Published in conjunction with a retrospective of Keaton films. In Italian.
Buster Keaton: A Rhetoric of Silents (Linda M. Miller). Charlottesville, VA: University of Virginia, 1987.
  A master's thesis.
Buster Keaton and His Role of Comedy in Silent Films (Richard O'Malley). University of Cincinnati, 1970.
  A Ph.D. thesis.
Buster Keaton and the Dynamics of Visual Wit (George Wead). New York: Arno Press, 1976.
  Based on a Ph.D. thesis.
Buster Keaton: Eine Dokumentation. Frankfurt, 1971.
  Issued in conjunction with a Keaton retrospective. Contains an interview with BK, a filmography, a bilbliography and synopses of the films shown at the retrospective. In German.
Buster Keaton: Mit Beitragen von Hans Helmut Prinzler... 2nd ed. Munich: Hanser, 1980.
  In German.
Buster Keaton mit Selbstzeugnissen und Bilddokumenten (Wolfram Tichy). Reinbek bei Hamburg: Rowohlt, 1983.
  In German.
Buster Keaton's Comic Vision: A Critical Analysis of Five Films (William Huie). Austin, TX: University of Texas at Austin, 1975.
  A Ph.D. thesis.
Buster, the Early Years: The Authorized Buster Keaton Film Festival Album (Don McGregor). Staten Island, NY: Eclipse Enterprises, 1982.
Butter with My Bread (Olga Petrova). Indianapolis, IN: Bobbs-Merrill, 1942.
  An autobiography.
Cads and Cavaliers: The Gentlemen Adventurers of the Movies (Tony Thomas). South Brunswick, NJ: Barnes, 1973.
  Lavishly illustrated career overviews of swashbuckling actors, including D. Fairbanks and J. Barrymore.
The Cast. Hollywood, CA: The Cast Ltd., 1932.
  A quarterly publication containing portrait photographs and brief biographies. The first volume included several silent performers. This may not have been published after 1932.
A Cast of Killers (Sidney D. Kirkpatrick). New York: Onyx, 1992.
  An account of the William Desmond Taylor murder in which M.M. Minter and M. Normand were investigated. Reprint of the Dutton edition (1986).
Catalog of the Jean Hersholt Collection of Hans Christian Andersen: Original Manuscripts, Letters, First Editions, Presentation Copies and Related Materials (Library of Congress). Washington, DC: Library of Congress, 1954.

Cecil Beaton: Memoirs of the 40s (Cecil Beaton). New York: McGraw-Hill, 1972.
Contains reminiscences about G. Garbo.
Celebrity Circus (Charles Higham). New York: Delacorte, 1979.
A series of interviews, one of which is with M.M. Minter.
Celebrity Homes: Architectural Digest Presents the Private Worlds of Thirty International Personalities. New York: Viking Press, 1977.
Color photos and descriptions of homes, including those of M. Pickford and D. Del Rio.
The Celluloid Mistress (Rodney Ackland). London: Columbus, 1989.
An account of Ackland's experiences with film and theater world personalities, including L. Gish. A reprint of the Wingate edition (1954).
The Celluloid Sacrifice: Aspects of Sex in the Movies (Alexander Walker). New York: Hawthorn, 1967.
Among the actresses discussed are T. Bara, C. Bow and G. Garbo.
Chaplin. New York: Dell, 1972.
Lavishly illustrated magazine format with articles on Chaplin's life and career.
Chaplin (Denis Gifford). Garden City, NY: Doubleday, 1974.
A well-illustrated description of Chaplin's films, with a filmography.
Chaplin (Roger Manvell) (Library of World Biography). Boston, MA: Little, Brown, 1974.
A biography.
Chaplin (Julian Smith). Boston: Twayne, 1984.
An analysis of Chaplin's career and films.
Chaplin and American Culture: The Evolution of a Star Image (Charles J. Maland). Princeton, NJ: Princeton University Press, 1989.
Chaplin's life and career as seen in the social context of his times.
Chaplin: Genesis of a Clown (Raoul Sobel and David Francis). London: Quartet, 1977.
A close analysis of the earliest films.
Chaplin: His Life and Art (David Robinson). New York: McGraw-Hill, 1985.
A lengthy and detailed opus.
Chaplin Imitators and Their Films: The Continuation of a Genre (Linda J. Obalil). Austin, TX: University of Texas at Austin, 1978.
A master's thesis.
Chaplin: The Immortal Tramp (R.J. Minney). London: Newnes, 1954.
Chaplin: Last of the Clowns (Parker Tyler). New York: Garland, 1985.
An analysis of the Chaplin persona. Reprint of the Vanguard edition (1948).
Chaplin Paa Jagt Efter Lykken. Copenhagen: Kosmofilm, 1916.
An early Chaplin commentary. In Danish.
Chaplin, the Mirror of Opinion (David Robinson). Bloomington, IN: Indiana University Press, 1983.
Chaplin, the Movies and Charlie (David Jacobs). New York: Harper & Row, 1975.
Both a biography and an analysis of the major films.
Chaplin vs. Chaplin (Ed Sullivan). Los Angeles: Marvin Miller Enterprises, 1965.
An account of Chaplin's "love life" including the proceedings of the Lita Grey–Charlie Chaplin divorce.
Chapliniana: A Commentary on Charlie Chaplin's 81 Movies, Vol. I: The Keystone Films (Harry Geduld). Bloomington, IN: Indiana University Press, 1987.
Chaplin's Films (Uno Asplund). South Brunswick, NJ: Barnes, 1976.
A critical analysis of the films. Translated from the Swedish edition.
Character People (Ken D. Jones, Arthur F. McClure and Alfred E. Twomey). South Brunswick, NJ: Barnes, 1976.
Very brief career summaries of numerous actors who began as, or became, character actors.

Charles Chaplin (Pierre Leprohon). Rev. ed. Paris: Seguier, 1988.
    In French.
Charles Chaplin (Marcel Martin) (Cinéma d'Aujourd'hui). Paris: Seghers, 1966.
    In French.
Charles Chaplin: A Guide to References and Resources (Timothy J. Lyons). Boston:
    G.K. Hall, 1979.
    A filmography and chronological listing of books and articles (1914–78), with some
    brief annotations.
Charles Chaplin: An Appreciation (Charles Silver). New York: Museum of Modern
    Art, 1989.
    A discussion of the major films, with a filmography.
Charles Chaplin and the Tradition of the Commedia dell'Arte (Anne Welsch). New
    Orleans, LA: University of New Orleans, 1975.
    A master's thesis.
Charles Chaplin: El Genio del Cine (Manuel Villegas Lopez). 4th ed. Barcelona:
    Planeta, 1978.
    In Spanish.
Charles Chaplin, Film Author (George E. Ebright). Trinity College, 1980.
    A master's thesis.
Charles Chaplin's City Lights, Its Production and Dialectical Structure (Gerard
    Molyneaux). New York: Garland, 1983.
    Adapted from a Ph.D. thesis.
Charles Chaplin's Limelight: A Socio-Cultural and Literary Analysis (Deborah D.
    Dierinzo). Los Angeles, CA: University of Southern California, 1978.
    A master's thesis.
Charlie Chan at the Movies: History, Filmography and Criticism (Ken Hanke). Jeffer-
    son, NC: McFarland, 1989.
    A survey of Charlie Chan films, with a discussion of W. Oland.
Charlie Chaplin (Maurice Bessy). New York: Harper & Row, 1985.
    English translation of the mainly pictorial French edition covering Chaplin's career.
Charlie Chaplin (Edouard Brasey). Paris: Solar, 1989.
    Includes filmography. In French.
Charlie Chaplin (Pam Brown). Watford, England: Exley, 1989.
Charlie Chaplin (Louis Delluc). New York: Lane, 1922.
Charlie Chaplin (Theodore Huff). New York: Arno, 1972.
    One of the first full-length biographies and analysis of Chaplin's films. Reprint of the
    Schuman edition (1951).
Charlie Chaplin (John McCabe). Garden City, NY: Doubleday, 1978.
    Contains a filmography and an extensive bibliography.
Charlie Chaplin (Robert F. Moss) (*Pyramid Illustrated History of the Movies*). New
    York: Pyramid, 1975.
    A relatively brief overview of Chaplin's career.
Charlie Chaplin: A Bio-Bibliography (Wes D. Gehring) (Popular Culture Bio-Bib-
    liographies). Westport, CT: Greenwood, 1983.
Charlie Chaplin: A Centenary Celebration (Peter Haining, editor). London: Foulsham,
    1989.
Charlie Chaplin: An Illustrated History of the Movies (Robert F. Moss). New York:
    Jove, 1977.
Charlie Chaplin: Biographie (Curt Riess). Rastatt, (Germany?): Verlagsunion E.
    Pabel-A. Moewig, 1989.
    Includes filmography. In German.
Charlie Chaplin: Early Comedies (Isabel Quigly). New York: Dutton, 1968.
Charlie Chaplin: His Life and Art (W. Dodgson Bowman). New York: Haskell House,
    1974.

Reprint of the Day edition (1931).

Charlie Chaplin in the Movies. Chicago, IL: Donohue, 1917.
Comic strips in full color.

Charlie Chaplin: King of Tragedy (Gerith Von Ulm). Caldwell, ID: Caxton, 1940.

Charlie Chaplin Sale (Christie's). Christie's, 1987.
Auction catalog of over 250 objects, all relating to Chaplin, including toys, books, programs, letters, photos, posters and ephemera.

Charlie Chaplin Story; ou, Charlot l'Immortel (Philippe Lemoine and François Pedron). Boulogne, France: Editions Alain Mathieu, 1978.
Profusely illustrated. In French.

Charlie Chaplin's Chatter and Funny Sayings: ... Over One Hundred Side Splitting Jokes (Charlie Chaplin). Baltimore, MD: Ottenheimer, 1916.
Comic strips in full color.

Charlie Chaplin's Funny Stunts. Chicago, IL: Donohue, 1917.
Comic strips in full color.

Charlie Chaplin's One Man Show (Dan Kamin). Carbondale, IL: Southern Illinois University Press, 1991.
In-depth analysis of the films and the Chaplin persona. Reprint of the Scarecrow edition (1984).

Charlie Chaplin's Own Story (Charlie Chaplin; edited by Harry Geduld). Bloomington, IN: Indiana University Press, 1985.
Reprinted from the 1916 edition.

Charlot (Philippe Soupault). Paris: Plon, 1957.
In French.

Charlz Spenser Chaplin (i.e., Charles Spencer Chaplin) (P. Atasheva) (Materials on the *History of the World Cinema Art*, v. 2: *American Cinematography*). Moscow: Goskinoizdat, 1945.
By the wife of Sergei Eisenstein? In Russian.

A Child of the Century (Ben Hecht). New York: Primus, 1985.
The autobiography of the famous writer includes a section about J. Barrymore. Reprint of the Simon and Schuster edition (1954).

Cinema: A Critical Dictionary: The Major Film-makers (Richard Roud, editor). New York: Viking, 1980.
Detailed career overviews of directors, including C. Chaplin, B. Keaton, H. Lloyd and H. Langdon, and a briefer account of R. Griffith, M. Pickford and D. Fairbanks.

Cinema: Practical Course in Cinema Acting in Ten Complete Lessons (Mary Pickford et al.). London: Standard Art Book Co., 1920(?).
Ten pamphlets containing acting tips from stars such as G. Brockwell, C. Chaplin, T. Mix and M. Pickford.

Le Cinéma Burlesque Américain au Temps du Muet: Etudes Documentaire (Jacques Chevallier). Paris, Institut Pedagogique National, 1960s(?).
A compilation of previously published data about silent comedians. Includes a chronology, filmography and bibliography. Most discussion is given to the major stars such as C. Chaplin, B. Keaton, H. Langdon and H. Lloyd.

Cinema Star Albums (A Series). Seattle, WA: Cinema Books by Post.
These pictorial volumes include C. Chaplin and G. Garbo.

Cinema Stylists (John Belton) (Filmmakers, no. 2). Metuchen, NJ: Scarecrow, 1983.
Analytical essays on several American and foreign directors, including C. Chaplin and H. Lloyd.

Cinq Mois à Hollywood avec Douglas Fairbanks: Films Muets, Films Parlant (Maurice Leloir). Paris: Peyronnet, 1929.
In French. Included in the Chadwyck-Healey microfiche series *History of the American Cinema, 1895-1940*.

Citizen Hearst: A Biography of William Randolph Hearst (W.A. Swanberg). New York: Scribners, 1961.
Reprinted several times. Contains much discussion of M. Davies.
The Civil War on the Screen, and Other Essays (Jack Spears). South Brunswick, NJ: Barnes, 1977.
Includes career overviews of A. Nazimova and L. Wolheim.
Clara Bow (Yvan Noe). Paris: Nouvelle Librairie Française, 1932.
Clara Bow: Runnin' Wild (David Stenn). New York: Doubleday, 1988.
A balanced biography.
Clara Kimball Young: In Her Most Successful Plays Produced by Her Own Company (Screen Favorites Library). 1910s(?).
Stills from three of her early films.
The Classic Cinema: Essays in Criticism (Stanley J. Solomon, editor). New York: Harcourt Brace Jovanovich, 1973.
Previously published essays on famous directors, among whom is C. Chaplin.
Classic Movie Comedians (Neil Sinyard). New York: Smithmark, 1992.
Lavishly illustrated career and biographical overviews of the major comic actors, including C. Chaplin, B. Keaton, H. Langdon and H. Lloyd.
Classics of the Silent Screen: A Pictorial Treasury (Joe Franklin). Secaucus, NJ: Citadel, 1959.
Descriptions of fifty "great" films and fairly brief accounts of the careers of seventy-five "great" stars. Profusely illustrated.
Close Ups: Intimate Profiles of the Movie Stars by Their Co-Stars, Directors, Screenwriters and Friends (Danny Peary, editor). New York: Workman, 1978.
Brief, lavishly illustrated pieces on stars, including T. Bara, J. Barrymore, L. Brooks, C. Chaplin, D. Fairbanks, G. Garbo, L. Gish, W.S. Hart, B. Keaton, H. Lloyd, M. Pickford, G. Swanson and R. Valentino. With filmographies.
Clown Princes and Court Jesters (Kalton C. Lahue and Samuel Gill). South Brunswick, NJ: Barnes, 1970.
Well illustrated career overviews of numerous comic actors, including many obscure individuals.
Colleen Moore: As She Is to Those Who Know Her (Little Movie Mirror Books). New York: Ross, 1920.
Brief, illustrated "puff piece."
Colleen Moore: The Jazz Age's Movie Flapper at San Simeon. San Simeon, CA: Hearst San Simeon State Historical Monument, 1991.
Two oral history interviews.
Colleen Moore's Doll House (Colleen Moore). Garden City, NY: Doubleday, 1971(?).
Lavishly illustrated with color photographs.
Colleen Moore's Doll House: The Story of the Most Exquisite Toy in the World (Colleen Moore). Garden City, NY: Doubleday, 1945.
An illustrated description of CM's famous "castle." Lavishly illustrated with color photos.
Colleen Moore's Fairy Castle. Chicago, IL: Museum of Science and Industry, 1981.
Another illustrated description of CM's doll house.
Col. Tim McCoy: The Last Plainsman (Mario DeMarco).
No publication information is available.
Col. Tim McCoy's Real Wild West and Rough Riders of the World (Fred D. Pfenig). Columbus, Ohio: Pfenig & Snyder, 1955.
An account of Tim McCoy's Wild West show.
Come to Judgment (Alden Whitman). New York: Viking, 1980.
Biographies of numerous prominent persons who died between 1965 and 1979, including C. Chaplin and M. Pickford.

Comedy/Cinema/Theory (Andrew Horton, editor). Berkeley, CA: University of California Press, 1991.
> Essays on the theory of film comedy, including one on C. Chaplin.

Comedy Films, 1894–1954 (John Montgomery). 2nd rev. ed. London: G. Allen & Unwin, 1968.
> Among the comic actors discussed are C. Chaplin, B. Keaton, H. Lloyd and L. Semon.

Comic Art of Charlie Chaplin: A Graphic Celebration of Chaplin's Centenary (Denis Gifford; edited by Mike Higgs). London: Hawk Books, 1989.
> A pictorial tribute on Chaplin's centenary, with reproductions of comic strips, posters, sheet music, toys and other artifacts contemporaneous with his career.

The Comic Mind: Comedy and the Movies (Gerald Mast). 2nd ed. Chicago, IL: University of Chicago Press, 1979.
> A detailed analysis of film comedy with sections on C. Chaplin, B. Keaton, H. Langdon and H. Lloyd.

Comic Technique of Pathos-Humor: Charlie Chaplin and the Gold Rush (Timothy J. Lyons). Santa Barbara, CA: University of California, Santa Barbara, 1968.
> A master's thesis.

The Complete Films of Charlie Chaplin (Gerald McDonald, Michael Conway, Mark Ricci). Secaucus, NJ: Citadel, 1988.
> A lavishly illustrated updating of *The Films of Charlie Chaplin* (1965).

The Complete Films of Greta Garbo (Michael Conway, Dion McGregor and Mark Ricci). New York: Carol, 1991.
> A reissue of the *Films of Greta Garbo* with a new introduction.

The Complete Films of William S. Hart: A Pictorial Record (Diane K. Koszarski). New York: Dover, 1980.

A Concise Encyclopedia of the Theatre (Robin May). Reading, England: Osprey, 1974.

Confessions of an Actor (John Barrymore). New York: Arno, 1980.
> A non-revealing autobiography. Reprint of the Bobbs-Merrill edition (1926).

Contemporary Dramatists (D.L. Kirkpatrick, editor). 4th ed. Chicago, IL: St. James, 1988.
> Brief personal data and bibliographies.

Contemporary Literary Criticism: Excerpts from Criticism of the Works of Today's Novelists... Detroit, MI: Gale Research, 1973–.
> Each lengthy entry contains numerous excerpts. Includes C. Chaplin.

Contemporary Theatre, Film and Television: A Biographical Guide... Detroit, MI: Gale Research, 1984–.
> Contains brief personal data, awards/honors information and filmographies/stageographies. Supersedes *Who's Who in the Theatre* (q.v.).

Continued Next Week: A History of the Moving Picture Serial (Kalton C. Lahue). Norman, OK: University of Oklahoma Press, 1964.
> A history and credits of serials through 1930. Includes information about G. Cunard, J. Hansen, H. Holmes, A. Ray, R. Roland and P. White.

Conversations with Greta Garbo (Sven Broman). New York: Viking, 1992.
> Broman is a Swedish journalist who claims to have had frequent talks with Garbo.

Corinne Griffith: As She Is to Those Who Know Her (Little Mirror Movie Books). New York: Ross, 1920.
> A brief illustrated pamphlet-style "puff piece."

Co-starring Famous Women and Alcohol (Lucy B. Robe). Minneapolis, MN: CompCare Publications, 1986.
> A study of alcoholism among women, including several silent stars.

The Cowboy: Six Shooters, Songs and Sex (Charles W. Harris and Buck Rainey, editors). Norman, OK: University of Oklahoma Press, 1976.

Included in this history of the American cowboy is an essay about film cowboys, including W.S. Hart, T. Mix and F. Thomson.

The Crazy Mirror: Hollywood Comedy and the American Image (Raymond Durgnat). New York: Horizon Press, 1970.
> This history and analysis of American comedy films contains sections on C. Chaplin, B. Keaton and H. Langdon.

Current Biography: Who's News and Why. New York: H.W. Wilson, 1940–.
> An encyclopedic work whose articles include C. Chaplin (1940), E. Ferguson, D. Gish and L. Gish (1944) and S. Hayakawa (1962), among several others.

Curtains: Selections from the Drama Criticism and Related Writings (Kenneth Tynan). New York: Atheneum, 1981.
> Contains a brief piece on G. Garbo. Reprint of the 1961 edition.

Customs and Characters: Contemporary Portraits (Peter Quennell). Boston, MA: Little, Brown, 1982.
> Contains a section on G. Garbo.

D. Quixote e Carlito (Tentativa de Interpretacao) (Francisco Silva). Rio de Janeiro: Aurora, 1959.
> About C. Chaplin. In Portuguese.

Dale Carnegie's Biographical Roundup: Highlights in the Lives of Forty Famous People. Freeport, NY: Books for Libraries, 1970.
> Brief anecdotal stories, one of which is about J. Barrymore. Reprint of the World edition (1944).

Dalmacio Carpio, Hearst Chef and Andrew Carpio, Hearst/Davies Beverly Hills Staff (Metta Hake). San Simeon, CA: San Simeon Region, 1990.
> An oral history interview about M. Davies, etc.

Damned in Paradise: The Life of John Barrymore (John Kobler). New York: Atheneum, 1977.

Dancing in the Sun: Hollywood Choreographers, 1915–1937 (Naima Prevots) (*Theater and Dramatic Studies*, no. 44). Ann Arbor, MI: UMI Research Press, 1987.
> Includes T. Kosloff.

Dark Lady of the Silents: My Life in Early Hollywood (Miriam Cooper). Indianapolis, IN: Bobbs-Merrill, 1973.
> Includes filmography.

Dark Star (Leatrice Gilbert Fountain). New York: St. Martin's, 1985.
> Biography of J. Gilbert by his daughter. Includes a filmography.

A Darling of the Twenties (Madge Bellamy). Vestal, NY: Vestal Press, 1989.
> Lavishly illustrated autobiography.

The Day the Laughter Stopped: The True Story of Fatty Arbuckle (David A. Yallop). New York: St. Martin's, 1976.
> Includes a filmography.

Debrett Goes to Hollywood (Charles Kidd). New York: St. Martin's Press, 1986.
> Biographical and career overviews, with family genealogies, of several performers including M. Astor, J. Barrymore, S. Carol, M. Davies, D. Fairbanks, G. Swanson.

A Deed of Death: The Story Behind the Unsolved Murder of Hollywood Director William Desmond Taylor (Robert Giroux). New York: Knopf, 1990.
> M.M. Minter and M. Normand were named possible suspects in the murder.

A Descriptive Study of the Acting of Alla Nazimova (Margaret McKerrow). Ann Arbor, MI: University of Michigan, 1974.
> A Ph.D. thesis.

Dictionary of American Biography. New York: Scribner's. 1927–.
> Articles include D. Fairbanks, J. Gilbert, T. Mix, B. Turpin, H.B. Walthall and P. White, all in Supplement 2.

Dictionary of Film Makers (Georges Sadoul). Berkeley, CA: University of California Press, 1972.

Career overviews and filmographies.

A Dictionary of the Cinema (Peter Graham). Rev. ed. New York: Barnes, 1968.
   Very brief entries and selected filmographies of major stars and other film people.

The Divine Garbo (Frederick Sands and Sven Broman). New York: Grosset & Dunlap, 1979.
   Focuses on the intimate details of Garbo's personal life.

Do You Sleep in the Nude? (Rex Reed). New York: New American Library, 1968.
   A collection of interviews, one of which is with B. Keaton.

The Doll House of Colleen Moore: A Fairyland Castle. Chicago, IL: Museum of Science and Industry, 1950.
   Illustrated description of C. Moore's fabulous doll castle.

Dolores Del Rio (Carlos Monsivais, Jorge Ayala and Gustavo Garcia). Huelva: Festival de Cine Iberoamericano, 1983.
   Includes a filmography.

Dolores Del Rio (Margery Wilson). Los Angeles, CA: Chimes Press, 1928.
   A pamphlet "puff piece" about Del Rio's current life and career.

Dolores Del Rio: La Triunfadora (Rafael Martinez Gandia). Madrid: Compania Ibero-Americana de Publicaciones, 1930.

Dolores Del Rio: XXIV Festival Internacional de Cine. San Sebastian, Mexico: IMEN, 1976.
   A survey of Del Rio's film career with numerous photographs and a filmography. In Spanish.

Dorothy and Lillian Gish (Lillian Gish). New York: Scribner's, 1973.
   A pictorial tracing, through numerous stills and photographs, of the Gish sisters' careers. Includes filmographies.

Doug and Mary: A Biography of Douglas Fairbanks and Mary Pickford (Gary Carey). New York: Dutton, 1977.

Doug and Mary and Others (Allene Talmey). New York: Macy-Masius, 1927.
   Sketches of several stars.

Douglas Fairbanks, 1883–1939 (Bernard Eisenschitz) (Supplement to *L'Avant Scène du Cinéma*, no. 98). Paris: Anthologie du Cinéma, 1969.
   Contains a filmography.

Douglas Fairbanks, 1883–1939 (Douglas Fairbanks Jr.). London: Academy Cinema.
   Written in conjunction with a festival of DF Sr.'s films.

Douglas Fairbanks; ou la Nostalgie de Hollywood (Charles Ford). Paris: France-Empire, 1980.
   A biography.

Douglas Fairbanks: The Fourth Musketeer (Ralph Hancock and Letitia Fairbanks). New York: Holt, 1953.
   An uncritical biography.

Douglas Fairbanks: The Making of a Screen Character (Alistair Cooke) (Museum of Modern Art Film Library Series, no. 2). New York: Museum of Modern Art, 1940.
   Contains biographical data and an analysis of Fairbanks's screen persona. Includes a detailed chronology.

A Dozen and One (Jim Tully). Freeport, NY: Books for Libraries, 1972.
   Brief sketches of famous men, one of whom is C. Chaplin. Reprint of Murray & Gee edition (1943).

Duglas Ferbenks (i.e., Douglas Fairbanks) (Nikita Verkhovsky). Leningrad: Tea-Kino-Pechat, 1929.
   In Russian.

Early American Cinema (Anthony Slide). New York: Barnes, 1970.
   A history of early film companies with brief discussion of performers.

Early Women Directors (Anthony Slide). New York: Da Capo Press, 1984.

A discussion of several pioneer women directors, including Dorothy Davenport. Reprint of Barnes edition (1977).

The Early Work of Charles Chaplin (Theodore Huff). 2nd rev. ed. New York: Gordon, 1978.
  Reprint of National Film Theatre edition (1961).

Eighty Silent Film Stars: Biographies and Filmographies of the Obscure to the Well Known (George A. Katchmer). Jefferson, NC: McFarland, 1991.
  A useful source of some otherwise not easily available information. Includes only a couple of women among the lengthy entries.

Eleanor Boardman d'Arrast: Remembering W.R. and Marion. San Simeon, CA: Hearst San Simeon State Historical Monument, 1991.
  An oral history interview held in 1987.

Encyclopedia of the Musical Theatre: An Updated Reference Guide to Over 2000 Performers... (Stanley Green). New York: Da Capo Press, 1980.
  An updating of the Dodd Mead edition (1976).

The Encyclopedia of World Theater. New York: Scribner's, 1977.
  Brief career summaries.

The Entertainers (Clive Unger-Hamilton, general editor). New York: St. Martin's Press, 1980.
  A lavishly illustrated survey of the performing arts from ancient Greece to modern times. Includes brief biographies of many hundreds of performers arranged chronologically by date of birth.

Ernest Torrens (i.e., Torrence) (B. Kolomarov). Moscow: Kinopechat, 1928.
  Brief pamphlet in Russian.

Essays in the Arts (Lord Dunsany et al.). Boston, MA: International Pocket Library.
  An essay on C. Chaplin by Elie Faure.

The Estate of Rudolph Valentino. Los Angeles, CA: A. H. Weil (Auctioneer), 1926.
  Catalog of the sale of RV's effects at auction.

Las Estrellas. Madrid: Urban, 19–.
  In Spanish. Contains numerous illustrations, career summaries and filmographies. Includes such performers as J. Barrymore (v. 5), C. Chaplin (v. 6), D. Del Rio (v. 3), D. Fairbanks (v. 3), G. Garbo (v. 1), P. Negri (v. 8), M. Pickford (v. 5), G. Swanson and R. Valentino (v. 1).

The Eubanks Family and San Simeon (Sherman Eubanks). San Simeon, CA: Hearst San Simeon State Historical Monument, 1988.
  Oral history reminiscences of the son of an electrician who worked at San Simeon from 1919 to 1952. Partly concerns M. Davies.

An Evening's Entertainment (See *History of the American Cinema*, vol. 3).

The Fabulous Holts: A Tribute to a Favorite Movie Family (Buck Rainey). Nashville, TN: Western Film Collector Press, 1976.
  An overview of the careers of Jack Holt and his children Tim and Jennifer, with filmographies.

The Fabulous Tom Mix (Olive S. Mix and Eric Heath). Englewood Cliffs, NJ: Prentice-Hall, 1957.

Faces, Forms, Films: The Artistry of Lon Chaney (Robert G. Anderson). South Brunswick, NJ: Barnes, 1971.
  Profusely illustrated overview of LC's career, including some biographical data.

The Faces of Hollywood (Clarence S. Bull and Raymond Lee). South Brunswick, NJ: Barnes, 1969.
  Basically a book of photographs of numerous silent stars with brief chapters on L. Chaney, G. Garbo, G. Swanson, J. Barrymore, C. Moore and R. Adorée.

The Fairbanks Album: Drawn from the Family Archives (Douglas Fairbanks Jr.; introduction and narrative by Richard Schickel). Boston, MA: New York Graphic Society, 1975.

340   Bibliography

Mainly pictorial, with a chronology of DF Sr.'s life.

Fallen Angel: Chronicles of L.A. Crime and Mystery (Marvin J. Wolf and Katherine Mader). New York: Facts on File, 1986.
Contains cases from 1847, including those concerning R. Arbuckle and W.D. Taylor in whose death M.M. Minter and M. Normand were investigated.

Famous Film Folk: A Gallery of Life Portraits and Biographies (Charles D. Fox). New York: G.H. Doran, 1925.
Brief biographies and photographs of numerous stars, some of whom it is difficult to find in other sources. Included in the Chadwyck-Healey microfiche *History of the Cinema, 1895–1940*.

Famous Movie Detectives (Michael R. Pitts). Metuchen, NJ: Scarecrow, 1979.
Brief synopses of the plots of detective films (mainly in series) including brief biographies of the leading actors with credits. Includes W. Baxter, B. Lytell, W. Oland.

Famous Stars of Filmdom (Men) (Elinor Hughes). Freeport, NY: Books for Libraries, 1970.
Career overviews and portrait photographs of several actors. Reprint of Page edition (1932). Included in Chadwyck-Healey microfiche *History of American Cinema, 1895–1940*.

Famous Stars of Filmdom (Women) (Elinor Hughes). Freeport, NY: Books for Libraries, 1970.
Career overviews and portrait photographs of several actresses. Reprint of Page edition (1931).

Fannie Ward: In Her Most Successful Plays Released Through Pathé Exchange (Screen Favorites Library). 1910s(?).
Stills from her film *Innocent*.

Fant'America 1: Tod Browning, Lon Chaney. Trieste: Azienda Autonoma di Soggiorno e Turismo, 1977.
Issued in conjunction with a festival of fantasy and horror films. In Italian.

Father Goose: The Story of Mack Sennett (Gene Fowler). New York, NY: Covici, Friede, 1934.
Among the Sennett performers mentioned in this biography are R. Arbuckle, C. Chaplin and M. Normand. Included in Chadwyck-Healey microfiche *History of American Cinema, 1895–1940*.

Fatti (i.e., Fatty) (B. Kolomarov). Moscow: Tea-Kino-Pechat, 1928.
A brief pamphlet in Russian about R. Arbuckle.

Fatty (Andy Edmonds). New ed. London: Futura, 1992.
A biography about R. Arbuckle.

The Fatty Arbuckle Case (Leo Guild). New York: Paperback Library, 1962.

The Fatty Arbuckle Scandal: The Man, the Crime, the Trials (Ronald Lilek). Tempe, AZ: Arizona State University, 1976.
A master's thesis.

Fifty Super Stars (John Kobal, compiler). New York: Bounty Books, 1974.
Lavish color illustrations (including some of lobby card size), with brief career descriptions and filmographies.

The Fifty-Year Decline and Fall of Hollywood (Ezra Goodman). New York: Simon and Schuster, 1961.
Goodman recounts his experiences as a publicist, columnist and writer in Hollywood. Includes a discussion of G.M. Anderson.

Film: An Anthology (Daniel Talbot, compiler and editor). Berkeley, CA: University of California Press, 1975.
A group of previously published essays and pieces; among the subjects are C. Chaplin, B. Keaton, H. Langdon and H. Lloyd. Reprint of the Simon and Schuster edition (1959).

The Film Acting of John Barrymore (Joseph Garton). New York: Arno, 1980.
Based on a Ph.D. thesis.

Film Actors Guide, Vol. 1: *Western Europe* (James R. Parish). Metuchen, NJ: Scarecrow, 1977.
  Filmographies include films made abroad. Not to be confused with *Film Actors Guide* published by Lone Eagle, 1991–.
The Film Answers Back: A Historical Appreciation (E.W. and M.M. Robson). New York: Arno, 1972.
  Among the actors discussed are C. Chaplin and M. Pickford. Reprint of the Lane edition (1939).
Film Biographies (Stan Brakhage). 2nd ed. Berkeley, CA: Turtle Island, 1979.
  Analysis of the careers and personas of several filmmakers and comedians, among them C. Chaplin and B. Keaton.
The Film Career of Buster Keaton (George Wead and George Lellis). Boston, MA: G.K. Hall, 1977.
  Contains synopses of the films and an extensive bibliography and filmography.
The Film Career of Pola Negri, 1914–1964 (Courtenay Beinhorn). Austin, TX: University of Texas at Austin, 1964.
  A master's thesis.
The Film Encyclopedia (Ephraim Katz). 2nd ed. New York: HarperCollins, 1994.
  Brief to lengthy career overviews with incomplete filmographies.
Film Essays, With a Lecture (Sergei Eisenstein). London: Dobson, 1968.
  One essay is on C. Chaplin.
The Film Handbook (Geoff Andrew) (G.K. Hall Performing Arts Handbooks). Boston, MA: G.K. Hall, 1990.
  For each director, there is a critique, "lineage"; i.e., what influenced his work, and a brief bibliography. Includes C. Chaplin and B. Keaton.
Film Makers on Film Making: Statements on Their Art by Thirty Directors (Harry M. Geduld, editor). Bloomington, IN: Indiana University Press, 1969.
  One of the directors is C. Chaplin.
Film 70/71: An Anthology by the National Society of Film Critics (David Denby, editor). New York: Simon and Schuster, 1971.
  Part of an annual series. One of the essays in this volume is about B. Keaton by Penelope Gilliatt.
Filmguide to the General (E. Rubinstein). Bloomington, IN: Indiana University Press, 1973.
  Data on the production of the classic Keaton film, with a lengthy analysis and critique.
The Filming of the West (Jon Tuska). Garden City, NY: Doubleday, 1976.
  A comprehensive history of film Westerns, with sections about W.S. Hart, T. McCoy, T. Mix, G. O'Brien and F. Thomson.
Filmlexicon degli Autori e delle Opere. Rome, Italy: Edizioni di Bianco e Nero, 1958–.
  Career summaries in Italian and filmographies which list the films' original titles. Includes many obscure performers and in some cases filmographies are more comprehensive than other sources.
The Films of Buster Keaton (Raymond Rohauer). New York: Audio Film Center, 1969.
  A catalog issued in conjunction with the release of several 16mm BK films. Contains synopses of those films and a filmography.
The Films of Dolores Del Rio (Allen L. Woll). New York: Gordon Press, 1978.
The Films of Gloria Swanson (Lawrence J. Quirk). Secaucus, NJ: Citadel, 1984.
  Profusely illustrated.
The Films of John Barrymore: As Shown in the Dryden Theatre Tribute Series (James Card). Rochester, NY: George Eastman House, 1969.
  Stills and synopses of the films shown at the 1969 retrospective. (For a related work, see *Tribute to John Barrymore* in this bibliography.)
The Films of Mary Pickford (Raymond Lee). South Brunswick, NJ: Barnes, 1970.

Mainly pictorial. MP's films are listed without description.

Final Placement: A Guide to the Deaths, Funerals and Burials of Notable Americans (Robert B. Dickerson). Algonac, MI: Reference Publications, 1982.
One of the "notables" is R. Valentino.

The First Film Makers (Richard D. McCann). Metuchen, NJ: Scarecrow; Iowa City, IA: Image & Idea, 1989.
A compilation of previously published articles that includes one on W.S. Hart.

First One Hundred Noted Men and Women of the Screen (Carolyn Lowrey). New York: Moffat, Yard, 1920.
Full page portraits and page-long synopses of careers with some personal data, some of which is inaccurate. Included in the Chadwyck-Healey microfiche *History of the Cinema, 1895–1940.*

First Person Plural: The Lives of Dagmar Godowsky (Dagmar Godowsky). New York: Viking, 1958.
An autobiography.

Five Films by Charles Chaplin: His Transition to Sound. 2 vols. (John Smead). Ann Arbor, MI: University of Michigan, 1974.
A Ph.D. thesis.

Focus on Chaplin (Donald W. McCaffrey, compiler). Englewood Cliffs, NJ: Prentice-Hall, 1971.
Essays and articles about aspects of Chaplin's career.

Folks Ushud Know: Interspersed with Songs of Courage (Lee Shippey). Sierra Madre, CA: Sierra Madre Press, 1930.
Brief career overviews of several Southern California notables, including B. Love, R. Novarro, I. Rich and G. Swanson.

Follywood [sic] *—and How!* (Sally O'Neil). Hollywood, CA: Sally O'Neil Publishing Co., 1929.
A publicity "puff piece" about SO'N's life and career.

Four Fabulous Faces: Swanson, Garbo, Crawford, Dietrich (Larry Carr). New York: Penguin, 1978.
Extensive photographic studies.

Four Great Comedians: Chaplin, Lloyd, Keaton, Langdon (Donald W. McCaffrey). New York: Barnes, 1968.
An analysis of many of their films.

The Fox Girls (James R. Parish). New Rochelle, NY: Arlington House, 1972.
Profusely illustrated lengthy career overviews and filmographies of several leading Fox actresses, including T. Bara and J. Gaynor.

Frame-Up! The Untold Story of Roscoe "Fatty" Arbuckle (Andy Edmonds). New York: William Morrow, 1991.

From Hollywood: The Careers of 15 Great American Stars (DeWitt Bodeen). South Brunswick, NJ: Barnes, 1976.
Lengthy career and personal details, with complete filmographies, of performers including M. Allison, T. Bara, J. Barrymore, M. Clark, B. Compson, D. Costello, B. Daniels, D. Del Rio, R. Dix, D. Fairbanks, H. Lockwood, W. Reid, A. Stewart and C. Talmadge.

From Hollywood with Love (Bessie Love). London: Elm Tree Books, 1977.
An autobiography, including a filmography.

Funny Men of the Movies (Edward Edelson). Garden City, NY: Doubleday, 1976.
Brief, rather superficial accounts of the careers of famous comedians, among them B. Keaton, C. Chaplin, H. Lloyd and H. Langdon.

Funny Women: American Comediennes, 1860–1985 (Mary Unterbrink). Jefferson, NC: McFarland, 1987.
Brief career summaries, including that of Mabel Normand.

The Funsters (James R. Parish and William T. Leonard). New Rochelle, NY: Arlington House, 1979.
>Lavishly illustrated lengthy career summaries of numerous comedians and comic actors, with filmographies.

Garbo (John Bainbridge). New York: Holt, Rinehart and Winston, 1971.
>Reissued version of the 1955 biography.

Garbo (Patrick Brion). Paris: Chene, 1985.
>Biography. In French.

Garbo (Antoni Gronowicz). New York: Simon and Schuster, 1990.
>A controversial biography by one who claimed to know Garbo intimately, a claim she vigorously denied.

Garbo (Screen Greats. A series, no. 8). New York: Barven, 1972.
>Lavishly illustrated in magazine format.

Garbo (Ture Sjolander). New York: Harper & Row, 1971.
>Mainly pictorial with numerous candid photographs.

Garbo (Brad Steiger and Chew Mank). Chicago, IL: Camerarts, 1965.
>Account of Garbo's career with a filmography.

Garbo (Norman Zierold). New York: Stein and Day, 1969.
>Discusses selected aspects of Garbo's life and career. Not a full biography.

Garbo: A Biography (Fritiof Billquist). New York: Putnam, 1960.
>Translated from the Swedish edition.

Garbo: A Biography (Barry Paris). New York: Knopf, 1993.

Garbo: A Portrait (Alexander Walker). New York: Macmillan, 1980.
>Profusely illustrated account of Garbo's career and later life.

The Garden of Allah (Sheilah Graham). New York: Crown, 1970.
>A gossipy account of life at the famous Hollywood residential complex. Includes information about its founder, A. Nazimova.

Gentlemen to the Rescue: The Heroes of the Silent Screen (Kalton C. Lahue). South Brunswick, NJ: Barnes, 1972.
>Well-illustrated career overviews of numerous screen leading men.

"Get Me Giesler" (John Roeburt). New York: Belmont Books, 1962.
>An account of attorney Jerry Giesler's most prominent cases, including C. Chaplin's paternity suit.

Giving Up the Ghost: A Writer's Life Among the Stars (Sandford Dody). New York: M. Evans, 1980.
>Interviews with several celebrities, including D. Godowsky.

Gloria and Joe (Axel Madsen). New York: Arbor House/W. Morrow, 1988.
>The story of the relationship between G. Swanson and Joe Kennedy.

Gloria Swanson (Richard Hudson and Raymond Lee). South Brunswick, NJ: Barnes, 1970.
>Basically pictorial, with brief synopses of her films.

Gloria Swanson at United Artists, 1925–1933 (Kenneth M. Mashon). Austin, TX: University of Texas at Austin, 1989.
>A master's thesis.

The Golden Age of Sound Comedy: Comic Films and Comedians of the Thirties. (Donald W. McCaffrey). South Brunswick, NJ: Barnes, 1973.
>Lavishly illustrated overview which includes C. Chaplin, B. Keaton, H. Langdon and H. Lloyd.

The Golden Days of San Simeon (Ken Murray). Garden City, NY: Doubleday, 1971.
>Lavishly illustrated work about W.S. Hearst's "castle" that includes information about M. Davies.

The Golden Gate and the Silver Screen (Geoffrey Bell). Rutherford, NJ: Fairleigh Dickinson University Press; New York: Cornwall Books, 1984.

History of movie-making in the San Francisco Bay area. Includes information about G.M. Anderson and H. Bosworth.

Good Night, Sweet Prince: The Life and Times of John Barrymore (Gene Fowler). San Francisco, CA: Mercury House, 1989.
  A biography by JB's great and good friend. Reprint of the Viking edition (1944).

Die Göttliche Garbo (Franz Blei). Giessen: Kindt & Bucher, 1930.
  Primarily stills from her early films, with a foreword supposedly written by Garbo. In German.

Graduating Exercises of the Paramount Pictures School Class of 1926.
  Portraits of the "graduates" with brief personal data. Includes J. Dunn and C. Rogers.

Great Companions: Critical Memoirs of Some Famous Friends (Max Eastman). New York: Farrar, Straus and Cudahy, 1959.
  Among the reminiscences is one about C. Chaplin.

The Great Cowboy Stars of Movies & Television (Lee O. Miller). New Rochelle, NY: Arlington House, 1979.
  Fairly lengthy career summaries and filmographies of numerous Western actors, including R. Dix, T. McCoy, W.S. Hart, T. Mix and G. O'Brien.

Great Film Directors: A Critical Anthology (Leo Braudy, Morris Dickstein, editors). New York: Oxford University Press, 1978.
  Articles on directors, including C. Chaplin and B. Keaton, by various film writers.

The Great Funnies: A History of Film Comedy (David Robinson). New York: Dutton, 1969.
  A brief lavishly illustrated account of such performers as C. Chaplin, B. Keaton, H. Langdon and H. Lloyd.

The Great Garbo (Robert Payne). New York: Praeger, 1976.
  A close analysis of Garbo's films.

The Great God Pan: A Biography of the Tramp Played by Charles Chaplin (Robert Payne). New York: Hermitage House, 1952.
  The English edition is called *The Great Charlie*.

The Great Lovers (Andrew Ewart). New York: Hart, 1968.
  An account of great historical lovers going back to Antony and Cleopatra. Includes M. Davies and Hearst. Originally published as *The World's Greatest Love Affairs* by Odhams (1968).

Great Lovers of the Movies (Jane Mercer). New York: Crescent Books, 1975.
  Fairly lengthy career overviews about many male matinee idols.

The Great Movie Comedians: From Charlie Chaplin to Woody Allen. Updated ed. (Leonard Maltin). New York: Harmony, 1982.
  Extensive discussion and complete filmographies of comedians including R. Arbuckle, C. Chaplin, C. Chase, R. Griffith, B. Keaton, H. Langdon, H. Lloyd and M. Normand.

The Great Movie Serials: Their Sound and Fury (Jim Harmon and Donald F. Glut). Garden City, NY: Doubleday, 1972.
  A discussion of some famous serials and their stars, such as T. Mix and P. White.

The Great Movie Series (James R. Parish, editor-in-chief). South Brunswick, NJ: Barnes, 1971.
  Background information and credits of many series, including the Charlie Chan and Dr. Christian films. There is very brief data on J. Hersholt and W. Oland.

The Great Movie Stars: The Golden Years (David Shipman). New York: Da Capo, 1985.
  Illustrated career overviews of numerous performers. Reprint of Hill and Wang edition (1979).

Great Names: And How They Are Made (Thoda Cocroft). Chicago, IL: Dartnell, 1941.
  A press agent's account of the stars she has known, including L. Gish.

Great Stars of Hollywood's Golden Age (Frank C. Platt, compiler). New York: New American Library, 1966.

Reprints of articles, some dating to the 1920s, about stars including J. Barrymore, C. Chaplin, G. Garbo and R. Valentino.

Great Stars of the American Stage: A Pictorial Record (Daniel Blum). New York: Grosset & Dunlap, 1954.
  Mainly pictorial with brief career overviews. Includes several stars who also appeared in silent films, including G. Arliss, J. Barrymore, E. Ferguson, D. Gish, L. Gish and A. Nazimova.

Great Times, Good Times: The Odyssey of Maurice Barrymore (James Kotsilibas-Davis). Garden City, NY: Doubleday, 1977.
  A biography of the 19th century matinee idol which contains much information about his son J. Barrymore.

Great Western Stars (James R. Parish). New York: Ace, 1976.
  Career descriptions and filmographies of several Western actors, including R. Dix, W.S. Hart, T. Mix, G. O'Brien.

Greta Garbo (Henri Agel). Paris: Seguier, 1990.
  Includes filmography. In French.

Greta Garbo (Richard Corliss) (*Pyramid Illustrated History of the Movies*). New York: Pyramid, 1974.
  Profusely illustrated discussion of Garbo's films.

Greta Garbo (Raymond Durgnat and John Kobal). New York: Dutton, 1965.
  Profusely illustrated, with analysis of Garbo's acting techniques.

Greta Garbo (Roland Wild) (Popular Lives Series). London: Rich & Cowan, 1933.

The Greta Garbo Collection. New York: Sotheby's, 1990.
  An auction catalog for GG's paintings.

Greta Garbo: Der Weg einer Frau und Kunstlerin (Richard Kuhn). Berlin: Arnold, 1941.
  In German (Garbo was supposedly a great favorite of Adolf Hitler). Included in Chadwyck-Healey microfiche *History of the Cinema, 1895-1940.*

Greta Garbo: La Somnambule (Françoise Ducout). Paris: Stock, 1979.

Greta Garbo: Paper Dolls in Full Color (Tom Tierney). New York: Dover, 1985.
  Contains costumes from GG's films.

Greta Garbo: Portraits 1920-1951. New York: Rizzoli, 1986.

Greta Garbo: The Development and Synthesis of Her Acting Philosophy (Charles Winstead). Chapel Hill, NC: University of North Carolina at Chapel Hill, 1967.
  A master's thesis.

Greta Garbo: The Story of a Specialist (E.E. Laing). London: Gifford, 1946.
  A biography.

Greta Garbo's Film Transformation of the Femme Fatale (Albert Agate). East Carolina University, 1987.
  A master's thesis.

Greta Garbo's Saga. Stockholm: Albert Bonniers Forlag, 1929.
  In Swedish.

The Griffith Actresses (Anthony Slide). South Brunswick, NJ: Barnes, 1973.
  Career overviews of several actresses who started in films with D.W. Griffith, including M. Cooper, C. Dempster, D. Gish, L. Gish, M. Marsh, M. Pickford and B. Sweet.

The Hall of Fame of Western Film Stars (Ernest N. Corneau). North Quincy, MA: Christopher, 1969.
  Photographs, stills, filmographies and brief career overviews of numerous actors who appeared in Westerns.

Halliwell's Filmgoer's Companion (Leslie Halliwell). 10th ed. London: HarperCollins, 1993.
  Very brief entries include selected films and performers.

Harlequin's Stick — Charlie's Cane: A Comparative Study of Commedia dell'Arte and Silent Slapstick Comedy (David Madden). Bowling Green, OH: Bowling Green University Popular Press, 1975.

Mainly pictorial, with much reference to C. Chaplin.

Harold Lloyd (Raymond Borde). Lyons: Société d'Etudes, Recherches et Documentation Cinématographiques, 1968.
  In French.

Harold Lloyd (Roland Lacourbe) (Cinéma d'Aujourd'hui, 66). Paris: Editions Seghers, 1970.
  Profusely illustrated. In French.

Harold Lloyd (Wolfram Tichy). Lucerne, SW: Bucher, 1979.
  In German?

Harold Lloyd: A Bio-Bibliography (Annette M. D'Agostino). Westport, CT: Greenwood, 1994.

Harold Lloyd: An American Film Institute Seminar on His Work. AFI(?), 1969.

Harold Lloyd Corporation (a Corporation), Pathe Exchange, inc. ... and Harold Lloyd, Appellants.... San Francisco, CA: Pernau-Walsh Printing Co., 1932.
  The account of a lawsuit.

Harold Lloyd Estate Pictorial Souvenir. 1970s(?).
  A pictorial pamphlet issued at the time Lloyd's renaissance-style mansion was open for public tours.

Harold Lloyd: Notes (Robert Miller). Chicago, IL: Film Center, 1976.

Harold Lloyd: The King of Daredevil Comedy (Adam Reilly). New York: Macmillan, 1977.
  A comprehensive look at Lloyd's films, containing much useful data about his co-stars and directors, including B. Daniels, B. Kent and J. Ralston.

Harold Lloyd: The Man on the Clock (Tom Dardis). New York: Viking, 1983.
  Detailed account of his life and films, with a filmography.

Harold Lloyd: The Shape of Laughter (Richard Schickel). Boston, MA: New York Graphic Society, 1974.
  An intimate account of Lloyd's personal life and a discussion of his career.

Harold Lloyd's World of Comedy (William Cahn). New York: Duell, Sloan and Pearce, 1964.
  An analysis of Lloyd's comedy techniques and persona.

Harry Langdon. Mount Vernon, NY: Audio Film Center, 1967.
  A film rental catalog containing interviews, information about HL's film company and a filmography.

Harry Langdon (William Schelly) (*Filmmakers*, no. 3). Metuchen, NJ: Scarecrow Press, 1982.
  Contains filmography.

Harry Langdon: A Biography (Wilbur O. Edmondson). San Francisco, CA: San Francisco State University, 1974.
  A master's thesis.

Harry Langdon: El Mejor de Todos (Francisco I. Taibo). Mexico: UNAM, 1966.
  In Spanish.

Harry Langdon: The Comedian as Metteur-en-Scène (Joyce Rheuban). Rutherford, NJ: Fairleigh Dickinson University Press, 1983.
  Contains filmography.

The Haunted Screen: Expressionism in the German Cinema and the Influence of Max Reinhardt (Lotte H. Eisner). Berkeley, CA: University of California Press, 1973.
  Among the films discussed are the German films in which Louise Brooks starred.

Headline Happy (Florabel Muir). New York: Holt, 1950.
  The Hollywood columnist relates her memories of various performers, including M. Astor and C. Chaplin.

Hearst and Davies at St. Donat's Castle: A Personal Memoir (Edgar Sheppard). San Simeon, CA: Hearst San Simeon State Historical Monument, 1989.
  An oral history by an employee at Hearst's Welsh estate from 1935 to 1937.

Hearst as a Host (Adela Rogers St. John). San Simeon, CA: Hearst San Simeon State Historical Monument, 1989.
The famous journalist reminisces about M. Davies and others.

The Hearsts: Family and Empire—The Later Years (Lindsay Chaney and Michael Cieply). New York: Simon and Schuster, 1981.
Contains much discussion of M. Davies.

Here Come the Clowns: A Cavalcade of Comedy from Antiquity to the Present (Lowell Swortzell). New York: Viking, 1978.
Includes C. Chaplin, B. Keaton, H. Langdon and H. Lloyd.

Here Lies the Heart (Mercedes de Acosta). Salem, NH: Ayer, 1990.
Memoirs which include much about her great and good friend, G. Garbo. Reprint of Reynal edition (1960).

Heroes, Heavies and Sagebrush: A Pictorial History of the "B" Western Players (Arthur F. McClure and Ken D. Jones). South Brunswick, NJ: Barnes, 1972.
Very brief descriptions and illustrations of numerous performers.

Heroes of the Horrors (Calvin T. Beck). New York: Macmillan, 1975.
Profusely illustrated and lengthy career overviews of several horror film stars, among them L. Chaney.

Heroes of the Range: Yesteryear's Saturday Matinee Movie Cowboys (Buck Rainey). Metuchen, NJ: Scarecrow, 1987.
Career overviews of several Western stars, with numerous photographs, and filmographies. Includes G. O'Brien and T. McCoy.

His Majesty the American: The Cinema of Douglas Fairbanks, Sr. (John C. Tibbetts and James M. Welsh). South Brunswick, NJ: Barnes, 1977.
Detailed synopses and analysis of Fairbanks's films.

His Picture in the Papers: A Speculation on Celebrity in America Based on the Life of Douglas Fairbanks Sr. (Richard Schickel). New York: Charterhouse, 1973.

L' Histoire de l'Art Cinématographique (Carl Vincent). 2nd ed. Brussels: Editions Trident, 1941(?).
A history of world film which contains information about C. Chaplin.

The History of Motion Pictures (Maurice Bardeche and Robert Brasillach). New York: Arno, 1970.
Includes information about C. Chaplin, D. Fairbanks, W.S. Hart, B. Keaton, H. Lloyd. Also known as *History of the Film*.

History of the American Cinema, vol. 3: *An Evening's Entertainment: The Age of the Silent Feature Picture, 1915–1928* (Richard Koszarski). New York: Scribner's, 1990.
Contains relatively brief career overviews of the major silent stars.

History of the American Film Industry: From Its Beginnings to 1931 (Benjamin B. Hampton). New York: Dover, 1970.
This survey contains information about C. Chaplin, D. Fairbanks and M. Pickford. Reprint of *A History of the Movies* (1931).

Hollywood: Stars and Starlets . . . (Garson Kanin). New York: Limelight, 1984.
Kanin's experiences in Hollywood with filmmakers, moguls and performers such as C. Chaplin and J. Barrymore. Reprint of the Viking edition (1974).

Hollywood: The Golden Era (Jack Spears). South Brunswick, NJ: Barnes, 1971.
Lengthy chapters on the careers of such silent performers as M. Pickford, N. Talmadge, C. Chaplin and C. Moore.

Hollywood: The Pioneers (Kevin Brownlow). New York: Knopf, 1979.
Profusely illustrated history of early Hollywood with sections about G. Garbo, J. Gilbert and R. Valentino.

Hollywood Album: Lives and Deaths of Hollywood Stars from the Pages of "The New York Times" (Arleen Keylin and Suri Fleischer, editors). New York: Arno, 1977–79.
Facsimiles of *The New York Times* obituaries for numerous performers.

Hollywood Album 2: Lives and Deaths of Hollywood Stars from the Pages of "The New York Times" (Arleen Keylin, editor). New York: Arno, 1979.
 A continuation of *Hollywood Album*.
Hollywood and the Great Stars: The Stars, the Sex Symbols, the Legend, the Movies and How It All Began (Jeremy Pascall, editor; Mundy Ellis, compiler). New York: Crescent Books, 1976.
 Lavishly illustrated career and biographical overviews of several stars, including L. Chaney, C. Chaplin, G. Garbo, B. Keaton, H. Lloyd, M. Pickford and R. Valentino.
Hollywood as Historian: American Film in a Cultural Context (Peter C. Rollins). Lexington, KY: University Press of Kentucky, 1983.
 Among the essays is one about three Chaplin films: *City Lights, Modern Times* and *The Great Dictator*.
Hollywood Be Thy Name: Random Recollections of a Movie Veteran from Silents to Talkies to TV (William Bakewell). (Filmmakers, no. 25). Metuchen, NJ: Scarecrow, 1991.
The Hollywood Beauties (James R. Parish with Gregory W. Mank and Don E. Stanke). New Rochelle, NY: Arlington House, 1978.
 Lengthy and profusely illustrated overviews of the careers of several actresses, including Dolores Del Rio.
Hollywood Character Actors (James R. Parish). New Rochelle, NY: Arlington House, 1978.
 Very brief illustrated descriptions and filmographies of numerous performers.
Hollywood Corral (Big Apple Film Series) (Don Miller). New York: Popular Library, 1976.
 Lavishly illustrated history of Western films, with sections about T. McCoy, T. Mix and G. O'Brien.
Hollywood Directors, 1914–1940 (Richard Koszarski, compiler). New York: Oxford University Press, 1976.
 Reprints of periodical articles and excerpts from books discussing such directors as C. Chaplin, W.S. Hart, B. Keaton, H. Langdon and H. Lloyd.
Hollywood Dynasties (Stephen Farber and Marc Green). New York: Delilah, 1984.
 Discusses studio heads, stars and their relatives who created "dynasties" in the film industry. Among them is Sue Carol, wife of Alan Ladd.
Hollywood Exiles (John Baxter). New York: Taplinger, 1976.
 Mainly brief discussions of the careers of various European and other foreign-born performers, including C. Chaplin, G. Garbo, P. Negri and M. Pickford.
Hollywood Goddesses: How the Stars Were Born... (Michael Jay, editor). New York: Galahad Books, 1982.
 Profusely illustrated brief stories about various actresses, including G. Garbo.
Hollywood Greats of the Golden Years: The Late Stars of the 1920s Through the 1950s (J.G. Ellrod). Jefferson, NC: McFarland, 1989.
 Very brief career summaries and incomplete filmographies of performers such as G. Arliss, M. Astor, J. Barrymore, W. Baxter, C. Chaplin, M. Davies, J. Gaynor and G. Swanson.
The Hollywood Hall of Fame: 50 All Time Great Stars of Motion Pictures (Johnny Roth). Los Angeles, CA: Richards Enterprises, 1968.
 Brief career summaries and photographs.
Hollywood Heartbreak: The Tragic and Mysterious Deaths of Hollywood's Most Remarkable Legends (Laurie Jacobson). New York: Simon and Schuster, 1984.
 Among the performers included are C. Bow, R. Novarro, W. Reid and W.D. Taylor, in whose death M. Normand and M.M. Minter were suspects.
Hollywood Heaven: From Valentino to John Belushi, the Film Stars Who Died Young (David Barraclough). New York: Gallery Books, 1991.

Lavishly illustrated brief (sometimes very brief) discussions of numerous performers, including R. Arbuckle, J. Gilbert, J. Murray, W. Reid, R. Valentino and P. White.
Hollywood Hunks and Heroes (Daniel and Susan Cohen). New York: Exeter Books, 1985.
 Brief profusely illustrated career overviews with filmographies. R. Valentino is the only silent star included.
Hollywood Kids: Child Stars of the Silver Screen from 1903 to the Present (Thomas Aylesworth). New York: Dutton, 1987.
 Very brief to lengthy career overviews of numerous performers.
Hollywood Lolitas: The Nymphet Syndrome in the Movies (Marianne Sinclair). New York: Holt, 1988.
 An account of how film portrays young girls. Includes several silent stars.
Hollywood Love Stories (Robyn Karney). London: Octopus Books, 1987.
 The careers and lives of several renowned Hollywood couples, including D. Fairbanks and M. Pickford.
The Hollywood Murder Casebook (Michael Munn). New York: St. Martin's, 1987.
 Some of these cases, which may not have actually been murders, include R. Arbuckle, R. Novarro and W.D. Taylor in whose death M.M. Minter and M. Normand were implicated.
Hollywood on Record: The Film Stars' Discography (Michael R. Pitts and Louis H. Harrison). Metuchen, NJ: Scarecrow, 1978.
 Includes recordings made wholly or in part by several stars.
Hollywood on the Palisades: A Filmography of Silent Features Made in Fort Lee, New Jersey, 1903–1927 (Rita Altomara). New York: Garland, 1983.
 Includes filmographies on T. Bara, C. Blackwell, J. Caprice, M. Clark, E. Clayton, I. Cummings, J. Elvidge, M. Evans, D. Fairbanks, E. Ferguson, P. Frederick, J. Hines, F. Lawrence, E. Lincoln, M. Marsh, A. Nazimova, M. Normand, O. Petrova, M. Pickford, V. Suratt, P. White, R. Warwick and C.K. Young.
Hollywood Players, the Thirties (James R. Parish and William T. Leonard). New Rochelle, NY: Arlington House, 1976.
 Career summaries and filmographies of numerous performers including J. Boles, M. Brian and A.M. Wong.
The Hollywood Reporter Star Profiles (Marc Wanamaker, general editor). New York: Gallery Books, 1984.
 Brief discussions about stars such as J. Barrymore, C. Bow, C. Chaplin, G. Garbo, L. Gish, B. Keaton, M. Pickford, G. Swanson and R. Valentino.
Hollywood R.I.P. (I.G. Edmonds). Evanston, IL: Regency Books, 1963.
 An account of the scandals, and in some cases the trials, involving some well-known Hollywood stars.
Hollywood Songsters (James R. Parish and Michael R. Pitts). New York: Garland, 1991.
 Ample career summaries, filmographies and, if applicable, discographies. Includes John Boles.
The Hollywood Style (Arthur Knight). New York: Macmillan, 1969.
 A glimpse, through color photographs, into the homes of many past and present Hollywood stars, including J. Barrymore, D. Fairbanks, M. Pickford, W.S. Hart and H. Lloyd.
Hollywood Tragedy (William H.A. Carr). Greenwich, CT: Fawcett, 1976.
 This account of several Hollywood scandals includes R. Arbuckle, M. Astor, C. Chaplin and W.D. Taylor, in whose death M. Normand and M.M. Minter were suspected.
Hollywood Without Make-up (Pete Martin). Philadelphia, PA: Lippincott, 1948.
 Interviews with several Hollywood personalities, one of whom is F.X. Bushman.
Hollywood's Children: An Inside Account of the Child Star Era (Diana Cary). Boston, MA: Houghton Mifflin, 1978.
 The stories of the author and other child stars, including M. Pickford.

Hollywood's Great Love Teams (James R. Parish). New Rochelle, NY: Arlington House, 1974.

Complete filmographies of the performers who were part of the "love teams," synopses of their films together and some background information. Includes V. Banky, C. Farrell, G. Garbo, J. Gaynor and J. Gilbert.

Hollywood's Other Women (Alex Barris). South Brunswick, NJ: Barnes, 1975.

An overview of various types of women as portrayed by Hollywood, including sirens, the best friend, mothers, etc. Includes M. Astor.

Hollywood's Unsolved Mysteries (John Austin). New York: S.p.i. Books, 1992.

Three of the "mysteries" involve R. Arbuckle, A. Rubens and W.D. Taylor, in whose death the names of M. Normand and M.M. Minter were mentioned.

Hommage à Lillian Gish. Cinémathèque Française, 1983.

Accompaniment to a retrospective of LG's films, with reprints of articles and a filmography. Mostly in French.

Horror Film Stars (Michael R. Pitts). 2nd ed. Jefferson, NC: McFarland, 1991.

Brief career overviews of numerous leading and supporting players, including L. Chaney.

The Horror People (John Brosnan). New York: St. Martin's, 1976.

This survey of horror films has a section on L. Chaney.

An Hour with the Movies and the Talkies (Gilbert Seldes). New York: Arno, 1973.

Includes discussion of C. Chaplin. Reprint of Lippincott edition (1929).

The House of Barrymore (Margot Peters). New York: Knopf, 1990.

A comprehensive biography that also contains much information about D. Costello.

How I Became a Successful Moving Picture Star (Jack [i.e., J. Warren] Kerrigan). Los Angeles, CA: Kellow & Brown, 1914.

Included in the Chadwyck-Healey microfiche *History of the Cinema, 1895-1940*.

How I Broke Into the Movies: Signed Autobiographies. Hollywood, CA: Hal C. Herman, 1929.

Full page portraits and stories of how 60 stars got into films.

I Couldn't Smoke the Grass on My Father's Lawn (Michael Chaplin). New York: Putnam, 1966.

An autobiography by C. Chaplin's son.

I Love You Clark Gable, Etc.: Male Sex Symbols of the Silver Screen (George Tashman). Richmond, CA: Brombacher Books, 1976.

Brief career summaries of leading actors, including J. Barrymore, D. Fairbanks, J. Gilbert and R. Valentino.

The "I" of the Camera: Essays in Film Criticism, History and Aesthetics (William Rothman). New York: Cambridge University Press, 1988.

One of the essays is about C. Chaplin.

The Idols of Silence (Anthony Slide). South Brunswick, NJ: Barnes, 1976.

Illustrations and career summaries of silent stars, including P. Bonner, H. Bosworth, B. Daniels, J. Goudal, R. Graves, B. Lyon, O. Petrova, B. Rhodes, A. Terry and K. Williams. Bibliographies of periodical articles are provided for these performers and numerous others in "checklists."

The Illustrated Encyclopedia of Movie Character Actors (David Quinlan). New York: Harmony Books, 1986.

Brief descriptions and filmographies of hundreds of performers, among whom are M. Blue, N. Beery, M. Love, P. Marmont, J. Miljan and H.B. Warner. Original title was *Illustrated Directory of Film Character Actors*.

The Illustrated Encyclopedia of the World's Great Movie Stars and Their Films (Ken Wlaschin). New York: Harmony Books, 1983.

Brief illustrated career overviews and "best films" of hundreds of stars.

An Illustrated History of the Horror Film (Carlos Clarens). New York: Putnam, 1979.

Includes data on L. Chaney.

The Illustrated Who's Who in British Films (Denis Gifford). Detroit, MI: Gale, 1978.
Brief entries with filmographies for British films only.
The Illustrated Who's Who of the Cinema (Ann Lloyd and Graham Fuller, editors).
New York: Portland House, 1987.
Brief entries, some with photographs or stills, and selective filmographies. Includes many British stars.
The Image Makers: Sixty Years of Hollywood Glamour (Paul Trent). New York: Harmony Books, 1982.
Photographic studies of numerous stars arranged by decade. Reprint of McGraw-Hill edition (1972).
"Image" on the Art and Evolution of the Film (Marshall Deutelbaum, editor). New York: Dover; Rochester, NY: International Museum of Photography, 1979.
Interviews with several stars and articles about others.
The Immediate Experience: Movies, Comics, Theatre and Other Aspects of Popular Culture (Robert Warshow). New York: Atheneum, 1979.
Lengthy essays, including two on C. Chaplin.
Immortals of the Screen (Ray Stuart, compiler). Los Angeles, CA: Sherbourne, 1965.
Very brief career summaries and stills of hundreds of performers.
Les Immortels du Cinéma. Ciné Revue.
Lavishly illustrated with numerous stills. Contains career overviews of stars such as C. Chaplin, G. Garbo and R. Valentino. Some entries contain filmographies. In French.
An In-Depth Analysis of Buster Keaton's "The General" (Noel E. Carroll). New York: New York University, 1976.
A Ph.D. thesis.
An Index to the Films of Charles Chaplin (Special Supplement to *Sight and Sound.* Index Series no. 3). 1945.
Chaplin films, through *The Great Dictator*, with brief plot summaries.
Initiative and Self-Reliance (Douglas Fairbanks). New York: Britton, 1918.
Another of a series of books by (or ghostwritten for) DF about how to gain success in life.
International Dictionary of Films and Filmmakers, vol. 2: *Directors*; vol. 3: *Actors and Actresses* (Nicholas Thomas, editor). 2nd ed. Detroit, MI: St. James, 1991–92.
Each entry contains a capsule career summary, a presumably complete filmography, photograph, brief bibliography and a commentary. Part of a five volume set.
The International Encyclopedia of Film (Roger Manvell, editor). New York: Bonanza, 1975.
Brief to lengthy entries about film terminology, personalities, national film industries, etc. Includes major stars only. Reprint of the Crown edition (1972).
International Motion Picture Almanac. New York: Quigley, 1956–.
Annual publication with brief career summaries, filmographies, stageographies and TV appearances.
Interviews with Film Directors (Andrew Sarris, editor). Indianapolis, IN: Bobbs-Merrill, 1968.
Among the directors interviewed at fairly great length are C. Chaplin and B. Keaton.
The Intimate Journal of Rudolph Valentino (Rudolph Valentino). New York: Faro, 1931.
Included in the Chadwyck-Healey microfiche *History of the Cinema, 1895–1940.*
The Intimate Life of Rudolph Valentino (Jack Scagnetti). Middle Village, NY: J. David, 1975.
A sketchy, profusely illustrated biography with a section on RV collectibles.
The Intimate Sex Lives of Famous People (Irving Wallace et al.). New York: Delacorte, 1981.
Among the celebrated persons included are J. Barrymore, C. Chaplin and R. Valentino.

352   Bibliography

Intimate Talks with Movie Stars (Edward Weitzel). New York: Dale, 1921.
Interviews with, and anecdotes about, several actors.
Introduction to the Photoplay, 1929: A Contemporary Account of the Transition to Sound in Film (John C. Tibbetts, editor). Shawnee Mission, KS: National Film Society, 1977.
A reprinting of lectures given in 1929 by individuals connected to the film industry. The actor is C. Nagel. Included in the Chadwyck-Healey microfiche *History of the Cinema, 1895-1940.*
Is That Who I Think It Is? (Patrick Agan). New York: Ace Books, 1975-.
Nostalgia pieces, including M. Bellamy (v. 3), S. Carol (v. 2), B. Love (v. 1), T. McCoy (v. 1), D. Del Rio (v. 3) and M. Nixon (v.3).
The "It" Girl: The Incredible Story of Clara Bow (Joe Morella and Edward Z. Epstein). New York: Delacorte, 1976.
The first full-length biography.
Janet Gaynor: A Bio-bibliography (Connie Billips). New York: Greenwood, 1992.
The J.M. Goodman Auction Gallery ... Presents the Auction of the Mary Pickford Estate. Glendale, CA: Goodman Gallery, 1981(?).
Joe Franklin's Encyclopedia of Comedians (Joe Franklin). New York: Bell, 1985.
Generally brief illustrated anecdotal overviews of the careers of numerous comedians, both well-known and obscure.
John Barrymore: The Legend and the Man (Alma Power-Waters). New York: Messner, 1941.
Just Me (Pearl White). New York: Doran, 1919.
Anecdotes about P. White's life. Included in Chadwyck-Healey microfiche *History of the Cinema, 1895-1940.*
Keaton (Rudi Blesh). New York: Collier, 1971.
Keaton et Cie: Les Burlesques Américains du "Muet" (Cinéma d'Aujourd'hui, 25) (Jean-Pierre Coursodon). Paris: Editions Seghers, 1964.
Contains discussions of several silent stars including C. Chase, L. Fazenda, B. Keaton, H. Langdon, H. Lloyd, M. Normand, L. Semon and B. Turpin, with a chronology of the silent period and incomplete filmographies. There are only filmographies for C. Chase and R. Arbuckle. In French.
Keaton: The Man Who Wouldn't Lie Down (Tom Dardis). New York: Limelight Editions, 1988.
A straightforward biography, with a filmography. Reprint of the Scribner edition (1979).
Keaton: The Silent Features Close Up (Daniel Moews). Berkeley, CA: University of California Press, 1977.
The Kindergarten of the Movies: A History of the Fine Arts Company (Anthony Slide). Metuchen, NJ: Scarecrow, 1980.
Contains a chapter about D. Fairbanks and a "Fine Arts Who's Who," including M. Blue, D. Gish, L. Gish, R. Harron, B. Love, W. Lucas, M. Marsh, T. Marshall, C. Myers, S. Owen, A. Rubens, P. Starke, C. Talmadge and N. Talmadge.
King Cowboy: Tom Mix and the Movies (Robert S. Birchard). Burbank, CA: Riverwood Press, 1993.
Lavishly illustrated with stills and photographs. Contains credits, and many plot synopses and excerpts of reviews for Mix's shorts and features.
King of Comedy (Mack Sennett). San Francisco, CA: Mercury House, 1990.
An autobiographical account with anecdotes about MS's studio and performers including C. Chaplin and M. Normand. Reprint of the Doubleday edition (1954).
King Vidor: Work and Play with Hearst and Davies (Rosie Wittig). San Simeon, CA: San Simeon Region, 1990.
An oral history interview.
Kings of Tragedy (Jane E. Wayne). New York: Manor Books, 1976.

Stories about "tragic" stars such as R. Arbuckle, J. Barrymore, J. Gilbert and R. Valentino. Contains some inaccuracies.

Kops and Custards: The Legend of Keystone Films (Kalton C. Lahue and Terry Brewer). Norman, OK: University of Oklahoma Press, 1972.
Among the silent players discussed are R. Arbuckle, C. Chaplin, C. Murray, M. Normand, M. Swain.

Ladd: The Life, the Legend, the Legacy of Alan Ladd: A Biography (Beverly Linet). New York: Arbor House, 1979.
Contains much information on S. Carol, the wife of Alan Ladd.

Ladies in Distress (Kalton Lahue). South Brunswick, NJ: Barnes, 1971.
Illustrated career overviews of a large number of silent film actresses.

Laugh and Live (Douglas Fairbanks). New York: Britton, 1917.
One of a series of books by (or ghostwritten for) DF about his upbeat philosophy of life.

The Laugh Makers: A Pictorial History of American Comedians (William Cahn). New York: Putnam, 1957.
Includes information on C. Chaplin and H. Lloyd.

The Laurel and Hardy Book (Leonard Maltin, editor). New York: Curtis, 1973.
Everything you always wanted to know about the famous duo including information on their "stock company," one of whom was M. Busch.

Leading Ladies: Photographs from the Kobal Collection (Don Macpherson, text). New York: St. Martin's Press, 1986.
Portrait photographs of numerous actresses, including M. Astor, T. Bara, E. Boardman, C. Bow, E. Brent, L. Brooks, M. Davies, D. Del Rio, G. Garbo, J. Gaynor, L. Gish, C. Moore, M. Murray, P. Negri, M. Pickford, G. Swanson, A.M. Wong.

Leading Men (Julie Welch). New York: Crescent, 1987.
Portrait photographs of actors from the silent era to modern times. Reprint of the Villard edition (1985).

Leatrice Joy (Vladimir Korolevich). Moscow: Kino-Press, 1927.
A brief pamphlet in Russian.

The Legend of Charlie Chaplin (Peter Haining, editor). Secaucus, NJ: Castle, 1982.
Profusely illustrated articles and essays by people who knew and/or worked with Chaplin.

The Legend of Garbo (Peter Haining). London: W.H. Allen, 1990.

Let Me Entertain You: Conversations with Show People (Jordan R. Young). Beverly Hills, CA: Moonstone Press, 1988.
Interviews of silent stars such as E. Boardman, L. LaPlante, M. MacLaren and D. Revier.

Life and Death in Hollywood. Cincinnati, OH: Zebra Picture Books, 1950.
Consists of photographs of stars, many of whom who were involved in scandal.

The Life and Legend of Tom Mix (Paul E. Mix). South Brunswick, NJ: Barnes, 1972.
Profusely illustrated, with a filmography and numerous factoids about Mix's family, etc.

Life and Lillian Gish (Albert B. Paine). New York: Macmillan, 1932.
An early biography. Included in Chadwyck-Healey microfiche *History of the Cinema, 1895–1940.*

The Life of Earle Williams (Oren C. Reel). New York: Shakespeare Press, 1915.
Included in Chadwyck-Healey microfiche *History of the Cinema, 1895–1940.*

A Life on Film (Mary Astor). New York: Dell, 1972.
Contains a filmography.

Life Stories of the Movie Stars (Mae Tinee, compiler). Hamilton, OH: Presto, 1916.
Photographs and brief narratives about numerous performers, some of whom are not found in many other sources.

Life Story of Conrad Nagel. Movie Weekly, early 1920s(?).

Brief "puff piece."

Life Story of Eugene O'Brien. Movie Weekly, 1920s(?).
    Brief "puff piece."

The Life Story of Greta Garbo (Mary Margaret McBride) (Screen Star Library). New York: Star Library Publications, 1932.
    Brief, profusely illustrated pamphlet. Included in Chadwyck-Healey microfiche *History of the Cinema, 1895–1940.*

Life Story of Richard Dix. Movie Weekly, early 1920s(?).
    A slim "puff piece" pamphlet.

Life with the Lyons: The Autobiography of Bebe Daniels & Ben Lyon (Bebe Daniels). London: Odham Press, 1953.

Lillian Gish. New York: Museum of Modern Art, 1980.
    A career overview, tributes and an appreciation by Edward Wagenknecht.

Lillian Gish: An Interpretation (Edward Wagenknecht) (University of Washington Chapbooks, no. 7). Seattle, WA: University of Washington Bookstore, 1927.
    Included in Chadwyck-Healey microfiche *History of the Cinema, 1895–1940.*

Lillian Gish: As She Is to Those Who Know Her (Little Movie Mirror Books). New York: Ross, 1920.
    A brief illustrated pamphlet-style "puff piece."

Lillian Gish: The Movies, Mr. Griffith and Me (Lillian Gish with Ann Pinchot). Englewood Cliffs, NJ: Prentice-Hall, 1969.
    An autobiography.

Lillian Gish: The Twelfth Annual American Film Institute Life Achievement Award. Los Angeles, CA: AFI, 1984.
    Lavishly illustrated, with reminiscences and tributes to LG's life and work.

Lina, DeMille's Godless Girl (Lina Basquette). Fairfax, VA: Denlinger's Publishers, 1990.
    An autobiography.

The Lion's Share: The Story of an Entertainment Empire (Bosley Crowther). New York: Dutton, 1957.
    This history of MGM contains a section about G. Garbo and a briefer discussion about J. Gilbert.

The Little Fellow: The Life and Work of Charles Spencer Chaplin (Peter Cotes and Thelma Niklaus). New York: Citadel, 1965.

Locklear: The Man Who Walked on Wings (Art Ronnie). South Brunswick, NJ: Barnes, 1973.
    A biography of pilot and stunt flier Ormer Locklear, containing some information about Viola Dana, his fiancée at the time of his death.

Lon Chaney: Master Craftsman of Make Believe (Nathaniel L. Ross). Los Angeles, CA: Quality RJ, 1988.
    Detailed career overview and biography, including a filmography.

Lon Chaney: The Man Behind the Thousand Faces (Michael F. Blake). Vestal, NY: Vestal Press, 1993.

Lon of 1000 Faces! (Forrest J. Ackerman). Beverly Hills, CA: Morrison, Raven-Hill, 1983.
    Profusely illustrated account of L. Chaney's films.

The Look of Buster Keaton (Robert Benayoun). New York: St. Martin's, 1983.
    Translation of the French edition, containing commentary on Keaton's life and work, with numerous illustrations.

Lotte Reiniger, David W. Griffith, Harry Langdon. Frankfurt am Main: Kommunales Kino, 1972.

Louise Brooks (Barry Paris). New York: Knopf, 1989.
    An extremely detailed biography.

Louise Brooks: Portrait of an Anti-Star (Roland Jaccard, editor). New York: Zoetrope, 1986.

Translation of the 1982 French edition containing analyses, by LB and others, of her most famous films, especially *Pandora's Box.*

Love Goddesses of the Movies (Roger Manvell). New York: Crescent Books, 1975.

Profusely illustrated career summaries of American and foreign actresses, including T. Bara, C. Bow, G. Garbo, M. Pickford and G. Swanson.

Love, Laughter and Tears: My Hollywood Story (Adela Rogers St. Johns). Garden City, NY: Doubleday, 1978.

The author remembers her days as the self-styled "Mother Confessor of Hollywood." Includes discussions of performers such as R. Arbuckle, C. Bow, L. Chaney, C. Chaplin, B. Daniels, D. Fairbanks, G. Garbo, J. Gilbert, B. LaMarr, T. Mix, C. Moore, M. Normand, M. Pickford, W. Reid, G. Swanson, R. Valentino.

Lulu in Hollywood (Louise Brooks). New York: Limelight, 1989.

A lively account of L. Brooks's experiences in Hollywood and in making films abroad. Reprint of Knopf edition (1982).

Mabel (Betty Harper Fussell). New York: Limelight, 1992.

A biography of M. Normand. Reprint of the Ticknor & Fields edition (1982).

Mack Sennett's Keystone: The Man, the Myth and the Comedies (Kalton C. Lahue). South Brunswick, NJ: Barnes, 1971.

Among the great comics and others discussed are R. Arbuckle, C. Chaplin, L. Fazenda, C. Murray, M. Normand, F. Sterling, M. Swain and G. Swanson.

Madam Valentino: The Many Lives of Natacha Rambova (Michael Morris). New York: Abbeville, 1991.

A biography of R. Valentino's second wife.

Mae West, Greta Garbo (Franz Blei et al.). Munich: Hanser, 1978.

Includes filmography. In German.

The Magic of Rudolph Valentino (Norman A. Mackenzie). London: Research Publ. Co., 1974.

Includes lengthy synopses of RV's best-known films.

Magill's Cinema Annual, 1983: A Survey of 1982 Films (Frank Magill, editor). Englewood Cliffs, NJ: Salem Press, 1983.

Contains a lengthy interview with L. Gish.

Major Film Directors of the American and British Cinema (Gene D. Phillips). Bethlehem, PA: Lehigh University Press, 1990.

Overviews of the careers of several directors, including C. Chaplin.

Making Life Worth While (Douglas Fairbanks). New York: Britton, 1918.

One of a series of books written by (or ghostwritten for) DF about his upbeat philosophy of life.

Marguerite Clark, America's Darling of Broadway and the Silent Screen (Curtis Nunn). Fort Worth, TX: Texas Christian University Press, 1981.

A lavishly illustrated and detailed overview of MC's career. Includes a filmography.

Marion Davies: A Biography (Fred L. Guiles). New York: McGraw-Hill, 1972.

Mark Twain and Buster Keaton: A Study in American Comic Attitudes (Karen Jo Reiber). Seattle, WA: University of Washington, 1984.

A Ph.D. thesis.

Mary Pickford, America's Sweetheart (Scott Eyman). New York: Fine, 1990.

A revealing biography which frankly discusses MP's alcoholism.

Mary Pickford and Douglas Fairbanks: The Most Popular Couple the World Has Ever Known (Booton Herndon). New York: Norton, 1977.

Mary Pickford, Comedienne (Kemp R. Niver). Los Angeles, CA: Locare Research Group, 1969.

Frame enlargements of, and advertisements for, some of MP's Biograph films, 1909–12.

Mary Pickfordova (Veroslav Haba). Prague: Ceskoslovensky Filmovy Ustav, 1983.
    An overview of MP's career, with a filmography. In Czech.
The Matinee Idols (David Carroll). New York: Galahad, 1974.
    A survey of theater and film matinee idols from Edmund Kean to J. Barrymore. Includes F.X. Bushman, D. Fairbanks, J. Gilbert, W.S. Hart, T. Mix, R. Novarro, W. Reid, L. Tellegen and R. Valentino.
Mayer and Thalberg: The Make-Believe Saints (Samuel Marx). Hollywood, CA: S. French, 1988.
    Among the performers discussed in this chronicle of MGM's great years are G. Garbo and J. Gilbert. Reprint of the Random House edition (1975).
Memoirs of a Star (Pola Negri). Garden City, NY: Doubleday, 1970.
    An autobiography.
Mexican American Biographies: A Historical Dictionary, 1836-1987 (Matt S. Meier). Westport, CT: Greenwood, 1988.
    Fairly brief entries, including one about R. Novarro.
Mexican Cinema: Reflections of a Society, 1896-1980. Rev. ed. (Carlos J. Mora). Berkeley, CA: University of California Press, 1989(?).
    Chronological history of Mexican films, including a little information about D. Del Rio.
The MGM Girls: Behind the Velvet Curtain (Peter H. Brown and Pamela A. Brown). New York: St. Martin's, 1983.
    The careers of leading MGM actresses, among them M. Davies, G. Garbo and M. Murray.
The MGM Stock Company: The Golden Era (James R. Parish and Ronald L. Bowers). New Rochelle, NY: Arlington House, 1973.
    Brief career summaries and filmographies of such MGM luminaries as M. Astor, J. Barrymore, M. Davies, M. Evans, G. Garbo and J. Hersholt.
The MGM Years (Lawrence B. Thomas). New York: Columbia House, 1972.
    An overview of MGM's great musicals from 1939 to 1971, with very brief biographies of some MGM musical stars such as J. Boles, B. Love and R. Novarro.
Mike Wallace Asks: Highlights from 46 Controversial Interviews ((Mike Wallace). New York: Simon and Schuster, 1958.
    Excerpts from the author's TV shows and newspaper interviews. Includes a segment on G. Swanson.
A Million and One Nights: A History of the Motion Picture (Terry Ramsaye). New York: Simon and Schuster, 1986.
    A seminal film history that discusses many of the early film stars, including C. Chaplin and M. Pickford. Originally published in 1926. Included in the Chadwyck-Healey microfiche *History of the Cinema, 1895-1940.*
Minutes of the Last Meeting (Gene Fowler). Mattituck, NY: Rivercity Press, 1976.
    A reminiscence about a group of Fowler's great friends, including J. Barrymore. Reprint of the Viking edition (1954).
Moments with Chaplin (Lillian Ross). New York: Dodd, Mead, 1980.
    Brief reminiscences.
Monsieur Chaplin; ou, Le Rire dans la Nuit (Maurice Bessy and Robert Florey). Paris: J. Damase, 1952.
    In French.
More Character People (Arthur F. McClure, Alfred E. Twomey and Ken D. Jones). Secaucus, NJ: Citadel, 1984.
    Very brief descriptions of numerous supporting players.
More Fabulous Faces: The Evolution and Metamorphosis of Dolores Del Rio . . . (Larry Carr). Garden City, NY: Doubleday, 1979.
    Extensive photographic studies of D. Del Rio and four other actresses from their

youth to the time of writing. Also contains brief discussions of their films and some anecdotes.

More from Hollywood!: The Careers of 15 Great American Stars (DeWitt Bodeen). South Brunswick, NJ: Barnes, 1977.
Lengthy career overviews and filmographies of performers and other Hollywood notables, including E. Ferguson, P. Frederick, G. Garbo, D. Gish, M. McAvoy, A. Moreno, A. Nazimova, R. Novarro, C. Ray and B. Sweet.

More Memorable Americans, 1750–1950 (Robert Downs, John T. Flanagan and Harold W. Scott). Littleton, CO: Libraries Unlimited, 1985.
Fairly brief biographies, among which are J. Barrymore and D. Fairbanks.

More of Hollywood's Unsolved Mysteries (John Austin). New York: Shapolsky, 1991.
Among the "mysteries" is the Thomas Ince death which possibly involved W.R. Hearst and M. Davies.

More Than a Cowboy: The Life and Films of Fred Thomson and Silver King (Edgar Wyatt). Raleigh, NC: Wyatt Classics, 1988.
A lavishly illustrated account with film synopses.

Motion Picture News Booking Guide and Studio Directory. Los Angeles, CA: Motion Picture News, n.d.
An annual(?) publication that appeared under slightly different titles. Most entries are brief but several are of greater length with photographs.

Movie Comedians: The Complete Guide (James Neibaur). Jefferson, NC: McFarland, 1986.
Although its completeness is in doubt, this contains brief discussions of the films and filmographies of C. Chaplin, C. Chase, B. Keaton and H. Lloyd.

Movie Comedy (see *The National Society of Film Critics on Movie Comedy*).

The Movie Makers (Sol Chaneles and Albert Wolsky). Secaucus, NJ: Derbibooks, 1974.
Brief career summaries with very sketchy filmographies. Illustrated.

The Movie Makers: Artists in an Industry (Gene D. Phillips). Chicago: Nelson-Hall, 1973.
Analysis of the oeuvres of several filmmakers, including C. Chaplin.

The Movie Musical from Vitaphone to 42nd Street: As Reported in a Great Fan Magazine (Miles Kreuger, editor). New York: Dover, 1975.
A collection of articles, photographs and advertisements which orginally appeared in *Photoplay* from 1926 to 1933. Among the performers profiled are J. Boles, B. Daniels, B. Love and R. Novarro.

The Movie Star (see *The National Society of Film Critics on the Movie Star*).

Movie Star: A Look at the Women Who Made Hollywood (Ethan Mordden). New York: St. Martin's, 1983.
Career overviews, some brief, of numerous actresses.

The Movie Stars (Richard Griffith). Garden City, NY: Doubleday, 1970.
A lavishly illustrated look at numerous Hollywood stars.

The Movie Stars Story (Robyn Karney, editor). New York: Crescent, 1984.
Brief career summaries and photographs of numerous performers.

The Movies Come from America (Gilbert Seldes). New York: Arno, 1978.
Includes commentary on Chaplin and M. Pickford. Reprint of the Scribner edition (1937). Included in the Chadwyck-Healey microfiche *History of the Cinema, 1895–1940.*

The Movies in the Age of Innocence (Edward Wagenknecht). New York: Ballantine, 1971.
An overview of the silent film era, with sections on L. Gish and M. Pickford. Reprint of the University of Oklahoma edition (1962).

My Autobiography (Charles Chaplin). New York: Plume, 1992.
Generally regarded to be less than accurate on many counts. Reprint of Simon and Schuster edition (1964).

My Father, Charlie Chaplin (Charles Chaplin Jr. with N. and M. Rau). New York: Random House, 1960.

My Hollywood: When Both of Us Were Young, the Memories of Patsy Ruth Miller (Patsy Ruth Miller). O'Raghailligh, 1988.
  Reminiscences of Miller's years in Hollywood, together with *The Hunchback of Notre Dame* (Philip Riley), the scenario and historical overview of the making of the 1923 film.

My Life East and West (William S. Hart). New York: B. Blom, 1968.
  An autobiography. Reprint of the Houghton Mifflin edition (1929). Included in the Chadwyck-Healey microfiche *History of the Cinema, 1895–1940.*

My Life in Pictures (Charles Chaplin). New York: Grosset & Dunlap, 1975.

My Life with Chaplin: An Intimate Memoir (Lita Grey Chaplin, with Morton Cooper). Bernard Geis Associates, 1966.

My Life with the Redskins (Corinne Griffith). New York: Barnes, 1947.
  The story of C. Griffith's life with George Marshall, owner of the Boston Redskins football team.

My Private Diary (Rudolph Valentino). Chicago, IL: Occult Publ. Co., 1929.

My Rendezvous with Life (Mary Pickford). New York: Kinsey, 1935.
  A brief inspirational tract. Included in the Chadwyck-Healey microfiche *History of the Cinema, 1895–1940.*

My Story: An Autobiography (Mary Astor). New York: Doubleday, 1959.

My Ten Years in the Studios (George Arliss). Boston, MA: Little, Brown, 1940.
  The English edition is entitled *George Arliss by Himself.* Included in the Chadwyck-Healey microfiche *History of the American Cinema, 1895–1940.*

My Trip Abroad (Charles Chaplin). New York: Harper and Row, 1922.
  Chaplin's reminiscences about his trip to Europe. The English edition is entitled *My Wonderful Visit.*

My Wonderful World of Slapstick (Buster Keaton with Charles Samuels). New York: Da Capo, 1982.
  An autobiography. A reprint of the Doubleday edition (1960).

The National Cyclopaedia of American Biography: Being a History of the United States.... New York: James T. White & Co., 1898–1984.
  The notables about whom there are articles include J. Hersholt (1942 and 1958) and B. Lytell (1961).

The National Society of Film Critics on Movie Comedy (Stuart Byron and Elisabeth Weis, editors). New York: Grossman, 1977.
  A compilation of previously published pieces on numerous stars.

The National Society of Film Critics on the Movie Star (Elisabeth Weis, editor). New York: Penguin, 1981.
  Generally brief essays on comic actors.

New York Times Great Lives of the Twentieth Century (Arthur Gelb, A.M. Rosenthal and Marvin Siegel, editors). New York: Times Books, 1988.
  One of the biographical entries is about C. Chaplin.

Norma Talmadge (Edmond Greville and Jean Bertin). Paris: Jean-Pascal, 1927.
  In French.

Norma Talmadge in Her Most Successful Plays Produced by Her Norma Talmadge Film Corp. (Screen Favorites Library). 1910s(?).
  Stills from a few of her early films.

Notable American Women, 1607–1950: A Biographical Dictionary (Edward T. James, editor). 3 vols. Cambridge, MA: Belknap Press of Harvard University Press, 1971.
  Lengthy entries with bibliographies, including the locations, if any, of archival materials.

Notable American Women: The Modern Period: A Biographical Dictionary (Barbara Sicherman et al., editors). Cambridge, MA: Belknap Press of Harvard University Press, 1980.

Lengthy entries with bibliographies, including the locations, if any, of archival materials.

Notable Hispanic American Women (Diane Telgen and Jim Kamp, editors). Detroit, MI: Gale Research, 1993.
   Contains a brief section on D. Del Rio.

Notable Names in the American Theatre. New and revised ed. Clifton, NJ: J.T. White, 1976.
   Brief biographies with stageographies, incomplete filmographies, TV appearances, awards and published works, if any. Earlier edition was titled *Biographical Encyclopaedia & Who's Who of the American Theatre* (q.v.).

Notable Women in the American Theatre: A Biographical Dictionary (Alice M. Robinson, Vera M. Roberts and Milly S. Barranger, editors). New York: Greenwood, 1989.
   Includes the Gish sisters and Nazimova.

The Oxford Companion to Film. New York: Oxford University Press, 1976.
   Fairly brief career summaries.

The Oxford Companion to the Theatre. 4th ed. London: Oxford University Press, 1990.
   Brief to lengthy career summaries. This is the 1983 edition reprinted with corrections.

The Parade's Gone By (Kevin Brownlow). London: Columbus, 1988.
   A lavishly illustrated and detailed history of the silent era, with sections on performers such as B. Blythe, L. Brooks, C. Chaplin, D. Fairbanks, B. Keaton, H. Lloyd, M. Pickford and G. Swanson. Reprint of Secker & Warburg edition (1968).

The Paramount Pretties (James R. Parish). New Rochelle, NY: Arlington House, 1972.
   Lengthy career summaries, many illustrations and filmographies of stars including C. Bow and G. Swanson.

La Passion de Charlie Chaplin (Edouard Ramond). Paris: Baudiniere, 1927.
   Included in the Chadwyck-Healey microfiche *History of the Cinema, 1895-1940.*

Passport to Hollywood: Film Immigrants: Anthology (Don Whittemore and Philip A. Cecchettini). New York: McGraw-Hill, 1976.
   The careers of several European filmmakers, among them C. Chaplin.

Pauline Frederick: On and Off the Stage (Muriel Elwood). Chicago, IL: Kroch, 1940.
   A biography. Included in the Chadwyck-Healey microfiche *History of the Cinema, 1895-1940.*

Pearl White, 1889-1938 (Jean Mitry). Paris: Anthologie du Cinéma, 1969.
   A supplement to *L'Avant-Scène du Cinéma.*

Pearl White, the Peerless, Fearless Girl (Manuel Weltman and Raymond Lee). South Brunswick, NJ: Barnes, 1969.
   Lavishly illustrated.

The Penguin Encyclopedia of Horror and the Supernatural (Jack Sullivan, editor). New York: Viking, 1986.
   Brief career overviews, some with stills or photographs, and selected films. Also includes entries on films, filmmakers and authors.

People in a Diary: A Memoir (S.N. Behrman). Boston, MA: Little, Brown, 1972.
   Brief mention of G. Garbo, for whom Behrman wrote some films.

People Will Talk (John Kobal). Rev. ed. London: Aurum, 1991.
   Includes interviews with L. Brooks, D. Gish, D. Godowsky, C. Moore, G. Swanson, O. Baclanova, E. Brent.

Personal Glimpses of Famous Folks: And Other Selections from the Lee Side o' L.A. (Lee Shippey). Sierra Madre, CA: Sierra Madre Press, 1929.
   Brief and chatty selections on famous Southern California residents, including performers such as J. Barrymore, C. Bow, B. Compson, W.S. Hart, H. Lloyd and C. Moore.

Pete Martin Calls on... (Pete Martin). New York: Simon and Schuster, 1962.
   Among the celebrities interviewed is F.X. Bushman.

Photostory of the Screen's Greatest Cowboy Star: Tom Mix (Mario DeMarco). 1970s(?).

Includes filmography. Also known as *A Photo Biography of the Screen's....*
Pickfair. Los Angeles, CA: Los Angeles Times-Mirror, 1937.
> A pictorial pamphlet about the home of D. Fairbanks and M. Pickford.
A Pictorial History of the Tarzan Movies: 50 Years of the Jungle Superman... (Ray Lee and Vernell Coriell). Los Angeles, CA: Golden State News Co., 1966.
> A lighthearted, lavishly illustrated look at film Tarzans, including E. Lincoln.
A Pictorial History of Westerns (Michael Parkinson and Clyde Jeavons). New York: Exeter, 1984.
> Several Western stars are included.
The Picture History of Charlie Chaplin (Gerald McDonald). Franklin Square, NY: Nostalgia Press, 1965.
> Photographs, stills, comic strips, etc. with explanatory text.
The Picturegoer's Who's Who and Encyclopedia of the Screen To-Day. New York: Gordon, 1977.
> Brief personal data and career overviews. Includes many people who are obscure today. Reprint of the Odhams edition (1933). Included in the Chadwyck-Healey microfiche *History of the Cinema, 1895–1940.*
Pictures of Movie Stars, with Stories (Mae Tinee). New York: Whitman, 1938.
> Mainly pictorial, with brief captions. Includes W. Baxter, J. Boles and J. Gaynor.
Polita (Wieslawa Czapinska). Warsaw: Wydawnictwa Radia i Telewizji, 1989.
> A biography of Pola Negri. In Polish.
Popcorn Venus: Women, Movies and the American Dream (Marjorie Rosen). New York: Coward, McCann and Geoghegan, 1973.
> A decade-by-decade analysis of how films reflected American mores. Includes discussion of C. Bow, G. Garbo, L. Gish, P. Negri and M. Pickford.
Popular Men of the Screen: Biographical Sketches of Twenty Outstanding Male Stars in Motion Pictures (Charles E. Donaldson). 1920s(?).
> A pamphlet with brief biographies of N. Asther, J. Barrymore, R. Barthelmess, L. Chaney, R. Dix, C. Farrell, J. Gilbert, W. Haines, C. Nagel, B. Norton, R. Novarro, G. O'Brien, B. Rogers.
The Primal Screen: Essays on Film and Related Subjects (Andrew Sarris). New York: Simon and Schuster, 1973.
> Two of the essays are about B. Keaton and H. Lloyd.
The Private Life of Greta Garbo (Rilla P. Palmborg). Garden City, NY: Doubleday, Doran, 1931.
> Basically a publicity "puff piece."
Profiting by Experience (Douglas Fairbanks). New York: Britton, 1918.
> Another in a series of DF's (or ghostwriter's) homilies on life and success.
Property from the Estate of Gloria Swanson. New York: William Doyle Galleries, 1983.
> Illustrated catalog of the effects of GS which were to be sold at auction.
The Public Is Never Wrong: The Autobiography of Adolph Zukor (Adolph Zukor). New York: Putnam, 1953.
> Contains some discussion of C. Bow, M. Clark, D. Fairbanks, M. Pickford and R. Valentino.
Quinlan's Illustrated Directory of Film Comedy Actors (David Quinlan). New York: Holt, 1992.
> Brief to lengthy career overviews and filmographies.
Quinlan's Illustrated Registry of Film Stars (David Quinlan). New York: H. Holt, 1991.
> Photographs, brief career overviews and credits for over 1,700 performers.
Ramon Novarro (Max Montagut). Paris: Publications Jean-Pascal, 1927.
> Brief account of RN's career and life. In French.
Ramon Novarro: En Filmens Romantiker. Stockholm: Ahlen & Akerlunds, 1932.
> In Swedish.

The Real Stars: Articles and Interviews on Hollywood's Great Character Actors (Leonard Maltin, editor). New York: Curtis Books, 1973.
Previously published articles from *Film Fan Monthly* which include career summaries and filmographies. One is about L. Littlefield.
The Real Tinsel (Bernard Rosenberg and Harry Silverstein). New York: Macmillan, 1976.
Reminiscences of individuals who were involved in various aspects of filmmaking. Actors include B. Bletcher, D. Godowsky, R. LaRocque, M. Marsh, C. Nagel and B. Sweet. Originally published in 1970.
The Real Valentino (S. George Ullman). London: Pearson, 1927.
Included in the Chadwyck-Healey microfiche *History of the Cinema, 1895–1940.*
Reel Women: Pioneers of the Cinema, 1896 to the Present (Ally Acker). New York: Continuum, 1991.
Brief career summaries and filmographies, including G. Cunard, D. Davenport, H. Gibson, L. Gish, H. Holmes, M. Normand, M. Pickford, R. Stonehouse and P. White.
Reference Point: Reflections on Creative Ways... (Arthur Hopkins). New York: S. French, 1948.
Based on papers read at a seminar. One of the pieces is about J. Barrymore.
Reinhold Niebuhr and Charles Chaplin: A Comparative Study Through the Ironic Ingredients of Niebuhr's Thought (Thomas M. Martin). Syracuse, NY: Syracuse University, 1972.
A Ph.D. thesis.
Religion in Film (John R. May and Michael Bird, editors). Knoxville, TN: University of Tennessee Press, 1982.
Previously published articles and essays, one of which is about C. Chaplin.
Remember Valentino: Reminiscences of the World's Greatest Lover (Beulah Livingstone). New York?: Livingstone, 1938.
Remembering Aunt Marion (Marion R.L. Canessa). San Simeon, CA: Hearst San Simeon State Historical Monument, 1989.
An oral history by M. Davies's grandniece.
Remembering Charlie: A Pictorial Biography (Jerry Epstein). New York: Doubleday, 1989.
A lavishly illustrated biography by one of C. Chaplin's closest associates.
Remembering Dorothy Gish (Harold Casselton, editor). Minneapolis, MN: Society for Cinephiles, 1986.
An illustrated career overview and reminiscences, with a filmography.
Return Engagement: Faces to Remember Then and Now (James Watters). New York: Clarkson Potter, 1984.
Contrasts of female stars as they looked during the height of their fame and as they appeared at the time of writing. Includes descriptions of the current lives of the actresses.
The Return of Rudolph Valentino (Carol E. McKinstry). Los Angeles, CA: Kirby & McGee, 1952.
Another lengthy account of RV's messages from the "beyond."
The Revealing Eye: Personalities of the 1920s (Nickolas Muray, photographs; Paul Gallico, text). New York: Atheneum, 1967.
Full page portraits and brief text about performers such as R. Barthelmess, S. Blane, C. Bow, B. Daniels, D. Fairbanks, G. Garbo, D. and L. Gish, T. Meighan, C. Moore, A. Nazimova, M. Pickford, G. Swanson, C. and N. Talmadge, F. Ward and L. Wolheim.
The Reverend Goes to Hollywood. New York: Crowell-Collier, 1962.
These reminiscences include a section on C. Chaplin.
Richard Diks (i.e., Dix) (B. Kolomarov). Moscow: Tea-Kino-Pechat, 1928.
A brief pamphlet in Russian.
Riders of the Range: The Sagebrush Heroes of the Sound Screen (Kalton C. Lahue). South Brunswick, NJ: Barnes, 1973.

362   Bibliography

Illustrated career summaries of Western stars including G. O'Brien.

Ridolini e la Collana della Suocera e Ridolini Esploratore, di Larry Semon. Milan: Editoriale Domus, 1945.

Two motion picture scripts. In Italian.

The Rise and Fall of the Matinee Idol: Past Deities of Stage and Screen, Their Roles, Their Magic and Their Worshippers (Anthony Curtis, editor). New York: St. Martin's, 1974.

Among the performers discussed are L. Gish and R. Valentino.

The Rise of the American Film: A Critical History (Lewis Jacobs). New York: Teachers College Press, 1968.

A history of film to the late 1930s which contains a section about C. Chaplin. Originally published in 1939. Included in the Chadwyck-Healey microfiche *History of the Cinema, 1895–1940.*

Rodolfo Valentino (Sergio Trinchero and Sergio Russo). Ivrea: Priuli & Verlucca, 1975. In Italian.

Rolling Breaks and Other Movie Business (Aljean Harmetz). New York: Knopf, 1983.

A collection of previously published articles, some about Hollywood finance, one of which is about M. Pickford.

Roscoe "Fatty" Arbuckle (Gerald Fine). 1971.

Roscoe "Fatty" Arbuckle: A Biography of the Silent Film Comedian, 1887–1933 (Stuart Oderman). Jefferson, NC: McFarland, 1994.

Interweaving of Arbuckle's life and career with the emergence of the art of film comedy.

Rudolfo Valentino: El Idolo de las Mujeres (Nicolas Barquet). Madrid: S.A.E. Graficos Espejo, 1963.

In Spanish.

Rudolph Valentino (Jeanne de Recqueville). Paris: Editions France-Empire, 1978.

In French.

Rudolph Valentino (Alexander Walker). New York: Stein and Day, 1976.

Lavishly illustrated.

Rudolph Valentino: His Romantic Life and Death (Ben-Allah, i.e., Ben-Allah Newman). Hollywood, CA: Ben-Allah Co., 1926.

Included in the Chadwyck-Healey microfiche *History of the Cinema, 1895–1940.*

Rudolph Valentino Paper Dolls (Tom Tierney). New York: Dover, 1979.

Features costumes from his most famous films.

Rudolph Valentino: The Man Behind the Myth (Robert Oberfirst). New York: Citadel, 1962.

Rudolph Valentino (Recollections): Intimate and Interesting Reminiscences of the Life of the Late World-Famous Star (Natacha Rambova). New York: Jacobsen-Hodgkinson, 1927.

Rudy: An Intimate Portrait of Rudolph Valentino (Natacha Rambova). London: Hutchinson, 1926.

Included in the Chadwyck-Healey microfiche *History of the Cinema, 1895–1940.*

Ruth Rolland (i.e., Roland) (K. Oganesov). Moscow, Kino Press, 1926.

In Russian.

Saddle Aces of the Cinema (Buck Rainey). San Diego, CA: Barnes, 1980.

Brief career overviews and filmographies of Western stars, including J. Holt, T. Mix, R. Stewart and F. Thomson.

Saint Cinema: Selected Writings on Film, 1929–1970. 2nd rev. ed. (Herman Weinberg). New York: Ungar, 1980.

Several of the brief essays are about C. Chaplin.

St. James Guide to Biography. Chicago, IL: St. James, 1991.

Each lengthy entry contains analyses of biographies written about the subject. Includes C. Chaplin.

The Salad Days (Douglas Fairbanks, Jr.). New York: Doubleday, 1988.
An autobiography that contains much discussion of his relationship with his famous father.
Saturday Afternoon at the Bijou (David Zinman). New Rochelle, NY: Arlington House, 1973.
An overview of popular movie series, with discussion of their stars. Includes W. Baxter, J. Hersholt and W. Oland.
The Saturday Evening Post Movie Book. Indianapolis, IN: Curtis, 1977.
A lavishly illustrated reprinting of articles about and by many film personalities.
Scandal! (Colin Wilson and Donald Seaman). New York: Stein and Day, 1986.
Scandals involving political, literary and other prominent figures, including R. Arbuckle.
Scandal! Headline Scandals of the Twentieth Century (Allen Lebrow). New York: Click, 1956.
Political, theatrical and Hollywood scandals, including those involving R. Arbuckle, M. Astor and M. Davies.
Schickel on Film: Encounters—Critical and Personal—With Movie Immortals (Richard Schickel). New York: Morrow, 1989.
Essays on filmmakers and stars, including C. Chaplin, D. Fairbanks, H. Lloyd.
Scream Queens: Heroines of the Horrors (Calvin T. Beck). New York: Macmillan, 1978.
Career overviews of numerous actresses who appeared in one or more horror films, including O. Baclanova, L. LaPlante, M. McAvoy and M. Philbin.
Screen Album: The Life Stories and Photos of the Screen Stars. New York: Theatre Publishing Corp., 1930(?).
Full page career overviews and full-page portraits of many stars, including E. Brent, C. Farrell, W. Haines, I. Keith, G. Swanson and A. White.
Screen Personalities (Vincent Trotta and Cliff Lewis). New York: Grosset & Dunlap, 1933.
Very brief career and personal data, with numerous drawings of each performer. Included in the Chadwyck-Healey microfiche *History of the Cinema, 1895–1940*.
Screening Out the Past: The Birth of Mass Culture and the Motion Picture Industry (Lary May). New York: Oxford University Press, 1980.
Among the performers included in this study of popular culture are D. Fairbanks and M. Pickford.
Secret Love-Life of Clara (Frederic H. Girnau). Los Angeles, CA: Girnau, 1931.
As "told by" Daisy DeVoe, C. Bow's former secretary.
Selected Short Subjects: From Spanky to the Three Stooges (Leonard Maltin). New York: Da Capo, 1983.
Contains career data and filmographies (of the shorts only) for C. Chase, B. Keaton and H. Langdon. Reprint of the Crown edition (1972).
The Self-Enchanted: Mae Murray, Image of an Era (Jane Ardmore). New York: McGraw-Hill, 1959.
The biography of M. Murray, with some discussion of R. Valentino.
The Serials: Suspense and Drama by Installments (Raymond W. Stedman). Norman, OK: University of Oklahoma Press, 1977.
This overview of the serial in all mediums includes discussions of R. Roland and P. White.
Serving Hearst and Davies as a Waiter and Butler (Charles Gates). San Simeon, CA: Hearst San Simeon State Historical Monument, 1989.
An oral history interview.
The Seven Lively Arts (Gilbert Seldes). New York: Barnes, 1962.
Essays on popular culture, including one on C. Chaplin. Originally published in 1924. Included in the Chadwyck-Healey microfiche *History of the Cinema, 1895–1940*.

Sex Goddesses of the Silent Screen (Norman Zierold). Chicago, IL: Regnery, 1973.
Lengthy career narratives about five "sex symbols": T. Bara, C. Bow, B. LaMarr, M. Murray and P. Negri.

Sex Psyche Etcetera in the Film (Parker Tyler). New York: Horizon Press, 1969.
Several essays, one of which is about C. Chaplin.

Sherlock Holmes on the Screen: The Motion Picture Adventures of the World's Most Popular Detective (Robert W. Pohle Jr. and Douglas C. Hart). South Brunswick, NJ: Barnes, 1977.
Contains biographies of actors who appeared in the films, including J. Barrymore and C. Blackwell.

Shooting Stars: Heroes and Heroines of Western Film (Archie McDonald, editor). Bloomington, IN: Indiana University Press, 1987.
Essays on Western film stars, including W.S. Hart.

Show People: Profiles in Entertainment (Kenneth Tynan). New York: Simon and Schuster, 1979.
Among the performers and others profiled is Louise Brooks in Tynan's famous piece *The Girl in the Black Helmet*.

Showcase (Roy Newquist). New York: Morrow, 1966.
Interviews with theater and film personalities, including J. Gaynor.

Showman: The Life of David O. Selznick (David Thomson). New York: Knopf, 1992.
Contains a small amount of information about Marjorie Daw, the wife of Myron Selznick.

The Silent Clowns (Walter Kerr). New York: Da Capo, 1990.
Covers the major comedians like C. Chaplin, H. Lloyd, H. Langdon and B. Keaton in some detail, with smaller sections on R. Griffith and L. Semon, and briefer mentions of J. Hines and other "minor" comedians. Reprint of the Knopf edition (1975).

Silent Portraits: Stars of the Silent Screen in Historic Photographs (Anthony Slide). Vestal, NY: Vestal Press, 1989.
Portraits are accompanied by very brief career summaries.

Silent Star (Colleen Moore). Garden City, NY: Doubleday, 1968.
An autobiography.

The Silent Stars Speak. Beverly Hills, CA: Academy of Motion Picture Arts and Sciences, 1979(?).
Transcript of a symposium with panelists including W. Bakewell, P. Bonner, C. Myers, E. Ralston and L. Wilson.

The Silent Voice: A Text (Arthur Lennig). Albany, NY: Lane Press, 1969.
A survey of silent cinema in the United States and major European countries. Contains a section on some D. Fairbanks films.

Sir Charlie (Edwin P. Hoyt). London: R. Hale, 1977.
About C. Chaplin.

Six Gun Heroes: A Price Guide to Movie Cowboy Collectibles (Theodore Hake and Robert D. Cauler). Des Moines, IA: Wallace-Homestead, 1976.
Besides its stated purpose, this contains career overviews and filmographies. Included is T. Mix.

Six Men (Alistair Cooke). New York: Knopf, 1977.
Articles on famous men Cooke has known, one of whom was C. Chaplin.

Some Are Born Great (Adela Rogers St. Johns). Garden City, NY: Doubleday, 1974.
Reminiscences of Hollywood stars as the author knew them, including M. Davies, B. Dove, C. Moore and L. Tashman.

Someday We'll Laugh: An Autobiography (Esther Ralston) (*Filmmakers*, no. 11). Metuchen, NJ: Scarecrow, 1985.
Includes a filmography.

Spatial Disorientation and Dream in the Feature Films of Buster Keaton (Charles C. Wolfe). New York: Columbia University, 1978.

A Ph.D. thesis.

Speaking of Silents: First Ladies of the Screen (William M. Drew). Vestal, NY: Vestal Press, 1989.
> Lengthy interviews giving biographical and career data and filmographies on several actresses, including M. Bellamy, E. Boardman, L. Joy, L. LaPlante, M. McAvoy, P.M. Miller, C. Moore, E. Ralston, B. Sweet and L. Wilson.

Special People, Special Times (Irving Wallace). New York: Pinnacle Books, 1981.
> Stories from, and about, people Wallace knew in 1940s Hollywood, including H. Lloyd.

Spellbound in Darkness: A History of the Silent Film (George C. Pratt). Rev. ed. Greenwich, CT: New York Graphic Society, 1973.
> Discusses films of performers such as T. Bara, C. Chaplin, M. Pickford and G. Swanson.

Star Acting: Gish, Garbo, Davis (Charles Affron). New York: Dutton, 1977.
> Detailed analyses of the three actresses' acting styles. Profusely illustrated, with filmographies.

Star Babies (Raymond Strait). New York: St. Martin's, 1979.
> Offspring of famous stars talk about their parents, among whom was T. Mix.

Star Quality: Screen Actors from the Golden Age of Films (Arthur F. McClure and Ken D. Jones). South Brunswick, NJ: Barnes, 1974.
> Brief career summaries of numerous stars and supporting actors, including E. Lowe.

Star Stats: Who's Whose in Hollywood (Kenneth Marx). Los Angeles, CA: Price/Stern/Sloan, 1979.
> Lists of biographical data such as parents' names, birth places and dates, marriages and other "factoids."

Stardom: The Hollywood Phenomenon (Alexander Walker). New York: Stein and Day, 1970.
> A discussion of the nature of stardom from the earliest days of cinema.

Stars! (Daphne Davis). New York: Stewart, Tabori & Chang, 1983.
> Mainly pictorial with brief career summaries and filmographies of the major stars, including C. Chaplin, G. Garbo, M. Pickford, G. Swanson and R. Valentino.

The Stars (Edgar Morin) (*Evergreen Profile Book*, 7). New York: Grove, 1970.
> A sociological analysis of stardom, with a chapter on C. Chaplin.

The Stars (Richard Schickel). New York: Dial, 1962.
> Lavishly illustrated career overviews.

The Stars Appear (Richard D. MacCann) (American Movies). Metuchen, NJ: Scarecrow; Iowa City, IA: Image & Idea, 1992.
> A compilation of previously published pieces by and about stars.

Stars of the Silents (Edward Wagenknecht) (*Filmmakers*, no. 19). Metuchen, NJ: Scarecrow, 1987.
> Chapters on M. McAvoy, L. Gish, C. Bow, C. Chaplin and M. Pickford.

Starstruck: The Wonderful World of Movie Memorabilia (Robert Heide and John Gilman). Garden City, NY: Doubleday, 1986.
> Besides the illustration and description of memorabilia, career overviews are provided.

The Story of the Films: As Told by Leaders of the Industry... (Joseph P. Kennedy, editor). New York: Ozer, 1971.
> Consists of a series of lectures given by individuals from various phases of the film industry. The actor is M. Sills. Reprint of the Shaw edition (1927). Included in the Chadwyck-Healey microfiche *History of the Cinema, 1895–1940*.

Strangers in Hollywood: The History of Scandinavian Actors in American Films from 1910 to World War II (Hans J. Wollstein). Metuchen, NJ: Scarecrow, 1994.
> Includes such performers as G. Garbo, A.Q. Nilsson, N. Asther and S. Owen.

A Study of the Satire of Charles Chaplin (Leslie Londo). Los Angeles, CA: University of Southern California, 1949.
    A master's thesis.
Stunt: The Story of the Great Movie Stunt Men (John Baxter). Garden City, NY: Doubleday, 1974.
    Besides the professional stunt men, performers who performed many of their own stunts included M. Blue, D. Fairbanks, B. Keaton, H. Lloyd, B. Lyon, T. Mix, E. Polo, R. Talmadge, P. White.
Sunshine and Shadow (Mary Pickford). Garden City, NY: Doubleday, 1955.
    A not very revealing autobiography.
Swanson on Swanson (Gloria Swanson). New York: Random House, 1980.
    An autobiography.
The Swashbucklers (James R. Parish and Don E. Stanke). New Rochelle, NY: Arlington House, 1976.
    The careers of several action stars, including D. Fairbanks. Contains filmographies.
Sweetheart: The Story of Mary Pickford (Robert Windeler). New York: Praeger, 1974.
    Reissued in 1975 as *Mary Pickford, Sweetheart of the World*.
Sweethearts of the Sage: Biographies and Filmographies of 258 Actresses Appearing in Western Movies (Buck Rainey). Jefferson, NC: McFarland, 1992.
    Brief biographies and presumably complete filmographies from the early silents to the present.
Swordsmen of the Screen, from Douglas Fairbanks to Michael York (Jeffrey Richards). Boston, MA: Routledge and Kegan Paul, 1977.
    Includes a discussion of D. Fairbanks.
Take Them Up Tenderly: A Collection of Profiles (Margaret C. Harriman). Freeport, NY: Books for Libraries, 1972.
    A collection of pieces originally published in *The New Yorker*, one of which is about M. Pickford. Reprint of the Knopf edition (1944).
The Talmadge Girls: A Memoir (Anita Loos). New York: Viking, 1978.
    About Constance, Natalie and Norma Talmadge.
The Talmadge Sisters: Norma, Constance, Natalie: An Intimate Story of the World's Most Famous Screen Family (Margaret Talmadge). Philadelphia, PA: Lippincott, 1924.
    Written by their mother.
Tarzan of the Movies: A Pictorial History of More Than Fifty Years of Edgar Rice Burroughs' Legendary Hero (Gabe Essoe). New York: Citadel, 1968.
    A lavishly illustrated overview which includes E. Lincoln.
Theda Bara and the Vamp Phenomenon, 1915–1920 (Gayla J. Hamilton). University of Georgia, 1972.
    A master's thesis.
Their Hearts Were Young and Gay (Marc Best). South Brunswick, NJ: Barnes, 1975.
    Brief career descriptions and numerous illustrations of many child stars, among whom is M. Evans.
Then Came Each Actor: Shakesperean Actors... (Bernard Grebanier). New York: McKay, 1975.
    One of the actors discussed is J. Barrymore.
There Is a New Star in Heaven, Valentino. Berlin: Spiess, 1979.
    A biography, essays and filmography in conjunction with a retrospective of RV films. In German.
They Had Faces Then: Hollywood in the '30s, the Legendary Ladies (John Springer). Secaucus, NJ: Citadel, 1988.
    Photographs and stills, accompanied by brief commentaries and biographies, of numerous actresses.
They Went Thataway (James Horwitz). New York: Dutton, 1976.

A discussion of many western actors, with some interviews, including G.M. Anderson, W.S. Hart, T. McCoy and T. Mix.

The Thief of Bagdad (Achmed Abdullah). Norfolk, VA: Starblaze Classics, 1987.
A novelization of the 1924 Fairbanks film with stills.

This You Won't Believe (Corinne Griffith). New York: Fell, 1972.
A reminiscence.

Those Fabulous Movie Years: The 30's (Paul Trent). Barre, MA: Barre Publishing, 1975.
Lavishly illustrated synopses of major films with brief biographies, including G. Garbo.

Those Fabulous Serial Heroines: Their Lives and Films (Buck Rainey). Metuchen, NJ: Scarecrow, 1990.
Photographs, career data and filmographies about actresses who appeared in serials, including G. Cunard, G. Darmond, H. Ferguson, D. Gulliver, J. Hansen, H. Holmes, E. Johnson, N. Kingston, A. Ray, R. Roland, M. Sais, E. Sedgwick, M. Snow, R. Stonehouse, P. White, and K. Williams.

Those Scandalous Sheets of Hollywood (Ray Lee). Van Nuys, CA: Venice Books, 1972.
Accounts of several Hollywood scandals.

Those Who Died Young: Cult Heroes of the Twentieth Century (Marianne Sinclair). 2nd ed. London: Plexus, 1989.
The stories of several actors, politicians and musicians who died young, among them R. Valentino.

Three Classic Silent Screen Comedies Starring Harold Lloyd (Donald W. McCaffrey). Rutherford, NJ: Fairleigh Dickinson University Press, 1976.
A revision of a thesis which analyzes *Safety Last, Grandma's Boy* and *The Freshman*. Includes filmography.

Tim McCoy Remembers the West: An Autobiography (Tim McCoy). Lincoln, NE: University of Nebraska Press, 1988.
Reprint of the Doubleday edition (1977).

The Times We Had: Life with William Randolph Hearst (Marion Davies). Indianapolis, IN: Bobbs-Merrill, 1975.
Edited from taped notes left by Davies. Corrections and clarifications are provided by the editors.

Tom Mix and Tony: A Partnership Remembered (Richard F. Seiverling). Hershey, PA: Keystone Enterprises, 1980.
A pictorial work that commemorates the centenary of TM's birth and the fortieth anniversary of his death.

The Tom Mix Book (M.G. Norris). Waynesville, NC: World of Yesterday, 1989.
Everything you ever needed to know about TM, including biography, films, the radio program, collectibles and innumerable factoids.

Tom Mix Highlights (Andy Woytowich). Madison, NC: Empire, 1989.
A brief, highly illustrated biography.

Tom Mix, Portrait of a Superstar: A Pictorial and Documentary Anthology (Richard F. Seiverling). Hershey, PA: Keystone Enterprises, 1991.

Tom Mix, Riding Up to Glory (John H. Nicholas). Oklahoma City, OK: National Cowboy Hall of Fame and Western Heritage Center, 1980.
Lavishly illustrated overview of TM's career. Includes a filmography.

Too Much, Too Soon (Diana Barrymore and Gerold Frank). New York: Holt, 1957.
A biography by the daughter of John Barrymore.

Too Young to Die (Patricia Fox-Sheinwold). New rev. ed. New York: Crescent, 1991.
Profusely illustrated account of several performers who died young, including R. Valentino.

Tout Chaplin: Tous les Films, par le Texte, par le Gag, et par l'Image (Jean Mitry). Paris: Seghers, 1972.
An expanded version of the text that appeared in *Image et Son* (1957). In French.

Tres Comicos del Cine (Cesar Muñoz Arconada). Madrid: Castellote, 1974(?).
Discusses C. Bow, C. Chaplin, and H. Lloyd.
Tribute to John Barrymore (Spencer Berger). Rochester, NY: George Eastman House, 1969.
A lengthy career overview of JB given at a retrospective of his films. (For a related work, see *The Films of John Barrymore* in this bibliography.)
Tribute to Mary Pickford (Robert B. Cushman, notes and filmography). Beverly Hills, CA: American Film Institute Theatre, 1970.
Pamphlet, with notes on Pickford's career, especially her Biograph period, and a complete filmography. Contributions by C. Myers, B. Rogers and B. Sweet.
A Tribute to Mary Pickford (coordinated by Anthony Slide). Beverly Hills, CA: Academy of Motion Picture Arts and Sciences, 1981(?).
A panel discussion, one of whose participants was Douglas Fairbanks, Jr.
The Truth About the Movies by the Stars (Laurence A. Hughes, editor). New York: Gordon Press, 1976.
Articles "by" numerous performers and photographs of several hundred stars. Reprint of the Hollywood Publishers edition (1924). Included in the Chadwyck-Healey microfiche *History of the Cinema, 1895-1940*.
Twinkle Twinkle Movie Star! (Harry T. Brundige). New York: Garland, 1977.
"Puff piece" interviews of various stars, including R. Adorée, G. Bancroft, J. Barrymore, M. Blue, C. Bow, M. Brian, M. Busch, L. Chaney, B. Compson, R. Dix, C. Farrell, B. Keaton, M. Nolan, G. O'Brien, E. Ralston, B. Rogers, B. Turpin and R. Valentino. Reprint of the Dutton edition (1930). Included in the Chadwyck-Healey microfiche *History of the Cinema, 1895-1940*.
Two Reels and a Crank (Albert E. Smith and Phil A. Koury). New York: Garland, 1985.
A reminiscence of the early days of the Vitagraph Company, with sections on J. Bunny and M. Pickford. Reprint of the Doubleday edition (1952).
Unholy Fools: Wits, Comics, Disturbers of the Peace: Film and Theater (Penelope Gilliatt). New York: Viking, 1973.
A compilation of previously published pieces, including those on C. Chaplin and H. Langdon.
United Artists: The Company Built by the Stars (Tino Balio). Madison, WI: University of Wisconsin Press, 1976.
History of UA, with considerable discussion of its founders, among them C. Chaplin, D. Fairbanks and M. Pickford.
Universal Filmlexikon (Frank Arnau, editor). 2 vols. Berlin: Universal Filmlexikon, 1932-33.
Single page entries about European performers, with photographs. Parallel text in English and German. Included in the Chadwyck-Healey microfiche *History of the Cinema, 1895-1940*.
Universal Pictures: A Panoramic History in Words, Pictures and Filmographies (Michael G. Fitzgerald). New Rochelle, NY: Arlington House, 1977.
Brief career summaries and filmographies (Universal films only) of stars including R. Arlen and L. Chaney.
Up the Years from Bloomsbury: An Autobiography (George Arliss). Boston: Little, Brown, 1930.
Valentino (Alan Arnold). New York: Library Publishers, 1954.
Valentino (Irving Shulman). New York: Trident Press, 1967.
A biography.
Valentino (Brad Steiger and Mank Chaw). New York: Manor Books, 1975.
A biography with a strong emphasis on RV's sexuality. Originally published in 1966.
Valentino (Vincent Tajiri). New York: Bantam, 1977.
Valentino as I Knew Him (S. George Ullman). New York: Macy-Masius, 1926.
Valentino: The Love God (Noel Botham and Peter Donnelly). New York: Ace, 1977.
A biography which contains imaginary conversations. Includes a filmography.

Valentino the Unforgotten (Roger C. Peterson). Los Angeles, CA: Wetzel, 1937.
    A conglomeration of biography, handwriting analysis, numerology, tributes and dream interpretation. Included in the Chadwyck-Healey microfiche *History of the Cinema, 1895–1940.*

Values, a Philosophy of Human Needs (Milton Sills and Ernest Holmes). Chicago, IL: University of Chicago Press, 1932.
    Consists mainly of conversations between the co-authors which had been stenographically transcribed.

Variety Who's Who in Show Business. Rev. ed. New York: Bowker, 1989.
    Very brief biographies and selective filmographies of performers still alive at the time of publication. Some performers in this book only may be listed in earlier editions which began publishing in 1983.

Venus in Hollywood: The Continental Enchantress from Garbo to Loren (Michael Bruno). New York: Lyle Stuart, 1970.
    A witty account of Hollywood's "sex symbols," and some of their leading men, which includes performers such as V. Banky, G. Garbo, J. Gilbert, P. Negri, M. Pickford and R. Valentino.

Vera Burnett (Shaw), Marion Davies' Movie Double... (Bob Board). San Simeon, CA: San Simeon Region, 1990.
    An oral history interview about M. Davies.

The Versatiles: A Study of Supporting Character Actors and Actresses in the American Motion Picture, 1930–1955 (Alfred E. Twomey and Arthur F. McClure). South Brunswick, NJ: Barnes, 1969.
    Extremely brief illustrated career highlights of supporting players.

Vida de Greta Garbo (Cesar M. Arconada). Madrid: Castellote, 1974(?).
    Originally published in 1929.

Vie de Charlot: Charles Spencer Chaplin, Ses Films et Son Temps (Georges Sadoul). Paris: Lherminier, 1991.
    Lavishly illustrated story of CC's life with a chronology and filmography. In French. Originally published in 1952.

Viliam (i.e., William) *Desmond i Triukovaia Filma* (N. Kaufman). 2nd ed. Leningrad: Tea-kino-pechat, 1928.
    Brief pamphlet in Russian.

Viola Dana: As She Is to Those Who Know Her (Little Movie Mirror Books). New York: Ross, 1920.
    Brief pamphlet-style illustrated "puff piece."

Virgins, Vamps and Flappers: The American Silent Movie Heroine (Sumiko Higashi). Montreal: Eden Press Women's Publications, 1978.
    A sociological study which includes discussions about T. Bara, L. Gish and M. Pickford.

The Voice of Valentino Through Leslie Flint (Lynn Russell). London: Regency Press, 1965.
    RV as he presumably revealed himself to a medium after death.

Walking with Garbo: Conversations and Recollections (Raymond Daum; edited by Vance Muse). New York: HarperCollins, 1991.

Wallace Neff, Architect of California's Golden Age (Wallace Neff, Jr., compiler/editor). Santa Barbara, CA: Capra Press, 1986.
    Plans, photos and text describe the homes designed by Neff in the 1920s for Hollywood celebrities such as C. Chaplin, D. Fairbanks, M. Pickford and F. Thomson.

Wallace Reid: As He Is to Those Who Know Him (Little Movie Mirror Books). New York: Ross, 1920.
    Brief illustrated pamphlet-style "puff piece."

Wallace Reid: His Life Story (Bertha Westbrook Reid). New York: Sorg, 1923.

A biography by his mother. Included in the Chadwyck-Healey microfiche *History of the Cinema, 1895–1940.*

The War, the West and the Wilderness (Kevin Brownlow). New York: Knopf, 1979.
A survey of silent films on World War I, the West and primitive cultures. Includes sections on G.M. Anderson, C. Chaplin, W.S. Hart and T. Mix.

We All Went to Paris: Americans in the City of Light, 1776–1971 (Stephen Longstreet). New York: Macmillan, 1972.
Contains some information about P. White's post-film life.

We Barrymores (Lionel Barrymore as told to Cameron Shipp). Westport, CT: Greenwood, 1974.
Reprint of the Appleton-Century-Crofts edition (1951).

We Three: Ethel, Lionel, John (John Barrymore). Akron, OH: Saafield, 1935.
A brief reminiscence rather than a true biography.

The West of Yesterday; and Tony's Story by Himself (Tom Mix). Los Angeles, CA: Times-Mirror Press, 1923.
Biographical reminiscences. Included in the Chadwyck-Healey microfiche *History of the Cinema, 1895–1940.*

The Western (Allen Eyles). South Brunswick, NJ: Barnes, 1975.
Brief career overviews and filmographies of the performers' western films only.

The Western, from Silents to the Seventies (George Fenin and William K. Everson). Rev. ed. New York: Penguin, 1977.
Profusely illustrated account of film Westerns which includes sections about G.M. Anderson, D. Fairbanks, W.S. Hart, T. Mix and F. Thomson.

What a Bunch of Characters! An Entertaining Guide to Who Played What in the Movies (Tom S. Cadden). Englewood Cliffs, NJ: Prentice-Hall, 1984.
A filmography that briefly describes the characters portrayed in each film. Includes G. Garbo.

What Is Cinema?: Essays (Andre Bazin). Berkeley, CA: University of California Press, 1974.
A translation of the four volume French work published from 1958 to 1965. Some of the essays are about C. Chaplin.

What the Fans Think of Rudy Valentino: A Memorial Book (Charles Mank Jr.). Staunton, IL: C. Mank, 1929.
A compilation of articles.

What the Stars Told Me: Hollywood in Its Heyday. Jericho, NY: Exposition Press, 1971.
The publicist for Goldwyn and other studios recounts his experiences with various stars during the 1920s, among them L. Chaney, C. Chaplin, R. Dix, D. Del Rio, G. Garbo, J. Gilbert, T. Mix, C. Nagel, P. Negri, B. Rogers, G. Swanson and R. Valentino.

Whatever Became of...? (Richard Lamparski). New York: Crown, 1967. (Some editions were published by Bantam Press and Ace Books; some editions were known as *Lamparski's Whatever Became of...? Giant Annual.*)
A series of eleven books, to date, which provide brief career overviews and discuss the later lives of former stars, supporting players and other notables, with "then" and "now" photographs.

When the Moon Shone Bright on Charlie Chaplin (Frederick Isaac). Melksham, England: Venton, 1978.
A brief biography.

When the Movies Were Young (Mrs. D.W. Griffith [Linda Arvidson]). New York: B. Blom, 1968.
The silent actress recalls the early days of filmmaking and gives much information on M. Pickford. A corrected reprint of the 1925 edition.

Who Was Who in the Theatre, 1912–1976: A Biographical Dictionary of Actors, Actresses.... 4 vols. Detroit, MI: Gale Research, 1978.

Contains stageographies, incomplete filmographies and very brief biographical data. Compiled from vols. 1–12 of *Who's Who in the Theatre*.

Whodunit? Hollywood Style (Charles Nuetzel). Beverly Hills, CA: Book Company of America, 1965.
Sensational view of several Hollywood murders.

Who's Who at Metro-Goldwyn-Mayer. Culver City, CA(?): Metro-Goldwyn-Mayer, 1930s–40s(?).
Biographical and career overviews of MGM stars and others, including G. Garbo.

Who's Who in Hollywood (David Ragan). Rev. ed. 2 vols. New York: Facts on File, 1992.
Contains brief career and personal data, with incomplete filmographies, on thousands of film personalities. This is probably the single best source for data on obscure performers.

Who's Who in the Film World: Being Biographies with Photographic Reproductions... (Fred C. Justice and Tom R. Smith, editors/compilers). Los Angeles, CA: Film World Pub. Co., 1914.
Photographs and brief, or in some cases no, career overviews. Included in the Chadwyck-Healey microfiche *History of the Cinema, 1895–1940*.

Who's Who in the Theatre: A Biographical Record of the Contemporary Stage. Various publishers, including Gale Research, 1912–1981(?).
Theater career overviews with brief summaries of film and TV appearances. Later titled *Contemporary Theatre, Film and Television* (q.v.).

Who's Who of the Horrors and Other Fantasy Films: The International Personality Encyclopedia of the Fantastic Film (David J. Hogan). San Diego, CA: Barnes, 1980.
Very brief career summaries of those who appeared in horror films, with sketchy filmographies. Illustrated.

Who's Who on the Screen (Charles D. Fox and Milton L. Silver, editors). New York: Gordon, 1976.
Brief descriptions and portrait photographs of performers about whom it may be difficult to find data elsewhere. A few stars have lengthier narratives. Reprint of the Ross edition (1920).

Who's Who on the Stage: The Dramatic Reference Book and Biographical Dictionary of the Theatre. New York: Browne & Austin, 1906–08.

Why Not Try God? (Mary Pickford). 2nd ed. New York: Kinsey, 1984.
A brief inspirational tract. Originally published in 1934.

Wicked Women of the Screen (David Quinlan). New York: St. Martin's, 1988.
Highly illustrated, with brief career overviews of filmdom's "bad" women, among them T. Bara and P. Negri.

Wild West Characters (Dale Pierce). Phoenix, AZ: Golden West, 1991.
This biographical study of Western history includes brief data about G.M. Anderson, W.S. Hart and T. Mix.

William S. Hart: As He Is to Those Who Know Him (Little Movie Mirror Books). New York: Ross, 1920.
Illustrated pamphlet-style "puff piece."

Winners of the West: The Sagebrush Heroes of the Silent Screen (Kalton C. Lahue). South Brunswick, NJ: Barnes, 1971.
Lavishly illustrated career summaries of numerous Western players.

With Eisenstein in Hollywood: A Chapter of Autobiography (Ivor Montagu). New York: International Publishers, 1969.
Among the people discussed in this reminiscence are C. Chaplin, D. Fairbanks and M. Pickford.

The Wizard of Mordialloc: The Life of Jack Holt (Maurice Cavanough). Melbourne: Cheshire, 1962.

Women and the Cinema: A Critical Anthology (Karyn Kay and Gerald Peary, editors). New York: Dutton, 1977.
    A compilation of previously published articles, including those by L. Brooks and G. Garbo.

Women Have Been Kind: The Memoirs of Lou Tellegen. New York: Vanguard Press, 1931.
    Included in the Chadwyck-Healey microfiche *History of the Cinema, 1895–1940.*

Women in Comedy (Linda Martin and Kerry Segrave). Secaucus, NJ: Citadel, 1986.
    Brief career summaries, including L. Fazenda and M. Normand.

Women Who Make Movies (Sharon Smith) (Cinema Studies Series). New York: Hopkinson and Blake, 1975.
    A survey of women directors worldwide, including a brief survey of American silent films.

The World Almanac Who's Who of Film (Thomas Aylesworth and John S. Bowman). New York: World Almanac, 1987.
    Brief biographies and incomplete filmographies of numerous performers, with some illustrations.

The World Encyclopedia of the Film (John M. Smith and Tim Cawkwell, editors). New York: Galahad Books, 1974.
    Very brief career summaries and selected filmographies. Previously titled *World Encyclopedia of Film.*

World Film Directors (John Wakeman, editor). 2 vols. New York: H.W. Wilson, 1987–88.
    Encyclopedic work with lengthy and detailed articles, including filmographies and bibliographies. Includes C. Chaplin and B. Keaton.

The World Film Encyclopedia: A Universal Screen Guide. New York: Gordon, 1976.
    Brief biographical and career information with selective filmographies. Includes now-obscure performers. Reprint of Amalgamated Press edition (1933).

The World of Comedy (Thomas Leeflang). Leicester, England: Windward, 1988.
    Overview of the careers of several comedians, including C. Chaplin, B. Keaton and H. Lloyd.

World of Laughter: The Motion Picture Comedy Short, 1910–1930 (Kalton C. Lahue). Norman, OK: University of Oklahoma Press, 1972.
    Includes sections on J. Bunny, C. Chaplin, H. Langdon, H. Lloyd, M. Normand and L. Semon.

Yesterday's Clowns: The Rise of Film Comedy (Frank Manchel). New York: Watts, 1973.
    Discusses the early careers (to the mid-1920s) of C. Chaplin, B. Keaton, H. Langdon and H. Lloyd. Profusely illustrated.

You Must Remember This (Walter Wagner). New York: Putnam, 1975.
    Interviews with several Hollywood notables, including Minta Durfee Arbuckle (about R. Arbuckle), R. Arlen, S. Carol, D. Fairbanks, Jr. (about DF, Sr.), M. Pickford and C. Windsor.

Youth Points the Way (Douglas Fairbanks). New York: Appleton, 1924.
    One in a series of books written by (or ghostwritten for) DF about his philosophy of life.

Zanies: The World's Greatest Eccentrics (Jay R. Nash). Piscataway, NJ: New Century, 1982.
    Brief anecdotes of such famous "eccentrics" as M. Astor, J. Barrymore, C. Bow, and C. Chaplin.

Zen Showed Me the Way to Peace, Happiness and Tranquility (Sessue Hayakawa). Indianapolis, IN: Bobbs-Merrill, 1960.
    An autobiography.

MEDIA (FILMS, VIDEOTAPES, ETC.)

The Birth of a Legend (video). Davenport, IA: Blackhawk Films, 1980s(?).
    M. Pickford's career in early films. Originally released in 1966 as a film.

Buster Keaton: A Hard Act to Follow (video) (Kevin Brownlow and David Gill). New York: HBO Video, 1987.
    In three parts: From Vaudeville to Movies; Star Without a Studio and a Genius Recognized.

Chaplin: A Character Is Born (video). Harmony Vision; distributed by Vestron Video, 1982.
    Also contains *Buster Keaton: The Great Stone Face.*

Colleen Moore Discusses Silent Star with Columnist Robert Cromie (recording). Tucson, AZ: Learning Plans, 1969.
    Silent Star is CM's autobiography.

Colleen Moore's Incredible Jewelled Castle (videotape). Scottsdale, AZ: Warbonnet, 1982.
    About CM's doll house.

Comedy: A Serious Business (videotape). New York: HBO Video, 1980.
    A celebration of silent comedy, featuring C. Chaplin, B. Keaton, H. Langdon and H. Lloyd. Also available as part of the series *Hollywood* (1990).

The Divine Garbo (video). Turner Home Entertainment, 1991.
    Contains numerous film clips and rare archival footage that trace her offscreen life.

Dorothy Gish, Actress (filmstrip). Society for Visual Education, 1975.
    Focuses on DG's comedic talent and her relationship with D.W. Griffith.

Early Women Directors on Directing (video) (Ally Acker). Roslyn Heights, NY: Ally Acker/Reel Women, 1991.
    In one segment, L. Gish discusses her role in directing a 1920 film.

Feinstein and Francis X. Bushman (recording). Berkeley, CA: Pacifica Tape Library, 1966.
    Bushman reflects on his long career. (Feinstein is the interviewer.)

Focus on Lillian Gish (recording). North Hollywood, CA: Center for Cassette Studies, 1980s(?).
    An interview in which LG discusses her books and her career, especially working with D.W. Griffith.

Francis X. Bushman: Hollywood's First Star Talks About His Life and Times (recording). Anaheim, CA: Mark 56 Records, 1975.

The Gentleman Tramp (film). RBC Films, 1975.
    Film clips, newsreels, still photos and archival footage tell the story of C. Chaplin's life from his early days.

Gloria Swanson/Laurel and Hardy (video). New York: Video Dimensions, 1980s(?).
    Two episodes from the TV show *This Is Your Life.*

Grace Kelly, Will Rogers, John Barrymore (video). Norwalk, CT: Easton Press Video, 1989.
    Three TV programs from the 1950s or 1960s.

The Great Stone Face (video) (Vernon P. Becker). New York: Mastervision, 1981.
    The story of Buster Keaton from his early show business childhood to his maturity. Includes clips from many of his films.

Harold Lloyd: The Third Genius (video) (Kevin Brownlow and David Gill). New York: Thames Television; HBO Video, 1989.
    Recounts HL's career, with interviews of many of the people who worked with him, and clips from many of his films.

Heroes: Men of Destiny (video). Westport, CT: Videorecord Corporation of America (distributor), 1972.
    A compilation of Pathé News newsreels with segments on J. Barrymore and R. Valentino.

Irving Berlin, John Barrymore, Rudolph Valentino (video) (Men of Destiny). Video-record Corp. of America, 1972.

Joe Louis/Bebe Daniels (video) (Video Yesteryear Recording, no. 334). Sandy Hook, CT: Video Images, 1981.
    Two episodes from the TV show *This Is Your Life*.

John Barrymore: From Matinee Idol to Buffoon (recording). Santa Monica, CA: Facet; distributed by Delos International, 1987.
    Two 1941 radio broadcasts with Rudy Vallee, etc.

Keaton Special (video). Davenport, IA: Blackhawk Films, 1960.
    A study of BK's career with excerpts from his films.

Keaton: The Great Stone Face (video) (Gerald A. Schiller). New York: Phoenix Films, 1982.
    Explores BK's growth as a film comedian by showing examples of his film techniques. Includes clips from several films.

Lillian Gish (video). New York: Worldvision Home Video, 1989.
    An overview of LG's career, with excerpts from her films.

Lillian Gish: The Actor's Life for Me (video). Santa Monica, CA: American Film Foundation, 1988.
    A segment from the TV program *American Masters*. LG talks about her career from 1902 to 1987.

Lulu in Berlin: The Story of Louise Brooks (video). New York: Louise Brooks Project; Kino on Video, 1990.
    Interview with LB and clips of several of her films.

Midwest Roots, Hollywood Dreams (video). Omaha, NE: University of Nebraska at Omaha, 1983.
    A series on Midwest actors and its other connections with the arts. Includes segments on H. Langdon and H. Lloyd.

Out West (video). New York: HBO Video, 1980.
    A large segment is on W. S. Hart's films. Also available as part of the series *Hollywood* (1990).

Portrait of Blanche Sweet (film). Studio City, CA: A. Slide, 1982.
    Interview by Anthony Slide in which BS discusses her life, career and politics.

Rudolph Valentino (video). Princeton, NJ: Films for the Humanities, 1988.
    Presents the famous actor during the 1920s.

Saddle Up (video). Evanston, IL: Wombat Films & Video, 1991.
    The early years of Hollywood westerns, especially the contrasting styles of Tom Mix and William S. Hart.

The Silent Language of the Plains: How to Speak Indian Sign Language (video) (Tim McCoy). Kingman, AZ: Harper and Wasson, 1985.
    In two parts. Tim McCoy's son reminisces about his father and TMcC demonstrates sign language. There was also a version produced in the 1950s entitled *Tim McCoy and the Silent Language of the Plains*.

Star Treatment (video) (David Gill and Kevin Brownlow). New York: HBO Video, 1980.
    An examination of the star system, with emphasis on the career of John Gilbert. Also available as part of the series *Hollywood* (1990).

Stars of the Silver Screen, 1929–1930 (recording). RCA Victor, 1967.
    Original recordings by many performers including G. Swanson.

Swanson & Valentino (video). New York: HBO Video, 1980.
    GS recalls her rise and fall in films. RV's career is examined with the insights of his brother. Also available as part of the series *Hollywood* (1990).

TV Variety (no. 13) (video). Van Nuys, CA: Shokus Video, 1985.
    Contains Buster Keaton's appearance on the TV show *This Is Your Life* (1957).

Unknown Chaplin (video) (Kevin Brownlow and David Gill). 3 cassettes. New York: HBO Video, 1983.
  By means of outtakes, long-lost film segments and interviews, CC's creative processes are shown.
Valentino (recording). Anaheim, CA: Mark 56, 1978.
  Interviews with people who knew RV; includes two songs actually sung by him.
A Very Public Private Affair (video). New York: Time-Life Video, 1982.
  Recounts the Hearst-Davies affair from its beginnings to their life at San Simeon.
Vi, Portrait of a Silent Star (video) (Anthony Slide). New York: Cinema Guild, 1990.
  V. Dana talks about her career, beginning with the Edison Company.
Why Ever Did They?: Hollywood Stars at the Microphone (CD recording). E. Sussex, England: Pavilion, 1990.
  Songs, originally recorded between 1923 and 1939, sung by several stars, including R. Valentino, N. Beery, D. Del Rio, G. Swanson and R. Novarro. Also released by Pearl (1991).
William S. Hart (film). New York: Sterling Educational Films, 1961.
  Traces WSH's career with highlights from his films.
Wm. S. Hart and the Sad Clowns (video). Davenport, IA: Blackhawk Films, 1970s(?).
  Two documentaries examine the career of W.S. Hart and the early works of C. Chaplin, B. Keaton, H. Langdon and H. Lloyd.

Index